COMPARATIVE
POLITICS

SIXTH EDITION

COMPARATIVE
POLITICS

Exploring Concepts
and Institutions
Across Nations

Gregory S. Mahler

LYNNE
RIENNER
PUBLISHERS

BOULDER
LONDON

Published in the United States of America in 2019 by
Lynne Rienner Publishers, Inc.
1800 30th Street, Boulder, Colorado 80301
www.rienner.com

and in the United Kingdom by
Lynne Rienner Publishers, Inc.
Gray's Inn House, 127 Clerkenwell Road, London EC1 5DB

Library of Congress Cataloging-in-Publication Data
A Cataloging-in-Publication record for this book
is available from the Library of Congress.

ISBN 978-1-62637-790-5

British Cataloguing in Publication Data
A Cataloguing in Publication record for this book
is available from the British Library.

Printed and bound in the United States of America

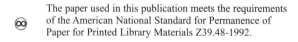

The paper used in this publication meets the requirements
of the American National Standard for Permanence of
Paper for Printed Library Materials Z39.48-1992.

5 4 3 2 1

Contents

Tables and Figures

Tables

Figures

Preface

The opportunity to write a textbook on comparative politics is the opportunity to introduce students to the world in which they live. We all know that we live in a noisy, confusing, chaotic world, and for the individual who has not had the chance to systematically learn about the myriad political institutions and political behaviors that exist, it can be difficult to comprehend. This book represents one effort to help bring that chaos into some degree of order.

Whether we are searching for an explanation of the Arab Spring of 2011, the centralization of power of such authoritarian figures as Vladimir Putin of Russia or Xi Jinping of China, the evolution of political institutions in Europe, the reasons for waves of immigrants coming from Latin America to the United States, or the coming to power and political machinations of Donald Trump, it is clear to all students of society that political institutions can affect the nation-states within which they operate. Among other things, they establish the political "rules of the game"—they determine who becomes a politically significant individual and how collections of politically significant individuals interact, and they determine the general style of politics in a regime. While there are a number of personal factors that can influence how and why individuals behave as they do in the political world, there is no doubt that political institutions are important.

Formal political institutions such as legislatures, executives, and judiciaries are ubiquitous in today's world. Constitutions, political parties, interest groups, bureaucracies, and a number of organized political behaviors such as participating in elections are similarly universal. It becomes clear as soon as we identify these types of institutions and start to look at how they fit together in the political world, however, that the details of precisely how these political structures operate vary widely on a nation-by-nation basis. In order to understand the Arab Spring, authoritarian rulers, the evolution of political institutions, causes of immigration, or unusual styles of political leadership, we need to understand these structures.

The world is changing. We must be able to observe the world, and we must be able to observe those changes. And, having observed those changes, we must make an effort to understand them. The purpose of a textbook such as this one is to help prepare citizens of the world to understand the settings in which they live and to help them respond in an enlightened way. We cannot do that if we do not know and understand how political systems are structured and how they operate.

This book offers both a cross-national view (Chapters 2–7) and a country-focused view (Chapters 8–16) of comparative politics. The logic for this approach is that the initial cross-national discussion will enable students to appreciate both the characteristics of political institutions and the variations of the institutions that can be found in the contemporary political world. Then, as we shift to a country-basis perspective, we can truly appreciate how the pieces all fit together when we look at them operating in a single national entity.

The study of comparative politics is a fascinating undertaking that cannot offer explanations for all of the truly bizarre behavior in the world around us, but can help to answer some of the questions about the political phenomena that we may observe, whether they take place far afield or near to home. I hope that the material in this text will help respond to some of the many questions we encounter on a daily basis.

* * *

I am delighted to be working with Lynne Rienner Publishers on the sixth edition of this textbook. I have very much appreciated the reactions of my students, and of students at other colleges and universities, in the years since the first edition of the book was published in 1992. A lot about the world has changed since that time, but the basic premises of the text have not.

I would like to acknowledge the assistance and encouragement of the outstanding professionals at Lynne Rienner Publishers who have been associated with this undertaking, starting with Lynne Rienner herself. Her enthusiasm for the project and her active participation in some key conversations about parts of the book have been really important and the kind of involvement that any author would appreciate. Thank you.

As I have in past editions, I thank those scholars who have been contacted over the years to review previous editions of the book and to make suggestions for changes. These scholars and teachers have made a number of very helpful suggestions for improvements, and although I cannot offer names here, I trust that you will recognize your suggestions in the pages that follow. Much of the book's improved comprehensiveness is because of these individuals' advice, which is much appreciated.

I also once again acknowledge the role of my students in the development of the book. Comments made by my students about other textbooks initially convinced me to try my hand at writing this one, and their subsequent comments over the years—at the University of Vermont, the University of Mississippi, Kalamazoo College, and Earlham College—have helped me a great deal in deciding what should be included in this type of work and the best way of presenting the material. Some of the organization of the book, and some specific topics covered, have been brought about by student suggestions, and I appreciate that assistance.

As in the past, I dedicate this book to my wife, Marjorie, who has been so tolerant as I have spent evenings, weekends, and vacations working on this project rather than being involved in other activities.

1

Comparative Political Analysis: An Introduction

Learning Outcomes

After reading this chapter, you will be able to

- Explain why we study politics.
- Describe the different approaches to how we study politics, and explain the relative value of each of the different approaches.
- Understand the nature of comparative political analysis, and explain the difference between comparative politics and area studies.
- Describe the concept of a political system, and give examples of different kinds of systems and subsystems.
- Appreciate the importance of the idea of a political culture, and explain why an understanding of a political culture is crucial to understanding how politics operates in a context.
- Offer illustrations for why an institutional approach to the study of comparative politics is important, and show how an institutional approach differs from other approaches to this study.

Politics. The word conjures up visions of political campaigns, voting, military action, subtle political influence by lobbyists, or a long and painfully drawn-out process of policy decisionmaking. For the student who is more politically experienced, the word may suggest other images—images such as legislatures, courts, and interest groups. The more advanced student may also associate concepts such as power, influence, socialization, or recruitment with the concept of politics.

One point that is clear to all students is that the term *politics* is an extremely broad one. It means all of the things just indicated, and more.[1] Political science as a discipline can be traced back to the time of Plato (c. 427–347 B.C.E.) and Aristotle (384–322 B.C.E.). Aristotle is often referred to as the first "real" political scientist—and we could add first "comparativist" as well—because of his study of the many political systems that he found in the political world of his time. His comparisons of constitutions and power structures contributed many words to our political vocabulary today—words such as *politics, democracy, oligarchy,* and *aristocracy.*[2]

The study of politics can be characterized as the study of patterns of systematic interactions between and among individuals and groups in a community or society.[3] This does not involve random interactions, but rather focuses upon those interactions that involve power, or authority. Aristotle saw many different types of relationships involved in this "political" association, but central to the concept was the idea of rule, or authority. In fact, one of the central criteria by which Aristotle classified constitutions in his study involved where power or authority to rule was located in the polis, the political system.[4] The seventeenth-century philosopher Thomas Hobbes felt that power had to do with the general capacity to attain goals in society.[5] Harold Lasswell put the question succinctly in the title of his classic book *Politics: Who Gets What, When, How?*[6] Much more recently, David Easton referred to politics as dealing with the "authoritative allocation of values for a society."[7] Thus, the study of politics may involve the study of legislatures, the study of the role of a minority group in a political system, more generally the study of how public policy is made, or all of these—and more.

Why Do We Study Politics?

It could be argued that political scientists since the time of Aristotle have been studying the same things—constitutions, rulers, the ruled, the behavior of political actors, and so on—and have not yet managed to come up with a formula for the establishment of a perfect society. Why do we continue to study politics, then? If we have not found what we are looking for by now, are we likely to? These are all good questions, and they are hard questions to answer, too.

What are we looking for? The subjects of inquiry are many. Some political scientists are trying to learn about justice. Others are concerned with how **social policy*** is made; they study political structures that are involved in the policymaking process. Others seek to understand why a given election is won by one political party rather than another. Still

---

*Terms that appear in the Glossary are shown in the text in boldface on first substantive use.

others study politics simply because political relationships seem to be important to our daily lives.

More than this, there is a remarkable range in how we study politics. Some studies approach politics from a philosophical perspective, perhaps asking questions related to whether political institutions or behavior are good or bad. Others approach politics from a more measurement- or data-oriented perspective, seeking to quantify different dimensions of politics. These different approaches contribute to the wide range of political perspectives in the literature.

In short, there are as many different reasons for studying political behavior as there are different aspects of political behavior to study. One thing, however, is clear: political science is only one of the social sciences concerned with helping us to understand the complex world around us. The others, including (but not limited to) economics, sociology, and anthropology, also study the same general types of social phenomena that political scientists study.

The same type of question can also be asked in relation to comparative politics: Why should we study comparative politics? Many American political scientists tend to label as comparative politics anything that does not fit into one of the subdisciplines of international relations, methodology, political theory, or US politics. For them, the subdiscipline of comparative politics would include politics in Japan, politics in Zimbabwe, and so on, with the general formula being politics in any nation other than the United States.

It should be added that American political scientists are not the only ones to have this perspective. If one were to travel to France, the study of US politics would be found within the subdiscipline of comparative politics; there, any area studies other than French politics would fall into the comparative basket. The same could be said for anything other than German politics in Germany, or anything other than Chinese politics in China.

But comparative politics should be more than that. Studying politics in other nations can more properly be referred to as area studies. Area studies, involving a detailed examination of politics within a specific geographical setting, are a legitimate kind of inquiry, but not one that necessarily involves any explicit comparison. Roy Macridis and Bernard Brown many years ago criticized comparative politics at the time for not being truly comparative, for being almost completely concerned with single cases (for example, politics in Egypt) and single area studies (for example, politics in the Middle East).[8] Comparative politics is—or should be—more than area studies. This is an area of debate in the discipline that continues to receive a great deal of attention and continues to cause a great deal of discussion.[9]

When we speak of comparative politics in this book, we are including the idea of the actual act of comparison. We all know what comparison is; it involves terms of relativity, terms like *bigger, stronger, more stable, less democratic,* and so on. Comparative politics, then, involves no more and no less than a comparative study of politics—a search for similarities and differences between and among political phenomena, including political institutions (such as legislatures), political behavior (such as voting), or political ideas (such as liberalism or Marxism). Everything that politics studies, comparative politics studies; it just undertakes the study with an explicitly comparative methodology in mind.

We could make the argument, in fact, that all of political science is comparative. The study of international relations compares diplomatic relations and strategies over time and between nations. The study of political behavior compares types of activity in different political contexts. The study of political philosophy compares perspectives of what ought to be and what is. Even the study of US politics is implicitly comparative: we study the power of the president as compared to the power of the Congress, or why one interest group is more powerful than another, and so on.

To return to the question of why we should study comparative politics, then, an answer now may be suggested. As Mattei Dogan and Dominique Pélassy observed, "Nothing is more natural than to study people, ideas, or institutions in relation to other people, ideas, or institutions. We gain knowledge through reference. . . . We compare to evaluate more objectively our situation as individuals, a community, or a nation."[10] The study of comparative politics is useful because it gives us a broader perspective of political phenomena and behaviors, and this broader perspective can contribute a great deal to both our understanding and our appreciation of the phenomena we are studying. We compare to escape from our ethnocentrism, our assumptions that everyone behaves the same way we do; we seek to broaden our field of perspective. We compare to discover broader rules of behavior than we might find in more narrow studies.

For example, the simplicity and brevity of the Constitution of the United States is more impressive when it is examined alongside longer constitutions of other nations.[11] We can better understand the significance of presidential government when we know about alternatives to presidential government. We can learn about those factors contributing to political stability by studying a country that is regarded as being politically stable. We can learn even more by including a country not regarded as stable in our study and looking for similarities and differences between the two countries.

How Do We Study Politics?

Broadly speaking, there are two paths on the road of inquiry: one is called the **normative approach to inquiry**, and the other is called the **empirical approach to inquiry**. The normative approach focuses upon principles, philosophies, or "shoulds." The empirical approach relies on data, measurement, and observation. Normativists might investigate the same questions as empiricists, but they go about their investigations differently. Normativists might study justice, equality, the "good society," and so on, and so might empiricists. The difference between the two groups is simply in how these questions would be approached.

Let us take an example to highlight differences in approach, studying the concept of justice. The normative approach might focus on the concept of justice itself: What is justice? Does the concept of justice ever change or vary? Should it do so? Should all citizens in a society have equal resources? Should there be free education? What policy would principles of justice demand?

The empirical approach would not ask many of these questions. The job of the empiricist is not to ask what should be, but simply to ask what is. The empirical approach might involve interviewing policymakers and ascertaining what they feel justice is. It might involve studying laws and their enforcement. It might involve examining economic distribution in order to observe patterns of material distribution. Do all people in a society have roughly equivalent resources? Do all people in a society have equal access to education? In brief, although both approaches would study the same general subject, the approaches would be different. In fact, the empirical approach does not utilize only one method of gathering information.[12] Arend Lijphart has suggested that there are four basic methods of discovering and establishing general empirical propositions. One of these methods is the **experimental method of inquiry**, while the other three are nonexperimental. The nonexperimental methods are the case study method, the statistical method, and the comparative method.[13]

The **case study method of inquiry** involves "the intensive study of individual cases. Case studies run the gamut from the most micro-levels to the most macro-levels of political phenomena."[14] Micro-level work might focus on individuals; macro-level work might focus on political interest groups, regional groups, or institutional groups. An area study, as described earlier, might be a case study (such as voting behavior in Lesotho), but clearly not all case studies involve area studies. In this method, the investigator picks one case—whether that case be a single nation, a single voter, or a single political structure—and studies it. Through the case study method one develops a certain amount of expertise in whatever one is studying, but the scope of one's study may be quite limited.[15]

The **statistical method of inquiry** involves more sophisticated forms of measurement and observation than the empirical method. Public opinion polls, survey research,[16] and various other forms of quantitative measurement are used to help make the measurements and observations that are characteristic of the empirical approach even more accurate.[17]

The **comparative method of inquiry** may be likened to two or more case studies put together. It focuses on a particular political structure or behavior and examines it in a comparative perspective. It looks for similarities and differences. The comparison may also be done in one setting, but across time—this is called diachronic comparison. For example, we may compare a given legislature in 2019 with the same legislature in 1919 in order to observe differences in the relative power and structures of that legislature. Or we may compare institutions or behavior at one point in time—synchronic comparison—but compare across national borders, for example by comparing the role of the legislature in Great Britain with the role of the legislature in Thailand or Jordan.[18]

These three nonexperimental methods are based exclusively upon observation and measurement. The experimental approach involves manipulation of variables. That is, whereas in the case study method one simply observes something, in the experimental method one manipulates one variable in order to observe its effect upon another variable. This is difficult to do in political research, because we are asking questions of extremely broad scope and usually cannot control the environment within which we are operating. We cannot, for example, set up two identical presidential elections at the same time in the same place—one with two candidates, and one with three candidates—in order to see the relationship between the number of candidates and voting turnout. Society is too complex to enable us to manipulate and experiment with many political structures and institutions.

Each of the methods in the empirical approach has its own advantages and disadvantages for the researcher. The chief advantage of the comparative approach is the broad perspective mentioned earlier. For example, studying the British Parliament in 2019 may tell us a great deal about that institution. We will learn more about the significance of what we are observing, however, if we compare our observations—either compare the observations with observations of the British Parliament of 1819 and 1919, or compare the British Parliament of 2019 with observations of the Indian Lok Sabha, the Japanese Diet, or the Israeli Knesset in the same year.

The study of comparative politics—or more properly, the comparative approach to the study of politics—is becoming more and more common in the discipline of political science today. We find comparative studies of legislatures, political elites, ideologies, women in politics, constitutions, legal cultures, revolutionary movements, political executives, and political parties. We also find comparative studies of the role of the military in government, of democracies, of new democracies, of political development, of political culture, and of political behavior.

The Nature of Comparative Political Analysis

How do we go about using the comparative method? If we start indiscriminately comparing every object on the political landscape with every other object, in a very short time we will find ourselves inundated with measurements of similarities and differences, most of which will turn out to be trivial distinctions either in scope or in significance. Suppose, for example, that we examine legislatures. One of the first things we will note is that legislatures are not physically the same. One legislature may have 100 seats, another may have 75 seats, and a third may have 500 seats. One building may be five stories high, another only two. One legislature may have its seats arranged in straight rows, while another may have its seats arranged in semicircles; indeed, one legislature may give its members individual desks, while another may only have long benches upon which many legislators must crowd.[19]

So what? Before we get bogged down in inconsequential detail (and of course detail need not be inconsequential), we need to plot a course of inquiry. We need to decide what questions we are interested in investigating, and why, and we need to understand the relationships between and among the objects of our scrutiny.

In this book we are interested in presenting an introduction to the comparative study of politics. What does this mean? We want to show how comparative analysis is undertaken, and why it is undertaken, and we want to provide examples of the types of things that one might look at while engaging in this kind of study.

In one very useful analysis of the values of comparative inquiry many years ago, Adam Przeworski and Henry Teune discussed two general approaches to the comparative method that they called the **most similar systems design** and the **most different systems design**. They argued that most comparativists use the most similar systems design. Investigators take two systems that are essentially similar, and subsequently study differences that exist between the two basically similar systems. They may then observe the impact of these differences on some other social or political phenomenon. These studies are based on the belief that "systems as similar as possible with respect to as many features as possible constitute the optimal samples for comparative inquiry."[20] If some important differences are found between two essentially similar countries, then "the number of factors attributable to these differences will be sufficiently small to warrant explanation in terms of those differences alone."[21]

An example may help to make this clear. We could study two essentially similar nations, say Canada and Australia. These two nations have similar political histories, similar political structures, and substantially similar political cultures. If we notice that in Australia public policy appears to be made easily and efficiently, while in Canada it appears to be very difficult to enact, we can conclude that the cause of this difficulty is probably not the substantial number of characteristics that they share in common. It must be something else that accounts for the difference, and we will be able to look at a relatively small list of possible factors for explanation.

In contrast, the most different systems approach directs us to select two or more systems to compare that are not essentially similar. Instead of looking for differences between two or more essentially similar nations, focusing upon nation-states, for example, we look for similarities between two or more essentially different nations.[22]

Let us take as an example the cases of the United Kingdom (UK) and the United Arab Emirates (UAE), two very different nations in terms of their political structures and behavior. If we find a political behavior that is similar in the two systems and we are interested in knowing why that behavior is the way that it is, we know that the explanation cannot lie in the many political structures and patterns of behavior that differ in the two nations; we must look elsewhere.

The point of all of this is to indicate that a number of different approaches are possible within the broad framework we call the comparative method. The important consideration in all cases is a theoretical rationale: Why are we undertaking the comparison that we are undertaking? What kind of objects do we want to study? The subjects of comparative political inquiry are as disparate and varied as one might imagine. Generally, it can be suggested that there are three broad categories of subjects of examination in the comparative study of politics: public policy, political behavior, and governmental structures.

In studies of comparative public policy,[23] the focus of attention is upon what governments do. Comparisons may be made between governments of different nations, governments in various stages of development (for example, developed nations versus underdeveloped nations), or governments and policy over time (for example, the government of Poland in 1969 and the government of Poland in 2019). Although the focus is upon what governments do, these studies will invariably pay some attention to the related questions of how and why governments act, as well as what the stimuli are that help governments to decide to act in the direction that they do at the time that they do.

A second general thrust of study is oriented to political behavior. Studies of this type may focus upon voting behavior, leaders in politics, and so on.[24] The central ideas of this approach involve the assumption that if one understands how people behave in a political system—and this includes all people, both the leaders and the led—then one will develop an understanding of the political systems within which that behavior takes place. This approach will include discussion of comparative public policy, primarily as an example of the behavior that is the focus of study, and also may include some study of the governmental institutions within which the behavior takes place.

The third general approach focuses upon governmental institutions themselves. This type of study may focus upon legislatures, constitutions, legal systems, and perhaps even political parties.[25] By studying the institutions of a regime, we are in a better position to understand how the regime operates than we would be with either the behavioral approach alone or the policy approach alone. This approach may well include some secondary subjects of scrutiny. It is possible that a study of governmental institutions might include a subject of policy output as an example of what it is that governmental institutions produce. In addition, a study of governmental institutions might include discussion of political behavior—both behavior of governmental officials as well as behavior of the public that may influence the government to act.

Often in comparative analysis we focus our attention on countries. Countries are important to study for a number of reasons, not the least of which is that they happen to be the units into which the contemporary world is divided. That is, it would be difficult to engage in comparative research without touching upon the political structure that we call the nation-state. Beyond this, however, nation-states often are useful bases for analysis because of what they represent.

A **nation**, a **state**, and a **nation-state** are not, strictly speaking, the same thing, although often these terms are used somewhat interchangeably.[26] The concept of nation has been used in an anthropological way to denote a group of people with shared characteristics, perhaps a shared language, history, or culture. A state, on the other hand, is an explicitly political entity, created and alterable by people, based upon accepted boundaries. It implies the notion of sovereignty, having the ability to make final decisions regarding policy, as well as the concept of legitimacy, the idea that the citizens of the state owe allegiance to the government, and that other states diplomatically recognize the state and consider that the government in question has a right to exist. A nation-state involves an instance in which the nation and the state overlap, where the unit that is found on the map corresponds to a meaningful use of the term *nation*.

Political borders can (and do) change, either as a result of war, as a result of agreement between parties involved, or perhaps as a result of both. For example, the United States and Mexico have reached agreement over a method of having periodic meetings between the two countries to "correct" the mapping of their border because of the gradual movement of the river that serves as a part of their common border, the Rio Grande.[27]

It is possible to find self-proclaimed nations that are not states as the term has just been defined. For example, many Canadian citizens today who are living in the province of Québec argue that there is a French nation in Canada that should be given independence. They are not content with being a self-perceived nation within a state (Canada), having an identifiably different language, with the powers that the Canadian federal balance gives to Québec alone; many citizens of Québec want to formalize their perceived differences with the rest of Canada and become an independent nation-state.[28] Similarly, the notion of Zionism at the turn of the twentieth century was based upon the idea that there was a nation of Jewish people who were stateless in a number of nation-states around the world, and that a Jewish state was needed for them to call their home. This Zionist concept subsequently gave birth to the state of Israel.[29] It is indeed ironic that in a very similar manner today Palestinians are claiming the need for a state of their own, independent of Israel, Jordan, Egypt, Lebanon, Syria, Saudi Arabia, and other Middle Eastern states.[30]

In any type of comparative political inquiry there are certain analytical problems of which we should be aware that might make our work more difficult than it otherwise might be. The first of these problems involves what we call the **levels of analysis**, and relates to the types of observations and measurements we are using and the types of conclusions that we can draw from those observations and measurements.[31] Generally, we can speak of two levels of data, or observation: an **individual level of analysis**, and an aggregate or **ecological level of analysis**. As the names suggest, the former focuses on individuals, the latter on groups.

We have all met what can be called problems of overgeneralization in our lives. This is the case when an individual takes an observation made at the general level and assumes that it can be validly applied to every case in a general setting. For example, to take a nonpolitical case, let us imagine that an individual has had negative experiences with fast-food restaurants in the past and does not like them. One day this person is traveling, looking for a place to have lunch; the only places available are fast-food restaurants. She enters, expecting to hate the food, and finds to her surprise that the food in *this* establishment is better than her past experiences would have led her to expect. What we have here is an instance in which the person has made a general observation (that is, food in fast-food restaurants is not very good), and she has encountered an individual case for which the general rule simply is not valid, or correct.

In political science we refer to this type of error as an ecological fallacy. That is, we take data, a measurement or an observation from the broad, ecological level, and apply it incorrectly to an individual case. The observation may be quite correct over a large population, as a generalization (for example, as a general rule food in fast-food restaurants is not very good), but this does not mean that it will be correct in every individual case within that population, and we need to be aware that when we make generalizations of this kind we may be making an error of this type.

More broadly, we have here a problem of two different levels of analysis—the individual level and the ecological, or aggregate, level. To take a political example, if we find on a national (aggregate) level that Republicans tend to vote more frequently than Democrats, this does not guarantee that every individual Republican that we might meet is going to vote, or that every individual Democrat that we might meet is not going to vote. It means that, on the whole, over the large population, Republicans as a group are more likely to vote than Democrats as a group.

To take another example, if we find in our cross-national research that the population of Côte d'Ivoire has overall a lower level of education than does the population of the United States (two aggregate-level observations), this does not mean that every citizen of Côte d'Ivoire is less educated than every citizen of the United States. It might in fact be the case that if we took a random sample from each nation, we might select an American with a sixth-grade education and a citizen of Côte d'Ivoire with a PhD from Duke University. In short, an ecological fallacy involves taking what may be a perfectly valid observation or generalization on the aggregate level and incorrectly assuming that it will always apply to every case on the individual level. It may apply in most cases (which may be why it is a general observation), but we may be leaving ourselves in a vulnerable position—and we may be drawing incorrect conclusions from our data—if we assume that it will always apply in every case.

We must also be aware of the reverse of the ecological fallacy: the individualistic fallacy. This occurs when we make an individual-level observation and incorrectly generalize from it to the aggregate level. For example, to stay with the example just introduced, it would clearly be incorrect to conclude from meeting one Duke-educated PhD from Côte d'Ivoire that all citizens of Côte d'Ivoire have PhD degrees from Duke, or that all PhD recipients from Duke come from Côte d'Ivoire. To be sure, there may be several individuals in this category, but we would be incorrect to generalize from this individual case to the entire population.

The importance of the "levels of analysis" problem can be summed up, then, by stating that observations made on one level of analysis, either the individual level or the aggregate (or ecological) level, are safely used only on that level. It does regularly happen, of course, that we will undertake a study in a situation in which we are forced to use data from one level to learn about another level. We may not be able to afford to question every individual in Côte d'Ivoire about their level of education, and we may have to rely on ecological or aggregate data. If all we have available to us is aggregate-level data about education (for example, average number of years of education), or health care (for example, number of hospital beds per population unit), or some similar characteristic, then we have to do our best with the data we have. We simply must keep reminding ourselves that conclusions we draw from one level of data must be used carefully on another level.

Another major pitfall in comparative analysis that we want to avoid involves making assumptions about the functions performed by political structures. It is possible that we will find two institutions, or patterns of behavior, that look alike in two different settings, but that perform entirely different functions in their respective settings. We might study, for example, the House of Commons in Britain, and see that the legislature in that setting is most important in the process of selecting government leaders and in establishing governmental legitimacy. In another setting, however, a similarly structured legislature may not be at all significant in the creation of a government or in the establishment of legitimacy, and to assume that because the British House of Commons is significant in this regard, all legislatures are significant in this regard, would be an example of an individualistic fallacy: incorrectly generalizing from the individual level (i.e., "it works that way in Britain") to the aggregate level (i.e., "it works that way everywhere").

The converse of this is true, too. Whereas we might find one structure (for example, a legislature) that performs two entirely different functions in two different nations, we might also find two entirely different structures in two different nations that perform similar or identical functions. Although the Congress performs the legislative function in the United States, the real designing of legislation in East Germany was done by the Central Committee of the Communist Party, not the legislature (although the legislature did subsequently give its approval to the measure prior to its becoming official).

This type of error of over-assuming can be especially troubling when students from stable, established Western democracies turn their attentions to non-Western systems. The problem of **political ethnocentrism**—of assuming that because political institutions or relationships work one way in stable Western democracies, they must work the same way in all political systems—is a real one, and we must be continuously on guard against making these types of assumptions, or falling victim to cultural bias. This is especially true when we turn our attention to political systems that are not stable, or not Western.[32] Indeed, this paragraph would represent an example of Western ethnocentrism in its own right if we did not observe that in many settings the very institutions or patterns of behavior that we take for granted in the West—such as legislatures or elections—may simply be irrelevant to other political cultures. Many critics of US foreign policy dealing with Iraq in the recent past have noted that the articulated US goal of "exporting democracy" to Iraq was too simplistic: democracy is very complex and cannot be exported like commercial goods, or transplanted like a plant from one pot to another. Iraq does not have a history of stable Western democracy, and because democratic institutions work in the United States does not necessarily mean that they will work in Iraq.

When we undertake comparative political analysis, then, we need to keep our eyes open for errors that we can make by simply assuming too much. We must take the political environment into consideration before drawing conclusions or making broad generalizations; we must make sure to "scout out the landscape" to make sure that we have included in our analysis all of the factors that may be of significance in that particular political system. In some systems the list of significant factors may be very long; in others it might be very short.

The Political System

We have been discussing comparative political analysis, and problems that may ensue in the research process, but we have not as yet laid out any framework for establishing the ground upon which we will base our research. The central concept in discussions of political analysis is that of the political system. Generally speaking, not confining ourselves only to the political, there are two types of systems that we can discuss: analytic systems and concrete systems.

We are all familiar with the concept of a system. Such terms as "nervous system," "electrical system," or even "solar system" are all examples of instances in which we use the term *system* in our daily lives. When we speak of a system such as one of these, we are speaking of a **concrete or real system** we can actually see (or touch, or feel, or measure). For example, we could actually touch the components of a skeletal system if we wanted to. In an electrical system we can touch wires involved and follow them along from one object to another. The solar system is a bit more difficult, since we cannot directly touch the force connecting the member units, but it can be measured with sophisticated instruments and observations.

Much more interesting for us as political scientists, however, are **analytic systems**. We can define analytic systems as groups of objects that are connected with one another in an analytic way. That is, it is our theories and perceptions that provide the links between the objects in question. The political system that we refer to as US government is not real or concrete in the same manner that the plumbing system of a house is. We cannot actually touch or feel the links between and among the House of Representatives and the Senate and the Supreme Court and the White House. (Literally, of course, we probably could make the argument that one could touch a telephone wire and trace it to a central switchboard where all Washington, D.C., telephones are connected, and thereby claim that these institutions are, in fact, physically connected, but that would be stretching the point.) The important and meaningful connection among these institutions is power, and the power relationship that is to be found in the Constitution of the United States and in US political tradition.[33]

When we talk about "developing nations" or the "political left" or "legislatures" or "interest groups" or the "Middle East," we are using analytic concepts to bring together groups of objects—in many cases individuals, in other cases regions, nations, or institutions—that we perceive to have something in common. These are political systems, sets of political objects or political concepts that are theoretically related to each other in some analytic way. These systems of objects—analytic systems—are the basis of comparative political research.

We cannot stop at the level of the system, however. Systems can be broken down into subsystems. A subsystem is an analytical component of a political system that is a system in its own right. The US political system has many subsystems, each of which could be studied on its own. To begin, of course, are the fifty subsystems that we call states. If we wanted to, we could study the political system of one state on its own; if our focus is on the United States, however, the state would be perceived as a subsystem, not a system. Other subsystems of the US political system might be the bureaucracy, the legislature, political parties, and so on.

Similarly, we can use the term *supersystem* to refer to that collection of objects of which our focus is only a part. If our focus is still on the US political system, then a supersystem might be Western governments, or democracies, or presidential systems—all groups of objects of which our focus is simply an example. Table 1.1 provides an illustration of the way in which we can use these terms.

We can shift our point of focus, too. If our focus is the US political system, then the Congress is a subsystem, and the House of Representatives is a sub-subsystem, and the Foreign Affairs Committee of the House of Representatives is a sub-sub-subsystem, and Republicans on the Foreign Affairs Committee are a sub-sub-sub-subsystem. If our focus were the House of Representatives, the Congress would be a supersystem, the US political system would be a super-supersystem, and the Foreign Affairs Committee would be a subsystem. And so on.

Although these terms may seem confusing at first, they can be extremely valuable in our analysis of politics. Unlike chemists or physicists who may use sophisticated physical instruments to help them in their measurement and analysis, we political scientists have to rely on concepts and theoretical frameworks to help us with our measurement, observation, and analysis. Terminology, then, is important for us.

Just as with many of the other terms we have introduced in this chapter, the concept of a system is not as simple as it first appears. There have been many different approaches to political systems over the years, each developing its own vocabulary and literature. Probably the two biggest contributions to systems theories, in terms of their subse-

---

Table 1.1   Using Systems as Frames of Reference

Level	Set 1	Set 2
Super-supersystem	World governments	Constitutional systems
Supersystem	Democracies	Presidencies
System	US political system (focus)	US political system
Subsystem	A state	Congress
Sub-subsystem	A county	Senate

quent generation of literature in the discipline, have been made by David Easton and Gabriel Almond.

Easton's variation on the political system, first introduced in the mid-1960s, has been referred to as **input-output analysis**.[34] Although many political scientists today feel that Easton's variation never realized its potential as a framework capable of explaining the operation of the political system, it did give rise to a great deal of literature on **systems theory**, and it can still be cited as one way of looking at the political system, even if it does not provide all of the answers that earlier theorists had hoped it might.

Easton's analytic framework viewed the political system as a continuously operating mechanism, with demands and supports going in (inputs), and authoritative decisions and actions coming out (outputs). Demands are defined as "an expression of opinion that an authoritative allocation with regard to a particular subject matter should or should not be made by those responsible for doing so."[35] Supports are those inputs between the political system and its environment that remain after demands have been subtracted.[36] The framework includes very elaborate regulatory mechanisms for preventing demand overloads and for maintaining the smooth operation of the system.

One of the major criticisms of Easton's framework involved its ethnocentrism, a concept introduced earlier. Many of the assumptions of Easton's model suggest that there will inevitably be the types of political structures and behaviors found in stable Western democracies (such as legislatures, bureaucracies, and so on), assumptions that are clearly not always valid. Further, the model was criticized by many because of what they suggested was an implied goal of "system maintenance" that put too much emphasis on political stability and that was inherently conservative.

The other major variation on systems theory was suggested by Gabriel Almond and is referred to as **structural-functional analysis**.[37] This analysis focuses upon what Almond refers to as political structures, by which he means either political institutions or behavior, and political functions, by which he means the consequences of the institutions or the behavior. This kind of analysis asks the basic question, What structures perform what functions and under what conditions in a political system? While the term *function* may be interpreted to mean "consequence," the framework introduced a new term as well, *dysfunction*. Simply put, a function is a good consequence, and a dysfunction is a bad consequence.

Both of these approaches, it should be explicitly noted, are quite sophisticated and quite substantial—far beyond what can be adequately discussed in this context. In addition, they are not the only variations on what is referred to as systems theory. They are, however, significant, and the test of time has indicated their impact on the discipline of political science. The concept of the political system, whether we use Easton's input-output framework, or Almond's structure-function framework, or any of a number of other variations on the theme, is another tool we have at our disposal to help in our cross-national comparison.

It is important that we observe that a political system need not be the same thing as a nation or a state. It may be convenient to use a nation or state as a point of departure in comparative analysis, but a system may be something else, as well. We may want to study a legislative system—that is, a collection of objects that are in some analytical way related and whose relationship is based upon legislation or the legislature. We may want to study the Organization of Eastern Caribbean States (OECS). We may want to study electoral systems. In short, although nation-states are convenient to study because we can find them on a map and their borders are (relatively) clearly defined, many of the subjects of comparative political analysis do not lie clearly within one set of national borders.

Political Culture

The concept of **political culture** is important in the study of comparative politics. As Gabriel Almond has noted, "something like a notion of political culture has been around as long as men have spoken and written about politics,"[38] and related concepts—such as subculture, elite political culture, political socialization, and cultural change—have also been used in a variety of settings since time immemorial. Indeed, Almond argues that the concept of political culture played a very important role in Plato's *Republic* when Plato observed "that governments vary as the dispositions of men vary, and that there must be as many of the one as there are of the other. For we cannot suppose that States are made of 'oak and rock' and not out of the human natures which are in them."[39] The concept of a political culture can be traced from Plato through Aristotle, Machiavelli, Montesquieu, Rousseau, Tocqueville, and up to modern times.[40]

Political culture, Almond tells us, "is not a theory; it refers to a set of variables that may be used in the construction of theories."[41] As Sidney Verba notes, it consists of "the system of empirical beliefs, expressive symbols, and values which defines the situation in which political action takes place."[42] As Carole Pateman notes, it "is concerned with psychological orientation toward social objects . . . the political system as internalized in the cognitions, feelings, and evaluations of citizens."[43] Among the major dimensions of political culture are included a sense of national identity, attitudes one holds toward one's fellow citizens, attitudes about governmental performance, and knowledge and attitudes about the political decisionmaking processes.

In fact, scholars tell us, we can refer to three different directions in which political culture runs: a system culture, a process culture, and a policy culture.[44] The system dimension of political culture is made up of attitudes toward the nation, the regime, and the authorities who control power at any given time. This includes values related to national identity, regime legitimacy, institutional legitimacy, and the effectiveness of individuals who hold significant political positions. The process dimension of political culture is made up of attitudes toward the role that the individual plays in the political arena, and attitudes about other political actors. The policy dimension of political culture focuses upon the results of politics, the outputs of the political system.

As suggested earlier, the importance of the political culture is that it refers to a number of political variables that we may use in our analysis of the political world and in our construction of political theories. Political culture has been argued to be significant in the process of political development, in the development of regime legitimacy, in economic and industrial development, and in social integration and regime stability. It is a concept that we shall use on a number of occasions in this book, especially in Part 2 when we turn our attention to area studies to illustrate the importance of the political institutions and political behaviors that we shall examine in the first part of this book.

When we consider political culture we must be aware of the danger of an ethnocentric approach to our study. We should not make the assumption that the way social relationships and institutions exist in our culture and society is necessarily the same way they exist in all other societies, or is the standard for institutions and behavior that other cultures strive to develop. There are many characteristics of what can be called Western culture that are definitely not sought by non-Western societies. Indeed, there are many characteristics of contemporary Western society that we do not like ourselves, such as contemporary crime rates, drug problems, the weakening of the nuclear family unit, and so on. We must keep in mind that Western capitalist democracies are not always the model chosen by others in the world, and whether we agree with this or not, we must be careful not to assume that our way is the only way.

Globalization

While the term *culture* refers to the way people or groups of people interact and the values that they may hold, there is another broad-ranging term that we should meet at this point in our study that also deals with ways that people or groups of people interact, and that is the term *glob-*

alization, increasingly used today as a shorthand for a huge range of impressive and important issues. The World Bank has noted that globalization "is one of the most charged issues of the day," although it notes that "there does not appear to be any precise, widely-agreed definition" of the term.[45] While there are clear supporters and opponents of the process—the former seeing globalization as the key to the future for the developing nations and the latter seeing it as a sure-thing destroyer of the environment and economic oppressor of citizens of have-not nations—there is no consensus on its meaning or on exactly how it should be measured.

Students of the process believe the core sense of the concept of economic globalization refers to the observation that a quickly rising share of economic activity in the world recently seems to be taking place between people who live in different countries rather than in the same country. This includes such topics as international trade, foreign direct investment, environmental policy, human rights, and a variety of other issues. The position of the World Bank in this debate is that

- it is necessary to distinguish between globalization's different forms, including trade, investment, market behavior, regulation, and so on;
- it is necessary to recognize that globalization does not affect all nations in the same way or to the same extent—participation in globalization varies widely;
- we must be careful to distinguish between the times that we use "globalization" in its economic sense and the times that we use it in other ways.[46]

The fact is that nation-states in today's environment are interrelated in ways that could only have been dreamed about in years past. Not only are nations connected by Internet and email in a way that wasn't imaginable, but their economies are integrated and interdependent in a way similarly unimaginable even a decade ago. In his book *The World Is Flat,* Thomas Freedman shows how buying a computer in the United States directly affects the economies of a half dozen nations—all in a way that may be invisible to the American consumer.[47]

There are several different dimensions of what we can today refer to as globalization. These include the movement of money around the world, multinational corporations, and international trade. Each of these merits brief discussion here.

Capital moves around the world today as if there were no such thing as the nation-state. The Chinese government, which we shall discuss in considerably more depth later in this book, owns a considerable share of the US national debt, and this worries many US policymakers in terms of the potential problems this might create in future years. People in one nation, whether that nation is the United States, Japan, China, or India, have the ability to invest in industry and business in other nations. While this is a good thing for those businesses and industries that are seeking outside investment, it may have the consequence of making it more difficult for national governments to plan—and control—their economies.

Multinational corporations (MNCs) may have the same effect. The behavior of most MNCs is focused on increasing their "bottom line," the profits that they earn for their shareholders. This means that in most situations the MNC has very little or no loyalty to the community or nation in which it is operating. If it can make more money by paying lower wages, it will do so. If this requires the MNC to move, so be it. For many years this behavior was relatively invisible to most Americans in an international context, although they were often aware of mills and factories in the northern states closing in order to move to southern states where labor was cheaper and labor unions were less powerful or nonexistent. Today, of course, even those southern factories have closed, and the jobs have moved to Mexico, or Asia, or Ireland, or other settings around the world, where the MNC involved can pay lower wages, with lower benefits (such as less health insurance), and increase their profits.

And at the end of the day, the balance sheet of globalization can be summarized by international trade figures. Today's de-industrialization in the United States and in the wealthier nations of the world (as industry moves to the poorer nations of the world where wages are lower) means that significant consuming funds are flowing outward, to nations where goods are produced. Increasingly, of course, this means China.

So, while globalization in the abstract may have many different definitions, its net effects can be seen in terms of jobs and trade, which in the final analysis pits all governments against other governments, and states against states, to attract business and capital to their settings.

The Institutional Approach

The approach to comparative politics that is used in this volume is an institutional one. Although there is no doubt that an emphasis on either public policy or political behavior would be a vehicle that would work in an introduction to comparative politics, the institutional approach has been selected here for several reasons. First, it lends itself to generalization more readily than do the other approaches. When we learn how a Westminster-model parliamentary system works in Britain, and we subsequently learn that Grenada, Tuvalu, and India have essentially Westminster-model parliamentary systems, we can relatively easily, and relatively accurately, transfer a good deal of what we have learned about one system to another. An emphasis on public policy (e.g., British housing policy) or political behavior (e.g., British voting patterns) would not permit this transferability.

Second, the institutional approach is more enduring. Although it is true that individual nation-states do change their basic political institutions on occasion, it is much more often the case that political institutions do not change either as radically or as frequently as either individual policies or aggregate behavior. The French electoral system was changed in 1985, and subsequently changed again shortly thereafter, but this was a true deviation from the French norm and from the norm we shall see in other settings. On the other hand, housing policy, health policy, foreign policy, and environmental policy are subject to political change as the corresponding political climate changes.

Third, the institutional approach lends itself to observation and measurement more readily than do other approaches. Although polities such as Britain, France, or Germany have been the subject of a great deal of policy analysis and examination of political behavior, there are many polities in the world in which sophisticated policy analysis is simply not done, nor is detailed analysis of political behavior undertaken. We can, on the other hand, undertake an examination of their political institutions.

To be sure, the institutional approach does not work all of the time; thus we will not restrict ourselves to only its use here. We shall discuss aspects of public policy and political behavior in our analysis here, but the primary vehicle for analysis will be that of political institutions. In the case of our description of Russia, for example, we shall begin by observing that it is a polity in which an institutional approach has not appeared to work very well in recent history, and there we shall focus our efforts in alternative directions. However, on balance, the institutional approach seems to be the best vehicle for an introduction to comparative politics.

The Comparative Method in Perspective

Throughout the remainder of this book we shall endeavor to follow the guidelines that we have set down thus far as to the comparative method of inquiry. The value of the comparative method is in the broad perspective that it offers the student of political science; we will focus upon this broad perspective as we continue.

In the next several chapters we will develop a base for further inquiry. We will present a number of different political structures and behaviors comparatively, looking first at the existence of a structure in one setting and then at the same structure elsewhere. We will also search for similarities and differences in the structures under examination, to try to understand how the political environments within which they exist have influenced them. Subsequently, we will turn our attention to a number of brief area studies to give ourselves the opportunity to better understand the political contexts within which the various political structures operate.

Discussion Questions

1. Can you explain why we study politics? How does the study of politics compare with other social sciences?
2. Describe the different approaches to how we study politics, and explain the relative value of each of the different approaches. When is a normative approach to inquiry more productive than an empirical approach?
3. What are the principle characteristics of comparative political analysis? How does a comparative approach differ from an area studies approach?
4. Can you describe the concept of a political system? What is the relationship between a political system, a political subsystem, and a political supersystem? In what way can these concepts be of analytic value?
5. What is a political culture? Why is the political culture of a polity an important thing to study and to understand?
6. What are the major advantages of an institutional approach to the study of comparative politics? What are the strengths of the institutional approach? What are its weaknesses?

Notes

1. Three very good recent general texts that show the range of concepts related to the term *politics* are Nigel Jackson and Stephen Tansey, *Politics* (London: Routledge, 2014); David Walsh, *Politics of the Person as the Politics of Being* (Notre Dame: University of Notre Dame Press, 2016); and Steven Bilakovics, *Democracy Without Politics* (Cambridge: Harvard University Press, 2012).

2. See Ernest Barker, ed. and trans., *The Politics of Aristotle* (New York: Oxford University Press, 1970), pp. xi–xix.

3. See Joel S. Migdal, *State in Society: Studying How States and Societies Transform and Constitute One Another* (New York: Cambridge University Press, 2001).

4. Ibid., p. 111.

5. See the classic essay by Talcott Parsons, "On the Concept of Political Power," *Proceedings of the American Philosophical Society* 107, no. 3 (June 1963): 232.

6. Harold Lasswell, *Politics: Who Gets What, When, How?* (New York: McGraw-Hill, 1936). See also Michael Saward, *Democracy: Critical Concepts in Political Science* (London: Routledge, 2007).

7. David Easton, *A Framework for Political Analysis* (Englewood Cliffs, NJ: Prentice Hall, 1965), p. 50.

8. See Roy C. Macridis and Bernard E. Brown, eds., *Comparative Politics: Notes and Readings* (Homewood, IL: Dorsey, 1977), pp. 2–4. This criticism is still the focus of debate.

9. The January 10, 1997, issue of the *Chronicle of Higher Education* introduced a new version of a long-running debate over the value of area studies as distinct from comparative politics; see Christopher Shea, "Political Scientists Clash over Value of Area Studies," p. A13. Harvard University's Robert Bates suggests in this essay that a focus on individual regions leads to work that is "mushy and merely descriptive." See also several of the essays in Margaret Levi, *Designing Democratic Government: Making Institutions Work* (New York: Russell Sage, 2008).

10. Mattei Dogan and Dominique Pélassy, *How to Compare Nations: Strategies in Comparative Politics* (Chatham, NJ: Chatham House, 1990), p. 3. See also Anthony Peter Spanakos and Francisco Panizza, *Conceptualising Comparative Politics* (New York: Routledge, 2016).

11. See, for example, the historical work by Howard Gillman, Mark Graber, and Keith Whittington, *American Constitutionalism* (New York: Oxford University Press, 2017); or Daniel Franklin and Michael Baun, *Political Culture and Constitutionalism: A Comparative Approach* (London: Routledge, 2015).

12. See Janet Ruane, *Introducing Social Research Methods* (Hoboken, NJ: Wiley, 2016); or Janet Buttolph Johnson, H. T. Reynolds, and Jason Mycoff, *Political Science Research Methods* (Thousand Oaks, CA: Congressional Quarterly, 2016).

13. Arend Lijphart, "The Comparable Cases Strategy in Comparative Research," *Comparative Political Studies* 8 (1975): 159. See also Theodore Meckstroth, "'Most Different Systems' and 'Most Similar Systems': A Study in the Logic of Comparative Inquiry," *Comparative Political Studies* 8 (1975): 132. See Dogan and Pélassy, *How to Compare Nations,* for a very good job of discussing these issues at greater length.

14. See Harry Eckstein, "Case Study and Theory in Political Science," in Fred Greenstein and Nelson Polsby, eds., *Handbook of Political Science: Strategies of Inquiry* (Reading, MA: Addison-Wesley, 1975), p. 79.

15. Examples of this kind of work can be found in John Gerring, *Case Study Research: Principles and Practices* (New York: Cambridge University Press, 2017); or Benjamin Most and Harvey Starr, *Inquiry, Logic, and International Politics* (Columbia: University of South Carolina Press, 2015).

16. A very good essay on this is by Richard Boyd and Herbert Hyman, "Survey Research," in Greenstein and Polsby, *Handbook of Political Science,* pp. 265–350. See also Willem Saris and Irmtraud Gallhofer, *Design, Evaluation, and Analysis of Questionnaires for Survey Research* (Hoboken, NJ: Wiley Interscience, 2007).

17. For a good introductory-level example of this approach, see Dvora Yanow and Peregrine Schwartz-Shea, *Interpretation and Method: Empirical Research Methods and the Interpretive Turn* (Armonk, NY: Sharpe, 2006); or Charles Ragin and Claude Rubinson, "The Distinctiveness of Comparative Research," in Todd Landman and Neil Robinson, eds., *The SAGE Handbook of Comparative Politics* (Thousand Oaks, CA: Sage, 2009), pp. 13–33.

18. A good essay on the comparative method may be found in Todd Landman, *Issues and Methods in Comparative Politics: An Introduction* (New York: Routledge, 2008). See chap. 2, "How to Compare Countries," pp. 30–55.

19. For an incredible collection of comparative data dealing with legislatures, see Valerie Herman, ed., *Parliaments of the World* (London: Macmillan, 1976). There is an entire section of this 985-page book dealing with seating arrangements in legislatures; note Table 21, on seating arrangements, which itself is seven pages long.

20. Adam Przeworski and Henry Teune, *The Logic of Comparative Social Inquiry* (New York: Wiley, 1970), p. 32.

21. Ibid. See also Dogan and Pélassy, *How to Compare Nations*, chap. 16, "Comparing Similar Countries," pp. 117–126.

22. See Dogan and Pélassy, *How to Compare Nations,* chap. 17, "Comparing Contrasting Nations," pp. 127–132.

23. For example, Anne Marie Cammisa and Paul Christopher Manuel, *The Path of American Public Policy: Comparative Perspectives* (Lanham: Lexington, 2014); or Isabelle Engeli and Christine Rothmayr Allison, *Comparative Policy Studies: Conceptual and Methodological Challenges* (New York: Palgrave Macmillan, 2014).

24. For example, see Fathali M. Moghaddam, *Sage Encyclopedia of Political Behavior* (Thousand Oaks, CA: Sage, 2017).

25. There are few integrated and structural comparative studies. One is left to rely on more specific comparative studies, such as comparative studies of legislatures (Gerring, *Case Study Research*; Most and Starr, *Inquiry, Logic, and International Politics*) or comparative studies of executives (Dogan and Pélassy, "Comparing Contrasting Nations"), for example.

26. See, for example, Ailsa Henderson, Charlie Jeffery, and Daniel Wincott, *Citizenship After the Nation State: Regionalism, Nationalism, and Public Attitudes in Europe* (New York: Palgrave Macmillan, 2014); or D. L. Hanley, *Beyond the Nation-State: Parties in the Era of European Integration* (New York: Palgrave Macmillan, 2007).

27. See the article by Douglas Littlefield, "The Rio Grande Compact of 1929: A Truce in an Interstate River War," *Pacific Historical Review* 60, no. 4 (November 1991): 497–516.

28. A very good discussion is provided by Wayne Reilly, "The Quebec Sovereignty Referendum of 1995: What Now?" *American Review of Canadian Studies* 25, no. 4 (1995): 477–496. See also my essay Gregory S. Mahler, "Canadian Federalism and the 1995 Referendum: A Perspective from Outside of Quebec," *American Review of Canadian Studies* 25, no. 4 (1995): 449–476.

29. A very good discussion of the concept of Zionism as a nationalist movement can be found in the study by Shlomo Avineri, *The Making of Modern Zionism* (New York: Basic, 1981).

30. For discussion of the Palestinian case, see Noam Chomsky, Ilan Pappe, and Frank Barat, *On Palestine* (Chicago: Haymarket, 2015); or Elise G. Young, *Gender and Nation-Building in the Middle East: The Political Economy of Health from Mandate Palestine to Refugee Camps in Jordan* (New York: Tauris, 2012).

31. Good discussions of problems of levels of analysis and other methodological difficulties can be found in Paul Pennings and Hans Keman, *Doing Research in Political Science* (London: Sage, 2005); or W. Phillips Shively, *The Craft of Political Research* (Englewood Cliffs, NJ: Prentice Hall, 2004).

32. Two very good—but different—illustrations of this concept can be found in Alessandro Ferrara, *The Democratic Horizon: Hyperpluralism and the Renewal of Political Liberalism* (New York: Cambridge University Press, 2014); and Mitchell Young and Eric Zuelow, *Nationalism in a Global Era: The Persistence of Nations* (New York: Routledge, 2007).

33. See Andreas Wimmer, *Ethnic Boundary Making: Institutions, Power, Networks* (New York: Oxford University Press, 2013).

34. David Easton, *A Systems Analysis of Political Life* (New York: Wiley, 1965).

35. Ibid., p. 38.

36. Ibid., p. 159.

37. Gabriel Almond, "Introduction," in Gabriel Almond and James Coleman, eds., *The Politics of the Developing Areas* (Princeton: Princeton University Press, 1960).

38. Gabriel Almond, "The Intellectual History of the Civic Culture Concept," in Gabriel Almond and Sidney Verba, *The Civic Culture Revisited* (Boston: Little, Brown, 1980), p. 1.

39. Quoted in ibid., p. 2.

40. Almond and Verba, *Civic Culture Revisited*. See also Jan-Erik Lane and Svante O. Ersson, *Politics, Culture, and Globalization: A Comparative Introduction* (London: Sage, 2001); and Irene Thomson, *Culture Wars and Enduring American Dilemmas* (Ann Arbor: University of Michigan Press, 2010).

41. Almond, "Intellectual History," p. 26.

42. Sidney Verba, "Comparative Political Culture," in Lucian Pye and Sidney Verba, eds., *Political Culture and Political Development* (Princeton: Princeton University Press, 1965), p. 513.

43. Carole Pateman, "The Civic Culture: A Philosophic Critique," in Almond and Verba, *Civic Culture Revisited*, p. 66.

44. This is a summation of much more detailed discussion in Almond, "Intellectual History," pp. 27–29.

45. PREM Economic Policy Group and Development Economics Group, "Assessing Globalization, Part I: What Is Globalization?" *Briefing Papers: What Is Globalization*, http://www.worldbank.org/html/extdr/pb/globalization/paper1.htm. See, as illustrative of a growing literature in this area, Ernesto Verdeja and Jackie Smith, *Globalization, Social Movements, and Peacebuilding* (Syracuse: Syracuse University Press, 2013); or Lane Crothers, *Globalization and American Political Culture* (Lanham: Rowman and Littlefield, 2012).

46. PREM Economic Policy Group, "Assessing Globalization."

47. Thomas Freedman, *The World Is Flat: A Brief History of the Twenty-First Century* (New York: Farrar, Straus, and Giroux, 2005). For a very good, more "academic" study, see Donald Boudreaux, *Globalization* (Westport: Greenwood, 2008).

PART 1

The Structures of Politics

2

Constitutions

Learning Outcomes

After reading this chapter, you will be able to

- Describe constitutions as political structures, and explain what a constitution is and its significance.
- Understand the difference between written and unwritten constitutions, give examples of each, and explain the significance of differences between them.
- Explain what constitutions do for the political systems in which they are found.
- Show the importance of the idea of the separation of powers, and explain how the separation of powers works in different regimes.
- Distinguish between federal and unitary political systems, give examples of each, and explain why the difference is significant.
- Articulate what an ideology is and how ideologies are reflected by political structures.
- Explain Aristotle's classification of political regimes, and evaluate his categories in a contemporary context.

As we study the principles behind political institutions and political behavior, one of the sets of relationships that we need to understand involves the sources of political power. What is political power, and where does it come from? Why do individuals want political power? We saw in Chapter 1 that the study of politics includes many subjects and that there are many different ways of undertaking such a study. In this chapter we shall seek to understand how the concept of power operates in politics, both through political institutions and constitutional structures and through political ideology.

Constitutions as Political Structures

One of the first things that an interested student of comparative politics will find in perusing the literature in the discipline is the emphasis placed on the state or the nation as the unit of analysis. While not all research takes place on this level, the state is a common subject of study.

Many characteristics of the state can be the focus for a basis of power in a comparative study—we will examine a number of them in this book—including structural characteristics (such as constitutions or legislatures) and behavioral characteristics (such as ideology or political participation). The initial area of our study should focus upon the structures that describe the system, the boundaries of the component structures found within the political system. In this way we turn our attention first to a brief examination of constitutions, and subsequently to a brief discussion of ideology and its place in political regimes.

It may be useful to think of **constitutions** as "power maps"[1] for political systems. It is often constitutions that tell us about the environment within which governments operate and describe how power is distributed among the actors involved. We look to constitutions for an explanation of who has power, and of the limitations on power. While these may change over time for a specific individual in a position of authority, or may change over time as different individuals occupy positions of authority, they are significant markers for the regime. Although it is true that in some systems the constitution is not of much help in understanding how the regime operates, in most of today's nation-states the constitution provides us with information that will help us understand the operation of politics.

Written and Unwritten Constitutions

Studies of constitutional governments often rely on the written documents that we call constitutions. Yet a government with a written constitution is not the same thing as a constitutional government. A written constitution is an expression of the ideas and organization of a government that is formally presented in one document. Some constitutions are quite short, such as the US Constitution, while others are much longer, such as the constitution of India, the (now nonexistent) constitution of the former Soviet Union, or the constitution of Switzerland.[2]

On the other hand, **constitutional government** can be described as limited government, specifically a limitation on governmental power. There are certain things that the government may not do, whether it wants to or not. The First Amendment to the US Constitution is a clear example of this, stating in part that "Congress shall make no law . . . abridging the freedom of speech." This is an explicit limitation upon the powers of government to act. Here we see a linkage between political institutions (in this case a constitution) and political power: the constitution controls the right, the ability, of the government to act.

We can find governments without written constitutions that can properly be called constitutional regimes, and conversely we can find governments that have written constitutions that do not properly fit the parameters we have set for a regime to be called a constitutional government. Several examples may help to make this clear.

The British government does not possess a document called "The Royal Constitution." British political history points to many different documents that are part of what is referred to as British constitutional law. These documents include the Magna Carta (1215), the **Bill of Rights** (1689), the Act of Settlement (1701), and other special acts of the British Parliament. On the other hand, scholars agree that Britain practices constitutional government: there are limits beyond which the government may not go. We may refer to Britain as a system with an **unwritten constitution**, a collection of constitutional principles that are widely accepted in the regime that are not formally approved as law.

The same thing can be said for Israel. Although there was no single document called a constitution when the state of Israel came into existence in 1949, Israel has been writing a constitution one chapter at a time over the past seven decades. Israelis believe that Israel's constitution is now almost complete, but Israelis have been living without a formally written constitution and an entrenched bill of rights until this time.[3]

To take another example from the Middle East, the entity referred to today as the Palestinian Authority, the transitional power that seeks to be the recognized government of a Palestinian state, is devoting much time to the creation of a constitution. A special committee of the Palestinian Legislative Assembly meets regularly to discuss what should be in its constitution.

Although the Union of Soviet Socialist Republics (USSR) had until its demise in 1991 a relatively new (1977) constitution that was highly specific,[4] many argued that the Soviet regime was not a constitutional government because there were no effective limitations on governmental power. Rights were conditional. To take three examples, Article 39 of the Soviet Constitution stated that "the exercise of rights and liberties of citizens must not injure the interests of society and the state";[5] Article 47 stated that USSR citizens, "in accordance with the goals of communist construction, are guaranteed freedom of scientific, technical, and artistic creation";[6] and Article 51 stated that "in accordance with the goals of communist construction, USSR citizens have the right to unite in public organizations."[7] These examples show that expressions of rights did exist; however, they were conditional, with the implication that if the government believed that the "goals of communist construction" were not being served, the rights in question might be lost.

There is another, more subtle distinction between these regimes that should be made explicit. One type of constitution gives rights, and the other recognizes rights. This is not merely a semantic difference. The Soviet Constitution, in stating that the government gave citizens certain rights, implied that the government also had the power to take away these rights. In the (unwritten) British Constitution, or the (written) US Constitution, rights are not given by the government; they are recognized as already existing. The US Constitution does not state that "citizens are given the right to free speech," although some people assume that it does. What is written is that "Congress shall make no law . . . abridging freedom of speech, or of the press"; these rights and freedoms appear to *already* exist and belong to the people, and the Constitution recognizes this fact by forbidding the Congress to limit them. This is quite different from what was the case in the Soviet Union.

Even the existence of a written constitution in a constitutional culture of limited governmental power (constitutional government) does not absolutely guarantee either limited or unlimited individual rights. Freedom of speech is not absolute in either the United States or Britain, to take two examples; in both systems there is substantial judicial precedent documenting instances in which government can, in fact, restrict individuals' speech.[8]

Even when we examine a polity with a history of constitutional protection of individual rights, short-term forces may occasionally motivate that polity to abrogate those rights: Japanese Americans who lived in California shortly after Japan attacked Pearl Harbor in World War II were denied due process, lost their homes and possessions, and were sent to relocation camps for the duration of the war. The US Supreme Court ruled at that time that this action was permissible because of the emergency situation posed by the war.[9]

When we discuss constitutional governments, then, we are not really talking about whether there exists a single document; rather we are interested in a kind of political behavior, culture, or tradition. The British Constitution is really a collection of documents and traditions, bound together in an abstract way. The US Constitution is a single document, with subsequent judicial interpretation and expansion. The forms may vary, but the behavioral results are the same: limits are imposed upon what governments may do.[10]

What Do Constitutions Do?

"Constitutions are codes of rules which aspire to regulate the allocation of functions, powers, and duties among the various agencies and officers of government, and define the relationship between these and the public."[11] Do constitutions make a difference? We have seen that having a written constitution may not guarantee the behavior of a regime; does having *any* constitution matter? Today, more and more political scientists are putting less emphasis on a constitution as a significant structure in politics. They argue that too often constitutions—whether written or unwritten—are not true reflections of the manner in which a political system operates, and, therefore, the constitution is of little use or value.[12]

Furthermore, constitutions may omit discussion of key political structures. For example, political parties are nowhere mentioned in the (written) US Constitution, yet it is difficult to conceive of the government operating without political parties in the United States. To take another example, the (written) Canadian Constitution fails to mention the prime minister as a significant actor in the political system at all,[13] yet there is no doubt that this is the single most important office in the Canadian political arena. The (written) constitution of the former Soviet Union guaranteed certain rights, but practice indicated that these guarantees were hollow. Much the same thing can be said in China today. Given all of this, why is it that constitutions seem to be universally accepted as necessary to a political system?

Several functions can be attributed to constitutions, whether written or unwritten, followed or not, wherever they may be found. First, they serve as an expression of ideology, a subject to which we shall return. Very often ideological expression is found in a preamble to the constitution. For example, the preamble to Canada's Constitution Act of 1867 indicated that Canada would have a constitution "similar in principle" to that of Britain. This "similar in principle" clause was seen by scholars as incorporating—all by itself—all of the hundreds of years of British constitutional tradition into the Canadian political realm, and accordingly it was regarded as being quite significant.[14]

Second, constitutions serve as an expression of basic laws. These laws play a central role in the regime and are often so special that they can be modified only through extraordinary procedures. Sometimes they cannot be amended at all, for example the clause in the German Constitution guaranteeing human rights. Whereas an ordinary law can usually be passed with a "simple majority" approval of the legislature— a majority of those present and voting in the legislature at the time— basic laws of the regime expressed in the constitution usually require special majorities of the legislature (two-thirds or three-quarters, for example) for approval.

Third, constitutions provide governmental organizational frameworks. These are often explained in the text of the document. It is common for constitutions to contain several sections, and to devote a section each to the legislative branch, the executive branch, the judicial branch, and so on. Constitutions discuss power relationships among actors, covering the legislative process, the role of the executive in policy formation, and checks and balances among actors. They may include discussion of impeachment of the executive and dissolution of the legislature, and perhaps discussion of succession as well.

Fourth, constitutions usually outline the levels of government of the political system. They discuss how many levels of government there will be and whether nations will be unitary, confederal, or federal. They often describe what powers fall within the jurisdiction of the national government and what powers it does not have.

Finally, constitutions usually have an amendment clause. No matter how insightful the authors of a constitution try to be, they recognize that they cannot foretell the future. Constitutions invariably need to be amended at some point down the road and must contain directions for modifications; failure to do so might mean that when change becomes necessary, the entire system could collapse for want of a mechanism of change.

Constitutions play an important role in regimes. Some constitutions will be more important in one of the functions just described than in others. For example, the constitution of the Islamic Republic of Iran may be more important as an expression of ideology (and theology) than as a real organizational diagram of the government.[15] Similarly, the US Constitution is more important as an expression of governmental organization and as a guideline for regime power relationships than as an expression of regime philosophy; the latter is usually said to be better expressed in the Declaration of Independence and the *Federalist Papers* than in the Constitution.

Constitutionalism and Federal Governmental Power

Another dimension of our study of politics and political power involves how systems and power are organized. We can identify several major frameworks, including unitary, confederal, and federal political systems. It is important to understand the distinctions among these organizational forms so as to appreciate some of the differences between governmental systems.

A **unitary system** has only one level of government above the local level. In Great Britain, although there are city governments and county governments, true **sovereignty**—the real power to make political decisions—resides with the national parliament; it has the right to control whatever powers the cities or counties might exercise. Parliament has the power to grant the cities and counties more influence, or to take away policy jurisdiction they may already control.

The chief advantage of these systems is their simplicity—there is only one responsible government. Unitary governments, however, are less effective for large nations than for small nations and do not allow for ethnic and regional groups to exercise some degree of autonomy. Britain's unitary government has periodically been the subject of tension over the years because some in Wales, Scotland, and Northern Ireland have argued that it does not give regional and ethnic groups as much power as they deserve. France, Italy, and Japan are other contemporary examples of unitary nations.

A **confederal system**—called a confederation—is a union of sovereign states that each retain their powers but agree to coordinate their activities in certain respects. A group of sovereign states may agree to coordinate trade barriers, or fishing activities, or oil production. The degree to which the units coordinate their behavior can vary greatly, as can the range of areas in which this coordination takes place.

The major advantage of confederations is their loose structure, which leaves flexibility and autonomy to member units. This allows units to retain individual characteristics and, to varying degrees, their own sovereignty to chart the policy directions they want. This same characteristic can be seen as a drawback of confederations as well: the inability to reconcile the varied interests of various member units. A confederation's citizens tend to identify most strongly with the member units, not the "national" unit, and priorities tend to be sectional, not broad. Often, action is taken only when all member units agree, which may mean that often no action is taken at all because unanimity is notoriously hard to achieve among large political units. Notable experiments in confederation that failed—the United States (1781–1787), Germany (1815–1866), and Switzerland (1815–1874)—were all reorganized as federations after it became clear that the confederal system would not further necessary common objectives.[16]

The European Community (EC)—often referred to today simply as Europe—began as an organization regulating tariffs among a small number of European nations. It has grown in power over the past several decades and has become a real political entity in the region with a common currency. European nations not only elect their own national legislators but also elect members of the European Parliament to represent their regions and nations.[17]

With the "Brexit" movement developing in Britain—a British exit from the EC—the future strength and composition of the European

Community is a topic of active discussion by many. Some say that Europe will survive Brexit and be more integrated and economically powerful than before, while others say that the British exit from Europe is the first step in a long-term diminishing of European influence. Only time will tell.

In a **federal system** there are two levels of government above the local level, both enjoying sovereignty in certain areas. The central government may have the sole authority to coin money, raise an army, or declare war; the intermediate level of government (such as the states or provinces) may have sole authority to regulate education, criminal law, or civil law; citizens deal with both levels of government.

Federal governments have been shown to have numerous advantages over other types of governments.[18] Federalism allows for both the expression of regional goals and a coordinated expression of national goals. One of the advantages of a federal system for member states is that the national level of government can absorb, through economic redistribution among member units, some of the costs of new technology or programs that would have to be absorbed completely by member units in a unitary or confederal system.[19]

The concept of federalism can be seen to have its roots early in political history—as far back as the Greek city-states. These early federations, for the most part, were not very stable or long-lived.[20] Modern federalism is usually dated from the American Constitutional Convention in Philadelphia in 1787.[21]

There are few federal states in the contemporary world. Of the approximately 193 nation-states today,[22] only 21 claim to be federal.[23] These twenty-one nations, however, cover more than half of the land surface of the globe and include almost half of the world's population.[24] Federalism is a significant element "in situations in which sheer size, involving the separation and divergence of communities, has been the dominating feature."[25]

Some authors argue that there is a direct correlation between large size and the advisability of federalism, and they quote Thomas Jefferson in support of their argument: "Our country is too large to have all its affairs directed by a single government."[26] Of the six largest nations in the world, only China is unitary, and even China has some characteristics of federal government.[27] (The five other largest nations are Russia, Canada, the United States, Brazil, and Australia.)

There are many smaller federations, as well, including Venezuela and Argentina in Latin America, and Switzerland in Europe. Many of these nations opted for federalism not because of their large land area but because of regional, ethnic, or linguistic characteristics of component groups that made a federal type of organization necessary. In general, federalism allows countries to maximize economic growth and political strength while at the same time allowing for the expression of regional characteristics.[28]

Switzerland, for example, chose the federal system because it was best-suited to the needs of that country's three language groups, German, French, and Italian. The Swiss Constitution, in fact, recognizes three official languages. Of the twenty-two Swiss cantons, there are eighteen unilingual cantons, three bilingual cantons, and one trilingual canton; the Constitution guarantees citizens the right to communicate with the central government in any of the three languages.[29]

The federal system has also been adapted in Germany. Rather than establishing clear divisions between areas of jurisdiction of the Bund (the central parliament) and the Lander (the member units), the German Constitution allows for broad areas of concurrent or shared jurisdiction.[30]

There does not appear to be a universally accepted theory of federalism or, for that matter, a clear definition of precisely what behavioral attributes are characteristic of federal government.[31] The most common characterization of a federal government is that it is organized on two levels above the local level, with one national unit and a number of intermediate units. Both levels of government rule over the same constituents, and both levels of government have the power to make certain decisions independently of the other.[32]

William Riker has suggested a useful framework within which the many federal governments of the world may be measured. He has suggested that federations can be measured along a "centralized-decentralized" dimension. This dimension may be defined by the following minimum and maximum, illustrated in Figure 2.1. At the minimum, the rulers of the federation can make decisions in only one narrowly restricted category of action without obtaining the approval of the rulers of the constituent units. At the maximum, the rulers of the federation can make decisions without consulting the rulers of the member governments in all but one narrowly restricted category of action.[33] The closer to the minimum end of the scale a federal government is, the more it can be described as a **peripheral federation**. The closer to the maximum end of the scale a federal government is, the more it can be described as a **centralized federation**.

Not all experiments with federation since the eighteenth century have been successes. The more decentralized or peripheral a federation is, the weaker the center is, the greater the centrifugal forces acting on the system, and the greater the likelihood that the federation will not endure. Cases such as the United Arab Republic, the Federation of the

Figure 2.1   A Scale of Federalisms

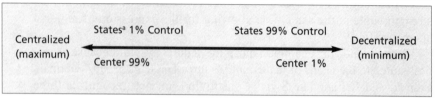

Note: a. States or provinces, cantons, lander, etc.

West Indies, or the Federation of Malaysia[34] are all illustrations of premature federations—unifications that took place before sufficient national integration was attained—and are examples of unifications that did not last.

However, the federal balance in a polity often influences the making of public policy.[35] For example, it is often difficult for the Canadian federal (national) government to set policy because many issues—such as health, education, and much resource policy—fall within the jurisdiction of the intermediate units, the provinces. Accordingly, if the federal government wants to enact a new health policy or a new job training program, it must convene a meeting of the federal prime minister and the provincial premiers, or the federal education minister and the provincial education ministers (or comparable officials depending upon the policy area involved) to negotiate a policy that will be acceptable to their respective governments. The provincial representatives will then return to their respective capitals and introduce the policy in their provincial legislatures.[36]

The Separation of Powers

The notion that centralized power is dangerous—that there must be a check on power—reached maturity in the eighteenth century, and its first full-scale application was to be found in the Constitutional Convention in Philadelphia in 1787. Delegates to the convention regularly cited "the celebrated Montesquieu," John Locke, Thomas Hobbes, and others[37] in support of the idea that political power, in order to be safe, had to be divided; the principle of the **separation of powers** was important to government. The legislature needed to have a check on the executive, and the executive on the legislature. Many of the ideas of John Locke were adopted in *The Federalist* (especially Number 47), among other documents, and expressed the philosophy that the executive force had to be kept separate from the legislative force.[38]

Constitutions express the power relationships among the many actors in political regimes. The US Constitution is explicit about the degree to which the president can take control of the work of the legislature (he or she cannot) and the degree to which the Congress can take control of the work of the president (it cannot). The situation is one that can devolve into a stalemate: the president can veto work of Congress, and Congress can refuse to pass legislative requests of the president, but neither can force the other to do anything. In recent years this has frequently led to a frustrating lack of action by US national government in key policy areas, and it has led recent presidents to rely more on executive agreements and executive orders than had been the case in the past. In other regimes the lines are less clearly drawn. For example, in France the president can, under circumstances that we shall examine later in this volume, issue decrees that have the force of legislation.

The Importance of Constitutions

Constitutions can be examined on two levels. On one hand, we can look at constitutions on a "piece" level and examine them section by section to see what structures and behaviors they prescribe for a given political system. On the other hand, we can look at constitutions from the level of the political system and ask the same question: What do constitutions do? David Easton's framework of analysis is useful in examining this type of question.

In Chapter 1 we examined the concept of the political system, and we noted that Easton offered a variation of the general systems approach referred to as input-output analysis.[39] Demands and supports are fed into the political system as inputs. They are "processed" by the system; the system is a giant conversion mechanism that takes demands and supports from the environment, digests them, and issues "authoritative allocations of values" in the forms of decisions and actions—outputs. These outputs filter through the environment as "feedback" and are subsequently reintroduced as new inputs, either demands or supports, and the cycle continues. The "digesting" and the "processing" phase of the system, what Easton labels the "political system," is what government is all about: responding to demands and supports, making decisions, providing information, establishing legitimacy, and so on.

Instead of looking at constitutions from the perspective of what they say about the separation of powers, about the federal or unitary natures of systems, about checks and balances, and about basic laws, we could ask the question of how constitutions help political systems to survive. To use Gabriel Almond's terminology introduced in Chapter 1, what are the functions (consequences) of the structures that we refer to as constitutions?

Ivo Duchacek has performed just such an analysis; his work offers answers to the question "What do constitutions do?" Constitutions help political systems in the function of "system maintenance," by helping them respond to demands and supports that are directed to them in the form of inputs. The constitutional framework of powers helps to process demands and supports and to convert them into outputs, which are reintroduced as inputs. Demands and supports are processed more smoothly because of commitment to responsiveness; specific institutions for rule-making, enforcement, and adjudicating; and commitment to goals, all of which are found in a constitution.[40]

Constitutions in a Comparative Perspective

The political structure that we call a constitution is a good place for us to begin cross-national comparison, because it presents for us examples of some of the problems that we first discussed in Chapter 1. We cannot be rigid when examining constitutional frameworks in comparative perspective. Sometimes we will find a piece of paper titled "The Constitution," and sometimes we will not. The mere existence of a piece of paper is no guarantee that a political system is constitutional, as we defined the term at the beginning of this chapter.

We have, then, the structures-and-functions problem mentioned in Chapter 1: the structure of a written constitution may perform different functions (have different consequences) in different political systems. Furthermore, different structures (in some places a written constitution, elsewhere tradition and custom) may perform the same function in different political systems. This is a scenario that we will see repeated in the next several chapters.

Ideologies

One of the functions that we ascribed to constitutions was that they might serve as an expression of ideology. The term *ideology* is often emotionally charged, and *ideologue* is often used as a description for an individual no longer having a rational perspective. Originally, the term *ideologue* referred to a student of how ideas were formed, and ideology was "a study of the process of forming ideas, a 'science of ideas.'"[41] The purpose behind the introduction of the concept of ideology was "to provide the new secular educators with a systematic educational theory. The unashamed view of the ideologues . . . was that the minds of the young should be bent to new, more healthy purposes."[42]

Furthermore, the term *ideology* has a number of meanings and connotations:

1. One meaning is that of "deception," "distortion," or "falseness." It conveys the notion of *subjectivity* as opposed to objectivity.
2. Ideology also conveys the notion of a *dream,* an impossible or unrealizable quest.
3. Ideology means also what may be called the *consciousness* of a society at any given moment, the values and beliefs and attitudes that hold it together.
4. Ideologies often correspond to *social criticism,* confronting existing beliefs and attempting through argument and persuasion to challenge and change them.
5. Ideology also provides a *set of concepts* through which people view the world and learn about it.
6. Ideologies can be a call for *committed action.*
7. Ideologies often become, under certain circumstances, a powerful *instrument of manipulation.*[43]

Ideologies, then, involve ideas that relate to the social/political world and provide a general guideline for action. One scholar has indicated that "an ideology represents a practical attitude to the world";[44] another has suggested that "ideologies are actually attempts to develop political accommodations to the economic and social conditions created by the Industrial Revolution."[45] Ideologies can unite groups, help to articulate philosophies, or serve as tools of political manipulation. In each of these we can see the same two critical components: a relation to political ideas, and a relation to political behavior.[46]

Ideologies give the regime its raison d'être, its sense of purpose, and serve as a point of reference for political behavior and the exercise of power in the political system. Political theorist Michael Curtis has suggested that ideologies are amalgams of "facts, values, and mythology that provide some understanding of history and the supreme significance of or necessary leadership by a particular individual, group, class, or nation."[47]

Many different ideologies have existed in the modern political world. Some have come and gone in a brief period of time; others have long been in existence. Some have had much influence on world events; others have not. What we could call classical liberalism was a significant ideology at about the time of the American Revolution, and it continues to be significant today. Certainly Marxism is an example of an ideology that has had a very broad and profound influence in society, one that has lasted for many years. Other "isms," including socialism, fascism, conservatism, and so on, have also become part of our vocabulary over the years.

Ideologies are often related to attitudes toward political change and the exercise of power, often conceived as fitting along a "left-right" spectrum, as illustrated in Figure 2.2. The "left-right" metaphor dates back to 1798, at which time the French legislative Council of 500 was arranged in a semicircular hall of representatives according to their self-determined place in the political spectrum.[48] Those generally supporting the monarch's policies sat on his right, while those who proposed changes in his policies sat on his left; hence, "leftists" favored change and "rightists" preferred the status quo. These same general labels are used today. It should be kept in mind that the positions in Figure 2.2 and the descriptions that follow relate to *classical* political values: those who consider themselves conservative in the United States today do not necessarily hold the same values as would a classical conservative in the 1790s.

Radical ideology is often associated with violence, although that need not be the case.[49] Generally, radicals are extremely dissatisfied with the way society (and politics) is organized and are impatient to undertake fundamental changes in society. Of course, not all radicals are alike, and we could certainly distinguish among more or less "radical" radicals, depending upon the intensity of their beliefs, the strategies they might wish to employ (including more or less violence), the immediacy with which they want changes undertaken, and so on.

The position of classical **liberal ideology** is one of more content with society compared to the position of radical ideology, but the liberal still believes that reform is possible, perhaps necessary. Among differences between liberals and radicals are their views toward law: "Radicals find it hard to respect the law. Liberals, on the other hand, generally respect the concept of the law, and although they may want to change certain specifics of the law, they usually will not violate it. Instead they try to change the law through legal procedures."[50] Liberalism includes a belief in human potential, in the ability of individuals to change institutions for the better, in human rationality, and in human equality.

The moderate position is one that is basically satisfied with the way society is operating and insists that changes that might be made in social rules and social values should be made slowly, gradually, and in a way that will not be disruptive.

Figure 2.2   The Liberal-Conservative Spectrum

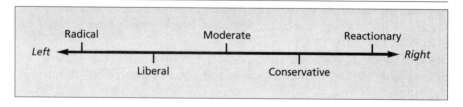

The position of classical **conservative ideology** can be described as being the most satisfied with the way society is operating, satisfied with the status quo. The major difference between conservatives and liberals is that "conservatives support the *status quo* not so much because they like it but because they believe that it is the best that can be achieved at the moment."[51] Classical conservatives do not share the optimism of liberals that individuals can improve society. They are more skeptical of human nature, and believe that human nature may be selfish. They place more emphasis on respecting institutions and traditions and are not sure that they (or others) are capable of devising a better system. They believe in elitism.

Finally, the position of classical **reactionary ideology** corresponds to that of the radical, only on the right end of the spectrum. The reactionary position proposes radical change backward—that is, "retrogressive change" favoring "a policy that would return the society to a previous condition or even a former value system."[52]

It is important to note before we leave our discussion of the left-right spectrum that it is very much a relative scale. Someone who is a "radical liberal" may view a "moderate liberal" as "ultraconservative." Indeed, in a classic study Louis Hartz essentially suggested that *all* American politics is "liberal" politics: "There has never been a 'liberal movement' or a real 'liberal party' in America: we have only had the American Way of Life, a nationalist articulation of Locke which usually does not know that Locke himself is involved."[53]

Thus, while the American "left" is part of the "classical liberal" tradition, so too is the American "right," which Hartz suggests "exemplifies the tradition of big propertied liberalism in Europe."[54] America's entire "left-right" scale may be seen as existing within a very small range of the "traditional left-right" scale, as illustrated in Figure 2.3.

What is a radical today may be moderate tomorrow; what is radical in one society may not be radical in another. To take one example, it

Figure 2.3   US Ideology on the Liberal-Conservative Spectrum

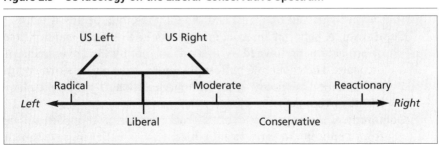

was not long ago—relatively speaking—that talk of a social security system in the United States in which government became involved in retirement pensions was perceived as a radical socialist proposal, completely unthinkable. Yet in 2018 few in American society seriously advocate doing away with social security; individuals may propose changing the way the system works, but most would not do away with the system completely. Another example could be found in proposals for socialized medical care. Socialized medicine may be seen by some today as a radical policy proposal in the United States—although clearly less so than it was fifty years ago—but such may not always be the case. Socialized medicine is not seen as radical in virtually all industrialized countries outside of the United States and has been incorporated in most advanced industrialized nations as part of the public sector.

Classification of Regimes

Care should be taken to avoid confusing ideologies—philosophies or values of political regimes—with the constitutional bases of regimes. The former concept asks the question "What does the regime stand for and what does it want to accomplish?" The latter asks the question "Who governs, and how is power distributed in the political system?" As a general rule, "isms" refer to ideology—the principles of what regimes stand for—while the suffix "-ocracy" refers to governance, how governments operate or behave.[55] Calling the contemporary government of the Islamic Republic of Iran a "theocracy" tells us that its constitution is based upon religious precepts; it does not tell us about the values of the regime (other than those of Islam).

Apart from the "isms" that we have already met that are related to the classical liberal-conservative spectrum (that is, radicalism, liberalism, conservatism, reactionism), there are many other "isms." Some of them are related to purely ideological considerations; others are related to economic arguments. Among these "isms" could be included the following:

Anarchism. A belief that all forms of government interfere with individual rights and freedoms and should, therefore, be abolished.[56]

Capitalism. A belief in an economic system in which the major means of production are owned by individuals, not by the government of the state. The economic philosophy emphasizes private ownership and a market economy—that is, nonregulation of the marketplace by the government.[57]

Communism. A theory that evolved from Marxism with modifications from Lenin in the early twentieth century. A belief in government ownership of the major means of production, and of the general "primacy of politics over economics,"[58] that the government should actively regulate and control all sectors of the economy with little or no private property.[59]

Corporatism. A belief that advocates a close degree of cooperation and coordination between the government and labor and business groups in the formation of economic policy.[60]

Fascism. A belief that includes national socialism, which usually is said to include seven components: "irrationalism, Social Darwinism, Nationalism, glorification of the state, the leadership principle, racism (more important in national socialism than in fascism), and anticommunism."[61]

Feminism. A system of beliefs that has emerged primarily in the West in opposition to oppression of women, and opposition to sexism in general. Has developed different schools including liberal or reform feminism, Marxist feminism, socialist feminism, and radical feminism.[62]

Marxism. A complex framework describing the economic system and the inevitable conflict between the working class and the owners of the means of production. Suggested the inevitability of class conflict, and was adopted and modified by Lenin to create Soviet communism.[63]

Nationalism. Includes identification with a national group and support for actions that will support and benefit the national group. This may or may not correspond to borders of a particular state as defined in Chapter 1.[64]

Socialism. An ideology that developed out of the industrial revolution advocating governmental concern with individuals' quality of life, including education, medical care, and standard of living. May be found in democratic versions—as in Great Britain or Sweden—or in authoritarian versions—as in Nazi ("Nazi" was short for "national socialist) Germany or fascist Italy.[65]

Totalitarianism. A system in which the government controls individual political behavior and political thought. This is distinguished from authoritarianism by its degree: the focus of authoritarian rule is individual behavior that affects the stability of the regime; the focus of totalitarian rule is virtually total.[66]

This brief introduction to some ideological frameworks is intended to demonstrate the range of approaches to politics and ideas that are available to the student. We shall see applied versions of many of these issues later in this volume as we examine specific problem areas or specific political systems.

Constitutions, Ideologies, and Classification

Aristotle provided us with terms that are still used today to discuss both "good" government and "bad" government. Good government included the polity (rule by many in the general interest), the aristocracy (rule by a few in the general interest), and kingship (rule by one in the general interest). Bad government included tyranny (self-interest rule by one), the oligarchy (self-interest rule by a few), and democracy (self-interest rule by many). Aristotle provided the "classical" division of systems of government, based upon two dimensions: the number of rulers in a system, and in whose interest the rulers rule. This framework is summarized in Table 2.1.

While knowledge of the constitutional structure of a regime and its ideology does not tell us everything that is important to know about that system, it tells us a great deal. It gives us an indication of the type of public policy that we can expect to see in that setting, and how that public policy is likely to be enacted. It also indicates the range and amount of political behavior that we are likely to encounter. It is a good beginning. Before we turn our attention to more of the constitutional/political structures of the regime, however, it is important to examine the environment within which the institutions of the regime operate. It is to this task that we turn our attention in the next chapter.

Table 2.1   The Aristotelian Classification of Regimes

Number of Rulers	Rule in General Interest ("Right" Type)	Selfish-Rule Rulers ("Wrong" Type)
One	Kingship	Tyranny
Few	Aristocracy	Oligarchy
Many	Polity	Democracy

Discussion Questions

1. What is a constitution? How do constitutions differ from other important political documents?
2. What are the key differences between written and unwritten constitutions? Give an example of each, and show what the effect of having a written or an unwritten constitution is in the political behavior of that system.
3. What functions do constitutions perform for the political systems in which they are found?

4. What does the concept of separation of powers mean? What is separated? How do we know if true separation of powers exists? Give examples.
5. What are the differences between federal, confederal, and unitary governments? Give a contemporary example of each. What are the strengths of each? The weaknesses?
6. What do we mean by an ideology? Give several examples of significant ideologies, and explain how they differ from each other. Why are they important?
7. What was Aristotle's classification of political regimes? How does his framework compare with political categories today?

Notes

1. Ivo Duchacek, *Power Maps: Comparative Politics of Constitutions* (Santa Barbara: Clio, 1973). See also the recent work by Kaarlo Tuori and Suvi Sankari, *The Many Constitutions of Europe* (Burlington, VT: Ashgate, 2010).
2. See Dawn Oliver and Carlo Fusaro, *How Constitutions Change: A Comparative Study* (Oxford: Hart, 2011).
3. This is discussed in a very good book by Suzi Navot, *The Constitution of Israel: A Contextual Analysis* (Portland: Hart, 2014).
4. See Robert Sharlet, *Soviet Constitutional Crisis: From De-Stalinization to Disintegration* (New York: Routledge, 2015).
5. Robert Sharlet, *The New Soviet Constitution of 1977* (Brunswick, OH: King's Court Communications, 1978), p. 89.
6. Ibid., p. 92.
7. Ibid., p. 93.
8. This is a very important issue. See Michael Gilmore, *The War on Words: Slavery, Race, and Free Speech in American Literature* (Chicago: University of Chicago Press, 2010); and Thomas Healy, *The Great Dissent: How Oliver Wendell Holmes Changed His Mind—and Changed the History of Free Speech in America* (New York: Holt, 2013).
9. For discussion of this episode of US history, see Jeff Hay, *The Internment of Japanese Americans* (Detroit: Greenhaven, 2012); or Gordon K. Hirabayashi, James Hirabayashi, and Lane Hirabayashi, *A Principled Stand: The Story of* Hirabayashi v. United States (Seattle: University of Washington Press, 2013).
10. Two good examples of recent comparative study of constitutions are Jeffrey Goldsworthy, *Interpreting Constitutions: A Comparative Study* (Oxford: Oxford University Press, 2007); and Richard Allen Epstein, *The Classical Liberal Constitution: The Uncertain Quest for Limited Government* (Cambridge: Harvard University Press, 2014).
11. S. E. Finer, ed., *Five Constitutions* (Sussex: Harvester, 1979), p. 15.
12. Ibid.
13. The position of prime minister is mentioned in the Prime Minister's Residence Act—which established an official residence for the prime minister—and the Prime Minister's Salary Act—which authorizes the prime minister to receive a higher salary than other cabinet members—but the precise method of selection, powers, and similar important descriptions of the position are not included in constitutional documents. See Robert J. Jackson and Doreen Jackson, *Canadian Government and Politics in Transition* (Toronto: Prentice Hall Canada, 2016).
14. Richard Van Loon and Michael Whittington, *The Canadian Political System* (Toronto: McGraw-Hill Ryerson, 1976), pp. 169–170. See also Stephen Tierney, *Multi-

culturalism and the Canadian Constitution (Vancouver: University of British Columbia Press, 2007).

15. See, for example, Said Amir Arjomand and Nathan Brown, *The Rule of Law, Islam, and Constitutional Politics in Egypt and Iran* (Albany: State University of New York Press, 2013); and Amirhassan Boozari, *Shi'i Jurisprudence and Constitution: Revolution in Iran* (New York: Palgrave Macmillan, 2011).

16. Thomas D. McGee, *Notes on Federal Governments: Past and Present* (Montreal: Dawson Brothers, 1865).

17. Literature on the European Parliament is increasing in size. See, for example, *The European Parliament* (Luxembourg: Publications Office of the European Union, 2012). Two good books on unification are Stephen Wood and Wolfgang Quaisser, *The New European Union: Confronting the Challenges of Integration* (Boulder: Lynne Rienner, 2008); and John McCormick and Jonathan Olsen, *The European Union: Politics and Policies* (Boulder: Westview, 2013).

18. A very good study is that by Erwin Chemerinsky, *Enhancing Government: Federalism for the 21st Century* (Stanford: Stanford University Press, 2008). See also Michael Burgess, *Comparative Federalism: Theory and Practice* (New York: Routledge, 2006).

19. See Jonathan Klick, *The Law and Economics of Federalism* (Cheltenham: Elgar, 2017); Sean Nicholson-Crotty, *Governors, Grants, and Elections: Fiscal Federalism in the American States* (Baltimore: Johns Hopkins University Press, 2015); and Michael Doonan, *American Federalism in Practice: The Formulation and Implementation of Contemporary Health Policy* (Washington, DC: Brookings Institution, 2013).

20. Jennifer Smith, *Federalism* (Vancouver: University of British Columbia Press, 2014); and William Riker, *Federalism: Origin, Operation, Significance* (Boston: Little, Brown, 1964), p. 5. See also Nicholas Aroney, *The Constitution of a Federal Commonwealth: The Making and Meaning of the Australian Constitution* (New York: Cambridge University Press, 2009).

21. See Max Edling, *A Revolution in Favor of Government: Origins of the U.S. Constitution and the Making of the American State* (New York: Oxford University Press, 2003).

22. One indicator of the number of nations is the number of members of the United Nations. While there were 51 member states in 1945, there were 99 by 1960, 127 in 1970, 154 in 1980, 159 in 1990, 189 in 2000, and as of October 2017 the United Nations indicated that it had 193 members. See http://www.un.org/en/member-states/index.html.

23. Duchacek, *Power Maps,* p. 111.

24. Riker, *Federalism,* p. 1.

25. Arthur R. M. Lower, "Theories of Canadian Federalism—Yesterday and Today," in A. R. M. Lower, ed., *Evolving Canadian Federalism* (Durham, NC: Duke University Press, 1958), p. 3.

26. Ivo Duchacek, *Comparative Federalism: The Territorial Dimension of Politics* (New York: Holt, Rinehart, and Winston, 1970), p. 198.

27. Ibid.

28. See Willem Maas, *Multilevel Citizenship* (Philadelphia: University of Pennsylvania Press, 2013); and Ronald Watts, *New Federations: Experiments in the Commonwealth* (Oxford: Clarendon, 1966).

29. See Clive Church and Randolph Conrad Head, *A Concise History of Switzerland* (Cambridge: Cambridge University Press, 2013); or Ursula K. Hicks, *Federalism: Failure and Success* (New York: Oxford University Press, 1978), pp. 144–171.

30. Hicks, *Federalism.*

31. Duchacek, *Comparative Federalism,* p. 189; Charlie Jeffery, *Federalism* (New York: Routledge, 2014).

32. Duchacek, *Comparative Federalism,* p. 191. See also Michael Pagano and Robert Leonardi, *The Dynamics of Federalism in National and Supranational Political Systems* (New York: Palgrave Macmillan, 2007).

33. Riker, *Federalism,* p. 6.

34. See Roland Sturm, Charlie Jeffery, and Arthur Benz, *Federalism, Unification, and European Integration* (New York: Routledge, 2013); and Daniel Halberstam and

Mathias Reimann, *Federalism and Legal Unification: A Comparative Empirical Investigation of Twenty Systems* (Dordrecht: Springer, 2014).

35. See Lori Riverstone-Newell, *Renegade Cities, Public Policy, and the Dilemmas of Federalism* (Boulder: Lynne Rienner, 2014); or Jordi Diez and Susan Franceschet, *Comparative Public Policy in Latin America* (Toronto: University of Toronto Press, 2012). Two recent studies of this problem in Canada are Ian Peach, *Constructing Tomorrow's Federalism: New Perspectives on Canadian Governance* (Winnipeg: University of Manitoba Press, 2007); and Garth Stevenson, *Unfulfilled Union: Canadian Federalism and National Unity* (Montreal: McGill-Queen's University Press, 2004).

36. One of the best studies of this is by Richard Simeon, *Federal-Provincial Diplomacy: The Making of Recent Policy in Canada* (Toronto: University of Toronto Press, 2006). Simeon discusses pensions, financial reform, and constitutional amendment as three case studies. See also Donald Doernberg and Keith Wingate, *Federal Courts, Federalism, and Separation of Powers: Cases and Materials* (St. Paul, MN: Thomson/West, 2008).

37. See especially Paul Spurlin, *Montesquieu in America: 1760–1801* (Baton Rouge: Louisiana State University Press, 1940); and Clinton Rossiter, *1787: The Grand Convention* (New York: Macmillan, 1966). Two good studies are Roger Masterman, *The Separation of Powers in the Contemporary Constitution: Judicial Competence and Independence in the United Kingdom* (New York: Cambridge University Press, 2010); and Christoph Mollers, *The Three Branches: A Comparative Model of Separation of Powers* (Oxford: Oxford University Press, 2013).

38. See John Locke, *Second Treatise on Civil Government* (especially chap. 13, "Of the Subordination of the Powers of the Commonwealth," pp. 87–94), in Ernest Baker, *Social Contract: Essays by Locke, Hume and Rousseau* (New York: Oxford University Press, 1970). See also Maxwell Cameron, *Strong Constitutions: Social-Cognitive Origins of the Separation of Powers* (New York: Oxford University Press, 2013); and Charles Manga Fombad, *Separation of Powers in African Constitutionalism* (Oxford: Oxford University Press, 2016).

39. See David Easton, *A Systems Analysis of Political Life* (New York: Wiley, 1965), p. 32.

40. Duchacek, *Power Maps,* p. 236.

41. Leon Baradat, *Political Ideologies: Their Origins and Impact* (Englewood Cliffs, NJ: Prentice Hall, 2009), p. 6. See also H. B. McCullough, *Political Ideologies* (Don Mills, Ontario: Oxford University Press, 2017).

42. Howard Williams, *Concepts of Ideology* (New York: St. Martin's, 1988), p. xi. See also Amy Wendling, *The Ruling Ideas: Bourgeois Political Concepts* (Lanham: Lexington, 2012).

43. Roy C. Macridis, *Contemporary Political Ideologies* (Cambridge, MA: Winthrop, 1980), pp. 3–4.

44. Williams, *Concepts of Ideology,* p. 122.

45. Baradat, *Political Ideologies,* p. 20.

46. Very good studies of comparative political ideology are István Mészáros, *The Power of Ideology* (New York: Palgrave Macmillan, 2005); and Terence Ball and Richard Dagger, *Political Ideologies and the Democratic Ideal* (New York: Pearson, 2009). An applied example is Majid Mohammadi, *Political Islam in Post-Revolutionary Iran: Shi'i Ideologies in Islamist Discourse* (New York: Tauris, 2015).

47. Michael Curtis, *Comparative Government and Politics* (New York: Harper and Row, 1978), p. 41. See also Alan Ryan, *The Making of Modern Liberalism* (Princeton: Princeton University Press, 2012).

48. Curtis, *Comparative Government and Politics,* p. 158. See also William Safran, *The French Polity* (New York: Routledge, 2016).

49. This discussion of the left-right spectrum and the five general attitudes to be found on it is based upon much more extensive discussion in Baradat, *Political Ideologies,* pp. 27–40.

50. Ibid., p. 30.

51. Ibid., p. 35.

52. Ibid., p. 39.

53. Louis Hartz, *The Liberal Tradition in America: An Interpretation of American Political Thought Since the Revolution* (New York: Harcourt, Brace, 1955), p. 11.

54. Ibid., p. 15. See also Byron Shafer and Richard Spady, *The American Political Landscape* (Cambridge: Harvard University Press, 2014); and Andrew Levine, *The American Ideology: A Critique* (New York: Routledge, 2016).

55. See Alan Ebenstein, William Ebenstein, and Edwin Fogelman, *Today's ISMs: Socialism, Capitalism, Fascism, Communism, Libertarianism* (Upper Saddle River, NJ: Prentice Hall, 2000); or Arthur Goldwag, *Isms and Ologies: All the Movements, Ideologies, and Doctrines That Have Shaped Our World* (New York: Vintage, 2007).

56. See Paul McLaughlin, *Anarchism and Authority: A Philosophical Introduction to Classical Anarchism* (Burlington, VT: Ashgate, 2007); or George Woodcock, *Anarchism* (Toronto: University of Toronto Press, 2015).

57. See Paul Bowles, *Capitalism* (Hoboken, NJ: Taylor and Francis, 2013); or Nelson Lichtenstein, *American Capitalism: Social Thought and Political Economy in the Twentieth Century* (Philadelphia: University of Pennsylvania Press, 2006).

58. William Ebenstein, *Today's ISMs: Communism, Fascism, Capitalism, Socialism* (Englewood Cliffs, NJ: Prentice Hall, 1970), p. 31.

59. For a recent discussion of modern communism, see Mark Sandle, *Communism* (New York: Routledge, 2014); or Vladimir Tismaneanu, *The Devil in History: Communism, Fascism, and Some Lessons of the Twentieth Century* (Berkeley: University of California Press, 2012).

60. See Debra Chapman, *The Struggle for Mexico: State Corporatism and Popular Opposition* (Jefferson, NC: McFarland, 2012); or Eva Hartmann and Poul Kjaer, *The Evolution of Intermediary Institutions in Europe: From Corporatism to Governance* (New York: Palgrave Macmillan, 2015).

61. Lyman Tower Sargent, *Contemporary Political Ideologies: A Comparative Analysis* (Chicago: Dorsey, 1987), p. 162. See also Madeleine Albright, *Fascism* (New York: HarperCollins, 2018); and Stefan Jonsson, *Crowds and Democracy: The Idea and Image of the Masses from Revolution to Fascism* (New York: Columbia University Press, 2013).

62. See Shamillah Wilson and Anasuya Sengupta, *Defending Our Dreams: Global Feminist Voices for a New Generation* (New York: Palgrave Macmillan, 2005); or June Hannam, *Feminism* (New York: Pearson/Longman, 2007).

63. For examples of this literature, see Geoff Boucher, *Understanding Marxism* (London: Routledge, 2014); or Colin Barker, *Marxism and Social Movements* (Leiden: Brill, 2013).

64. See Philip Roeder, *Where Nation-States Come From: Institutional Change in the Age of Nationalism* (Princeton: Princeton University Press, 2007); or Ben Wellings, *English Nationalism and Euroscepticism: Losing the Peace* (New York: Lang, 2012); or Glenda Sluga, *Internationalism in the Age of Nationalism* (Philadelphia: University of Pennsylvania Press, 2013).

65. See Roger Burback, Michael Fox, Federico Fuentes, *Latin America's Turbulent Transitions: The Future of Twenty-First-Century Socialism* (London: Zed, 2013); or Anatole Anton and Richard Schmitt, *Taking Socialism Seriously* (Lanham: Lexington, 2012); or Nina Bandelj and Dorothy Solinger, *Socialism Vanquished, Socialism Challenged: Eastern Europe and China, 1989–2009* (New York: Oxford University Press, 2012).

66. The "classic" in this area is Carl Friedrich, *Totalitarianism in Perspective* (New York: Praeger, 1969). See also Hannah Arendt, *The Origins of Totalitarianism* (New York: Schocken Books, 2004); and A. James Gregor, *Totalitarianism and Political Religion: An Intellectual History* (Stanford: Stanford University Press, 2012).

3

Legislatures

Learning Outcomes

After reading this chapter, you will be able to

- Describe legislatures as one of the three key branches of government as described by John Locke.
- Understand the importance of legislatures to their political systems.
- Distinguish between unicameral and bicameral variations of legislatures, and why they are that way.
- Appreciate the power relationship between two houses in a bicameral system.
- Explain the relationship of federalism to bicameralism.
- Perceive the functions of political parties in legislatures.
- Articulate how legislators are selected—the single-member-district model and the proportional representation model, as well as some less common variations.
- See what legislatures do and the functions they perform for their political systems.
- Explain the accuracy of representation in legislatures for minority groups.
- Depict the role of legislative committees.
- Highlight the legislative process.
- Evaluate many of the issues related to legislative-executive relations.

In this chapter we turn our attention to one of the three governmental structures that were identified in the late seventeenth century by John Locke as key to the creation of a stable political system, the legislature. We will turn to a discussion of executives and courts and judicial structures in the next two chapters. We examine legislatures and executives before we examine courts because they are—to varying extents—interrelated. Indeed, in the parliamentary model of government the executive *comes from* the legislature. In the presidential model of government, although the two branches are nominally separate, they interact in very important ways requiring an understanding of both sets of functions if one is to understand the operation of politics.

In 1690 John Locke published his *Second Treatise on Government,* in which he discussed the "true original, extent, and end of civil government." In his discussion of why individuals would leave the "state of nature" and join society, Locke suggested that the prime motivation for people doing such a thing was the preservation of "their lives, liberty, and estates, which I call by the general name, property."[1] (This phrase was subsequently amended by Thomas Jefferson in the Declaration of Independence to read "life, liberty, and the pursuit of happiness.")

There are "many things wanting" in the state of nature, Locke suggested, and it was these missing structures that would prompt individuals to join society:

> (Section 124) First, there wants an established, settled, known law. . . .
> (Section 125) Secondly, In the state of nature there wants a known and indifferent judge, with authority to determine all differences according to the established law. . . .
> (Section 126) Thirdly, In the state of nature there often wants power to back and support the sentence when right. . . .
> (Section 127) Thus mankind notwithstanding all the privileges of the state of nature, being but in an ill condition while they remain in it, are quickly driven into society. . . . And in this we have the original right and rise of both the legislature and executive power as well as of the governments and societies themselves.[2]

Legislatures are popular subjects of analysis by political scientists.[3] Among other reasons for this phenomenon is that legislatures are usually important structures in their governmental systems.[4] In addition, legislatures are among the oldest political institutions. Although the functions of legislatures within their political systems have varied, and vary today on a country-by-country basis,[5] they are universally regarded as significant institutions.[6]

It has been suggested that legislatures may be more important in some contexts than in others, much as has been suggested in relation to constitutions. One example of this can be seen in the central role parliaments play in promoting regime stability,[7] or their effectiveness—or lack of it—in developing nations or in the process of modernization.[8] Although legislatures may have more direct impact upon some subjects or processes (such as regularizing group interaction in society)[9] than others (such as land reform), it is not difficult to imagine ways in which legislatures can affect wide areas of human concern.

One House or Two?

One of the initial characteristics of the legislative institution that we note when we look at a given legislature is whether it is a **unicameral legislature** or a **bicameral legislature**—whether it has one or two houses.[10] The number of unicameral and bicameral legislatures around the world is about even,[11] but the distribution of unicameral and bicameral legislatures around the world is not random: bicameral legislatures are more prevalent in some areas than in others, as Table 3.1 indicates.

If we want to explain why some nations have bicameral legislatures while others have unicameral legislatures, we must be careful about making broad generalizations. Why are some legislatures bicameral while others are unicameral? What do the second chambers do, where they exist? Before we can answer these questions, we must introduce a very important distinction in conceptual terms. This is the distinction between that which exists by legal establishment, by law, and that which exists by actual fact, although perhaps not by legal establishment. We refer to the former situation—establishment in law—as a de jure case, and to the latter situation—establishment in fact—as a de facto case.

In a number of instances we will see political structures that simply are not the same in fact as they are in law. We will see, for example, that de jure (in law), the **upper house of a legislature** may have the power to delay or veto a bill passed by the **lower house of a legislature**. How-

---

Table 3.1 Houses in Legislatures

	Unicameral		Bicameral	
Region (number)	Number	Percentage	Number	Percentage
Africa (54)	32	59.2	22	40.7
Americas (35)	15	42.8	20	57.1
Asia (41)	25	61.0	16	39.0
Europe (48)	31	64.6	17	35.4
Pacific (15)	13	86.7	2	13.3
Total (193)	116	60.1	77	39.8

Source: Inter-Parliamentary Union, "Parline Database," http://archive.ipu.org/parline-e /ParliamentsStructure.asp?LANG=ENG&REGION_SUB_REGION=All&Submit1=Launch +query.

ever, although the power may exist de jure, it may not exist de facto; that upper house may not have used its power of veto in over 200 years, and in the real world, de facto, no matter what the law says it *may* do, custom and tradition in fact prohibit the upper house from exercising what may be its legitimate legal power. In many cases, the de facto rule of custom and tradition is stronger than any de jure rule.

Countries that are small in size are more likely to have one chamber than two, because "the problem of the balance of political power is less difficult to solve in them than it is in big countries."[12] Bicameral systems are often regarded in socialist countries as leading to complications and delays, and as contributing few advantages to offset these costs. With the exception of Norway, all of the Scandinavian countries have, in the twentieth century, replaced bicameral systems with unicameral ones.

According to a study undertaken by the Inter-Parliamentary Union, the earliest example of a bicameral system occurred in England toward the end of the thirteenth century:

> It began with the institution of a Chamber for the high aristocracy and brought together the feudal magnates, the Lords Spiritual and Temporal. This arrangement has been maintained to the present day, although the aristocratic characteristic of the House of Lords has been reduced by the appointment to it of Life Peers. [Appointments good only for the life of the holder that cannot be passed from one generation to another, as could traditional Peerage.] Furthermore, the power of the House of Lords has been greatly restricted in favour of the popular House, the House of Commons.[13]

Bicameral systems are justified primarily by two arguments. First, in federal states (as we shall develop shortly) bicameralism reflects the split-government nature of the state. Second, in unitary states, bicameralism provides a "revising" chamber for legislation.[14]

The American "Great Compromise" in Philadelphia in 1787 is one example of the development of a bicameral legislature. The large states wanted representation based upon population, while the small states wanted representation based upon equal representation for the member units (that is, an equal number of representatives per state). The Great Compromise meant that there would be a bicameral legislature, with one house based on population and the other based on an equal number of representatives for each state.[15]

Where we find federal states we will almost always find a bicameral legislature in which the lower house represents the national, popular jurisdiction, while the upper house represents the intermediate political structures or territories.[16] The United States, Mexico, and Germany are all examples of federal states with bicameral legislatures in which the lower houses are national and the upper houses are regional.[17]

Although federal regimes are typically bicameral, not all bicameral systems are federal. There are other reasons for bicameral structure besides federal status. A nation might adopt a bicameral legislative structure because that is the structure that its colonial "parent" had, and because it simply seemed the most normal alternative after independence was achieved. (See Table 3.2.)

The fact that virtually all federal systems are bicameral but not all bicameral systems are federal is illustrated in Table 3.3. We can see in this table that federal systems are in a clear minority and that unicameral and bicameral systems are just about evenly divided.

The representational bases of upper chambers vary. They may represent territorial units. (In Canada the provinces of Ontario and Quebec each receive twenty-four senators, while all of the four western provinces together receive twenty-four senators, and all of the maritime provinces together receive twenty-four senators, excluding Newfoundland, which joined the confederation last and, therefore, received six senators of its own. The three northern territories each have an additional senator.) Upper houses may provide equal representation for member units of a federation (for example, two senators each for US states) or weighted representation for member units of a federation (for example, in Germany, some Lander have three deputies in the Bundesrat, some have four, some have five, and some have six, depending upon their size). Upper houses may simply provide an extra house in the legislature for a "sober second

Table 3.2   Some Bicameral Systems

Nation	Lower House	Represents	Upper House	Represents
United States	House of Representatives	Districts (people)	Senate	States
Canada	House of Commons	Districts (people)	Senate	Regions
India	Lok Sabha	Districts (people)	Rajya Sabha	States
Australia	House of Representatives	Districts (people)	Senate	States
Bahamas	House of Commons	Districts (people)	Senate	Appointed
Britain	House of Commons	Districts (people)	House of Lords	Appointed

Table 3.3   Systems and Houses

Area	Number Unicameral	Number Bicameral
Unitary		
Atlantic area	7	9
East Europe and North Asia	10	—
Middle East and North Africa	6	4
South and East Asia	8	7
Sub-Saharan Africa	16	8
Latin America	7	10
Total	54	38
Federal		
Atlantic area	—	6
East Europe and North Asia	—	3
Middle East and North Africa	—	—
South and East Asia	—	2
Sub-Saharan Africa	1	—
Latin America	—	3
Total	1	14
Total	55	52

Source: Jean Blondel, *Comparative Legislatures* (Englewood Cliffs, NJ: Prentice Hall, 1973), pp. 144–153.

thought" on legislation, a house that is elected in the same manner as the lower house. Finally, they may provide several jurisdictions at once; the upper house in Japan represents both local and national units, and the British House of Lords represents hereditary positions, new political positions, judicial positions, and ecclesiastical positions.[18]

The terms *upper* and *lower* as adjectives for legislative houses are strictly a product of convention. The terms date from early in British parliamentary history, when the House of Lords was felt to be superior to the House of Commons, even though (perhaps because) it was not elected by the people. It was felt that the aristocratic nature of the House of Lords, the fact that it was *not* chosen by the public, made it the superior, or "upper" house. Today, we use the term *lower* to describe that house in a bicameral system (most) directly elected by the people, and the term *upper* to describe that house further from direct public control, although today many upper houses are elected directly by the public as well.

Where we find a unicameral legislature, whatever power may reside in the legislature in that particular system resides in the single house. In bicameral settings the situation is not so simple. We may find instances in which the two houses act as equal partners in a cooperative venture; or the two houses have equal powers but are constantly feuding so that little is ever accomplished; or power is not balanced, and one house dominates the other.

When we speak of a power relationship between any two actors, three possibilities appear. One can have more power than the other, the same power as the other, or less power than the other. The same options can be said to exist if these two actors are two houses of a national legislative body. Let us briefly examine each of these possibilities, where bicameral legislatures exist. Table 3.4 shows us the frequencies with which these alternatives exist in the world today.

The first relationship, in which the lower house is stronger than the upper house, is the most common relationship today. Because many second chambers are not elected by the public, but are either appointed or hereditary bodies, many theorists argue that in principle upper houses *should* be weaker than lower houses; they are in essence "undemocratic" institutions.

It must be noted, however, that many of the settings described in Table 3.4, in which upper houses are indicated as being legally equal to the lower houses, do not practice this relationship. For example, although the Canadian Senate is in most respects legally equal to the House of Commons and must approve all bills before they become laws, it has been described as having "retained a full set of legislative muscles, but consistently has refused to make real use of them,"[19] and should not be considered as the de facto equal of the House of Commons.

In other legislatures, the upper house is both legally and behaviorally an equal partner in the legislative process (although even if it is equal it may not have identical powers). Certainly among the best examples of this type of relationship is the case of the US Senate.

Table 3.4 Powers of Second Chambers

Category	Number of Countries
Upper house weaker than lower house	26
Upper house equal to lower house	22
Upper house stronger than lower house	0
Upper house only advisory	1
No upper house	58

Source: Jean Blondel, *Comparative Legislatures* (Englewood Cliffs, NJ: Prentice Hall, 1973), pp. 144–153.

Although the Senate is legally prohibited from certain legislative acts (under the Constitution, for example, it cannot introduce tax bills), overall it is an equal partner in the legislative process. A bill cannot become a law without the Senate's approval. Similar situations, de jure and de facto, may be found in Italy, Switzerland, Liberia, Mexico, and Jordan.

Although we might find a legislature in which the upper house is actually stronger than the lower house, in practice this is not common today. In some cases people might argue that the US Senate is stronger and more important than the US House of Representatives. The focus of attention, however, must be the question "Can the Senate pass laws without the approval of the House?" The answer is clearly no. There are no contemporary cases in which the power relationship is dominated by the upper house (although remember that if we go back far enough in history, at one time the House of Lords dominated the House of Commons in Great Britain, for example).[20]

Finally, there are a few variable cases. Germany is a good example of this. When legislation affects the Lander, or states, the upper house has an **absolute veto** over legislation. Members of the upper house, the Bundesrat, are not elected by the public but are chosen by the governments of the states. If a bill that will affect the states (such as transportation policy) is not approved by a majority of the representatives of the states in the upper house, it cannot become law. When legislation does not affect the states, such as foreign policy, the negative vote of the upper house may be overridden by the lower house.

Some upper houses, then, can be seen to have an absolute veto in the legislative process (for example, the US Senate), in which their refusal to approve legislation results in failure of the legislation in question. Other upper houses can be said to have a **suspensory veto**; their refusal to approve legislation is only guaranteed to slow the legislative process down a bit. Subsequent re-passage by the lower house either with a regular majority (as in Great Britain) or a special majority (as in Germany) can create laws without the approval of the upper house. Still other upper houses may be said to have **rubber stamp power**—formal approval—only.

While legislatures vary in terms of the number of houses they have, they also vary in terms of the number of members they have. Legislatures range in size from lows of 16 in the Caribbean island-nation of St. Vincent, and 24 in Barbados, to highs of about 3,000 in China.[21]

Size of a legislative body may be determined by a number of factors, some philosophical and intentional, others accidental. Some legislative bodies continue to grow until it is clear that there simply is no room for them to grow more, and their size (number of members) is then frozen. The US House of Representatives is a good example of this. The representative-to-population ratio was one for every 30,000 people in 1787; by 1970 it was approximately one for every 500,000 people. The ratio has changed because the size of the House was frozen.

In 1787, there were 66 members in the House of Representatives; there were 242 in 1833. In 1921 a reapportionment based on the 1920 census would have pushed the size of the House to 483. The House decided at that time to keep its membership at 435, arguing that "the great size of the membership had already resulted in serious limitations on the right of debate and an overconcentration of power in the hands of the leadership."[22] It took eight years until this view was incorporated in law, but in 1929 a law was passed and signed by President Herbert Hoover establishing the maximum size of the House of Representatives at 435 members.

The size of a legislative body may also be symbolic. The size of the unicameral Israeli Knesset was determined by history: the Great Assembly—the first supreme legislative authority elected by the Jews in the fourth and fifth centuries B.C.E.—had 120 members, ten representatives for each of the twelve tribes of Israel. When the modern state of Israel was created in 1949, it was determined that the new national assembly should also have 120 members.[23]

Political Parties in Legislatures

One of the legislative structures about which we *can* generalize is the political party. Parties are, as a general rule, highly significant structures in legislative systems, in terms of both their organizational influence and their influence over legislative behavior.[24]

Parties provide the basis around which organization of legislatures takes place.[25] In this context the concept of **party discipline** is central; it relates to the cohesion of the body of party members within the legislature. In a legislature with high party discipline, we expect legislators to act (and this includes voting, making speeches, introducing bills, or other possible activities) in concert with their party leader's directions.[26] In legislatures with low party discipline, the concept of party label is less significant in its usefulness in helping us to predict legislative behavior; individuals will act as they see fit, with little regard for directions from party leaders.

Two examples can illustrate the idea of party discipline. In the British House of Commons, party discipline is strong. Members invariably vote as their leaders tell them to.[27] We would expect all members of the majority Conservative Party to vote as a bloc, all the time. Any member who votes against his or her party may be subject to party sanctions, including withdrawal of campaign funds, being given poor committee assignments in the legislature (or no assignment at all, for that matter), and the like.[28] On occasion "free votes" take place in the House of Commons, during which the member of parliament (MP) may vote as he or she wants. This, however, is the only time the MP is expected to follow his or her own will in voting.

The United States offers a good example of a legislature with considerably weaker party discipline. This is not to say that there is *no* party discipline in the Congress, for as a general rule, if we know legislators' party identifications, and if we know the position of the party leaders on a bill, we will be correct more often than we will be incorrect in predicting how legislators will behave. However, it is not at all uncommon to find a group of southern Democrats voting with Republicans, or a group of liberal Republicans voting with Democrats.

How Legislators Are Selected

There are a number of different "pathways to parliament."[29] Some legislators, of course, are not elected by the public at all but are appointed by some individual or political body. Others are elected. Here we want to examine how elected legislators come to play their roles.[30]

There are two major methods by which the public elects legislators (see Box 3.1). One method we can refer to as district-based elections; the other method can be called proportional representation elections. Each of these methods affects the political system in which it is found.[31] There are a number of variations for each of these general methods (which vary on a country-by-country basis, as we shall see later), but the broad principles are the same.

Single-Member-District Voting

Among the most common forms of district-based representation is the system that is referred to as a **single-member-district plurality voting system**. In this kind of system, the entire nation is divided into a number of electoral districts. Each district corresponds to a seat in the legislative house. Within each district, a contest is held to determine the representative for that district, with the individual receiving the most votes (a **plurality**) being elected. Usually all of the districts in the nation hold their elections on the same day, although special elections may be held to replace a representative who has resigned or died.

The single-member-district plurality system, which exists in the United States, Canada, Great Britain, Mexico, Russia, and many other nations, does not require that any of the candidates win a majority of the vote in their districts. (A majority is defined as one vote more than 50 percent of the total votes cast.) All that is required for an individual to win

---

Box 3.1   Methods of Selection for Legislatures

1. Direct election by public.
   (a) District-based elections, either single-member-district or multiple-member-district (this tends to produce a two-party system and a one-party majority government).
   (b) Proportional representation elections (this tends to produce a multi-party system and minority or coalition government).
2. Appointment by head of state.
3. Indirect election by electoral college, convention, local notables, and the like.

---

is that he or she wins more than anyone else (a plurality); this is why it is sometimes called a "first past the post" system. So, in a contest with four candidates, it would be possible for someone to be elected with only 32 percent of the vote, if the other three candidates each received less.

Like other political structures we might examine, the single-member-district system has both advantages and disadvantages. An advantage is that representatives have specific districts that are "theirs" to represent, and people know who "their" representatives are. A disadvantage is that this system over-represents majorities, hides minorities, and promotes a two-party system at the expense of third and minor parties. Three examples will help to make this clear.

First, let us take four imaginary electoral districts, each with 100 voters, shown in Table 3.5. Suppose that in each of these districts, in which there are two political parties, Party A wins 51 votes and Party B wins 49 votes. When we total up the results in the four districts, Party A will have won 204 votes to 196 for Party B, a 51 to 49 percent margin; but Party A will have won four seats in the legislature to zero seats for

---

Table 3.5   A Two-Party Single-Member-District System

District	Party A	Party B	Total
District 1	51	49	100
District 2	51	49	100
District 3	51	49	100
District 4	51	49	100
Total votes	204	196	400
Total seats	4	0	4

Party B, with a very slight majority in popular votes turning into a huge majority in legislative seats. In short, the votes for Party B are unrepresented or hidden. This is an extreme example, yet the principles it demonstrates are not uncommon.

The second example, shown in Table 3.6, illustrates how in a multiparty system (here three parties, but the principle would apply to four or more parties) a very small margin—in this case bare pluralities in place of bare majorities—in a number of districts can make a party appear very strong, when in fact that is not the case. Here, although the plurality party wins only 34 percent of the popular vote, that 34 percent will yield 100 percent of the seats in the legislature.

The third example, illustrated in Table 3.7, uses the same setting as Table 3.6: four districts of 100 voters, and three parties. We can see that in the most mathematically extreme case a shift of only two votes (or half a percent in this case) from Party A to Party B results in Party B winning two seats—that is, 50 percent—in the legislature where it previously had none. In other words, a shift in popular support of as little as half a percent of the popular vote has the potential to change the composition of the legislature by 50 percent. Party C is still shut out of the legislature, despite the fact that it received 33 percent of the vote, one vote out of three, and only half a percent less than either Party A or Party B. Clearly this is the most extreme example we could design in a 100-person district, but the principles it illustrates would apply just as forcefully in an electoral district with 100,000 voters.

Although these examples are simpler than the reality of electoral politics, the patterns of bias that they demonstrate are real. In the British general election of June 2017, to take the most recent election, the Labour Party won 40.0 percent of the popular vote, and received 40.3 percent of the seats in the House of Commons, a bonus of just 0.3 percent. Yet the Scottish National Party received 3 percent of the vote and

Table 3.6   A Three-Party Single-Member-District System

District	Party A	Party B	Party C	Total
District 1	34	33	33	100
District 2	34	33	33	100
District 3	34	33	33	100
District 4	34	33	33	100
Total votes	136	132	132	400
Total seats	4	0	0	4

Table 3.7   A Second Three-Party Single-Member-District System

District	Party A	Party B	Party C	Total
District 1	34	33	33	100
District 2	34	33	33	100
District 3	33	34	33	100
District 4	33	34	33	100
Total votes	134	134	132	400
Total seats	2	2	0	4

received 5.4 percent of the seats. The Conservative Party received 42.3 percent of the popular vote and received 48.8 percent of the seats in the House of Commons, a bonus of 5.5 percent. The bias most severely affected the smaller parties, however, as demonstrated in Table 3.8. The Liberal Democratic Party received 1.8 percent of the seats in the House of Commons in exchange for 7.4 percent of the votes (5.6 percent less than it "should" have received). The "earned less received" losses to many of the very small parties (and there were many other parties that didn't even win a single seat) were not as great as they were for the Liberal Democrats because, as noted earlier, many of the other small parties

Table 3.8   The British General Election, June 2017

Party	Percentage Votes Won	Number of Seats Won	Percentage Seats Won
Conservative Party	42.3	317	48.8
Labour Party	40.0	262	40.3
Scottish National Party	3.0	35	5.4
Liberal Democrats	7.4	12	1.8
Democratic Unionist Party			
Sinn Fein			
Plaid Cymru			
Social Democratic and Labour Party	7.3	24	3.7
Green Party of England and Wales			
Alliance Party of Northern Ireland			
Other			
Total	100	650	100

Source: Inter-Parliamentary Union, "Parline Database," http://archive.ipu.org/parline-e/reports /2335_E.htm.

were regionally concentrated (for example, the Scottish Nationalists, Sinn Fein, or Plaid Cymru), and *where they ran candidates* they won significantly more frequently than did the Liberal Democrats.

The problem with the single-member-district plurality system is that if a party can't get more votes than any of the other parties in a district, it might as well not run there, because it will get no representation at all, illustrated by the British Liberal Democrats. This happened because, although they could count on some votes from many districts, in most districts they did not have more votes than their competitors, and so they ended up with no representation. One by-product of the single-member-district system is a two-party system, because generally speaking it is extremely hard for third parties to win seats in single-member-district systems, so two major parties tend to dominate the political landscape.[32]

Proportional Representation Voting

An alternative to the single-member-district system is called the **proportional representation voting system**. The proportional representation system is not based upon districts. Rather, the members of the electorate vote for the single party they prefer, not for candidates. The proportion of votes that a party receives in the election (for example, 23 percent of the total votes cast) determines the proportion of seats it will receive in the legislature (in this example, 23 percent of the legislative seats).

An example may help to clarify this. The Israeli system for electing the legislature has a "pure" proportional representation electoral framework. Voters cast their ballots for the political party they support. After the election, if the Labour Party has received 25 percent of the votes, it receives 25 percent of the 120 seats (that is, 30 seats) in the Israeli parliament, the Knesset.

How are the individual winners determined? Prior to the election, parties deposit lists of their candidates with a national election board, and these lists are made public. The parties may submit lists of 120 names—one for each possible seat in the Knesset (even though they can be sure that they will not win 100 percent of the vote). After the election, if Labour has won 30 seats (25 percent of 120 seats), it simply counts down the top 30 names on its electoral list: positions 1 through 30 are declared elected, positions 31 through 120 are not elected. This system has an added advantage, too: if a member of Knesset dies during the term, or if someone resigns, a special election is not necessary; the next name on the party list enters the Knesset.[33]

The proportional representation system, like the single-member-district system, has its advantages and disadvantages.[34] Its advantages center on the fact that it is highly representative. Parties in Israel need to win only

3.25 percent of the vote to win a seat in the legislature. This means that groups that are not pluralities can still be represented in the legislature. To take our example in Table 3.5, if all districts in a 100-seat legislature voted in the same 51 to 49 percent manner as the four districts we have drawn, in a proportional representation system Party A would receive 51 seats and Party B would receive 49 seats. In a comparable single-member-district system, Party A would receive 100 seats and Party B would receive none.

The disadvantage of the proportional representation system is that proportional representation legislatures tend to be multiparty legislatures—since it is easy for small parties to win seats—which means that they tend to be more unstable and to contain more groups than single-member-district, two-party legislatures. To use our example from Table 3.6, in a proportional representation system Party A would win 34 of 100 seats in the legislature, Party B would win 33 seats, and Party C would win 33 seats. This will require the formation of a coalition government, something to be discussed later, since no single party would control a majority of the legislative seats on its own. On the other hand, we might want to argue that this is not really a disadvantage at all—in fact, it is a real advantage, since groups that exist should be represented in the legislature.

Variations on Electoral Models

There are variations on both the single-member-district and proportional representation models. One variation on the single-member-district plurality system requires a majority for election. The single-member-district majority system invariably involves runoff elections, since, given the many political parties that might exist, few districts give a majority to a candidate on the first round of voting. Voting might be scheduled on two consecutive Sundays (we will see later that this is the case in France), with the top two vote-getters from the first round having a runoff election on the second Sunday. Generally, few districts would elect candidates on the first round (that is, have candidates that can win majority margins); the other 85 to 90 percent of the districts have runoff elections.

Another variation on the district-based model involves the number of representatives per district. A number of legislatures use a **multiple-member-district voting system**, in which the top vote-getters are elected. In elections for the lower house in Japan (the House of Representatives) prior to the mid-1990s when a new system was instituted, each district elected from three to five representatives, depending upon the size of the district. Voters voted for one candidate, and the top three vote-getters (or four, or five, depending upon the population living in the district) were elected. Japan utilized an even more complex multiple-member-district scheme for its upper house, the House of Councilors.

Some might argue that technically, US states fall into this multiple-member category, since each state is represented in the US Senate by two senators and is, therefore, not a single-member district but rather a multiple-member district. The method of selection of US senators is the single-member-district method rather than the multiple-member-district method, however, since election of senators is staggered, and only one senator is elected at a time.[35]

Legislative Functions

There is consensus in the discipline as to the structures and functions of legislatures, as well as their common attributes.[36] In general, five functions that legislatures perform for political systems may be sifted from the lists in the literature. These are, not necessarily in order of importance, (1) criticism and control of the other branches of government, most notably the executive; (2) debate; (3) lawmaking or legislation; (4) communication with the public, representation, and legitimation; and (5) recruitment, education, and socialization.

Much research on legislatures mentions the "criticism and control" function as being necessary for the maintenance of a stable political system.[37] This function has its roots in seventeenth- and eighteenth-century democratic political theory; at that time the role of the legislature as a check upon the powers of monarchs was first practiced. Legislatures have, in modern times, been less and less able to perform this very important function satisfactorily.[38]

A second function is that of debate, or discussion of values for the political system. In many nations the legislature's role in legislation is rather modest. It might discuss a bill proposed by the executive or the bureaucracy, but the bill might become law even if it is never actually voted on and passed by the legislature. In such instances, a legislature may appear to be performing a debating and a legislating function, but de facto its function is limited to debate.[39]

The function most frequently ascribed to legislatures in Western countries is that of lawmaking. As Jean Blondel observed, "From the theorists of the 17th Century to those of the contemporary world, it has been held as axiomatic . . . that the function of legislatures was to make laws."[40] The lawmaking function is no longer considered the litmus test by which a legislature is judged: "in formal terms, the principal function of the Parliament . . . is to pass legislation. But, legislation is only a part of the Parliament's business."[41]

The fourth function suggested is that of communication with the public, representation, and legitimation. The relationship between legislatures and big business, lobbies, and pressure groups is just as important for democratic government as is the representation of individual views and opinions.[42] The collective actions of legislators in these matters help build support not only for the legislature as an institution but also for the regime itself.[43]

There is a chain of three interconnected concepts at work here. First, legislators are necessarily aware of communications, both supportive and demanding, from their constituents. Second, by performing actions in response to these communications, the legislators can be said to be acting in a representative manner. Finally, by acting in a representative manner, the legislators can contribute significantly to the legitimacy of the governmental structure.

The fifth function that has been attributed to legislatures is that of recruitment, education, and socialization. Through the process of attracting individuals to politics, giving them experience, and enabling them to attain higher office, legislatures draw people into the political arena.[44] By serving as role models and by developing and maintaining political norms, legislatures actively participate in the process of political socialization, the transmission of political values.[45]

In some circumstances, legislatures are invested with special functions as a result of a particular constitutional framework or historical background. For example, the British Parliament (and many parliaments like it) also has an elective function—choosing the prime minister. The US House of Representatives has a similar elective function (choosing the president), but because of the nature of the electoral college and historical situations faced by the United States, the House has rarely been called upon to perform this task. The presidential election of 2000 came precariously close to being decided in the House of Representatives; ultimately a decision by the US Supreme Court made the House's participation in the election unnecessary.

As indicated earlier, one of the most important functions usually ascribed to the legislature as an institution is that of representation.[46] Whether or not legislatures are truly representative in a demographic sense, the need for legislatures to *appear* representative is central to their mission.

Central to this issue, however, is the very idea of being a "representative." In the late eighteenth century British member of parliament Edmund Burke introduced the idea of "virtual representation," in which he claimed that he could represent the views of the American colonies in the "no taxation without representation" controversy without actually *being from* the colonies. After all, he claimed, he *knew* what their view was, and he was capable of presenting it to the British Parliament (thus the idea of representation).[47] He didn't actually need to be from the American colonies at all.

Must the distribution of population groups in the legislature accurately reflect their distribution in the general population? It is clear that legislatures do not accurately reflect the demographic makeup of their settings.[48] To take the most obvious example, women are systematically underrepresented in their national legislatures.[49]

Table 3.9 shows the disproportionate percentage of seats women fill in many countries' governments compared with the percentage of the total population they compose in that country. Women's lack of representation in the world's governments—in both low-income and high-income countries—is clearly problematic for those who value representative, democratic government.

Similarly, ethnic, religious, and racial minorities tend to be significantly underrepresented in national parliaments. Even in settings in which there are no legal barriers to representation, this is a function of

Table 3.9   Underrepresentation of Women in Legislatures

		Percentage Women Represented			
Country	Election Year	Lower or Single House	Upper House	Inter-Parliamentary Union Rank for Lower or Single House[a]	Female Population (percentage of total)
Rwanda	2013	61.3	38.5	1	51.0
Norway	2013	39.6	—	13	49.6
Ethiopia	2015	38.8	32.0	17	50.1
Switzerland	2015	32.5	15.2	36	50.5
Poland	2015	28.0	14.0	53	51.7
Canada	2015	26.3	43.0	64	50.4
China	2013	24.2	—	73	48.5
Venezuela	2015	22.2	—	83	50.2
United States	2016	19.4	21.0	101	50.5
Russia	2016	15.8	17.1	130	53.5
India	2014	11.8	11.1	149	48.2
Bahrain	2014	7.5	22.5	172	37.9
Kuwait	2016	3.1	—	184	42.6

Sources: Inter-Parliamentary Union, "Women in National Parliaments: World Classification," September 1, 2017, http://archive.ipu.org/wmn-e/classif.htm. Population data from World Bank Group's GenderStats, "Population, Female," http://data.worldbank.org/indicator/SP.Pop.totl.fe.zs.
Notes: This table was originally conceived by Kate Thomas.
a. The Inter-Parliamentary Union ranking shows the international rank of the lower house in terms of the percentage of members of the lower or single house who are women. Rwanda, with 61.3 percent of its lower house being women, is ranked first; the United States, with under 20 percent of the membership of its lower house being women, is ranked 101st.

educational, financial, career, and other sociological patterns of bias reflected in the electoral machinery of the nation.

Many argue that the important point is not the gender, ethnic identity, age, religious, or racial characteristics of the representative, but the degree to which he or she understands the views of his or her constituency.[50] The true role of the representative, some would argue, is to represent the *interests* of his or her constituency, since obviously one representative cannot actually belong to all of the many demographic groups he or she represents.

The role that legislators play in the generation of legislative output varies in different political systems. A *political role,* as the term is used here, consists of "a pattern of expected behavior for individuals holding particular positions in a system."[51] One author lists seventeen possible roles that legislators can play; others list twenty-three.[52] The possibilities are numerous.

Certainly one of the major distinctions in legislative roles comes in the description of a legislator as a **frontbencher** or **backbencher**. The names come from positions in the British House of Commons, in which seats were, and still are, arranged in two sets of rows facing each other. Party leaders sit on the frontbenches of their respective sides; nonleaders, or followers, sit on the backbenches (see Figure 3.1). The prime minister and members of the cabinet sit on the frontbench of the Government side of the House. Members who sit on the frontbench of the Opposition side of the House are party leaders who *would* be in the cabinet if their party were in power.

Although the terms *frontbencher* and *backbencher* are positional terms designating the actual location of where one sits in the chamber, they are also terms of power.[53] This is because as their seniority and power increase, they tend to move to their party's frontbench. Those seated on the frontbench have more power and influence than those not on the frontbenches.

Although the British model of the legislature places an emphasis—because of its physical organization—on the "Government versus Opposition" conflict in the legislature, not all legislatures are organized in this way. We noted in our discussion of ideology that "left" and "right" were simply holdovers from 1798, at which time the French Council of 500 was arranged in a semicircular hall of representatives according to their self-determined place in the political spectrum.[54] Those generally supporting the monarch's policies sat on his right, while those who proposed changes in his policies sat on his left—hence we noted that "leftists" today tend to favor change and "rightists" tend to prefer the status quo. Like the French Council of 500, US legislative bodies also sit in a semicircular pattern.

Figure 3.1   House of Commons Seating in a British Model Legislature

Interior of the British House of Commons. General view from the Opposition benches looking toward the Speaker's chair (rear center) and the Government benches (left). The clerk's table is in the center. *Source:* UK Parliamentary Education Unit.

Legislative Committees

Another of the major structures that we find in legislative bodies is that of the committee.[55] Committees exist to meet a real need in legislatures: legislative bodies as a whole are too large for complex discussion on highly specialized matters to take place involving all of the members at one time. If, however, the entire legislative body is divided into groups, with each group specializing in a different aspect of the legislature's business, the work of the legislature can be performed more efficiently. The idea of a division of labor and specialization serves as the primary justification for the legislative committee's existence.[56]

Let us imagine a legislature with 200 members. Each legislator could not possibly develop expertise in all of the business of the legislature (everything from defense weapons systems to taxation to national parks policy to agriculture subsidies) to enable the legislature to function effectively. Accordingly, the members will establish, say, twenty committees dealing with the issues that the legislature must address. Each member may serve on two committees, and each committee will have twenty members. It is usually the case that the committees engage further in the "division of labor-specialization" behavior, too, forming a number of subcommittees so that committee members can specialize in very narrow aspects of the committee's work.

Thus our imaginary legislature might have an Agriculture Committee, a Defense Committee, and a Finance Committee, to take three examples. These committees will have subcommittees. Members of the Agriculture Committee, who will all be generally well informed about all aspects of agriculture, will each be very well informed about some specific aspect of the Agriculture Committee's work (such as the wheat crop, or price subsidies, for example).

Legislatures tend to have a number of different types of committees. A **standing or permanent committee** is one that is established at the opening of the legislative term and that lasts for the life of the legislature. A **select committee** is one that tends to be given a specific scope of inquiry, or a special problem, to address, as well as a specific duration. Some bicameral systems also make use of the **joint committee**, which is made up of members from both houses. A **committee of the whole**, often found in legislatures, is a technical device used to establish a different set of procedural rules; a legislative body can dissolve itself into a committee of the whole, and without anything physically changing (the same legislators are still sitting in the same seats), there is a different set of rules governing debate time, how motions may be introduced, and so on, that applies to their proceedings.

The relative importance of committees varies on a national basis. In some systems (such as the US legislature), legislative committees are very important and have a significant role in the legislative process. In other systems (such as that of Great Britain), the role of committees is weaker; they are not as active in the oversight function as are committees in the United States, and they do not play as significant a role in the legislative process as their US counterparts.[57] The ability of committees to examine, modify, delay, or even kill legislative proposals can be very significant and can be quite important in determining the amount of power the executive branch can exercise over the legislative branch of government.

The Legislative Process

As David Olson has argued, the most common pattern among parliaments in the process of handling legislation is to alternate the focus of activity between the **plenum**—the floor of the legislative house—and committee stages of legislation.[58] Box 3.2 shows the procedures for handling legislation in a typical legislative body; the description is generalized from actual procedures in a number of legislative bodies.

Box 3.2   Steps in Legislative Procedure in Selected Countries

1. Introduction
   - First reading: presentation of bill and discussion of its contents
   - Debate
   - Vote
   - The bill is sent to committee(s)
2. When (and if) the bill emerges from committee(s)
   - Second reading: often presented by members of committee(s) who held hearings on the bill
   - Debate
   - Vote
3. Third reading
   - Debate
   - Final vote
4. In a bicameral system, the bill would then go to the second house, and usually go through the same procedure there.

When we speak of sources of legislation, we do not distinguish just between frontbenchers and backbenchers, because this would group the Government frontbench with the Opposition frontbench, and the Government backbench with the Opposition backbench. Instead, we leave the Government frontbench standing alone, and group the Government backbench with the Opposition frontbench and backbench. A bill originating in the Government frontbench—where the members of the cabinet sit—is called a **Government bill**. A bill originating from any other member of parliament, either in the Government backbench or the Opposition frontbench or backbench, is called a **private members' bill**.[59]

In a classic study of the relative difference in efficacy between Government bills and private members' bills, Sheva Weiss and Avraham Brichta found a marked, though predictable, difference in legislative effectiveness between the chances of passage of Government bills and private members' bills.[60] Bills introduced by the Government invariably pass and become law; bills introduced by private members do not usually enjoy the same fate.

Legislatures and Executives

Much has been made in recent years about the "decline of the legislature" as a viable political structure[61] that is effectively able to counterbalance the growing structure of the political executive. The argument is made that in the modern political world the executive structure has grown at an alarming rate in terms of the increase in and centralization of its power, and the legislative structure has correspondingly lost power. This means that the legislature is less able today to provide a meaningful check on the power of the executive.[62]

Some have argued that there is nothing wrong with this and suggested that the legislature *ought* to expedite this process by voluntarily ceding to the executive many of its own powers. The legislature can remain as an institution, according to these advocates, but it should permit the executive to lead, with the legislature's proper role being to follow.[63]

The question of the relationship between the legislature and the executive is one that can be addressed on two levels. On the normative level, we can ask about what the relationship *should* be. More precisely, which alternative best promotes democratic, representative government? On the empirical level, we can ask about the validity of the observations that legislatures *are* declining in significance while executives are on the ascent. Is it true? What happens to the executive structure when the legislature loses its power?

Evidence seems to show that the executive institutions are winning the battle for power with the legislative branch. The legislature cannot keep up with a rapidly expanding executive bureaucracy in terms of information, personnel, and ability to formulate policy. To take the example of foreign policy, it simply is not possible for the Committee on Foreign Affairs (with a staff of less than a dozen) of the British House of Commons to oversee successfully the Ministry of External Affairs (with a staff of literally thousands); the same could be said of the ability of the US Senate's Foreign Relations Committee to oversee the policy of the US State Department (although the US Senate committees have far more in the way of committee staff than do committees of most other national legislatures). In fact, what often ends up happening is that legislative committees become dependent upon executive agencies—whether they are external affairs, defense, or agriculture ministries—to supply them with information, and the ability to control the information to which the legislature will have access gives the executive branch of government a permanent and overwhelming advantage in the legislative-executive power competition.

Although it may be the case that legislatures are generally regarded as having lost the battle for expanded power to executives, this does not mean that they have surrendered completely.[64] Indeed, in recent years we have seen a number of calls for reform, and in many instances some changes have been made in the legislative process that were designed to strengthen the legislature in relation to the executive, and to regain some of the traditional powers of the legislature, although there have been some very clear limitations to this reform.[65]

We should note that the subject of legislative reform is not a new one; it has been discussed by legislatures for well over a hundred years.[66] The problem has been, of course, that parliamentary reform—that is, an increase in the de facto power of parliament in relation to the executive—is seen as being in a zero-sum game with the executive: any gains on the part of parliament must come at the expense of the executive. It is to an examination of the executive structure that we now turn our attention.

Discussion Questions

1. How would you compare Locke's view of legislative institutions with the common view of legislatures today?
2. What do you believe are the most important functions that legislatures perform in their respective political systems today?
3. Which type of legislative system—unicameral or bicameral—seems to you to be most effective? Why?
4. What is the most compelling reason for a legislative system to be bicameral? Why would a system opt to be unicameral?
5. How important are political parties for legislative institutions? Could we have a nonpartisan legislature today?
6. Which do you think are more effective for legislatures: single-member-district elections or proportional representation elections? Why?
7. How could legislatures become more accurate in representation of minority groups in society? Is this important?
8. What do legislative committees do in legislative bodies?
9. What are the key "choke points" in the legislative process? If you were redesigning the legislative process, what would you do differently?

Notes

1. In Sir Ernest Baker, ed., *Social Contract: Essays by Locke, Hume and Rousseau* (New York: Oxford University Press, 1970), p. 73.

2. Ibid., pp. 73–77.

3. What has become a definitive resource in the field appeared in 1985 and reviewed the state of the art of legislative studies until that time; see Gerhard Loewenberg, Samuel Patterson, and Malcolm Jewell, eds., *Handbook of Legislative Research* (Cambridge: Harvard University Press, 1985). A more recent compendium is M. Steven Fish and Matthew Kroenig, *The Handbook of National Legislatures: A Global Survey* (New York: Cambridge University Press, 2009). See also Shane Martin, Thomas Saalfeld, and Kaare W. Strøm, eds., *Oxford Handbook of Legislative Studies* (Oxford: Oxford University Press, 2016); and Peverill Squire, *The Evolution of American Legislatures: Colonies, Territories, and States, 1619–2009* (Ann Arbor: University of Michigan Press, 2012).

4. Jean Blondel once wrote that "of the 138 countries which exist in the world today, only five, all in the Middle East, have never had a legislature"; in Jean Blondel, *Comparative Legislatures* (Englewood Cliffs, NJ: Prentice Hall, 1973), p. 7. According

to the United Nations, the count today is 193 nations; see Claudia Hefftier, *The Palgrave Handbook of National Parliaments and the European Union* (New York: Palgrave Macmillan, 2015).

5. The national legislature has been the most common level of study in recent years. Recent examples of such studies include the following: Mark Freeman, *Making Reconciliation Work: The Role of Parliaments* (Geneva: Inter-Parliamentary Union, 2005); Mohamed Abdel Rahim Salih, *African Parliaments: Between Governance and Government* (New York: Palgrave Macmillan, 2005); and Reuven Hazan, *Cohesion and Discipline in Legislatures: Political Parties, Party Leadership, Parliamentary Committees, and Governance* (New York: Routledge, 2013).

6. Very good recent studies are Philip James Giddings, *The Future of Parliament: Issues for a New Century* (Houndmills: Palgrave Macmillan, 2005); and Magnus Blomgren and Olivier Rozenberg, *Parliamentary Roles in Modern Legislatures* (New York: Routledge, 2012).

7. Joseph LaPalombara, *Politics Within Nations* (Englewood Cliffs, NJ: Prentice Hall, 1974), p. 177. See also David Farrell and Roger Scully, *Representing Europe's Citizens? Electoral Institutions and the Failure of Parliamentary Representation* (New York: Oxford University Press, 2007); and David Arter, *Comparing and Classifying Legislatures* (Hoboken, NJ: Taylor and Francis, 2013).

8. See Nicholas Baldwin, *Legislatures of Small States: A Comparative Study* (London: Routledge, 2013); Salih, *African Parliaments;* and Gavin Barrett, *National Parliaments and the European Union* (Dublin: Clarus, 2008).

9. For examples of the range of issues that can be affected by legislatures, see Roger Congleton and Birgitta Swedenborg, eds., *Democratic Constitutional Design and Public Policy: Analysis and Evidence* (Cambridge: Massachusetts Institute of Technology Press, 2006); David Olson and Michael Mezey, *Legislatures in the Policy Process: The Dilemmas of Economic Policy* (New York: Cambridge University Press, 2008); or Murray Hunt, Hayley Hooper, and Paul Yowell, *Parliaments and Human Rights: Redressing the Democratic Deficit* (Portland: Hart, 2015).

10. See Heather Evennett, *Second Chambers* (London: House of Lords Library, 2014). For discussion of US state legislatures, see Tom Todd, *Unicameral or Bicameral State Legislatures* (St. Paul: Minnesota House of Representatives, 1999). For those who enjoy exceptions to general rules, there are, in fact, tricameral legislatures, too. To offer one example, the national legislature of the Isle of Man, the oldest continuously operating legislative body in the world, operates in three different situations, a lower house, an upper house, and both houses sitting together as a distinct third house. See also Peverill Squire and Keith Hamm, *101 Chambers: Congress, State Legislatures, and the Future of Legislative Studies* (Columbus: Ohio State University Press, 2005); and Alan Rosenthal, *Engines of Democracy: Politics and Policymaking in State Legislatures* (Washington, DC: Congressional Quarterly, 2009).

11. Data come from Blondel, *Comparative Legislatures,* pp. 144–153. To illustrate different nation counts, note that Michael Curtis says that 47 out of 144 nations in the world are bicameral; see Michael Curtis, *Comparative Government and Politics* (New York: Harper and Row, 1978), p. 195. See also Betty Drexhage, *Bicameral Legislatures: An International Comparison* (The Hague: Ministry of the Interior, 2015).

12. Valerie Herman, ed., *Parliaments of the World* (London: Macmillan, 1976), p. 3. See also Arter, *Comparing and Classifying Legislatures*; and Baldwin, *Legislatures of Small States*.

13. Herman, *Parliaments*, p. 3.

14. See Donald Shell and David Beamish, *The House of Lords at Work: A Study with Particular Reference to the 1988–1989 Session* (New York: Oxford University Press, 1993). See also Meg Russell, *The Contemporary House of Lords: Westminster Bicameralism Revived* (Oxford: Oxford University Press, 2013).

15. See Adrienne Koch, "Introduction," in James Madison, *Notes of Debates in the Federal Convention of 1787* (Athens: Ohio State University Press, 1966), pp. vii–xxiii.

16. These vary on a country-by-country basis.

17. See Jan Erk, *Explaining Federalism: State, Society, and Congruence in Austria, Belgium, Canada, Germany, and Switzerland* (New York: Routledge, 2008); or Herbert Obinger and Stephan Leibfried, *Federalism and the Welfare State: New World and European Experiences* (New York: Cambridge University Press, 2005).

18. See Russell, *Contemporary House of Lords.* See also Jorg Luther and Paolo Passaglia, *A World of Second Chambers: Handbook for Constitutional Studies on Bicameralism* (Milan: Giuffre, 2007).

19. Allan Kornberg, *Canadian Legislative Behavior* (New York: Holt, Rinehart, and Winston, 1967), p. 19. See also J. Patrick Boyer, *Our Scandalous Senate* (Toronto: Dundurn, 2014).

20. See *The Work of the House of Lords* (London: House of Lords Information Office, 2005); Kenneth Clarke, *Reforming the House of Lords: Breaking the Deadlock* (London: University College, 2005); or Meg Russell, *Reforming the House of Lords: Lessons from Overseas* (Oxford: Oxford University Press, 2000).

21. Blondel, *Comparative Legislatures,* pp. 144–153. Blondel's data are out of date, and also a bit inaccurate. Caribbean data come from my own research there in 1985. See the Inter-Parliamentary Union, "Parline Database," http://www.ipu.org/parline-e /parlinesearch.asp. See also David Olson, *Democratic Legislative Institutions: A Comparative View* (New York: Routledge, 2015).

22. Robert Diamond, ed., *Origins and Development of Congress* (Washington, DC: Congressional Quarterly, 1976), pp. 127–128.

23. Asher Zidon, *The Knesset* (New York: Herzl, 1967), p. 27.

24. See Carol Mershon and Olga Shvetsova, *Party System Change in Legislatures Worldwide: Moving Outside the Electoral Arena* (Cambridge: Cambridge University Press, 2013); and Hazan, *Cohesion and Discipline in Legislatures.*

25. Kaare Strøm and Wolfgang Müller, *Delegation and Accountability in Parliamentary Democracies* (Oxford: Oxford University Press, 2006); Kristin Kanthak and George Krause, *The Diversity Paradox: Political Parties, Legislatures, and the Organizational Foundations of Representation in America* (New York: Oxford University Press, 2012).

26. One of the best recent books on the subject is by Blomgren and Rozenberg, *Parliamentary Roles in Modern Legislatures.* See also Hazan, *Cohesion and Discipline in Legislatures.*

27. See J. Richard Piper, "British Backbench Rebellion and Government Appointments, 1945–1987," *Legislative Studies Quarterly* 16 (1991): 219–238. See also Shane Martin and Olivier Rozenberg, *The Roles and Function of Parliamentary Questions* (Hoboken, NJ: Taylor and Francis, 2014).

28. Mark Franklin, Alison Baxter, and Margaret Jordan, "Who Were the Rebels? Dissent in the House of Commons, 1970–1974," *Legislative Studies Quarterly* 11, no. 2 (1986): 143–160. See also Marjorie Randon Hershey, Barry Burden, and Christina Wolbrecht, *U.S. Political Parties* (Thousand Oaks, CA: Congressional Quarterly, 2014).

29. See Larry Diamond and Marc Plattner, eds., *Electoral Systems and Democracy* (Baltimore: Johns Hopkins University Press, 2006). The classic on this subject is Austin Ranney, *Pathways to Parliament* (Madison: University of Wisconsin Press, 1965). Good reviews of women and elections are in Sue Thomas and Clyde Wilcox, *Women and Elective Office: Past, Present, and Future* (New York: Oxford University Press, 2005); and Didier Ruedin, *Why Aren't They There? The Political Representation of Women, Ethnic Groups, and Issue Positions in Legislatures* (Colchester: ECPR, 2013).

30. See the collection of articles in Joan DeBardelben and Achim Hurrelmann, eds., *Democratic Dilemmas of Multilevel Governance: Legitimacy, Representation, and Accountability in the European Union* (New York: Palgrave Macmillan, 2007).

31. See Anthony McGann, *The Logic of Democracy: Reconciling Equality, Deliberation, and Minority Protection* (Ann Arbor: University of Michigan Press, 2006); and Thomas Lundberg, *Proportional Representation and the Constituency Role in Britain* (New York: Palgrave Macmillan, 2007). See also Susan Carroll and Kira Sanbonmatsu,

More Women Can Run: Gender and Pathways to the State Legislatures (Oxford: Oxford University Press, 2013).

32. For discussions of past British general elections, see Pippa Norris and Christopher Wlezien, *Britain Votes, 2005* (Oxford: Oxford University Press, 2005); and Philip Norton, *Parliament in British Politics* (New York: Palgrave Macmillan, 2005).

33. See Gregory Mahler, *The Knesset: Parliament in the Israeli Political System* (Rutherford, NJ: Fairleigh Dickinson University Press, 1981), especially chap. 2. On Israeli elections, see Gregory Mahler, *Politics and Government in Israel: The Maturation of a Modern State,* 3rd ed. (Lanham: Rowman and Littlefield, 2016).

34. See Norman Schofield, *Multiparty Democracy: Elections and Legislative Politics* (New York: Cambridge University Press, 2006); Keren Ben-Zeev and Jochen Luckscheiter, *Do Parliaments Matter? African Legislatures and the Advance of Democracy* (Cape Town: Heinrich Boll Stiftung, 2012).

35. An interesting comparative study of this subject is Lois Duke Whitaker, ed., *Voting the Gender Gap* (Urbana: University of Illinois Press, 2008). See also Ruedin, *Why Aren't They There?*

36. Gerhard Loewenberg, *Modern Parliaments: Change or Decline* (Chicago: Atherton, 1971), p. 3. See also Cristina Leston-Bandeira, *Parliaments and Citizens* (London: Routledge, 2014).

37. Lord Ponsonby of Shulbrede, "The House of Lords: An Effective Restraint on the Executive," *Parliamentarian* 69, no. 2 (1988): 83–86. See also the very good study by William Aydelotte, *The History of Parliamentary Behavior* (Princeton: Princeton University Press, 2015).

38. See Richard Bauman and Tsvi Kahana, eds., *The Least Examined Branch: The Role of Legislatures in the Constitutional State* (New York: Cambridge University Press, 2006).

39. Michael Mezey, "The Functions of a Minimal Legislature: Role Perceptions of Thai Legislators," *Western Political Quarterly* 25 (1972): 686–701.

40. Blondel, *Comparative Legislatures,* p. 4.

41. Laxmi Singhvi, "Parliament in the Indian Political System," in Allan Kornberg, ed., *Legislatures in Developmental Perspective* (Durham, NC: Duke University Press, 1970), p. 217.

42. See Christopher Grill, *The Public Side of Representation: A Study of Citizens' Views About Representatives and the Representative Process* (Albany: State University of New York Press, 2007); or Tracy Sulkin, *Issue Politics in Congress* (New York: Cambridge University Press, 2005).

43. See Anthony Nownes, *Total Lobbying: What Lobbyists Want (And How They Try to Get It)* (New York: Cambridge University Press, 2006).

44. See Cliff Zukin, *A New Engagement? Political Participation, Civic Life, and the Changing American Citizen* (New York: Oxford University Press, 2006).

45. Eldin Fahmy, *Young Citizens: Young People's Involvement in Politics and Decision Making* (Burlington, VT: Ashgate, 2006); or Jennifer Lawless, *It Takes a Candidate: Why Women Don't Run for Office* (New York: Cambridge University Press, 2005).

46. Malcolm Jewell covers the literature in this area in his essay "Legislators and Constituents in the Representative Process," in Loewenberg, Patterson, and Jewell, *Handbook of Legislative Research,* pp. 97–134.

47. For discussion of Burke's views, see George H. Sabine, *A History of Political Theory* (New York: Holt, Rinehart, and Winston, 1961), p. 610; or Ian Crowe, *An Imaginative Whig: Reassessing the Life and Thought of Edmund Burke* (Columbia: University of Missouri Press, 2005).

48. A good example of such an issue is Johanna Birnir, *Ethnicity and Electoral Politics* (New York: Cambridge University Press, 2007). See also David Docherty, *Legislatures* (Vancouver: University of British Columbia Press, 2014).

49. See Margaret Conway, Gertrude Steuernagel, and David Ahern, *Women and Political Participation: Cultural Change in the Political Arena* (Washington, DC: Congressional Quarterly, 2005); Drude Dahlerup, *Women, Quotas, and Politics* (New York: Routledge, 2006); and Manon Tremblay, *Sharing Power: Women, Parliament, Democracy* (Burlington, VT: Ashgate, 2005).

50. See Gary Segura and Shaun Bowler, eds., *Diversity in Democracy: Minority Representation in the United States* (Charlottesville: University of Virginia Press, 2005); or Christina Wolbrecht and Rodney Hero, *The Politics of Democratic Inclusion* (Philadelphia: Temple University Press, 2005).

51. Raymond Hopkins, "The Role of the M.P. in Tanzania," *American Political Science Review* 64 (1970): 754.

52. LaPalombara, *Politics Within Nations,* pp. 180–182; and Malcolm Jewell and Samuel Patterson, *The Legislative Process in the United States* (New York: Random, 1973), respectively.

53. This is discussed in Trish Payne, *Backbenchers and the Press Gallery* (Canberra: Department of the Parliamentary Library, 1997).

54. Curtis, *Comparative Government and Politics,* p. 158.

55. See Reuven Hazan, *Reforming Parliamentary Committees: Israel in Comparative Perspective* (Columbus: Ohio State University Press, 2001), for one good case study on committees with a very good theoretical introduction. For a good description of the British case, see Patrick Dunleavy, *Developments in British Politics* (New York: St. Martin's, 2000).

56. See David Judge, *Backbench Specialization in the House of Commons* (Burlington, VT: Ashgate, 1982).

57. John Baughman, *Common Ground: Committee Politics in the U.S. House of Representatives* (Stanford: Stanford University Press, 2006).

58. Olson quoted in Walter Oleszek, *Congressional Procedures and the Policy Process* (Washington, DC: Congressional Quarterly, 2007); or Jack Davies, *Legislative Law and Process in a Nutshell* (St. Paul, MN: Thomson/West, 2007).

59. See David Marsh and Melvyn Read, *Private Members' Bills* (New York: Cambridge University Press, 1988).

60. See Sheva Weiss and Avraham Brichta, "Private Members' Bills in Israel's Parliament," *Parliamentary Affairs* 23 (1969): 25.

61. See William Howell and Jon Pevehouse, eds., *While Dangers Gather: Congressional Checks on Presidential War Powers* (Princeton: Princeton University Press, 2007); or James Thurber, ed., *Rivals for Power: Presidential-Congressional Relations* (Lanham: Rowman and Littlefield, 2006).

62. For an example of this argument, see Pendleton Herring and Sidney Pearson, *Presidential Leadership: The Political Relations of Congress and the Chief Executive* (New York: Routledge, 2017).

63. See especially the classic argument of Samuel P. Huntington, "Congressional Responses to the Twentieth Century," in Ronald Moe, ed., *Congress and the President* (Pacific Palisades, CA: Goodyear, 1971), pp. 7–31.

64. See John Garrett, *Westminster: Does Parliament Work?* (London: Orion Publishing, 1993).

65. For issues related to economic development, see Alex Brazier, *Parliament at the Apex: Parliamentary Scrutiny and Regulatory Bodies* (London: Hansard Society, 2003); and Leslie Seidle and David Docherty, *Reforming Parliamentary Democracy* (Montreal: McGill-Queen's University Press, 2003).

66. On this note see David Judge, "Why Reform? Parliamentary Reform Since 1832: An Interpretation," in David Judge, ed., *The Politics of Parliamentary Reform* (Rutherford, NJ: Fairleigh Dickinson University Press, 1984), pp. 9–36.

4

Executives

Learning Outcomes

After reading this chapter, you will be able to

- Discuss various roles that are played by the political executive.
- Explain the distinction between presidential and parliamentary executive models.
- Illustrate the bases of power of presidential systems.
- Articulate the role of political parties in presidential systems.
- Trace the development of the parliamentary executive.
- Highlight the changing role of the monarchy.
- Offer an analysis of constitutional monarchy.
- Understand the process of the selection of the chief executive in a parliamentary system.
- Give details about the relationship of power between legislative supremacy and cabinet supremacy.
- Make clear the process of formation of coalition governments.
- Offer a comparison of presidential and parliamentary executive structures to determine which is better.
- Describe the potential role of the military in politics.
- Understand the role of public administration and the bureaucracy in politics.

When John Locke wrote that the state of nature was wanting "power to back and support" the sentence of a national judiciary,[1] he was speaking of an executive power. There is much difference, however, between the kind of executive power that Locke had in mind and the kind of political executive that we find in contemporary political systems.

What does an executive do in a political system today? In his classic study of the US presidency, Clinton Rossiter[2] listed ten distinct, identifiable roles that the president is expected to play in the US political arena; these roles transfer to the parliamentary system, too:

1. Chief of state
2. Chief executive
3. Commander-in-chief
4. Chief diplomat
5. Chief legislator
6. Chief of party
7. Voice of the people
8. Protector of peace
9. Manager of prosperity
10. World leader

When we look at this list of duties that the president performs, we must marvel that anyone is able to handle the demands of the office. Indeed, this was one of the major themes of Rossiter's study. Wouldn't a political system be more efficiently run if it hired a crew of executives to handle these jobs? The concept of such a multiple executive is not new; in many different contexts in history the multiple executive has been tried. At the Federal Convention in Philadelphia in 1787, where the US Constitution was created, the idea of a multiple executive was suggested. It was rejected, however, because history had shown that it might tend to cause divisiveness when a difficult decision needed to be made and obscure responsibility, or culpability, since blame for a bad decision might be difficult to attribute to a single individual.[3]

In fact, Rossiter's list of ten roles for the president may be longer than is necessary. Political history has shown that we really only need to separate the executive role into two components: a symbolic role and a political role.[4] As a symbol the executive represents the dignity of the state. The executive lays wreaths on tombs, makes national proclamations, and generally serves a ceremonial function. In the political role, the chief executive "manages the national business" and makes the hard political decisions that need to be made; this person is the owner of the desk where "the buck stops."[5]

There are, generally speaking, four approaches to the executive institution that are found in political systems around the world, two of which we shall examine at this time. We will see in Part 2 of this volume that all political systems have their idiosyncratic differences, but at this stage of our study we are concerned with explaining the general models.

One general type of political executive can be referred to as the presidential model of executive, and the other type of political executive can be referred to as the "Westminster" parliamentary-cabinet form of executive. Later in this text we will add discussion of the French parliamentary-cabinet model and the collective executive model (although the model that was developed in the former Soviet Union has become virtually extinct in recent years); these are variations on the two models we shall discuss at this time. As with our discussion of legislatures, what we are about to explore will vary in specific detail from country to country.

The Presidential Executive

The type of political executive that American students know best is the presidential executive. American students are often surprised to learn, however, that the presidential model of executive behavior is in a minority once we go beyond the borders of the United States.

The **presidential model** centralizes political power and symbolic authority in one individual, the president. The president presides at ceremonial functions, and it is the president who symbolizes the nation in the eyes of the rest of the world. The president is the head of state. Foreign diplomats present their credentials to him. (Although a number of countries have had women presidents, we will use the masculine pronoun here.) He presents the State of the Union message to the Congress each year. He throws out the first baseball to open the baseball season.[6]

Presidential systems do not separate the symbolic and the business functions of the office. Some have suggested that since the US government has the institution of the vice presidency, which has few constitutional duties and the primary significance of which is not in what it is but in what it might become,[7] a good use of the vice president might be to assign to that person the ceremonial duties of office, and leave the president to important decisionmaking duties. The problem is that vice presidents do not like the idea of spending all of their time at funerals and ceremonies. Moreover, the public does not like it either; the vice president is, after all, the second officer of US government, not the first, and the public wants to see the president.[8]

The strength of the presidency is in its independence. In the US system, the model for presidential systems elsewhere, the chief executive is elected independently from the legislature. Presidential elections in the United States are held every four years, no more frequently and no less frequently. It is the fixed term of the president and the corresponding security in office that comes with the fixed term that contribute to the president's base of power.[9]

As indicated in Figure 4.1, the president is independently elected on the basis of popular election. The US political system has an additional structure between the populace and the president, the Electoral College, which officially elects the president. The genesis of the Electoral College is based upon the Founding Fathers' distrust of popular will. The Founders felt that by having voters choose electors, who would subsequently cast ballots for the presidency, their concern could be resolved.[10] Recent US political history—including the quite extraordinary presidential election of 2000 and the election of 2016, in which the winner of the popular vote did not win the presidency—has shown the Electoral College to be an anachronistic institution, and efforts are regularly undertaken to do away with the institution and to have the president directly elected by the public. Most other presidential systems do not have such a structure, but instead have voters cast their votes directly for the presidential candidates campaigning for office.

The fact that the American public votes in several different electoral contests—once for the president and vice president (literally for electors for the president and vice president), once for the House of Representatives (all seats in the House of Representatives come up for reelection every two years), and, where a contest is held, once for the Senate (Senate seats have six-year terms and are staggered so that both seats in any given state are not up for election at the same time)—is quite significant for a number of reasons. First, it gives the president an independent power base. Short of the process of impeachment, which history had shown, until the term of President Bill Clinton, could be instituted only

Figure 4.1 Presidential Systems' Bases of Power

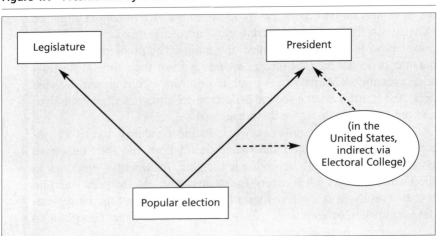

for high crimes and treason and not simply for reasons of political opposition,[11] the president does not depend upon either the legislature or public opinion for continuation of his four-year term. Once he is in office, this individual remains in office until the term is completed. This allows the president to take actions that may be unpopular with both the public and the legislature in the short term but that the president feels, nonetheless, are the right actions to take.

A second point is that this relationship works in the other direction, too. That is, legislators are chosen by the people, not by the president; as long as they keep their constituencies happy they can act independently of the president, and there is virtually nothing that the president can do to them.[12] Members of the House of Representatives are elected for two-year terms, and although the president may threaten to not campaign for them in the next election (or even may threaten to campaign against them) if they don't do what he wants, the president cannot directly affect the duration of their time in office. He cannot "fire" them. And, their more frequent election allows the public the opportunity to "send a message" to the government with the more frequent turnover of the House, such as took place in 2010 with the electoral repudiation of some of the policies of President Barack Obama.

Senators are elected to six-year terms, and they, in a similar manner, are secure in their office.[13] A president might be angry when a senator from his party fails to support his legislation in the Senate, but there is little the president can do to directly punish a recalcitrant senator, short of threatening to withhold future support.[14]

A third significant point to note is that this structural independence of the branches of government (depicted in Figure 4.1) can have negative consequences. Because both the executive and legislative branches of government have secure tenure in office, they can frustrate each other, but that is all they can do. The president can veto acts of Congress, but Congress can override the presidential veto. (The president of the United States does not have an "absolute" veto that is impossible to override, although presidents in some other systems do possess such absolute vetoes.) Congress can refuse to pass a legislative request of the president, but the president can try to accomplish his goals through executive decrees, executive agreements, and similar unilateral executive actions.

It is important to recall that the president is not part of the legislative branch of government and cannot, literally cannot, take part in the legislative process. Only senators can introduce bills in the Senate, and only representatives can introduce bills in the House. If the president is unable to find a legislative sponsor for a bill (something that, realistically, is unimaginable), he is unable to generate new legislation. This situation can deteriorate to a point of **immobilism**; each actor has enough power to block the other but not enough to achieve its own objectives over the opposition of the other, which means that it is possible that nothing will be accomplished.

This situation is most evident in the United States when the executive and legislative branches of government are controlled by the two different major political parties. When Richard Nixon (a Republican) was president, he faced a Senate and House controlled by Democrats; the relationship between the two branches of government was often tense.[15] This was repeated during the term of (Republican) Ronald Reagan in the 1980s. For some of that time, Congress was partly controlled by Democrats (a Republican-controlled Senate and a Democrat-controlled House), and for some of that time it was fully controlled by a Democratic majority in both houses. This situation continued through the Presidency of George H. W. Bush. Although Nixon, Reagan, and Bush were able to get the support of some southern (and other more conservative) Democrats, as a general rule much tension existed between the two branches. The same general situation existed with (Democrat) Bill Clinton facing Republican majorities in both Houses of Congress through most of the 1990s.

Following the midterm election of 2010, the Democratic control of the White House and both houses of Congress ended, and the Republican Party controlled the House of Representatives with a significant majority. This had significant results in terms of President Barack Obama's inability to press forward with legislation on a strictly partisan basis as he had done during his first two years as president.

Party difference is not a requirement for this kind of tension, however. The four years of Jimmy Carter (a Democratic president with a Democratic Congress) were not very productive either, and often witnessed the same tension, despite the fact that both branches were controlled by Democrats. After his inauguration, Carter proposed an energy program, which he labeled as "the moral equivalent of war." By the time the Congress acted (over two years later), Carter's original legislative proposals bore little resemblance to the legislation produced by the Congress.[16]

The Parliamentary Executive

The **parliamentary executive** is more complex than its presidential alternative, if for no other reason than it features a multiple executive.[17] The ceremonial function and the decisionmaking function are performed by two separate individuals, whose titles vary by political system (see Table 4.1) and to whom we can generically refer as the **head of state** and the **chief executive**, respectively.

Table 4.1   Executive Titles

Nation	Model of Government	Head of State	Chief Executive
Australia	Parliamentary	Governor-general[a]	Prime minister
Canada	Parliamentary	Governor-general[a]	Prime minister
Germany	Parliamentary	President	Chancellor
India	Parliamentary	President	Prime minister
Israel	Parliamentary	President	Prime minister
Italy	Parliamentary	President	Prime minister
Japan	Parliamentary	Emperor	Prime minister
Mexico	Presidential	President	President
United Kingdom	Parliamentary	Queen	Prime minister
United States	Presidential	President	President

Note: a. Serving on behalf of the monarch in his or her absence.

The head of state symbolizes the state and the dignity of the political regime. The head of state receives ambassadors, hosts receptions, and performs many of the ceremonial tasks government requires. Heads of state, generally, are chosen one of three ways. First, in a number of political systems—about a third of all parliamentary systems—the head of state is a hereditary position, one that "belongs" to a royal family. Certainly among the best-known examples of this manner of selection is the British monarchy, with a clearly delineated line of succession.

A second pattern of selection is one in which the head of state is selected by a governmental body, often the legislature. The president of India is elected by the combined membership of the Indian Parliament. A third method of selection has been referred to as self-selection and is characteristic of political systems in which power has been seized, such as the position of the late Fidel Castro in Cuba, or the now-toppled position of Idi Amin as president-for-life in Uganda.[18]

The chief executive, on the other hand, is the chief of the executive branch of government.[19] The chief executive is a full-time politician, devoting less time to ceremonial duties of office. Generally speaking, the chief executive in a parliamentary regime performs the same executive tasks as the chief executive in a presidential regime but not the symbolic activities. Both executives coordinate government policymaking. Both executives are assisted by cabinets of individuals heading separate departments or ministries of government. Both executives are responsible for the day-to-day operation of government.

In many political systems, the position of chief executive is totally without legal basis, but instead it is founded upon years of political custom and tradition—which we have noted can be just as important as written constitutional measures. In other systems the position is legally entrenched and described in detail in constitutional documents.[20] The manner in which the office of the chief executive in a parliamentary system was created tells us a great deal about both the position of the chief executive and its relationship to the position of the head of state.

The Changing Role of the Monarchy

When we discuss the development of parliamentary government, we are in fact discussing British political history (just as we are discussing US political history when we speak of the development of the presidential model of government). Although many parliamentary systems today differ from the contemporary British system, the parliamentary system of government as we know it was born in England, and it is regarded as starting with Robert Walpole as prime minister in 1741. A very brief survey of nine centuries of political history may help us to understand and appreciate the role of the monarchy today.[21]

When William, Duke of Normandy, took the English throne in 1066, there existed a political structure called the Witenagemot, an assembly of sorts, which formally elected him king. William the Conqueror (as he became known) extended and formalized the feudal system during his tenure and institutionalized the Curia Regis, the King's Court, as a political body. At this time there was no distinction among the legislative, executive, and judicial functions of government: all government was the king (John Locke was not to come onto the scene for another 600 years). The king used both the Curia Regis and the Witenagemot as sources of funds, and in return for members' financial support he listened to their counsel and advice, although he was clearly not bound to accept it.

In 1215, the group of barons of the realm that had made up the Curia Regis drew up a document called the Magna Carta, describing what the barons considered to be the proper relationship between the king and themselves. It is important to note that this was not a declaration of new rights and privileges; rather, it was an expression of what the barons asserted already to have been the relationship for some time. They argued that the king had been forgetting some of the powers that kings had already given to barons and the public. This "Great Charter" was a significant constitutional document. It expounded upon major political obligations of the time: people's obligations to the king, the king's obligations to the people, and how law and justice should be administered.

During the thirteenth century the financial resources of the barons of the Curia Regis proved to be insufficient for the needs of government, and the Curia Regis called upon representatives of towns and counties for "aids"—financial contributions to the budget. In exchange for their financial contributions, representatives of the towns and counties were admitted to the Curia Regis alongside the barons, thus giving the Curia Regis two classes of members: the earlier baronial membership, which became the House of Lords, and its new (and often elected) membership, which became the House of Commons. The term *parliament* was first used during the thirteenth century to refer to the debating function of these bodies.

Because the king received financial assistance from both groups, he was now obligated to discuss public affairs not only with the nobility but also with the representatives of the commoners. The public's representatives had a major weapon in their hands to ensure that they were listened to: the right to assent, or refuse to assent, to the king's proposals for raising and spending money. Parliament, especially the House of Commons, used this power as a condition with the king: its approval of royal financial proposals in exchange for the king's attention to public grievances. By about the year 1500, the Commons had grown in political strength to the point that it could introduce proposals on its own to change laws, and it could offer amendments to bills that had originated in the House of Lords, the superior house of the legislature.

The seventeenth century saw the legislature's power grow in relation to that of the monarch, and it was a period of much stress. King James I, who reigned from 1603 to 1625, was an advocate of the **divine right of kings** theory,[22] which argued that the monarch derived his power directly from God, not from the people. James had little need for Parliament as an institution, and he argued that any privileges of Parliament were gifts from the king, not rights of Parliament. During James's twenty-two-year reign, Parliament sat for only eight years. On a number of occasions he dissolved the House of Commons, declared that its members were not "truly" elected, and sent them home—in effect, he fired them.

Charles I succeeded his father, James I, in 1625, and followed his father's practice of imprisoning members of Parliament (especially, of course, members of the House of Commons) who opposed him. When Charles could not control a Parliament, he dissolved it and called for new elections after a period of time. By 1640, Charles was in need of funds and convened Parliament to authorize new taxes. The Commons refused; only three weeks later Charles again dissolved Parliament. This became known as the "Short Parliament."

Six months later another Parliament assembled; it became known as the "Long Parliament." The issue upon which the election for the House of Commons had been held was whether the king should rule Parliament or Parliament should rule the king. Within two years an armed struggle ensued (referred to as the English Civil War, 1642–1648) between supporters of the king and supporters of the Parliament. Eventually the royal army was defeated, and Charles was captured and sentenced to death as "a tyrant, traitor, murderer, and public enemy" following a trial in 1649. The Commons dissolved the monarchy and established a republic, led by Oliver Cromwell. In 1660, the Long Parliament dissolved itself, and the Convention that was elected to take its place restored the Stuart family to the throne; Charles II became king of England.

Through the reign of Charles II (1660–1685) and his brother James II (1685–1688) the tensions between Parliament and the monarch grew again, and in 1688 James II was pressured into abdicating—resigning his position as monarch. Parliament then invited William, Prince of Orange, and grandson of Charles I, to rule, and William and his wife, Mary, were proclaimed king and queen by Parliament in 1688.

During the reign of William and Mary, the English constitutional system became much more stable; indeed, it laid much of the groundwork for stable constitutional government to come. The British Bill of Rights (1689)—which asserted that taxes could be raised only with the assent of Parliament, guaranteed the people the right to petition the king, limited the use of the army without the consent of Parliament, guaranteed free elections and freedom of speech and debate in Parliament, limited excessive bail, prohibited cruel and unusual punishment, and asserted that Parliament ought to meet frequently—became law. Parliament became institutionalized as a significant political actor in the English system of government.

Constitutional Monarchy

Over the past three centuries, the relationship between the monarch and Parliament has evolved to a point that not even William and Mary would recognize it. De jure, under law, most powers of the British government (and in a parallel fashion parliamentary governments, generally) are still exercised in the name of the king or queen, but today they are invariably exercised "on the advice" of the chief executive.

In the eighteenth and nineteenth centuries, the king relied more and more on his **cabinet**, a group of advisers, for guidance. In the early eighteenth century the role of the cabinet was only that of providing advice; the king still could do as he pleased. As ideas of democratic and republican government grew over the next two centuries, the power relationship changed so that the king and queen were now obligated (although not legally required) to accept the advice of their cabinets.

The cabinet by now was primarily chosen from the house of Parliament elected by the public, the House of Commons. Now the cabinet was in reality governing in the name of the king or queen, and without consulting him or her.

Among the most striking characteristics of parliamentary government today is the duality of its executive leadership referred to earlier. The monarch is the official (de jure) head of state, but the active (de facto) head of government is the prime minister. Appointments are made, acts of Parliament or the legislature are proclaimed, and all government is carried on in the name of the monarch, although it is the prime minister and his or her cabinet who make all of the selections for appointments, who author or sponsor legislative proposals, and who make the administrative decisions that keep government running.

The legal bases for the prime minister and cabinet are rare, as noted earlier, and in many political systems both the prime minister and cabinet are (legally) constitutionally nonexistent institutions. In the case of Great Britain (and many Commonwealth nations), the legal claim to power of the cabinet rests in the fact that ever since the seventeenth century the monarch has had the advisement of a **Privy Council**—a kind of present-day cabinet. Today, although the Privy Council is no longer active, cabinet members are first made members of the Privy Council and then are appointed to the cabinet. The cabinet meets as a "subcommittee" of the (inactive) Privy Council and acts in the name of the Privy Council, a body that *does* have constitutional and legal status. Discussing the relationship between the Canadian cabinet and the Queen's Privy Council for Canada, R. MacGregor Dawson noted,

> Those appointed to the Privy Council remain members for life, and hence will include not only ministers from the present Cabinet, but also all surviving ministers of past Cabinets as well. The Privy Council would therefore, if active, be a large and politically cumbersome body with members continually at cross-purposes with one another; but it has saved itself from this embarrassment by the simple device of holding no meetings.
>
> The Cabinet, lacking any legal status of its own, masquerades as the Privy Council when it desires to assume formal power; it speaks and acts in the name of the entire Council.[23]

The Selection of the Chief Executive

Although the British monarch may have felt free to choose whomever he or she wanted as advisers in the seventeenth and eighteenth centuries, such is no longer the case today. The process by which the head of state in a parliamentary system selects the chief executive is one of those patterns of behavior that may legally (de jure) be entirely up to the head of state, but practically and politically (de facto) the head of state usually has little or no choice in the matter.

In the model found in most parliamentary nations, unlike their presidential counterparts, there is no special election to select the chief executive.[24] The chief executive is elected as a member of the legislature, just as all of the other members of the legislature are elected. Elections for the legislature are held on a regular basis, which varies with the political system. In Britain, the term of the House of Commons is limited to five years.

After the elections for legislative seats have taken place, it is the duty of the head of state to "invite" someone to create a Government. (It should be noted at this point that the term *Government* with a capital *G* has a specific meaning in this volume: the prime minister and the cabinet; *government* with a lowercase *g* refers to the general structures of the political system.) Although the head of state in most systems is technically free to select whomever he or she wants for the Government, in practice and custom (de facto) heads of state are required to invite the leader of the largest political party in the legislature—a recognition of the will of the people—as indicated in Figure 4.2.[25]

Once the head of state designates an individual to create a Government, that individual will subsequently advise the head of state as to whom to appoint to the cabinet. After the new Government (the new

Figure 4.2   Selection of the Parliamentary Chief Executive

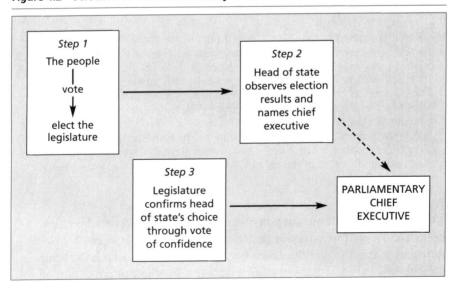

prime minister and the new cabinet) has been assembled, in most political systems that Government must first receive a **vote of confidence** from the legislature before it assumes power. The vote of confidence is a vote by a majority of the legislature indicating its confidence in, or support for, the prime minister and his or her cabinet. (Keep in mind that the vote of confidence will typically involve only the lower house of the legislature—the House of Commons in Britain—and will generally not involve the upper house at all.)

In most political systems, if the Government does not receive a vote of confidence—if it receives the support of less than a majority of the legislature in a vote—it cannot take office, and another Government must be designated by the head of state. Britain represents an exception to the general rule that newly designated Governments need votes of confidence. In Britain, and many other Commonwealth nations, the designation by the head of state *assumes* legislative confidence (that is, the head of state wouldn't make the appointment without making sure of legislative support first), and the Government assumes power immediately, without first needing an expression of confidence from the legislature.

The institution of the vote of confidence is an indication of **legislative supremacy** in the political system. That is, the legislature technically "hires" the chief executive (although the head of state may "nominate" him or her) or invests him or her with power. The chancellor in Germany, as well as the prime minister in Japan or India, to cite just a few examples, assumes power only *after* receiving a majority vote of support in their respective legislatures.

This legislative power works in the other direction, too. Just as the legislature "hires" the executive, by expressing support in one of its members forming a Government, it can "fire" the executive by expressing a lack of support or confidence in the Government. Whenever the chief executive loses the confidence of the legislature, whenever the legislature passes a **vote of no confidence** (or, conversely, fails to pass a legislative expression of confidence if asked to do so), the chief executive is in fact fired. Even if the legislature expresses a lack of confidence in the chief executive only a week after that person has assumed office, he or she must resign. In some systems this resignation is a legal requirement; elsewhere it is simply a custom that has the force of law.[26] In some systems a vote of no confidence is not even required to fire a chief executive: if the Government is defeated on *any* major piece of legislation, that is considered to be an expression of a lack of confidence in the Government. It should be added that in most parliamentary systems votes of no confidence are very rare. They do, however, happen from time to time, especially if the Government does not control a substantial legislative majority.

When the prime minister resigns, we say that the Government has "fallen." A Government falls when either of two things happens: it loses on a question of confidence or a major piece of legislation, leading the prime minister to resign, or the prime minister resigns for some other reason. The resignation of an individual minister does not cause a Government to fall, but the resignation of the prime minister does cause the Government to fall.[27]

The prime minister in a parliamentary system, then, does not have the job security of a president in a presidential system. The prime minister is selected by the head of state to be chief executive precisely because he or she is the leader of the largest party in the legislature. If this individual's party controls a majority of the legislative seats, and if the prime minister can maintain that majority through party discipline, this person should be able to remain prime minister for the entire term of the legislature (and perhaps several terms of the legislature, since there are usually no term limits in parliamentary government). If, however, the prime minister does not control a majority, or if the prime minister is not able to retain the support of a majority of the legislature, his or her tenure might be brief.

Of course, if there is a party with a majority, the head of state will have to appoint its leader to be prime minister. (Obviously, if the head of state appointed anyone else, the majority party would make sure that the new Government failed to receive a vote of confidence.) If there is no majority party, one of three situations is possible. First, the head of state may appoint someone to head a **minority government**, one in which the prime minister does not control over 50 percent of the seats in the legislature. Minority governments tend to be short-lived. They usually obtain an initial vote of confidence through a temporary understanding among a number of parties who do not want to have to contest another election right away, and who see a minority government as the least unattractive alternative at the time. These understandings usually break down after a short while and result in a no-confidence vote and the fall of the Government.[28]

A second alternative to a majority party is for the head of state to appoint someone to form a **coalition government**. A coalition government is one in which two or more nonmajority parties pool their legislative seats to form a majority parliamentary bloc. There may well be a formal agreement drawn up among the participants in the coalition, in which they agree to team up and create a majority in the legislature to support a Government. We will discuss coalition governments shortly.

The third alternative, one usually not taken right away, is for the head of state to not form any Government, but instead to dissolve the newly elected legislature—fire the newly elected legislators—and call for new elections in the hope that the next elections will result in one party winning a clear mandate. This usually is not taken as a first resort, but if the head of state appoints a minority government that falls within a short period of time, it may be clear to him or her that political stability is simply not possible with the legislature constituted in its current form. If such is the case, the head of state may dissolve the legislature and call for new elections by issuing a **writ of dissolution**.[29]

The chief executive, then, is selected by the head of state *from* the legislature. The chief executive retains his or her position as long as the legislature continues to express support for the Government by approving the proposals of the Government. The concept of party discipline is very important in all of this, for it is party discipline that enables the prime minister to control the legislature. There is a circular relationship at work here. The prime minister is selected to be prime minister precisely because he or she is the chosen leader of the largest party in the legislature. This person will remain prime minister as long as he or she can control a majority of the legislature. When a majority cannot be controlled, a motion of no confidence will be passed, or at least threatened, and the prime minister will be forced (through either law or custom) to resign.

At this point it is typically not necessary that new elections be held. The head of state must now reassess the situation and may invite someone else (or perhaps even the same person who last failed) to try to form a new Government and receive an expression of legislative confidence. This process—a Government being designated, receiving a vote of confidence, surviving for a period of time, falling, and then a new Government being designated, and so on—can go on until the term of the legislature is completed, over and over again, until the head of state decides that there is no point in trying again. At that point the head of state will issue a writ of dissolution, dissolving the legislature (much as we noted Charles I did in 1640), and will call for new elections. Thus the entire process starts again, as indicated in Figure 4.3.

We should note that there are some systems in which the head of state does not have the power to dissolve the legislature and call for new elections; only the legislature has that power. Thus, in Israel, only the Knesset has the power to dissolve itself and call for new elections before its term of office is over.

It occasionally happens that a chief executive will *cause* his or her own Government to fall, for what we can describe as reasons of electoral advantage. Let us suppose that in a hypothetical political system the constitution requires that elections be held at least every five years (as is the case in Great Britain), and elections are held in January 2017

Figure 4.3 The Government-Formation Process

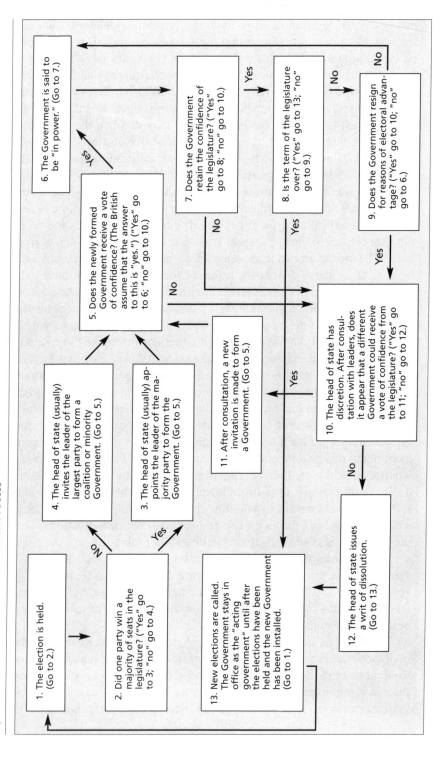

that result in the Liberal Party winning 56 of the 100 seats in the legislature, and the Conservative Party winning the remaining 44 seats. The leader of the Liberal Party becomes prime minister. As time goes by, that person's popularity, and correspondingly the popularity of the Liberal Party, fluctuates up and down, depending upon economic factors, world events, and so on.

This prime minister knows that if the present Government can keep the majority in the legislature satisfied, the constitution will require that elections be held by January 2022 (five years after the last election). In early 2020, three years into the term of the legislature but almost two years before elections must be held, this prime minister's popularity is at an all-time high, as depicted in Figure 4.4. After some discussion with political advisers, this prime minister's Government resigns and asks the head of state to dissolve the legislature and call for new elections. They do this because they feel that if the elections are held now, they may win control of the legislature by an even bigger margin than they did in 2017. The head of state has no real choice in the matter: the prime minister's Liberal Party controls a majority in the legislature and supports the decision to call for early elections. If the head of state were to refuse to dissolve the legislature and try to name some other leader (such as the leader of the opposition Conservative Party) to form a Government, the Liberal group would vote the new Government down by a 56–44 vote. The head of state, then, grants this prime minister a dissolution and calls for new elections to be held, typically in six to ten weeks. During the interim period, this prime minister's Government continues in office as the "acting" Government, and the prime minister's title is "acting prime minister" until the next election is held and a new prime minister (likely the now acting prime minister) is designated by the head of state.

Although the example just presented is hypothetical, the situation it depicts happens regularly in parliamentary systems. In recent years, dissolutions of this type have taken place in Japan, France, Great Britain, Belgium, and India, among other nations.

Coalition Governments

In political systems that have more than two major political parties, it regularly is the case that no single party controls a majority in the legislature. (Clearly, in a two-party system we don't have this problem. Unless there is a tie—which is quite rare—one of the two parties must, by definition, have more than half of the legislative seats.) Where no party has a majority, several options are available to the head of state in the creation of a Government. The most commonly utilized option is the creation of a coalition government.

Figure 4.4   Government Falling as a Result of Fluctuation in Public Opinion, 2016–2022

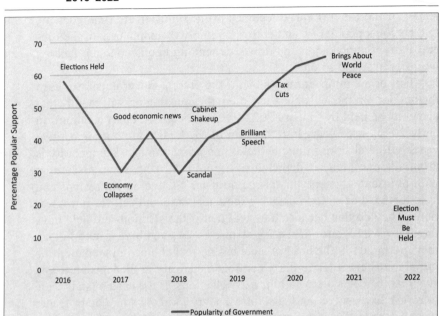

Let us take a hypothetical newly elected legislature to use as an example as we discuss the process of coalition formation. Imagine a 100-seat legislature with five political parties, as described in Table 4.2. In this instance, the head of state would most likely invite the leader of Party A to form a Government, since Leader A has the largest popular mandate. We should note, however, that in most systems the head of state is not required to invite Leader A; the head of state can invite anyone that she or he feels has the best chance to form a coalition successfully. In this example, Leader A needs to find an additional eighteen seats in order to form a majority of fifty-one to support her Government in the legislature. In this case, Leader A could go to either the leader of Party B or the leader of Party C to find a partner. As well, of course, Leader A could go to more than one other party, to try to form an ABC coalition, for example.

Usually, Leader A will have to promise the leaders of other parties involved in the coalition some reward for joining the coalition. In most instances, this reward is a cabinet position (or several cabinet positions). Sometimes the payoff is a promise that a certain piece of legislation that the prospective coalition partner has drafted will be passed as part of the Government's program.[30] Sometimes both types of payoff are required.

Table 4.2 A Hypothetical Legislative Composition

Party A	33 seats
Party B	20 seats
Party C	18 seats
Party D	16 seats
Party E	13 seats

If Leader A can reach an agreement with one or more partners to form a coalition that will control a majority of the seats in the legislature, then Leader A will receive his or her vote of confidence, and the Government can be said to be installed. If, however, Leader A cannot find sufficient coalition partnership within a constitutionally mandated period of time, usually two to three weeks, then Leader A must return her "mandate" to the head of state and inform the head of state of her inability to form a coalition.

At this point, as indicated earlier, the head of state makes a decision. The head of state could dissolve the legislature and call for new elections, with the hope that in another election a party seeking seats in the next legislature might win a majority, or at least a large enough plurality to be able to form a coalition easily; or the head of state could invite some other party leader to try to form a government. In our hypothetical example, the head of state at this point might turn to Leader B to see whether that person could form a coalition.

The process then goes on and on in this fashion. At each occasion that a Government fails to retain the confidence, or support, of a majority in the legislature—that is, a motion of no confidence introduced by the opposition passes, or a motion of confidence introduced by a Government supporter fails—the head of state must decide whether another leader might be able to succeed. Elections, after all, are expensive, and often divisive, and one doesn't want to have a national election every six months.

Coalition majority governments tend to be less stable than single-party majority governments in parliamentary systems.[31] In a single-party majority system, the prime minister must be concerned with party discipline, keeping followers in the party in line. In a coalition system, the flow of power is more diffuse. The prime minister exercises party discipline over party followers and counts on the leaders of the partner coalition party or parties to do the same. Coalitions usually fail because of differences between party leaders—in our example, because Leader B has a disagreement with Leader A and pulls the support of Party B out of the AB coalition—not because of a failure of party discipline within either Party A or Party B.[32]

As might be expected, the complexity of the coalition-formation process is a direct function of the number of political parties in a legislature.[33] In the example in Table 4.3, it is clear that Situation I is most simple, Situation II more complex, and Situation III even more complex. The more parties there are, the more possibilities there are for a winning coalition to form; the more partners there are in a coalition, the more possibilities there are for intracoalition conflict to cause a coalition to fall apart.

Presidential and Parliamentary Systems: Comparisons

Clearly there are a number of major and significant differences in structure between the presidential system and the parliamentary-cabinet system. A question for us to ask at this time is, What are the *behavioral* implications of the differences between the two systems, and how will the two systems differ in terms of policy output and day-to-day operation? Several significant dimensions of difference are mentioned here.

The first distinction has to do with the idea of **responsible government**. Responsible government in this context does not mean trustworthy

Table 4.3   The Complexity of the Coalition-Formation Process

Party	Seats	Majority Possibilities
Situation I: Simplest		
Party A	44 seats	AB, AC, BC, ABC
Party B	42 seats	
Party C	14 seats	
Situation II: More Complex		
Party A	38 seats	AB, AC, AD, ABC,
Party B	20 seats	ABE, ACD, ACE, etc.
Party C	17 seats	
Party D	15 seats	
Party E	10 seats	
Situation III: Most Complex		
Party A	30 seats	ABC, ABD, ABE,
Party B	19 seats	ABG, BCDE,
Party C	12 seats	etc.
Party D	9 seats	
Party E	8 seats	
Party F	8 seats	
Party G	7 seats	
Party H	7 seats	

or rational government, but instead it refers to the Government's ability to deliver on its promises. Responsible government comes about in parliamentary systems through some of the structural characteristics we have already met. The idea of party discipline suggests that legislators will vote (and speak and act) in the manner that their party leader suggests. The selection of the prime minister as leader of the largest party in the legislature and the notion of the vote of confidence ensure that the prime minister will always have the support of (and, therefore, because of party discipline, be able to control) a majority of the legislature. Consequently, whatever the prime minister wants will have the approval of a majority of the legislature. If the prime minister's proposals do not receive a parliamentary majority, the prime minister will of course have to resign.

This means that when the prime minister promises the public that his or her Government will act in a certain way, that person is in a position to follow through on that promise. In addition to being the leader of the executive branch of government, the prime minister is also (by definition) the leader of the legislative branch of government.

Contrast this with the presidential system, in which the notion of separation of powers and checks and balances—something that explicitly does not apply in a parliamentary system—is so important. One of the central principles of presidential government is that the legislature is free to deny requests of the president. Consequently, although a presidential candidate may run for office on the basis of his or her position on a single issue or a number of issues, in most cases the candidate cannot guarantee delivery of campaign promises. To enact policy, the legislature must be convinced that the president's policy preferences are the right ones.

Which system is "better"? It is hard to say, and the answer depends upon certain value judgments, since each system has its own strengths and weaknesses. On one hand, the parliamentary system does have a real advantage in rapid policy delivery, through the notions of party discipline and cabinet leadership. On the other hand, if good policy can be passed quickly, so can bad policy—"good" and "bad" here reflecting the values of specific constituencies in the public. Many in parliamentary systems bemoan the overwhelming influence of party discipline and corresponding "prime ministerial dictatorship," however, and some have even suggested that their respective systems consider conversion to the presidential model.[34]

The corresponding weakness/strength of the presidential system is precisely its slower, more deliberative legislative process. The argument suggested is that whereas it may (and usually does) take longer to pass policy, groups that are in a minority in an issue area have more opportunity to protect their interests, and the policy that is ultimately passed is more likely to be a good one. Put slightly more cynically, the policy that is ultimately passed is likely to offend as few as possible. On the other hand, a policy decision that is urgently needed may go unanswered for a long period of time while the legislature deliberates and argues with the president.

Another major area of difference between the two systems has to do with stability and tenure of office. In the presidential system, both the president and the legislature have fixed terms of office. They can be secure in their knowledge of their fixed terms in these positions, barring extraordinary occurrences (such as impeachment and conviction of the president in the United States, for example). This security permits both the president and the legislature to take either an unpopular position or an antagonistic position in relation to the other branch of government if it is believed that such a position is the proper one to take.

The parliamentary system offers no such job security. The chief executive can lose his or her position at any time, depending upon the mood of the legislature. A chief executive worried about keeping his or her job, then, would be less likely to take a position that is clearly disapproved of by the legislature than would a president, although an individual "out of step" with the legislature would not be likely to become chief executive in a parliamentary system. Moreover, the legislature would be less likely to rebel against executive leadership: party discipline would tend to force party members to follow the instructions of their leader (and the leader of the majority party, of course, would be the chief executive). If the legislature became too contentious, the chief executive could request a writ of dissolution from the head of state, effectively firing the legislature and calling for new elections.

As indicated earlier, it is easy to see that each of these systems has advantages and disadvantages as far as stability, policy output, protection of minority rights, ability to deliver on campaign promises, responsiveness to public opinion, and so on, are concerned.[35] Some of these values are simply inverses of others: responsiveness to majority public opinion may infringe on minority rights, for example. What is seen as an advantage to one observer may be a distinct disadvantage to another.

Both the presidential and parliamentary models of executive structure are conducive to democratic government. Both models can be responsive to public opinion, both can provide effective leadership, and both can provide for the general welfare of the political system. The differences between the two types of systems are differences of structure and process, not ideology. As such, it is difficult to argue that one type of system is, overall, "better" than the other; they are simply different.

The Military

The military is another structure of the executive branch of government that is significant in both the socialization and recruitment processes. It is sometimes regarded as *the* "elite" in developing nations, and it is also a structure that can be significant on its own in shaping the type and style of political participation that is permitted in the political arena. Although the military is not perceived as a politically significant actor in most stable Western democracies, we should not let a pervasive Western ethnocentrism (and here we really mean an Anglo-American ethnocentrism, since the military has clearly played significant political roles in modern French and German history) blind us to the fact that the military, as an institution, is a highly significant political actor in many developing regimes.

One need only look at a military or military-supported **coup d'état**[36] —a military takeover of the government—or attempted coups in recent history—in Thailand (2006), Mauritania (2005), Nepal (2005), the Central African Republic (2003), or Pakistan (1999), to take but a few examples—to see that in many instances political leaders are more concerned with what the military reaction will be to their decisions than they are with what the reactions of their respective legislatures or courts will be to their decisions.[37] In fact, even in countries such as India or Guatemala, where civilian governments "are clearly in control," the armed forces have been shown to exert considerable political influence.[38] "They are symbols of state sovereignty and the primary defenders against possible external or internal attack against the government. Given their prestige, responsibilities, and the material resources needed to fulfill these responsibilities, all military establishments exercise a significant degree of political influence."[39]

The study of what has been called praetorianism, or the **military coup**, has been justified on many counts, including the fact that such events happen frequently; as Chairman Mao said in China, power "grows out of the barrel of a gun." Among twenty Latin American nations, only two—Costa Rica and Mexico—have not experienced at least one attempted coup since 1945. In one study, it was suggested that 57 percent of the third world states examined had been under military rule for half or more than half of their respective periods of independence.[40] According to one observer, "Between 1945 and 1976, soldiers carried out successful coups in half of the eighteen Asian states," and more generally "it turns out that the military have intervened in approximately two-thirds of the more than one hundred non-Western states since 1945."[41]

Although coups may be motivated "for public-spirited reasons on behalf of constitution and nation," research has shown that "almost all coups are at least partly, and usually primarily, inspired by the military's own interests."[42] One result of a military takeover is almost invariably a significant increase in the defense budget of the regime.[43] Examined more broadly, research shows that "military rule was found to have negative or zero-order correlations with economic development." Moreover, "'politicians in uniform' invariably caused political decay."[44]

The issue of civilian control of the military is a very important one, especially in developing societies in which (civilian) governments may not yet have acquired the same degree of legitimacy and stability that one finds in the older Western democracies. The key issue involved in the maintenance of civilian control involves finding ways to set limits within which military leaders, and all members of the armed forces, "accept the government's definition of appropriate areas of responsibility."[45]

This does not mean in the final analysis that the military is prohibited from lobbying for policies it supports, but it does mean that the military agrees to do this in acceptable ways, and that the military agrees to accept the consequences of the policymaking process. Thus the military accepts a subordinate role in the political system. Ironically, in military regimes the leaders face the same problems as previous civilian governments did: how to keep their military underlings loyal and prevent an overthrow of the (military) forces in power at the time.[46]

Remember that the military is a political institution in most countries. The military role in a political system is also significantly affected by that country's political culture, history, and tradition. In some Latin American systems the idea of a military coup, if not desirable, is certainly recognized as a statistical possibility—in fact a probability—over the course of time.

Public Administration and the Bureaucracy

Apart from the creation of a cabinet, one of the key functions of the political executive is to administer public policy. In this respect, this volume would be seriously remiss if we did not discuss, even briefly, the comparative study of public administration and a comparative analysis of the structure that has come to be called the **bureaucracy**. Public bureaucracies are perhaps the most common political structures in the world today; they exist in all political systems, whether they are democratic or authoritarian, presidential or parliamentary, developed or underdeveloped. They are as nearly a universal political structure as one can find. As a specialized structure, "bureaucracy is common to all contemporary nation-states."[47]

The term *bureaucracy* itself is something of a problem, because it has a number of definitions, some value-free and some quite judgmental.

The scholar whose work is most closely associated with the term, and who contributed most to its development, is Max Weber (1864–1920). Weber's concern was "less with organizational efficiency than . . . the expansion of bureaucratic power, and with the implications of that expansion for fundamental liberal values."[48]

Weber saw "modern officialdom" as having characteristic patterns of behavior:

1. It has "fixed and official jurisdictional areas," which are "generally ordered by rules or administrative regulations."
2. The authority to give orders is also limited by rules, and officials have "coercive means" that they may use to enforce those rules.
3. The management of the office "is based upon written documents ('the files')," which requires a substantial staff to keep records.
4. Management "presupposes thorough and expert training."
5. Office activity requires the full attention of the official.
6. "The management of the office follows general rules."[49]

Generally, bureaucracies have been studied from several different perspectives.[50] First, they can be studied from an organizational perspective, focusing upon structures, organizational charts, lines of communication, hierarchical organization, a bureaucracy's formal rules, and how it operates.[51] Second, bureaucracies can be studied from a behavioral perspective, seeking to understand what bureaucracies do, how they behave, and what behavioral characteristics distinguish bureaucracies from other hierarchically organized structures.[52] A third approach focuses upon how well bureaucracies achieve their goals, and discusses their efficiency, specialization, rational activity, and role in the framework of democratic government.[53]

Bureaucracies (and here we speak of public bureaucracies, although most of what is said here about public bureaucracies applies to private bureaucracies as well) are typically complex systems of personnel, usually organized in a hierarchical fashion. That is, bureaucracies are usually pyramidally shaped, with the number of employees in higher positions being fewer than the number in lower positions.

The nature of a bureaucracy is usually that specialized jobs are performed by different divisions of the organization, and the organization is divided into functional categories. Bureaucracies are also well known for having well-institutionalized sets of rules or procedures and a relatively rigid set of precedents that govern their behavior.[54]

Bureaucracies often claim to be based upon some kind of merit system, in which one takes an examination to receive a position, or receives a position based upon perceived objective skills. This is characteristic of more developed nations[55] and is a reaction to practices dating back to the early years of the American Republic. President Andrew Jackson coined the phrase "spoils system," referring to a chief executive's right to appoint public personnel as one of the spoils of an electoral victory.

It is often the case in political bureaucracies that some type of civil service system exists to protect lower-level bureaucrats from political interference in their jobs; if they have been working for several years under one political party, they need not fear that they will lose their jobs should the opposition party gain control of the government. The other side of this coin, of course, is that a party that is new to government does not have the ability to put an unlimited number of its followers into positions of power when it wins an election. They must compete for positions through the established civil service system that exists at the time. Parties that have been out of power for a long time often claim that the bureaucracy "represents" the interests of the "old order," and that it is "resisting" their proposed changes. Often this is, in fact, actually the case.

Top-level positions in the bureaucracy often are political appointments; there is an expectation that after an election is held, all officials at this level will submit their resignations and permit a new cohort of political appointees to direct the administration of policy. Thus in a typical government ministry the minister and the deputy ministers will clearly be political appointments, with the minister being an MP and the deputy ministers being party loyalists, but the director-general (or an official with a similar title) will be a civil servant who remains in office even with a change of administrations.

The function of the bureaucracy is theoretically to administer the policy of the executive and to offer specialized advice to the executive,[56] not to make policy of its own. As indicated earlier, however, one of the frequent complaints about bureaucracies is that they do, in fact, make policy in an "irresponsible" way—irresponsible because nobody elected them.[57] As society has grown increasingly complex, resulting in the gradual expansion of the executive branch of government over the legislative branch of government—as discussed in Chapter 3—this administration has required more and more personnel, leading to a rapid growth of public bureaucracies.[58] Often the growth of bureaucracy in modern society is decried, but it has been demonstrated to be necessary to administer more and more complicated social policy.

Discussion Questions

1. What are the various roles that are played by the political executive?
2. Can you offer a distinction between presidential and parliamentary executive models?
3. What are bases of power of presidential systems?
4. What is the role of political parties in presidential systems?
5. Trace the development of the parliamentary executive structure and the changing role of the monarchy.
6. How would you explain the concept of constitutional monarchy?
7. Explain the selection of the chief executive in a parliamentary government.
8. What is the relationship of power between legislative supremacy and cabinet supremacy?
9. Explain the establishment of coalition governments.
10. How would you compare presidential and parliamentary executive structures: which is better?
11. What are the potential roles of the military in politics?
12. What is the role of public administration and the bureaucracy in politics?

Notes

1. See Locke's Section 126 in Sir Ernest Baker, ed., *Social Contract: Essays by Locke, Hume and Rousseau* (New York: Oxford University Press, 1970).

2. Clinton Rossiter, *The American Presidency* (New York: Mentor, 1960). A new edition of this was published by Johns Hopkins University Press in 1987.

3. See James Madison, *Notes on Debates in the Federal Convention of 1787* (Athens: Ohio University Press, 1966).

4. See Joel Aberbach and Mark Peterson, eds., *The Executive Branch* (New York: Oxford University Press, 2005); and David Orenticher, *Two Presidents Are Better Than One: The Case for a Bipartisan Executive Branch* (New York: New York University Press, 2013).

5. "The Buck Stops Here" was an unattributed quote on a sign that was kept on the desk of President Harry Truman.

6. See Sidney Milkis and Michael Nelson, *The American Presidency: Origins and Development, 1776–2007* (Washington, DC: Congressional Quarterly, 2008); or Guy Burton and Ted Goertzel, *Presidential Leadership in the Americas Since Independence* (Lanham: Lexington, 2016). For descriptions of the US presidency, see Adam L. Warber, *Executive Orders and the Modern Presidency: Legislating from the Oval Office* (Boulder: Lynne Rienner, 2006). A classic study of the presidency can be found in Rossiter, *American Presidency*; or Richard Neustadt, *Presidential Power* (New York: New American Library, 1964).

7. The famous quote by John Adams, the first vice president of the United States, is as follows: "I am possessed of two separate powers, the one *in esse* and the other *in posse.* I am Vice President. In this I am nothing, but I may be everything"; Rossiter, *American Presidency,* p. 131. See also Robert Gilbert, *Managing Crisis: Presidential Disability and the Twenty-Fifth Amendment* (New York: Fordham University Press, 2006).

8. On the powers of the vice president, see Marilyn Anderson, *The Vice Presidency* (Philadelphia: Chelsea House, 2001). See also Timothy Walch, *At the President's Side: The Vice Presidency in the Twentieth Century* (Columbia: University of Missouri Press, 1997).

9. On presidential elections, see Mark Halperin and John Harris, *The Way to Win: Taking the White House in 2008* (New York: Random, 2006); and *Presidential Elections, 1789–2004* (Washington, DC: Congressional Quarterly, 2005). An interesting approach is found in D. Grier Stephenson, *Campaigns and the Court: The U.S. Supreme Court in Presidential Elections* (New York: Columbia University Press, 1999), a book that is especially interesting since it was written before the election of 2000, the outcome of which was substantially affected by a decision of the Supreme Court.

10. *Federalist* Number 68 by Alexander Hamilton discusses the rationalization of this structure. See *The Federalist Papers* (New York: New American Library, 1961), pp. 411–415. See also John Fortier and Walter Berns, *After the People Vote: A Guide to the Electoral College* (Washington, DC: AEI, 2004).

11. There were crimes involved in his impeachment, of course, but there was substantial debate over whether sexual offenses and covering them up were the "high crimes and misdemeanors" suggested by the Constitution. See Leonard Kaplan and Beverly Moran, *Aftermath: The Clinton Impeachment and the Presidency in the Age of Political Spectacle* (New York: New York University Press, 2001); and *Proceedings of the United States Senate in the Impeachment Trial of President William Jefferson Clinton* (Washington, DC: Superintendent of Documents, 2000).

12. See Pendleton Herring and Sidney Pearson, *Presidential Leadership: The Political Relations of Congress and the Chief Executive* (New York: Routledge, 2017); or Riccardo Pelizzo and Frederick Stapenhurst, *Parliamentary Oversight Tools: A Comparative Analysis* (New York: Routledge, 2012).

13. See Steven Calabresi and Christopher Yoo, *The Unitary Executive: Presidential Power from Washington to Bush* (New Haven: Yale University Press, 2008); and Benjamin Kleinerman, *The Discretionary President: The Promise and Peril of Executive Power* (Lawrence: University Press of Kansas, 2009).

14. See Michael Nelson, *Guide to the Presidency and the Executive Branch* (Thousand Oaks, CA: Congressional Quarterly, 2013); and Mark Rozell, *Executive Privilege: Presidential Power, Secrecy, and Accountability* (Lawrence: University Press of Kansas, 2010).

15. See Christopher Kelley, *Executing the Constitution: Putting the President Back into the Constitution* (Albany: State University of New York Press, 2006); Milkis and Nelson, *The American Presidency.*

16. See Charles O. Jones, *The Trusteeship Presidency: Jimmy Carter and the United States Congress* (Baton Rouge: Louisiana State University Press, 1988); and Burton Kaufman, *The Carter Years* (New York: Facts on File, 2006).

17. Some good comparative works include Gretchen Bauer and Manon Tremblay, *Women in Executive Power: A Global Overview* (New York: Routledge, 2011); and Arend Lijphart, *Parliamentary vs. Presidential Government* (New York: Oxford University Press, 1992).

18. See the data in Jean Blondel, *Comparative Legislatures* (Englewood Cliffs, NJ: Prentice Hall, 1973), pp. 144–153, col. 39.

19. See Richard Rose, *The Prime Minister in a Shrinking World* (Cambridge: Blackwell, 2001); and Peter Hennessy, *The Prime Minister: The Office and Its Holders Since 1945* (London: Penguin, 2001).

20. See, for example, *The Saint Vincent Constitution Order, 1979* (Kingstown, Saint Vincent: Government Printing Office, 1979), pp. 38–39, establishing a constitution for the new nation of St. Vincent. Sections 50 and 51 outline the executive power: Section 50 states that "the executive authority of Saint Vincent is vested in Her Majesty [and] . . . may be exercised on behalf of Her Majesty by the Governor-General." Section 51 notes, "(1) There shall be a Prime Minister of Saint Vincent who shall be appointed by the Gov-

ernor-General. (2) Whenever the Governor-General has occasion to appoint a Prime Minister he shall appoint a Representative who appears to him likely to command the support of the majority of Representatives. . . . (6) The Governor-General shall remove the Prime Minister from office if a resolution of no confidence in the Government is passed by the House and the Prime Minister does not within three days either resign from his office or advise the Governor-General to dissolve Parliament."

21. This section is based upon a much longer discussion of the same subject in the now classic study by Sydney Bailey, *British Parliamentary Democracy* (Boston: Houghton Mifflin, 1958), pp. 12–20.

22. This argument was expounded at length in his *True Law of Free Monarchies* in 1603.

23. R. M. Dawson, *The Government of Canada* (Toronto: University of Toronto Press, 1965), pp. 184–185.

24. The election in Israel in 1996 created a unique variation on the general parliamentary model after a constitutional change there, one in which the legislature was directly elected by the people (in proportional representation voting), and the prime minister was also directly elected by the people. In addition, following the general parliamentary model, the head of state—in Israel called the president—is elected by the Knesset, the legislature. After two elections with this model, Israel changed its constitution again back to the model it had used prior to 1996 because it found the changes to be more destabilizing than the older system had been. See Gregory Mahler, *Politics and Government in Israel: The Maturation of a Modern State,* 3rd ed. (Lanham: Rowman and Littlefield, 2016).

25. In fact, most cabinet members come from the legislative body. See Patrick Malcolmson and Richard Myers, *The Canadian Regime: An Introduction to Parliamentary Government in Canada* (Toronto: University of Toronto Press, 2009).

26. One system with a legal requirement is Barbados. See the *Barbados Independence Order, 1966,* pp. 62–63, Section 66: (1) "The Office of Prime Minister shall become vacant . . . ; (2) If the House of Assembly by a resolution which has received the affirmative vote of a majority of all the members thereof resolves that the appointment of the Prime Minister ought to be revoked."

27. Blondel, *Comparative Legislatures,* pp. 144–153, col. 42.

28. See Kaare Strøm, "Deferred Gratification and Minority Governments in Scandinavia," *Legislative Studies Quarterly* 11, no. 4 (1986): 583–606.

29. Blondel, *Comparative Legislatures,* pp. 144–153, col. 41.

30. See Kaare Strøm, Wolfgang Müller, and Torbjörn Bergman, eds., *Cabinets and Coalition Bargaining: The Democratic Life Cycle in Western Europe* (New York: Oxford University Press, 2008); or Catherine Moury, *Coalition Government and Party Mandate: How Coalition Agreements Constrain Ministerial Action* (New York: Routledge, 2013).

31. See Ian Budge and Hans Keman, *Parties and Democracy: Coalition Formation and Government Functioning in Twenty States* (New York: Oxford University Press, 1990). See also Peter Russell, *Two Cheers for Minority Government: The Evolution of Canadian Parliamentary Democracy* (Toronto: Emond Montgomery, 2008); or Nicolo Conti and Francesco Marangoni, *The Challenge of Coalition Government: The Italian Case* (New York: Routledge, 2015).

32. A very good comparative study is Simon Hix, Abdul Noury, and Gerard Roland, *Democratic Politics in the European Parliament* (New York: Cambridge University Press, 2007). See also Daniela Giannetti and Kenneth Benoit, *Intra Party Politics and Coalition Governments* (New York: Routledge, 2009).

33. See Strøm, Müller, and Bergman, *Cabinets and Coalition Bargaining.* See also Vernon Bogdanor, *The Coalition and the Constitution* (Oxford: Hart, 2011).

34. See, for example, Alan Arian and David Nachmias, *Executive Governance in Israel* (New York: Palgrave, 2002). See also Steven Levitt, *Power in the Balance: Presidents, Parties, and Legislatures in Peru and Beyond* (Notre Dame, IN: University of Notre Dame Press, 2012).

35. Some discussion of this is found in Riccardo Pelizzo and Frederick Stapenhurst, *Government Accountability and Legislative Oversight* (New York: Routledge, 2014).

36. See, for example, George Kieh and Pita Agbese, *The Military and Politics in Africa: From Intervention to Democratic Control* (Burlington, VT: Ashgate, 2004); or Gordon Tullock and Charles Rowley, *The Social Dilemma: Of Autocracy, Revolution, Coup d'État, and War* (Indianapolis: Liberty Fund, 2005).

37. See, for example, Anthony F. Lang, *Agency and Ethics: The Politics of Military Intervention* (Albany: State University of New York Press, 2001); or Paul Drake and Ivan Jansic, eds., *The Struggle for Democracy in Chile, 1982–1990* (Lincoln: University of Nebraska Press, 1991).

38. See William Maley and C. J. G. Sampford, *From Civil Strife to Civil Society: Civil and Military Responsibilities in Disrupted States* (New York: United Nations University Press, 2003); Husain Haqqani, *Pakistan: Between Mosque and Military* (Washington, DC: Brookings Institution, 2005); and Michael Drake, *Problematics of Military Power: Government, Discipline, and the Subject of Violence* (Portland: Cass, 2002).

39. Eric Nordlinger, *Soldiers in Politics: Military Coups and Governments* (Englewood Cliffs, NJ: Prentice Hall, 1977), p. 3. See also Hasan-Askari Rizvi, *Military, State, and Society in Pakistan* (New York: Macmillan, 2000) for an example.

40. Theo Farrell, Frans Osinga, and James Russell, *Military Adaptation in Afghanistan* (Stanford: Stanford University Press, 2013), p. 18. See also Jimmy D. Kandeh, *Coups from Below: Armed Subalterns and State Power in West Africa* (New York: Palgrave Macmillan, 2004).

41. Nordlinger, *Soldiers,* pp. 5–6. For examples of this kind of literature, see Aqil Shah, *The Army and Democracy: Military Politics in Pakistan* (Cambridge: Harvard University Press, 2014); or Jerry Davila, *Dictatorship in South America* (Chichester: Wiley-Blackwell, 2013).

42. Nordlinger, *Soldiers,* p. 192. See also Carlos Maria Vilas, *Shaky Democracies and Popular Fury: From Military Coups to Peoples' Coups* (Tampa: University of South Florida Press, 2004); and Michael Kiselycznyk and Phillip Saunders, *Civil-Military Relations in China: Assessing the PLA's Role in Elite Politics* (Washington, DC: National Defense University Press, 2010).

43. Talukder Maniruzzaman, *Military Withdrawal from Politics: A Comparative Study* (Cambridge, MA: Ballinger, 1987), p. 3.

44. Ibid., p. 205.

45. Claude E. Welch Jr., *Civilian Control of the Military: Theory and Cases from Developing Countries* (Albany: State University of New York Press, 1976), p. 2; and Marcus Mietzner, *Military Politics, Islam, and the State in Indonesia* (Singapore: Institute of Southeast Asian Studies, 2009).

46. Christopher Clapham and George Philip, *The Political Dilemmas of Military Regimes* (Totowa, NJ: Barnes and Noble, 1985). See also Risa Brooks, *Shaping Strategy: The Civil-Military Politics of Strategic Assessment* (Princeton: Princeton University Press, 2008).

47. Ferrel Heady, *Public Administration: A Comparative Perspective* (New York: Marcel Dekker, 1984), p. 59. See also B. Guy Peters and Jon Pierre, *Handbook of Public Administration* (Thousand Oaks, CA: Sage, 2003); and Kevin Smith and Michael Licari, *Public Administration: Power and Politics in the Fourth Branch of Government* (Los Angeles: Roxbury, 2006).

48. David Beetham, *Bureaucracy* (Minneapolis: University of Minnesota Press, 1987), p. 58. More recent works on Weber include Fritz Ringer, *Max Weber: An Intellectual Biography* (Chicago: University of Chicago Press, 2004).

49. Max Weber, "Bureaucracy," in H. H. Gerth and C. Wright Mills, eds., *From Max Weber: Essays in Sociology* (New York: Oxford University Press, 1978), p. 196.

50. This section is based upon much more detailed analysis in Heady, *Public Administration,* pp. 61–64. See Michael Spicer, *In Defense of Politics in Public Administration* (Tuscaloosa: University of Alabama Press, 2010).

51. This is the approach of Edward Schneier, *Crafting Constitutional Democracies: The Politics of Institutional Design* (Lanham: Rowman and Littlefield, 2006). See Patricia Ingraham, Jon Pierre, and B. Guy Peters, eds., *Comparative Administrative Change and Reform: Lessons Learned* (Montreal: McGill-Queen's University Press, 2010).

52. To a substantial degree this approach is illustrated in Walter Kickert, ed., *The Study of Public Management in Europe and the U.S.: A Comparative Analysis of National Distinctiveness* (New York: Routledge, 2008). See also Dennis Riley and Bryan Brophy-Baermann, *Bureaucracy and the Policy Process* (Lanham: Rowman and Littlefield, 2006).

53. An example of this might be J. Michael Martinez, *Public Administration Ethics for the 21st Century* (Santa Barbara: Praeger, 2009). See also B. Guy Peters and Jon Pierre, *Politicization of the Civil Service in Comparative Perspective* (New York: Routledge, 2004).

54. See Jan-Erik Lane, *State Management: An Enquiry into Models of Public Administration* (New York: Routledge, 2009).

55. See the discussion by Heady, "Relating Bureaucratic and Political Development," in his *Public Administration,* pp. 409–417.

56. A very good study of the advising function is by Norma Riccucci, *Public Administration: Traditions of Inquiry and Philosophies of Knowledge* (Washington, DC: Georgetown University Press, 2010).

57. A very good discussion of some of the philosophical dimensions of this problem, and how democratic control can coexist with bureaucracy, can be found in David Rosenbloom, Rosemary O'Leary, and Joshua Chanin, *Public Administration and Law* (Boca Raton, FL: CRC, 2010).

58. This point is discussed at some length in the study by Peters in B. Guy Peters, *The Politics of Bureaucracy* (London: Routledge, 2009). Peters's second chapter is titled "The Growth of Government and Administration," and he discusses the growth of administration not only in the executive branch, but also in the legislature and in other areas of the government.

5

Judiciaries

Learning Outcomes

After reading this chapter, you will be able to

- Understand judiciaries as one of the three key Lockean institutions of government.
- Appreciate the comparative study of judiciaries, with their playing significantly different roles in different systems.
- Explain courts as nonpolitical institutions.
- Articulate the idea of law as an output of government.
- Describe the different types of law (scientific, moral, natural, positive).
- Evaluate the concept of a legal culture.
- Distinguish between common law legal systems and code law legal systems.
- Appreciate non-Western legal systems and their differences from Western models.
- Explain sources of law.
- Highlight key structures of legal systems.
- Summarize judicial functions in political systems.
- Place the concept of judicial review in its appropriate context in terms of governmental structures.

Having examined the key Lockean political institutions of legislatures and executives, it is appropriate for us to discuss another group of political institutions that can be very significant for the political systems in which they are found. These institutions, judiciaries, can play absolutely crucial roles in their respective political systems, and there are many,

many examples that we can cite of instances in which they are singularly responsible for the success—or failure—of the political system in which they might be found. Although these institutions are less often the focus of comparative political analysis, it is important that students understand the significance they can have in the successful operation of politics around the world.

On the Comparative Study of Judiciaries

After our discussion of legislative and executive structures, the structure of government suggested by John Locke in 1690 that remains to be discussed is "a known and indifferent judge, with authority to determine all differences according to the established law."[1] One of the functions that was ascribed to constitutions in our discussion in Chapter 2 was that they serve as an expression of the basic laws of the regime. At this point we should say something about the function of legal systems in political processes and the importance of legal culture in general, as well as something about the role of judges and courts in political systems.

Of the three major Lockean governmental structures—the legislature, the executive, and the judiciary—that can be observed on a crossnational basis, courts and legal systems generally receive the least attention in introductory texts and comparative studies,[2] unless, of course, the study in question explicitly focuses upon the judiciary or the law.[3] Why is this the case? Two possible suggestions can be offered here.

First, as far as systemic characteristics and political institutions go, legal systems and courts may be the most system-specific. That is, although both executives and legislatures have structural idiosyncrasies, and have behaviors that vary on a country-by-country basis, we can still make a number of useful generalizations about both their structures (for example, presidential systems as compared with parliamentary systems) and their behavior (for example, a system with high party discipline compared with a system with low party discipline). This level of generalization is hard to achieve with legal systems and courts. Although we can speak of constitutional regimes—governments of laws, not ruled by individual whim—we very quickly get to the point at which individual system-level characteristics of judiciaries must be discussed; consequently generalizability is low.[4]

Second, while executives and legislatures are undoubtedly part of the political process, in many political systems the courts are explicitly excluded from the political arena.[5] This is not a refutation of Locke's argument that courts (judges) are necessary to society; it simply limits the role of the judges and the courts to one of arbitration or mediation.

They are not, it is claimed, part of the lawmaking or policymaking process specifically, or of the political arena generally. (It should be noted, in fact, that Locke suggested that the function of the judge was to "determine all differences according to the established law," not to actually make the law or public policy.) Accordingly, many political scientists have left the judiciary out of their studies of the political arena and the policymaking process generally.

In explaining the almost nonpolitical role of the courts, one study pointed out that courts, "logically and historically, have been undemocratic institutions. An increased role for the courts, then, could render a political order less democratic."[6] Thus, although the courts have often been significant in maintaining individual rights, they have often kept a low profile in their respective polities, thereby generating relatively little scholarship on their comparative political impact.

Although courts are often nonpolitical in nature, they do play a significant role in political systems. As we shall see, in many systems courts play a role through judicial review in shaping the law.[7]

The Idea of Law

The idea of law tends to be assumed whenever we think of politics. That is, there is an implicit (Western, ethnocentric) assumption that political systems are based, to varying degrees, upon the rule of law. This assumption is made because so many of our contacts with government come in relation to governmental rules, regulations, and administrative guidelines. It is almost impossible to think of government existing without laws; the "authoritative allocation of values" with which politics is concerned deals with laws.

Law is generally regarded as one of the greatest achievements of civilization.[8] It is concerned with basic rules of conduct that reflect to some degree the concept of justice. An ideal of justice frequently expressed is that the government should be "a government of laws and not of men."[9] This means that there should be some consistency in expectations of behavior, and that when deviations from this behavior take place, the social response will be more or less consistent. In practice, this ideal is generally interpreted to mean a legal system that treats everyone equally, and that is not subject to change through the arbitrary acts of a dictator, or even the whim of transient majorities.[10] Even in the seventeenth century, John Locke saw law as being the principal attraction of society: "Thus mankind, notwithstanding all the privileges of the state of nature, being but in an ill condition while they remain in it, are quickly driven into society. . . . [They] take sanctuary under the established laws of government."[11]

There are a number of different kinds of law to which the interested student can find reference, including scientific law, moral law, divine law, natural law, and positive law,[12] among others (see Box 5.1). **Scientific law** refers to observations and measurements that have been empirically determined and that focus upon physical, biological, and chemical concepts, not social questions. **Moral law** refers to precepts or guidelines that are based upon subjective values, beliefs, and attitudes, focusing upon behavior: the proper way of doing things. **Divine law**, as well, will be seen to vary depending upon the religious or theological conceptual framework from which it is said to be derived.

The two major approaches to law with which we as social scientists are concerned are natural law and positive law. **Natural law** refers to a body of precepts governing human behavior that is "more basic than man-made law, and one that is based on fundamental principles of justice."[13] The type of law with which governments are most concerned is **positive law**, which can be said to have three major identifiable characteristics: it is human-made, it is designed to govern human behavior, and it is enforceable by appropriate governmental action. Positive law gets its name not from the fact that it is necessarily "good," but from the fact that it requires "positive action" by people to bring it into being (whereas natural law exists in the state of nature and is said to exist whether the state "creates" it or not, and religious law is believed to have been given by a higher power, and similarly exists independent of the state).

Conflict has erupted throughout human history when natural law and positive law appear to disagree. Political philosophers from the time of Cicero (106–143 B.C.E.)—including John of Salisbury, Thomas Aquinas, Thomas Hobbes, John Locke, Jean-Jacques Rousseau, David Hume, Jeremy Bentham, and Karl Marx—through to philosophers of the present day, have dealt with this thorny issue.[14] What is the individual to do when the law of the state says to do one thing, but one's perception of natural law, of the fundamental standard of "rightness," says to do something else? Many have argued that human laws (positive laws) that conflict with

---

Box 5.1   Different Kinds of Law

- Scientific law: empirical; observations and measurements.
- Moral law: subjective; values, beliefs, attitudes.
- Divine law: religious or theological conceptual framework.
- Natural law: perceived fundamental principles.
- Positive law: human-made, governing behavior, enforceable by the state.

natural laws (or religious laws) are null and void. St. Augustine's "two sword" theory in the early fifth century was one attempt to resolve this conflict.[15] Augustine argued that natural law and divine law were the same thing: the laws of nature are God's laws. Individuals are required to obey earthly (positive) law only insofar as it does not conflict with natural law. When natural law and positive law conflict, it is the law of God that must be obeyed, according to Augustine.

Legal Culture

The concept of a "culture" is one that has been developed primarily by sociologists and anthropologists. A **legal culture** can be considered to be "a set of deeply rooted, historically conditioned attitudes about the nature of law, about the role of law in the society and the polity, about the proper organization and operation of a legal system, and about the way law is, or should be made, applied, studied, perfected, and taught. The legal tradition relates the legal system to the culture of which it is a partial expression."[16] The concept of a legal culture, then, focuses upon the beliefs, attitudes, and values of society relative to the law and politics.[17]

We discussed the idea that political systems should be "governments of law and not of men." The reader will recall that in our discussion of constitutions and constitutional government, one of the dividing lines between (behaviorally) constitutional and unconstitutional regimes was the degree to which the behavior of regimes was limited or controlled by law. Are there limits beyond which the government absolutely may not go? Or conversely, is the function of law perceived to be primarily that of controlling individual behavior, keeping individuals "under control," while the government may do whatever it wishes?

A nation's legal culture will shape the role that the law and legal institutions play in the political realm. For example, the fact that the United States is "the most litigious country in the world"[18] suggests that Americans are more likely to look to the courts for the resolution of conflict than might citizens of other polities. On the other hand, "the Japanese legal culture puts a premium on informal settlement of legal disputes based on informal controls and social sanction without legal procedure."[19]

Although political cultures do vary on a nation-by-nation basis, there are certain "families" or groupings of legal cultures that may be suggested here for purposes of generalization: (1) the Romano-Germanic family; (2) the family of the common law; (3) the family of socialist law; and (4) the non-Western legal families.[20]

The **Romano-Germanic approach to law**, sometimes referred to as code law, has developed from the basis of Roman law at the time of Justinian (C.E. 533).[21] This type of law, as contrasted with common law, is based upon comprehensively written legislative statutes, often bound together as codes. The **Code Napoleon** was just such a bound collection; the Emperor Napoleon (reigned 1804–1815) decided that law throughout his empire needed to be standardized, and he had a single, comprehensive set of laws assembled and disseminated. The Code Napoleon influenced legal structures from Europe to North America to Asia. The French legal system is characteristic of a code law system, and in North America today the legal systems of Louisiana and Quebec have similar characteristics, evidence of their (French) colonial heritage.

The **common law system**, found in England and countries modeled on English law (including the United States), is sometimes called Anglo-American law[22] and has been referred to as "judge-made law."[23] This is not to suggest that today's laws in these political systems are not made by the legislatures of those systems, or that, conversely, today's laws are made by judges in those systems. Rather, the term suggests that when the science of the law was being developed in England in the twelfth century, it was the judges who made decisions. Today, **judicial precedent** plays a major role in common law nations—the process is referred to as *stare decisis* ("to stand by things decided").[24] A judge may use a previously adjudicated case as a guide for his or her decision, but the judge may decide that there are new characteristics involved in the case at hand that require deviation from earlier decisions. Of course, today, the legislature plays a highly significant role in designing the laws the judge is applying to the specific situation.

The differences between the code law systems and the common law systems can easily be overstated, but two main characteristics should be pointed out. First, judges play a slightly less significant role in decision-making in the code law systems, with correspondingly greater influence exercised by the legislature. Second, the common law systems, characteristic of Anglo-American nations, try to minimize the likelihood of an innocent person being convicted by setting up various procedural and substantive safeguards. The code law systems, characterized by the system found in France, place "more stress on preventing a guilty person from escaping punishment."[25]

Socialist law derives from a different philosophical root.[26] Karl Marx and his philosophy assumed that law was a tool of the state in capitalist societies and that it was used to oppress the working class. Marx argued that in a perfect socialist state there would be no need for law at all, once the economic ills of society were cured. In fact, of course, things have not turned out to be quite as simple as Marx thought they would. Law in the former Soviet Union, perhaps the best example of such a system, played, if anything, a greater role than in Western democracies.[27]

In the second and third quarters of the twentieth century, Soviet Marxists saw law as a tool of the state, to be used to work toward a socialist society: The state could (and should) use law to further its ends. Law exists to further the interests of citizens. The state knows better than any individuals what the interests of the citizens are. Thus anything the state does must be legal. Therefore, law becomes simply another instrument of state policy.

In non-Western legal systems, such as those of some developing nations, legal cultures are quite different and depend upon (1) local traditions and customs, (2) the legal culture of the colonizing power (if any) that controlled the political infrastructure prior to independence, and (3) the degree to which the colonizing power permitted autonomy and development during the colonial era. In some non-Western systems, religious law, especially Islamic law, now has a major role in the general legal framework of the regime. In others, religious and tribal laws are blended with colonial legal values. Elsewhere, developing nations have completely forsaken their traditional legal cultures and have opted instead for modern legal structures and processes.[28] To take just one example, the legal culture found in Israel today is a blend of Turkish law and British law (former colonial powers in the Middle East), religious law (including Jewish, Muslim, and Christian components), as well as contemporary legal and judicial values.[29]

Sources of Law

For as long as political systems have been based upon the rule of law, there have been a variety of sources for the laws that have existed. At one point in time, patterns of behavior were governed by religious or *moral values*. This kind of law generally comes in entire bodies, often in a specifically delineated set. Thus the Mosaic Law—the Ten Commandments said to be brought down from Mount Sinai by Moses—was a body of law. Similarly, the Quran, the sacred book of the Muslim religion, contains a body of laws. This religious law often is interpreted to be natural law, as we distinguished the terms earlier, although some might argue that religious law may contain elements much more specific than natural law. For example, religious laws may prohibit the consumption of certain foods, regulate men's or women's dress, or govern working on a certain day of the week, when there is no immediately apparent reason why this should be considered to be part of a "law of nature." Depending upon the nature of a society, this type of religious or moral value may become entrenched in the legal framework of a political system.[30]

Some monarchs, notably James I of England (reigned 1603–1625), used religion as a basis of their power. In his *True Law of Free Monar-*

chies,[31] James I developed his theory of "divine right of kings," arguing that rulers derived their powers from God and that policies they designed would have the force of law. James I was not the only monarch to believe this, and "the will of the monarch" became a major source of law for a long time.

Another source of law is tradition or custom. We made the distinction in our discussion of legislatures and executives between de jure (in law) and de facto (in fact) political power, and it has been argued that tradition may develop the force of law, even if it never becomes law. The tradition in England, for example, that the monarch selects the leader of the largest party in the House of Commons to be prime minister, has become so established that it is taken as part of the "Westminster model" constitutional regime there and elsewhere. Similarly, the tradition that the prime minister "must" resign if he or she receives a vote of no confidence may take on the force of law, even if it hasn't become actual law.

Sometimes traditions are left unwritten, as the parliamentary case of the head of state acting "on the advice" of the chief executive illustrates. On other occasions, traditions are actually formalized and made part of the constitutional or legal framework of a political system. For example, the tradition of US presidents serving no more than two terms of office was firmly entrenched in US politics prior to World War II. George Washington started the tradition, and if a president did not bow out of politics at the end of his first term of office, he consistently did so at the end of his second term. When Franklin Delano Roosevelt violated this tradition and successfully ran for a third term, and then a fourth term, some reacted quite strongly. This reaction led to the Twenty-Second Amendment to the Constitution, limiting presidential terms of office.[32]

Certainly, a major source of law in contemporary regimes is the constitution of the regime. Some national constitutions include specific legal proscriptions that must be followed in the political system, as well as more general descriptions of the structures and institutions to be found in the regime. The US Constitution, for example, contains a number of specific limitations and guidelines that not only are laws in their own right (for example, "Congress shall make no law . . . abridging the freedom of speech"), but also have generated an entire body of supplementary law.

In many settings this happens through yet another source of law, the judiciary. Judicial decisionmaking, including the interpretation of constitutional dogma and legislative statutes, and the application of judicial precedents to new circumstances, has resulted in a great deal of judge-made law.

Another governmental structure directly concerned with the creation of law is, of course, the legislature. The legislature as an institution derives its name from the law (*legis*), and certainly one of the functions most commonly attributed to the legislature is the lawmaking function. In some settings, though, we need to remember that the legislature may be more important in the political system in some other capacity—its legislative function may be primarily that of a rubber stamp.

More and more often today, we see arguments that legislatures are in a decline as far as their legitimate legislative powers are concerned. The argument suggests that, in both presidential and parliamentary systems of government, legislatures are surrendering their legislative powers to the executive branch in exchange for the rubber stamp function. The question important to ask is, Why is this so?[33]

Theodore Lowi has argued that part of this problem stems from the complexity of modern society and government. To develop this reasoning, it was easy for legislatures in 1690 to perform their legislative tasks—for example, to pass laws forbidding poaching on the king's land. It is much harder for legislatures to address the complex social problems of the twenty-first century that governments must address: For example, how can a legislature fight poverty? It could pass a law making it illegal to be poor, but that would not solve the fundamental problem. Lowi suggests in his book *The End of Liberalism* that problems such as these may be beyond the competence of legislatures. Often, the only response to these complex problems that is available to a legislature is to pass on leadership on the issue to an executive agency, appropriate adequate funding, and give the executive agency authority to set rules and policy by itself.[34]

This leads to yet another source of law—administrative decisions. A legislature may decide, for example, that it does not have either the time or the capacity to make highly specialized policy decisions regarding food and drugs. Its response to this quandary, given a feeling that some regulation in this area is clearly necessary, might be to establish a national agency on food and drugs, giving commissioners on the agency authority to set standards and regulations ensuring a constant quality of both food and drugs. The actions of a majority of commissioners, then, may have the force of law (violations of their decisions and rules could result in fines or imprisonment) and could have the same effect as legislated laws, even though the legislature really was not responsible for specific policy set by the agency.[35]

We can see, then, that although positive laws may derive from a number of sources, their effects can be the same. Whether these laws stem from religious or moral values, tradition or custom, a constitution, judicial interpretation, legislation, or administrative actions and decisions, all may serve the functions of regulating behavior in society.

Structures in Legal Systems

The heart of a judicial system's structure is to be found in its network of courts. Theodore Becker, a significant contributor to the cross-national literature on judiciaries, has characterized courts as having seven components. A court is

1. An individual or group of individuals;
2. With power to make decisions in disputes;
3. Before whom the parties or their advocates present the facts involved in the dispute and cite principles (in statutes, or other forms) that
4. Are applied by that individual or those individuals;
5. Who *believe* that they should listen to the facts and apply cited principles impartially, and;
6. That they may so decide, and;
7. As an independent body.[36]

The main service of modern courts, then, is to serve as an arena in which controlled conflict may take place. The controls exercised upon this conflict are very rigid, emphasizing verbal, conceptual, legal, and philosophical strengths rather than physical strength. (Let us not forget that at the time of King Arthur, conflicts were often resolved by "champions" in physical combat.)

To process the disputes as smoothly and efficiently as possible, judicial structures are established in political systems. The actual structures of these courts vary tremendously on a system-by-system basis. Federal political systems may have legal infrastructures that reflect their federal makeup; unitary systems may be more simply organized. Some systems may have very specialized courts as part of their judicial structure, while others may not.

Judiciaries tend to be organized in a pyramidal fashion, with a larger number of courts of initial adjudication, fewer appeals courts, and a single, ultimate, supreme court. In many judicial systems, all cases must begin on the "ground floor" and work their way up through the judicial system. There are instances in some judicial systems, however, in which the appeals courts and supreme court may have some original jurisdiction—some cases may start at the intermediate or top level and not have to work their way up on appeal to that point.

The question of **jurisdiction**, of which court (or level of court) has authority to adjudicate a specific question, can be complex.[37] For example, in the US judicial system, jurisdiction is divided between federal courts and state courts, reflecting the federal nature of the polity. Sometimes jurisdiction might overlap. In the United States today, for example, it is not a federal crime to rob a bank, but a state crime. It is, however, a federal crime to rob a bank insured by the federal government (and, it turns out, virtually all banks today are federally insured).

So, the individual who robs a federally insured bank actually commits two crimes—robbing a bank (a state crime) and robbing a federally insured bank (a federal crime)—and can, accordingly, face two trials. (It should be noted that this liability to face two trials is not the same thing as "double jeopardy," against which the individual is protected under the Fifth Amendment to the US Constitution. The Fifth Amendment says that no person shall "be subject for the same offense to be twice put in jeopardy of life or limb." If a person commits two offenses, even in the same act, he or she may be tried twice; he or she may not be tried twice for the same offense.)

The US federal judicial structure, then, consists of a single federal judicial pyramid and fifty separate state judicial pyramids. This double-structured judicial framework was designed to accommodate the federal nature of the US political arena, although this does occasionally make determination of jurisdiction more difficult.

Other federal political systems manage to allow for reflection of their federal character in their judicial systems without this parallel structure. In the case of Canada, for example, there is no double-pyramid structure.[38] Courts are "constituted, maintained, and organized" by the provinces in both the areas of civil and criminal law. At the same time, however, to balance the grant of exclusive power over civil procedure given to the provinces, the federal government has exclusive jurisdiction over criminal procedure, and it is the federal government that controls the appointment, salary, and tenure of the judges in the courts that are established by the provinces. Thus, the Canadian federal judicial structure appears as ten separate provincial pyramids, designed by the provinces and staffed by federal appointments. Civil procedure is established by the provinces (so that, for example, civil procedures in Ontario might be different from civil procedures in British Columbia), but criminal procedure will be standardized through its control by the federal government. There is, moreover, a single Supreme Court of Canada that acts as an appeals court for the entire nation.[39]

We can see, then, that the actual structural design of judicial systems varies on a nation-by-nation basis. Questions of jurisdiction, appeals, and procedure are so tailored to individual national characteristics that even members of the same legal cultural "families" that we saw earlier—the common law family, for example, or the code law family—may differ significantly in terms of specific political structures. Not only do Canada and the United States differ significantly in the manner in which their judicial structures reflect their federal natures, but even within a nation judicial structures can vary. For example, the court structure in Massachusetts differs from courts in California, and courts in Alberta differ from courts in Newfoundland.

Judicial Functions

The judicial function has been characterized by one scholar of comparative politics as consisting of "the determination of the meaning of laws and rules, the imposition of penalties for violating those rules, the deciding on the relative rights and obligations of individuals and the community, the determination of the area of freedom to be allowed persons within the political system, and the arbitration of disputes between individuals and officials."[40] With such a list of functions, it is no wonder that courts or judiciaries are important political structures. Given a focus upon functions, the structure of a judiciary can vary, as we have just seen.

Judges are often in an invaluable position to protect minority rights. Most judicial systems offer some degree of protection for judges, shielding them from political consequences of their actions. Judges not only can take a nonpolitical view of conflicts, but they are also free to act; in most systems judges cannot be fired for unpopular decisions. Judges have the power to hand down decisions that might be so unpopular, socially or politically, that legislators or executives might hesitate to act, and judges should not need to be worried about losing their positions. Short of treason or a major criminal offense, judges are often "irresponsible" to majority opinion.

An "irresponsible" judiciary, of course, can be seen as either good or bad, depending upon one's view of the particular policy question under consideration. Some citizens might view a court decision giving individual women the right to decide whether or not to have an abortion as a victory for individual rights and freedom of choice; others might see the same decision as an affront to (their) religious values. One constituency might cry that a court's decision banning prayer in public school is an act of atheism, while others might argue that the decision has nothing to do with religion at all, simply with religion in school, and is, therefore, a protection of the rights of a minority in the school who don't want to follow the majority's religious preferences.

Judiciaries in the Political Arena

The judiciary may, in many political systems, engage in a lawmaking function of a sort, by interpreting laws made by other actors. As a general rule, however, the courts prefer to stay out of the political arena.[41] Even in the United States, where the US Supreme Court is among the most politically active high tribunals in the world, the Court is hesitant to inject itself into the political arena.

Although the US Supreme Court has endeavored to avoid highly visible and highly politicized cases throughout the history of the United States, on occasion it has not been possible to avoid the spotlight completely. The presidential election of 2000 was one such instance in which the Court had to play a highly visible, highly political, and highly significant role in the outcome of the election. While many decried the Court's role as an "undemocratic" institution in making a decision that effectively decided who would be the victor in the election, most commentators were agreed that the legitimacy of the Court was very significant for most Americans in helping to provide a (relatively) swift and definitive outcome to the controversy.[42]

In many political systems, however, the most direct interaction between the courts and other political structures in the regime comes through the pattern of behavior that we refer to as **judicial review**. This is the process by which courts are in the position to rule upon the propriety or legality of action of the legislative and executive branches of government.[43] More specifically, "judicial review refers to the judicial power to decide on the constitutionality of activities undertaken by other governmental institutions, most notably those decisions, laws, and policies advanced by executives and legislatures."[44]

As is indicated in Table 5.1, the concept of judicial review exists in only a minority of the nations in the world, and where it does exist, the extent of its scope and ability to review the actions of other governmental structures varies. That is, not all of the countries listed in Table 5.1 have courts as powerful in their respective political systems as is the Supreme Court in the United States.[45]

The idea of judicial review, although most strongly institutionalized today in the United States, was not, as some scholars have suggested, "invented" in American colonial days, or with the decision of Chief Justice John Marshall in the case of *Marbury v. Madison* in 1803.[46] We can go back to the time of Plato to find discussion of judicial review, in a primitive sense, when Plato discussed the establishment of a "nocturnal council of magistrates" to be the "guardians of our god-given constitution."[47]

Although judicial review may not exist at the present time in all judicial systems,[48] there is an ingredient of change that we must keep in mind. For example, most studies assert as a given that there is no judicial review in Great Britain, and that the fundamental principle underlying the operation of British politics is that of parliamentary supremacy. While this is

| Table 5.1   Some Countries Whose Political Systems Include Judicial Review ||||
Western Europe and North America	Latin America	Asia and the Pacific	Other
Austria	Argentina	Australia	Ghana
Canada	Brazil	India	Israel
Denmark	Colombia	Japan	Nigeria
Ireland	Mexico	Pakistan	
Norway		Philippines	

Sources: Monte Palmer and William Thompson, *The Comparative Analysis of Politics* (Itasca, IL: Peacock, 1978), p. 136; Theodore Becker, *Comparative Judicial Politics* (Chicago: Rand McNally, 1970), pp. 137, 209, 213, 219–222.

true, it also has recently been pointed out that the role of the courts in the British political culture has changed, and that this reflects "deep-seated changes occurring in the institutional fabric of British government," especially in the realm of administrative law. It has been shown that "until twenty years ago judges took an extremely restrained position vis-à-vis administrative agencies," but more recently scholars have noted "an embryonic move toward judicial activism."[49] Although this is not meant to suggest that British courts will soon be nullifying Acts of Parliament, it does illustrate the fact that all political institutions, courts included, can change over time.

There are two major types of judicial review mechanisms today. One, in the US model, uses the regular courts to make decisions. The other major type of judicial review structure comes from Europe and provides a special constitutional court or reviewing body to perform the judicial review function. The Constitutional Court found today in France is a good example of this.[50]

Political systems vary as well in the question of who can initiate lawsuits. In the United States, only someone "injured" by an act can initiate suit. The US Supreme Court will not issue an advisory opinion or permit an uninvolved party to commence litigation; the Supreme Court of Canada will. In other political systems, those affected by an act are specifically not permitted to initiate a suit. Rather, only specific governmental agencies may apply for judicial review. In still other systems, access to the judicial review process is very liberal, and anyone can bring a case into the reviewing process. In Colombia, for example, "anyone could introduce a petition of unconstitutionality directly to the

Supreme Court, without even having to prove a case or controversy existed, or that he had any real or personal interest in the constitutionality of the law in question."[51]

The justification of judicial review—a practice many condemn as undemocratic in that it permits an (often) unelected and, therefore, "irresponsible" judiciary to reverse or nullify actions of democratically elected legislators and executives—is basically that there is inevitably some degree of uncertainty about constitutional matters, whether they be powers of an executive or parameters of permissible legislation. As well as being structural blueprints of a regime, constitutions, as indicated in Chapter 2, also in effect provide limitations upon what government may or may not do in a political environment. The authors of a constitution do not have unlimited foresight, and so it is inevitable that eventually even sincere, honest, ethical individuals of goodwill (not to mention dishonest and unethical individuals) will disagree over what is permissible and impermissible governmental behavior, especially over the passage of time. At that time the court is the appropriate organ of government to step into the picture and help to resolve the conflict.

Courts in Comparative Perspective

We began this chapter by observing that courts, as the third of the Lockean three branches of government, tend not to receive the same amount of attention in introductory cross-national studies as either legislatures or executives. It was suggested that this is so primarily because, first, legal systems and legal cultures are more system-specific and hence more difficult to generalize about; and second, in many political systems courts and judiciaries are specifically excluded from the political process and, therefore, are not really of direct relevance to discussions of political behavior.

We have seen, however, that judiciaries as well as legal cultures are highly significant to the political systems of which they are a part. The legal culture sets the tone, at a minimum, for the operation of the political regime. Even if the legal culture does not describe specific political structures, it does include the essential philosophical and theoretical principles that will underlie the daily operation of the regime. The judiciary, as a governmental structure, may be more or less political in its operation. Even when it is at its minimum political dimension, however, it is important for the regime in terms of the services it provides in areas of mediation, conflict resolution, and the promotion of regime legitimacy and stability.

Discussion Questions

1. How do judiciaries interact with the other two key Lockean institutions of government?
2. It has been said that the impact of judiciaries may vary widely in different political systems. How is this so? Where are they most significant?
3. What kind of nonpolitical roles do courts play as political institutions?
4. What are the different types of law?
5. What is the importance of the concept of a legal culture?
6. How would you distinguish between common law legal systems and code law legal systems?
7. What are the several sources of law?
8. What do you believe are the key structures of legal systems?
9. Can you place the concept of judicial review in its appropriate context in terms of governmental structures?

Notes

1. See Locke's Section 125 in Sir Ernest Baker, ed., *Social Contract: Essays by Locke, Hume and Rousseau* (New York: Oxford University Press, 1970), p. 73.

2. For example, Joseph LaPalombara's *Politics Within Nations* (Englewood Cliffs, NJ: Prentice Hall, 1974) had fourteen chapters, with chapters on legislatures, executives, bureaucracies, interest groups, political parties, participation, and so on, but judiciaries and courts were not discussed.

3. See, for example, Glendon Schubert and David J. Danelski, eds., *Comparative Judicial Behavior* (New York: Oxford University Press, 1969); or Theodore L. Becker, *Comparative Judicial Politics* (Chicago: Rand McNally, 1970). A more recent book is Cristina Ruggiero, *Judicial Power in a Federal System: Canada, United States, and Germany* (El Paso: LFB, 2012).

4. See, for example, Kermit Hall and Kevin McGuire, *The Judicial Branch* (New York: Oxford University Press, 2005); and Hiram Chodosh, *Global Justice Reform: A Comparative Methodology* (New York: New York University Press, 2005).

5. For some different types of discussions of this issue, see Robert Badinter and Stephen Breyer, *Judges in Contemporary Democracy: An International Conversation* (New York: New York University Press, 2004); or Robert Bork, *Coercing Virtue: The Worldwide Rule of Judges* (Toronto: Vintage Canada, 2002).

6. Jerold Waltman and Kenneth Holland, "Preface," in Jerold Waltman and Kenneth Holland, eds., *The Political Role of Law Courts in Modern Democracies* (New York: St. Martin's, 1988), p. vi. See also Patrick Garry, *Limited Government and the Bill of Rights* (Columbia: University of Missouri Press, 2012).

7. Jerold Waltman, "Introduction," in Waltman and Holland, *Political Role of Law Courts*, p. 5.

8. This is one of the central premises of the work of John Rawls, perhaps the best known of contemporary scholars in this area. See John Rawls, *A Theory of Justice* (Cambridge: Harvard University Press, 1971); and John Rawls, *Justice as Fairness* (Cambridge: Harvard University Press, 2001). See also Ronald Kahn, *The Supreme Court and American Political Development* (Lawrence: University Press of Kansas, 2006).

9. This passage became well known when it was used by John Adams in 1774 in the *Boston Gazette* Number 7. Adams credited this formulation to the philosopher James Harrington (1611–1677), the author of the work *The Commonwealth of Oceana* (1656). See also Austin Sarat and Lawrence Douglas, *The Limits of Law* (Stanford: Stanford University Press, 2005).

10. Herbert Winter and Thomas Bellows, *People and Politics* (New York: Wiley, 1977), p. 307. See also Kate Malleson, *The Legal System* (New York: Oxford University Press, 2005); or Mary Sarah Bilder, *The Transatlantic Constitution: Colonial Legal Culture and the Empire* (Cambridge: Harvard University Press, 2008).

11. See Locke's Section 127 in Baker, *Social Contract*, p. 74.

12. For an example of writing on natural law, see Paulo Ferreira da Cunha, *Rethinking Natural Law* (New York: Springer, 2013). On positive law, see James Murphy, *The Philosophy of Positive Law: Foundations of Jurisprudence* (New Haven: Yale University Press, 2005); or Ralph Rossum and G. Alan Tarr, *American Constitutional Law* (Boulder: Westview, 2013). On moral law, see Owen J. Anderson, *The Natural Moral Law: The Good After Modernity* (New York: Cambridge University Press, 2012). On divine law, see Christine Hayes, *What's Divine About Divine Law? Early Perspectives* (Princeton: Princeton University Press, 2015).

13. Winter and Bellows, *People and Politics*, p. 308.

14. See George Sabine, *A History of Political Theory* (New York: Holt, Rinehart, and Winston, 1961), p. 942.

15. Ibid., pp. 194–196.

16. John Merryman, *The Civil Law Tradition*, quoted in Henry Ehrmann, *Comparative Legal Cultures* (Englewood Cliffs, NJ: Prentice Hall, 1976), p. 8. See also Ejan Mackaay, *Law and Economics for Civil Law Systems* (Cheltenham: Elgar, 2014).

17. See Roger Cotterrell, *Law, Culture, and Society: Legal Ideas in the Mirror of Social Theory* (Burlington, VT: Ashgate, 2006); David Nelken, *Using Legal Culture* (London: Wildy, Simmonds, and Hill, 2012); or Genevieve Helleringer and Kai Purnhagen, *Towards a European Legal Culture* (Portland: Hart, 2014).

18. Kenneth Holland, "The Courts in the United States," in Waltman and Holland, *Political Role of Law Courts*, p. 7. See also Michael Grossberg and Christopher Tomlins, *The Cambridge History of Law in America* (New York: Cambridge University Press, 2008).

19. Hiroshi Itoh, "The Courts in Japan," in Waltman and Holland, *Political Role of Law Courts*, p. 211. See also Daniel Foote, *Law in Japan: A Turning Point* (Seattle: University of Washington Press, 2007).

20. Ehrmann, *Comparative Legal Cultures*, p. 13. This and the following several paragraphs are based on more extended material in Ehrmann, *Comparative Legal Cultures*; and Winter and Bellows, *People and Politics*, pp. 309–310, 319–322.

21. A good discussion of this can be found in William Gordon, *Roman Law, Scots Law, and Legal History: Selected Essays* (Edinburgh: Edinburgh University Press, 2007).

22. A thorough discussion of the assumptions of the Anglo-American legal process can be found in Allan C. Hutchinson, *Evolution and the Common Law* (New York: Cambridge University Press, 2005).

23. On common law more generally, see Hamar Foster, *The Grand Experiment: Law and Legal Culture in British Settler Societies* (Vancouver: University of British Columbia Press, 2008).

24. See Michael Gerhardt, *The Power of Precedent* (New York: Oxford University Press, 2008); or Thomas Hansford and James Spriggs, *The Politics of Precedent on the U.S. Supreme Court* (Princeton: Princeton University Press, 2006).

25. Winter and Bellows, *People and Politics*, p. 316.

26. See Christine Sypnowich, *The Concept of Socialist Law* (New York: Oxford University Press, 1990), for a full discussion.

27. For discussion of this relationship, see Olufemi Taiwo, *Legal Naturalism: A Marxist Theory of Law* (Ithaca: Cornell University Press, 2015).

28. See Luis Franceschi and Andrew Ritho, eds., *Legal Ethics and Jurisprudence in Nation-Building* (Strathmore: Strathmore University Press, 2005); Timothy Lindsey, *Law Reform in Developing and Transitional States* (London: Routledge, 2006); or Simon Butt, *The Constitutional Court and Democracy in Indonesia* (Leiden: Brill, 2015).

29. See Gregory Mahler, *Politics and Government in Israel: The Maturation of a Modern State* (Lanham, MD: Rowman and Littlefield, 2011), p. 230. See also Setsuo Miyazawa et al., *East Asia's Renewed Respect for the Rule of Law in the 21st Century: The Future of Legal and Judicial Landscapes in East Asia* (Leiden: Brill, 2015).

30. On religion and law, see Marci Hamilton, *God vs. the Gavel: Religion and the Rule of Law* (New York: Cambridge University Press, 2005); or Kent Greenawalt, *Religion and the Constitution* (Princeton: Princeton University Press, 2006).

31. Sydney Bailey, *British Parliamentary Democracy* (Boston: Houghton Mifflin, 1958), pp. 15–16.

32. See Kenneth Thompson, ed., *The Presidency and the Constitutional System* (Lanham: University Press of America, 1990); or Richard Neustadt, *Presidential Power and the Modern Presidents: The Politics of Leadership from Roosevelt to Reagan* (New York: Free Press, 1990).

33. See the references to the "decline of legislatures" literature discussed in Chapter 4. For more specific discussion of this issue in the United States, see Alan Rosenthal, *The Decline of Representative Democracy: Process, Participation, and Power in State Legislatures* (Washington, DC: Congressional Quarterly, 1999).

34. Theodore Lowi, *The End of Liberalism* (New York: Norton, 1969), especially chap. 5, pp. 128–156. See also Detlef Nolte, *New Constitutionalism in Latin America: Promises and Practices* (Farnham: Ashgate, 2012); and Richard Allen Epstein, *The Classical Liberal Constitution: The Uncertain Quest for Limited Government* (Cambridge: Harvard University Press, 2014).

35. See Alfred C. Aman and William T. Mayton, *Administrative Law* (St. Paul, MN: West, 2001); or Richard Clements and Jane Kay, *Constitutional and Administrative Law* (London: Blackstone, 2001).

36. Becker, *Comparative Judicial Politics,* p. 13. See John Bell, *Judiciaries Within Europe: A Comparative Review* (Cambridge: Cambridge University Press, 2010); and Nils Engstad, Astrid Frosetg, and Bard Tender, *The Independence of Judges* (The Hague: Eleven International, 2014).

37. There are a number of very good discussions of this issue. See J. Woodford Howard, *Courts of Appeals in the Federal Judicial System: A Study of the Second, Fifth, and District of Columbia Circuits* (Princeton: Princeton University Press, 2014); or Andrew Harding and Peter Leyland, eds., *Constitutional Courts: A Comparative Study* (London: Wildy and Hill, 2009).

38. See the British North America Act (Canada Act) of 1867, Section 92(14), for provincial legislative jurisdictions, and Section 91(27) for federal legislative jurisdiction. See Nadia Verrelli, *The Democratic Dilemma: Reforming Canada's Supreme Court* (Montreal: McGill-Queen's University Press, 2013).

39. See Robert Jackson and Doreen Jackson, *Politics in Canada: Culture, Institutions, Behaviour, and Public Policy* (Scarborough: Prentice-Hall Canada, 1990), pp. 197–201. See also Donald Songer, *Law, Ideology, and Collegiality: Judicial Behaviour in the Supreme Court of Canada* (Montreal: McGill-Queen's University Press, 2012).

40. Michael Curtis, *Comparative Government and Politics* (New York: Harper and Row, 1977), p. 102. See Kenneth Miller, *Direct Democracy and the Courts* (New York: Cambridge University Press, 2009). See also Harold J. Sullivan, *Civil Rights and Liberties* (London: Taylor and Francis, 2016).

41. Curtis, *Comparative Government,* p. 107. See Matthew Taylor, *Judging Policy: Courts and Policy Reform in Democratic Brazil* (Stanford: Stanford University Press, 2008); and Richard J. Regan, *A Constitutional History of the U.S. Supreme Court* (Washington, DC: Catholic University of America Press, 2015).

42. The literature in this area is still growing. See Abner Greene, *Understanding the 2000 Election: A Guide to the Legal Battles That Decided the Presidency* (New York: New York University Press, 2005); Christopher Banks and David Cohen, *The Final Arbiter: The Consequences of Bush v. Gore for Law and Politics* (Albany: State University of New York Press, 2005); and Lance Smith-DeHaven, ed., *The Battle for Florida: An Annotated Compendium of Materials from the 2000 Presidential Election* (Gainesville: University of Florida Press, 2005).

43. See Donald Jackson and Neal Tate, eds., *Comparative Judicial Review and Public Policy* (Westport, CT: Greenwood, 1992); Lee Epstein, William Landes, and Richard Posner, *The Behavior of Federal Judges: A Theoretical and Empirical Study of Rational Choice* (Cambridge: Harvard University Press, 2013). See also Mark Miller, *Judicial Politics in the United States* (Boulder: Westview, 2015).

44. Monte Palmer and William Thompson, *The Comparative Analysis of Politics* (Itasca, IL: Peacock, 1978), p. 136. See also James Heckman, Robert Nelson, and Lee Cabatingan, eds., *Global Perspectives on the Rule of Law* (New York: Routledge, 2010).

45. See David O'Keeffe and Antonio Bavasso, *Judicial Review in European Union Law* (London: Edward Elgar, 2000). The classic work here is Charles Grove Haines, *The American Doctrine of Judicial Supremacy* (New York: Russell and Russell, 1959).

46. Two good references to this decision and its impact can be found in Bernard Schwartz, *A History of the Supreme Court* (New York: Oxford University Press, 1993); and Edward White, *The Marshall Court and Cultural Change* (New York: Oxford University Press, 1991).

47. Becker, *Comparative Judicial Politics,* p. 206. See Tom Ginsburg and Tamir Moustafa, eds., *Rule by Law: The Politics of Courts in Authoritarian Regimes* (New York: Cambridge University Press, 2008).

48. See the new journal published by John Wiley and Sons titled *Judicial Review: Mapping the Developing Law and Practice of Judicial Review,* edited by Michael Fordham in London. See Justin Crowe, *Building the Judiciary: Law, Courts, and the Politics of Institutional Development* (Princeton: Princeton University Press, 2012).

49. Jerold Waltman, "The Courts in England," in Waltman and Holland, *Political Role of Law Courts,* pp. 119–120. See the book by the Network of the Presidents of the Supreme Judicial Courts of the European Union, *Regulating Judicial Activity in Europe: A Guidebook to Working Practices of the Supreme Courts* (Northampton, MA: Elgar, 2014).

50. This is discussed in Andrew Knapp and Vincent Wright, *The Government and Politics of France* (New York: Routledge, 2006); and Susan Milner and Nick Parsons, *Reinventing France: State and Society in the 21st Century* (Basingstoke: Palgrave Macmillan, 2003).

51. Becker, *Comparative Judicial Politics,* p. 208.

6

Political Behavior and the Political Environment

Learning Outcomes

After reading this chapter, you will be able to

- Explain what political socialization is, and give illustrations of how it might be important for the political system.
- Discuss some of the key agents of the socialization process.
- Understand how different agents of socialization can be more or less important at different points of an individual's life.
- Highlight key segments of the process of political recruitment.
- Explain how political institutions and regulations can affect the political recruitment process.
- Understand the importance of political recruitment for nations and political causes.
- Appreciate the way that individual characteristics such as social class or gender can affect an individual's participation in politics.
- Describe the role of the political elite.
- Evaluate the consistency of the idea of a political elite with some of the key principles of democracy.
- Offer a definition of what constitutes political violence, and explain how the different types of political violence can be distinguished from each other.
- Explain the difference between a revolution and a coup d'état.

In Chapter 1 we introduced the concept of the political system, a set of related objects connected with one another in an analytic way. We indicated that the relationships of these objects were *perceived* by the observer: sometimes the links between objects are clear and distinct, and sometimes they are not. The links between the British House of Commons and the British House of Lords are reasonably clear; the links between a particular multinational corporation (for example, British Petroleum) and a third world nation's political stability (or instability) may be less so.

Thus far we have focused our attention upon the central structures of regimes: constitutional frameworks, legislatures, executives, and judiciaries. We must keep in mind, though, that these structures, however similar or varied they may be and however they may relate to other constitutional structures in their regimes, all operate within a political context or a political environment, not in a vacuum. Although it is possible for us to speak abstractly about constitutional structures, we cannot be content to end our cross-national political analysis at that point; the political environment introduces a broad range of variables into our examination.

The Political System Revisited

There are a number of variables—some individual-level and some political-level—that should be considered as part of the environment within which an individual operates. A general description of these would use the term *political behavior* to describe our interests: we want to understand how the individual acts as he or she does, and why. Questions focus on the development of attitudes, called political socialization, and the process by which individuals come to be active in politics, political recruitment. We also need to describe the nature of political elites in the polity and a specific kind of political behavior—political violence—and its role in politics, and then turn our attention to environmental factors, such as the general idea of pluralism, the interaction between and among interest groups in politics, and the role of political parties in the system.

On the individual level, we need to understand how individual political attitudes are developed and passed from generation to generation so as to appreciate the political culture of the regime. Moreover, preliminary examination may indicate a need to understand the process of political recruitment: How are leaders and elites selected from among the ranks of the masses? We also want to understand how some key types of characteristics—social class and gender, specifically—can affect opportunities to participate in politics and advance in the political world.

At the level of the political system, we need to understand several other possible influences on political behavior. The subject of political recruitment introduces questions related to the relation of the political elite to the masses. We know that the recruitment process serves to separate an elite from the masses, but how "open" is the elite? We also need to briefly discuss the subject of political violence, since it is a type of political behavior that is of significance to the political system in the context of "systems maintenance" as discussed in Chapter 1.

All of this is a big assignment for the beginning student. In this chapter we will briefly discuss several individual and systemic structures and behaviors just referred to. We will discuss their potential impact upon the political systems of which they are a part. They will not, however, be the primary focus for our area studies chapters in Part 2 of this book. The student will be better prepared for further cross-national study following an introduction emphasizing political structures and political institutions and placing less emphasis on the many variables in the political environment, compared to an introduction that emphasizes the many variables in the political environment but gives short shrift to the decisionmaking processes of political regimes.

The Study of Political Socialization and Political Attitudes

Contemporary studies focusing upon political actors are often based upon the assumption that *who the actors are* affects politics. This includes the study of values, beliefs, and skills that actors bring with them to the political arena, and leads us to a discussion of **political socialization**.[1] Many scholars believe that the study of political socialization has value as a factor contributing to a greater understanding of how individual political behavior is motivated.

Interest in political socialization is not a creation of contemporary political scientists. Plato dealt with the problem of political education in his *Republic,* as did Aristotle in his *Politics* and *Ethics*; the debate has continued from the time of Jean-Jacques Rousseau to B. F. Skinner: "From time immemorial, social philosophers have thought that political education should have an early start. For Plato and Rousseau there was also little question about the feasibility of such early instruction; to them it was common sense that young children could be educated in fundamental political matters."[2]

Political socialization has been conceptualized as the process by which "the individual acquires attitudes, beliefs, and values relating to the political system of which he is a member and to his own role as a citizen within that political system."[3] The important thing to note here is that socialization is conceived as a progression; that is, it is an ongoing process, which is not finished as long as the individual is still able to perceive his or her environment and respond to it.

While the idea of formal political socialization has negative connotations for many because of similarity to "brainwashing" in authoritarian systems, it is still the case that there are many societal actions that are directly politically socializing that exist even in "democratic" regimes—including civics courses in school and learning the "Pledge of Allegiance," for example.

Many gaps need to be filled in research about the importance of political socialization. In the introductory essay to his now classic book *Socialization to Politics,* Jack Dennis suggested ten "central problem dimensions" related to socialization research. These include the system relevance of political socialization; varieties of the content of political socialization; socialization across the life cycle and generations; cross- and subcultural aspects and variations in socialization; the political learning process; the agents and agencies of political socialization; the extent and relative effects of political socialization upon different individuals; and finally, problems related to specialized political socialization, especially socialization of political elites.[4]

Dennis suggested that "the question about what effects political socialization has upon political life" is "the most important aspect of political socialization research for the development of a theory of politics."[5] It has been argued that political socialization is important to politics because it generates support for the system in which it takes place. What is not known, however, is what proportion of the support for a system that exists may be attributed to socialization. There are other factors that generate diffuse support[6] in a political system—such as popular leaders, popular decisions or policies, and the like—and it has not yet been shown that it is the process of political socialization that plays a significant role in the creation of diffuse support.[7]

It is interesting to note that socialization has been shown to have a negative effect on diffuse support to some degree. In one study, investigators have shown a relationship between the cynicism of parents toward government and an increased occurrence of such cynicism in their children, with clear implications for diffuse support for government, generally.[8]

A key question related to political socialization and the development of political attitudes and values is related to the "what" of the process: What is the object, the content, of political socialization that is of significance for the political system? Perhaps the best-known exposition on political culture and the passing of political cultures from one generation to another is to be found in Gabriel Almond and Sidney Verba's classic work *The Civic Culture*: "When we speak of the political culture of a society, we refer to the political system as internalized in the cognitions, feelings, and evaluations of its population. People are induced into it just as they are socialized into non-political roles and social systems."[9] Similarly, Gabriel Almond has written elsewhere that political socialization is "the process of induction into the political culture. Its end product is a set of attitudes—cognitions, value standards, and feelings—toward the political system."[10]

Political roles, as well as a political culture, are suggested as being taught by political socialization. As the term is used here, a *political role* is "a pattern of expected behavior for individuals holding particular positions in a system."[11] Roles and role behavior are clearly not established from the time of birth but are taught phenomena. As such, they are a part of the content of political socialization. General knowledge of the political system and the manner in which it operates is also included in the content of political socialization. How the system works, the functioning of different branches of the government, the role of political parties in the political system, and so on—all are introduced to individuals through the socialization process.

Another area given considerable attention in investigation is the "when" of the process—a temporal dimension of socialization. Political socialization is a process, and it is not a process to be studied merely in individuals at a single age, with no consideration given to earlier and later years. Studies examining political socialization have focused on such questions as when the process begins, which are the most important years for later political attitudes, and how long the political socialization process can be said to continue.

Research has shown that there is a strong relationship between the *time* of initial socialization to politics and the *agents* of initial political socialization. One study found that legislators could be placed along a bi-dimensional continuum "ranging from those who were socialized early (childhood or grammar school) by the family, through those socialized as adolescents by self (self starters), to those whose socialization was delayed until the post-adolescent period and occurred because of external events and conditions."[12] While we can say that different agents of socialization are most effective at different times, problems appear when we try to translate this fact into its effect on legislative behavior, for example.

Different points in the life cycle are significant in terms of *what* will be learned, as well as *by what agent* the socialization will be influenced. It has been demonstrated that children first become aware of executive positions in government, such as the president or a mayor, and that not until they grow older do they perceive legislators as anything but "the president's helpers."[13] Jean Piaget has shown that certain concepts are more difficult than others for a child to learn.[14] For example, in some studies there was much confusion for young children as to whether they were citizens of Switzerland or citizens of Geneva; it was not until the children reached a later level of cognitive development that they saw that these two possibilities were not mutually exclusive.

Cross-cultural differences and similarities in the socialization process may be among the most valuable types of socialization studies, because they have implications for many problem dimensions.[15] By finding differences in the socialization processes in two different cultural settings, implications can be drawn relating not only to the effectiveness of various agents of socialization but also to system relevance of the study of political socialization.

Studies of subcultural and group variations in political socialization may have the same value as cross-national research. One example of this type of research is a study led by Dean Jaros. Through a study of a specific American subculture, in this case the "Appalachian personality," Jaros not only learned about the effectiveness of some agents of socialization in Appalachia as compared with an earlier study in New Haven, Connecticut,[16] but also made several suggestions about the effects of socialization on political cynicism and thereby its relevance for system maintenance. Similar studies have been undertaken investigating other subcultural or group characteristics, including race, gender, ethnic group membership, and social class.[17]

The actual question of how learning takes place—the "how" of the socialization question that asks "Who learns what from whom, how, and when?"—is certainly no less important. This "how" question encompasses several components and can be seen to often include both the "when" and the "from whom" aspects of socialization theory.

When many people ask how political learning takes place, what they are in fact asking is what the *agents* are that are active in the political learning process, rather than really inquiring about learning theory:

QUESTION: "How did Alden come to believe that?"
ANSWER: "Oh, she was in the Peace Corps and saw that behavior for herself. After the Peace Corps she was a graduate student and read more about that topic. Then she worked in the news media and her views matured. She also talks about politics with her husband, Scott, quite a bit."

In many cases this "from whom or what" response to our "how" question is the only response possible. That is, the questioner in this case is not *really* looking for an answer couched in terms of learning theory; the individual is interested in the active elements involved in the process of Alden coming to believe something that she does.

In other instances, the "how" is answered in temporal terms, employing such implicit concepts as maturation, for example:

QUESTION: "How did Darcy come to believe that?"
ANSWER: "She is now a teacher in elementary school and is much more perceptive of the world around little children."

Or an answer in terms of both the "when" and the "from whom":

QUESTION: "How did Darcy come to believe that?"
ANSWER: "Now that she is married to Chris, who is very interested in politics, she talks about politics a great deal. Her children, Miriam and Thomas, are also teaching her a lot about how children perceive the world around them."

Thus, we can see that often in political socialization research, the question being answered, which is ostensibly our "how" question, frequently is not answered in "how" (learning theory) terms at all. Rather, it is answered in terms of either the agents of socialization involved ("from whom or what"), or temporal-chronological factors ("when"), or both.[18]

The most attention in political socialization research has been given to the "by whom or what" question, examining agents and factors most influential in the socialization process. It has been almost traditionally accepted that the family is foremost among agents of socialization influential during childhood. Aristotle wrote of the overriding importance of the family; a more recent author suggests that "the most important source of children's conceptions of authority undoubtedly is the civic instruction which goes on incidental to normal activities in the family."[19]

Research also shows that one product of the socialization process is that the child is likely to form impressions and even opinions before he or she has any real political *knowledge* upon which to base those feelings. Children develop party identification early, with no good reason for preferring one party over another. In a now classic study, Fred Greenstein wrote that by the fourth grade more than 60 percent of the children could give a party identification, even if they could not give a good reason for why they had chosen that party or what party label really meant.[20]

Another key set of issues suggested by Jack Dennis concerns the "extent" of political socialization—that is, to what degree one is politicized when one is socialized to politics. Does political socialization merely involve imparting a sensitivity or awareness of issues upon an individual, or does it imply a true politicization of the individual? That is, not only is the individual aware of issues, but he or she also has opinions on all the issues involved.

A final area of research involves specialized political socialization. This has focused upon elite socialization, specifically upon those who are politically active, including legislators.[21] By studying the socialization of legislators or other political elites, we know better what kind of individuals attain formal office, for example, and thereby we have some basis for predicting how political elites will perform. As political socialization theory becomes more developed, we should better be able to predict how those political elites will behave once they are in office.

The Study of Political Recruitment

The study of **political recruitment** has not been subjected to the same questions of "relevance for the political system" as has political socialization research. Potential critics and challengers have been satisfied that the channels that are open for people to enter the political elite level, and subsequently to become officeholders, influence which people become political elites and subsequent officeholders. This has de facto significance for the political system.[22]

Political recruitment research, however, suffers from several of the same theoretical problems as political socialization research. Significant among those problems is that theorists are not in agreement as to exactly what political recruitment is. Although theorists agree that political recruitment is a process, definitions suggested in the literature differ. One author, for example, suggested that "political recruitment refers to the processes that select from among the several million socially favored and politically motivated citizens comprising the political stratum those several thousand who reach positions of significant national influence."[23]

The most broadly applicable definition is that of Gabriel Almond. He defines recruitment as the function of the political system that draws upon members of the society and inducts them "into the specialized roles of the political system, trains them with political cognitive maps, values, expectations, and affects." Thereby, he writes, the recruitment function "takes up where the general political socialization function leaves off."[24]

Part of the definition problem is that the term *recruitment* is used to cover two actual processes, initial recruitment *to* politics, and promotion *within* the political infrastructure. Lester Milbrath broke down the overall recruitment process into several levels of participation.[25] He argued that there is a hierarchy of political involvement and participation in the United States, ranging from the individual who is merely a "spectator," to someone who is a "gladiator" who is actively involved in the political arena, with "transitionals" in the middle.

A number of studies of political recruitment have been done, and several areas of research may be identified as a basis for an examination of this area. To take one example, Moshe Czudnowski suggested a six-fold framework to study political recruitment: (1) social background characteristics, (2) political socialization and recruitment factors, (3) initial activity and apprenticeship, (4) occupations, (5) motivations, and (6) the selection process itself.[26]

A broader examination of the literature seems to indicate the existence of two major points of focus of study here: studies examining the backgrounds of those who are recruited, and studies focusing upon the recruitment process itself. While most theorists do recognize political recruitment as a process, the bulk of the attention in research is not focused upon the "how" aspect, but rather upon the "who" of the question—background studies of those who are recruited.

The rationale for gathering background data is based upon two assumptions. The first is that "relationships exist between social background characteristics and opportunities to gain access to political offices"; the second is that "the social background characteristics are related to variations in the attitudes and behavior of political elites."[27]

Generally speaking, the literature has substantiated the first assumption underlying the study of social background data; there *is* a relationship between background and the opportunity to gain political office. Individuals from the middle and upper classes of some societies appear to be disproportionately recruited in relation to their size in populations. This bias exists not only in national office but also in all aspects of the political system.[28]

One interesting finding of social background research has been the discovery of an association between certain occupations and subsequent elective office. The relationship between legislators and the practice of law prior to election has been cited; in the United States "it is proverbial that U.S. Congressmen are lawyers."[29] Studies show that this American affinity is not universal. It has been shown that whereas 58 percent of US legislators were lawyers at one point in time, only about 2 percent of Swedish legislators were lawyers. In fact, of twenty-two nations examined in one study, the average share of legislators who previously were lawyers was 16 percent, a far cry from a universally "proverbial" relationship.[30]

In addition to the "who" of the recruitment process, considerable attention has been paid to the questions of how and why individuals are recruited. A number of studies have focused on the role that parties and other groups play in the recruitment process. Still others are oriented toward psychological factors involved in the recruitment process and the roles that the electoral system and opportunity in general play in the process.

Studies focusing on the role of parties in recruitment have shown that their significance varies on a country-by-country basis. In the United States, parties have lost much influence that they once had over recruitment. The loss of influence can be attributed to changes in the primary election system and increased openness of party conventions.[31] Outside of the United States, one need not look far to see evidence of the importance of the party in the recruitment process, although it, too, varies on a country-by-country basis.[32]

Other groups have been shown to have an impact on the recruitment process, sometimes through the political party itself. Czudnowski demonstrated the conditions under which political parties may become very group-oriented in their selection procedures for candidates for the national legislature, to the extent of permitting groups to dictate who "their" representatives on the party electoral list will be.[33] It was suggested that group-oriented recruitment is positively associated with a proportional representation electoral system.

Yet another important factor that can influence the recruitment process is opportunity. Regardless of the size of the political strata or the number of "self-starters" ready to run for office, recruitment cannot take place if vacancies in office are not present.[34] Moreover, different recruitment rates exist for different offices; in the United States, recruitment to the presidency is more difficult than recruitment to the Senate because turnover in the Senate is greater, and there are more opportunities there. Similarly, recruitment will be greater for the House of Representatives than the Senate, and greater for state legislative offices than for national legislative office.

Social Class and Gender Influences on Political Behavior

As noted earlier, there are often formal, political, legal barriers that affect the way individuals behave in politics. We will note later in this text that the president of Mexico must be male. Women need not apply. In some settings there is an age requirement in order to vote, or to hold office. In some settings there are legal restrictions that follow religious lines.

In this section of this chapter we want to discuss some more indirect ways of influencing political behavior, and we will specifically focus on three kinds of factors: those related to social class, those related to religion, and those related to gender. Our interest here is not to address the formal/legal restrictions that may affect these identifying attributes. Rather, we are interested in social class and gender and their indirect influences upon attitudes and behavior.

Social Class

Social class refers to some kind of ordering of groups in society, often including such objective characteristics as income, education, or occupation.[35] The point of these characteristics is not only to identify the characteristics themselves, but also to give individuals the opportunity to *infer* rankings about individuals: one group is *better than* another in some respects. The importance of a class approach to understanding politics is that it is based upon the notion of stratification: some classes have more (rights, benefits, resources) than others simply because of their class identity. Certainly one good example of this was the work of Karl Marx,[36] who distinguished between the workers (the proletariat); members of a middle class, a group of business workers and self-employed individuals (the petite bourgeoisie); and the economic elite (the bourgeoisie). One's economic standing affected their power in society and in politics.

Social class is often strongly associated with ethnic identity.[37] In both developing and underdeveloped nations, ethnic-based conflict has developed based on language, religion, or race. Whether we look at settings such as the Ibos battling with the Hausa in Nigeria, or the Catholics battling with the Protestants in Northern Ireland, ethnic (which would include religious) identity has served as the basis for much violence and sadness in society. In settings where ethnic identity has not resulted in so much violent action, it still is possible to identify competition between and among ethnic groups—Anglo-Saxons, Irish, Hispanic, Jewish, Italian, African American—that results in social tension.

One of the key uses of the construct of class is the idea of class conflict.[38] This suggests not only that different classes exist, but also that they are in competition with each other for power, access to resources, or security. Higher classes fight to keep what they have; lower classes fight to get more of what they don't have. Sometimes these struggles transfer neatly to the political arena (so that British blue-collar workers are more prone to vote for Labour, while British middle- and upper-class voters are more prone to vote for the Conservatives). Sometimes the association between politics and class isn't so neat. It has often been the case that the most intense conflict involving social and economic class has involved the rural poor in developing nations against the landlord class, often well represented in the national government.

Social class can be affected by religious identity, too.[39] Many societies have dominant and minority religious identities. The key question is what happens with those identities: Are they essentially "private" labels, or do they open or close doors of opportunities for individuals? For many years in the United States some of the nation's premier institutions of higher education had quotas on the number of Jewish students they would admit. This was not based upon ability, or likely success, but was an example of social discrimination against a religious group.

Gender

We have already seen in other sections of this text that gender is a significant political construct.[40] That is, it makes a difference in terms of an individual's political behavior whether the individual is a man or a woman in society. In most nations women make up more than half of the population. Yet, as we have already seen and will see again, women tend to hold far less than half of the leadership positions in governments. Why is this?

In some societies there are legal limitations on what women can do.[41] That is, women may be legally excluded from participation in some structures, such as the presidency in Mexico, where the law says that the president must be a male. In some societies there may be both formal (legal) and informal (cultural) limitations placed upon women's opportunities. Although these are examples of gender-limiting behavior, exactly the same thing can be said for attitudes, too. As individuals are growing up in society and are developing beliefs and attitudes about politics, and about political behavior, they develop different attitudes depending upon their gender. In these settings girls may "learn"—either formally or informally—that political behavior and political leadership is "just not something that girls do." Other cultures may be gender-blind, and girls may be closer to boys in the kinds of attitudes they develop.

Some scholars have argued that colonialism played an important role in breaking traditional gender roles in colonized systems. Although it is hard to generalize, because different colonial systems had different sets of relationships, some argue that imperialism and colonialism brought increased access to education to women, thereby increasing their relative equality in society.[42] Others argue that the reverse actually occurred, that gender roles were actually more flexible before colonial powers appeared and set very rigid social structures into place.

In modern and postmodern societies, gender roles have changed significantly from those of the developing world. Women have more opportunities outside of the home, more access to education, to career opportunities that they want to pursue. They are more politically active.[43]

Much research has been done on gender and political attitudes. In the early 1990s the United Nations (UN) released a study focusing upon gender, and the annual *Human Development Report* regularly has data on women in different areas of the world. Girls increasingly have similar opportunities to boys in terms of primary education, and although the equality of the genders decreases as education progresses, this is a pattern that is changing as time goes on, although slowly.

The UN's 2016 *Human Development Report* (see Figure 6.1) shows that "gender equality and women's empowerment are now mainstream dimensions of any development discourse. And there is no denying that with an intention to overcome them constructively, space for discussions and dialogues on issues once taboo is slowly opening—as with sexual orientation; discriminations faced by lesbian, gay, bisexual, transgender and intersex people; and female genital mutilation and cutting."[44] The report further indicates that "in all regions women have a

Figure 6.1   Global Discrimination Against Women

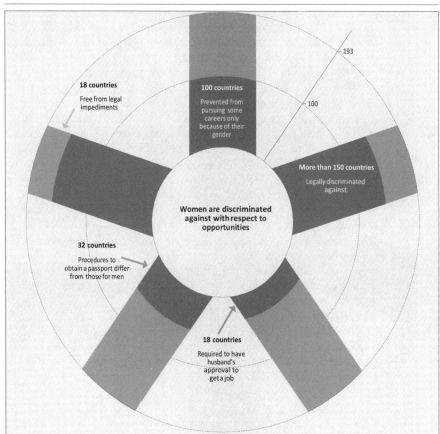

Source: United Nations, *Human Development Report 2016,* "Overview: Human Development for Everyone," http://hdr.undp.org/en/2016-report/download, p. 6.

longer life expectancy than do men, and in most regions girls' expected years of schooling are similar to those of boys. Yet in all regions women consistently have, on average, a lower Human Development Index (HDI) value than do men. The largest difference is in South Asia, where the female HDI value is 20 percent lower than the male HDI value."[45]

The *Human Development Report* offers what it calls "Five Misconceptions About Women's Economic Empowerment" (see Box 6.1) that suggest that much work has yet to be done before true gender equality

---

**Box 6.1 Five Misconceptions About
Women's Economic Empowerment**

- *Women's economic contribution is limited when women are not employed.* While women are less engaged in paid employment than men (in 2015, 36 percent of women and 44 percent of men worked full time), women's economic contribution in unpaid work is significant. A 2011 survey found that, on average, 28 percent of women and 6 percent of men spent three to five hours a day on household work.
- *Women's economic participation equals women's economic empowerment.* Increasing the number of women in the workforce would be a significant objective but not necessarily if women enter the paid economy under poor conditions. Exploitation, low pay, and job insecurity are unfavorable terms often encountered by women.
- *There is an automatic win-win between gender equality and wider development outcomes.* Gender equality has been found to promote economic growth, poverty reduction, and economic and human development, but the reverse is not always true. Governments need to pay attention to gender equality and not rely solely on growth to achieve it.
- *What works for one group of women will work for another.* Women across the world often face similar obstacles, but demographic, economic, and cultural contexts make women's experiences different from each other. Women are not a homogeneous group, and tailored approaches are required.
- *Increasing women's individual skills and aspirations is the main challenge.* Women's capacity to seize economic opportunities can be improved through individual support such as training in business management skills, but structural causes of gender inequality must be addressed simultaneously.

Source: United Nations, *Human Development Report 2016*, p. 42. Based upon data in Abigail Hunt and Emma Samman, *Women's Economic Empowerment: Navigating Enablers and Constraints*, https://www.odi.org/sites/odi.org.uk/files/resource-documents /10683.pdf.

can be said to exist in today's society, or even before we start to approach such a state.

The *Human Development Report* sorts nations by what it calls the Human Development Index into four categories: very high, high, medium, and low. The HDI looks at both the total amount of wealth in a society and the consequences of that wealth, what we might call the national quality of life. This includes such measures as literacy, life expectancy, education, and gross domestic product (GDP). It answers the question of whether the wealth created results in a quality standard of living for all. The data show, as indicated in Table 6.1, that even within HDI categories there is still remarkable variation in the degree of loss of achievement due to gender inequality.[46]

We saw in Chapter 2 that one relatively modern ideology, feminism, has sought to remove this characteristic of contemporary society.[47] Feminist theory is often used to explain why politics operates as it does, why political institutions are as they are, and why political behavior has developed as it has developed. Feminists argue that attitudes about women that limit their rights and opportunities must be opposed, and advocate removing barriers to the equality of women. The feminist agenda wants more than simply removing restrictions; it wants true opportunity, including equal pay for equal work. It includes several health issues, including abortion and birth control, because it relates to the idea that a woman should have control of her own body. It includes numerous other economic and noneconomic issues, too.

We should note that while there is a problem with women having full participation in the developing world, progress is being made. Economic development is bringing with it more opportunity for girls and women, rising educational levels, rising economic opportunities, and increasing opportunities to participate in leadership positions in society. While it is true that the majority of women who have become political leaders of their respective nations have come to power as either daughters of leaders or widows of leaders, it is increasingly the case that women are in fact having opportunities today that were simply not available to them a generation ago.

Group Membership and Attitude Formation

We have seen in the preceding paragraphs that although there are occasionally legal barriers to participation by specific groups in society, there are also informal barriers to participation that can be associated with social characteristics and that affect attitudes, which in turn affect behavior. As we look at political case studies later in this volume we should keep these factors in mind and ask whether the explanation for

Table 6.1   United Nations Gender Inequality Index

Overall Rank and Country	Gender Inequality Index Rank	Maternal Mortality Ratio (2015) (deaths per 100,000 live births)	Births per 1,000 Adolescent Women (ages 15–19)	Percentage Seats in Parliament Held by Women
Very high human development				
1 Norway	6	5	5.9	39.6
10 United States	43	14	22.6	19.5
17 Japan	21	5	4.1	11.6
29 Greece	23	3	7.5	19.7
42 United Arab Emirates	46	6	29.7	22.5
High human development				
54 Barbados	59	27	40.7	19.6
66 Serbia	40	17	19.0	34.0
78 Brazil	92	44	67.0	10.8
90 China	37	27	7.3	23.6
Medium human development				
107 Moldova	46	23	22.6	21.8
115 Vietnam	71	54	38.6	24.3
127 Guyana	117	229	88.0	30.4
139 Bangladesh	119	176	83.0	20.0
Low human development				
151 Tanzania	129	398	118.6	36.0
163 Haiti	142	359	39.3	3.5
177 Liberia	150	725	108.8	10.7
188 Central African Republic	149	882	91.9	12.5

continues

political phenomena is formal and legal—including political institutions, for example, or rules of behavior—or whether the explanation for political phenomena is informal, sometimes cultural, in nature.

The Role of the Political Elite

Now that we have briefly examined how the elite often become the elite, it is important to understand the role of the **political elite**. An interesting question is whether "elitism" is compatible with democratic government. How should the elite behave, and how should the masses

Table 6.1   continued

Overall Rank and Country	Female Population with at Least Some Secondary Education (% ages 25 and older)	Male Population with at Least Some Secondary Education (% ages 25 and older)	Female Labor Force Participation (% ages 15 and older)	Male Labor Force Participation (% ages 15 and older)
Very high human development				
1 Norway	96.1	94.6	61.2	68.5
10 United States	95.4	95.1	56.0	68.4
17 Japan	93.0	90.6	49.1	70.2
29 Greece	63.7	71.7	43.9	60.0
42 United Arab Emirates	77.4	64.5	41.9	91.6
High human development				
54 Barbados	93.0	90.6	62.4	70.7
66 Serbia	82.3	91.6	43.4	60.1
78 Brazil	59.1	55.2	56.3	78.5
90 China	69.8	79.4	63.6	77.9
Medium human development				
107 Moldova	95.2	97.3	38.8	45.6
115 Vietnam	64.0	76.7	73.8	83.2
127 Guyana	68.1	53.2	41.8	77.2
139 Bangladesh	42.0	44.3	43.1	81.0
Low human development				
151 Tanzania	10.1	15.3	74.0	83.3
163 Haiti	25.7	38.7	61.5	71.4
177 Liberia	17.3	39.7	58.0	63.9
188 Central African Republic	12.3	29.8	71.7	84.6

Source: United Nations, *Human Development Report 2016*, Statistical Annex, tab. 5, "Gender Inequality Index," p. 214, http://hdr.undp.org/en/2016-report.

relate to the elite?[48] The concept of a political elite means different things to different people. On one hand, the term *elite* simply means "best," and there is very little that is objectionable in that. On the other hand, *elite* is sometimes interpreted more broadly to refer to those who wield power in politics, with a distinctively negative connotation.

The question is, How does the existence of a political elite fit with the idea of democratic government? We know that democracy places many requirements (or expectations) on citizens, including that they be informed, have principles, and be rational, and we know that not all voters are like that. Fortunately, we have been told that not all voters *need* to have these characteristics for a democratic system to survive.[49] If enough individuals are adequately motivated and informed, the system can continue to operate.

Philosophers who have written about elitism, including Vilfredo Pareto (1848–1923) and Gaetano Mosca (1858–1941), have focused on uneven distribution of power in society. Modern theorists, such as Robert Michels (1876–1936), have argued that an uneven distribution of power cannot be avoided; the question is how organizations (and society) respond to this uneven distribution of power. Perhaps the best-known modern study, *The Power Elite* by C. Wright Mills,[50] suggested that politics in the United States was dominated by a small number of military, political, and corporate leaders.

Elite theory suggests that society is not controlled by a range of groups, each competing with other groups to have access to power, but suggests instead that society is a closed system controlled by a relatively small group. It might recognize that **pluralism**—having many different groups in society—would suggest that many different groups in society compete for power, but its view is that real power is kept controlled by a relatively small group, the same individuals that Mills referred to as the "power elite." In this sense "elite theory" is really about how power is distributed in society, and about how individuals get control of power.

Is there an association between elitism and political development? Will a politically underdeveloped nation have more, or less, equality in access to power, resources, and opportunities? As a general rule, scholars have argued that with economic and political development comes greater opportunity, so that we are more likely to find a more open elite, with more opportunities for nonelite individuals to become members of the elite.

Elite theory is usually represented as a pyramid of power, as shown in Figure 6.2. This suggests that the number of individuals at the lower levels of the pyramid is large, and as we move up the pyramid—in terms of power and in terms of resources and in terms of opportunity—the number of individuals becomes smaller. At the end of the day, elite theory tells us, political decisions are made by a relatively small number of individuals.

The key ingredient here is what are called elite-mass linkages, the relationships that exist between the elite and the masses that allow the elite to govern on behalf of the masses. The elite can govern by force, such as we find in military regimes. The political system will be more stable, however, and will have to expend less on coercive measures, if it

Figure 6.2 The Political Elite and the Masses

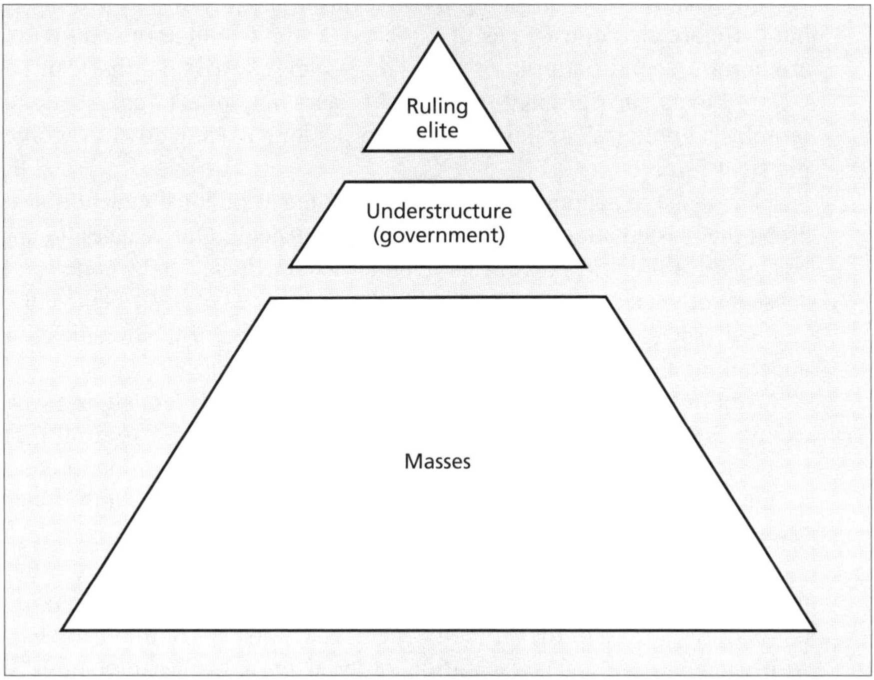

can govern through a sense of legitimacy on the part of the public, not through coercion. This will be based upon the degree to which the mass public shares the views of the political and socioeconomic elite.

The existence of elites can be compatible with democratic government under the right circumstances.[51] The most important single characteristic appears to be that of an open elite: the possibility for the masses to become part of the elite. Again, this ties in with our discussion of recruitment processes in a regime. Where there are effective recruitment structures, a relatively open elite can exist; where sufficient opportunities do not exist, and where we find a relatively closed elite, we will invariably find a system of lower legitimacy and less stability.

Political Participation and Political Violence

Our discussion of the role of the military in politics (see Chapter 4) shows that it is not only participation that is crucial for regimes but also the type of participation that takes place. One kind of participation that we should mention briefly here can be of great significance in the political arena: political violence.

Violence is a term that means different things to different people.[52] We might agree that throwing a brick through a window is violence, but there are also other types of violence. Some would argue that there are certain social patterns of behavior—such as racism—that can be referred to as "institutional violence." Others may reject "unjust social or political policies" as being "violence" as long as they do not involve physical force.

The range of actions that might be classified as political violence is so broad that systematic theory construction is difficult. One recent attempt began with a framework focusing upon "who" did "what" to "whom," and subsequently tried to study the "symbolic addressee" of the violence, the claimed "social basis" of the act of violence, the size of the organization undertaking the violence, and "why" the action took place.[53]

Among the many types of behavior that we can consider to be examples of political violence might be a riot or a demonstration that turns violent, an assassination, a kidnapping, a mass revolution, a coup d'état, guerrilla warfare, terrorism, and of course conventional war. Motivations for these actions might be ideological (e.g., a Marxist revolution or Marxist-inspired coup), religious (e.g., the Islamic revolution in Iran, or the Sikh separatist battles in the Punjab in India), nationalistic (e.g., resistance of the Afghan guerrillas against US military forces), or personal (e.g., an assassination ordered by a leader to remove a potential political competitor). Alternatively, the motivation could come from some combination of these and other reasons.

Consistent with other warnings about ethnocentrism in this text, it is important to remember that US politics in recent years has not been completely confined to peaceful constitutional discourse. Political assassinations are acts of political violence. Much Ku Klux Klan action in the southern United States involved (and still involves) political violence.[54] The Ohio National Guard fired on college students at Kent State University who were participating in a demonstration against the Vietnam War in May 1970, resulting in the deaths of four students.[55] Police violence, still frequent in the United States against minorities, has been considered by many as political violence, too. This is not meant to suggest that all of US politics is violent, but it should serve as a reminder that political violence can exist even in stable, democratic societies.

Because space is limited here, we shall confine our discussion to only a few types of violence. We shall briefly discuss two types of revolution: revolution from above, the **coup d'état**, and revolution from below, otherwise known as the **jacquerie**. We shall also briefly discuss **guerrilla warfare** and **terrorism** and attempt to point out similarities and differences between the two.

Most simply, a revolution typically involves a dramatic changing of one government, or type of government, for another.[56] One definition that has been offered argues that a revolution involves a "relatively sudden violent and illegal attempt to change the regime of a state or other political organisation, in which large sections of the population are involved as participants."[57] Others might disagree with this view, however, claiming that revolutions often seek to restore legality against a regime that has voided the country's law and thus cannot be "illegal" actions.

A mass-based revolution is sometimes referred to as a jacquerie and involves significant and radical changes in the ruling class. Four "great" revolutions of modern times are the American Revolution (1776), the French Revolution (1789), the Russian Revolution (1917–1921), and the Chinese Revolution (1927–1949).

Another type of revolutionary change, although not one directly involving large sections of the population, is the coup d'état, a seizure of power from above, instead of action from the masses. Coups are usually carried out by individuals near the center of power who have access to resources and political support. The most common type of coup is called a military coup, sometimes called a "generals' coup," which involves military leaders taking over because of their dissatisfaction with civilian control. This has happened recently in Argentina, Thailand, Chad, Pakistan, Myanmar, and Nigeria, among other settings.

Other types of coups are the **palace coup** and the **reform coup**. In the former, the forces behind the coup are typically members of a royal family; one member of the royal family tries to push out those in office so that he or she can take power. In the latter case, the sudden political takeover is often done in the name of reform, and the seizure of power may be undertaken by a labor leader or someone holding political office.

The distinction between terrorism and guerrilla action can sometimes become unclear. Generally, we can define terrorism as using violence, the threat of violence, or coercion to influence political behavior or induce fear. There is often a symbolic dimension to the terrorist act, as well, often involving civilian casualties. The terrorist seeks to influence political behavior of a government through extranormal means, often having tried conventional political options. "Terrorism" is a relatively recent political label in its common usage, although phrases such as "Reign of Terror" (in the French Revolution in 1794) demonstrate that the concept certainly existed long ago.[58]

If we look at groups labeled as terrorists today, we often find self-ascribed "national liberation" groups. They become labeled as terrorists because their strategy involves violence and (often) civilian victims. This highlights one very problematic characteristic of the label "terrorist": it is strongly influenced by perspective, as the following example shows.

Menachem Begin, the prime minister of Israel from 1977 to 1984, was once asked how he responded to charges that there was really no difference between his actions against the British in Palestine preceding Israeli independence in 1948—the British referred to him at the time as a "terrorist" and offered a reward of 10,000 pounds sterling, dead or alive, for his capture—and the actions of Yassir Arafat and the Palestine Liberation Organization (PLO) against Israel in the 1980s. Begin's response illustrated the importance of perspective perfectly. He said, "Of course there is a difference. He is a terrorist. I was a freedom fighter."[59]

"Terrorism" is also used to label some situations of cross-border violence. Al-Qaeda in the Middle East, Boko Haram in Africa, and other regional and cross-regional groups are often mentioned in this context. In these cases, the terrorist motive may be not a national liberation movement but instead directed at some policy-related goal, such as the presence of foreign multinationals, environmental concerns, foreign policy issues, the release of political prisoners, and the like.

We should also note that although objected to by some, the label "terrorism" has also been used in the US context in critical comments about those who use unusual or violent practices to protest against abortions, to protest against logging in the northwest of the country, to protest the fur industry, or to protest against whaling by the Japanese, to take just a few examples. Again, the use of the label "terrorist" is a very subjective one, and as the example of former prime minister Begin showed, one man's terrorist can be another man's hero, and vice versa.

Guerrilla action, on the other hand, tends to be a bit different in terms of the targets sought by the participants. The usual distinction drawn suggests that guerrillas tend to focus their attention on government targets, usually military targets, rather than the often random civilian targets focused upon by terrorists.

These and other types of political violence are of significance for the political system because they offer fundamental challenges to the institutions of the regime. They operate outside of the system, as it were, simply rejecting the ability of the institutions and behaviors of the political system to handle their demands.

Political Behavior and the Environment in Perspective

Political structures, like constitutions, cannot be examined in a vacuum. While constitutions might inform us about the behavior of a political regime and the relationships among the various actors and structures within that regime, there may be a number of significant details of the political regime that are not included in the constitution (such as customs, traditions, political culture, political parties, and the like). In this chapter we have seen some of the factors that are key to understanding why individuals participate in politics: those factors that influence not only who participates in politics but how they come to believe what they believe. The process of political socialization and political recruitment, the importance of social class and gender, and the role of the political elite all tell us a great deal about who is active in politics, and why.

We have also seen in this chapter that political participation is not always constructive or positive. Political violence is a kind of political behavior. Similarly, just studying the constitutional structures of a regime may omit a number of significant political details, and to this extent other variables must be included in area studies to make them complete.

In the next chapter we shall turn our attention to some key organizing structures of politics in contemporary society: interest groups and political parties. Why these types of groups form and how they form are key questions that we will meet. As we discuss several different dimensions of what is called "group theory" we will have the opportunity to think about how politics and political behavior are organized, and what the key structures are that help individuals to behave politically.

Discussion Questions

1. To what does the process of political socialization refer? How is it important for the operation of politics?
2. What are some of the key agents of the political socialization process? How might these differ from one country to another?
3. What do we mean when we refer to the process of political recruitment? To whom does the term apply?
4. How do political institutions and regulations affect the political recruitment process? Give examples from both developed and underdeveloped nations.
5. Who are the political elite? What makes someone part of the political elite? Is this the same in all political settings?
6. Can you describe the relationship between the idea of the existence of a political elite and the existence of a democratic government? Can we have an identifiable political elite in a democracy?
7. What is political violence? How do we distinguish (if indeed we can) between political violence and "regular" violence? Are there different kinds of political violence?
8. What is the difference between a revolution and a coup d'état?

Notes

1. See, for example, Edward S. Greenberg, *Political Socialization* (New York: Routledge, 2017).

2. David Easton and Jack Dennis, *Children in the Political System* (New York: McGraw-Hill, 1969), p. 76. See also Bjorkman Bennich, *Political Culture Under Institutional Pressure: How Institutional Change Transforms Early Socialization* (New York: Palgrave Macmillan, 2007).

3. Greenberg, *Political Socialization,* p. 3. See also Robert Hess and Judith Torney-Purta, *The Development of Political Attitudes in Children* (New Brunswick, NJ: Aldine Transaction, 2006).

4. Jack Dennis, ed., *Socialization to Politics* (New York: Wiley, 1973), p. 4. See also Rosalee Clawson and Zoe Oxley, *Public Opinion, Democratic Ideals, and Democratic Practice* (Washington, DC: Congressional Quarterly, 2008).

5. Dennis, *Socialization,* p. 5.

6. Diffuse support is very general support for the regime, not for specific leaders or specific policy, but system-level support.

7. See David Easton, *A Framework for Political Analysis* (Englewood Cliffs, NJ: Prentice Hall, 1965), pp. 124–125.

8. Dean Jaros et al., "The Malevolent Leader: Political Socialization in an American Subculture," *American Political Science Review* 62 (1968): 564–575. See J. Celeste Lay, *A Midwestern Mosaic: Immigration and Political Socialization in Rural America* (Philadelphia: Temple University Press, 2012).

9. Gabriel Almond and Sidney Verba, *The Civic Culture* (Boston: Little, Brown, 1965), p. 14. Some more recent work that has built upon Almond and Verba's scholarship includes David Jackson, *Entertainment and Politics: The Influence of Pop Culture on Young Adult Political Socialization* (New York: Lang, 2009).

10. Gabriel Almond, "Introduction," in Gabriel Almond and James Coleman, *The Politics of the Developing Areas* (Princeton: Princeton University Press, 1960), p. 27. See also David C. Barker and Christopher Carman, *Political Representation in Red and Blue America: How Cultural Differences Shape Democratic Expectations and Outcomes* (New York: Oxford University Press, 2012).

11. Raymond Hopkins, "The Role of the MP in Tanzania," *American Political Science Review* 64 (1970): 756. See also Tawnya J. Adkins Covert, *Making Citizens: Political Socialization Research and Beyond* (New York: Palgrave Macmillan, 2017).

12. Allan Kornberg and Norman Thomas, "The Political Socialization of National Legislative Elites in the United States and Canada," *Journal of Politics* 27 (1965): 761–775.

13. See, for example, Jens Qvortrup, *Studies in Modern Childhood: Society, Agency, Culture* (New York: Palgrave Macmillan, 2005); or Orit Ichilov, *Political Learning and Citizenship Education Under Conflict: The Political Socialization of Israeli and Palestinian Youngsters* (New York: Routledge, 2004).

14. The classic article is by Jean Piaget and Anne-Marie Weil, "The Development in Children of the Idea of the Homeland," *International Social Science Bulletin* 3 (1951): 561–578. More recent work includes Sonia Livingstone and Kirsten Drotner, eds., *International Handbook of Children, Media, and Culture* (London: Sage, 2008).

15. An example of such a study would include John Schumaker and Tony Ward, *Cultural Cognition and Psychopathology* (Westport: Praeger, 2001); or Esther Thorson, *Political Socialization in a Media-Saturated World* (New York: Lang, 2016).

16. Jaros et al., "Malevolent Leader," pp. 564–575; and Fred Greenstein, "The Benevolent Leader: Children's Images of Political Authority," *American Political Science Review* 54 (1960): 934–943.

17. Other studies include Micha de Winter, *Socialization and Civil Society: How Parents, Teachers, and Others Could Foster a Democratic Way of Life* (Boston: SensePublishers, 2012); or Russell Francis Farnen, *Political Culture, Socialization, Democracy, and Education: Interdisciplinary and Cross-National Perspectives for a New Century* (New York: Lang, 2008).

18. Krista Jenkins, *Mothers, Daughters, and Political Socialization: Two Generations at an American Women's College* (Philadelphia: Temple University Press, 2013).

19. Fred Greenstein, *Children and Politics* (New Haven: Yale University Press, 1965), p. 44. A good example of a different target population is by Janette Habashi, *Political Socialization of Youth: A Palestinian Case Study* (New York: Palgrave Macmillan, 2016).

20. Greenstein, *Children and Politics,* p. 71.

21. For illustrations of this type of literature, see Sue Thomas and Clyde Wilcox, *Women and Elective Office: Past, Present, and Future* (New York: Oxford University Press, 2005); and Margaret Conway, Gertrude Steuernagel, and David Ahern, *Women and Political Participation: Cultural Change in the Political Arena* (Washington, DC: Congressional Quarterly, 2005).

22. See Matevz Tomsic, *Elites in the New Democracies* (New York: Lang, 2016); and Volker Perthes, *Arab Elites: Negotiating the Politics of Change* (Boulder: Lynne Rienner, 2004).

23. Robert Putnam, *The Comparative Study of Political Elites* (New York: Prentice Hall, 1976), p. 46. See also Masamichi Sasaki, *Elites: New Comparative Perspectives* (Boston: Brill, 2008).

24. Almond, "Introduction," p. 31. See also Katherine Opello, *Gender Quotas, Party Reform, and Political Parties in France* (Lanham: Lexington, 2006); and Elizabeth Evans, *Gender and the Liberal Democrats: Representing Women?* (Manchester: Manchester University Press, 2011).

25. Lester Milbrath, *Political Participation* (Chicago: Rand McNally, 1965). See also Marian Sawer and Manon Tremblay, *Representing Women in Parliament: A Comparative Study* (New York: Routledge, 2006); and Jennifer Lawless, *Becoming a Candidate: Political Ambition and the Decision to Run for Office* (New York: Cambridge University Press, 2012).

26. Moshe Czudnowski, "Political Recruitment," in Fred Greenstein and Nelson Polsby, eds., *Handbook of Political Science* (Reading, MA: Addison-Wesley, 1975), p. 179. See also Meryl Kenny, *Gender and Political Recruitment: Theorizing Institutional Change* (Basingstoke: Palgrave Macmillan, 2013).

27. Harold Clarke and Richard Price, "Political Recruitment: Theoretical Overview and Review of the Literature," in Harold Clarke and Richard Price, eds., *Recruitment and Leadership Selection in Canada* (Toronto: Holt, Rinehart, and Winston, 1976), p. 7.

28. For an example of such studies, see Kay Lehman Schlozman, Sidney Verba, and Henry Brady, *The Unheavenly Chorus: Unequal Political Voice and the Broken Promise of American Democracy* (Princeton: Princeton University Press, 2012).

29. M. Pederson, "Lawyers in Politics: The Danish Folketing and United States Legislatures," in Samuel Patterson and John Wahlke, eds., *Comparative Legislative Behavior: Frontiers of Research* (New York: Wiley, 1972), p. 25.

30. Patterson and Wahlke, *Comparative Legislative Behavior,* p. 25. See also Peter Siavelis and Scott Morgenstern, eds., *Pathways to Power: Political Recruitment and Candidate Selection in Latin America* (University Park: Pennsylvania State University Press, 2008); or Harold Kerbo and John McKinstry, *Who Rules Japan? The Inner Circles of Economic and Political Power* (Westport: Praeger, 1995).

31. See Roger Davidson and Walter Oleszek, *Congress and Its Members* (Washington, DC: Congressional Quarterly, 2006); and Gerhard Loewenberg and Peverill Squire, *Legislatures: Comparative Perspectives on Representative Assemblies* (Ann Arbor: University of Michigan Press, 2002).

32. A very good review of the literature on political parties can be found in Frank Belloni and Dennis Beller, eds., *Faction Politics: Political Parties and Factionalism in Comparative Perspective* (Santa Barbara: ABC-Clio, 1987).

33. Moshe Czudnowski, "Sociocultural Variables and Legislative Recruitment," *Comparative Politics* 4 (1972): 561–587; and Moshe Czudnowski, "Legislative Recruitment Under Proportional Representation in Israel: A Model and a Case Study," *Midwest Journal of Political Science* 14 (1970): 216–248.

34. Malcolm Jewell and Samuel Patterson, *The Legislative Process in the United States* (New York: Random, 1973), p. 88.

35. See Marjorie Cohen and Jane Pulkingham, *Public Policy for Women: The State, Income Security, and Labour Market Issues* (Toronto: University of Toronto Press, 2009); or Stephen Parks, *Class Politics: The Movement for the Students' Right to Their Own Language* (Anderson, SC: Parlor, 2013).

36. See John Seed, *Marx: A Guide for the Perplexed* (New York: Continuum, 2010); Paul Hirst, *Marxism and Historical Writing* (New York: Routledge, 2010); or Pnina Werbner, *The Making of an African Working Class: Politics, Law, and Cultural Protest in the Manual Workers Union of Botswana* (London: Pluto, 2014).

37. Thomas Barfield, *Afghanistan: A Cultural and Political History* (Princeton: Princeton University Press, 2010); Roland Hsu, *Ethnic Europe: Mobility, Identity, and Conflict in a Globalized World* (Stanford: Stanford University Press, 2010); and Neal Jesse and Kristen Williams, *Ethnic Conflict: A Systematic Approach to Cases of Conflict* (Washington, DC: Congressional Quarterly, 2011).

38. Irene Thomson, *Culture Wars and Enduring American Dilemmas* (Ann Arbor: University of Michigan Press, 2010); or Thomas Bramble and Rick Kuhn, *Labor's Conflict: Big Business, Workers, and the Politics of Class* (New York: Cambridge University Press, 2011).

39. See Brian Grim and Roger Finke, *The Price of Freedom Denied: Religious Persecution and Conflict in the 21st Century* (New York: Cambridge University Press, 2011); or Richard Brian Miller, *Terror, Religion, and Liberal Thought* (New York: Columbia University Press, 2010).

40. See Mona Lena Krook and Sarah Childs, *Women, Gender, and Politics: A Reader* (New York: Oxford University Press, 2010); or Sarah Henderson and Alana Jeydel, *Women and Politics in a Global World* (New York: Oxford University Press, 2010).

41. Jennifer Lawless and Richard Fox, *It Still Takes a Candidate: Why Women Don't Run for Office* (New York: Cambridge University Press, 2010); or Anna Manasco Dionne, *Women, Men, and the Representation of Women in the British Parliaments: Magic Numbers?* (Manchester: Manchester University Press, 2010).

42. See Clinton Bennett, *Muslim Women of Power: Gender, Politics, and Culture in Islam* (New York: Continuum, 2010); Anna Korteweg and Jennifer Selby, *Debating Sharia: Islam, Gender Politics, and Family Law Arbitration* (Toronto: University of Toronto Press, 2012); or Georgina Waylen, *Gender in the Third World* (Boulder: Lynne Rienner, 1996).

43. See Susan Henneberg, *Gender Politics* (New York: Greenhaven, 2017); or Ronald Inglehart and Pippa Norris, *Rising Tide: Gender Equality and Cultural Change Around the World* (Cambridge: Cambridge University Press, 2003).

44. United Nations, *Human Development Report 2016*, "Human Development for Everyone," http://hdr.undp.org/en/2016-report/download, p. 3. See the data from the Gender Development Index (GDI) at http://hdr.undp.org/en/composite/GDI.

45. United Nations, *Human Development Report 2016*, p. 5.

46. Ibid., "Statistical Annex: Table 5: Gender Inequality Index," http://hdr.undp.org /en/2016-report/download.

47. Jonathan Dean, *Rethinking Contemporary Feminist Politics* (New York: Palgrave Macmillan, 2010); Catherine Redfern and Kristin Aune, *Reclaiming the F Word: The New Feminist Movement* (New York: Palgrave Macmillan, 2010); or Myra Marx Ferree, *Varieties of Feminism: German Gender Politics in Global Perspective* (Stanford: Stanford University Press, 2012).

48. For examples of recent work in this area, see Richard Zweigenhaft and G. William Domhoff, *Diversity in the Political Elite: How It Happened, Why It Matters* (Lanham: Rowman and Littlefield, 2006); or Tomsic, *Elites in the New Democracies*.

49. Kenneth Good, *Trust in the Capacities of the People, Distrust in Elites* (Lanham: Lexington, 2014); Charles Kadushin, *The American Intellectual Elite* (New Brunswick, NJ: Transaction, 2006); and Daniel C. Lynch, *China's Futures: PRC Elites Debate Economics, Politics, and Foreign Policy* (Stanford: Stanford University Press, 2015).

50. C. Wright Mills, *The Power Elite* (Oxford: Oxford University Press, 1956).

51. A very good discussion of these issues can be found in G. William Domhoff, *Who Rules America? Power and Politics and Social Change* (Boston: McGraw-Hill, 2006). See also John Jackson, *The American Political Party System: Continuity and Change over Ten Presidential Elections* (Washington, DC: Brookings Institution, 2014).

52. For examples of recent discussion of this nature, see Erica Chenoweth, *Political Violence* (Los Angeles: Sage, 2014); or Virginia Held, *How Terrorism Is Wrong: Morality and Political Violence* (New York: Oxford University Press, 2008).

53. Peter Merkl, ed., *Political Violence and Terror: Motifs and Motivations* (Berkeley: University of California Press, 1986), pp. 32–33. See Haroon K. Ullah, *Vying for Allah's Vote: Understanding Islamic Parties, Political Violence, and Extremism in Pakistan* (Washington, DC: Georgetown University Press, 2013).

54. See Antoni Abat I Ninet, *Constitutional Violence: Legitimacy, Democracy, and Human Rights* (Edinburgh: Edinburgh University Press, 2013).

55. See Kim Sorvig, *To Heal Kent State: A Memorial Meditation* (Portland, OR: Worldview, 1990). See also Brad Lucas, *Radicals, Rhetoric, and the War: The University of Nevada in the Wake of Kent State* (New York: Palgrave Macmillan, 2006).

56. See Jorg Le Blanc, *Political Violence in Latin America* (Newcastle upon Tyne: Cambridge Scholars, 2012); or Zahia Smail Salhi, *Gender and Violence in Islamic Societies: Patriarchy, Islamism, and Politics in the Middle East and North Africa* (London: Tauris, 2013).

57. John R. Thackrah, *Encyclopedia of Terrorism and Political Violence* (London: Routledge and Kegan Paul, 1987), p. 215. See also David Whittaker, *The Terrorism Reader* (New York: Routledge, 2007).

58. Edgar O'Ballance, *Language of Violence: The Blood Politics of Terrorism* (San Rafael, CA: Presidio, 1979), pp. 1–8. See also Philip Herbst, *Talking Terrorism: A Dictionary of the Loaded Language of Political Violence* (Westport: Greenwood, 2003).

59. Interview with author in the Knesset, April 3, 1975. The distinction between being a hero of national liberation and being a terrorist is often one of perspective, as this interview indicated. See Gerald Cromer, *A War of Words: Political Violence and Public Debate in Israel* (New York: Cass, 2004).

7

The Institutions of Civil Society

Learning Outcomes

After reading this chapter, you will be able to

- Appreciate the importance of political behavior for the political system.
- Describe the political environment within which political structures operate.
- Understand the difference between pluralism and corporatism and be able to explain the significance of both for the political system.
- Explain what rational choice theory is and how it explains individual behavior.
- Understand the importance of the concept of civil society.
- Distinguish between political parties and interest groups (and pressure groups) and explain why they are important for democratic politics.
- Explain the difference between social movements and interest groups.

In this chapter we will investigate some of the ways that the political environment is organized in its operation. We begin with some discussion of a pluralist theory of democracy and discuss the relationship between pluralism and corporatism in politics. We then discuss the concept of collective action and the way that it might influence the operation of politics and individual political behavior, followed by some attention given to the distinctions between democratic and nondemocratic rule and their implications for the political environment.

We then turn our attention to two major organizing structures in the political environment: the interest group and the political party. Both of these structures play key roles in both democratic and nondemocratic politics, and both affect in significant ways the political contexts within which they operate.

Pluralism and Corporatism

Among the most basic concepts in modern political science is the idea of pluralism. The idea suggests that "multiple, competing elites (including interest groups) determine public policy through bargaining and compromise."[1] Although referred to as "factions" and not called "pluralism" at the time, this topic was present at the time of the establishment of American political institutions as the theme of one of James Madison's contributions to *The Federalist Papers,* Number 10.[2] Central to the concept of pluralism are the ideas of individual rationality and individual choice, and the premise that a rational individual will act in his or her own self-interest.

According to what is called pluralist theory,[3] interest groups could be called "advantage groups." People join them because they see an advantage to doing so. Policy outcomes are perceived as a result of group competition, not necessarily a product of majority rule: a well-organized minority can defeat a less-well-organized majority in the process of competition for policy outcomes.

The original group theorist was Arthur Bentley, whose 1908 work on the subject[4] was very popular in the 1950s; it was expanded upon by David Truman, whose 1951 book *The Governmental Process* became one of the classics of political science. Truman took the idea of interest groups further than had Bentley, suggesting that individuals belong to several different interest groups, the group loyalties reflecting different aspects of their interests and personalities. This gave rise to Truman's idea of "overlapping" group affiliations. According to Truman, "'Interest group' refers to any group that, on the basis of one or more shared attitudes, makes certain claims upon other groups in the society for the establishment, maintenance, or enhancement of forms of behavior that are implied by the shared attitudes."[5] Truman also considered "potential" interest groups as part of the process.

Mancur Olson's work *The Logic of Collective Action,* as we will note shortly, helped to explain the problems with Truman's theory, because Olson pointed out that it was not logical, or rational, for an individual to invest his or her time or effort in joining an organization if that organization was working for a **collective good**. He defined this as "any good such that, if any person X in a group . . . consumes it, it cannot feasibly be withheld from the others in that group."[6] By this definition, it would not be "rational" for an individual to contribute funds to a clean air fund, because if the goal were achieved it would also be available for free to persons who had not contributed. And if enough other people supported the goal then the individual might share in the rewards (i.e., the good public policy of clean air) without having to absorb any of the costs. Olson's work showed that if there already was an interest group to further a certain goal, it might not be the case that all individuals interested in that goal would join the group: they could enjoy the benefits of the group without contributing to the efforts of the group.

Another collection of theories regarding political interaction among groups of individuals involves **corporatism**. The idea of corporatism implies for many a close interaction of groups and government. For some it suggests "a situation where the interest organizations are integrated in the governmental decision-making process of a society."[7] Modern development of the idea of corporatism, called **neocorporatism**, "emphasizes the characteristics of the interest associations entering a relationship with the state apparatus, and the nature of this relationship, i.e., the ways in which they are recognized and granted a representational monopoly by the state."[8]

The theory of neocorporatism takes up where the theory of pluralism leaves off. It suggests that groups are significant for the political system, although it accepts Olson's suggestion that not all individuals with shared interests will necessarily join those groups. There are a number of common elements in the several variations of neocorporatist theory today:

1. Monopolies of interest representation exist and are important to explain political behaviour and policy outcomes.
2. Hierarchies emerge among associations and they may subordinate and coordinate the activities of whole economic sectors and/or social classes.
3. Membership in associations is not always voluntary . . . arrangements exist both to bind members to "their" associations and to prevent the emergence of competing ones.
4. Interest associations are not just the passive recipients of already formed member interests, but may play an active role in identifying and forming those interests.
5. Interest associations do not merely transmit member preferences to authorities, but may actively and coercively govern the behaviour of their members, especially through devolved responsibility for the implementation of public policy.
6. The state may not be either an arena for which interests contend or another interest group with which they must compete, but a constitutive element engaged in defining . . . the activities of associations. . . .
7. Interest associations are not always autonomous entities pressuring the state from without and seeking access wherever they can find an opportunity.[9]

The idea of conflict is found at the center of neocorporatist theory just as it is found at the center of pluralist theory.[10] This involves disagreement between and among different groups regarding social, economic, and political goals—what goals should be, and how they should be achieved. Pluralism and corporatism (or neocorporatism) are at different ends of a continuum, because both argue for the significance of the *group* in the political process. Where they differ is on the relationship between government and groups—perhaps put another way, the degree to which the government establishes a patron-client relationship with specific interest groups.

The Logic of Collective Action

One of the key assumptions of democratic politics is that individuals will participate if given the opportunity to do so. They *will* communicate with the government to be certain that their preferences come about. They *will* vote. They *will* participate in other ways. We know, however, that this is empirically not correct. People often, commonly, do not participate in politics, even when they can, and even when it is relatively easy to do so in stable and secure democratic regimes. We might understand why someone would refrain from participating in situations of danger (such as being shot at in a demonstration) or great expense (such as having to pay huge fees to participate). Why, however, do individuals not participate when there is no threat to them personally and there is essentially no cost?

One now classic study of US politics examined political participation and found that nearly 30 percent of American adults knew virtually nothing about politics. These individuals were labeled "apathetic." Another 60 percent of adults paid some attention to politics but participated only moderately. They were called "spectators." Only about 5 to 7 percent of the public were active participants in politics, routinely engaging in discussion and participation in presidential election years, and this number fell to 1 to 2 percent in non–presidential election years. These individuals were referred to as "gladiators."[11] Why were there so few gladiators?

This question can be expanded to focus on the broader political landscape. Why is it in situations when it is easy to vote that individuals do not vote in some nations? Why do individuals not invest the modest time and effort necessary to participate in democratically choosing their leaders when given the opportunity to do so?

One of the best explanations for why this is the case, as suggested earlier, was offered by Mancur Olson in his seminal book *The Logic of Collective Action*, published in 1965.[12] Olson argued that although the traditional interpretation of democratic government is that people will participate when given the opportunity to do so, by joining political parties or operating in interest groups, in fact individuals usually do not do this.

Further, Olson argued that this inaction was a rational position to take: personal inaction often makes more sense than participation in collective action through political parties or interest groups.

Olson argued in terms of **rational choice theory**. Individuals will participate when it is in their personal interest to do so, when individual participation will make a difference in terms of benefits (e.g., public policies) to them, personally. Olson suggested that individuals are rational actors in deciding whether to participate or not, and will ask some version of the question, Are the potential benefits of this action greater than the potential costs of this action? If the anticipated benefits of an action (e.g., voting, demonstrating) are not greater than the anticipated costs (e.g., time spent, possible arrest), then an individual might not participate, even if he or she could do so.

If the individual thinks that the costs of a potential action could be very high, and the benefits relatively lower, she or he might not participate. If a group is already going to participate in the direction that the individual would prefer, and this person perceives that their participation wouldn't make a significant difference in any event, they might not participate. It is all a matter of costs and rewards, calculated very objectively.

From the point of the logic of collective action, participation often is wasted energy. This is especially true in what can be called collective goods, either material or nonmaterial goods that are shared by a number of people or that will be available to all. Should one join a group that is going to work hard to clean up a polluted lake? While it may be a good thing to do so, the rational actor may say no, and be happy to let the group go ahead. If the group is successful in cleaning the lake, then the benefits of the clean lake are available to all. If the group is not successful in cleaning the lake then their efforts were wasted, and the nonparticipating citizen didn't incur the cost of time and effort that being a member of the group would have demanded.

There are many different forms of political participation, ranging from joining a group to voting to organizing to protest a government action to even more violent and dangerous options. Each of these types of participation can be examined from a rational choice perspective: Is my personal participation likely to make a difference that will benefit me? It certainly may be the case from a philosophical perspective that participation is a good and necessary thing. Democracy will work only if the people (the *demos*) actually participate. On the other hand, while some individuals may derive enough satisfaction from participation to make it worthwhile to them, others participate only out of a sense of citizen duty, and for them the costs may exceed the benefits. An individual who doesn't care a good deal about politics may be willing to walk to the nearby polling station to vote out of a sense of duty, but if the weather is especially bad she or he might decide to stay home. An individual who feels moderately pleased about new democratization and elections taking place might be willing to stand in line for hours to vote, until he or she sees gangs attacking potential voters. Participation, in short, is not always automatic.

Democratic and Nondemocratic Rule

The perspective of rational choice theory reminds us of a very important point: the act of political behavior is a function of its context. In some places it is very easy to participate. Elsewhere it is much more difficult. Sometimes the costs are low or nonexistent. Other times the costs may be very high, including possible death. The same act, for example walking into a voting booth and casting a vote, can have very different implications in two different systems, and very different consequences, too. Voting in the United States may take time but is likely to be safe. We do not hear of individuals being killed while voting. Voting in the recent election in Tanzania, on the other hand, had the potential to result in an individual being killed, or at least injured, by others trying to prevent voters from voting against the incumbent.

There are many kinds of political structures in democratic nations that are designed to serve as a form of **linkage mechanism** to connect the voice of the people to the political leaders of the regime. A list of these structures might include interest groups, political parties, ad hoc social movements, and nongovernmental organizations (NGOs). In democratic government these structures listen to the public and pass along some message to the leaders in a way that in some manner parallels the formal legislative representative relationship.

In nondemocratic regimes the government is usually not interested in encouraging individual political participation by the public, at least not *free* individual participation. The government does want people to participate—it wants them to obey laws, to pay taxes, to come to political rallies, and so on—but it doesn't want them doing so on their own or without government sanction. Some of these regimes have structures that roughly approximate structures in democratic settings, including elections, political parties, interest groups, and so on, but the structures are controlled by the government, and spontaneous political expression is not encouraged.[13]

Nondemocratic regimes are usually defined as political systems in which power is controlled by a small group that exercises power without being responsible to the public.[14] In this sense the word responsible means "answerable": the people do not have an opportunity to remove leaders from office, and the public does not play a role in selecting leaders to hold office. Leaders in nondemocratic regimes may come to power through a military, palace, or reform coup, and among their major concerns is staying in power. We generally observe that nondemocratic regimes limit individual freedom in order to stay in power. While this may result in limitations on individual freedom, it is not the same thing as curtailing all political participation.

Authoritarian governments in fact encourage public participation in order to develop legitimacy for themselves. They will claim a 100 percent participation rate in elections—contrasted with half to two-thirds of that in most democratic governments—thereby showing that they are *more* democratic than Western democracies. They will have larger legislatures, to show that more individuals are elected to office. They have active political parties (often only one is allowed). They have active and productive, but tightly controlled, media structures. In short, it is not the level of participation that differs from Western democratic regimes, but the nature of the participation and the freedom of the individual interacting with government.

It turns out that there is a strong association between modernization and democracy. Societies that do not have modern institutions—reflected by measures of urbanization, education, equal rights, and the like—are not likely to have democratic rule. Modernization is not the same thing, of course, as equal access to resources. These associations are not absolute, however. It is possible to find high standards of living in both democratic and nondemocratic nations, and it is possible to find low standards of living in both democratic and nondemocratic nations.

The Notion of Civil Society

This brings us back to the idea of **civil society**. Civil society can be defined as the way that the population of a nation organizes into associations or organizations that are independent of formal institutions of the state, the way that people organize groups to define their interests.[15] Civil society includes traditional interest groups (to be discussed shortly), as well as social movements and nongovernmental organizations. The most important point to note about civil society and what is not included in civil society is that civil society is distinct from government institutions. It refers to organizations that citizens form on their own, without governmental guidance or regulation. Some of these groups may have political goals or interests, and some may have no political goals at all. The point is that citizens become involved in society and organize with other citizens to form groups and networks that permit them to interact with others.[16]

In this way civil society is a key ingredient of a democratic political culture, providing some of the networks and support mechanisms that permit democratic political behavior to take place. The idea of a "loyal opposition" was developed in Britain in the early nineteenth century to suggest that it was possible to *oppose* the government of the day but still be *loyal* to the monarch.[17] In much the same way, the concept of a civil society *permits* criticism of a particular regime while still being committed to operating *within* the particular regime.

Two of the pioneers in scholarship in this area in the 1950s were Gabriel Almond and Sidney Verba, who did field research in a number of nations and concluded that there was something that they called a "civic culture" that could be found in democracies, a term that referred to individuals' accepting both the "rules of the game" of the political system and also the individuals who were their leaders. A civic culture and a civil society are two kinds of sets of relationships that make it possible for government to work in a stable way, even if individuals may be unhappy with individual political decisions from time to time. Whether we are talking about religious organizations, sports organizations, fraternal organizations, or other kinds of networks, these gathering structures are important to politics because they help individuals to articulate what is important to them and to interact with others.

A contemporary study of the notion of civil society was undertaken at the end of the twentieth century by Robert Putnam. In *Bowling Alone,*[18] Putnam sought to understand the state of American civil society, and he showed that there had been for years a consistent decline in membership in a wide range of associations, everything from educational associations to bowling leagues (hence the title of his book). Putnam argued that this suggested a serious decline of American "social capital," a decline in social networks and the social trust that is developed in them.

Interest Groups

Although political systems may contain political structures designed to ensure popular representation in the governmental policymaking process, most notably the legislature, it is entirely likely that the formal governmental (constitutional) structures of representation will not prove to be sufficient for representing all shades of public opinion.

Two additional structures are available in the political environment to supplement the formal (constitutional) representative structures, and they are quite effective in many political regimes. Both the **interest group** and the **political party** can play significant roles in political systems in assisting formal-legal structures in the processing of political demands and the communication of public beliefs, attitudes, and values.

Although interest groups and political parties have many characteristics in common,[19] we should be careful to distinguish between them, for they really are quite different. As indicated earlier, group theory suggests that all public opinion can be described in group terms and that individual opinion is essentially unimportant, save for the fact that individuals make up groups. Public opinion either originates with groups or is articulated by groups, and so we do not need to worry about individual representation as long as a mechanism for group representation exists.[20]

Interest groups are collections of individuals who share common beliefs, attitudes, or values. The shared concerns may focus upon a variety of issues, such as concern about nuclear weapons, gun control, air pollution, or minimum wage or work conditions. The shared concerns may also be a bit more frivolous, such as love of miniature schnauzers, Parker fountain pen collecting, or appreciation of antique wall clocks.

Interest groups come into existence because individuals see something to be gained by such an association, including material gains (higher wages by joining a union, or free auto towing by joining an automobile club); psychological gains (a feeling of "brotherhood" from joining a fraternity, or a sense of theological fulfillment by joining a church); recreational gains (lower ski-lift fees by joining a ski association); and humanitarian gains (helping to promote civil rights by contributing to a civil rights organization).[21]

Interest groups may be highly organized, loosely organized, or not formally organized at all.[22] Their scope of concern may be quite broad, or quite narrow. Groups might be open to anyone interested, or limited in membership. They may, in short, vary greatly. Interest groups can be more or less active, and more or less effective, depending upon several different constraints on their behavior. These constraints include the group's resources, the group's objectives, and the political environment within which the group is operating.[23]

Different interest groups have different resources, although the types and nature of these resources can vary greatly. Financial resources can affect what a group does in terms of activity, publicity, travel, and outreach. The number of individuals who participate in the interest group is important, too. Groups that are small generally have less impact than groups that are large. It should be noted that the degree to which a group is tightly organized can make up for smaller numbers; the ability of the National Rifle Association (NRA) to generate mass mailings to the US Congress is legendary in explaining its ability to influence legislation, given the fact that its number of members isn't that large. The relationship between the interest group and key social and political institutions can affect how important an interest group will be. Labor unions have had for years a close relationship with the Democratic Party in the United States; when the Democrats control government, the union agenda is much more likely to be enacted than with the Republicans.

The group's objectives make a difference in how effective it is. There is a wide range of subjects of interest for interest groups, and a wide range of goals. Some seek to influence a tax code. Others may seek to entrench religious law as the law of the political system. "Green" organizations may be concerned about establishing public policy that deals with environmental issues. Some organizations may work for international peace. Others may simply be content to promote a group of individuals that gathers once a week to play a game of checkers. In short, the goal of the interest group may be easier to achieve or more difficult to achieve.

Finally, the political environment within which interest groups operate makes a difference. As suggested earlier, in nondemocratic regimes the government is far more concerned with social order and stability than with individual freedom and interests. This may make it more difficult for interest groups to organize and operate without the blessing of the regime. On the other hand, democratic regimes may be fairly wide open in terms of the organization and operation of interest groups, and might offer no resistance to the interest group at all.

Group theorists suggest that interest groups play an important function in the political arena (see Figure 7.1). They are important as linkage mechanisms, some argue, because they are effective communicators of segments of public opinion.[24] Because interest groups generally are of limited scope, they are able to communicate their collective opinion more effectively than can individuals. The NRA and the American Medical Association (AMA) are two examples of interest groups that, although numerically not overwhelmingly large, are very effective in exerting political pressure in the areas of concern to their members.

The argument for interest group utility suggests that political (formal, constitutional, legislative) representatives cannot represent all of their constituents. On any given issue in relation to which a legislator takes a position, it is almost inevitable that he or she will alienate some group. An American legislator voting in favor of gun control, for example, is going to irritate constituents who oppose gun control. What is more, once "their" representative has come out on the opposite side of an issue, the anti-gun-control

Figure 7.1   Interest Groups and Political Linkages

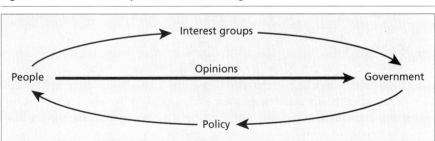

constituents (to use the same example) are no longer—strictly speaking—represented by their representative in the legislature. The existence of an interest group, in this case the NRA, affords these individuals recourse to an alternative representational structure that will voice their concerns and act on their collective behalf.

Many political scientists use the terms **interest group** and **pressure group** interchangeably. Others, however, make a distinction between the terms, and the student should be aware of the distinctions that are drawn.[25] Pressure groups, simply put, are said to be a subset of interest groups that are organized exclusively for the purpose of political lobbying. Thus we can say that all pressure groups are interest groups, but not all interest groups are pressure groups.

There are many kinds of interest groups (collections of individuals who share a common belief, attitude, value, or concern) whose activities are oriented around nonpolitical themes. A fountain pen collectors' club may meet once a month to have fountain pen shows and competitions, give prizes and award ribbons, and discuss articles of interest in the widely read publication *Pen World*. Their group is a nonpolitical concern. Other interest groups may be usually nonpolitical. The American Automobile Association (AAA) has as its primary raison d'être auto safety, and it provides its members with a number of benefits: maps, car insurance, tow service, and so on. On occasion, however, the AAA has become politically active, such as when the Congress was considering an extra tax on gasoline. The AAA, acting on behalf of its members (drivers), lobbied effectively against such a tax.

Still other interest groups are exclusively political, having as their primary reason for being a policy objective, for example a group to end US involvement in Iraq, or a group lobbying for reproductive rights. These groups, pressure groups, are narrower in scope—usually related to a single issue—and ostensibly temporary. Once their policy objective is achieved, they no longer have a reason for being. General interest groups, on the other hand, are much longer-lived, and their reason for being is not as transient. Pressure groups will often support any candidate—from whatever political party—who will pledge to support their particular cause. Pressure groups are usually single-issue groups and orient all of their political behavior around "their" issue. This is very different from the behavior of political parties.

Political Parties

This leads us to our next distinction, the difference between interest groups (and here the concept includes our pressure group subcategory) and political parties. Many differences between political parties and interest groups have been pointed out in detailed studies, including permanence and levels of organization (political parties tend to be more permanent and institutionalized than are interest groups) and breadth of issue concerns (political parties almost invariably are concerned with a large number of issues, while interest groups usually focus upon a more narrow range of issues).

The single most important difference between political parties and interest groups, however, relates to the goals of the organization. The goal of the interest group is to satisfy its members, either through the organization itself (for example, with the fountain pen collectors' club) or through political pressure resulting in a specific policy outcome (for example, the National Rifle Association helping to defeat gun-control legislation). The goal of a political party is to win political office, gain political power, and thereby control the policymaking process.[26] The interest group does not care which party or which individual wins an election as long as its specific policy concern prevails. The political party is much broader in scope and seeks to hold power (to the point of perhaps modifying some of its issue positions if that will help it to control power); the interest group is not so much concerned with power as with policy outcome.

Parties have been said to derive from many different sources.[27] One source is factions within a legislature. US political parties are examples of this; they originally formed as groups of legislative supporters of Thomas Jefferson and Alexander Hamilton, which subsequently established formal organizations leading to the creation of the Jeffersonian Democrats and the Federalists.[28] A second source of party organization is labor movements. The British Labour Party is a good example of this,[29] an already-existing labor organization (itself an interest group) deciding to develop a political identity, seeking not only to influence labor policy but also to control power. Still another point of origin of political parties is the national liberation movement. The Congress Party in India was not primarily a political party under British rule; rather it was organized to help India achieve independence, and to help drive the British from India. Once the British left, the conversion from liberation movement to political party was easily achieved.[30] Finally, parties may be created for ideological reasons, to represent a viewpoint not otherwise represented in the polity.[31]

Political parties vary in different respects, including membership and size, and structure of organization, not to mention variation in the number of parties active in the system itself.[32] One of the structural distinctions among parties is whether they are mass parties or cadre parties. Maurice Duverger, in his classic work *Political Parties,* suggested that "the difference involved is not one of size but of structure." For mass parties, the recruiting of members is a fundamental activity; "the members are therefore the very substance of the party, the stuff of its activity. Without members, the party would be like a teacher without pupils."[33] Also, mass parties are financially mass-based; party finances are, to a large extent, based upon member dues.

The cadre party is of a different sort. As Duverger suggested, "what the mass party secures by numbers, the cadre party achieves by selection; . . . it is dependent upon rigid and exclusive selection."[34] Sometimes the distinction between mass and cadre parties is made less clear because the cadre parties may admit numbers of the mass in imitation of a mass party; there are few pure cadre parties today. Contemporary US parties, for example, are disguised cadre parties. They have democratic constitutions and permit mass participation, but they are really steered by a much smaller group of individuals. Generally, then, cadre parties correspond to more caucus-organized types of parties, usually decentralized, while mass parties tend to correspond to parties based on branches, more centrally organized and firmly knit.

The number of political parties in an electoral system is a function of several factors, including ideology, political culture, electoral laws, and methods of election.[35] Duverger noted that the relationship between the electoral regime and the number of political parties is direct: "The simple-majority single-ballot system favours the two-party system."[36] There are a number of differently sized party systems: single-party systems, two-party systems, two-party-plus systems, and multiparty systems. The term *party system* refers not to a single party but instead to the framework of parties operating in a given nation. It discusses the number of parties that are competitive in a system (not the absolute number that can be said to exist, because that typically includes many parties whose success is grossly unrealistic in competition).

This is significant. The number of parties "realistically" competing in a political system (that is, that have a realistic chance of being elected and organizing power) tells us about that system. Countries that have a single party are less likely to be "democratic" by objective measures than countries with several parties. Countries with several parties, none of which controls a majority in the legislature, are more likely to be politically unstable than others. We want to know whether a political system is a single-party system, a two-party system, or a multiparty system to better understand the context within which political institutions are operating.

We should note at this point that the terms *single-party* and *two-party* are not meant to be taken literally. Even authoritarian single-party systems may have several parties that are active in elections. Party systems that we call two-party systems often have far more than two parties active and extant. What we are really asking about is the likelihood of winning election in electoral competition. Typically, single-party systems are systems in which one party will regularly win more than 65 percent of the vote; two-party systems suggest that the two (or two-plus such as Britain or Canada) parties will receive over 75 percent of the vote; and multiparty systems suggest that the two largest parties have a total of less than 75 percent of the vote.[37]

Single-party systems are often associated with nondemocratic rule, where the party and the state are often seen as the same. Authoritarian regimes, such as those found in China, Cuba, or formerly the Soviet Union or Nazi Germany, are examples of single-party systems. But single political parties may also operate in developing nations that are essentially democratic, with the single dominant party being the party that was associated with independence and freedom, for example the Kenyan African National Union in Kenya, the Independent Republican Party in Mexico, or the Congress Party in India.

We will see later in this volume, however, that Mexico's single-party system has evolved into a competitive two-party system, with the Institutional Revolutionary Party (PRI) candidate coming in third in the most recent presidential election.[38] The Congress Party has split and resplit in India and has lost national elections in recent years, and although it still exists and is a major player, it does not dominate national politics in the manner it did at India's independence or during India's early years.[39]

Two-party systems, or two-party-plus systems, are often the consequence of electoral systems, as we have seen earlier in this book. Where we have a single-member-district plurality voting system, we tend to have two political parties, or series of two political parties. The Canadian political system, as we will see later in this volume, has one system of party competition at the national level and a number of different systems of party competition in its provinces. Thus any given electoral contest may be a two-party or three-party competition, but there are a number of different parties in existence in Canada.

Political parties are an important part of a theory of pluralism. If political pluralism, as one author has put it, highlights the "existence of a 'plurality of groups that are both independent and non-inclusive,'" then parties are an important part of that pluralistic model.[40] Parties are crucial as an organizing structure in legislatures; obviously, party discipline could not exist in legislatures without political parties, and it is party discipline that is the vehicle for responsible government, for a government being able to deliver on its promises.[41]

Internal party organization varies on a party-by-party basis.[42] Some parties are highly unified, while others are collections of factions that may not have a great deal in common except their commitment to share power. Some parties are very democratic organizations, while others permit no internal competition at all and are simply organizations dedicated to following and supporting a single individual's political advancement.

Political parties, much as interest groups, serve a number of important functions in the political regime. They are, among other things, rather elaborate personnel services, serving as a mechanism for assisting in the hiring of political leaders.[43] They help to organize political groups. They help to articulate political demands.[44] They serve as a point of reference for bewildered voters who are overwhelmed by the political world: party label is often the only clue available to voters to guide their behavior, and it is widely used as such.

Another important function served by the political party as an organization is in the process of political development.[45] Parties are important vehicles in the process of political recruitment, helping to bring individuals into the political arena by offering a convenient vehicle for participation to the masses. They also serve as structures that mobilize the electorate—"get out the vote" and participate—through competition between parties (or within a party in one-party systems).[46] Through this action they contribute to a sense of "national integration,"[47] thus helping to develop a sense of political nationhood on the part of the masses.[48]

In short, research has shown that political parties can play significant roles in five important respects in the process of political development. First, parties encourage and facilitate political participation. Second, they help to stimulate a sense of governmental legitimacy through the campaign process and the debate that ensues. Third, they contribute to the development of a sense of national integration. Fourth, they play an important role in conflict management within the polity, providing a vehicle by which differences of opinion over policy preferences can be peacefully resolved. Finally, political parties play an important role in the political socialization function in society, helping to transmit attitudes and values from one generation to another.

Much as the interest group was seen to be a political structure that assists in the representation function in the political world, so, too, the political party serves as a linkage mechanism[49] in passing along public opinions from various groups in the electorate to government officials, as shown in Figure 7.2. Of course, the degree to which parties serve these several functions depends upon the individual party organization and the political system within which it is found. Depending upon the number of political parties in a system, the degree of party discipline found in the political system, and the ideology and constituency of the party in question, the role of the party will vary.

Scholars have speculated about the future of political parties and whether they can continue to be as central a political structure in their respective political systems as they have been in the past. The continual growth of executive power in political systems, combined with greater public attention to politics and increasingly aggressive media, means that traditional assumptions about political parties and political party behavior have to be rethought.[50]

Figure 7.2 Political Parties and Political Linkages

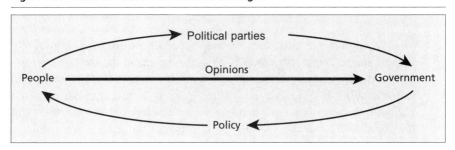

Social Movements

A **social movement** is defined as a broad group of individuals who share an interest in a given social issue. How do social movements differ from interest groups or political parties? Interest groups generally are organized and are collections of individuals who share common beliefs, attitudes, values, or concerns. They are "advantage groups," coming into existence because a number of individuals see something to be gained (either materially or psychologically) by doing so. And they serve as linkage mechanisms between the public and the state.[51] Pressure groups are a subset of interest groups that are organized for the purpose of political lobbying (and thus all pressure groups are interest groups, but not all interest groups are pressure groups). The important difference between interest groups and political groups is the breadth and the ultimate goal of the organization: the political party seeks to hold power and is broader in scope than the interest group.

As a general rule we can say that social movements share many characteristics of interest groups, in that they articulate group interests and seek to influence government (rather than hold power themselves). A key difference, though, is that social movements are likely to be less organized than an interest group, and possibly have a broader constituency, one that doesn't correspond to a particular political structure.[52] They also, similar to our description of interest groups, want to influence public policy, but not control power and exercise policy themselves. Another characteristic that they have in common with interest groups is that they are inclusive and that they help individuals to bring their concerns to the attention of political and social leaders outside of the political structures of the regime.

Anthony Giddens has argued that there are five general categories of social movements in modern society:

1. Democratic movements that work for political rights.
2. Labor movements that work for control of the workplace.
3. Ecological movements that are concerned with the environment.

4. Religious movements that work with more or less outreach.
5. Peace movements that work toward peace and less global conflict.[53]

We might argue that many interest groups flow out of, or conversely help to create, social movements. What can be called the women's movement has created many interest groups over time and around the world, and in some political systems even political parties dedicated to issues focusing upon women. The same can be said for the gay rights movement and the right-to-life movement. The environmental movement has similarly created many interest groups, and political parties for that matter (such as the Greens in Germany).

A **nationalist movement** can be seen as a special type of social movement, in which a group of individuals who are articulating a common set of beliefs (for example, that India should become independent of Britain) start to act within the political system to influence political policy. These movements create interest groups, and sometimes political parties, that work toward the common goal of the individuals involved.

We cannot write about social and political movements without mentioning the **Arab Spring**, which took place from December 2010 through the summer of 2011. Protests began in Tunisia, then spread to Egypt in January 2011, and took place for over two weeks. They spread through Libya, Bahrain, Syria, Jordan, to as far west as Morocco. Almost no country in the region was untouched. This was a protest that was a political movement in the purest sense of the term; organization was almost spontaneous, made possible by advances in technology and the ubiquity of cell phones. Although the protest in Tunisia started with an instance of self-immolation by an individual angry at being mistreated by the police, it rapidly—extremely rapidly—spread throughout the region (even into relatively stable countries such as Turkey) into a more general protest against authoritarian rule and a cry for democratic government.[54]

Social movements emerge as a result of several possible causes. One theory (social deprivation) suggests that people create social movements because they feel deprived of some resource, and they start to coalesce with others who share that feeling of deprivation.[55] A second theory (mass-society) argues that social movements are made up of individuals in large societies who feel insignificant or socially detached. Social movements, according to this theory, provide a sense of empowerment and belonging that the movement's members would otherwise not have.[56] Yet a third idea (structural strain) suggests that people believe that society has problems, and this is what draws them together into a common movement.[57]

One of the major scholars in the field of social movements today is Ronald Inglehart, who has written about the proliferation of social movements in contemporary society. His view is that traditional political parties are no longer adequate organizationally to represent citizen concerns, and that more ad hoc group activity is forming in response to the issues of the day. This activity, he suggests, is finding its outlet in social movements rather than political parties.[58]

Pluralism, Parties, Interest Groups, and Social Movements

The terms *groups, parties,* and *movements* are central in any discussion of democratic politics, and are even central in discussion of political participation in systems that may not, at a given time, be democratic. After all, the behavior of over a million Chinese students in Beijing in May 1989 showed the potential impact of an interest group: the "critical mass" that was present at the time was so large that even the Chinese army was not able to control students' behavior for a significant period of time. The more recent Arab Spring protests and democracy movement is another example of how spontaneous political movements may arise even in repressive and authoritarian contexts. Political parties, interest groups, and social movements are primary vehicles by which collective public opinion is communicated to the political elite in most political systems.

We have seen in this chapter that a pluralistic approach to the study of politics suggests that we need to look at (some kinds of) political groups to understand how much political behavior takes place. We saw in Chapter 6 how individuals develop their political beliefs and attitudes, and how the political elite comes to be the political elite. It is necessary to add to this—as we have done in this chapter—some understanding of pluralism theory, interest groups, political parties, and social movements to get a broad vision of what influences political behavior and how that political behavior appears in the political environment.

At this point in our study of comparative politics we will turn our attention to a series of country studies in order to see how the institutions and behaviors that we have described in the first part of this text fit together in single political settings. We have been looking at political structures and behaviors from an explicitly cross-national perspective, examining constitutional structures from a range of settings together, legislatures from a range of settings together, executives from a range of settings together, and so on. It is now time for us to pull the national threads out of these chapters to see how they fit together: the British constitution with the British parliament and the British executive and British political parties, and the like. This analysis will, it is hoped, provide the student with a better understanding of both institutions and behavior, as well as an appreciation for how these can be affected by the political settings in which they operate.

Discussion Questions

1. What is the importance of political behavior for the political system?
2. What are the key components of the political environment within which political structures operate?
3. Explain the difference between pluralism and corporatism. What is the significance of both for the political system?
4. What is rational choice theory, and how does it explain individual behavior?
5. What is the importance of the concept of civil society?
6. What are the key differences between political parties and interest groups (and pressure groups)? How are they different in democratic politics?
7. What are the differences between social movements and interest groups?

Notes

1. Harmon Zeigler, *Pluralism, Corporatism, and Confucianism: Political Association and Conflict Regulation in the United States, Europe, and Taiwan* (Philadelphia: Temple University Press, 1988), p. 3. See also Victor M. Muniz-Fraticelli, *The Structure of Pluralism: On the Authority of Associations* (Oxford: Oxford University Press, 2014).

2. Alexander Hamilton, James Madison, and John Jay, *The Federalist Papers* (New York: New American Library, 1961), pp. 77–83.

3. This section is based upon a much longer analysis in Zeigler, *Pluralism,* pp. 4–11. See also Douglas Farrow, *Recognizing Religion in a Secular Society: Essays in Pluralism, Religion, and Public Policy* (Montreal: McGill-Queen's University Press, 2004).

4. Arthur F. Bentley, *The Process of Government: A Study of Social Pressures* (Chicago: University of Chicago Press, 1908).

5. David Truman, *The Governmental Process* (New York: Knopf, 1951), p. 33. See also Michael Peletz, *Gender Pluralism: Southeast Asia Since Early Modern Times* (New York: Routledge, 2009); and Mark Bevir, *Modern Pluralism: Anglo-American Debates Since 1880* (New York: Cambridge University Press, 2012).

6. Mancur Olson, *The Logic of Collective Action: Public Goods and the Theory of Groups* (Cambridge: Harvard University Press, 1965), p. 14. See also Francesco Vanni, *Agriculture and Public Goods: The Role of Collective Action* (Dordrecht: Springer, 2014).

7. O. Ruin, "Participatory Democracy and Corporatism: The Case of Sweden," *Scandinavian Political Studies* 9 (1974): 171–186, as cited in Gerhard Lehmbruch and Philippe Schmitter, eds., *Patterns of Corporatist Policy-Making* (Beverly Hills: Sage, 1982), p. 4. See also Arend Lijphart, *Patterns of Democracy: Government Forms and Performance in Thirty-Six Countries* (New Haven: Yale University Press, 2012).

8. See Eva Hartmann and Poul Kjaer, *The Evolution of Intermediary Institutions in Europe: From Corporatism to Governance* (New York: Britannica Educational, 2013), p. 11; and George Fredrickson, *Diverse Nations: Explorations in the History of Racial and Ethnic Pluralism* (Boulder: Paradigm, 2008).

9. Philippe C. Schmitter, "Reflections on Where the Theory of Neo-Corporatism Has Gone and Where the Praxis of Neo-Corporatism May Be Going," in Lehmbruch and Schmitter, *Patterns,* pp. 260–261. See also Fraticelli, *Structure of Pluralism.*

10. Two examples of research dealing with corporatism and group conflict are Howard J. Wiarda, *Corporatism and Comparative Politics: The Other Great "Ism"* (Florence: Taylor and Francis, 2016); and Marina Ottaway and Amr Hamzawy, *Getting to Pluralism: Political Actors in the Arab World* (Washington, DC: Carnegie Endowment for International Peace, 2009).

11. Lester Milbrath, *Political Participation* (Chicago: Rand McNally, 1965). See also Lauren K. Hall, *Family and the Politics of Moderation: Private Life, Public Goods, and the Rebirth of Social Individualism* (Waco, TX: Baylor University Press, 2014).

12. Olson, *Logic of Collective Action.* See Angela Kallhoff, *Why Democracy Needs Public Goods* (Lanham: Lexington, 2011).

13. One of the classic studies of this subject is by William Kornhauser, *The Politics of Mass Society* (Glencoe, IL: Free Press, 1959). For an interesting case study, see Elizabeth Thompson, *Justice Interrupted: The Struggle for Constitutional Government in the Middle East* (Cambridge: Harvard University Press, 2013); or Ellen Wiles, *Saffron Shadows and Salvaged Scripts: Literary Life in Myanmar Under Censorship and in Transition* (New York: Columbia University Press, 2015).

14. A good discussion of nondemocratic rule is offered by Stein Ringen, *Nation of Devils: Democracy and the Problem of Obedience* (New Haven: Yale University Press, 2013). See also Eric Brousseau, Tom Dedeurwaerdere, and Bernd Siebenhuner, *Reflexive Governance for Global Public Goods* (Cambridge: Massachusetts Institute of Technology Press, 2012).

15. Karen Hagemann, Sonya Michel, and Gunilla Budde, *Civil Society and Gender Justice: Historical and Comparative Perspectives* (New York: Berghahn, 2008). For other examples of this literature, see Jon Shefner, *The Illusion of Civil Society: Democratization and Community Mobilization in Low-Income Mexico* (University Park: Pennsylvania State University Press, 2008); Ajay Gudavarthy, *Politics of Post–Civil Society: Contemporary History of Political Movements in India* (Los Angeles: Sage, 2013); or Wanda Krause, *Women in Civil Society: Women, Islamism, and Networks in the UAE* (New York: Palgrave Macmillan, 2008).

16. See Jeremy Walton, *Muslim Civil Society and the Politics of Religious Freedom in Turkey* (New York: Oxford University Press, 2017); or Sabine Fischer, *Civil Society in Central and Eastern Europe* (New York: Columbia University Press, 2014).

17. On the development of the concept of a loyal opposition, see Gerald Schmitz, "The Opposition in a Parliamentary System," published by the Political and Social Affairs Division of the Parliamentary Information and Research Service of the Parliament of Canada; it can be found at http://www.parl.gc.ca/Content/LOP/researchpublications/bp47-e.htm#GOV.

18. Robert Putnam, *Bowling Alone: The Collapse and Revival of American Community* (New York: Simon and Schuster, 2000). See also Rosa Sanchez Salgado, *Europeanizing Civil Society: How the EU Shapes Civil Society Organizations* (Basingstoke: Palgrave Macmillan, 2014).

19. One of the classics in this area is Norman Luttbeg, ed., *Public Opinion and Public Policy* (Homewood, IL: Dorsey, 1974), especially pp. 1–10, 109, 187. More recent work includes Christine Barbour et al., *Keeping the Republic: Power and Citizenship in American Politics* (Washington, DC: Congressional Quarterly, 2006); or Ken Godwin, Scott Ainsworth, and Erik Godwin, *Lobbying and Policymaking: The Public Pursuit of Private Interests* (Thousand Oaks, CA: Sage/Congressional Quarterly, 2013).

20. Truman, *Governmental Process,* especially pp. 129–139, offers the classic articulation of this argument. See also James R. Hudson, *Special Interest Society: How Membership-Based Organizations Shape America* (Lanham: Lexington, 2013).

21. See Robert Alexander, *The Classics of Interest Group Behavior* (Belmont, CA: Thomson/Wadsworth, 2006). See also Matthew Grossmann, *The Not-So-Special Interests: Interest Groups, Public Representation, and American Governance* (Stanford: Stanford University Press, 2012).

22. One of the classic typologies developed for the study of interest groups was developed by Gabriel Almond and can be found in his introduction to G. Almond and J. S. Coleman, eds., *The Politics of the Developing Areas* (Princeton: Princeton University Press,

1960), p. 33. See also Holly Brasher, *Vital Statistics on Interest Groups and Lobbying* (Los Angeles: Sage/Congressional Quarterly, 2014).

23. This threefold framework was offered by James Danziger, *Understanding the Political World: A Comparative Introduction to Political Science* (White Plains, NY: Longman, 1996), pp. 68–69. Another good source here is Paul Herrnson, Christopher Deering, and Clyde Wilcox, *Interest Groups Unleashed* (Thousand Oaks, CA: Sage/Congressional Quarterly, 2013).

24. There has been a great deal of work in this area. Among more recent work is John Ahlquist and Margaret Levi, *In the Interest of Others: Organizations and Social Activism* (Princeton: Princeton University Press, 2013). See Luttbeg, *Public Opinion and Public Policy*, pp. 187–188. The articles reprinted in this section of this reader that deal with the pressure groups model of political linkage are all very well done and provide illustrations of the linkage suggested by the theory.

25. This distinction is developed in Luigi Grazio, *Lobbying, Pluralism, and Democracy* (New York: Palgrave, 2001). See also Paul Herrnson, Ronald Shaiko, and Clyde Wilcox, eds., *The Interest Group Connection: Electioneering, Lobbying, and Policymaking in Washington* (Washington, DC: Congressional Quarterly, 2005).

26. See Richard Katz and William Crotty, eds., *Handbook of Party Politics* (Thousand Oaks, CA: Sage, 2005). For further distinctions, see Michael Curtis, *Comparative Politics* (New York: Harper and Row, 1978), pp. 143–144. See also Louis Sandy Maisel and Jeffrey Barry, eds., *The Oxford Handbook of American Political Parties and Groups* (New York: Oxford University Press, 2010).

27. One of the classic essays in this area is that by J. LaPalombara and M. Weiner, "The Origin and Development of Political Parties," in J. LaPalombara and M. Weiner, eds., *Political Parties and Political Development* (Princeton: Princeton University Press, 2015), pp. 3–6. See also Bill Cross, *Political Parties* (Vancouver: University of British Columbia Press, 2014).

28. A good discussion of this is found in James Sterling Young, *The Washington Community: 1800–1828* (New York: Harcourt, Brace, and World, 1966). See also Morton Keller, *America's Three Regimes: A New Political History* (Oxford: Oxford University Press, 2007); or Marjorie Hershey, Barry Burden, and Christina Wolbrecht, *U.S. Political Parties* (Thousand Oaks, CA: Congressional Quarterly, 2014).

29. See Meg Russell, *Building New Labour: The Politics of Party Organisation* (New York: Palgrave Macmillan, 2005). See also David Rubinstein, *The Labour Party and British Society: 1880–2005* (Brighton: Sussex Academic, 2006); and Matthew Cole, *Political Parties in Britain* (Edinburgh: Edinburgh University Press, 2012).

30. This is discussed in Stanley Wolpert, *Shameful Flight: The Last Years of the British Empire in India* (Oxford: Oxford University Press, 2006).

31. One of the best illustrations of ideological parties, of course, involves communist and Marxist parties. Arun Jana and Bhupen Sarmah, *Class, Ideology, and Political Parties in India* (Colorado Springs, CO: International Academic, 2002). See also Marc Guinjoan I. Cesena, *Parties, Elections, and Electoral Contests: Competition and Contamination Effects* (Burlington, VT: Ashgate, 2014).

32. Probably the best single reference book was compiled and edited by Katz and Crotty, *Handbook of Party Politics*. See also D. J. Sagar, *Political Parties of the World* (London: Harper, 2009).

33. This and material in the next paragraph come from Maurice Duverger, *Political Parties* (New York: Wiley, 1963), p. 63.

34. Ibid.

35. See David Farrell, *Electoral Systems: A Comparative Introduction* (New York: Palgrave, 2001).

36. Duverger, *Political Parties*, p. 217.

37. This framework is offered by Marcus Ethridge and Howard Handelman, *Politics in a Changing World: A Comparative Introduction to Political Science* (New York: St. Martin's, 1994), p. 133.

38. Larissa Adler de Lomnitz et al., *Symbolism and Ritual in a One-Party Regime: Unveiling Mexico's Political Culture* (Tucson: University of Arizona Press, 2010).

39. Paul Wallace and Ramashray Roy, *India's 2009 Elections: Coalition Politics, Party Competition, and Congress Continuity* (Thousand Oaks, CA: Sage, 2011).

40. Giovanni Sartori, *Parties and Party Systems: A Framework for Analysis* (Cambridge: Cambridge University Press, 1976), p. 15. See also Lucia Bonfreschi, Giovanni Orsina, and Antonio Varsori, *European Parties and the European Integration Process, 1945–1992* (Bruxelles: Lang, 2015).

41. See Stephen Taylor and David Wykes, *Parliament and Dissent* (Edinburgh: Edinburgh University Press, 2005); or Reuven Hazan, *Cohesion and Discipline in Legislatures: Political Parties, Party Leadership, Parliamentary Committees, and Governance* (London: Routledge, 2013).

42. One example of a study of internal party structure is Katz and Crotty, *Handbook of Party Politics*. See also Barry Steven Levitt, *Power in the Balance: Presidents, Parties, and Legislatures in Peru and Beyond* (Notre Dame, IN: University of Notre Dame Press, 2012).

43. One of the classics in this area is the work of Austin Ranney, *Pathways to Parliament: Candidate Selection in Britain* (Madison: University of Wisconsin Press, 1965). See also Frank Thames and Margaret Williams, *Contagious Representation: Women's Political Representation in Democracies Around the World* (New York: New York University Press, 2013).

44. See Kay Lawson, *The Comparative Study of Political Parties* (New York: St. Martin's, 1976), pp. 136–161; or her newer *Political Parties and Democracy* (Santa Barbara: Praeger, 2010).

45. See Victor Tonchi and Albertina Shifotoka, *Parties and Political Development in Namibia* (Johannesburg: EISA, 2005); Dafydd Fell, *Party Politics in Taiwan: Party Change and the Democratic Evolution of Taiwan, 1991–2004* (New York: Routledge, 2005); or Nathan J. Brown, *When Victory Is Not an Option: Islamist Movements in Arab Politics* (Ithaca: Cornell University Press, 2012).

46. In a US context this is discussed at some length by Donald P. Green and Alan Gerber, *The Science of Voter Mobilization* (Thousand Oaks, CA: Sage, 2005); and in David Brady and Mathew McCubbins, *Party, Process, and Political Change in Congress* (Stanford: Stanford University Press, 2007).

47. Myron Weiner and Joseph LaPalombara, "The Impact of Parties on Political Development," in LaPalombara and Weiner, *Political Parties and Political Development,* p. 413. This is also addressed by F. Michael Wuthrich, *National Elections in Turkey: People, Politics, and the Party System* (Syracuse, NY: Syracuse University Press, 2015).

48. See Stein Rokkan, "Electoral Mobilization, Party Competition, and National Integration," in LaPalombara and Weiner, *Political Parties and Political Development,* pp. 241–266. See also Anika Gauja, *Political Parties and Elections: Legislating for Representative Democracy* (Burlington, VT: Ashgate, 2010).

49. Luttbeg, *Public Opinion,* pp. 109–186. See also Kay Lawson, "When Linkage Fails," in Kay Lawson and Peter Merkl, eds., *When Parties Fail: Emerging Alternative Organizations* (Princeton: Princeton University Press, 1988), pp. 13–40. See also Roger W. Bowen, *Japan's Dysfunctional Democracy: The Liberal Democratic Party and Structural Corruption* (New York: Taylor and Francis, 2016).

50. An example of this kind of study is the work by Louis Sandy Maisel and Paul Sacks, eds., *The Future of Political Parties* (Beverly Hills: Sage, 1975).

51. See Immanuel Ness, Stephen Bronner, and Frances Fox Piven, *Encyclopedia of American Social Movements* (London: Routledge, 2015); or Jackie Smith and Dawn Wiest, *Social Movements in the World System: The Politics of Crisis and Transformation* (New York: Russell Sage, 2012).

52. Brian K. Grodsky, *Social Movements and the New State: The Fate of Pro-Democracy Organizations When Democracy Is Won* (Stanford: Stanford University Press, 2012). See also Catherine Corrigall-Brown, *Patterns of Protest: Trajectories of Participation in Social Movements* (Stanford: Stanford University Press, 2012).

53. Anthony Giddens, *The Nation-State and Violence* (Cambridge: Polity, 1985). See also Paolo Gerbaudo, *Tweets and the Streets: Social Media and Contemporary Activism* (London: Pluto, 2012).

54. See the article by Ray Takeyh in the *New York Times,* "A Post-American Day Dawns in the Mideast," June 8, 2011, http://www.nytimes.com/2011/06/09/opinion/09iht-edtakeyh 09.html?scp=3&sq=arab%20spring&st=cse. On this topic see Dafna Hochman Rand, *Roots of the Arab Spring: Contested Authority and Political Change in the Middle East* (Philadelphia: University of Pennsylvania Press, 2013); and Joel Beinin and Frederic Vairel, *Social Movements, Mobilization, and Contestation in the Middle East and North Africa* (Palo Alto, CA: Stanford University Press, 2013).

55. Denton Morrison, "Some Notes Toward Theory on Relative Deprivation, Social Movements, and Social Change," in Louis E. Genevie, ed., *Collective Behavior and Social Movements* (Itasca, IL: Peacock, 1978), pp. 202–209. See also Claudio Cattaneo, Miguel Martinez, and Thomas Aguilera, *The Squatters' Movement in Europe: Commons and Autonomy as Alternatives to Capitalism* (London: Pluto, 2014).

56. William Kornhauser, *The Politics of Mass Society* (New York: Free Press, 1959). See also Valentire Moghadam, *Globalization and Social Movements: Islamism, Feminism, and the Global Justice Movement* (Lanham: Rowman and Littlefield, 2013).

57. Neil Smelser, *Theory of Collective Behavior* (New York: Free Press, 1962). See also Martine Raibaud, *Cultures in Movement* (Cambridge: Cambridge Scholars, 2015).

58. Ronald Inglehart, *Culture Shift in Advanced Industrial Society* (Princeton: Princeton University Press, 1990), pp. 363–368. See also Ernesto Verdeja and Jackie Smith, *Globalization, Social Movements, and Peacebuilding* (Syracuse, NY: Syracuse University Press, 2013).

PART 2
Country Cases

8

China

Learning Outcomes

After reading this chapter, you will be able to

- Identify key themes in Chinese history that have shaped Chinese politics today.
- Discuss major crises in the development of the Communist Party of China.
- Discuss the parallels between formal state institutions in China and those in Western nations.
- Understand the structural components of the Communist Party of China and how power flows, both up and down, in the party.
- Explain the relationship between the structures of the Communist Party of China and the Chinese national government.
- Explain the relative importance of political institutions and political leaders in China.
- Clarify the forces that are pressing toward economic and political liberalization in China today.

China, as will quickly become clear, is different from other political systems we have seen and will see in this book. China is a political system with which the contemporary student of politics should be familiar, if for no other reason than over one-fifth of the population of the planet lives within its borders. It is noteworthy that for so many years (and still today) so many people have known so little about China.

A discussion of China in a textbook that puts an emphasis on political institutions and political structures faces some important challenges. This chapter will not be parallel to all of the other country studies chapters in this volume, primarily because such an approach to Chinese politics would not lead to an understanding of Chinese politics. China's political structure, and its political history, can be characterized as being dominated by charismatic and powerful individuals, and it has been those individuals and the patterns of behavior they have demonstrated that have guided and shaped Chinese political history.

China today is a strongly ideologically based system. What does this mean? Don't all nations have political ideologies at their foundations? They do, but those foundations are also influenced by the political structures that rest upon those foundations. In the case of China, while there is a clear foundation of Marxist-Leninist-Maoist ideology, that ideology has been interpreted by the leaders of the day—a relatively small number of extremely powerful individuals—rather than by the structures and institutions of the regime.

Scholars who specialize in the study of China and Chinese politics have long suggested that China must be studied differently from the way other nations can be studied; its unique history has created a political culture and political institutions that are not directly comparable to those of other nations. This will result in a relatively longer discussion of Chinese history and culture in this chapter than provided for national governments in other chapters, and a relatively shorter discussion of Chinese institutions and political structures than provided elsewhere.

The Middle Kingdom and Modern Chinese History

The history of China goes back over thousands of years, and China has been argued to be "imprisoned by her history."[1] China has been referred to as the **Middle Kingdom**, *Zhōngguó* in Mandarin Chinese, which can also be translated as "the center of civilization," and this perspective of Chinese culture has shaped the way China has seen its own role in the world. One historical characteristic of China has been its isolation from the rest of the world, especially from the West, and this has had an effect upon Chinese political development.

Many names have been used to describe China and eras of government and society in China as it evolved through dynasties, a republican period, and into and during the current Communist period. The history of China as a significant region is a very long and complex one, as illustrated in Box 8.1.

China's early dynasties were an important part of the growth of Chinese civilization, and they played an important role in the development of civilized society. Over the almost 3,000 years leading up to the collapse of the Qing Dynasty in 1911, there were twenty-five dynastic changes in China; they created the basis for an expectation that stable

---

Box 8.1   Eras in Chinese History

c. 21st–16th centuries B.C.E.	Xia
1700–1027	Shang
1027–221	Zhou
221–207	Qin
206 B.C.E.–C.E. 220	Han
220–618	Period of instability
618–907	Tang
907–960	Five dynasties
960–1279	Song
1279–1368	Yuan
1368–1644	Ming
1644–1911	Qing
1912–1949	Republic of China (mainland China and Taiwan)
1949–	Republic of China (Taiwan)
1949–	People's Republic of China (mainland China)

Source: Adapted from Robert L. Worden, Andrea Matles Savada, and Ronald E. Dolan, eds., *China* (Washington, DC: Library of Congress, Federal Research Division, 1988), p. 617, https://cdn.loc.gov/master/frd/frdcstdy/ch/chinacountrystud00word/chinacountrystud00word.pdf.

---

society required authoritarian rule.[2] Through the Xia and Shang Dynasties the idea of Chinese nationhood developed. It was during the Zhou Dynasty that China's great schools of intellectual thought—Confucianism, Legalism, Daoism, Mohism, and others—developed.

> Since the beginning of recorded history (at least since the Shang Dynasty), the people of China have developed a strong sense of their origins, both mythological and real, and kept voluminous records concerning both. As a result of these records, augmented by numerous archaeological discoveries in the second half of the twentieth century, information concerning the ancient past, not only of China but also of much of East, Central, and Inner Asia, has survived.[3]

Of the many influences upon Chinese culture, the teachings of **Confucius** (Kung Fu-tzu, c. 551–479 B.C.E.) may be the best known in the West. While the emperors based their power on a "mandate of heaven"— a Chinese variation on what would be known in Europe much later as the "divine right of kings" theory—Confucian theory suggested that even emperors had to follow ethical principles, including moral leadership.

Over the years the identity of a "Chinese" nation and culture developed. Assimilation and conquest helped China expand, and two general characteristics of the various imperial dynasties can be identified here that had implications for future (and present) Chinese attitudes and behavior. One of these generalizations was that an important characteristic of Chinese society and culture has been its agrarian nature, and "the unceasing struggle of the largely agrarian Chinese against the threat posed to their safety and way of life by non-Chinese peoples on the margins of their territory."[4] This is what gave rise to the image of China as the Middle Kingdom, or a central nation, standing up to periodic invasion from outside. The Great Wall of China, we should recall, was a defensive structure, designed to keep outsiders out.

Another general legacy of China's past has been that China has had a history of strong rulers, and not democratic government.[5] Chinese emperors are often characterized in the literature as being authoritarian[6]—sometimes "ruthless"—and this was significant:

> This tradition stretches back at least to the first emperor of the Qin Dynasty . . . who unified China in 221 B.C.E. A ruthless ruler, the emperor ended feudalism in China, starting China on a path remarkably different from that of Europe or Japan. The legacy of this crushing of local autonomy has been a powerful belief that China can be unified only under strong, central rule; the idea of federalism, although now advocated by some intellectuals, is alien to China's political tradition.[7]

As the Qing Dynasty weakened in the late nineteenth century, the global political environment was beginning to intrude on China in a way that had not happened in earlier years. Beginning with the **Opium War** (1839–1842), outside forces pressed Chinese authorities to make concessions that resulted in China suffering from increasing foreign domination and interference in its domestic policy. The Opium War ended with China having to cede Hong Kong to the British, as well as having to agree to grant **extraterritorial rights** to foreigners in China, which meant that foreigners could operate under their own national legal systems while in China and not have to operate under Chinese law.[8] From 1850 to 1865 a major peasant uprising took place, the Taiping Rebellion, which sought to overthrow the Qing Dynasty; the rebellion was ultimately defeated by the government of the day, but estimates suggest that 20 million Chinese may have been killed in the process. These signs of imperial weakness led many to start to question what form of government should come in China's future.

Chinese who had been exposed to Western education and Western politics were interested in taking advantage of the weakening Qing

Dynasty to undertake fundamental changes in China. **Sun Yat-sen** (1866–1925) was typical of these individuals, born middle-class, exposed to Western ideas, including Christianity, and educated overseas. A new class of political leaders was emerging, one that was not interested in a continuation of the old order.

When Chinese imperial rule ended in 1911 and the Republic of China was established led by Sun Yat-sen, there were still many who wanted to restore the throne to an emperor. However, a Western-style parliamentary democratic republic was established in 1912, one that struggled to provide stability for the regime; Japan, especially, was supporting those who were not interested in the success of the new regime. From 1911 through 1928, China struggled with weak republican government that proved to be unable to effectively control the nation. A network of **warlords** developed that dominated politics in that era, using private armies of regionally powerful individuals.

Sun Yat-sen turned to the new Soviet Union for assistance, and the Soviets provided advisers to the **Nationalist Party** (known as the **Guomindang** [GMD]). At the same time, a group of Chinese who were inspired by Marxist theory and the Soviet Revolution formed (in 1921) the Communist Party of China. In addition to supporting Sun and the Nationalists, however, Moscow was also providing advice and support to the new **Chinese Communist Party** (CCP) being established by **Mao Zedong** (1893–1976). There was, apparently, some thought that perhaps the CCP and the Nationalists would unite and create a new government. For a period of time (starting in 1923) they did join together under the auspices of the Communist International—Comintern—in China, led by Mikhail Borodin, who ordered the CCP to merge with the GMD, to fight the warlords and establish stability in China. "The GMD was the larger, older, and better-known party, while the CCP brought in a core of highly dedicated young activists—as well as foreign aid from the Soviet Union."[9]

Sun Yat-sen died in 1925 and was succeeded by **Chiang Kai-shek** (1887–1975), who broke with the Communists and the Soviet Union, and who militarily united China by 1927 by turning against the Communist Party organization. In April 1927 the GMD attacked their CCP allies in Shanghai, with fighting lasting until 1930—referred to as the era of "White Terror." Ultimately several hundred thousand Communists and sympathizers were killed by the Nationalists.[10] From 1927 to 1938 China was governed by the Nationalists from Nanjing (the word *Nanjing* means "southern capital"; *Beijing* means "northern capital").

After the 1927 split between Chiang Kai-shek and the CCP, the CCP started to engage in armed resistance against the Nationalists. Mao

Zedong, its leader, argued that unlike the Soviet Union's Marxist model, which called for the oppressed industrial workers to unite and lead the Communist struggle, what was needed in China was a significant modification: the CCP needed to organize the peasants to perform this task. In 1931 the CCP announced the establishment of the Chinese Soviet Republic, under the leadership of Mao Zedong, based in Jiangxi province in south-central China. The forces of Chiang moved against Mao, and because the Communist forces were no match for the Nationalists, Mao and his **People's Liberation Army** (PLA) fled from Jiangxi and undertook in 1934–1935 the **Long March** to Shaanxi province in the north to a new political base.

Although the Long March was a military disaster for the CCP, during which it lost most (some say as much as 90 percent) of its strength, it was significant for Chinese politics for three important reasons. First, in this period of time Mao strengthened his hold over the CCP, becoming chairman of the party in January 1936, a role he continued to control until his death in 1976. The development of other future leaders of China was significant, too; indeed, all Chinese leaders through Deng Xiaoping were drawn from that leadership pool. Second, during this period Mao reshaped the Communist Party as a militarized body and closely linked it with the Red Army. "Rural guerrilla struggle and the eventual encirclement of the cities, rather than the organization of the urban working class, became the formula for Communist victory."[11] Third, the Long March played a huge role in Chinese political mythology, providing the CCP with legends to support its leadership for years to come.[12]

From the early 1930s through 1946, China was focused on Japan and what was to become World War II, and from 1937 to 1945 the GMD and the CCP were again acting as if they were allies. Japan invaded Manchuria in 1931 and established a puppet government in what they called Manchukuo in 1932. Japan then pressed south into mainland China, and active conflict between China and Japan began in July 1937. Japan quickly conquered Shanghai and then in an effort to quickly crush the Nationalist government undertook what was called the **Nanjing Massacre** in December 1937, killing over 57,000 Chinese prisoners of war in one day; China reports over 340,000 deaths and 20,000 women raped in that campaign.

When, following US defeat of Japan, the war with Japan was ended in 1946, civil war between the Nationalists and the CCP broke out, eventually resulting in the Nationalists being driven off the mainland to the island of Taiwan in 1949, where the **Republic of China** was declared. Mao and the CCP established the new capital of the People's Republic of China (PRC) in Beijing on October 1, 1949.

Once the CCP had driven the Nationalists off of the mainland, their primary goal became the establishment of a Marxist-Leninist government. The government that was established was an authoritarian and highly centralized structure, one that remains highly centralized and tightly controlled today (although less so than under Mao).

The Constitutional System

China ratified its most recent constitution in 1982. We noted in Chapter 2 that constitutions play different roles in their respective systems, including serving as expressions of ideology, expressions of the basic laws of the regime, organizational frameworks for governments, frameworks for how government is organized, and frameworks for how constitutions can be changed. We observed that different constitutions perform these several tasks differently. In the Chinese case, the most important role of the constitution is clearly ideological; as we shall see throughout the rest of this chapter, basic laws and structures of the regime are changed as needed to meet the needs of the Chinese Communist Party. The importance of the Constitution of the People's Republic of China is to serve as a document of educational and symbolic value for the nation.

In earlier chapters in this volume when we have discussed the constitutional system we have focused on the political structures that are established to assist in the operation of state government. In China, although those state institutions and structures exist, they are clearly secondary to the political institutions, structures, and ideology of the Chinese Communist Party. As Figure 8.1 shows later in the chapter, the unofficial and informal linkages from the party structure to the state structure are the key determinants of power.

In describing the Chinese constitutional system, we can note that China is a unitary and socialist state based upon Marxist-Leninist thought as modified by "Mao Zedong thought and Deng Xiaoping theory."[13] The Preamble to the Constitution includes text stating that "the basic task of the nation in the years to come is to concentrate its effort on socialist modernization," and that it will operate "under the leadership of the Communist Party of China and the guidance of Marxism-Leninism and Mao Zedong Thought."

We will see later that Chinese political structures include a 3,000-member National People's Congress (NPC), elected indirectly from regional congresses, which in turn elects the president and the State Council (the Chinese equivalent of a cabinet), which in turn selects the premier. Those structures in themselves are not so very different from structures we have met in other political systems, and they seem like a variation on a parliamentary model government, but their operation and importance is radically different compared to other nations.

The major difference in Chinese constitutional operation is the role of the Chinese Communist Party, which in fact is the key political institution in the regime. Essentially all political decisions are made and undertaken with the guidance and approval of the CCP, and not only the state constitution but also the CCP constitution must be considered in an understanding of how Chinese politics works.

> Both constitutions stress the principle of democratic centralism, under which the representative organs of both party and state are elected by lower bodies and in turn elect their administrative arms at corresponding levels. Within representative and executive bodies, the minority must abide by decisions of the majority; lower bodies obey orders of higher-level organs. In theory, the National Party Congress ranks as the highest organ of party power, but actual power lies in the CCP Central Committee and its even more exclusive Political Bureau. At the apex of all political power are the members of the elite Standing Committee of the Political Bureau.[14]

Unitary Government:
The Chinese Communist Party in Politics

The Chinese Communist Party is the core of Chinese politics today.[15] China's 1982 Constitution states that "the People's Republic of China is a unitary multi-national state," and indicates that its philosophical orientation is "under the leadership of the Communist Party of China and the guidance of Marxism-Leninism and Mao Zedong Thought."[16] Accordingly, rather than discussing the party's structures later in this chapter, it is appropriate to discuss this here in the context of China's approach to unitary government and its vehicle for organizing all governmental and political activity. The Chinese Communist Party is so close to being equivalent with the Chinese state in power and scope that the two institutions are, for all intents and purposes, the same thing. In December 2017 the CCP had nearly 88 million members, with over 4 million branches of the party.[17] This is not a political party in the same sense of the concept as political parties in Britain, France, the United States, or even Russia.

In its philosophy the Chinese Communist Party states that it follows Marxism-Leninism and Mao Zedong thought.[18] In a major speech at the sixteenth meeting of the National Congress of the Chinese Communist Party in June 2006, **Jiang Zemin** (1926–),[19] who was General Secretary of the Communist Party of China from 1989 to 2002, as well as president of the People's Republic of China from 1993 to 2003, added to this traditional characterization by saying that the party must "adhere to the important thought of **Three Represents**." This thought is a continuation and development of Marxism-Leninism, Mao Zedong thought, and Deng Xiaoping theory.[20] Jiang's Three Represents meant that China would follow the basic writings of Marx as interpreted by Lenin, but also modify those principles in their application to China by examining the writings and theories of both Mao Zedong and Deng Xiaoping. In recent years the current president of China, **Xi Jinping** (1953–), has come to be seen as developing power even greater than that of Deng in his day. We shall return to a discussion of this later in this chapter.

Maoist thought has several key components. James Hsiung has suggested that in traditional Chinese political culture, morality and authority are inseparable, and thus Marxist-Leninist thought as interpreted by Mao was a key moral foundation of the Communist Party in China.[21] Mao's view of society ascribed a key role to the peasants. It was rigidly egalitarian, and many actions of the government later (such as the Great Leap Forward, which will be further discussed shortly) turned out to be disastrous precisely because Mao insisted in treating all members of society equally, too equally in fact. Mao believed that even when Communists were in power they needed to be "ever vigilant against the dangers of bourgeois (capitalist) influences."[22] The class struggle was a continuing struggle.

China's unitary government is highly centralized, and most decisions that are made develop under the auspices of appropriate levels of leadership of the CCP. The CCP is highly hierarchical and is led by the **Supreme Leader**, who is the center of the party. The Supreme Leader has traditionally held the position of **General Secretary of the Party**, but in recent years it has become possible that someone else could hold this position; the Supreme Leader continues to be a member of the **Standing Committee of the Politburo**, a subgroup of the **Politburo** (Political Bureau) that is at the center of power. The most important political group within the CCP is the Politburo, most of whose members also hold other important offices in the formal state governmental structures. The actual powers of the Politburo and the functions of the Politburo as a policymaking group have varied over time, depending upon the individuals involved. The members of today's Politburo Standing Committee are indicated in Box 8.2.

There has traditionally been a great deal of overlap between formal party position and formal state position, although this is not legally required. Mao Zedong was president and also chairman of the CCP. Deng Xiaoping was Supreme Leader but never held either the General Secretary of the Party position or the presidency. Today, Xi Jinping is president of the People's Republic of China and also General Secretary

---

Box 8.2   Members of the Politburo Standing Committee of the Communist Party of China

January 2018

Xi Jinping, President, PRC; General Secretary of the CCP, Chairman of the Central Military Commission, Chairman of the National Security Committee, Full Member of the Central Committee of the CCP, Commander-in-Chief of the People's Liberation Army

Li Keqiang, Premier of the State Council, Vice Chairman of the National Security Committee, Vice Chairman of the Central Military and Civilian Integration Development Committee, Chairman of the National Defense Mobilization Committee, Director of the State Energy Committee

Li Zhanshu, Director of the General Office of the CCP Central Committee, Secretary of the Central Work Committee for Organs of the CCP Central Committee, Director of the Office of the National Security Committee, Secretariat Member of the Central Committee of the CCP

Wang Yang, Vice Premier of the State Council, Member of the Politburo, Full Member of the Central Committee of the CCP

Wang Huning, Executive Secretary of the Secretariat of the CCP Central Committee, Director of the Central Policy Research Center of the CCP Central Committee, Secretary-General and Director of the General Office of the Central Leading Group for Comprehensively Deepening Reforms

Zhao Leji, Secretary of the Central Commission for Discipline Inspection, Director of the Central Organization Department of the CCP Central Committee, Deputy Head of the Central Leading Group for Party Building Work, Deputy Head of the Central Leading Group for Inspection Work

Han Zheng, Party Secretary of Shanghai, Member of the Politburo, Full Member of the Central Committee of the CCP

Source: Brookings Institution, "China's 19th Party Congress," https://www.brookings.edu/interactives/chinas-new-politburo-standing-committee.

---

of the Party, and also chairman of the Central Military Commission and chairman of the National Security Committee, and his power in the regime is growing as time goes by.

Each member of the Politburo Standing Committee is responsible for a specific function—if the Politburo is the Communist Party equivalent of a cabinet, then each member would have equivalent responsibilities within the party organization of a cabinet minister in the government—such as the military, agriculture, industry, legal affairs, international relations, and so on. The nine members of the

Politburo Standing Committee are elected by members of the Politburo, which is composed of about twenty individuals and which is selected by the **Central Committee** of the CCP. The Central Committee is a body of about 200 individuals—most recently documented at 205 members and 171 alternate members[23]—elected by the **Party Congress**, which is supposed to meet every five years but meets irregularly. The Party Congress is designed to represent the lower levels of party organization, and it consists of 4,000 to 5,000 members who come together for a few days at a time, every five years or so, to ratify actions of the Central Committee (which in fact ratifies actions of the Politburo) and to elect members of the Central Committee.

Thus we can see that while in formal organization the Chinese Communist Party is organized from the lower level to the higher level—village committees electing county committees, county committees electing provincial committees, provincial committees participating in the National Party Congress, the National Party Congress selecting the Central Committee, the Central Committee selecting the Politburo of the Central Committee, and the Politburo selecting its own Standing Committee—in fact real power and decisionmaking flow in the opposite direction: individuals with power are on the Politburo; they decide who will be on the Central Committee in important positions (along with many others who are not politically significant); and so on.

This reflects a Chinese version of a Marxist-Leninist-Stalinist practice of **democratic centralism**. Democratic centralism means that key decisions are made at the center and then moved out to the more symbolically democratic bodies and structures to be ratified. Article 3 of the 1982 Constitution says that "the state organs of the People's Republic of China apply the principle of democratic centralism."[24] Although it is theoretically possible in this kind of setting for the larger, lower body to say no to plans that come down from above, it almost never happens. Democratic centralism is far more central than democratic in nature.

The CCP meets at National Congresses, and it is at those meetings that the national leadership sets the stage for the next several years. Since its founding in 1921 there have been nineteen meetings of the **National Party Congress**, as shown in Table 8.1. In recent years the party has met fairly regularly, approximately every five years, usually immediately before the meeting of the National People's Congress (the national legislature). Many members of the National Party Congress are also elected representatives to the National People's Congress.

The nineteenth National Congress of the Communist Party of China was held in October 2017. At that time party representatives from all over the nation assembled in Beijing for several days of party business.

**Table 8.1   Meetings of the National Congress of the Chinese
Communist Party**

Congress	Date	Location
1	July 1921	Shanghai
2	July 1922	Shanghai
3	June 1923	Guangzhou
4	January 1925	Shanghai
5	April 1927	Shanghai
6	June 1928	Moscow
7	April 1945	Yanan
8	September 1956	Beijing
9	April 1969	Beijing
10	August 1973	Beijing
11	August 1977	Beijing
12	September 1982	Beijing
13	October 1987	Beijing
14	October 1992	Beijing
15	September 1997	Beijing
16	November 2002	Beijing
17	October 2007	Beijing
18	November 2012	Beijing
19	October 2017	Beijing

Source: "The Communist Party of China," http://www.chinatoday.com/org/cpc.

President Xi Jinping gave the major address to the Congress that the president/general secretary normally gives at that time.[25]

Although China is a unitary political system, it is divided into many administrative districts because of the scale of government that is necessary for a country of 1.4 billion people. Article 30 of the 1982 Constitution says,

> The administrative division of the People's Republic of China is as follows: (1) The country is divided into provinces, autonomous regions and municipalities directly under the Central Government; (2) Provinces and autonomous regions are divided into autonomous prefectures, counties, autonomous counties and cities; (3) Counties and autonomous counties are divided into townships, nationality townships and towns. Municipalities directly under the Central Government and other large cities are divided into districts and counties. Autonomous prefectures are divided into counties, autonomous counties, and cities. All autonomous regions, autonomous prefectures and autonomous counties are national autonomous areas.

China has twenty-two provinces (*sheng*), five autonomous regions (*zizhiqu*), and four municipalities (*shi*). China also has two special administrative regions (SARs): Hong Kong, which reverted from British control in 1997, and Macau, which reverted from Portuguese control in 1999. Beijing also claims Taiwan as a province.

The governors of China's provinces and autonomous regions and the mayors of its centrally controlled municipalities are appointed by the central government in Beijing, although these positions, too, require approval from the National People's Congress. The political leadership of both Hong Kong and Macau have more local autonomy than the "normal" Chinese regions, since they have separate governments, legal systems, and basic constitutional laws, but they come under Beijing's control in matters of foreign affairs and national security, and their chief executives are handpicked by the central government.[26]

Political Culture and Political Participation

Chinese political behavior and political thought is often referred to as Mao Zedong thought, although as we have noted this has been modified to include Deng Xiaoping theory as well. At the meeting of the nineteenth National Party Congress in 2017 observers reported that President Xi Jinping's status had risen to almost the level of Deng Xiaoping, and that his positions on Chinese policy would soon achieve the status of those of China's most influential leaders. Mao's approach to Marxism-Leninism was to be pragmatic, and he actively practiced what analysts have referred to as the **Sinification of Marxism** over the years, rooting the abstract formulations of Marxism-Leninism in the specific reality of China.[27] Deng carried this even further. This included such strategies as mass mobilization—using groups of people to carry the message of the revolution to the population—and the idea of a united front—the idea of trying to bring the majority of people together in an initiative and thereby isolate those who were in opposition.

One of the manifestations of Mao's commitment to a Chinese version of Marxism was the collectivization of industry and agriculture in 1955–1956, when the CCP decided to eliminate private ownership of land. Across China nearly 110 million farms were converted to about 300,000 "cooperatives" run by the party; the party similarly took over factories and private businesses in cities, as well. This was followed in 1957 by the **Hundred Flowers Movement**, based upon a saying of Confucius—"Let a hundred flowers bloom, let a hundred schools of thought contend"—suggesting that the free and open exchange of ideas would be supported by Mao.[28]

Unfortunately for those who decided to freely exchange ideas that were critical of the government, Mao was apparently shocked by the amount of criticism that the government received under the Hundred

Flowers Movement, criticism about collectivization, criticism about taking away all private property and industry, and criticism about the decline of democratic rights and practices. Mao labeled the critics "rightists"—suggesting that they were anti-revolutionaries—and launched an anti-rightist campaign to clamp down on complaints against the government.[29]

During the years that Mao led China, Chinese popular culture suffered from several major dislocations, including three that should be mentioned here: the Great Leap Forward, the Red Versus Expert Debate, and the Cultural Revolution. The **Great Leap Forward** was the name given to a five-year plan announced in 1958 that was Mao's attempt to increase Chinese self-sufficiency and radically grow the Chinese economy by transforming the economy from an individualized agrarian one to an effective collective agricultural and industrial one.[30] The Great Leap Forward intended to rapidly grow agriculture and industry by collective efforts, and by dividing China into **communes** of about 5,000 families who would work together for greater efficiency than had been the case previously. Communes were in turn subdivided into working teams of twelve families, with twelve teams in a brigade. By the end of 1958, 700 million people had been placed into over 26,000 communes.[31] Private property was banned.

The Great Leap Forward was not a success, however. While the idea of decentralization had some merit, the overall plan had taken many workers away from their fields, so food shortages developed. Since workers were not trained for industrial tasks and supplies were irregular, industrial production fell drastically. Almost more important was the dimension of terror and authoritarianism that developed, with mass propaganda sessions commonplace, and killings not uncommon if groups of individuals didn't meet their assigned goals. Reports described individuals tortured or killed if they failed to meet their grain quotas.[32] Having so many decentralized groups meant that there was no coordination in providing resources, and material shortages were frequent. The first phase of collectivization that took place resulted in widespread famine. The official toll of deaths resulting from the Great Leap Forward is 14 million, but in 1987 some scholars had estimated the number of victims to be between 20 and 43 million.[33] One of the most often cited examples of failed policy in this era was the policy that required the development of backyard furnaces to produce steel:

> The campaign to develop backyard furnaces came to symbolize the wastefulness of the [Great Leap Forward]. Determined to surpass England and catch up with the United States in steel production, Chinese leaders called for the creation of thousands of small-scale iron

smelters. By late 1958, there were several hundred thousand small blast furnaces scattered throughout the country. Into these furnaces went every bit of scrap steel that peasants could locate—sometimes including their own cooking implements.

The result was wasteful in the extreme. The quality of the iron produced was so poor that most of it had to be discarded. In many instances, perfectly good iron and steel products had been dumped into the blast furnaces only to produce useless lumps of iron. Moreover, forests were destroyed in this ill-fated effort to industrialize, causing an ecological disaster from which China has yet to recover.[34]

The **Red Versus Expert Debate** was one of the most divisive issues in China in the early 1960s. The more pragmatic party leaders were labeled as the "Experts," and the more radical supporters of Mao and the People's Liberation Army were labeled as the "Red" faction, and they disagreed over the appropriate strategy for China's ongoing economic development after the Great Leap Forward failed. The moderates—the Experts—had managed to roll back some of the more extreme policies of the Great Leap, so that by 1962 peasants were again permitted their own private plots and farm animals. Premier Liu Shaoqi and Vice Premier Deng Xiaoping felt that Communist purity was less important than what worked: Deng's famous quote of the day was "it doesn't matter whether a cat is black or white as long as it catches mice."[35]

Although the Experts brought calm and some economic stability back to China, Mao and his more ideological supporters were troubled by the pragmatic approach. They felt that allowing private farming would inevitably lead to the kind of conflicts that were developing at the time in Eastern Europe (in East Germany, Poland, and Hungary, where criticism of communism was increasing and demonstrations were taking place). The Reds felt that the Experts were not sufficiently committed to the CCP. At the end of the day the Red faction proved victorious. Liu and Deng were removed from their posts in the party and government and placed under house arrest.

The **Cultural Revolution** took place between 1966 and 1976 and had as a goal further advancing socialism by removing aspects of capitalism from Chinese society, as well as more effectively imposing Maoist orthodoxy within the Chinese Communist Party.[36] In August 1966, Mao called for a Great Proletariat Cultural Revolution, more commonly known as the Cultural Revolution, to seek out and remove bourgeois (Western) influence from Chinese culture, and to push capitalist tendencies out of Chinese society. To do this he organized youth groups, the **Red Guard**, to be formed around the country. Their job was to purge society of individuals who were deemed to be deviating from the "true" socialist path; this frequently focused on teachers, artists, intellectuals, and individuals who were too oriented to non-Chinese values, but it included literally tens of thousands of others, too.[37] "Under the banner of opposing the 'four olds' (old customs, old habits, old culture, and old thinking), Red Guards ransacked people's homes, confiscating or destroying anything deemed 'feudal' in nature (including old books, paintings, and ceramics), persecuting individuals deemed 'bourgeois' or 'rightist,' and denouncing party leaders who were accused of opposing Chairman Mao."[38]

One observer noted that "just as the Great Leap Forward was an economic disaster, the Cultural Revolution was a political disaster."[39] A consequence of the Cultural Revolution was great damage, both societal and individual. Over 70 percent of the CCP Central Committee was removed from their positions, and Red Guard units were notorious for arresting, beating, and killing Chinese who had done little to deserve punishment.[40] Literally millions of people were persecuted, were imprisoned, and lost their homes and their property and their jobs. There is a massive literature by survivors who were forcibly displaced.

The Cultural Revolution ended officially in 1969, although its effects lasted for years after that, through the arrest of the Gang of Four (one of whom was Mao's wife), who were charged with treasonous crimes and for criminal excess during the Cultural Revolution. One result of the disaster of the Great Leap Forward was a reexamination of the role that Mao played in China, and a review of the "cult of personality" that surrounded him. Mao stepped down as state chairman of the People's Republic of China in 1959, although he did remain as chairman of the CCP.

One of the conclusions that we can reasonably draw from even a cursory examination of Chinese political history is that China has not developed institutions that can *gradually* respond to a need for change. Countries that are able to address problems gradually, while the problems are developing and before a major crisis comes about, are able to respond to issues more successfully than nations that have to lurch from crisis to crisis, undertaking major systemic modification at each lurch. We can see that both the Great Leap Forward and the Cultural Revolution were attempts to resolve a large number of issues in one package. The Chinese Communist Party looked for broad-ranging policies (e.g., the Great Leap Forward) that could respond to complex social problems (economic development, equitable distribution of goods, social equality) in simple ways (i.e., collectivization). What was clear from both the Great Leap Forward and the Cultural Revolution was that social challenges are too complex to be solved by this kind of all-encompassing

policy, and what is most likely to happen is that disastrous policy will
be applied in a disastrous way with disastrous results.

Politics and Political Structures

China's political tradition of having strong executive leadership over
the years has resulted in the executive branch of the formal political
system being much more important than the legislative branch of the
formal political system, although it must be said that the National People's Congress (not to be confused with the National Congress of the
Communist Party of China), the legislature, which is the highest organ
of state power according to the Chinese constitution, has become more
active and visible in recent years.

In theory, formal governmental administrative structures are completely separate from structures of the Chinese Communist Party. In
reality, however, there is a huge overlap between party membership and
formal state political leadership positions, and as one moves higher up
the state political hierarchy the overlap becomes stronger and stronger,
until it is complete at the upper levels of political participation. Thus, an
official organizational chart of the leadership of the People's Republic
of China would be unhelpful without a description of the unofficial
leadership, too. Individuals with the most political power may hold formal positions of power, but that need not always be the case. As one
observer has noted, "sometimes leaders have remained in seemingly
insignificant positions yet exercised enormous power. This is easier in
an authoritarian system than in a democratic one, for in the former, the
public has virtually no way of protesting the accretion of power in a
particular individual or institution."

> A good example of this is the case of Hua Guofend: from 1977 to
> 1980, Hua simultaneously held the three most powerful institutional
> positions in China (CCP Chairman, Premier of the State, and CCP's
> Chairman of the Military Affairs Commission), whereas Deng Xiaoping
> held the position of a mere Vice-Premier. Yet, by 1979, Deng exercised
> far greater power than Hua, and was even able to shift the locus of
> power away from the CCP Chairman (a position Deng was powerful
> enough to abolish) to the CCP's General Secretary, who at that point
> was a long-time ally of Deng's.[41]

Figure 8.1 shows the official state government leadership structure
on the left and the party leadership structure on the right. The president
of the People's Republic of China today is Xi Jinping, who is the seventh president of the PRC. He assumed office as General Secretary of
the Party in November of 2012 and was first elected president of the

Figure 8.1 How China Is Ruled

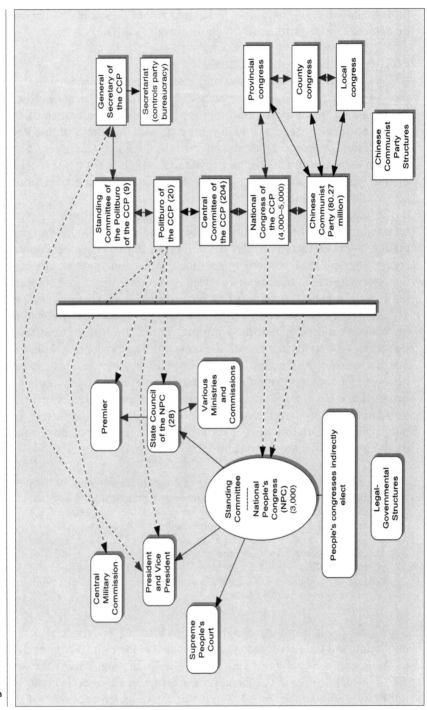

PRC in March 2013. He was reelected in 2017 for a second (and at the time final) term as president. This limitation to two terms in office has now been lifted, as we will further describe shortly, so he is eligible for further terms in office. Although the position of president is symbolically important, Xi's more important base of power is that he also serves as General Secretary of the Party and chairman of the party's Central Military Commission, the top party/military position.

Executive Branch

The executive branch of government is led by the **State Council**, the equivalent of the cabinet in most Western democratic governments. The State Council is chaired by the **premier**, who is formally reviewed by the National People's Council after being appointed to office by the president. The State Council also typically has four or five vice premiers, as well as several state councilors, ministers in charge of ministries, the auditor-general, and the Secretary General of the Party. Other members of the State Council are nominated by the premier and reviewed by the NPC or its Standing Committee, and appointed and removed by the president. Today's State Council has twenty-eight members, including the premier. Members of the State Council have a term of office concurrent with the term of the NPC. State Council members are limited to no more than two consecutive terms on the State Council.[42]

As is the case with members of cabinet in Western nations, the members of the State Council each oversee the work of a ministry. A list of ministries and commissions that make up the State Council can be found in Box 8.3 and looks very much like lists of ministries in other nations we are studying.

The position of president of the People's Republic of China is described in the Constitution as having the same term as that of the NPC. The president is elected by the NPC. His duties as described in Articles 80 and 81 are unremarkable: "in pursuance of decisions of the National People's Congress and its Standing Committee" he

- promulgates statutes;
- appoints and removes the Premier, Vice-Premiers, State Councilors, Ministers in charge of Ministries or Commissions, and the Auditor-General and the Secretary-General of the State Council;
- confers state medals and titles of honour;
- issues orders of special pardons;
- proclaims martial law;
- proclaims a state of war;
- issues mobilization orders;

**Box 8.3   Ministries and Commissions
Represented on the State Council**

Ministry of Agriculture
Ministry of Civil Affairs
Ministry of Commerce
Ministry of Culture
Ministry of Education
Ministry of Environmental Protection
Ministry of Finance
Ministry of Foreign Affairs
Ministry of Health
Ministry of Housing and Urban-Rural Development
Ministry of Human Resources and Social Security
Ministry of Industry and Information Technology
Ministry of Justice
Ministry of Land and Resources
Ministry of National Defense
Ministry of Public Security
Ministry of Railways
Ministry of Science and Technology
Ministry of State Security
Ministry of Supervision
Ministry of Transport
Ministry of Water Resources
National Audit Office
National Development and Reform Commission
National Population and Family Planning Commission
People's Bank of China
State Ethnic Affairs Commission

Source: Chinese Government Web Portal, "State Council Organization Chart,"
http://english.gov.cn/state_council/2014/09/03/content_281474985533579.htm.

- receives foreign diplomatic representatives on behalf of the People's Republic of China;
- appoints and recalls plenipotentiary representatives abroad; and
- ratifies and abrogates treaties and important agreements concluded with foreign states.

Until 2018 in modern Chinese constitutional history the president was constitutionally prohibited from serving more than two consecutive terms. This was a political structure that was added to the Chinese Constitution in 1982 as a response to the "culture of personality" that had placed so much power and influence in the hands of Mao Zedong. Chinese leaders at the time thought that the best way to prevent that concentration of power in the future would be to prohibit whoever was serving as president from serving more than two terms in office: it would force a change in leadership every ten years and would guarantee that any leader would know when they assumed power that this power would be only temporary. "The politicians and legal experts who drafted China's 1982 Constitution saw lifelong tenure as a recipe for tyranny, especially in a one-party state."[43]

In March 2018 the National People's Congress voted to amend the Chinese Constitution so that the president could hold power longer than two five-year terms.

> If the term limit remained, Mr. Xi would have to step down as president at the end of his next five-year term, in 2023. Any successor could potentially become a rival.
>
> Mr. Xi seems determined to remain "three-in-one" leader because he sees himself on a historic mission to make China into a great power. Achieving that will take more than a decade, Xi has said.
>
> Last year, Mr. Xi showed his intent to stay in power by declining to promote a potential successor into the new Politburo Standing Committee, the party's most powerful body. Mr. Xi and Mr. Hu both served political apprenticeships in the Standing Committee before taking over.[44]

Legislative Branch

There is no doubt that legally, constitutionally, the **National People's Congress** is the legislative branch of the national government of the People's Republic of China. The question is, What does it do? What is the relationship between the NPC and the parallel, although unofficial, body of the National Congress of the Chinese Communist Party? The answer is that since its creation in 1954 the NPC has played a variety of roles, none central, some less important than others. It has never really been a significant body, but it has seen its role change from being less to more frequently cited as a symbolic player in Chinese politics. Through the Mao-driven campaigns of the Great Leap Forward (1958–1960) and the Cultural Revolution (1966–1976), power was very centralized in Mao's hands, and the NPC was essentially irrelevant. Since Mao's death in 1976, however, the NPC has become more visible, it has been convened regularly, and its involvement in lawmaking, oversight, and constituency representation has increased.[45]

Under China's 1982 Constitution, the National People's Congress is the "highest organ of state power."[46] The primary function of the National People's Congress is ratification and legitimation of party decisions. The NPC exercises "the legislative power of the state," but actually what it does is to meet on an annual basis for two or three weeks and approve actions that either have already been taken in its name or approve proposals coming from the CCP for actions that will be taken in its name.

When the NPC is not in session (which is typically fifty weeks out of each year), every two months or so the **Standing Committee of the National People's Congress** will meet to "supervise" the government and to approve proposals that cannot wait until the next regularly scheduled meeting of the NPC. The NPC Standing Committee consists of a chairman, fifteen vice chairmen, a secretary-general, and 153 members, so in fact the Standing Committee looks like a small national legislative body, which is what it is. Standing Committee members are often senior CCP and former state leaders and officials. The Standing Committee is elected for the same term as the National People's Congress (Article 66), and it acts in the name of the NPC when the latter is not in session.

The members of the NPC are elected for terms of five years, according to Article 60 of the Constitution. It is constitutionally charged to meet in session once a year and has statutory responsibility (Article 62)

(1) To amend the Constitution;

(2) To supervise the enforcement of the Constitution;

(3) To enact and amend basic statutes concerning criminal offences, civil affairs, the state organs and other matters;

(4) To elect the President and the Vice-President of the People's Republic of China; [previously translated as Chairman and Vice-Chairman of the People's Republic of China—translator's note]

(5) To decide on the choice of the Premier of the State Council upon nomination by the President of the People's Republic of China, and to decide on the choice of the Vice-Premiers, State Councilors, Ministers in charge of Ministries or Commissions and the Auditor-General and the Secretary-General of the State Council upon nomination by the Premier;

(6) To elect the Chairman of the Central Military Commission and, upon his nomination, to decide on the choice of the other members of the Central Military Commission;

(7) To elect the President of the Supreme People's Court;

(8) To elect the Procurator-General of the Supreme People's Procuratorate;

(9) To examine and approve the plan for national economic and social development and the reports on its implementation;

(10) To examine and approve the state budget and the report on its implementation;

(11) To alter or annul inappropriate decisions of the Standing Committee of the National People's Congress;

(12) To approve the establishment of provinces, autonomous regions, and municipalities directly under the Central Government;

(13) To decide on the establishment of special administrative regions and the systems to be instituted there;
(14) To decide on questions of war and peace; and
(15) To exercise such other functions and powers as the highest organ of state power should exercise.

Elections of members to the NPC are indirect. Deputies are elected by people's congresses in twenty-three provinces, five autonomous regions, and four municipalities directly under the central government. Representatives are also chosen from special administrative regions (Hong Kong and Macau) and by the armed forces. The minimum number of deputies from provinces or regions is fifteen, but the size of groups varies with the population of the unit being represented. Elections take place in a multicandidate format (i.e., there are always more candidates than seats to be filled); top vote-getters in each race are elected.

> The allocation of the number of Deputies to the NPC—which may not exceed 3,000—is decided by its Standing Committee in accordance with the principle that the number of citizens represented by each rural Deputy is four times that represented by each urban Deputy (880,000 people to 220,000). The number of Deputies elected by minority nationalities—which, according to the Constitution, are all entitled to appropriate representation—is also allocated by the Standing Committee, in light of the population and distribution of each nationality; they are chosen by the respective people's congresses and their number totals approximately 12% of that of the NPC. Nationalities with exceptionally small populations have at least one Deputy.[47]

Legal System

China has a very conventional system of courts, with the highest level of court being the Supreme People's Court in Beijing.[48] Other courts include the Higher People's Courts in provinces, autonomous regions, and special municipalities, as well as Intermediate People's Courts at the prefecture level and in parts of provinces, autonomous regions, and special municipalities. A series of Basic People's Courts also exist in counties, towns, and municipal districts.

The Supreme People's Court supervises the administration of justice by local courts and special courts, while courts at higher levels oversee the administration of courts at lower levels. At each level, the courts are "responsible to the organs of state power which created them." Judges are limited to two consecutive terms running concurrently with the National People's Congress or local people's congresses.

The court system is paralleled by a hierarchy of prosecuting organs called people's procuratorates; at the apex stands the Supreme People's

Procuratorate. The procurators serve as prosecutors, or district attorneys, and are limited to two consecutive terms running concurrently with the NPC or local people's congresses.

One of the legal characteristics that the People's Republic of China has taken directly from the Marxist-Leninist model of the old Soviet Union is that it sees the value of a close interaction of the legal system with its ideological and political cultural system. China is a system in which law is very important, as a way for the state to regulate the behavior of citizens, but lawyers and litigation are not at all as common or visible as in the West, since "the Chinese have historically had a distaste for lawyers and for resorting to law to settle disputes."[49]

A key characteristic of the Marxist-Leninist model was that law was seen to be a tool of the state. Marx's view was that in capitalist societies, despite what the governments said, the legal system was not equitable in terms of the resources available to the different actors involved, with the workers having far fewer resources than the property-owning class, and that it was, therefore, appropriate in a Marxist state for the state to use the legal system to further the goals of the state. In China, like in the Soviet Union, law is used as a tool of the state to further the goals of the state. "In short, while in the American legal system the emphasis is on process, in China it is on serving the state and society. Murderers must be executed, regardless of how evidence was acquired, because the protection of societal interests takes precedence over the rights of any single individuals."[50]

This means, unfortunately, that protection of individual rights and liberties is not a high priority for either the legal system or the government more broadly conceived. As we noted in Chapter 2 when discussing written and unwritten constitutions and the role of law, in a system in which the law serves as a tool of the state, and where the dominant political party can be identified with the state, the goals of the party can start to become identified as the law, and individuals who come in conflict with these goals can find themselves subject to what may seem to be arbitrary enforcement of the law. Many felt that the treatment of the participants in the **Tiananmen Square massacre** in 1989 (see Box 8.4) was a gross miscarriage of justice, and that the violent response of the government to the demonstrations by the participants was the real crime at the time, and this has led to much discussion about the state of civil society in China today.[51]

Political Reform and Liberalization

One of the patterns of Chinese politics that we identified at the outset of this chapter is the pattern of strong—sometimes overly strong—

**Box 8.4   The Tiananmen Square
Massacre, 1989**

During the 1980s the Chinese government was interested in economic expansion and growth, but it was less concerned about political reforms. By the mid-1980s, many in China, especially students and intellectual leaders, were frustrated at government policy and the pace of political in Shanghai began a series of public demonstrations about student living conditions, and these demonstrations grew to include other criticism of the government and government policy in other areas.

The immediate cause of the Tiananmen Square massacre was a demonstration that was sparked by the death on April 15, 1989, of the former General Secretary of the Party, who had been associated with support of political liberalization but who had been forced from his position because he was too supportive of reform—Hu Yaobang. Huge popular demonstrations developed to protest past repressive government decisions and to call for further political reform. Although the demonstrations were focused on inflation and government corruption, the government at the time saw the real focus of the demonstrations being the overthrow of the government. As the demonstrations increased, the focus of the demonstrations shifted and included fundamental changes in China's political system, labor unions, and even the removal of Li Peng (the premier) and Deng Xiaoping (the vice premier).

By the time of Hu's funeral, it was estimated that 100,000 people were in Tiananmen Square. The demonstrations lasted seven weeks after Hu's death. Premier Li Peng declared martial law on May 20 but took no other action. Finally, late on June 3, 1989, the government clamped down on the demonstrators with a sudden and surprisingly extreme response to the peaceful mass protest. Tanks and People's Liberation Army troops were summoned to Tiananmen Square in central Beijing, and hundreds (700 was the estimate most commonly used) of peaceful demonstrators were shot dead by seeming random firing from the troops. An iconic photograph of a lone student standing in the square in front of a tank came to symbolize the tragedy, despair, and rage associated with the event.

Sources: James Miles, *The Legacy of Tiananmen: China in Disarray* (Ann Arbor: University of Michigan Press, 1997), p. 28; Merle Goldman, "The 1989 Demonstrations in Tiananmen Square and Beyond: Echoes of Gandhi," in Adam Roberts and Timothy Garton Ash, eds., *Civil Resistance and Power Politics: The Experience of Non-Violent Action from Gandhi to the Present* (New York: Oxford University Press, 2009), pp. 247–259; Zhao Dingxin, *The Power of Tiananmen: State-Society Relations and the 1989 Beijing Student Movement* (Chicago: University of Chicago Press, 2001), p. 82. See also British Broadcasting Corporation, "1989: Massacre in Tiananmen Square," http://news.bbc.co.uk/onthisday/hi/dates/stories/june/4/newsid_2496000/2496277.stm.

leadership that has resulted in modern times in authoritarian leadership. We have seen the consequences of the Great Leap Forward, and the Cultural Revolution, two illustrations of Maoist policy that were disastrous for the nation.

The modern Chinese leader most closely associated with reform was **Deng Xiaoping** (1904–1997). In 1977, Deng Xiaoping (who had been purged during the Cultural Revolution) was restored to his position as vice premier and led China in discussion of modernization. From 1977 through 1985 the most radical groups in the CCP were either moved out of power or purged completely from CCP positions, and by 1981 public pronouncements were being made that were critical of past actions: "A 1981 pronouncement by the Communist Party Central Committee called the Cultural Revolution 'the most severe setback [to] . . . the Party, the state and the people since the founding of the People's Republic.' It assigned Mao chief responsibility for the disaster and accused the once-revered leader of arrogance."[52]

During the 1980s, many problems were identified by Chinese leaders as well as issues that had been inherited from the Mao era that needed to be reformed.[53] These included the problem of the overconcentration of political power, the lack of development of formal institutions, the state of health of the Chinese Communist Party, a weak bureaucracy, and the need for a reconciliation of the CCP and the public.

We have noted earlier several instances of too much political power resting in the hands of Mao. While this may have been consistent with the way Chinese leaders have exercised political power for literally thousands of years, by the 1980s it was seen to be increasingly problematic for modern times. The Chinese attempted to resolve this by doing away with the title of "party chairman," in the hope that it might provide some modest diminution of power held by the party leader, although it is not clear that "general secretary" is a significantly weaker title, and the more basic problem of the Chinese Communist Party exercising control on the organs of state government was not touched at all.

The Chinese tradition of having power exercised by strong individuals rather than flowing through stable and regulated political institutions has also been a concern in modern times. Mao clearly preferred to rule by virtue of his personal charisma, so formal state titles and lines of organizational reporting were not significant in his era. In the time since Mao there have been some efforts made to restore standing to formal political bodies, with greater consultation of the National People's Congress and the Politburo, for example. This, too, only resulted in very marginal change, since the political leaders of the day, from Deng through Hu, have consistently held on to their own personal political power. This has continued to change in post-Deng years, though, and today China has more discussion that looks like Western policy debate than ever before.[54]

By the time that Deng took control of the Chinese Communist Party, party members "on the whole were too old, too uneducated, and too radical."[55] The party saw this as a major challenge and set upon a new path of recruitment of members to the party. By 2005 almost one-quarter of members were under the age of thirty-five (compared to less than 5 percent being under twenty-five when Deng assumed power), and over 56 percent had a high school or higher level of education (compared with under 18 percent in 1984).

During the early Deng years a variety of reforms started to appear, including a reduction of CCP ideological positions and a corresponding increase in more pragmatic policy. The state began to liberalize its views about privacy, individual rights, communication, education, and a variety of different areas that affected individuals.[56] This reform began to put great stress on the system—because China was still not a democracy, by any means—and in 1989 violence erupted as thousands of Chinese citizens started to demonstrate in Tiananmen Square in Beijing, demanding a more open political system. After several weeks of confrontation the government eventually sent in the army and tanks; over 700 individuals were killed in the event, and the reform movement in China was stopped and reversed, with reform advocates losing their positions of political leadership.

The significance of the liberalization of the Deng years, however, is that it opened the door to the contemporary world in which the Chinese population wants to move even further forward.[57] Although the government of the day clamped down on the Tiananmen Square demonstrators, it was relatively shortly thereafter that liberalization started again. What Bruce Gilley has called a "democratic breakthrough" has been imagined by the public, and while the political leadership of the CCP has the power to regulate individuals' behavior at the present time, it does not have the power to regulate what the individuals think. While it can regulate some of their communication, it cannot regulate all of their communication. As quickly as the government blocks websites and tries to censor email, individuals develop techniques for getting around the government barriers. Gilley imagines what China will look like without the Chinese Communist Party in control, noting,

> The CCP will have ruled China for 60 years in 2009. The previous records for a party's unbroken tenure in office were just over 70 years by both the Russian Communist Party and Mexico's Institutional Rev-

olutionary Party. Whatever the exact date of democratic transition, the CCP will go down in history as one of the world's longest lived ruling parties. It will be a reign that ends for the same reason that other dynasties in China ended: the court lost touch with the people, was starved of resources, and finally rotted from the inside.[58]

The Chinese bureaucracy needed help, too, since it suffered from many of the same problems as did the CCP. In the Deng years the government actively recruited for the state bureaucracy, seeking young and more highly educated officials for that structure.

Finally, the party has tried to help restore relations between itself and the public through less regulation of individuals. Certainly in recent years the party has opened the doors to capitalism, to private property, and to many different manifestations of Western behavior—including music, art, and so on. The Chinese government has established special economic zones to encourage foreign investment and employment, and it has vigorously encouraged Western investment in China.[59]

The post-Mao economic goals of the Chinese government have been wildly successful. China's leaders wanted to develop technology and become competitive with the West. They also wanted to develop a middle class and create material prosperity in China. "In the post-Mao period, China's leaders have based their legitimacy on their ability to create economic growth and better living standards rather than on political correctness."[60]

Government in the Twenty-First Century

China's role in the world has changed significantly, to some extent as a result of changing Chinese leadership and to some extent as a result of a changing geopolitical context within which China is operating. The Chinese economy has become among the strongest in the world, and China has shown an interest in using that economy, and the influence that comes with it, in making friends around the world and to exert influence in its part of the world. This has come at a time when the political leadership of the United States has shown a radical change in the direction that it intends to go as a global leader: withdrawal, inwardness, and isolationist.

Thus as the United States under President Donald Trump withdrew from the Trans-Pacific Partnership, a new trade agreement negotiated under the presidential administration of Barack Obama that was intended at least in part to help Asian nations control the impact of China's economy in the region, China stepped forward and called for an expansion of free trade, with China being the largest actor in the region. As the United States announced that it would not sign the Paris Agreement, on climate change, China announced that it would provide even greater leadership and more vigorous pursuit of the goals of that agreement. President Xi Jinping has set China on a path to greater global influence and interaction,[61] although it is not yet clear what the domestic implications of that international role will end up being.

The Chinese System in Perspective

The final chapter of a recent collection of essays on contemporary Chinese politics began with the observation that

> China seems to be a paradox: on the one hand, it has a thriving capitalist economy; on the other hand, the catalyst behind its phenomenal growth has been none other than the Chinese Communist Party. Economic liberalization and socialist authoritarianism have marched hand in hand. Unlike many ailing post-Soviet states with weakly institutionalized democratic structures and fragile economies, the Chinese Communist Party has unleashed a tide of economic entrepreneurialism, raising living standards and making China a major economic global player, while at the same time maintaining territorial power.[62]

We have seen in this chapter that the approach we have used in this text for understanding the way that political systems operate in other parts of the world doesn't work well in China. The Chinese approach to politics—involving a highly ideological regime and highly personalistic following of executive-centered leadership—does not recognize the important role for political institutions that is the key to understanding politics elsewhere. Whereas in most nations—developed and underdeveloped, Northern and Southern, Eastern and Western—it is important to know what a constitution says, and how the political structures of the regime are organized, in China both of these factors take a decidedly secondary role to the behavior of the one-party state, the ideology of Chinese Communism, and the attitudes of the Supreme Leader of the day.

But it is important to understand and appreciate that Chinese politics is changing. The opening to a market economy that was undertaken—or at least tolerated—by Deng Xiaoping has had, and will continue to have, very significant consequences for the Chinese regime. It appears to be inevitable that doing business with the West means having more social and cultural contact with the West, and this in turn will result in increased demands by the Chinese public for more political rights and liberties than have been the case in China's recent and extended past as they see and hear and read more about life outside of China. The growth of a Chinese middle class oriented toward Western markets is having an effect upon Chinese politics and society.

Recent months and years have shown that this increased contact with the West is indeed having an effect upon Chinese society and culture. There is a vibrant and growing middle class in China today, not only in the largest cities but indeed also growing across the nation. The middle class is, increasingly, in touch with the West electronically—sometimes to the consternation of a Chinese government that tries to regulate communication between Chinese citizens and those outside of China—and that contact is resulting in greater demand for Western-style freedoms. Although the pressures of the Arab Spring[63] did not ignite in China, there is no doubt that the Chinese government is aware of the patterns of behavior that are flourishing around the world, and this is being reflected in the government's increasing sensitivity to the need for political as well as economic reform in the way the Chinese government operates.

Discussion Questions

1. What would you suggest are the four most important themes in Chinese history that have shaped Chinese politics today?
2. Can you identify several major crises in the development of the Communist Party of China? What have been the effects of each of these crises?
3. How would you compare the formal state institutions in China to those in Western nations? Do Western models work in China? Why or why not?
4. What are the key structures of the Communist Party of China, and how does power flow both up and down in the party?
5. What is the relationship between the structures of the Communist Party of China and the Chinese national government? Where is the more important base of power? Why?
6. What is the relationship between political institutions and political leaders in China? Do individuals have power because of the positions they hold, or do they hold certain positions because they control power?
7. What are the forces that are pressing toward economic and political liberalization in China today?

Notes

1. John K. Fairbank, *China: The People's Middle Kingdom and the U.S.A.* (Cambridge: Belknap, 1967), pp. 3–4. See Rinn-Sup Shinn and Robert Worden, "Historical Setting," in Robert L. Worden, Andrea Matles Savada, and Ronald E. Dolan, eds., *Country Profile: China* (Washington, DC: Library of Congress, Federal Research Division, 1987), https://www.loc.gov/item/87600493; or Morris Rossabi, *A History of China* (Malden, MA: Wiley, 2014).

2. Charles Hauss, *Comparative Politics: Domestic Responses to Global Challenges* (Belmont, CA: Wadsworth/Thomson Learning, 2000), chap. 11, "China," p. 297.

3. Worden, Savada, and Dolan, *Country Profile: China.*

4. Ibid., p. 2. See also Kerry Brown, *Contemporary China* (New York: Palgrave Macmillan, 2013).

5. Bruce J. Dickson, "China," in Michael J. Sodaro, ed., *Comparative Politics: A Global Introduction* (New York: McGraw-Hill, 2008), p. 656.

6. A good essay on contemporary authoritarianism is by Yan Jiaqi, "The Nature of Chinese Authoritarianism," in Carol Lee Hamrin and Suisheng Zhao, eds., *Decision-Making in Deng's China: Perspectives from Insiders* (Armonk, NY: Sharpe, 1995), pp. 3–14. See also Yingshi Yu, Michael Duke, and Josephine Chiu-Duke, *Chinese History and Culture* (New York: Columbia University Press, 2016).

7. Joseph Fewsmith, "The Government of China," in Michael Curtis, ed., *Introduction to Comparative Politics* (New York: Pearson, 2003), p. 452.

8. James Townsend and Brantly Womack, *Politics in China* (Boston: Little, Bown, 1986), p. 46.

9. Fewsmith, "Government of China," p. 456. See also Yongnian Zheng, *Contemporary China: A History Since 1978* (Hoboken, NJ: Wiley, 2014).

10. Maurice Meisner, *Mao's China and After* (New York: Free Press, 1987), p. 27. See also Hui Wang and Michael Hill, *China from Empire to Nation-State* (Cambridge: Harvard University Press, 2014).

11. Marcus Ethridge and Howard Handelman, *Politics in a Changing World: A Comparative Introduction to Political Science* (New York: St. Martin's, 1994), p. 412.

12. In Edgar Snow's book *Red China Today* he notes that Premier Zhou Enlai and other leaders looked back on the Long March as their personal struggle. See Edgar Snow, *Red China Today* (New York: Vintage, 1970), pp. 111–112. See also Jean-Philippe Béja, Hualing Fu, and Eva Pils, *Liu Xiaobo, Charter 08, and the Challenges of Political Reform in China* (Hong Kong: Hong Kong University Press, 2012).

13. The full text of the Chinese Constitution can be found at http://en.people.cn /constitution/constitution.html. See also Sebastian Heilmann, *China's Political System* (Lanham: Rowman and Littlefield, 2017).

14. Worden, Savada, and Dolan, *Country Profile: China,* p. 26. This is also discussed in Flemming Christiansen and Shirin M. Rai, *Chinese Politics and Society: An Introduction* (Hoboken, NJ: Taylor and Francis, 2014).

15. The website of the Chinese Communist party is http://english.cpc.people.com.cn.

16. See http://english.peopledaily.com.cn/constitution/constitution.html.

17. "The Communist Party of China," http://www.chinatoday.com/org/cpc /index.htm.

18. Ibid.

19. Jiang Zemin became leader in China following the Tiananmen Square protests of 1989. With the waning influence of Deng Xiaoping and the other members of China's senior leadership, Jiang effectively became the Supreme Leader in the 1990s.

20. "News of the Communist Party of China: The Three Represents," http://english .cpc.people.com.cn/66739/4521344.html.

21. James Chieh Hsiung, *Ideology and Practice: The Evolution of Chinese Communism* (New York: Praeger, 1970), p. 107. See also Ning Fang, *China's Democracy Path* (Berlin: Springer, 2015).

22. Ethridge and Handelman, *Politics in a Changing World,* p. 414. See also William Joseph, *Politics in China: An Introduction* (New York: Oxford University Press, 2014); and Hecheng Tan, Stacy Mosher, and Jian Guo, *The Killing Wind: A Chinese County's Descent into Madness During the Cultural Revolution* (New York: Oxford University Press, 2017).

23. "List of Members of the 19th CPC Central Committee," http://www.chinatoday .com/org/cpc/index.htm. See Guoguang Wu, *China's Party Congress: Power, Legitimacy, and Institutional Manipulation* (Cambridge: Cambridge University Press, 2015).

24. Constitution, Article 3. See also Teresa Wright, *Party and State in Post-Mao China* (Malden, MA: Polity, 2015).

25. "The 19th National Congress of the Communist Party: Xi Urges Study, Implementation of CPC Congress Spirit," http://english.gov.cn/news/top_news/2017/10/28 /content_281475924262128.htm. See also Cheng Li, *Chinese Politics in the Xi Jinping Era: Reassessing Collective Leadership* (Washington, DC: Brookings Institution, 2016).

26. Worden, Savada, and Dolan, *Country Profile: China,* pp. 25–28.

27. Fewsmith, "Government of China," p. 457. See also Yang Zhong, *Political Culture and Participation in Urban China* (Singapore: Palgrave Macmillan, 2018).

28. See Harry Harding, *Organizing China: The Problem of Bureaucracy, 1949–1976* (Stanford: Stanford University Press, 1981), chap. 5, "The First Crisis: The Hundred Flowers, 1956–1957," pp. 116–151. See also Wenfang Tang, *Populist Authoritarianism: Chinese Political Culture and Regime Sustainability* (New York: Oxford University Press, 2016).

29. Dickson, "China," p. 667. See Shanruo Ning Zhang, *Confucianism in Contemporary Chinese Politics: An Actionable Account of Authoritarian Political Culture* (Lanham: Lexington, 2015).

30. See Harding, *Organizing China,* chap. 6, "The Great Leap Forward and Its Aftermath, 1957–1962," pp. 153–194. See also Xiaobing Li and Xiansheng Tian, *Evolution of Power: China's Struggle, Survival, and Success* (Lanham: Lexington, 2014).

31. Chris Trueman, "The Great Leap Forward," in *China: 1900–1976,* http://www .historylearningsite.co.uk/great_leap_forward.htm.

32. Benjamin Valentino, *Final Solutions: Mass Killing and Genocide in the Twentieth Century* (Ithaca: Cornell University Press, 2004), p. 127.

33. Frank Dikotter, *Mao's Great Famine: The History of China's Most Devastating Catastrophe, 1958–1962* (London: Walker, 2010), p. 70. *Time* magazine wrote, "It is now established that at least that number [20,000] died in China during the famine that followed the Great Leap between 1959 and 1961." See Jonathan Spence, "Mao Zedong," *Time,* April 13, 1998, http://www.time.com/time/magazine/article/0,9171,988161-1,00.html.

34. Fewsmith, "Government of China," p. 461.

35. Ethridge and Handleman, *Politics in a Changing World,* p. 416.

36. See Harding, *Organizing China,* chap. 8, "The Second Crisis: The Cultural Revolution, 1966–1968," pp. 235–265. See Aminda M. Smith, *Thought Reform and China's Dangerous Classes: Reeducation, Resistance, and the People* (Lanham: Rowman and Littlefield, 2013).

37. There is a large literature on the Cultural Revolution. See, among others, K. S. Karol, *The Second Chinese Revolution* (New York: Hill and Wang, 1974).

38. Fewsmith, "Government of China," p. 462.

39. Dickson, "China," p. 669.

40. Ethridge and Handleman, *Politics in a Changing World,* p. 417. See Joseph Fewsmith, *The Logic and Limits of Political Reform in China* (New York: Cambridge University Press, 2013).

41. Lawrence Mayer, John Burnett, and Suzanne Ogden, *Comparative Politics: Nations and Theories in a Changing World* (Upper Saddle River, NJ: Prentice-Hall, 1996), p. 309. See Xiaoping Deng, *On Reform* (New York: CN Times, 2013).

42. "The State Council," http://english.gov.cn/statecouncil.

43. Chris Buckley and Adam Wu, "Ending Term Limits for China's Xi Is a Big Deal: Here's Why," *New York Times,* March 11, 2018, p. 1.

44. Ibid.

45. Kevin O'Brien, *Reform Without Liberalization: China's National People's Congress and the Politics of Institutional Change* (New York: Cambridge University Press, 1990).

46. Constitution, Article 57.

47. Inter-Parliamentary Union, "Parline Database: China—National People's Congress," http://www.ipu.org/parline-e/reports/2065_B.htm.

48. This section is based upon a much more detailed discussion in Worden, Savada, and Dolan, *Country Profile: China,* pp. 25–28. See also Yuwen Li, *The Judicial System and Reform in Post-Mao China: Stumbling Towards Justice* (Burlington, VT: Ashgate, 2014).

49. Mayer, Burnett, and Ogden, *Comparative Politics,* p. 312. A very good study of the Chinese legal system is by Victor Li, *Law Without Lawyers: A Comparative View of Law in China and the United States* (Boulder: Westview, 1978). See also Pitman Potter, ed., *Domestic Law Reforms in Post-Mao China* (Armonk, NY: Sharpe, 1994). See also Zhu Sanzhu, "Reforming State Institutions: Privatizing the Lawyers' System," in Jude Howell, ed., *Governance in China* (Boulder: Rowman and Littlefield, 2004), pp. 58–77.

50. Mayer, Burnett, and Ogden, *Comparative Politics,* p. 313.

51. See Baogang He, *The Democratic Implications of Civil Society in China* (New York: St. Martin's, 1997); and Jude Howell, "New Directions in Civil Society: Organizing Around Marginalized Interests," in Howell, *Governance in China*, pp. 143–171.

52. Ethridge and Handelman, *Politics in a Changing World,* p. 419. See Michael Dillon, *Deng Xiaoping: The Man Who Made Modern China* (London: Tauris, 2014); or David M. Lampton, *Following the Leader: Ruling China, from Deng Xiaoping to Xi Jinping* (Berkeley: University of California Press, 2013).

53. This section is based upon a much longer discussion in Dickson, "China," pp. 672–674.

54. See John P. Burns and Stanley Rosen, eds., *Policy Conflicts in Post-Mao China: A Documentary Survey, with Analysis* (Armonk, NY: Sharpe, 1986).

55. Dickson, "China," p. 673. See Yu Zhou, William Lazonick, and Yifei Sun, *China as an Innovation Nation* (Oxford: Oxford University Press, 2016).

56. A very good discussion of how the human rights agenda squares with traditional Chinese values can be found in William Theodore de Bary, "Confucianism and Human Rights in China," in Larry Diamond and Marc Plattner, eds., *Democracy in East Asia* (Baltimore: Johns Hopkins University Press, 1998), pp. 42–54. See also Suisheng Zhao, *Debating Political Reform in China: Rule of Law vs. Democratization* (Hoboken, NJ: Taylor and Francis, 2014).

57. See Joseph Fewsmith, *China Since Tiananmen: The Politics of Transition* (New York: Cambridge University Press, 2001).

58. Bruce Gilley, *China's Democratic Future: How It Will Happen and Where It Will Lead* (New York: Columbia University Press, 2004), p. 136.

59. Yumei Zhang, *Pacific Asia: The Politics of Development* (New York: Routledge, 2003), p. 34.

60. Dickson, "China," p. 677.

61. See Binhong Shao, *China Under Xi Jinping: Its Economic Challenges and Foreign Policy Initiatives* (Leiden: Brill, 2015); and Jonathan Sharp, *The China Renaissance: The Rise of Xi Jinping and the 18th Communist Party Congress* (Hackensack, NJ: World Scientific, 2013).

62. Jude Howell, "Getting to the Roots: Governance Pathologies and Future Prospects," in Howell, *Governance in China,* p. 226.

63. This refers to the pattern of demonstrations and protests and demands for increased democratization that broke out across the Arab world in the period from January through June 2011. Several governments in the Middle East were toppled—including Tunisia and Egypt—while others were moved to make what could be significant political reforms—including Jordan and Morocco—while others started and continue to be in revolutionary turmoil—including Libya, Syria, and Yemen.

9

France

Learning Outcomes

After reading this chapter, you will be able to

- Understand how French political history in the Third and Fourth Republics helped to shape the creation of the Fifth Republic.
- Appreciate the unique role of Charles de Gaulle in the creation of the Fifth Republic.
- Understand the unique nature of French unitary government.
- Explain the special characteristics of the French presidency, and understand its particular powers.
- Understand how the role of political parties has changed in France over time, and how the coalition nature of French politics affects the way public policy is made.
- Compare the French legislature and legislative process to those of other democratic systems and appreciate unique characteristics that exist in France.

We saw in Chapter 4, and will see in greater detail in Chapter 15 on the United Kingdom, that the constitutional system of Great Britain is the product of a gradual process taking place over a period of several hundred years; the same cannot be said of the French constitutional system. In the British case, we can point to specific dates of constitutional significance—for instance the signing of the Magna Carta in 1215—but the general constitutional system has remained intact and has changed only slowly over a long period of time. The French system is more properly characterized as experiencing a number of (more or less) sudden alterations of the entire political regime, not merely evolutionary modifications of aspects of the system.

France's Constitutional History

We refer to the current system of government in France as the Fifth Republic. This suggests, of course, that earlier republics have come and gone. Many of these arrivals and departures have not been slow and moderate, but have been abrupt and violent substitutions of one system of government for another—revolutions in fact and sometimes in name. It behooves us at this point to examine briefly the recent constitutional history of France that has led to the establishment of the Fifth Republic.

The Third Republic

We will begin our discussion of modern French political structures with the **Third Republic**,[1] which has been referred to by some as a "republic by default."[2] Although the Third Republic dates from 1870, its constitution was not assembled until 1875. The bicameral parliament was composed of a Chamber of Deputies and a Senate, the deputies elected by the people and the senators elected indirectly and over-representing rural areas.[3] The combined legislature, called the **National Assembly**, elected a president for a seven-year term. Ministers were responsible to the legislature, and with the consent of the Senate the president could dissolve the Chamber of Deputies before its four-year term expired.

The fact that the Third Republic lasted as long as it did—seventy years, from 1870 until 1940—is an anomaly of French political history. One should not deduce from the relative longevity of that Republic that its life was placid and stable. A number of crises arose during the life of that Republic that caused many people to fear that the Republic was in danger of extinction.[4]

Interestingly, World War I did not appear to have a deleterious effect upon the French regime. Rather, the economic depression in Europe after the war severely affected the French Government. In 1935 a temporary electoral alliance of a number of political parties helped elect Leon Blum premier. The Spanish Civil War in 1936 affected the stability of the Blum regime, as did a number of other social issues, and the Government resigned after a year.

From 1936 through 1940 several governments were created and dissolved. The Spanish Civil War, the Munich Agreement of 1938 between Neville Chamberlain (the British prime minister) and Adolph Hitler over the annexation of Czechoslovakia by Germany, the Nazi-Soviet Nonaggression Pact of 1939, and the German invasion of Norway and the Low Countries all left French governments powerless to act.

The phenomenon that most people associate with French politics under the Third and Fourth Republics is no doubt **ministerial instability**, the frequent turnovers of cabinets. The phenomenon can be illustrated by comparing the number of French and British cabinets and premiers (or prime ministers) during similar periods, as indicated in Table 9.1.

The major explanation for the frequency of new cabinets in France during the Third Republic can be found in the Chamber of Deputies. There were usually eight to ten parties in the legislature, which invariably meant that coalitions were necessary to form government majorities. These coalitions (as we have seen is often the case with coalitions) were not durable enough to withstand the short-term pressures brought about by rapidly evolving political events, which resulted in the collapse of government after government.

In June of 1940 a new cabinet was formed, which was led by the World War I hero Marshal Henri Petain. The hope was that Petain, as a military hero, would be able to provide strong leadership in the face of powerful external pressure from Hitler's Nazi Germany. He did provide leadership, but in an unexpected direction. Immediately after taking power on June 16, 1940, Petain opened negotiations with the Nazis; less than a week later (on June 22) he signed an armistice with Germany dividing France into an occupied northern half and an unoccupied southern half, governed from the city of Vichy. From this time until November 1942, when Germany occupied all of France, the Vichy regime governed the southern half of France without a constitution, a legislature, or presidential elections. The Third Republic was dead.[5]

Table 9.1   Ministerial Instability in France: A Comparative Perspective

	Third Republic France, 1879–1940	Britain, 1880–1940	Fourth Republic France, 1947–1958	Britain, 1945–1963
Number of cabinets	94	21	18	5
Average cabinet life (months)	8	36	8	43
Number of premiers	44	11	15	4
Average tenure of premier (months)	16	60	9	54

Source: Adapted from Roy Pierce, *French Politics and Political Institutions* (New York: Harper and Row, 1968), pp. 19–21.

The Fourth Republic

When France was liberated from German occupation in 1944, General **Charles de Gaulle**, who had led a National Council of Resistance from London during the war, became head of the new Government.⁶ In October 1945, "French voters by an overwhelming majority of 18,600,000 to 700,777 decided to leave the Third Republic in its grave."⁷ The first postwar legislature was subsequently elected, and one of its first tasks was to construct a new constitution for the **Fourth Republic**; this combination legislature-constitutional convention was called the Constituent Assembly. There was no agreement, however, on the direction that should be followed in France's constitutional future.⁸

The first draft constitution was presented to the voters in May 1946 for ratification and was rejected by a narrow margin: 10.6 million to 9.5 million. This plan proposed abolition of the Senate as an essentially "undemocratic" institution (since it was not directly elected by the public) and proposed a weak executive, with virtually all powers vested in a unicameral National Assembly. The draft had the support of the leftist parties, the Communists and the Socialists, but was opposed by moderate parties and a new political organization, the Popular Republican Movement (MRP).

The second Constituent Assembly, elected in June 1946, produced a draft constitution that resembled the first proposal in many respects. It placed almost complete authority in the elected lower house, the National Assembly, a name previously used to describe the entire two-house parliament, with a weak Council of the Republic as a second legislative house.

Members of the National Assembly were to be elected from multimember districts, averaging five deputies per district, by proportional representation. The executive was to remain weak. In October 1946 this plan was presented to the French public, and it received an unenthusiastic approval: 9.3 million votes in favor to 8.2 million against, with 7.8 million eligible voters not voting. General de Gaulle and his supporters, who had argued for a stronger executive and opposed the plan, claimed that the new constitution would never last, since it was supported by only slightly more than a third of the electorate.⁹

A number of devices were included in the constitution to promote governmental stability, such as the 1954 change making the investiture of a prime minister easier by requiring a relative, or simple, majority (a majority of those present and voting) rather than an absolute majority (a majority of all members of the legislature). Despite this, the multiparty system encouraged by the proportional representation electoral framework led to an absence of stable parliamentary majorities, producing a change in cabinets averaging once every six months.

Although domestic issues were the primary source of political conflict in the early postwar years, by the mid-1950s it was international events that consumed governmental attention. The Government was able to handle almost all of the crises it faced. The war in Indochina (Vietnam) was ended in 1954. France accepted West Germany into the North Atlantic Treaty Organization (NATO) in 1957 and joined the European Economic Community (the Common Market). Both Morocco and Tunisia were granted independence in 1956. Also in 1956 the French Government passed legislation to "set France's African colonies south of the Sahara on the road to real, and not sham, self-government."[10] The question of Algeria, however, proved to be too much for the Government.

In April 1958 the French army stationed in Algeria supported a revolt launched by European settlers in Algiers and called for the formation of a "Government of Public Safety" in Paris. They demanded that the present Government resign, and that General de Gaulle be called out of political retirement to take power.[11] The Government in power accepted General de Gaulle as "the only possible savior-assassin of the regime. On June 1, 1958, by a vote of 329 to 224, the Assembly accepted de Gaulle as Prime Minister, and the next day empowered him to supervise the drafting of a new constitution."[12] The Fourth Republic was dead.

The Constitutional System of the Fifth Republic

When on June 1, 1958, the Fourth Republic's National Assembly invested de Gaulle as prime minister, many deputies in the assembly were suspicious of de Gaulle and feared that his selection would lead to the creation of another Napoleon-like empire. In June 1946 de Gaulle had delivered in the town of Bayeux what would prove to be one of his most famous speeches. He set forth his notion of the type of strong, vigorous executive leadership that he thought France needed.[13]

Despite de Gaulle's protestations that at the age of sixty-seven he did not pose a threat to French liberty, when the legislature authorized him to draft a new constitution for a fifth French republic it attached two significant conditions. First, the constitution of the new Fifth Republic had to retain the two distinct offices of the president and the premier. Second, the new constitution had to retain the characteristic of having the premier "responsible to" the legislature: the legislature would have the power to fire the premier. The latter requirement was included on the assumption that de Gaulle himself would seek the premier's office once the new constitution was established, and thus the legislature would still have some degree of control over any future acts of de Gaulle.

It is interesting to note that although de Gaulle was given authority by the legislature to draft a new constitution that he would subsequently submit to the public in a referendum for approval, many have argued that this grant of power was illegal. The Constitution of the Fourth Republic, in effect when de Gaulle worked on his draft constitution, provided that constitutional amendments could be initiated only in parliament. Thus it has been argued by anti-Gaullists that the de Gaulle Constitution of the Fifth Republic was simply a "coup d'état that had only a thin veneer of legality."[14]

The **de Gaulle constitution** does not fit neatly into either of the two major models of executive leadership (presidential or parliamentary) introduced earlier in this text. The presidential model has a single individual playing the roles of both head of state and chief executive, elected independently of the legislature, with a base of power independent of the legislature. The parliamentary model separates the two executive roles: with a weak figurehead as head of state chosen by one of a number of different mechanisms (such as heredity or election) and a powerful chief executive coming from, being a part of, and being responsible to the legislature. The de Gaulle constitution bridges the two systems, and is accordingly sometimes referred to as either a **quasi-presidential** or **quasi-parliamentary executive**.

The de Gaulle constitution brought together elements of both the Bonaparte era and the republican era. "The Constitution established a strong Executive in the form of a President with independent power to govern and a cabinet headed by a Prime Minister responsible to a popularly elected assembly."[15] To put the institution of the French president in a comparative perspective, the president of France had both in theory and in practice the power that the British prime minister had in practice but not in theory. The French model, unlike the standard Westminster-model power relationship, produced a politically significant head of state and a weak chief executive.

The so-called de Gaulle constitution of 1958 was actually drafted by a small group of individuals, led by **Michel Debré**, the future prime minister.[16] No person other than de Gaulle had more influence on the 1958 constitution than Debré. The new constitution was submitted to a constitutional advisory committee, primarily made up of legislators, and subsequently presented to the public for approval in a national referendum.

A strong presidency, coupled with some structural changes in the powers of the legislature, was the major thrust of changes that the Fifth Republic would make to the political system of the Fourth Republic. This was clearly in response to what was seen as the fundamental weaknesses of the Fourth Republic: a lack of leadership and parliamentary instability.

Unitary Government

French politics is built on three levels of government: the commune, the department, and the national government.[17] Just as French parliamentary government is a variation of the "normal" parliamentary model, so, too, the French style of unitary government appears to be different from other unitary governments.

Remember that while unitary governments and federal governments both have local as well as national levels, they differ in the existence of an intermediate level of government. The United States, Canada, Mexico, and Germany are examples of federal governments in which power is shared (to different degrees) between the "central" or "national" governments and the intermediate governments—states, provinces, or Lander. The primary alternative to the federal system is the unitary regime, in which there is no intermediate level of government. The "typical" unitary government (if such can be said to exist) is found in Great Britain, in which a national government and a local government divide functions that would be of concern to the intermediate level of government in a federal regime, although all sovereignty resides with the national government.

The French system includes twenty-two administrative regions containing ninety-six departments (this is usually referred to as **metropolitan France**). There are also four overseas departments (Guadeloupe, Martinique, French Guiana, and Reunion Island), five overseas territories (New Caledonia, French Polynesia, Wallis and Futuna Islands, and French Southern and Antarctic Territories), and two "special status" territories (Mayotte, and St. Pierre and Miquelon).

The 1982 law affecting the twenty-two administrative regions—setting up elected regional councils with the power to elect their executives—also gave the regional authorities many powers that had previously belonged to the national government.

The French system is an odd form of unitary government because although there is much sharing of power between the national and local levels of government, there are intermediate levels of government designed to assist in the administration of policy.[18] Locally, the mayor and municipal council deal with two kinds of decisions: how to carry out and finance state-mandated services, and priority-setting decisions in areas not controlled by the state. The commune, the lowest-level political organization of the state, is the central administrative unit of the state.

The second level of French government is the department. The prefect is the representative of national government in the department. This individual has "wide-ranging powers over local government."[19] A good deal of the commune's legislation cannot go into effect without the prefect's approval. There are ninety-six departments in France, most of which have the same borders today that they did at the time of the French Revolution in 1789.

Departments are governed by a council; for purposes of administration, departments are divided into subunits called cantons, and each canton elects one member to the department council. Like the commune, the department is both a self-governing structure and an administrative level of the state. The chief executive of government at the department level is not an elected official at all, but is the prefect, who is appointed.

It can be seen, then, that although France is invariably—and correctly —classified as a unitary regime, it is a unitary regime with many characteristics that might be thought to be more appropriate for a federal system than a unitary system. Departments and cantons both exist above the local (commune) level and, particularly in regard to the Senate, play a significant role in the French political system.

Executive Structures

The Presidency
When de Gaulle returned to power in 1958, it was generally expected that the presidency would be crucial.[20] It was by making the president— usually the weak figurehead actor in split-executive parliamentary systems—the keystone of the system, rather than the prime minister— usually the dominant figure in parliamentary systems—that de Gaulle and the coauthors of the new constitution were able to put so much power in the hands of a single political actor and yet still be able to stay within the conditions set down by Fourth Republic legislators permitting a new constitution to be written and submitted to the public for approval.

The system of executive power in the Fifth Republic is similar in many respects to those found today in Austria, Finland, Ireland, and Iceland, in which the president is popularly elected. In those systems, however, the president is significantly weaker than in the French system "because his role is circumscribed by his being subject to ouster by Parliament (as in Iceland), by strong legislative powers that Parliament possesses (as in Finland), or by the role of strong, disciplined parties (as in Austria). The French president, in contrast, suffers from none of these limitations."[21]

As suggested earlier in this volume, constitutions are often written in response to political regimes of the past. This is certainly true in France. The Constitution of the Fifth Republic was written in response to French political history.

De Gaulle's goal in designing the constitution was "to free the executive from legislative domination and so to make possible greater governmental stability."[22] The president was given absolute power, without needing the consent of either the Government or the parliament, to

1. Appoint the Prime Minister
2. Dissolve Parliament
3. Assume Emergency Powers under Article 16
4. Ask Parliament to reconsider a law just passed
5. Refer a law to the Constitutional Council for judgment on its constitutionality
6. Preside over the Council of Ministers (the Cabinet)
7. Serve as Commander-in-Chief
8. Exercise the right of Pardon
9. Decide whether or not to submit a bill to popular referendum when the Parliament or the Prime Minister suggest it.[23]

We should note the presidential power to dissolve the National Assembly (the lower house of the bicameral legislature) at any time the president wished, except while exercising emergency powers under Article 16 or if the National Assembly had already been dissolved once within a year. It is not unusual to find this power in the hands of the head of state in other political systems; the British monarch has the same power. The difference, and a significant one, is that although de jure (in law) the British monarch may use this power at any time, de facto (in fact) she or he will use it only "on the advice" of the prime minister. The French president possessed this power both de jure and de facto—in law and in fact—and French presidents since the time of de Gaulle have used the power on their own initiative, without seeking approval of, or acting on request of, the prime minister and cabinet.

A major set of presidential powers included in the de Gaulle constitution of the Fifth Republic dealt with **Article 16 powers** of the president. This article stated that "when the institutions of the Republic, national independence, the integrity of national territory, or the application of international commitments are threatened in a serious and immediate fashion, and the normal functioning of public institutions is interrupted," the president is authorized to "take the measures required by these circumstances."[24]

The measures that the president could take were, and have been in practice, virtually unlimited. The only checks on his or her power were that (1) the president must consult with the prime minister, the presidents of the two houses of legislature, and the Constitutional Council; and (2) the legislature must remain in session during the period of the declared emergency. It should be noted that the first item required the president only to consult with others, not seek their approval or permission, so these "checks" really did nothing to limit what the president did.

Article 16 has been used six times during the Fifth Republic, as indicated in Table 9.2. Four of these instances were a result of challenges in overseas territories related to "independentist" issues in Algeria and New Caledonia. Two were a result of domestic disturbances, one of these related to race-related rioting, and one a result of an instance of domestic terrorism. To take one illustration, in April 1961 a group of French generals in Algeria who opposed governmental policy leading to Algerian independence from France threatened to invade the French mainland and take over the Government. De Gaulle acted under Article 16, announced that "the institutions of the Republic" were threatened, and declared a state of emergency. The attempted coup was put down within a very few days, but de Gaulle let his Article 16 powers remain in force for over five more months; only the president decides when to deactivate the Article 16 powers.

There really are no checks and balances in the traditional sense over the president's use of the emergency powers in Article 16. The president needs no countersignature, no advice and consent, no one's permission to declare the state of emergency, and the state of emergency remains until the president, and only the president, decides to declare the emergency over.

Yet another set of powers exclusively reserved for the president had to do with justice-related issues. Again, without the permission or countersignature of either the Government or the legislature, the president had the power to appoint three of the nine members of the Constitutional Council. Moreover, the president had the right of pardon.

Beyond these powers, anything the president wanted to do in the French political system could be done only in collaboration with others.

Table 9.2 Uses of Article 16 in France

Date	Cause
1955	Algeria: independentist unrest
1958	Algeria: independentist unrest
1961	Algeria: failed coup attempt to overthrow President Charles de Gaulle
1984	New Caledonia: independentist unrest
2005	Race-related violence in which a break-in at a building site in Clichy-sous-Bois, an eastern suburb of Paris, led to the deaths of two young people, which in turn led to three weeks of rioting throughout France
2015	Terrorist attacks and related events in Paris; four extensions lasted until November 2017

For example, only the president has the power to call for a **referendum**, to submit a political issue to the voters, but theoretically the president may call a referendum only if asked to do so by either the Government or the legislature. In September 2000 a question put before the French voters in a referendum was overwhelmingly approved; in that ballot 72 percent of the voters approved a measure to shorten the president's term of office from seven to five years. Only about 30 percent of the voters participated in the referendum, however, the lowest turnout ever recorded for a referendum.[25]

This theoretical control over the referendum was in response to the history of its use—or abuse—in French politics. Napoleon frequently used the referendum, often to achieve a goal that the legislature would not permit, and the public at the time did not prove to be very discriminating in its approval of Napoleon's ideas. The founders of the Fifth Republic, while giving the president great emergency powers, did not want to give a charismatic president license to regularly circumvent the duly elected legislators in the policymaking process.

Given that the president has only the aforementioned powers (even though they are significant powers), which he can perform independently of all others, what has caused the French political leadership system to evolve to a point that it arguably resembles the US presidency as much as, if not more than, the Westminster model of parliamentary government?

The answer can only partially be attributed to the constitutional grant of special powers to the president. There is in French politics a "fundamental difference between the role which the constitution and those who actually drafted it assigned to the presidency and the actual significance which the office has taken on in the process of decision making."[26]

Certainly a major reason for the evolution of the presidency as a significant political institution was the first holder of the office, Charles de Gaulle.[27] De Gaulle was a charismatic leader who favored strong executive leadership, and in the same way that initial incumbents of many political offices leave lasting impressions on the institutions they helped to create (such as Chairman Mao in China, for example), de Gaulle's role in the development of the French presidency cannot be overstated.

A second reason for the growth of the relative power of the French presidency can be found in the constitutional amendment of October 1962, which established the direct popular election of the president.[28] In the 1958 Constitution, the president was to be elected by an electoral college made up of local and provincial officials and national legislators. By having the president directly elected by the people and, therefore, responsible to them and not to the legislators, de Gaulle gave the presidency a tremendous infusion of power and legitimacy.

As a result of the 1962 referendum the president's term of office was seven years, making him one of the most secure chief executives in any Western democracy. The September 2000 referendum in which the term was shortened from seven years to five years was seen as the most radical change to the French constitution in decades.[29]

The issue of whether the seven-year term for the president should be shortened had been on the political agenda since **Georges Pompidou** assumed the presidency in 1969, but most presidents opposed having their terms shortened and would not submit the issue to a referendum or to the parliament in a special session. **Jacques Chirac**, the president at the time of the referendum, had been on record as opposing the change in the length of the presidential term until the summer before the vote. The new policy went into effect at the end of Chirac's term, in 2002; some reporters suggested that Chirac believed that his chances to win reelection would be increased if voters knew that he would not serve seven more years, but only five more years.[30]

Direct popular election "endowed the presidency with the legitimacy of a direct popular vote which, it was hoped, would accrue to the office when it was occupied by a less charismatic personality than General de Gaulle."[31] The apparent similarity to the US system can be overstated, however. Apart from the strong head of state, which is a single deviation from "normal" parliamentary systems, the French system is still much closer to the parliamentary model than to the US presidential model. This is so for a number of reasons:

1. By holding the power of dissolution (Article 12) over parliament, the French President can "interfere directly" with parliamentary organization and activity. The American President, of course, cannot.
2. By dissolving parliament the French President can, like the British Prime Minister, create a plebiscitary situation to receive popular support for his actions. The American President, of course, cannot dissolve the legislature.
3. The President has vast emergency powers under Article 16, with no judicial oversight as exists in the United States with the judicial review of the Supreme Court.[32]

The Prime Minister

The role of the prime minister in the Fifth Republic is of less significance than in most parliamentary systems. (It should be noted that the formal title of the chief executive in France is "prime minister," not "premier." "Premier" was used in the Third and Fourth Republics and is still often used today as an incorrect holdover from former regimes.)

The role of the prime minister "has been limited to a joint formulation of policy with the President (in which the premier has played an increasingly subordinate role) and to manage the legislature so that it will accept the government's program."[33] One student of the French political system has suggested that in the Fifth Republic the prime minister is "merely the 'head of government,' while the president is the actual decision-maker. He leaves to the premier the role of being a link between the president and Parliament, particularly on matters the president is not interested in."[34]

The President, Prime Minister, and Cohabitation

The model of French politics described here seemed to operate reasonably well until the election of 1986. To understand the significance of the 1986 election it is necessary to go back to April and May 1981, at which time **François Mitterrand** was elected president, the first time a Socialist had been elected president of France. One of his first actions was to dissolve the National Assembly (at that time conservative-dominated) and call for new elections, producing a Socialist-dominated legislature. At that point he appointed a Socialist prime minister, Pierre Mauroy, and everything continued normally until the next elections.

By the time of the next elections for the National Assembly, the Socialists had lost much of their glamour, and in the election they captured only 216 out of 577 seats in the National Assembly. (Socialist) President Mitterrand invited Jacques Chirac, leader of the largest party within the majority (conservative) coalition to become prime minister. He and Chirac agreed to a new power-sharing arrangement between the (Socialist) president and the (conservative) prime minister, something that came to be called **cohabitation**—"living together."[35] For the duration of Mitterrand's term as president, his powers were considerably reduced from their pre-1986 level, and correspondingly the powers of Prime Minister Chirac were considerably greater than the powers of the prime minister had been previously.[36]

Legislative Structures

The Legislature and the Government

The executive branch dominates the legislative process in a number of ways. Two of these are functions of direct limitation on the power of the legislature. First, the legislature cannot propose "increasing expenditures or lowering revenue in relation to the details of and total range of government budgetary proposals."[37] Second, the legislature can pass laws dealing only with matters that are specifically delegated to it in the French Constitution.

The budgetary process in any political system is a point of vulnerability for the Government. Governments that are unable to have their budgets passed find themselves at the mercy of their respective legislatures, literally unable to carry on the business of governing. The Fifth Republic's Constitution places strong restrictions on the legislature's ability to obstruct or delay the Government in the budgetary arena.[38]

The knowledge that the essence of the Government's budget will become law in any case, and the limitations imposed upon the legislature in terms of changes it can and cannot propose to the Government's budget, place the legislature at a severe disadvantage in relation to the Government.

In addition, the 1958 Constitution departed from "the traditional French republican principle of unrestricted parliamentary sovereignty" by specifically listing the legislative powers of parliament (Article 34), indicating those areas in which parliament could legislate; fields not specifically reserved for the legislature were left to the Government "to decide by decree."[39]

There are a number of other ways in which the executive is able to influence the legislative process. First, the Government controls the agenda of the National Assembly, and "by means of its power to determine the agenda the government can insure that its bills have priority over 'private members.'" The Government also has the power to stipulate which portions of its legislative proposals can be amended, and how much time can be spent on each section of the bill. Moreover, the Government can call for a **blocked vote** requiring the legislative chambers to vote on a bill in its original text "incorporating only those amendments proposed or accepted by the government."[40] As a more severe action, the Government can announce that it is making the passage of a bill into a question of confidence. If it does this, the bill automatically passes "unless a censure motion is filed by one-tenth of the deputies within 24 hours and an absolute majority of the deputies vote in support of censure."[41]

The question of the relation between the Government and the National Assembly over the concept of "censure" or "confidence" is interesting, because it is another area in which the usual vulnerability of the executive branch to the will of the legislature has been modified from the "standard" model. Although some texts declare that "if a motion of censure is adopted by the National Assembly, the Government must resign,"[42] history has shown that this rule of thumb has not always been followed.

The censure process is more difficult to operate in France than it is in many parliamentary systems, although it is not as difficult as the German "positive vote of no confidence." Opposition members can introduce motions of censure if the motion is signed by one-tenth of the deputies of the National Assembly (totaling 491). After the motion is introduced, forty-eight hours must pass before it can be debated and voted on; in order for it to pass, the motion must receive an absolute majority of deputies' support (half plus 1 of the 491 deputies, i.e., 246 deputies), not just a majority of deputies present and voting. Opposition members who sign a motion of censure are enjoined from being co-signatories of another such motion during the same legislative session; this is designed to prevent a constant stream of motions that are sure to be defeated.[43]

The Senate

In 1947 the founders of the Fourth Republic decided to do away with the Senate as the second half of the legislative body in the then new regime. Their argument was that the Senate was (1) undemocratically selected, since it was not directly elected by the people; (2) over-representative of rural areas; and (3) either redundant or antidemocratic—if it agreed with the lower house it was redundant and, therefore, unnecessary, and if it disagreed with the popularly elected lower house it was antidemocratic, because the lower house was popularly elected and the Senate was not. After some discussion, a weak Council of the Republic was substituted for the Senate in the Fourth Republic. In 1958 Charles de Gaulle brought back the second house to the French legislative system of the Fifth Republic.

The Senate is sometimes referred to as the "agricultural" chamber of the legislature because it heavily represents rural areas of France. As noted earlier, the unit of representation in the Senate is the department; the number of senators representing a given department varies from one or two to over five, depending upon the size and population of the department.

Generally speaking, the Senate is the inferior of the two legislative bodies in France today, although it does have some real responsibilities. Senators are indeed legislators, and their responsibilities include voting on issues that will become law in France. Senators have the right to table legislative proposals, but the Government has priority in setting the agenda for both the National Assembly and the Senate, and there are specific times reserved for an agenda chosen by the Senate.

> The Senate's right to take the initiative is expressed primarily in its right to amend bills. This enables both Senators and members of the National Assembly, as well as the government, to modify texts that are under discussion. Non-governmental bills are naturally discussed first by the house to which their authors belong. Government bills may receive their first examination by either the Senate or the National

Assembly. But the government's financial bills, including those that concern funding of the social security system, must first be tabled before the National Assembly. Since 2003, the government's bills concerning territorial organization or representation of French citizens living outside France must first be tabled before the Senate.[44]

The Senate introduces about 8,000 amendments per year.

However, the Senate sometimes can be an effective legislative body in terms of its ability to provide a "sober second thought" to legislative proposals, especially to Government proposals.[45] This is true for very much the same reason as it is for the House of Lords in Great Britain. Because the Government is responsible to the lower house, and can be fired by the lower house, party discipline will keep criticism in that body to a minimum. The upper house, to which the Government is not responsible, often has more freedom to inquire and criticize than does the lower house. An additional basis of power for the Senate in France is more parallel to the upper house in Germany (the Bundesrat) than to the House of Lords in Great Britain; although France is not a federal regime, senators represent geographical districts, or departments, and when Government bills deal with regional issues, agriculture, or similar questions, the Senate is likely to play a more significant role in the legislative process than it otherwise would.

The Legislative Process

The Senate of the Fifth Republic is not an equal partner in the legislative process. The legislative process is clearly dominated by the Government in the National Assembly, with the Senate often not much more than an afterthought in the process.

As in the Fourth Republic, and in Britain, West Germany, and Italy, a distinction is made between government bills (*projets de loi*) and private members' bills (*propositions de loi*), with the former accounting for most of the bills introduced in the Assembly. When a bill is introduced, it is sent first to the *bureau*; and the speaker, who heads that unit, transmits the bill directly to a legislative committee. When the committee has done its work, the *rapporteur* formally reports the bill to the floor for what is technically the initial "reading" of it. The ensuing debate, which provides an opportunity for the introduction of amendments, is followed by a vote. After its passage by the Assembly, the bill is transmitted to the Senate. If that chamber accepts the original version of the bill, it is sent to the government for signature. If the Senate rejects the bill, the subsequent procedure varies. There can be a resort to the shuttle (***navette***)—the sending of a bill back and forth between the two chambers until a common version is achieved; second, the government may request the establishment of a conference committee (*commission mixte paritaire*); third, the government may ask each chamber for a "second reading" (i.e., a reconsideration and new vote on the original bill); and fourth, if disagreement persists, the government may ask the Assembly to determine the final version of the bill by simple majority vote.[46]

The Government's ability to select among these several options when interchamber disagreement arises in the legislative process gives it a great deal of power. Ultimately, the Government can choose to simply ignore the Senate and ask the National Assembly to determine the final version of a bill. If the National Assembly wants to pass a bill that the Government does not want, it can simply let the navette go on endlessly, or keep the bill off the agenda. Finally, of course, if the Government finds both chambers noncompliant, it has the ultimate power to couple a blocked vote with a question of confidence to force its proposals through the legislative process.

The Constitutional Council

As is the case in most parliamentary systems of government, France has no active tradition of judicial review in politics.[47] Despite this, the Constitutional Council of the Fifth Republic was designed (Articles 56–63 of the Constitution) "to ensure that constitutional provisions would possess a certain superiority over ordinary laws." Its function is to rule on the standing orders of the legislature and, on request of the Government majority (but not a legislative minority), to determine the boundaries of executive and legislative competence and "whether laws . . . or treaties are in conformity with the constitution."[48] It also is required to supervise presidential and parliamentary elections, as well as referenda.

Many in 1958 feared the creation of a Constitutional Council because it sounded very much like the US Supreme Court; the powers of the US Supreme Court were thought to be too sweeping to transplant to the French system. The fears of an activist judiciary have not been realized, however, primarily because the members of the Constitutional Council were generally sympathetic to Government policy. Three of the nine regular judges are appointed by the president, three by the president of the National Assembly, and three by the president of the Senate. The nine judges serve nine-year terms. Former presidents of the Republic are on the Constitutional Council for life terms, as well.

The bulk of the Constitutional Council's work has been in adjudicating jurisdictional disputes between the presidency and the legislature "over boundaries of law and regulation." The Constitutional Council so consistently ruled on behalf of the president's point of view that it became perceived as an "auxiliary of executive authority."[49]

The Council is most frequently consulted today on the questions of the constitutionality of legislation. This is one dimension of its power that has grown in recent years, increasing the status of the Constitutional Council to more nearly that of the US Supreme Court.

Political Parties and Elections

There have traditionally been a number of political parties active in the French political system. In modern times, it was not until the Fifth Republic that a true majority party existed in France, the Union for a New Republic–Democratic Union for the Republic (UNR-UDR).[50] Throughout French history, the political party systems that existed failed to provide a basis for stable elections; the parties failed to govern.[51]

General Charles de Gaulle, in his criticisms of the Government in the Fourth Republic, described this anarchic situation of no responsible government and no responsible opposition as *"le regime des partis."*[52] It was, strictly speaking, a regime *with* parties, not a regime *of* parties. Party *control* (in the sense of stable party government) of the regime did not come until de Gaulle's supporters won parliamentary majorities in the Fifth Republic.

Gaullism and Presidential Leadership

Certainly among the most significant phenomena in the French party system was the rise of the Gaullist "nonparty" that became the significant political organization of the regime. Originally, **Gaullism** was a movement of support for Charles de Gaulle that claimed to be an alternative to divisive political parties; both organizationally and ideologically it insisted upon being regarded simply as a following for de Gaulle. Its ideology was the ideology of de Gaulle; its organization was designed to further the interests and goals of de Gaulle. It "pretended not to be a party at all, but rather a national *movement,* an alternative to parties."[53]

The Gaullist ideology was perceived as a rightist ideology, but it was able to draw from the political left as well as the right, because of de Gaulle's antiparliamentary attitudes, shared with the French Communist Party (PCF), his positive view of the Church, which was shared with the Popular Republican Movement, and his commitment to plebiscitary democracy and frequent referenda, generally a left-wing attitude. In 1962 the Union for a New Republic, in fact the Gaullist party of its day, combined with a generally conservative working-class party called the Democratic Union of Labor to form the Democratic Union for the Republic.

When de Gaulle left the political scene and Georges Pompidou, his former prime minister, became president, the Gaullist movement weakened somewhat, but not as much or as rapidly as many had predicted would be the case.[54] Many had claimed that the UDR—the Democratic Union for the Republic, the descendent of the UNR—and Gaullism in general were simply personalistic followings for de Gaulle; as soon as de Gaulle left politics, the critics said, the Gaullists as a political bloc would fall apart.

Pompidou reigned over the demise of the UDR between 1970 and 1974. By the time of the parliamentary elections in 1973, the UDR had so weakened that it joined with the Independent Republicans and the Center of Democracy and Progress (CDP) in an electoral alliance called the Union of Republicans for Progress (URP), but even with that its parliamentary representation fell from 273 seats in 1968 to 185 in 1973.

With the election of **Valérie Giscard d'Estaing** as president in 1974, the UDR became an "also-ran." Giscard, an Independent Republican, drew a good deal of what was left in the UDR to his party, the Independent Republican Party. The Giscard years were associated with economic liberalism, a theme of national unity, and a "more liberal functioning of institutions,"[55] the latter including a slight increase of the power of the parliament compared to earlier regimes.

The year 1981 saw the rise to prominence of the Socialist Party under President François Mitterrand. In the 1981 campaign many of the principle issues were economic, and Mitterrand was able to convince a majority of the French voters that they should give the political left a chance to lead France. Mitterrand became the first Socialist to be elected president, and as indicated earlier he immediately dissolved the National Assembly and called for new elections so that he could have a Socialist-dominated Assembly to help enact his program. The Socialists, riding on the coattails of the newly elected president, won a clear majority (262 of the 491 seats), and with their non-Communist allies controlled 285 seats in the National Assembly. With a clear majority in the legislature, Mitterrand was able to implement a number of socialist policies.[56]

The perception at the time was that the "intention of the French Socialist administration, presided over by Mitterrand, was 'to give the state back to the people.'"[57] Mitterrand believed that centralization had been necessary in the creation of France, but at the time of his election decentralization was necessary for the future of France. Mitterrand was a political realist, recognizing that the forces that elected him were as much a response to the economic climate of the time as they were indications of fundamental agreement with his ideology.[58]

Public reaction against the Mitterrand Government and some of its policies led to a decline in public support for the Socialists. In local elections in 1982 and 1983 many of the supporters who had worked so hard for Mitterrand in 1981 supported conservative candidates, and the conservative parties made great progress. In the long view, "the years of socialist government did not produce the revolution of which many of its supporters dreamed."[59] Social inequality and injustice did not disappear; the economy did not expand as promised.

In March 1986 the "French socialist experience"[60] came to an end with a conservative victory in the elections for the National Assembly, resulting in the cohabitation arrangement between Socialist president Mitterrand and conservative Prime Minister Chirac discussed earlier. The conservatives thought that this was a foreshadowing of a presidential victory for their candidate in 1988, but such was not the case: President Mitterrand, with a much more economically moderate and ideologically toned-down campaign than he had run in 1981, defeated Prime Minister Chirac, who was running against him for the presidency, and won reelection in 1988.

Mitterrand's term in office was followed in 1995 by the election of Chirac as president. Chirac ran for office promising tax cuts, but the economy did not cooperate, and he and his prime minister, Alain Juppé, were not able to honor their campaign promises. In 1997 Chirac dissolved parliament prematurely and called for early elections in a bid to increase support for his economic program. Unfortunately, the public did not approve of this course of action and the strategy backfired; in the subsequent election of 1997 the Socialist Party and other parties on the left defeated Chirac's conservative allies, forcing Chirac into a new period of cohabitation with Socialist leader Lionel Jospin as prime minister.

In 2002, at age sixty-nine, Chirac ran for a second term as president. He received the support of less than 20 percent of the voters in the first round of voting in April 2002. Most observers had expected that he would face incumbent (Socialist) prime minister Lionel Jospin in the second round of voting; instead, the candidate receiving the second-highest vote total in the first round was controversial far-right politician Jean-Marie Le Pen of the law-and-order, anti-immigrant National Front. When the second round took place, Chirac won reelection by a landslide, receiving over 80 percent of the vote; most parties outside the National Front had called for opposing Le Pen, even if it meant voting for Chirac. Following his reelection, Chirac sought to reorganize politics on the right, establishing a new party, initially called the Union of the Presidential Majority, then the Union for a Popular Movement (UMP), to take the place of the former Rally for the Republic. The UMP won the parliamentary elections that followed the presidential poll with ease, a point to which we shall return shortly.

The 2007 election was seen as a generational election. Both **Nicolas Sarkozy** (UMP) and Ségolène Royal (Socialist) were born after

World War II. The results of the first round of voting saw Sarkozy and Royal qualify for the second round, with Sarkozy getting 31 percent and Royal 26 percent of the votes. In the voting for the second round, Sarkozy received 53 percent of the votes to Royal's 47 percent.[61] Sarkozy's term in office included such challenges as the financial crisis of the late 2000s and economic recession in Europe, and the Arab Spring (with France having significant relations with three of the key nations, Tunisia, Libya, and Syria).

In 2012 Sarkozy sought reelection but was defeated by **François Hollande**, the candidate of the Socialist Party, by a margin of 52 to 48 percent.[62] Two years later Sarkozy ran for the position of leader of the UMP and was elected; shortly thereafter the UMP changed its name to the Republicans. In 2016 Sarkozy announced his candidacy for the 2016 Republican presidential primary, but he came in third in the party primary behind François Fillon and Alain Juppé; he subsequently retired from politics.

François Hollande's major achievements during his five-year term of office involved legalizing same-sex marriage, pulling France out of the Afghanistan military conflict, and guiding France's response to the 2015 Paris terrorist attacks. In 2016 he announced that he would not seek reelection in 2017, and he later endorsed Emmanuel Macron for the position.

Emmanuel Macron is of a new generation of French politicians; he rose through business and political positions to serve as deputy secretary-general in François Hollande's first government in 2012, and served as minister of economy, industry, and digital affairs in 2014 under the second government of Hollande. He ran for president in 2017 as a member of En Marche!, a political party he created in April 2016. As we will see, he won the election in May 2017, and a month later his party (renamed La République En Marche!) won the parliamentary elections, giving him a majority in the National Assembly.

French Political Parties

Most contemporary texts dealing with French politics[63] discuss the party system in terms of component parties and move from left to right (or right to left) along the political spectrum describing the respective ideologies and policy positions of the many contemporary French parties.[64] Because of the nature of the electoral system—a point to which we return shortly—many parties have decided that although they are not going to merge permanently with one another, their views are sufficiently similar so that they should not compete against one another in elections. This kind of attitude gave rise to the Union of Republicans for

Progress in 1973, leading to a coordination of candidacies around France among the Independent Republican Party, the Democratic Union for the Republic, and the Center for Democracy and Progress. The same thing happened in the elections of 1978 and 1981 with the French Democratic Union (UDF), resulting from coordination between the Republican Party (PR, formed by Giscard from the Independent Republican Party in 1977), the Center for Social Democrats (CDS, a new party organized from the earlier CDP), and some others. In both 1988 and 1993 the Union for French Democracy and the Rally for the Republic contested the elections jointly as the Union of the Rally and of the Center (URC). Subsequently, many of the various right-wing parties joined the URC prior to the second ballot.

Another more recent phenomenon involved the development of the National Front (FN), led originally by Jean-Marie Le Pen and now by his daughter Marine Le Pen.[65] The National Front has been variously labeled as "extreme right" and "neo-Nazi," and has campaigned strongly in favor of statism and against foreigners. The issues of ultra-nationalism, isolationism, and anti-immigrant policy are not limited to France, of course,[66] and Marine Le Pen has continued to be a vocal and visible political force in France. She was in the final round of voting for president in 2017 and, like her father in earlier elections, was defeated by the combined force of all major French political parties, even those that had opposed Macron in the first round of voting.

Elections to the National Assembly

If France were a "typical" parliamentary system, we would have only elections to the national legislature to study at this point, because the selection of the head of state would not be politically significant, and the selection of the chief executive would automatically follow the leader of the majority in the lower house of the national legislature. However, because of the 1962 referendum—deciding to have the president directly elected by the citizenry rather than indirectly elected by a complex electoral college—any discussion of French elections must include both presidential and parliamentary elections. We will begin our brief discussion with the National Assembly, move to the presidency, and conclude with a discussion of selection of senators.

French elections for the National Assembly are for terms of five years (or less if the Assembly is dissolved early) and for the most part have been based upon a majority approach to voting rather than a plurality approach (the latter being the case in Great Britain or the United States). That is, in electoral contests for the National Assembly the initial question that is asked on election day after the polls close is not

"Who received the most votes?" The reader will recall that in single-member-district plurality voting systems, the candidate who receives the most votes is the winner; if there are six candidates and the candidate with the most votes receives only 25 percent of the total vote, that candidate is elected even though 75 percent of the public did not vote for him or her. In majority-based elections such as we find in France, unlike the plurality-based elections, to win a race on the first ballot one must receive a majority of the vote, one more than half of the votes cast.

As mentioned earlier, French elections for the National Assembly have "for the most part been based upon a majority approach" because for about one year—from March 1986 until June 1987—the electoral system was changed from universal direct election to a proportional representation electoral system (that is, proportional representation within departments, not nationally, with a 5 percent threshold necessary for election).[67] Proportional representation replaced the single-member-district model when it became clear to President Mitterrand that his Socialist Party faced an overwhelming rejection by the voters in the election of March 1986.

With the majority voting system and only 30 percent support from the public, the Socialists would very likely have become a very tiny minority in the Assembly. With a change of the rules for elections to a system of proportional representation voting, the Socialists won 206 out of 577 seats in the National Assembly, but the parties of the right still controlled a majority in the Assembly and a conservative Government was formed. This resulted in the period of cohabitation referred to earlier. The system of proportional representation elections angered the political elite and brought about a commitment by the new government to get rid of it again. Within a year of the election the new conservative-dominated Government restored the former majority-based district voting electoral system.

When the presidential elections were held in April and May 1988 and President Mitterrand was reelected, he again—much as he did immediately after his first electoral victory seven years earlier—dissolved the National Assembly and called for new elections. Again, as in 1981, the French public gave the left a majority in the Assembly, although the Socialist Party alone did not receive the outright majority in 1988 that it did in 1981, and it had to make arrangements with the Communists[68] to maintain a majority.

Two years after being elected president in 1995, President Jacques Chirac decided to dissolve the National Assembly in 1997 and call for early elections—a year before their "normal" time—feeling that he could revitalize the right-of-center majority in the National Assembly. The right believed that in taking the left by surprise they could minimize their losses and hold on to a clear majority for a new five-year term, enough time to meet the challenges of moving France into the European Union and meeting the strict criteria set up by the Maastricht Treaty for countries to meet to gain entry to the single European currency. As was also noted earlier, the strategy did not work and the 1997 Assembly was dominated by the Socialists.

In December 2000 the National Assembly—three years into its five-year term and controlled by the Socialist Party—voted to reverse the order of the next scheduled elections that had been planned for the spring of 2002, having the presidential election precede the parliamentary election rather than the other way around. As noted earlier, in the September 2000 referendum the voters of France decided to reduce the presidential term from seven years to five years. One of the arguments in favor of this change was that since the elections for the parliament and the president would be held in the same year (with both the National Assembly and the president having five-year terms, the assumption was that they would be held at nearly the same time), the likelihood was that cohabitation would disappear, since it would be less likely that one party would win the presidency and a different party would control the Assembly.

Analysts suggested that if the presidential election were held first the Socialists would be more likely to win, thereby increasing the likelihood that they would also control the Assembly. They also suggested that the (conservative) Rally for the Republic (RPR) was more likely to gain control of the Assembly if the elections for that body were held first, thereby helping the RPR to continue to control the presidency.

As noted earlier, because of the appearance of Jean-Marie Le Pen in the race, Chirac was overwhelmingly reelected to a second term, and he restructured the party system on the political right to replace the RPR as the major right-wing political party with a new organization called the Union for a Presidential Majority, later called the Union for a Popular Movement.[69]

Given the number of political parties in the French electoral system, it is clear that few candidates will win majorities outright. This has led to France's unique two-ballot simple-majority system of voting.[70] The first election is held on a Sunday, and any candidate who receives an absolute majority (50 percent of the vote plus one vote) of the total votes cast in their district is elected on the first round of voting, providing they receive the votes of at least one-quarter of the number of registered voters in the constituency.[71] If no candidate wins a majority on the first ballot—which is the case in most constituencies—a second ballot is held on the following Sunday. At that time, whichever candidate receives a plurality of the votes (that is, more votes than anyone else) is declared the winner. (See Table 9.3.)

Being elected to the National Assembly on the first ballot is the exception rather than the rule. In the Assembly election of 2017, the most recent elections, only 4 of the 577 races were resolved in the first round of voting, a bit under 1 percent of the total.[72]

When the second round of elections is held, no new candidate for office may register. In order to contest the second ballot, a candidate

Table 9.3   The Parliamentary Election in France of June 11 and June 18, 2017

Party	Percentage of Votes in First Round (number of seats won)	Percentage of Votes in Second Round (number of seats won)	Number of Seats After Second Round (% total)
Republic on the Move (REM)	28.1 (2)	43.1 (306)	308 (53.4)
Republicans (LR)	15.8	22.2 (112)	112 (19.4)
Democratic Movement, Modem (MDM)	4.1	6.1 (42)	42 (7.3)
Socialist Party (PS)	7.4	5.7 (30)	30 (5.2)
Union of Democrats and Independents (UDI)	3.0 (1)	3.0 (17)	18 (3.1)
France Unbowed (FI)	11.3	4.9 (17)	17 (2.9)
Other left-wing (DVG)	1.6 (1)	1.4 (11)	12 (2.1)
French Communist (COM)	2.7	1.2 (10)	10 (1.7)
National Front (FN)	13.2	8.8 (8)	8 (1.4)
Other right-wing (DVD)	2.8	1.7 (6)	6 (1.0)
Regionalist (REG)	0.9	0.8 (5)	5 (0.8)
Others (DIV)	2.2	0.6 (3)	3 (0.5)
Left Radical	0.5	0.4 (3)	3 (0.5)
Stand Up France (DLF)	1.2	0.1 (1)	1 (0.2)
Ecologist (ECO)	4.3	0.1 (1)	1 (0.2)
Far Right (EXD)	0.3	0.1 (1)	1 (0.2)
Far Left (EXG)	0.7	—	0
Total	100.1 (4)	100.2 (573)	577 (99.9)

Voter turnout
First round: 48.8% (23.2 million of 47.5 million eligible)
Second round: 42.7% (20.2 million of 47.3 million eligible)

Source: Ministry of the Interior, "Résultats des Élections Législatives 2017," https://www.interieur.gouv.fr/Elections/Les-resultats/Legislatives/elecresult__legislatives-2017/(path)/legislatives-2017/FE.html.

must have received 12.5 percent of the vote on the first round (this was raised from 10 percent in the 1978 election). If only one candidate receives over 12.5 percent of the votes cast on the first ballot, the person who receives the second largest number of votes on the first ballot may also participate in the second ballot, in which only a simple majority is needed to win. Although this means that technically several candidates could compete in the second round of voting (since more than two candidates could receive 12.5 percent of the vote on the first round), most second ballots turn out to be duels between two parties because of the alliances mentioned earlier.

Preelectoral alliances/agreements have had the effect in many cases of turning the first ballot into a type of primary election, in which a number of candidates from the left may compete, and a number of candidates from the right may compete, with the understanding that the top vote-getter from the left will represent the left, and the top vote-getter from the right will represent the right.

In the most recent election, June 11 and 18, 2017, President Macron's Republic on the Move (République en Marche) won an outright majority in the National Assembly, winning 350 of the 577 seats with the support of the Democratic Movement (Modem). A record 224 women were elected to the body, up from a previous record of 155 women in 2012.

Presidential Elections

In presidential elections a candidate must receive an absolute majority of the public votes in order to win on the first ballot. This has never happened in Fifth Republic France; the most votes that Charles de Gaulle ever received on the first ballot was 44 percent of the total votes cast. As can be seen in Table 9.4, in the 2017 election to replace François Hollande as president for a five-year term, with eleven candidates in the race the winner Emmanuel Macron received just over 24 percent of the first-ballot votes, and Marine Le Pen received just over 21 percent of the votes. The second ballot is limited to the top two vote-getters from the first round and takes place two weeks after the first round of voting. In that race, with most of the major parties endorsing Macron because of strong objections to the nationalist, racist, and isolationist tone of Le Pen's positions, Macron received over 66 percent of the votes compared with Le Pen's almost 34 percent of the votes.

Election of Senators

The selection of senators differs from the single-member-district majority-voting selection of deputies to the National Assembly. Senators are intended to represent the administrative/territorial units of France, and

Table 9.4   France's Presidential Election of April 23 and May 7, 2017

Candidate	Party	Percentage of Votes
First round, April 23, 2017		
Emmanuel Macron	En Marche! (EM)	24.0
Marine Le Pen	National Front (FN)	21.3
François Fillon	Republicans (LR)	20.0
Jean-Luc Mélenchon	France Unbowed (FI)	19.6
Benoît Hamon	Socialist Party (PS)	6.4
Nicolas Dupont-Aignan	Stand Up France (DLF)	4.7
Jean Lassalle	Resist!	1.2
Philippe Poutou	New Anticapitalist (NPA)	1.1
François Asselineau	Popular Republican Union (UPR)	0.9
Nathalie Arthaud	Workers' Struggle (LO)	0.6
Jacques Cheminade	Solidarity and Progress (S&P)	0.2
Total: 37,003,728 votes cast		100.00
Second round, May 7, 2017		
Emmanuel Macron	En Marche! (EM)	66.1
Marine Le Pen	National Front (FN)	33.9
Total: 35,467,327 votes cast		100.0
Number of registered voters: 47,568,693		

Source: Ministry of the Interior, "Résultats de l'Élection Présidentielle 2017," https://www
.interieur.gouv.fr/Elections/Les-resultats/Presidentielles/elecresult__presidentielle-2017
/(path)/presidentielle-2017/FE.html.

the method of their selection reflects this. They are elected by *grands électeurs*—individuals who hold elected office in some other governmental structure (e.g., mayors, members of the National Assembly, local councilors, and the like)—and thus senators are only indirectly representative of the population.

The French Senate is currently going through an evolutionary transformation, moving from a structure in the past in which senators were elected for nine-year terms and one-third of the Senate was elected every three years, to a structure in which senators will serve a six-year term and half of the chamber will be replaced every three years.

Senators are elected from departments by electoral colleges. These electoral colleges range from 270 electors in smaller departments to over 6,000 electors in the larger departments, depending upon the population of the department. Deputies in the National Assembly from districts in a given department, departmental councilors, and delegates chosen by municipal councils all comprise these electoral colleges. Thus the Senate is elected by the 577 National Assembly deputies, about 3,000 *conseillers généraux,* and about 100,000 delegates from the municipal councils.[73] (See Table 9.5.)

The larger departments (seven in all) elect five or more senators; smaller departments choose fewer. In the departments that choose five or more senators, senators are chosen by proportional representation voting: electors vote for a party list, and parties receive a number of senatorial positions corresponding to the proportion of the vote they received. In the smaller departments, senators are elected on a two-ballot system very similar to elections for the National Assembly: a majority is required on the first ballot, and a plurality is required on the second ballot.

Within the Senate, senators belong to "political groups" for their work assignments. Political groups must have at least ten members in order to participate in organizational and formal responsibilities, so Table 9.5 reflects some combinations of political parties that have taken place to meet the ten-seat minimum.[74]

As mentioned, the Senate is often referred to as an "agricultural chamber" because of its uneven representation of the French population. "Rural France is overrepresented and urban France is under-represented in the Senate." For example, "the eight departments of the Paris Region, plus five other departments which each had more than one million inhabitants . . . contain one-third of the French population, and while

Table 9.5   The Senate in France in the October 2017 Election by Political Group

Political Group	Number of Seats
Republican	146
Socialist and Republican	78
Centrist Union	49
Republique en Marche!	21
European Democratic and Social Rally	21
Communist, Republican, Citizen, and Ecologist	15
Republic and Territories/Independents	11
Others	5
Total	348
Number of women: 75 (21.9% of total)	

Source: Government of France, Senate, "Groupes Politiques," http://www.senat.fr/grp/index.html.

they have 32 percent of the . . . seats in the National Assembly, they have only 26 percent of such seats in the Senate."[75]

The French System in Perspective

We have seen in this chapter that the French political system can almost be seen as a variation of the Westminster model of government in several respects, many of them quite significant. The dual executive, although resembling the British model on paper, is quite different in its actual day-to-day behavior and power structure. The French president is virtually unique in the parliamentary world (except for political systems modeled after France), having both in theory and in practice all of the power that the British monarchy has only in theory.

The French Constitution is partially responsible for this. When Charles de Gaulle and his colleagues designed the constitutional structures in the Fifth Republic, they took pains to provide for strong executive leadership—to a large extent to compensate for years of weak executives and strong, and uncontrollable, legislatures. The fact that the legislatures in both the Third and Fourth Republics were unstable foundations upon which to base a government was not lost on the founders of the Fifth Republic.

The legislative bodies of the Fifth Republic are typical of other parliamentary legislatures in a number of respects. First, of course, they are inferior to the executive branch of government. The legislature is not expected to be a major policymaking body in the political system. Its function is to approve the policies of the executive and, if the executive becomes too unpopular, to replace the Government. Second, the upper house of the legislature is inferior to the lower house of the legislature. Ultimately, the Senate can have only a suspensory veto over the actions of the National Assembly; it can slow down the actions of that house, but it cannot prevent National Assembly legislation from becoming law.

French elections differ from elections in other political systems because of the single-member-district majority-voting system used for the National Assembly, and the two-wave voting for the presidency. Again, we can see that the structure of the electoral system can have an impact upon the political party system in a country. France has a number of political parties, not just one or two, and these parties do their best to operate within the rules of the Fifth Republic's electoral system.

In the case of France, then, we have seen a number of applications of the material described in Part 1 of this volume. Constitutions, executives, legislatures, electoral systems, and political parties all matter in the day-to-day operation of a political regime. We will continue to see in the chapters that follow that some of the idiosyncratic features of political regimes are of tremendous significance in the daily operation of government.

Discussion Questions

1. What were the political behaviors from the Third Republic that France particularly wanted to avoid in the Fifth Republic? What from the Fourth Republic? Was there agreement on the problems of the earlier regimes?
2. How was de Gaulle's role in the creation of the Fifth Republic special? How did the de Gaulle constitution particularly reflect the values of de Gaulle? What were the issues that were most important to him?
3. What are the special characteristics of unitary government in France? How is French unitary government different from unitary government in Britain, for example?
4. How does the French executive structure compare with other parliamentary executives? What are the powers of the French president that are unusual for parliamentary heads of state? What are the president's most unusual powers?
5. How has the operation of cohabitation affected the way that French politics has operated in recent years? Is this a structure that is good for France?
6. How would you compare the French legislative process to the legislative process in other systems? Is the French model more or less efficient? Why?

Notes

1. For discussion of French political history prior to the Third Republic, see William Fortescue, *The Third Republic in France, 1870–1940: Conflicts and Continuities* (London: Routledge, 2000); and Edward Berenson, Vincent Duclert, and Christophe Prochasson, *The French Republic: History, Values, Debates* (Ithaca: Cornell University Press, 2011).

2. William Safran, *The French Polity,* 2nd ed. (New York: Routledge, 2016), p. 5. See also Robert Lynn Fuller, *The Origins of the French Nationalist Movement, 1886–1914* (Jefferson, NC: McFarland, 2012).

3. John Ambler, *The Government and Politics of France* (Boston: Houghton Mifflin, 1971), p. 7. See also Robert Young, *An Uncertain Idea of France: Essays and Reminiscence on the Third Republic* (New York: Lang, 2005).

4. Further discussion of this period can be found in Gwendolen Carter, *The Government of France* (New York: Harcourt, Brace, Jovanovich, 1972), pp. 22–23; and Ambler, *Government and Politics of France,* p. 7. See also James Lehning, *To Be a Citizen: The Political Culture of the Early French Third Republic* (Ithaca: Cornell University Press, 2001).

5. See Robert Paxton, *Vichy France: Old Guard and New Order, 1940–1944* (New York: Columbia University Press, 2001). See also Michael Curtis, *Verdict on Vichy: Power and Prejudice in the Vichy France Regime* (New York: Arcade, 2002).

6. Carter, *Government of France,* p. 25. See also N. J. G. Wright and H. S. Jones, *Pluralism and the Idea of the Republic in France* (New York: Palgrave Macmillan, 2012).

7. Ambler, *Government and Politics of France,* p. 10.

8. The best general discussions of problems and performances of the Fourth Republic are to be found in two sources: Philip Williams, *Crisis and Compromise: Politics in the Fourth Republic* (New York: Doubleday, 1966); and Duncan MacRae, *Parliament, Parties, and Society in France: 1946–1958* (New York: St. Martin's, 1967).

9. Ambler, *Government and Politics of France,* p. 11.

10. Roy Pierce, *French Politics and Political Institutions* (New York: Harper and Row, 1968), p. 44. See Tony Chafer, *The End of Empire in French West Africa: France's Successful Decolonization?* (New York: Berg, 2002); and Anthony Clayton, *The Wars of French Decolonization* (London: Routledge, 2013).

11. Safran, *French Polity,* p. 11. On the crisis in Algeria, see Martin Evans, *Algeria: France's Undeclared War* (New York: Oxford University Press, 2012). On DeGaulle, see Daniel Mahoney, *DeGaulle: Statesmanship, Grandeur, and Modern Democracy* (London: Transaction, 2000). De Gaulle's autobiographical *The Complete War Memoirs of Charles de Gaulle* (New York: Carroll and Graf, 1998) is also worth noting.

12. Ambler, *Government and Politics of France,* p. 13.

13. See the text of de Gaulle's Bayeux speech in Martin Harrison, ed., *French Politics* (Lexington, MA: Heath, 1969), pp. 24–28.

14. Safran, *French Polity,* p. 59. See Sophie Boyron, *The Constitution of France: A Contextual Analysis* (Portland: Hart, 2013); and David Marrani, *Dynamics in the French Constitution: Decoding French Republican Ideas* (Abingdon: Routledge, 2013).

15. Roy C. Macridis, *French Politics in Transition* (Cambridge, MA: Winthrop, 1975), p. 6. See also David Scott Bell, *Presidential Power in the Fifth Republic of France* (New York: Berg, 2000).

16. On the origins and drafting of the new constitution, see the article by Nicholas Wahl and Stanley Hoffman, "The French Constitution of 1958," *American Political Science Review* 53 (1959): 332–382.

17. Suzanne Berger, *The French Political System* (New York: Random, 1974), p. 126; much of the material in this section, and all quotes unless otherwise noted, derive from this Berger source, pp. 126–131. See Nicholas Atkins, *The Fifth French Republic* (New York: Palgrave Macmillan, 2004).

18. See John A. Rohr, "French Constitutionalism and the Administrative State: A Comparative Textual Study," *Administration and Society* 24, no. 2 (1992): 224–240.

19. Berger, *French Political System,* p. 127. See also Vincent Wright and Andrew Knapp, *The Government and Politics of France* (New York: Routledge, 2006).

20. Henry Ehrmann, *Politics in France* (Boston: Little, Brown, 1976), p. 267. See also Jonathan Fenby, *The General: Charles de Gaulle and the France He Saved* (New York: Skyhorse, 2013).

21. Safran, *French Polity,* p. 128. See also William R. Nester, *DeGaulle's Legacy: The Art of Power in France's Fifth Republic* (New York: Palgrave Macmillan, 2014).

22. Leslie Derfler, *President and Parliament: A Short History of the French Presidency* (Boca Raton: University Presses of Florida, 1983), p. 169. See also Michael Haskew, *DeGaulle: Lessons in Leadership from the Defiant General* (New York: Palgrave Macmillan, 2011).

23. Ambler, *Government and Politics of France,* p. 126.

24. For the full text of the Constitution, see Pierce, *French Politics and Political Institutions,* pp. 227–254; or Ambler, *Government and Politics of France,* pp. 237–248.

25. John-Thor Dahlburg, "French Deliver a Yawn on Shorter Presidential Term," *Los Angeles Times,* September 25, 2000, http://articles.latimes.com/2000/sep/25/news/mn-26504.

26. Ehrmann, *Politics in France,* p. 268. See also John Gaffney, *Political Leadership in France: From Charles de Gaulle to Nicolas Sarkozy* (Basingstoke: Palgrave Macmillan, 2012); and David Bell and John Gaffney, *The Presidents of the French Fifth Republic* (Houndmills: Palgrave Macmillan, 2013).

27. See de Gaulle's essay "Charles de Gaulle and the Presidency," in Harrison, *French Politics,* pp. 48–54.

28. On the change to a five-year term of office, see the book by Olivier Duhamel, *France's New Five-Year Presidential Term* (Washington, DC: Brookings Institution, 2001). See Michael Lewis-Beck, Richard Nadeau, and Eric Bélanger, *French Presidential Elections* (New York: Palgrave Macmillan, 2012).

29. Olivier Duhamel, "France's New Five-Year Presidential Term," March 1, 2001, http://www.brookings.edu/articles/frances-new-five-year-presidential-term/.

30. Ibid.

31. Ehrmann, *Politics in France,* p. 269. See also Michael S. Lewis-Beck, *The French Voter: Before and After the 2002 Elections* (New York: Palgrave Macmillan, 2004).

32. Ehrmann, *Politics in France,* pp. 270–272.

33. Carter, *Government of France,* p. 81. See also Serge Berstein and Jean-Pierre Rioux, *The Pompidou Years, 1969–1974* (New York: Cambridge University Press, 2000).

34. Safran, *French Polity,* p. 130; or Carter, *Government of France,* p. 83.

35. See John Frears, "Cohabitation," in Howard Penniman, ed., *France at the Polls, 1981 and 1986: Three National Elections* (Durham: Duke University Press, 1988). See also Sebastien Lazardeux, *Cohabitation and Conflicting Politics in French Policymaking* (New York: Palgrave Macmillan, 2015).

36. See Christiane Gouaud, *La Cohabitation* (Paris: Ellipses, 1996).

37. Carter, *Government of France,* p. 75. See also Connie Doebele and Kevin King, *French Politics and the French Parliament* (West Lafayette, IN: C-SPAN Archives, 2003).

38. Carter, *Government of France,* p. 75. See also Pierce, *French Politics and Political Institutions,* p. 87.

39. Pierce, *French Politics and Political Institutions,* pp. 78–79. See also Gerhard Loewenberg, *British and French Parliaments in Comparative Perspective* (New Brunswick, NJ: Aldine, 2010).

40. Philip E. Converse and Roy Pierce, *Political Representation in France* (Cambridge: Harvard University Press, 1986), p. 533. See also Magnus Blomgren and Olivier Rozenberg, *Parliamentary Roles in Modern Legislatures* (New York: Routledge, 2012).

41. Carter, *Government of France,* p. 72.

42. Pierce, *French Politics and Political Institutions,* p. 91.

43. Carter, *Government of France,* p. 72. See also Pierce, *French Politics and Political Institutions,* p. 91; or Olivier Costa, *Parliamentary Representation in France* (London: Routledge, 2013).

44. "The Senate's Role: The Senate Votes the Law," https://www.senat.fr/lng/en/the_senates_role/the_senate_votes_the_law.html.

45. See Paul Smith, *A History of the French Senate* (Lewiston, NY: Mellen, 2005–2006).

46. Safran, *French Polity,* p. 165.

47. See Alec Stone, "Where Judicial Politics Are Legislative Politics: The French Constitutional Council," *West European Politics* 15, no. 3 (1992): 29–43; or Carter, *Government of France,* p. 324.

48. Carter, *Government of France,* pp. 32–33.

49. Berger, *French Political System,* p. 57; or Pierce, *French Politics and Political Institutions,* p. 80.

50. Carter, *Government of France,* p. 39. See Andrew Knapp, *Parties and the Party System in France: A Disconnected Democracy?* (New York: Palgrave Macmillan, 2004).

51. J. R. Frears, *Political Parties and Elections in the French Fifth Republic* (New York: St. Martin's, 1977), p. 12. See also Robert Elgie, *The Changing French Political System* (Portland: Cass, 2000); Ehrmann, *Politics in France,* pp. 223–224; and David Scott Bell, *Parties and Democracy in France* (Brookfield, VT: Ashgate, 2000).

52. Frears, *Political Parties,* p. 12. See D. L. Hanley, *Party, Society, and Government: Republican Democracy in France* (New York: Berghahn, 2002).

53. Safran, *French Polity,* p. 68. See also Alistair Cole, Patrick le Galès, and Jonah D. Levy, *Developments in French Politics,* vol. 3 (New York: Palgrave Macmillan, 2005).

54. D. L. Hanley, A. P. Kerr, and N. H. Waites, *Contemporary France: Politics and Society Since 1945* (Boston: Routledge and Kegan Paul, 1979), p. 41. See also Berstein and Rioux, *Pompidou Years.*

55. J. R. Frears, *France in the Giscard Presidency* (London: Allen and Unwin, 1981), p. 162. See also Vincent Wright, ed., *Continuity and Change in France* (London: Allen and Unwin, 1984), for a collection of essays offering a general description of the Giscard years.

56. A very good book about François Mitterrand written before his candidacy is that by C. L. Manceron and B. Pingaud, *Francois Mitterrand: L'Homme, les Idees, le Programme* (Paris: Flammarion, 1981).

57. Michael Keating and Paul Hainsworth, *Decentralisation and Change in Contemporary France* (Brookfield, VT: Gower, 1986), p. 15. See also Philip Short, *Mitterrand: A Study in Ambiguity* (London: Bodley Head, 2013).

58. Maurice Larkin, *France Since the Popular Front: Government and People, 1936–1986* (Oxford: Clarendon, 1988), p. 356; and John Tuppen, *France Under Recession, 1981–1986* (Albany: State University of New York Press, 1988), p. 1.

59. Tuppen, *France Under Recession,* p. 257.

60. Sonia Mezey and Michael Newman, eds., *Mitterrand's France* (London: Croom Helm, 1987), p. 4.

61. Nick Hewlett, *The Sarkozy Phenomenon* (Exeter: Societas, 2011).

62. Irwin M. Wall, *France Votes: The Election of Francois Hollande* (New York: Palgrave Macmillan, 2014). See also Jocelyn Evans and Gilles Ivaldi, *The 2012 French Presidential Elections: The Inevitable Alternation* (Basingstoke: Palgrave Macmillan, 2013); or Pascal Perrineau and Chantal de Barra, *The 2012 French Election: How the Electorate Decided* (New York: Palgrave Macmillan, 2016).

63. See David Hanley, *Party, Society, Government: Republican Democracy in France* (Oxford: Berghan, 2001).

64. A very good survey of French parties is by David S. Bell, ed., *Contemporary French Political Parties* (New York: St. Martin's, 1981). See also Richard Gunther, Jose Montero, and Juan Linz, *Political Parties: Old Concepts and New Challenges* (New York: Oxford University Press, 2002).

65. See N. Mayer and Pascal Perrimeau, "Why Do They Vote for LePen?" *European Journal of Political Research* 22, no. 1 (1992): 123–137; on Marine Le Pen, see Daniel Stockerner, *The Front National in France: Continuity and Change Under Jean-Marie Le Pen and Marine Le Pen* (Cham, Switzerland: Springer, 2017).

66. See Gabriella Lazaridis, Giovanna Campani, and Annie Benveniste, *Rise of the Far Right in Europe: Populist Shifts and "Othering"* (London: Palgrave Macmillan, 2016); or Andrea Mammone, Emmanuel Godin, and Brian Jenkins, *Varieties of Right-Wing Extremism in Europe* (New York: Routledge, 2013).

67. A description of the exact operation of this proportional representation system can be found in John Frears, "The 1986 Parliamentary Elections," in Penniman, *France at the Polls,* pp. 211–214.

68. A very good article on the French Communist Party is by George Ross, "Party Decline and Changing Party Systems: France and the French Communist Party," *Comparative Politics* 25, no. 1 (1992): 43–62.

69. "The French Political System: From 'Cohabitation' to a Five-Year Term," http://www.diplomatie.gouv.fr/en/france_159/institutions-and-politics_6814/the-french-political-system_6827/from-cohabitation-...to-five-year-term_12291.html.

70. See "France: Elections," http://www.ipu.org/parline-e/reports/2113_B.htm.

71. Unless turnout is very small and the candidate has received the votes of less than one-quarter of all of the registered electors.

72. See "Résultats des Élections Législatives 2017," https://www.interieur.gouv.fr/Elections/Les-resultats/Legislatives/elecresult__legislatives-2017/(path)/legislatives-2017//FE.html.

73. Frears, *Political Parties,* p. 224. Each department has a council, called the *conseil general,* which consists of from about twenty to seventy members who are elected from subdivisions of the department called *cantons.* Elections of departmental councilors (*conseillers generaux*) are called *elections cantonales.* Each city and town in France has a municipal council. Election of municipal councilors are called *elections municipales.* See Pierce, *French Politics and Political Institutions,* p. 75.

74. "The Political Groups," http://www.senat.fr/lng/en/organisation/the_political_groups.html.

75. Pierce, *French Politics and Political Institutions,* p. 75.

10

Germany

Learning Outcomes

After reading this chapter, you will be able to

- Explain how German political history, including the unification of the "two Germanys," affected the way politics operates in contemporary Germany.
- Understand how German federalism differs from other federal systems.
- Discuss the special nature of German executive structures.
- Appreciate how the German legislative process is different from other democratic legislatures' processes, and how it effectively represents German federalism.
- Explain the nature of coalition government in Germany.

When World War II ended in 1945, the four occupying powers (the United States, the United Kingdom, France, and the Soviet Union) agreed to work toward a reunification of occupied Germany. By December 1947, however, at the London Conference of the Council of Foreign Ministers of the four occupying powers, it was clear to the British, French, and Americans that the Soviet Union was not prepared to move to a reunification of Germany. Accordingly, the three Western powers decided to move forward and attempt to restore normal civilian government on their own.

Germany's Constitutional System

Many German leaders were concerned about this; they believed that such an action would result in a permanent division of Germany, with the Soviet Union controlling the eastern half of the country. Many West German leaders opposed the creation of a West German constitution until such time as Germany was reunified. After discussion, a compromise was reached: the West Germans agreed to construct a "temporary" constitution until Germany was reunified.

In September 1948, the Parliamentary Council met in Bonn and drafted a document called the **Basic Law** for the three Western-occupied zones. The Basic Law was to "give a new order to political life for a transitional period," and was not only for West Germans, but also "on behalf of those Germans to whom participation was denied." Article 146 stated that the Basic Law "shall cease to be in force on the day on which a constitution adopted by a free decision of the German people comes into force."[1] The document was drafted by representatives of the three Western occupying powers and West German leaders who were acceptable to the occupying powers.

The construction of the Basic Law was finally completed in May 1949. To avoid the appearance of establishing a permanent political system, it was never submitted to the West German people for ratification. Rather, it was submitted to legislatures of the West German states, the **Lander**, winning the endorsement of all of the West German Lander except Bavaria.[2] The West German Basic Law was finally approved on May 23, 1949. And just as many of the West German leaders had feared, the German Democratic Republic (East Germany) came into existence less than a month later.

Just over forty-one years later, on October 2, 1990, East and West Germany reunited after four decades of partition. The early years of the separation included a blockade of West Berlin; the most dramatic sign of the partition was a wall dividing the Eastern and Western parts of the city of Berlin. The reunited Germany, now the most populous and economically powerful nation in the European Community, adopted West Germany's constitutional system; the highly centralized political structures of communist East Germany disappeared. Many Germans were excited about reuniting East and West Germany, but at the same time were concerned about the costs of reunification.[3] In fact, among the challenges facing the newly reunited nation was the task of bringing the standard of living of Germans in the former German Democratic Republic (East Germany) up to that of the Federal Republic of Germany (West Germany). They also feared that their reunification and their new role as the largest and most economically powerful European nation might engender concern among other European nations.

Many details can be pointed out that distinguish the 1949 Basic Law from the 1919 Constitution of the **Weimar Republic**—the parliamentary republic established in Germany in 1919 to replace the imperial government—that preceded it. One of the major perceived shortcomings of the Weimar Constitution was that it promoted internal discord through a number of supposedly democratic structures, especially the power of the presidency and the mass plebiscites that were so frequently utilized. The Basic Law sought, through a number of political structures, to remedy the defect of "too much democracy"[4] in the earlier regime.

The Basic Law sought to modify German direct democracy while at the same time emphasizing the protection of human rights, individual liberty, and division of powers in a federal structure. Except in extraordinary circumstances, elections would be held every four years. Moreover, the public would vote only for representatives to the lower house of the legislature. The president, the chancellor, and members of the upper legislative house would all be chosen indirectly. Structures were established to make it more difficult to overthrow the chancellor—the chief executive in Germany.

Although the Basic Law sought to "dampen" many of the (perceived) "overly democratic" structures of the Weimar regime, it did not intend to restrict individual freedoms. To the contrary: articles of the Basic Law that deal with civil and political rights (Articles 1–19) are given a "preferred position"; as one scholar noted, "for the first time in German history, there were no loopholes left in the protection of individual rights."[5] Both Article 1, which focuses on human dignity, and Article 20, which guarantees Germans the "right to resist any person or persons seeking to abolish [the German] constitutional order," cannot be amended. Other articles dealing with civil and political rights cannot be suspended except after a ruling by the Federal Constitutional Court (Article 18).[6] The Basic Law can be amended by a two-thirds majority vote of each house of the federal legislature (subject to the limitations just mentioned), and it "has been altered more often in twenty-five years than the American [Constitution] in two hundred."[7]

Germany today has five key constitutional bodies that are significant in the political process. These are the Federal Constitutional Court, the federal presidency, the federal cabinet and chancellor, and the two chambers of the legislature, the Bundestag and the Bundesrat. After a brief discussion of German federalism we shall discuss each of these institutions here.

Federalism

Germany is the only major state of Western Europe that has a federal rather than a unitary political structure.[8] However, German federalism should not be a surprise. This is so for several reasons, including (1) a general fear of centralized government that developed during the Nazi period; (2) a history of federal and confederal relations in Germany, with the exception of the centralized Nazi era, going back to 1871 when the German Reich was formed and "composed of twenty-five 'historic' German states that 'voluntarily' entered into a federation";[9] and (3) the pattern of administration of the occupying powers from 1945 to 1949 that led to the creation of seven of today's sixteen states or Lander (the singular of the word *Lander* is *Land*). Three of today's Lander existed as separate political entities prior to 1945.[10] German federalism was "a device which perpetuated into the era of a single national state the particularist habits and traditions of the dynasties and estates which were dominant in the separate states of Germany."[11]

The federal nature of Germany has resulted in wide disparities among the intermediate levels of political organization. The Lander vary greatly in size and in population, as illustrated in Table 10.1, and these disparities increased significantly following unification of East and West Germany in 1990.[12]

There are both advantages and disadvantages to the German style of federalism. The drawbacks are that policy can vary from state to state, providing unequal opportunities across the nation. It is a complex system, resulting in a situation in which it is sometimes difficult to form an accurate picture of the seventeen different decisionmaking centers (sixteen states and the federal capital) in the Federal Republic of Germany.[13] It is time-consuming, requiring more discussion between government actors in the process of making policy. And it is more costly, because there is a required level of redundancy that doesn't exist in unitary systems. The advantages of federalism are that political power is divided, thus making it easier to protect against abuse of power. It is more democratic. It offers the public more choices where the selection of leadership is concerned. And it "guarantees a multiplicity of centres of economic, political and cultural influence."[14]

The German federal system, often referred to as an example of **cooperative federalism**,[15] gives the intermediate level components of the regime, the Lander, a great deal of political power—far more power than is found in US states, for example. Article 28 of the Basic Law requires that the Lander "conform to the principles of republican, democratic, and social government based on the rule of law," but leaves questions of specific governmental structure up to the state governments. The state of Bavaria has a bicameral legislature; all others have unicameral legislatures. States are allowed to determine their own electoral structures.

It can be suggested that a major reason that the Lander are as powerful as they are in the German political system is due to the different types of legislation discussed in the Basic Law. The Basic Law essen-

Table 10.1   Lander in the German Federal System

Land	Area (square miles)	Population (million)	Number of Bundesrat (Upper Chamber) Seats	Parties in Land (State) Government
Baden-Wurttemberg	13,739	10.89	6	CDU/Greens
Bavaria	27,114	12.84	6	CSU
Berlin[a]	184	3.52	4	SPD/Left/Greens
Brandenberg[a]	10,036	2.48	4	SPD/Left
Bremen	155	0.67	3	SPD/Greens
Hamburg	287	1.79	3	SPD/Greens
Hesse	8,113	6.18	5	CDU/Greens
Mecklenburg-Vorpommern[a]	8,685	1.61	3	SPD/CDU
Lower Saxony	18,127	7.78	6	SPD/CDU
N. Rhine–Westphalia	13,084	17.87	6	CDU/FDP
Rhineland-Palatinate	7,621	4.05	4	SPD/FDP/Greens
Saarland	987	1.00	3	CDU/SPD
Saxony[a]	6,562	4.08	4	CDU/SPD
Saxony-Anhalt[a]	9,650	2.24	4	CDU/SPD/Greens
Schleswig-Holstein	6,018	2.86	4	CDU/Greens/FDP
Thuringia[a]	5,983	2.17	4	Left/SPD/Greens
Total		82.03	69	

Sources: Most recent data come from the Government of Germany website dealing with the Bundesrat, http://www.bundesrat.de/cln_179/nn_11400/EN/organisation-en/stimmenverteilung -en/stimmenverteilung-en-node.html?__nnn=true. See also "Germany: States and Major Cities," http://www.citypopulation.de/Deutschland-Cities.html.
Note: a. Formerly part of the German Democratic Republic

tially balances centralized and decentralized powers by distinguishing among three different types of legislation.

Article 73 gives exclusive federal jurisdiction over legislation involving foreign affairs, citizenship, money, customs, federal railroads, telecommunications, federal employees, copyrights, and cooperation of the central government and Lander in criminal matters. The Lander are given **residual powers** in Article 70: "The Länder shall have the right to legislate insofar as this Basic Law does not confer legislative power on the Federation." Finally, Articles 72 and 74 list twenty-three specific areas in which jurisdiction is a **concurrent power**: the Lander may legislate in these areas "as long as, and to the extent that, the Federation does not exercise its right to legislate." Among areas of concurrent jurisdiction are civil and criminal law; registration of births, deaths, marriages; issues related to public welfare; labor laws; regulation of education; road traffic and highways; and some health-related matters.[16]

The Lander have maintained a great deal of influence in the German political system for several reasons. One is that there are many legislative powers left residually to them. Another is the constitutional provision that stimulates the "cooperative federalism" by requiring that the states administer most national policy, although this does not include foreign affairs and defense matters.[17]

Certainly another factor that must be considered is the role of the upper house of the federal parliament, the Bundesrat, in politics. This is a structure that we will discuss later in this chapter; here we mention that all deputies in the upper house are chosen by the Lander legislatures, not the people, and are correspondingly perceived to represent the Lander governments.

Legislation within the federal jurisdiction that affects the Lander, even if the Lander themselves cannot legislate on the issue, must be approved by a majority of the Land representatives in the Bundesrat, or it does not become law. The Lander, therefore, have sole jurisdiction through the residual clause of Article 70 over any subject matter not given to the federal government. They have concurrent (shared) jurisdiction over a number of subject matters in areas specified by the Basic Law. Even in the areas that are described in the Basic Law as exclusively federal jurisdiction, the Lander are not without influence, because issues that might affect them must be approved by their representatives in the Bundesrat.

The Constitutional Court

Another structure in Germany that reinforces the federal nature of the polity is the Constitutional Court. Unlike the Supreme Court of the United States, the Constitutional Court of Germany is not a court of appeal for either criminal or civil cases. Rather, the Constitutional Court "is a watchdog for the Basic Law. Its mission is not only to defend individual liberty and civil rights but to protect the legislature from the courts applying laws incorrectly. The Court is the final arbiter of disputes between the federal executive and the Bundestag, between the federal government and the states, between the different states, and between other courts."[18] On a number of occasions over the years, the Constitutional Court has ruled against the federal government, supporting an interpretation of the Basic Law favoring expansion of the powers of the Lander.[19]

Germany has an independent judicial structure reflecting its federal character, with (in addition to the Constitutional Court) a High Court of Justice and four systems of courts with jurisdictions in administrative, financial, labor, and social issues. While all courts have the ability to review the constitutionality of government action and legislation in their particular areas of jurisdiction, only the Constitutional Court can declare legislation unconstitutional. If the other courts find a constitutional problem they must refer the case to the Constitutional Court.

Executive Structures

The Parliamentary Council that drafted the Basic Law in 1948 felt that the institution of the presidency in the Weimar period was, to some degree, responsible for the weakness of the chancellor at that time and thus responsible for the use of "emergency rule" that led to the rise of Hitler and the corresponding abuse of law. So, when the members of the Parliamentary Council met in 1948 to construct new political structures, there was little sense that a strong head of state was necessary. Their goals with respect to executive powers were straightforward and dealt with a "neutralized" presidency, a strengthened chancellorship, and controls on Parliament.[20]

First, members of the Parliamentary Council believed that the president should be "neutralized," which meant that she or he should have few, if any, significant political powers and should play the figurehead role in office that the constitutional monarchs of Britain or Scandinavia play. This meant that the presidency should be an explicitly nonpolitical office.

Second, members felt that the position of the head of the government, the **chancellor**, should be strengthened. The chancellor should not be as vulnerable to short-term political pressures as he had been in the Weimar regime, and his base of power should be more secure.[21]

Third, members of the council wanted to design a structure in which there would be "penalties" imposed on the legislature if it started to use its power in relation to the chancellor "irresponsibly"—in this case referring to the type of behavior observed in the Weimar regime in which several small parties would get together to vote no confidence in a chancellor and subsequently not be able to agree on a replacement. The penalty structure designed was part of a "constructive" vote of no confidence, described later.

The Federal President

Articles 54 through 61 of the Basic Law deal with the office of the federal president. The president is elected by a Federal Convention, made up of members of the Bundestag (the lower house of the federal legislature) and an equal number of members elected by the legislative assemblies of the states. The vote in the special convention must be by an absolute majority of the delegates on the first two ballots; if no one wins a majority on either of the first two ballots, the candidate receiving a plurality on the third ballot is elected.

The most recent Federal Convention took place in February of 2017 to elect the twelfth president, as stipulated by the Basic Law thirty days before the end of the federal president's term of office, at the latest. Frank-Walter Steinmeier of the Social Democratic Party (SDP) was elected on the first ballot. He took office on March 19, 2017.[22]

The federal president has very few real powers. Orders and decrees of the federal president must be countersigned by the federal chancellor or an appropriate federal minister to be valid. This is significantly different from the relationship between most heads of state and their chief executives and cabinets. In most systems, legally (de jure) the head of state has a great deal of power, although actually (de facto) it is recognized that the head of state will only act "on the advice" of his or her chief executive. In Germany, the head of state is legally (de jure) restricted to the passive role. That the head of state must have all orders and decrees countersigned is a legal acknowledgment of their lack of power. The two exceptions to the countersignature rule are the appointment and dismissal of the federal chancellor, and the dissolution of the Bundestag, both of which we will address later.

The president appoints and dismisses ministers, federal judges, and civil servants; promulgates laws; represents the federation in its international relations; and concludes treaties, all "on the advice," of course, of the federal chancellor. Above all, the federal president is expected to be "above politics," to be nonpartisan, and to represent Germany to the world.

The Chancellor and the Cabinet

What is officially referred to as the federal government in Germany refers to the federal chancellor and his or her cabinet (the first female chancellor, Angela Merkel, was elected in 2005).[23] The present cabinet is composed of the chancellor and fifteen ministers.[24] The chief executive in Germany is the chancellor, and it is the chief executive, not the head of state, to whom we must turn to see the real locus of power in the political arena. The chancellor "has been seen as the keystone of the political system, the guarantee of stability and coherence in the democratic structure of German politics."[25] The chancellor is more powerful than most parliamentary chief executives, primarily because the chancellor has greater job security than most. This has led the German system to be referred to as "chancellor democracy."[26]

Elections are held for the Bundestag at least every four years. According to Article 39, "The Bundestag . . . term shall end four years after its first meeting or on its dissolution. The new election shall be held during the last three months of the term or within sixty days after dissolution." The Bundestag must assemble within thirty days after the election. The Bundestag determines the termination and resumption of its meetings, but it may be called into special session by the federal president, the federal chancellor, or one-third of the Bundestag members.

After the elections of the members of the Bundestag, the president proposes a chancellor-designate, which in the German case has either been the leader of the majority party in the Bundestag (in 1957) or has been the leader of the apparent majority coalition. Article 63 of the Basic Law states that "the Federal Chancellor shall be elected, without debate, by the Bundestag upon the proposal of the Federal President."

If the federal president makes a designation not supported by a majority in the Bundestag, the Bundestag has the power to reject the candidate. If the person proposed by the president is not supported by a majority, "the Bundestag may elect within fourteen days of the ballot a Federal Chancellor by more than one-half of its members."

If the Bundestag rejects the federal president's nominee, and cannot agree on majority support for its own candidate within fourteen days, a new vote in the Bundestag must be taken "without delay, in which the person obtaining the largest number of votes shall be elected." If this person has been elected by a majority of Bundestag members, the federal president must appoint him or her within seven days. If this newly elected person has not been elected by a majority, but only by a plurality, the federal president must either appoint him or her within seven days, or else dissolve the Bundestag and call for new elections within sixty days. (To date, all chancellors have been those approved as initial presidential designations, indicating the degree to which federal presidents make only "realistic" nominations.)

Once a chancellor has been confirmed by the Bundestag, it is extremely hard to "fire" that individual. One of the major distinctions between presidential and parliamentary systems observed earlier in this text was in respect to tenure, or job security: presidents generally have fixed terms of office, whereas prime ministers can lose their positions at any time through votes of no confidence by the legislature. The Parliamentary Council of 1948 did not want the chancellor to be in a vulnerable position and developed a new political structure to help protect the chancellor's job security: the **positive** or **constructive vote of no confidence**.

> The positive vote of no confidence is described in Article 67 of the Basic Law: The Bundestag can express its lack of confidence in the Federal Chancellor only by electing a successor with the majority of its members and by requesting the Federal President to dismiss the Federal Chancellor. The Federal President must comply with this request and appoint the person elected. . . . Forty-eight hours must elapse between the motion and the vote thereon.[27]

In short, having a majority of members of the Bundestag express their lack of confidence in a chancellor is not sufficient to dismiss that chancellor; they must at the same time (actually prior to that time) agree on a successor that a majority of the Bundestag can support. This can be a very difficult task and has helped the federal chancellor weather strife and complaints that might have much more serious consequences—such as causing the Government to fall—in other political systems.

This positive vote of no confidence has led some to refer to the German political system as a semi-parliamentary system rather than a parliamentary system, arguing that a "genuine parliamentary system, in the sense of enforceable responsibility of the executive to parliament, existed in Germany only as long as the Weimar Constitution functioned."[28] The difficulty of obtaining a positive vote of no confidence is so great that the Government is virtually no longer responsible to the Bundestag.

In September 1982, for the first time, such an unusual incident did arise. After constant feuding within the Social Democratic Party/Free Democratic Party (FDP) coalition, the FDP minor partner decided to withdraw support for the Government of **Helmut Schmidt**.[29] In itself, this guaranteed only a **simple vote of no confidence** and not a positive vote of no confidence. After consultation, however, it became clear that the leader of the more conservative Christian Democratic Union/Christian Socialist Union (CDU/CSU) bloc—**Helmut Kohl**—was willing to make policy concessions to the Free Democrats, which convinced the FDP deputies to join with the CDU/CSU deputies in a positive vote of no confidence, voting Helmut Schmidt out and Helmut Kohl in.[30]

In addition to the unlikelihood that the chancellor will be thrown out of office, the chancellor has the added leverage of being able to use a vote of confidence as a weapon. Article 68 states that if the chancellor asks for a vote of confidence and does not receive it, he or she can ask for a dissolution of the Bundestag and call for new elections. This has been used in the past by chancellors either to push a piece of legislation through the Bundestag that might have difficulty otherwise by referring to the vote on the bill as a question of confidence, or to bring about an early dissolution for electoral gain. Newly selected Chancellor Kohl used this vehicle after his accession to the chancellorship in September 1982 to seek a popular mandate from the German people, since his party had not won a majority with him as leader. He received the mandate he sought in the March 1983 elections.

Unlike other political systems, in Germany the head of state does not possess the legal power to dissolve the Bundestag at will. (Of course, although most heads of state have this power legally, they really only exercise it "on the advice" of their chief executives. In Germany the head of state does not even possess the power merely legally.) The federal president can dissolve the Bundestag only under one of two circumstances: first, if her or his nominee for chancellor is not approved by the Bundestag, and the chancellor eventually chosen by the Bundestag does not have majority support and is not acceptable to the president; and second, if the chancellor requests a vote of confidence in the Bundestag, and the Bundestag fails to give him or her one, *and* the chancellor subsequently requests a dissolution.

Chancellors who know that elections must be held within the next year or so, and who see their popularity as being very high, have been known to use the "confidence mechanism" to secure an early dissolution. They do this by asking for a vote of confidence and instructing their own party supporters to vote against them, thereby ensuring that they will lose the vote of confidence. (Note, however, that this is not the same as a positive vote of no confidence; in this case the Bundestag has not agreed on a replacement for the chancellor.) The chancellor's supporters will go along with this, of course, since it is in their own interest to have elections held at a time when their party and their leader are both popular.

We can see, then, that the German chancellor is stronger in their political system than virtually any other parliamentary chief executive we can imagine. The chancellor not only has the usual tool of party discipline at their disposal, but also is extraordinarily difficult to dismiss, and is able to threaten the legislature with dissolution if it is not cooperative.

Ministers in the Federal Republic share in collective responsibility, as do ministers in other parliamentary regimes, but they have more individual authority than do ministers in many other parliamentary systems because they tend to manage their individual departments "on their own responsibility," with less collective input than in many other parliamentary systems. The cabinet tends to be smaller than in many nations; recent cabinets have consisted of fifteen or sixteen members. The major limitation on the cabinet as a policymaker has been that governments have involved coalitions, and in many instances the coalition partners have not been able to agree in-cabinet and "many policy issues have to be prepared outside the Government."[31]

Legislative Structures

Several aspects of the federal legislature have already been introduced. We have seen how the members of the Bundestag (the lower house of the legislature) are elected.[32] We have seen the relationship between the Bundestag and the federal chancellor; the chancellor is dominant and is beyond the normal reach of the legislature in terms of the usual meaning of "responsible government." We also saw in a very introductory manner that the Bundesrat (the upper house of the legislature) is important in the federal structure of the regime, although some discussions of German politics do not consider it a chamber of the legislature since it is not elected.

The Bundestag

The **Bundestag** is perceived in the Basic Law to be the center of legislative activity in German politics. The German political system is essentially designed to be managed by the chancellor and their cabinet. The job of the Bundestag is to choose its leader; once this is accomplished, it is expected that the Bundestag will permit itself to be led by the Government. The difficulty of the positive vote of no confidence is an indication that the framers of the Basic Law did not intend for the Bundestag to exercise its role as the ultimate authority in the regime very often.

The Bundestag is today composed of 709 members. The Bundestag nominally has 598 members, of whom 299 are elected in fixed single-member districts, and another 299 are elected by statewide party proportional lists. The complex electoral system also allows for some extra seats to be created—called "overhang" seats and "balance" seats—and in the current Bundestag there are 111 of these, bringing the total to 709 members.[33]

The Bundesrat

Article 50 of the Basic Law indicates that "the Länder shall participate through the **Bundesrat** in the legislation and administration of the Federation." The Bundesrat, the upper house, is important insofar as the federal distribution of powers is concerned. As seen in Table 10.1, the sixteen Lander each have either three, four, five, or six deputies in the Bundesrat, depending upon their size, yielding a total of sixty-nine members. A majority in the Bundesrat is thirty-five votes. Article 51 of the Basic Law indicates that every Land shall have at least three seats in the Bundesrat; Lander with between 2 and 6 million inhabitants shall have four; Lander with between 6 and 7 million inhabitants shall have five; and Lander with more than 7 million inhabitants shall have six votes.[34]

This difference in the size of Bundesrat delegations, however, does not alleviate disproportionate representation. To take two examples, the city-state of Bremen (with three delegates) has one Bundesrat representative for each 223,000 people, and the state of North Rhine–Westphalia (with six delegates) has one Bundesrat representative for each 3 million people.

The Land governments (the legislative assemblies of the Lander) choose their three, four, five, or six delegates to the Bundesrat. Since the Bundesrat delegates are chosen by the Land governments, they will all be of the political party that controls the majority in the Land legislature. Bundesrat delegates from a Land must cast their votes as a bloc; they may not divide their three, four, five, or six votes.

The role of the Bundesrat in the German legislative process varies, depending upon the specific piece of legislation involved. According to the Basic Law (Articles 77 and 78), bills intended to become federal laws require adoption by the Bundestag. Bills can be introduced in the Bundestag by either the Bundesrat, the Bundestag, or the federal Government (the chancellor and the cabinet).

The Legislative Process

The legislative process is complex.[35] All bills begin their legislative journey in the Bundestag. Bills introduced by the Bundesrat (a small number) go first to the Government for comment before being introduced in the Bundestag.[36] Bills being introduced by the Government (more than half of the total)[37] go first to the Bundesrat for comment before being introduced in the Bundestag. In each of these cases, scrutiny is implied, not veto power; the goal is for government actors to let other government actors know what is happening. Bills starting in the Bundestag (almost half) are simply introduced there; they do not go to either the Bundesrat or the Government for advance scrutiny. Currently almost 50 percent of all laws passed require the approval of the Bundesrat.[38]

Once bills are introduced, they first go through the Bundestag phase of the legislative process, including a first reading, a vote in the Bundestag, assignment to committee followed by a committee report, a second reading and vote in the Bundestag covering specific details of the proposed legislation, followed by a third reading and vote.

If a bill passes the Bundestag phase of the legislative process—and many do not—it goes to the Bundesrat. This is the first opportunity for the Bundesrat to see bills that were initiated in the Bundestag (other bills either were initiated in the Bundesrat, or were initiated in the Government and first sent to the Bundesrat for review and comment prior to going to the Bundestag). The Bundesrat can either approve the bill, in which case it is sent on to the federal president to sign and to the chancellor or appropriate minister to countersign, or within two weeks the Bundesrat may ask for a meeting of the Bundestag-Bundesrat Mediation Committee to try to find a compromise.

At this point an important distinction must be made. Bills that "affect the Lander" require the approval of the Bundesrat. It has an absolute veto over this kind of legislation; if it doesn't approve the bills, the bills don't pass.[39] Bills that do not directly affect the Lander—to take one example, questions dealing with foreign policy—do not require Bundesrat approval; over these bills the Bundesrat has only a suspensory veto.

In cases over which the Bundesrat has an absolute veto, and in which it does not approve of the Bundestag bill, a compromise must be reached by the Mediation Committee and must be approved by both houses before it can be handed down as law. Failing this, the bill does not become law. Laws that affect the interests of the states are called "consent bills," because they cannot come into force unless the Bundesrat explicitly consents to them. "Objection bills" are bills that can come into effect over the objection of the Bundesrat, because they do not directly affect the interests of the states.[40]

In cases over which the Bundesrat does not have an absolute veto, and in which the Bundesrat does not approve of the Bundestag bill,

> it may enter a suspensive veto, but only after an effort at compromise through the Mediation Committee has been made. . . . If the Bundesrat enters its objection by a vote of a majority of its members, then the Bundestag can override it by the same majority; if the Bundesrat has entered its objections by a vote of two-thirds of its members, it can only be overridden in the Bundestag by a vote of two-thirds of the Members present, but these two-thirds must also constitute at least a majority of the total membership. If the Bundesrat fails to act within the prescribed time limits, bills which do not specifically require its approval are ready for promulgation.[41]

The structure of the Mediation Committee is modeled after the conference committee of the US Congress. Members are appointed from each house of the legislature. Unlike the US conference committee, however, which is only a temporary political structure and which is created anew for each bill over which a compromise is necessary, the Mediation Committee is a standing committee—permanent for the life of the legislature. It is composed of Bundesrat members (one from each Land) and Bundestag members, divided proportionally to reflect party distribution in that house. The Bundesrat, then, while not having an absolute veto in all cases, as is the case with the US Senate, is a reasonably powerful upper house.

Over the years the Bundesrat's veto power has expanded to include a substantial proportion of all federal legislation. To some degree this expansion occurred through judicial decisions. Article 84 of the Basic Law gave the states the task of administering much federal legislation; the states argued before the courts—successfully—that since they had to administer the law, they were affected by the law, and accordingly the Bundesrat should have absolute veto power. Accordingly, states currently argue that even if a law affects them only because they must administer it, the entire law may be vetoed by the Bundesrat in the legislative process.

Political Parties and Elections

The Electoral Process

Germany is a political system with many political parties, but one that has been dominated by just a few parties over the past seventy years;[42] the system has evolved since the 1949 election to become a two-coalition, if not a two-party, system. In the elections of October 5, 1980, although twenty political parties appeared on West German ballots, the five major parties (CDU, CSU, FDP, SPD, Greens) won 99.5 percent of the votes;[43] in the 2017 election these parties won 87 percent of the votes, with a new party—the Alternative for Germany (AfD)—winning 12.6 percent of the vote and 13 percent of the seats in the Bundestag.[44] The reasons for this are complex, and to explain the pattern of the parties' election returns over the years we must know something of the manner in which the German electoral system operates.[45]

In 1949, at the time of the creation of the Federal Republic, each citizen voted only once in each election. This system was changed in 1953 when a second vote for each citizen in each election was added.[46] When Germans go to the polls they receive a ballot with two columns, as illustrated in Figure 10.1. In the left-hand column, known as the first vote, the citizen votes directly for a candidate who has been nominated by a local political party organization (there are no primary elections in Germany), in a single-member-district plurality-voting electoral framework. This is sometimes referred to as the **constituency vote**. Germany is now divided into 299 single-member districts,[47] from which deputies are selected by simple-plurality margins: whichever candidate in a district receives the most votes, wins. If two or more candidates receive the same number of votes, the returning officer (the official in charge of administering the election) for the electoral district draws lots to decide the winner.

In the right-hand column the citizen casts a second vote for a political party, not a candidate, in a proportional representation electoral competition. Parties receive seats on the basis of the percentage of votes they receive in the election. At least another 299 deputies are elected to the Bundestag through this electoral route, bringing the total number of seats in the Bundestag to at least 598.

Some argue that the second ballot is in many ways more important than the first, direct ballot because it is the second ballot that determines the final proportion of parliamentary seats that each party will receive in the Bundestag. In each Land every party is entitled to the number of

Figure 10.1 A Sample First Vote/Second Vote Ballot

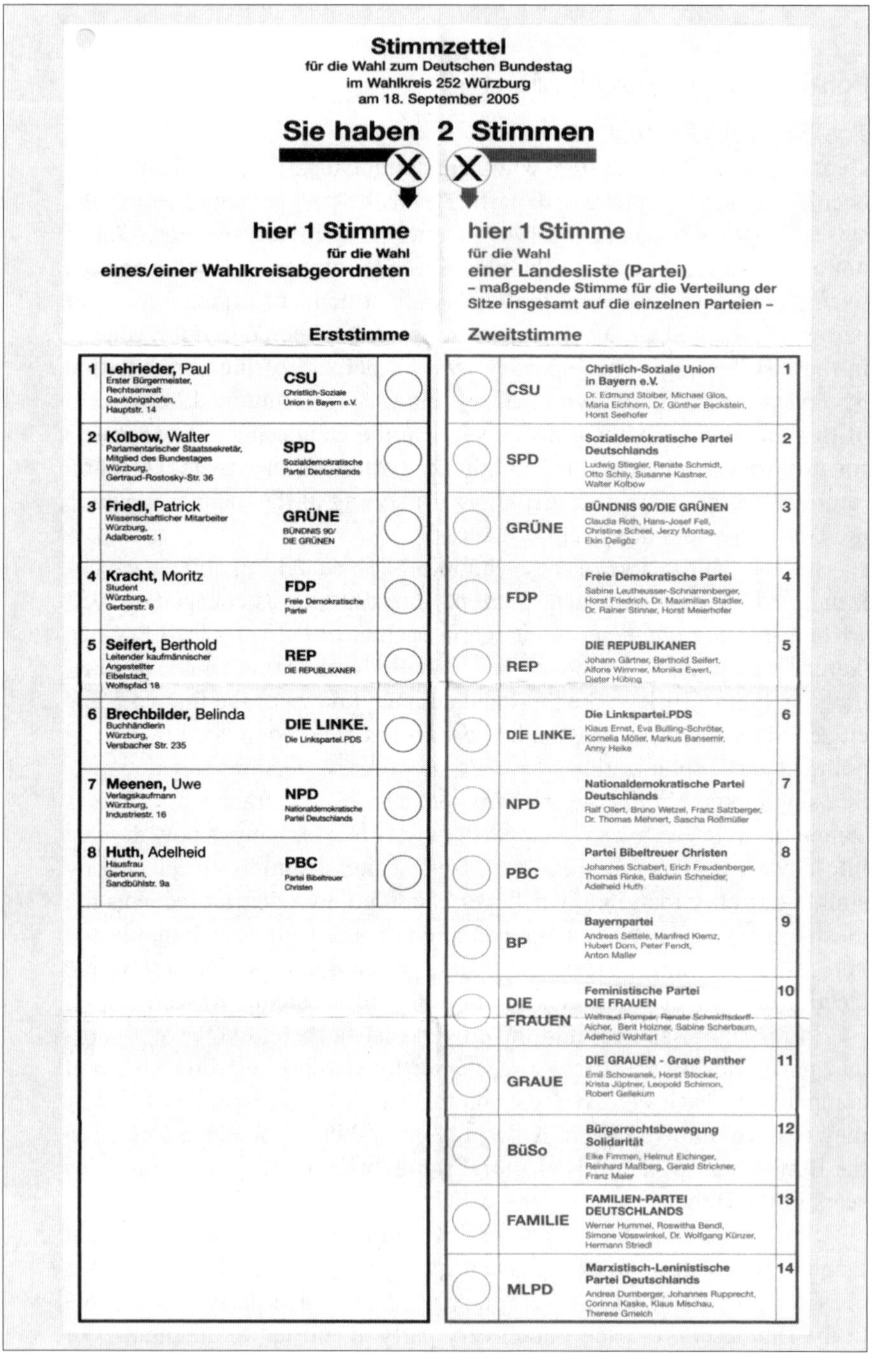

Stimmzettel
für die Wahl zum Deutschen Bundestag
im Wahlkreis 252 Würzburg
am 18. September 2005

Sie haben 2 Stimmen

hier 1 Stimme
für die Wahl
eines/einer Wahlkreisabgeordneten

Erststimme

1	**Lehrieder,** Paul Erster Bürgermeister, Rechtsanwalt Gaukönigshofen, Hauptstr. 14	**CSU** Christlich-Soziale Union in Bayern e.V.	◯
2	**Kolbow,** Walter Parlamentarischer Staatssekretär, Mitglied des Bundestages Würzburg, Gertraud-Rostosky-Str. 36	**SPD** Sozialdemokratische Partei Deutschlands	◯
3	**Friedl,** Patrick Wissenschaftlicher Mitarbeiter Würzburg, Adalberostr. 1	**GRÜNE** BÜNDNIS 90/ DIE GRÜNEN	◯
4	**Kracht,** Moritz Student Würzburg, Gerberstr. 8	**FDP** Freie Demokratische Partei	◯
5	**Seifert,** Berthold Leitender kaufmännischer Angestellter Eibelstadt, Wolfspfad 18	**REP** DIE REPUBLIKANER	◯
6	**Brechbilder,** Belinda Buchhändlerin Würzburg, Versbacher Str. 235	**DIE LINKE.** Die Linkspartei.PDS	◯
7	**Meenen,** Uwe Verlagskaufmann Würzburg, Industriestr. 16	**NPD** Nationaldemokratische Partei Deutschlands	◯
8	**Huth,** Adelheid Hausfrau Gerbrunn, Sandbühlstr. 9a	**PBC** Partei Bibeltreuer Christen	◯

hier 1 Stimme
für die Wahl
einer Landesliste (Partei)
– maßgebende Stimme für die Verteilung der Sitze insgesamt auf die einzelnen Parteien –

Zweitstimme

◯	**CSU**	**Christlich-Soziale Union in Bayern e.V.** Dr. Edmund Stoiber, Michael Glos, Maria Eichhorn, Dr. Günther Beckstein, Horst Seehofer	1
◯	**SPD**	**Sozialdemokratische Partei Deutschlands** Ludwig Stiegler, Renate Schmidt, Otto Schily, Susanne Kastner, Walter Kolbow	2
◯	**GRÜNE**	**BÜNDNIS 90/DIE GRÜNEN** Claudia Roth, Hans-Josef Fell, Christine Scheel, Jerzy Montag, Ekin Deligöz	3
◯	**FDP**	**Freie Demokratische Partei** Sabine Leutheusser-Schnarrenberger, Horst Friedrich, Dr. Maximilian Stadler, Dr. Rainer Stinner, Horst Meierhofer	4
◯	**REP**	**DIE REPUBLIKANER** Johann Gärtner, Berthold Seifert, Alfons Wimmer, Monika Ewert, Dieter Hübing	5
◯	**DIE LINKE.**	**Die Linkspartei.PDS** Klaus Ernst, Eva Bulling-Schröter, Kornelia Möller, Markus Bansemir, Anny Heike	6
◯	**NPD**	**Nationaldemokratische Partei Deutschlands** Ralf Ollert, Bruno Wetzel, Franz Salzberger, Dr. Thomas Mehnert, Sascha Roßmüller	7
◯	**PBC**	**Partei Bibeltreuer Christen** Johannes Schabert, Erich Freudenberger, Thomas Rinke, Baldwin Schneider, Adelheid Huth	8
◯	**BP**	**Bayernpartei** Andreas Settele, Manfred Klemz, Hubert Dorn, Peter Fendt, Anton Maller	9
◯	**DIE FRAUEN**	**Feministische Partei DIE FRAUEN** Waltraud Pomper, Renate Schmidtsdorff-Aicher, Berit Holzner, Sabine Scherbaum, Adelheid Wohlfart	10
◯	**GRAUE**	**DIE GRAUEN - Graue Panther** Emil Schowanek, Horst Stocker, Krista Jüptner, Leopold Schimon, Robert Gellekum	11
◯	**BüSo**	**Bürgerrechtsbewegung Solidarität** Elke Fimmen, Helmut Eichinger, Reinhard Maßberg, Gerald Strickner, Franz Maier	12
◯	**FAMILIE**	**FAMILIEN-PARTEI DEUTSCHLANDS** Werner Hummel, Roswitha Bendl, Simone Vosswinkel, Dr. Wolfgang Künzer, Hermann Striedl	13
◯	**MLPD**	**Marxistisch-Leninistische Partei Deutschlands** Andrea Dumberger, Johannes Rupprecht, Corinna Kaske, Klaus Mischau, Therese Gmelch	14

seats that corresponds to its share of the second votes. The number of "district" seats is subtracted from the total number of seats due to the party on the basis of its performance in the proportional representation elections, determining the number of "at large" seats the party will receive. For example, if a party wins 25 percent of the vote on the proportional ballot—thus earning a total of 150 seats in the new Bundestag (25 percent of 598 total "normal" official seats available yields 150 seats)—and it wins 70 district seats, it will be awarded 80 at-large seats to bring its total to the percentage it earned in the election. Individual candidates will be selected, in order, from party lists that have already been filed with the government.

Two calculations are involved in the decisions regarding representation for the right side of the ballot. First, the proportion that each German state has of the total German population is calculated, determining the percentage of the 299 proportional seats it will receive. If it has 10 percent of the national population it should receive 10 percent of the proportional seats. After the number of seats for the state are determined, each state determines the distribution of "its" seats based upon the proportion of the vote that a party receives. If a party receives 20 percent of the vote in a state with thirty Bundestag seats, the party will receive six of those seats.

> The minimum number of seats for each party at federal level is then determined. This is done by calculating, for each party Land list, the number of constituency seats it won on the basis of the first votes, as well as the number of seats to which it is entitled on the basis of the second votes. The higher of these two figures is the party's minimum number of seats in that Land. Adding together the minimum number of seats to which the party is entitled in all of the Lander produces a total representing its guaranteed minimum number of seats in the country as a whole.[48]

There may, however, be more than the "normal" 598 seats elected to the Bundestag, and there regularly are. Indeed, as noted earlier, today there are a total of 709 members. What are called "overhang mandates" are awarded when parties win more seats on the first ballot in the constituencies than they are entitled to according to the second-vote proportions.

> It is generally necessary to increase the size of the Bundestag to ensure that each party receives its guaranteed minimum number of seats when the seats are allocated using the Sainte-Laguë/Schepers method. Then it must be ensured that the seats are distributed to the parties in line with their national share of the second votes.
>   Additional "balance seats" are created to ensure that the distribution of the seats reflects the parties' share of the second votes and that

no party receives fewer than its guaranteed minimum number of seats. Balance seats are also necessary to ensure that each party requires roughly the same number of second votes per seat. Once the number of seats which each party is entitled to receive across the country has been determined, the seats are allocated to the parties' individual Land lists. Each Land list must receive at least as many seats as the number of constituencies which the party won in the Land in question.[49]

One of the classic studies of German politics has described the second ballot's importance as follows:

The second ballot provision made the system basically proportional, with two important exceptions. A party had to secure at least five percent of the second ballot vote, or win three "direct" district (first ballot) contests in order to share in the proportional distribution of parliamentary seats. Secondly, if a party won more district contests (first ballot) than it was entitled to according to its totals on the second ballot, it was allowed to keep the extra seats and the parliament was enlarged accordingly. In the last West German parliament, for example, there was one of these "excess mandates" and the Bundestag had 497 members in addition to 22 from West Berlin.[50]

The rationale behind the two-vote electoral system is that it allows for the accuracy of proportional representation while still allowing for the "personal representation" of the single-member-district electoral structure. Another function of the system has to do with interest groups and representation. One study has suggested that for individual candidates who seek to enter parliament from outside political party organizations, it is "virtually impossible to gain nomination as a party candidate for a direct seat"[51]—that is, for a seat for which voters ballot directly for an individual candidate. However, significant interest groups may have sufficient influence at the Lander level to be able to influence the Lander political parties to include "their" candidates on the party's proportional representation part of the ballot.

Voting turnout is regularly high in Germany, as shown in Table 10.2; 89 percent of the electorate voted in 1983, and in the most recent election, in 2017, over 76 percent of the eligible voters voted.[52] (To draw a comparison, in the United States 55.7 percent of the voting-age population voted in 2016. The United States trails most developed countries in voting turnout.)[53] Every citizen over the age of eighteen years has a vote, and eligibility certificates are mailed by the Federal Board of Elections to lists of eligible voters prepared by the local census bureau.

We might think that the proportional representation component of the electoral system would encourage a large number of political parties

Table 10.2   Voting Turnout in German Parliamentary Elections Since Unification

	2017	2013	2009	2005	2002	1998	1994	1990
Bundestag number	19	18	17	16	15	14	13	12
Voting turnout (%)	76.2	71.5	70.8	77.7	79.1	82.2	79.0	77.8

Source: Adam Carr's Election Archive, http://psephos.adam-carr.net/countries/g/germany.

to flourish in the Federal Republic of Germany, as was the case in Weimar Germany. There was much discussion about this possible consequence when the authors of the Basic Law met in 1948; the structure that has evolved to prevent the proliferation of parties in Germany is called the **Five Percent Clause**.

Proportional representation electoral systems, as we saw earlier in this text, can have the negative effect in a political system of providing too much representation. If every party that receives, say, 1 percent of the vote is given representation in the legislature, we may find a legislature with so many political parties that coalition governments are necessary, leading to what can be less stable governments. (This is the case in Israel, which has a pure proportional representation electoral system that regularly results in over a dozen political parties in the Knesset, Israel's unicameral parliament.) Under the Weimar Constitution, which preceded World War II, a proportional representation system existed that resulted in a large number of political parties. In fact, fourteen different parties successfully competed for the Reichstag election of September 14, 1930. Many Germans thought that it was wrong that although nine parties had less than 5 percent of the total vote, they still took part in deciding who was to form the Government.[54]

There is a difficult tradeoff involved in this policy, as discussed earlier. On one hand, single-member districts fail to represent small minority blocs in electoral districts; on the other hand, proportional representation systems may result in too much influence for minor parties. To limit the danger of tiny parliamentary blocs gaining a disproportionate amount of political influence and resulting in political instability through resultant coalition governments, the Federal Election Law introduced the Five Percent Clause.[55]

The Five Percent Clause indicates that parties can win seats from the proportional representation second votes only if they poll at least 5 percent of the second votes, or either (1) if they have won at least three constituency seats, or (2) if they represent an officially registered national minority (such as the party of the Danish minority in Schleswig-Holstein).[56]

The Five Percent Clause has been of significance for Germany. In the first Bundestag, in 1949, there were ten parties represented, but ever since the Five Percent Clause was introduced, there have been only four until the 1983 election added a fifth. The 1990 post-unification election expanded this slightly. The Five Percent Clause serves as a real psychological barrier for voters that dampens enthusiasm for new parties, as well as a legal or structural barrier; many voters feel that voting for a minor party is "throwing away" their votes, since the minor parties will probably not win 5 percent of the vote. The major parties can be counted upon to remind the voters of this principle. This is undoubtedly why we have not seen the appearance of many new parties in the Bundestag since the Five Percent Clause came into force.

When East and West Germany were reunified in 1990, there was concern expressed by many parties in (what had been) East Germany that they would not be able to compete with the larger, better-organized parties in (what had been) West Germany in the 1990 elections. The Constitutional Court, in fact, threw out the Five Percent Clause as unconstitutionally discriminating against the smaller (formerly) East German parties. On the advice of the Constitutional Court, the law was amended at that time so that political parties in the former German Democratic Republic (East Germany) could form alliances and run on joint tickets, and so that votes for the proportional seats would be counted separately in what were once East Germany and West Germany,[57] thereby allowing smaller East German parties to compete against smaller East German parties rather than against the larger West German parties.

The Five Percent Clause continues to have an effect on elections. The Free Democratic Party was kept out of the 2013 Bundestag because it won only 4.8 percent of the votes, and that year's newcomer party, the right-wing AfG, received only 4.7 percent and was also ineligible for Bundestag membership at that time. In the 2017 election the Free Democrats won 10.7 percent of the votes, and the Alternative for Germany received 12.6 percent.[58]

Political Parties

As is the case in most democratic systems, it is impossible to discuss the German political system without an explicit discussion of political parties.[59] Unlike many democracies, however, in Germany parties are constitutionally included in the political system: the Basic Law specifically refers to political parties, and in Article 21 "guarantees the legitimacy of parties and their right to exist—if they accept the principles of democratic government."[60] The Federal Republic has thoroughly institutionalized political parties, and we describe the working of German politics as "party government," as we do with other parliamentary democracies.

Although a large number of political parties have consistently competed in German elections, various structures in the political system—most notably the Five Percent Clause—have made it extremely difficult for minority or splinter parties to form and flourish. The Five Percent Clause has been successful in this goal, and in the elections in West Germany since the Five Percent Clause came into effect, support for political parties other than the five large parties has decreased markedly.

In 2005, the Christian Democratic Union party won 180 seats. The CDU's sister party in Bavaria, the CSU, won 46 seats. The CDU/CSU bloc, with 226 seats, had very slightly more seats than the Social Democratic Party of then-chancellor **Gerhard Schröder**, which won 222 seats. After a very long post-election negotiation period, the (conservative) CDU/CSU bloc formed a Grand Coalition with the (liberal) SPD, and **Angela Merkel** became Germany's first female chancellor.[61]

The Grand Coalition had difficulty governing, however, because the CDU (and CSU) and the SPD disagreed on many issues.[62] In the 2009 elections, Chancellor Merkel's CDU hoped to win by a larger margin so that either it could govern by itself or that it would be able to form a coalition government with the Free Democratic Party, ideologically more similar to its goals. The FDP is a more business-oriented party, and it had been a member of the CDU-led coalition government between 1982 and 1998.

In the 2009 campaign, Chancellor Merkel argued for a continuation of the status quo. During the campaign the CDU and the SPD were very, very close to each other in polls. The results were surprising, however. The CDU gained 14 seats over its results in 2005, going from 180 to 194, while the partner CSU held constant at 45 seats. The CDU/CSU's hoped-for partner, the FDP, increased its results by 50 percent, winning 93 seats rather than 61. This gave the CDU/CSU/SPD coalition a comfortable majority of 332 in the Bundestag. On the other hand, the SPD had its worst election since the end of World War II, winning only 146 seats, down 76 from its 2005 performance. The Green Party slightly increased its population, from 51 to 68, and the Left Party increased its population from 54 to 76 seats.

In the October 2009 election for the Bundestag, twenty-nine parties competed for the voters' attention. There were 43.2 million valid votes cast. The parties received from 32 percent of the first votes cast (the Christian Democratic Union, receiving 13.8 million votes) to less than 1 percent of the first votes cast (seventeen parties received less than 1 percent of the vote total, for instance with "The Center" receiving 369 votes).[63]

The September 2013 German election was a referendum on Chancellor Angela Merkel's policies, and the CDU/CSU alliance had its best performance since 1990, winning 41.5 percent of the vote, and almost 50 percent of the seats in the Bundestag, just five seats short of a majority. Merkel's party reached an agreement with the SPD, the main opposition party, to form a Grand Coalition, for the third time in Germany's history.[64]

The most recent German election, in September 2017, returned Merkel to power, but this time with a much reduced mandate. One of the most interesting dimensions of this election was the appearance of the AfD, the Alternative for Germany, which won 12.6 percent of the votes (see Table 10.3) and more than ninety seats in the Bundestag. It was created in 2013 as an anti-euro party, but in the 2017 campaign its focus was anti-immigration and anti-Islam, and was generally far-right in perspective.[65]

Four political parties have proven over time to play a significant political role in the German political system, all participating in government coalitions at one point or another. A fifth party, the Greens, has regularly won seats, but it has not yet participated in government. From

Table 10.3 Federal Election Results in Germany, September 2017

	Percentage of Votes	+/– 2013 Percentage	Number of Seats	Percentage of Seats
CDU/CSU	32.9	– 8.6	246	34.7
SPD	20.5	– 5.5	153	21.6
Radical Left	9.2	+ 0.6	69	9.7
The Greens	8.9	+ 0.5	67	9.4
FDP	10.7	+ 6.0	80	11.3
AfD	12.6	+ 7.9	92	13.0
Independents	—	—	2	0.3
Total	94.8		709	100.0
Voter turnout: 76.2%				

Source: "Germany's Election Results in Charts and Maps," https://www.ft.com/content/e7c 7d918-a17e-11e7-b797-b61809486fe2.

Note: The total number of seats won includes the "overhang" seats. The simple number of seats to be elected is 598.

1949 through 1956, and from 1961 through 1965, West Germany was governed by a coalition of the Christian Democratic Union and Christian Socialist Union (the CSU is the CDU in the state of Bavaria—they act as one party in the government), and the Free Democratic Party. In 1957 the CDU/CSU had an outright majority in the Bundestag, the only time an outright majority has been obtained by a political party, and formed a government without a coalition, which lasted until elections in 1961. From 1965 through 1969 a Grand Coalition existed, in which all the major parties including the Social Democratic Party participated in the Government. From 1969 until 1982, all governments were SPD and FDP coalitions.[66]

In September 1982, primarily as a result of economic pressure exerted on the Government, the FDP/SPD coalition came apart, and the FDP gave its support instead to the CDU/CSU bloc. Accordingly, Chancellor Schmidt of the Social Democratic Party resigned, and Helmut Kohl of the Christian Democratic Union/Christian Socialist Union bloc became chancellor. This coalition stayed in power until 2005, when a new Grand Coalition came into existence, headed by Angela Merkel and the conservative CDU/CSU bloc.

The CDU/CSU bloc is a conservative party, founded in 1945 based upon Christian, conservative, social principles.[67] The CSU was also founded in 1945 and appears on the ballot only in Bavaria, while the CDU is a more national party, appearing on all ballots except in Bavaria. The CDU and CSU are almost always in agreement on major issues and are considered as one party in the Bundestag, although each party maintains its own structure. The Christian Democratic Union has a federal party conference at least every two years, consisting of 1,001 delegates from the local, regional, and state associations, as well as delegates from foreign associations. The federal party conference comes to a decision as to what the basic party principles will be and thereby creates the party platform.[68] The Christian Socialist Union is divided into ten district associations, 108 area associations, and about 2,900 local associations. The CSU is present in practically every Bavarian municipality. It is Bavaria's strongest party and the most powerful force in the municipalities.[69]

The Free Democratic Party is the liberal-center party in Germany, and it is much more active in the German political system than its relatively small size might suggest. It has been referred to as the "party of coalition,"[70] having served as a coalition partner with both the CDU/CSU and the SPD. It is perceived as a centrist party, mainly composed of middle- and upper-class Protestants who consider themselves "independents" typifying European liberalism, and thus has been in most elections the only acceptable partner for the more conservative CDU/CSU and for the more liberal SPD. The 2005 election was an exception to this pattern. Although the SPD did well—receiving 9.8 percent of the vote and sixty-one federal deputies—because the CDU/CSU did less well than predicted the FDP-CDU/CSU bloc didn't have enough support in the Bundestag to form a new government. Instead, the CDU formed a Grand Coalition with the SPD, and the FDP entered the opposition.[71] In 2009, as we have seen, the FDP reappeared as a "natural" partner to the CDU/CSU plurality winner. In 2013 the Free Democrats did not clear the Five Percent Clause threshold, winning 4.8 percent of the vote, and were not entitled to Bundestag membership, but they reentered the Bundestag in 2017 when they won 10.7 percent of the vote.

The Social Democratic Party dates back to the 1860s, is one of the oldest political parties in the world, and was a traditional working-class social democratic party.[72] The SPD is a left-of-center political party. Historically the SPD was associated with Marxist policies, but since 1959 this association has been less clear. Its economic policies are a very moderate version of socialist thought, more sympathetic to free-market economic policies than to Marxist thought. The SPD first participated in a cabinet in the Grand Coalition of 1965; in 1969 the SPD led the cabinet formation process for the first time, joining in a coalition with the FDP. This alliance continued through the elections of 1972, 1976, and 1980, dissolving in October 1982, as indicated earlier.[73] The SPD, as already noted, was a partner in the Grand Coalition with the CDU/CSU following the 2005 election, but following the 2009 election it was back in the opposition, and it has continued to be in the opposition since that time.

As mentioned, the Green Movement in Germany has become a parliamentary political party only in recent years.[74] The Green Movement emerged in Germany in 1975, and for many years it existed as a lobby in West Germany opposing expanded use of nuclear power, opposing NATO strategy, and applying pressure for changes in society that "did not pose an immediate threat to the established 'people's' or 'catch-all' parties."[75] Membership in the Greens rose from 3,000 in October 1979 to over 10,000 in January 1980; in March 1980 the Greens met to formulate a formal political party program.[76]

The Greens were especially important as a demonstration that views that were outside the mainstream of West German political thought could win representation in parliament.[77] Although there had been several protest movements with various degrees of popular support in West Germany between the formation of the Federal Republic and 1983,[78] the Greens' victory in 1983 offered the first instance of parliamentary political victory for an organization that could be called a "protest movement."

The Greens have not been a typical German party, and their parliamentarians have not been typical legislators, in either behavior or demeanor.[79] The average Green legislator was almost ten years younger than other legislators, and "six of the ten youngest deputies in Parliament were Greens."[80]

In the 1980 federal elections the Greens did not cross the threshold required for representation. In the 1983 federal election they received 5.6 percent of the vote and entered the federal parliament for the first time.[81] They increased their voter support in 1987 with 8.4 percent of the vote.[82] The (former West German) Greens did not get enough votes in the 1990 election to clear the 5 percent threshold and win any seats in the new legislature, but the (former East German) Alliance 90/Greens did win sufficient votes to be represented, so the Green Movement has continued to be represented in the federal legislature. In 1994 the Greens from East and West returned to the Bundestag with over 7 percent of the vote, winning forty-nine seats; this figure held almost constant at forty-seven seats and 6.7 percent of the votes in the 1998 election. The Greens' support increased to almost 9 percent of the vote in 2002, although in the 2005 election their support dropped slightly to just below 7 percent of the vote. It increased to almost 11 percent in 2009. As noted earlier, the Greens passed the Five Percent Clause requirement with 8.4 percent of the vote in 2013 and 8.9 percent in the most recent 2017 elections.

The newest significant actor in the German party system is the Alternative for Germany, which is now the third largest parliamentary group in the Bundestag. It was created in 2013 as a result of right-wing criticism of Chancellor Merkel's decision to commit German funds to assist Greece in its fiscal crisis. Its focus shifted to immigration policy in 2015 after Germany accepted nearly a million immigrants from the Middle East, and "its tone became increasingly nationalistic, populistic, and—its critics said—racist."[83]

The German Political System in Perspective

We see in Germany, then, a political system that is similar to others that we have already seen, but one that differs in a number of aspects from those other systems. Although many idiosyncratic structural and procedural differences exist between Germany and other nations, the most significant differences that we have highlighted in this chapter number four.

First, Germany is federal, and the role of the states (Lander) in the German political system is quite significant. Through the veto power of the Bundesrat, the Lander exercise a great influence in the policymaking process generally, and in the legislative process specifically. The federal distribution of power in Germany makes Germany unlike any other European political system we will see here.

Second, the "normal" responsibility of the chief executive to the (lower house of the) legislature is different in the German political system. The political structure of the positive vote of no confidence has many implications for the degree to which the chancellor must worry about the likelihood that they will be dismissed by the Bundestag.

Third, the German electoral structure offers a unique blend of methods of selection for a national legislature. By combining single-member-district voting with proportional representation selection, the Germans have attempted to blend the advantages of each: the minority representation of proportional representation with the stability and orientation of district-based representation. Moreover, by establishing the Five Percent Clause the Germans have attempted to resolve the major drawback of proportional representation—a proliferation of political parties and the ensuing political instability of the regime.

Fourth, from a legislative point of view the German case is quite interesting. In some political systems (such as that of the United States, for example) the upper house has, both in law (de jure) and in fact (de facto), an absolute veto. Laws cannot be made without the approval of the upper house. In other political systems (such as those of Britain and France, for example) the upper house has only a suspensory veto, in both law and fact. If both the Government and the lower house want a piece of proposed legislation passed, it will become law, and the most that the upper chamber can do is to slow down the process. In Germany, on the other hand, in both law and fact, the upper house sometimes has an absolute veto and sometimes has a suspensory veto, depending on the focus of legislation under consideration.

This brief discussion of the German political system, then, although covering only a small portion of all the significant structures of the political regime, points out some of the interesting, significant, and in some cases unique characteristics of the German polity. We will see in the several chapters that follow that many of these political structures that are so appropriate to the German political culture would not work elsewhere. Other regimes have developed their own mechanisms and structures for processing political demands and supports.

Discussion Questions

1. What were the most important changes that had to be made in West Germany to allow for the addition of East Germany to the German constitutional system?
2. What are the special federal institutions and political practices in Germany? How do they influence German politics?
3. What is special about the German chancellor? What special powers does this person have? What is special about their relationship with the German parliament?
4. What is the relationship between the Bundestag and the Bundesrat in the legislative process in Germany? Do they have equal roles? What is particularly representative of the principle of federalism in their procedures?
5. Is the German coalition-formation process substantially different from coalition formation in other democratic nations? How? Why?

Notes

1. Guido Goldman, *The German Political System* (New York: Random, 1974), pp. 157, 214; the full text of the Basic Law can be found here. See also Dietrich Orlow, *A History of Modern Germany: 1871 to Present* (New York: Routledge, 2015).

2. According to Hancock, a majority of the members of Bavaria's Parliament opposed the Basic Law "because it provided for a more centralized form of government than they would have wished. Nonetheless, the Bavarian Landtag endorsed the Basic Law as binding on the state"; see M. Donald Hancock, *West Germany: The Politics of Democratic Corporatism* (Chatham, NJ: Chatham House, 1989), pp. 29–30. See also Margaret Crosby, *The Making of the German Constitution: A Slow Revolution* (Oxford: Berg, 2004).

3. For a brief discussion of the costs of reunification and problems immediately following unification, see "Economic Affairs of Germany" under "Germany" in *Europa World Yearbook 1993,* p. 1208. See also Stephen Redding and Daniel Sturm, *The Costs of Remoteness: Evidence from German Division and Reunification* (London: Centre for Economic Policy Research, 2005).

4. On this note, an interesting study was published in 1966 by Karl Jaspers, a well-known German philosopher, who argued that "the Federal Republic of Germany is well on its way to abolishing parliamentary democracy and may be drifting toward some kind of dictatorship"; see Karl Jaspers, *The Future of Germany,* trans. E. B. Ashton (Chicago: University of Chicago Press, 1967), p. v.

5. Klaus von Beyme, *The Political System of the Federal Republic of Germany* (New York: St. Martin's, 1983), p. 12.

6. See Goldman, *German Political System,* pp. 157–164. All quotes from the Basic Law are taken from the text in Goldman and will not be given individual citations.

7. Lewis Edinger, *Politics in West Germany* (Boston: Little, Brown, 1977), p. 11. See Werner Heun, *The Constitution of Germany: A Contextual Analysis* (Oxford: Hart, 2011).

8. See Cristina Fraenkel-Haeberle et al., *Citizen Participation in Multi-Level Democracies* (Leiden: Brill, 2015); and Daniel Ziblatt, *Structuring the State: The Formation of Italy and Germany and the Puzzle of Federalism* (Princeton: Princeton University Press, 2006).

9. David Conradt, *The German Polity,* 3rd ed. (New York: Longman, 1986), p. 210.

10. The three were Bavaria, Hamburg, and Bremen. See ibid., p. 212.

11. Nevil Johnson, *State and Government in the Federal Republic of Germany: The Executive at Work* (New York: Pergamon Press, 1983), p. 7. See also Jan Erk and Wilfried Swenden, *New Directions in Federalism Studies* (New York: Routledge, 2010).

12. See Simon Green and William Paterson, eds., *Governance in Contemporary Germany: The Semisovereign State Revisited* (New York: Cambridge University Press, 2005); or Arthur Gunlicks, *The Lander and German Federalism* (New York: Manchester University Press, 2003).

13. See the *CIA World Factbook,* https://www.cia.gov/library/publications/the-world -factbook/geos/gm.html. See also R. Daniel Keleman, *The Rules of Federalism: Institutions and Regulatory Politics in the EU and Beyond* (Cambridge: Harvard University Press, 2004).

14. CIA World Factbook. See Chad Rector, *Federations: The Political Dynamics of Cooperation* (Ithaca: Cornell University Press, 2016); and Dietmar Braun, Christian Ruiz-Palmero, and Johanna Schnabel, *Consolidation Policies in Federal States: Conflicts and Solutions* (New York: Routledge, 2017).

15. Hancock, *West Germany,* p. 49. See also Jan Erk, *Explaining Federalism: State, Society, and Congruence in Austria, Belgium, Canada, Germany, and Switzerland* (New York: Routledge, 2008); and Sergio Ortino and Mitja Zagar, eds., *The Changing Faces of Federalism: Institutional Reconfiguration in Europe from East to West* (New York: Palgrave, 2005).

16. See John M. Quigley and Konrad Stahl, *Fiscal Competition and Federalism in Europe* (Amsterdam: North-Holland Press, 2001); and Carolyn Rowe and Wade Jacoby, *German Federalism in Transition: Reforms in a Consensual State* (New York: Routledge, 2010).

17. Hancock, *West Germany,* p. 49. See also Wilfried Swenden, *Federalism and Second Chambers: Regional Representation in Parliamentary Federations—The Australian Senate and German Bundesrat Compared* (New York: Lang, 2004).

18. Peter Katzenstein, *Policy and Politics in West Germany: The Growth of a Semisovereign State* (Philadelphia: Temple University Press, 1987), pp. 17–18. See also Florian Profitlich, *The Federal Constitutional Court of Germany* (London: Springer, 2004).

19. See Tom Ginsburg and Robert Kagan, eds., *Institutions and Public Law: Comparative Approaches* (New York: Lang, 2005); Ralf Rogowski and Thomas Gawron, *Constitutional Courts in Comparison: The U.S. Supreme Court and the German Federal Constitutional Court* (New York: Berghahn, 2016).

20. Johnson, *State and Government,* pp. 49–50. See also Nevil Johnson, *Government in the Federal Republic of Germany: The Executive at Work* (New York: Pergamon, 2013).

21. See the discussion "The Elevation of the Chancellor" in Gordon Smith, *Democracy in Western Germany: Parties and Politics in the Federal Republic* (New York: Holmes and Meier, 1986), p. 56; or the chapter by Thomas Poguntke, "A Presidentializing Party State? The Federal Republic of Germany," in Thomas Poguntke and Paul Webb, eds., *The Presidentialization of Politics: A Comparative Study of Modern Democracies* (New York: Oxford University Press, 2005).

22. See "Parliament: Election of the Federal President," http://www.bundestag.de /en/parliament/function/federal_convention/federal_convention/201836.

23. Johnson, *State and Government,* p. 50. A very good profile of Angela Merkel, Germany's first female chancellor, can be found on the British Broadcasting Corporation website at http://news.bbc.co.uk/2/hi/europe/4572387.stm.

24. See https://www.bundesregierung.de/Webs/Breg/EN/FederalGovernment/Cabinet /_node.html.

25. Johnson, *State and Government,* p. 54. See Hans Kundnani, *The Paradox of German Power* (New York: Oxford University Press, 2015). See also https://www.bundeskanzlerin .de/Webs/BKin/EN/Chancellery/Federal_Cabinet/federal_cabinet_node.html;jsessionid =E248A46268A0DEA1796E579E6E62E6C4.s5t2.

26. For example, see Conradt, *German Polity,* p. 162; or Joyce Marie Mushaben, *Becoming Madam Chancellor: Angela Merkel and the Berlin Republic* (Cambridge: Cambridge University Press, 2017). See "Tasks of the Federal Chancellor," https://www .bundeskanzlerin.de/Webs/BKin/EN/Chancellery/Tasks_of_the_Chancellor/tasks_of_the _chancellor_node.html;jsessionid=E248A46268A0DEA1796E579E6E62E6C4.s5t2.

27. See the publication by the German Bundestag, *Basic Law for the Federal Republic of Germany* (Berlin, 2010).

28. John Herz, *The Government of Germany* (New York: Harcourt, Brace, Jovanovich, 1972), p. 123. See also Katja Ziegler and Denis Baranger, eds., *Constitutionalism and the Role of Parliaments* (Oxford: Hart, 2007).

29. A good analysis of this period can be found in the book by Gert-Joachim Glaessner, *German Democracy: From Post–World War II to the Present Day* (New York: Berg, 2005). For a good description, see Kristina Spohr, *The Global Chancellor: Helmut Schmidt and the Reshaping of the International Order* (Oxford: Oxford University Press, 2016).

30. This is discussed in some detail in Hancock, *West Germany,* pp. 121–124.

31. Johnson, *State and Government,* pp. 68–69. See also Eric Langenbacher, ed., *Launching the Grand Coalition: The 2005 Bundestag Election and the Future of German Politics* (New York: Berghahn, 2006); and Geoffrey K. Roberts, *German Politics Today,* 3rd ed. (Manchester: Manchester University Press, 2016).

32. Articles 38–39 of the Basic Law. See also Horst Willi Schors, Klemens Vogel, and Raymond Kerr, *Facts: The Bundestag at a Glance* (Berlin: German Bundestag, Public Relations Division, 2010); and Susanne Linn and Frank Sobolewski, *The German Bundestag: Functions and Procedures, Organization and Working Methods—The Legislation of the Federation* (Rheinbreitbach: Kürschners Politikkontakte, 2015).

33. See "Distribution of Seats in the 19th German Bundestag," https://www.bundestag .de/en/parliament/plenary/19thbundestag/245692.

34. See https://www.bundesrat.de/EN/organisation-en/organisation-en-node.html. See also Gunlicks, *The Lander and German Federalism*; and Bjorn Erik Rasch and George Tsebelis, *The Role of Governments in Legislative Agenda Setting* (Hoboken, NJ: Taylor and Francis, 2013).

35. See http://www.bundestag.de/en/parliament/function/legislation.

36. See Gerhardt Loewenberg, *Parliament in the German Political System* (Ithaca: Cornell University Press, 1967), p. 269.

37. Ibid., p. 270.

38. See "Competencies of the German Federation and the Lander," http://www .bundestag.de/en/parliament/function/legislation/competencies/245700.

39. Loewenberg writes that about 60 percent of important measures require Bundesrat approval. The Basic Law sections that determine which subjects are subject to Bundesrat approval are "scattered over many sections of the document." Loewenberg, *Parliament,* pp. 365–366, n. 214.

40. A good discussion of the role of the Bundesrat in the passage of legislation can be found at http://www.bundestag.de/en/parliament/function/legislation.

41. Loewenberg, *Parliament,* p. 366. See also "Deutscher Bundestag, CDU/CSU Remains Strongest Parliamentary Group in the Bundestag Despite Losses," http://www .bundestag.de/en/#url=L2VuL2RvY3VtZW50cy90ZXh0OYXJjaGl2ZS9lbGVjdGlvbi0y MDE3LzUyNzI4NA==&mod=mod453306.

42. See Peter James, *The German Electoral System* (London: Taylor and Francis, 2017); or Geoffrey K. Roberts, *German Electoral Politics* (Manchester: Manchester University Press, 2013).

43. An archive of past results can be found at http://www.ipu.org/parline-e/reports /2121_arc.htm.

44. See "Deutscher Bundestag, CDU/CSU Remains Strongest Parliamentary Group."

45. A very good source is by the German federal foreign office in Berlin, "This Is the Way Federal Elections Work," https://www.deutschland.de/en/node/5023. See also Roberts, *German Electoral Politics.*

46. Von Beyme, *Political System of the Federal Republic of Germany,* p. 26.

47. In the twelfth electoral term of the Bundestag (1990–1994) the number of constituencies was increased from 248 to 328 as a consequence of the unification of Germany in 1990 and the increase in population and electoral size. As noted earlier, the number of districts was changed in 2001 from the 656 seats of the previous Bundestag (328 district representatives and 328 electoral list representatives) by the Federal Electoral Law of April 27, 2001. Today it comprises 299 single-member constituencies and a "normal" 299 proportional seats, although the latter can change. See http://www.bundestag.de /htdocs_e/bundestag/elections/electionresults/election_mp.html.

48. See https://www.bundestag.de/en/parliament/elections/arithmetic.

49. Ibid.

50. David P. Conradt, *Unified Germany at the Polls: Political Parties and the 1990 Federal Election* (Baltimore: Johns Hopkins University Press, 1990), pp. 23–24.

51. Eva Kolinsky, *Parties, Opposition, and Society in West Germany* (New York: St. Martin's, 1984), p. 40.

52. See "Voter Turnout at General Elections in Germany from 1949 to 2017," https://www.statista.com/statistics/753732/german-elections-voter-turnout. See also Harald Schoen, *Voters and Voting in Context: Multiple Contexts and the Heterogeneous German Electorate* (Oxford: Oxford University Press, 2017).

53. See "U.S. Trails Most Developed Countries in Voter Turnout," http://www .pewresearch.org/fact-tank/2017/05/15/u-s-voter-turnout-trails-most-developed -countries.

54. Helmut Gobel and Herbert Blondiau, eds., *Procedures, Programmes, Profiles: The Federal Republic of Germany Elects the German Bundestag on 5 October 1980* (Bonn: Inter-Nationes, 1980), p. 13.

55. For a discussion of the evolution of this point, see Karl H. Cerny, ed., *Germany at the Polls: The Bundestag Election of 1976* (Washington, DC: American Enterprise Institute, 1978), pp. 3–17. For a complete list of the parties participating in the 2017 Bundestag elections, including a full list of parties not winning enough seats for representation in the Bundestag, see "Bundestag Election 2017," https://www.bundeswahlleiter.de /en/bundestagswahlen/2017/ergebnisse/bund-99.html.

56. Gobel and Blondiau, *Procedures,* p. 13.

57. "Germany: Elections, Parliament, and Political Parties," p. 8. See also David Patton, *Out of the East: From PDS to Left Party in Unified Germany* (Albany: State University of New York Press, 2011).

58. "Deutscher Bundestag, CDU/CSU Remains Strongest Parliamentary Group."

59. See Charles Lees, *Party Politics in Germany: A Comparative Politics Approach* (New York: Palgrave Macmillan, 2005); and John Kincaid, Wolfgang Renzsch, and Klaus Detterbeck, *Political Parties and Civil Society in Federal Countries* (Don Mills, Ontario: Oxford University Press, 2015).

60. Russell J. Dalton, *Politics: West Germany* (Boston: Little, Brown, 1989), p. 246. See also Edward Turner, *Political Parties and Public Policy in the German Länder: When Parties Matter* (New York: Palgrave Macmillan, 2011).

61. See the report by the British Broadcasting Corporation, "Merkel Becomes German Chancellor," appearing on November 22, 2005, http://news.bbc.co.uk/2/hi/europe /4458430.stm.

62. Silvia Bolgherini and Florian Grotz, *Germany After the Grand Coalition: Governance and Politics in a Turbulent Environment* (New York: Palgrave Macmillan, 2010).

63. See the results of the election at http://www.ipu.org/parline-e/reports/2121_E.htm.

64. See Eric Langenbacher, *The Merkel Republic: An Appraisal* (New York: Berghahn, 2015).

65. See "German Election: How Right-Wing Is Nationalist AfD?" *BBC News,* October 13, 2017, http://www.bbc.com/news/world-europe-37274201. Interesting context can be found in Jean-Yves Camus, Nicolas Lebourg, and Jane Marie Todd, *Far-Right Politics in Europe* (Cambridge: Harvard University Press, 2017).

66. There is much good discussion of the evolution of the party system in the chapter by Gerhard Loewenberg, "The Remaking of the German Party System," in Karl Cerny, ed., *Germany at the Polls* (Washington, DC: American Enterprise Institute, 1990).

67. See Geoffrey Pridham, *Christian Democracy in Western Germany* (New York: St. Martin's, 1977). Another good source on Christian Democratic movements is Thomas Kesselman and Joseph Buttigieg, *European Christian Democracy: Historical Legacies and Comparative Perspective* (Notre Dame, IN: University of Notre Dame Press, 2003).

68. See http://www.cdu.de/en/3440.htm.

69. See http://www.csu.de/dialog/infomaterial.

70. See Christian Soe, "The Free Democratic Party," in H. Peter Wallach and George Romoser, eds., *West German Politics in the Mid-Eighties* (New York: Praeger, 1985).

71. See the discussion of coalition negotiation in the British Broadcasting Corporation coverage of the event on November 15, 2005, "Analysis: German Coalition Deal," http://news.bbc.co.uk/2/hi/europe/4438212.stm.

72. See http://www.spd.de/aktuelles. Unfortunately the party no longer maintains a website in English.

73. A very good study of the role of the Social Democrats while in power can be found in the work by Dan Hough, Michael Koss, and Jonathan Olsen, *The Left in Contemporary German Politics* (New York: Palgrave Macmillan, 2007).

74. See Stephen Milder, *Greening Democracy: The Anti-Nuclear Movement and Political Environmentalism in West Germany and Beyond, 1968–1983* (New York: Cambridge University Press, 2017); Werner Reutter, *Germany on the Road to "Normalcy": Policies and Politics of the Red-Green Federal Government (1998–2002)* (New York: Palgrave Macmillan, 2004).

75. Elim Papadakis, *The Green Movement in West Germany* (New York: St. Martin's, 1984), p. 13.

76. Ibid., pp. 159, 161.

77. Rob Burns and Wilfried van der Will, *Protest and Democracy in West Germany: Extra-Parliamentary Opposition and the Democratic Agenda* (New York: St. Martin's, 1988), p. 230.

78. Among these might be included the opposition to remilitarization and nuclear weapons (1950–1969), the movement of students against authoritarianism (1965–1969), the women's movement (1968–1985), environmentalism (1970s–1980s), and mass opposition to nuclear arms (1980–1986). See ibid., which has chapters on each of these protest movements.

79. A good analysis of the Greens can be found in Werner Hulsberg, *The German Greens: A Social and Political Profile,* trans. Gus Fagan (London: Verso, 1988), especially chap. 7, "The Greens: A Preliminary Assessment," and chap. 8, "The Crisis of Orientation." See also http://www.gruene.de/startseite.html; unfortunately the website is not available in English.

80. Dalton, *Politics: West Germany,* p. 293, n. 15.

81. Papadakis, *Green Movement,* p. 196.

82. Hulsberg, *German Greens,* p. 247. In the first appendix of his study, Hulsberg provides election results for the Greens in Land and federal elections between 1978 and 1987.

83. Melissa Eddy, "Alternative for Germany: Who Are They, and What Do They Want?" *New York Times,* September 25, 2017, https://www.nytimes.com/2017/09/25/world/europe/germany-election-afd.html.

11

India

Learning Outcomes

After reading this chapter, you will be able to

- See the impact of the creation of the modern Indian state on current Indian politics.
- Understand the pressures on the world's largest democracy today.
- Compare India's current political system with that of its colonial founder, Britain, and explain why India's political structures differ from those of Britain.
- Discuss the importance of religion, class, and caste in India.
- Understand the unique characteristics of Indian federalism and their effect upon the operation of Indian politics.
- Explain the institutions of Indian government.
- Discuss the role of political parties in India, and appreciate their role in the challenges facing Indian government.

India's political legacy stretches back over 5,000 years to the earliest civilizations in the Indus Valley.[1] Here, however, we begin by noting that by the eighteenth century, from 1757 to 1857, it was British trade—specifically in the form of the **British East India Company**—that dominated Indian politics, society, and economy. (The British East India Company, founded in London in 1600,[2] exercised much influence in the American colonies, too.)

India's Political Heritage
In 1857 the "Indian Rebellion" (the name given to it by British historians), also known as the First War of Indian Independence (the name

given to it by Indian historians), or the "Indian Mutiny," broke out as Indians protested their treatment at the hands of the British East India Company and the ultimate domination of British trade.[3] The outcome was an end to the rule of the British East India Company, but in its place came direct rule by the British government that became known as the **British Raj**. Britain controlled virtually all Indian land for the next ninety years, with the exception of a few princely states ruled by rajahs (but under the ultimate control of the British rule).[4]

In the early 1900s an Indian nationalist movement started to develop in earnest, and between 1918 and 1922 the **Indian National Congress** began to undertake an active movement to encourage the British to leave India.[5] Under the leadership of **Mohandas** (called Mahatma—"teacher") **Gandhi**, the movement emphasized a nonviolent style of civil disobedience to demonstrate to the British that they (the British) were in fact an occupying power, and that the Indians did not want the British to continue in that role.[6] It was a long-term process, however, with most British officials absolutely convinced that India should "belong" to Britain. The Congress movement continued to lead mass demonstrations through the period of World War I, and during that period of time the Congress led in the development of a "Home Rule" movement, through a noncooperation movement that started in 1918. A British military massacre at Amritsar, in the Punjab, in 1919 fueled the anti-British sentiment in India and helped the Congress's nationalist movement, which grew through more noncooperation as well as through active, but nonviolent, civil disobedience—called Satyagraha— in the 1920s and 1930s. In the 1940s a "Quit India" movement was undertaken, seeking to drive the British out of India completely.

The events of World War II had an effect on this, of course; although Indians were unhappy that the British government had committed India to the war effort by declaring a Commonwealth-wide position without appropriate consultation of India, the British reaction to Indian nationalism during the war was even more intense when the Japanese started to move west across Asia, toward Burma and India.[7] Although the British refused to consider any discussion of Indian nationalism during the war, by the time of the war's end it became clear through the vibrancy of the "Quit India" movement that such an eventuality would have to be considered after the war was over.

In early 1946 a group of British cabinet members visited India and participated in a conference dealing with India's future. While the conference ended up being unable to resolve the issue of how to handle the Hindu-Muslim tensions in India, it did conclude in May 1946 that "immediate arrangements should be made whereby Indians may decide the future constitution of India and an Interim Government be set up until the new constitution could be brought into being."[8] The Congress Party, led by **Jawaharlal Nehru** (1889–1964),[9] was set as the organization that would lead the new government. Later in 1946 the Muslim League,[10] led by **Muhammed Ali Jinnah**, was brought into the interim government with the (Hindu-dominated) Congress in the hope that such an action would lead to cooperation between the two religious groups.

In June 1947, **Viscount Lord Louis Mountbatten**, the representative of the British government in India and the last British governor-general of India, announced what came to be known as the **Mountbatten Plan**: India would be divided into two nations, one Hindu-dominated and one Muslim-dominated. Through the end of 1946 and into 1947, rioting and intercommunal conflict grew worse as the time of independence approached, with Hindus in what would become Pakistan moving to what would become India, and Muslims in what would become India moving to what would become Pakistan. Based on a 1951 census of displaced persons, 7.2 million Muslims went to Pakistan from India while approximately the same number of Hindus, Sikhs, and Muslims were forced to move to India from Pakistan immediately after partition.[11] Unfortunately, during this period of time there were numerous instances of horrible violence, including occasional ambushes by Hindus of departing Muslims, and by Muslims of departing Hindus. By the middle of 1947 tensions between the two groups were very strained. In July 1947 the India Independence Act was passed by the British Parliament, taking effect on August 15, 1947, but it was an India without the Muslim-majority territories that became part of Pakistan. A constituent assembly worked on a new constitution for India through 1949, and in January 1950 the Republic of India was formally declared to exist.

The Constitutional Structure

India's political structure, known as the Union Government, is based upon the British parliamentary model, to which we have been introduced and with which we will become more familiar later in this book. Cabinet government is the model by which politics operates in India. Although India is generally based upon the British model, one very significant difference of the Indian structure is that India is federal, not unitary as is the case of Britain, and this has very important implications for the operation of Indian politics. We will return to the topic of Indian federalism shortly.

> [India's Constitution] is among the longest in the world, with 395 articles and 8 schedules. It continued the constitutional development that took place under the British, retaining the basic precepts of the Government of India Act of 1935, and taking from it approximately 250

articles, verbatim or with minor changes. At the time of its adoption in 1950, the "borrowed" constitution was attacked as "un-Indian" and unsuited to a people inexperienced in democratic self-rule.[12]

India has the same three distinct but interrelated branches of government that we have met elsewhere: legislative, executive, and judicial. As in the British parliamentary model, the true (de facto as distinct from formal or de jure) political leadership of the executive branch of government—the prime minister—comes from the lower house of the bicameral legislature, and the **Council of Ministers** (which corresponds to the body called the cabinet in Britain) is also responsible to the legislature, meaning that the legislature has the right to fire the prime minister and the Council of Ministers. Also as is the case in Britain, the prime minister is the leader of the Council of Ministers. India's bicameral legislature consists of one chamber directly elected by the people and another chamber elected by members of the state legislatures.

Because India is a **republic**, and not a monarchy, the powers of the (symbolic) head of state are exercised by a president, who is elected for a five-year term of office by members of state legislatures and the national legislature.[13] These structures of the national government are essentially replicated on the state level, with each state having a governor as head of state, a chief minister serving the role of head of government, a Council of Ministers to run the business of state government, and a state legislature (some are unicameral, some are bicameral).

Although the Constitution specifically indicates that the judicial branch of government is to be independent of the other two branches, the fact is that since the executive controls judicial appointments, the judiciary has a difficult time ignoring the executive. India's network of courts is interesting because it reflects the fact that India is federal, not unitary:

> One of the unique features of the Indian Constitution is that, notwithstanding the adoption of a federal system and existence of Central Acts and State Acts in their respective spheres, it has generally provided for a single integrated system of Courts to administer both Union and State laws. At the apex of the entire judicial system, exists the Supreme Court of India below which are the High Courts in each State or group of States. Below the High Courts lies a hierarchy of Subordinate Courts . . . to decide civil and criminal disputes of petty and local nature. Different State laws provide for different kinds of jurisdiction of courts.[14]

Federalism

In addition to being the world's largest democracy, India also has the world's largest federal government. The national government shares power with twenty-eight states and seven union territories, although many have described India as quasi-federal in nature, with the central government far more powerful than the governments of the states.[15] Earlier in this volume we discussed why a political system might become federal; India is an example of a country that became federal both because of its size and also because of the diversity of its population.[16] The sheer scale of being a subcontinent means that having one government administer all policies would be almost an impossibility simply in terms of the infrastructure of administering policy across such distances. When this is combined with the incredible diversity of a population of 1.3 billion people,[17] we can see why more than one level of government makes good sense.

To take only one indication of how the Indian population is extremely diverse, let us look at language. Although Hindi and English are the two formal languages of Indian national government, many of India's twenty-eight states have their own official languages, different from these. Overall,

> Sir George Grierson's twelve-volume Linguistic Survey of India, published between 1903 and 1923, identified 179 languages and 544 dialects. . . . The 1981 census—the last census to tabulate languages—reported 112 mother tongues with more than 10,000 speakers and almost 1 million people speaking other languages. . . . In the early 1990s, there were thirty-two languages with 1 million or more speakers. . . . The Indian . . . constitution's Eighth Schedule, as amended by Parliament in 1992, lists eighteen official or Scheduled Languages.[18]

India's states vary greatly in size, population, and development. Some of the state legislatures are bicameral, based upon the model of the bicameral national parliament, while some are unicameral, having only one chamber.

The leaders of the state governments are called chief ministers, corresponding to the prime minister at the national level, and they are responsible to their respective legislatures in the same manner that the prime minister is responsible to the Lok Sabha—the lower house—on the national level. In fact, in some respects these chief ministers have more of a direct impact on the lives of Indian citizens than does the much more visible national prime minister. As James Manor has observed about the states' chief ministers, "Their role is similar to that of the prime minister at the national level. But since state governments loom large in the implementation of most of the national government's policies, and since the states have immense powers in their own right, chief ministers are much more intimately involved in the day-to-day dilemmas of governance than anyone in New Delhi."[19]

As we might expect in a federal, parliamentary system,[20] while each state has its own chief executive, it also has its own head of state, called a governor, who is appointed for a five-year term by the president of India (on the advice of the prime minister of India). The state governors play the same generally symbolic role in their respective states that the president plays at the national level in New Delhi, including choosing the chief minister of the state following state elections.[21]

India also has seven national union territories in addition to the twenty-eight states, including the national capital territory of Delhi. The territories are administered by lieutenant governors or administrators, each of whom is appointed by the president of India. The territories of Delhi and Pondicherry also have elected state assemblies of their own, and their own chief ministers, as well as heads of state known as lieutenant governors.

Executive Structures

The President

Although we have included India's president as one of its "executive structures" here, it is interesting to note that in India's Constitution the presidency is considered part of the legislative branch of government: India's Parliament is defined as comprising the upper house, the lower house, and the president. India's president is elected by what is called an electoral college made up of members of both houses of the national legislature—the Lok Sabha and the Rajya Sabha—as well as the members of all of the legislatures of the states. He (the president has always been a man, although there is no constitutional requirement that this be the case) is elected for a five-year term. The current president, **Shri Ram Nath Kovind**, was elected to become India's eleventh president in July 2017 and will serve until July 2022.

As is often the case in the selection of heads of state whose positions are primarily symbolic, President Kovind had a distinguished career before assuming his current office, as a lawyer, veteran political representative, and longtime advocate of egalitarianism in Indian society. He served as governor of the state of Bihar prior to being chosen to serve as president of India.[22]

India's president has some specific responsibilities related to the legislative branch of government.[23] He must approve all legislation before it becomes law (although this is not interpreted to mean that he can veto legislation that he doesn't like; he is expected to sign all legislation passed by the legislature), and like the British monarch, he also delivers a regular address to the opening of each session of Parliament—the speech is primarily drafted by the prime minister and Council of Ministers, much as we will see is the case for the British Speech from the Throne—describing the intentions of government for the coming term.[24]

India also has a vice president, who is also elected for a five-year term by a special electoral college of the members of both houses of the national legislature.[25] The vice president serves as the chair of the upper house of the legislature—the Rajya Sabha—unless he is serving as acting president. The vice president does not automatically become president in case of the death or resignation of the president, but would become acting president until a new president is chosen by a newly commissioned electoral college.

The Prime Minister

In Britain and most of the other parliamentary systems we have seen or will see in this book (with the exception of France), the true (de facto) leader of the executive branch of government is the prime minister, working with the cabinet, known in India as the Council of Ministers.[26] The prime minister is the leader of a party—or bloc of parties—that can command a majority in the Lok Sabha (see Box 11.1).

This, we will recall, enables us to say that India has responsible government—that is, government that is able to deliver on its promises because it controls a majority in the legislature and *can* do so. As we have seen to be the case elsewhere, the prime minister is appointed by the president, after the president consults with leaders of the national legislature and determines who will be able to command a majority in the directly elected house of the legislature. The prime minister must be a member of the Lok Sabha. There have been instances, such as the election of 1991, when the leader of a political party is not already a member of the Lok Sabha, and after their party has won a majority in the Lok Sabha they must ask one of their colleagues to resign so that they can run for a seat in the legislature to meet the constitutional requirement that the prime minister be a member of the lower house. This was the case when **Narasimha Rao** was chosen to be the Congress (I) Party's leader in 1991 and the Congress subsequently was chosen to form the Government. He ran for a special election to replace a colleague who was asked to resign, and he became prime minister in 1991.

When no single party can command a majority in the Lok Sabha—such as was the case for the Bharatiya Janata Party (BJP)–led coalition of over a dozen parties from 1999 to 2004, and the Congress-led thirteen-party coalition from 2004 to 2014—then the president invites the leader of a group of parties, referred to as a coalition, to form a Government.[27] After the president appoints the prime minister, the prime minister provides the

Box 11.1   Prime Ministers of India

Jawaharlal Nehru	August 1947–May 1964, Congress
Gulzari Lal Nanda	May 1964–June 1964, Congress
Lal Bahadur Shastri	June 1964–January 1966, Congress
Gulzari Lal Nanda	January 1966–January 1966, Congress
Indira Gandhi	January 1966–March 1977, Congress
Morarji Desai	March 1977–July 1979, Janata Party
Charan Singh	July 1979–January 1980, Janata Party
Indira Gandhi	January 1980–October 1984, Congress (I)
Rajiv Gandhi	October 1984–December 1989, Congress (I)
Vishwanath Pratap Singh	December 1989–November 1990, Janata Dal
Chandra Shekhar	November 1990–June 1991, Janata Dal (S)
P. V. Narasimha Rao	June 1991–May 1996, Congress (I)
Atal Bihari Vajpayee	May 1996–June 1996, Bharatiya Janata Party
H. D. Deve Gowda	June 1996–April 1997, Janata Dal
Inder Kumar Gujral	April 1997–March 1998, Janata Dal
Atal Bihari Vajpayee	March 1998–May 2004, Bharatiya Janata Party
Manmohan Singh	May 2004–May 2014
Narendra Modi	May 2014–present

Source: Government of India, "Former Prime Ministers of India," http://archive pmo.nic.in.

president with a list of names of individuals to appoint to the Council of Ministers, and the ministries to which they should be assigned.

The creation of the Council of Ministers is an important power of the prime minister, even though it is technically the president who names individuals to the Council of Ministers (see Box 11.2). This is true because it gives the prime minister the power to pull individuals from among a much larger group of aspiring politicians into formal leadership positions. And of course the reverse is also true: the prime minister has the power to remove anyone from their Council of Ministers and replace them if their performance is not satisfactory.

Legislative Structures

The Bicameral Parliament

As noted earlier, India has a bicameral parliament generally based upon the British Westminster model of government, with an upper house called the Rajya Sabha (Council of States) and a lower house called the Lok

286

Box 11.2   The Indian Union Council of Ministers, January 2018

Narendra Modi	Prime Minister; other portfolios
Raj Nath Singh	Minister of Home Affairs
Sushma Swwaraj	Minister of External Affairs
Arun Jaitley	Minister of Finance; Minister of Corporate Affairs
Nitin Jairam Gadkari	Minister of Road Transport and Highways; Minister of Shipping; Minister of Water Resources, River Development, and Ganga Rejuvenation
Suresh Prabhu	Minister of Commerce and Industry
D. V. Sadananda Gowda	Minister of Statistics and Program Implementation
Uma Bharati	Minister of Drinking Water and Sanitation
Ramvilas Paswan	Minister of Consumer Affairs, Food, and Public Distribution
Maneka Sanjay Gandh	Minister of Women and Child Development
Ananth Kumar	Minister of Chemicals and Fertilizers; Minister of Parliamentary Affairs
Ravi Shankar Prasad	Minister of Law and Justice; Minister of Electronics
Jagat Prakash Nadda	Minister of Health and Family Welfare
Ashok Gajapathi Raju Pusapati	Minister of Civil Aviation
Anant Geete	Minister of Heavy Industries and Public Enterprises
Harsimrat Kaur Badal	Minister of Food Processing Industries
Narendra Singh Tomar	Minister of Rural Development; Minister of Mines
Chaudhary Birender Singh	Minister of Steel
Jual Oram	Minister of Tribal Affairs
Radha Mohan Singh	Minister of Agriculture and Farmer Welfare
Thaawar Chand Gehlot	Minister of Social Justice and Empowerment
Smriti Zubin Irani	Minister of Textiles; Minister of Information and Broadcasting
Harsh Vardhan	Minister of Science and Technology; Minister of Earth Sciences
Prakash Javadekar	Minister of Human Resource Development
Dharmendra Pradhan	Minister of Petroleum and Natural Gas; Minister of Entrepreneurship
Piyush Goyal	Minister of Railways; Minister of Coal
Nirmala Sitharaman	Minister of Defense
Mukhtar Abbas Naqvi	Minister of Minority Affairs

Source: Government of India, "Portfolios of the Union Council of Ministers," http://www.pmindia.gov.in/en/news_updates/portfolios-of-the-union-council-o-ministers-2.
Notes: This list does not include eleven ministers of state (independent charge), nor thirty-seven ministers of state attached to various ministries.

Sabha (House of the People). The prime minister and Council of Ministers are drawn from and are responsible to the lower house, the Lok Sabha.

We saw in Chapter 3, in studying how legislatures are selected, that in bicameral legislatures the lower house is typically the "people's house," larger than the upper house and directly elected by the people, while the upper house may not be directly chosen by the people at all and is typically smaller. Both of these characteristics apply in India. The 233 elected members of the upper house, the Rajya Sabha, are chosen by members of the legislatures of the twenty-eight states and seven territories, and the president appoints another twelve "distinguished citizens" as members, bringing the total membership to 245.[28] Members of the Rajya Sabha serve six-year terms of office, with one-third of the members being elected every two years. By contrast, the members of the lower house, the Lok Sabha, are elected to five-year terms of office from single-member districts.

We also saw earlier in this volume that legislatures have been gradually losing the battle with executives for domination in the policy-formation process. This is so for a variety of reasons,[29] not the least of which is that policy issues are increasingly complex today and do not lend themselves to easy legislating as did issues in a much earlier time (the example used earlier was that it is much more difficult to effectively legislate the end of poverty than it was legislating against poaching on a king's land). The Indian Parliament is often criticized for not being particularly effective as a representative body, but it probably should be observed in the Parliament's defense that with a population of over 1.3 billion people, with pressures of poverty and lack of education limiting what can be done, it is really quite impressive that a stable democratic government has survived in India for over six decades.

The Lower House

The lower house of the national parliament is called the **Lok Sabha**, the House of the People. Its members are chosen by direct popular election in single-member districts. The Constitution allows for up to 552 members of the lower house. This means that there are up to 530 members coming from single-member districts in the twenty-eight states, and up to twenty members coming from single-member districts in the seven union territories. As well, the president has the right to appoint not more than two more members of the Lok Sabha to represent the "Anglo-Indian Community" if, in his opinion, there is not adequate representation of that group in the body.[30]

The single-member-district system is designed so that states get their share of seats in the Lok Sabha in proportion to their share of the national population. State legislatures are responsible for actually drawing district boundaries to create the districts for electoral contests.

Representation in the current sixteenth Lok Sabha is divided among the twenty-eight states and the seven union territories as indicated in Table 11.1. Representation in the Lok Sabha reflects the quite extraordinary diversity of India, both geographically and in terms of interest groups. There are over three dozen different political parties represented in the Lok Sabha, as indicated in Table 11.2.

As is the case in other bicameral parliamentary systems, although the Lok Sabha and the Rajya Sabha are nominally equal in the legislative process, the lower house in Indian federal parliament has some powers that give it in many respects more power than the upper house. First, because members of the Government (the prime minister and the

Table 11.1   States and Representation in the Lok Sabha, January 2018

State	Number of Representatives	State	Number of Representatives
Andhra Pradesh	25	Manipur	2
Arunachal Pradesh	2	Meghalaya	2
Assam	14	Mizoram	1
Bihar	40	Nagaland	1
Chhattisgarh	11	Orissa	21
Goa	2	Punjab	13
Gujarat	26	Rajasthan	25
Haryana	10	Sikkim	1
Himachal Pradesh	4	Tamil Nadu	39
Jammu and Kashmir	6	Telangana	17
Jharkhand	14	Tripura	2
Karnataka	28	Uttar Pradesh	80
Kerala	20	Uttaranchal	5
Madhya Pradesh	29	West Bengal	42
Maharashtra	48		
			State total: 530
Union territories			
Andaman and Nicobar Islands	1	Delhi	7
Chandigarh	1	Lakshadweep	1
Dadra and Nagar Haveli	1	Pondicherry	1
Daman and Diu	1		
			Territories total: 13
Nominated members from the Anglo-Indian Community	2		
			Total seats: 545
Women members: 66 (12%)			

Source: Government of India, Lok Sabha, "Sixteenth Lok Sabha, Statewise," http://164.100.47.194/Loksabha/Members/StatewiseList.aspx.

Table 11.2   Representation in the Lok Sabha by Party and Vote Percentage, January 2018

	Number of Seats	Percentage of Vote
Bharatiya Janata Party (BJP)	276	51.49
Indian National Congress (INC)	46	8.58
All India Anna Dravida Munnetra Kazhagam (AIADMK)	37	6.90
All India Trinamool Congress (AITC)	33	6.16
Biju Janata Dal (BJD)	20	3.73
Shiv Sena (SS)	18	3.36
Telugu Desam Party (TDP)	16	2.99
Telangana Rashtra Samithi (TRS)	11	2.05
Yuvajana Sramika Congress Party (YSR Congress)	9	1.68
Communist Party of India (Marxist) (CPI(M))	9	1.68
Lok Jan Shakti Party (LJSP)	6	1.12
Nationalist Congress Party (NCP)	6	1.12
Samajwadi Party (SP)	5	0.93
Shiromani Akali Dal (SAD)	4	0.75
Aam Aadmi Party (AAP)	4	0.75
All India United Democratic Front (AIUDF)	3	0.56
Independents (Ind)	3	0.56
Rashtriya Janata Dal (RJD)	3	0.56
Rashtriya Lok Samta Party (RLSP)	3	0.56
Indian National Lok Dal (INLD)	2	0.37
Indian Union Muslim League (IUML)	2	0.37
Janata Dal (Secular) (JD(S))	2	0.37
Janata Dal (United) (JD(U))	2	0.37
Jharkhand Mukti Morcha (JMM)	2	0.37
Apna Dal (Apna Dal)	2	0.37
Parties winning 1 seat and 0.19% of votes	12	
Total	536	97.75

Source: Parliament of India, Lok Sabha, "Sixteenth Lok Sabha, All Members Partywise," http://www.loksabha.nic.in/members/PartyWiseStatisticalList.aspx.

Council of Ministers) must come from the Lok Sabha, the Lok Sabha has more prominence. Second, because the Government is responsible to (that is, can be fired by) the Lok Sabha, and not the Rajya Sabha, the Lok Sabha ends up having more influence over the Government. Government coalitions are based upon representation in the Lok Sabha, not the Rajya Sabha. Third, money bills or financial bills containing clauses dealing with funding cannot be introduced in the Rajya Sabha, but are constitutionally required to start their legislative journey in the lower house. (This, too, is fairly typical of parliamentary practice in British-model systems, the usual justification being that the lower house is the house directly elected by the people, so any spending decisions should be made by those representatives directly chosen by the people.)[31]

The Upper House

With Britain as the colonial power in India prior to independence, it should come as no surprise that the model for a legislature that would be designed in India would reflect many characteristics of the Parliament at Westminster. However, the key to understanding the structure of India's upper house, the **Rajya Sabha**, does not lie in British politics, but rather in US politics. More specifically, we can understand the Rajya Sabha's role in the Indian Parliament in terms of the idea of representation of federal principles of government. The notion of hereditary membership for the upper house that exists in Britain was clearly inappropriate for India, but the federal nature of India suggested (as it did in the United States and Germany, among others) that representation in the upper house should be based upon the states, and (unlike the case in the United States) should be roughly proportional to the share of the national population that each state controlled.

In India's British colonial times, a chamber known as the Council of States was established in 1919 to represent some of the interests of the states in the colonial government. In modern times, the Rajya Sabha was set up in April 1952, and its first session took place in May 1952.[32] As noted earlier, the members of the Rajya Sabha are chosen by the members of the state legislatures for six-year terms, with one-third of the members being elected every other year. The Rajya Sabha has 233 members representing the states and union territories, as well as up to twelve presidential appointees, for a total of 245 members. As is typical of many upper houses that are not directly elected at one time by the people, it is referred to as a permanent body, which means that it is never dissolved and replaced by an entirely new Rajya Sabha, although its actual composition changes every two years.

Representation in the Rajya Sabha is based upon population. Each state is given a number of seats in the house that corresponds to the proportion of the national population found within its borders. Representation in the current Rajya Sabha is shown in Table 11.3.

As upper houses go, the Rajya Sabha is an active partner in the government process of India and, as Table 11.4 shows, reflects the wide range of political parties active in the political arena.[33] While the Government (i.e., the prime minister and the Council of Ministers) is responsible to (i.e., can be fired by) the lower house, the Lok Sabha, the upper

Table 11.3   Representation of the States in the Rajya Sabha, January 2018 (number of representatives)

Andhra Pradesh: 11	Karnataka: 12	Sikkim: 1
Arunachal Pradesh: 1	Kerala: 9	Tamil Nadu: 18
Assam: 7	Madhya Pradesh: 11	Telangana: 7
Bihar: 16	Maharashtra: 19	Tripura: 1
Chattisgarh: 5	Manipur: 1	Uttar Pradesh: 31
Goa: 1	Meghalaya: 1	Uttarakhand: 3
Gujarat: 11	Mizoram: 1	West Bengal: 16
Haryana: 5	Nagaland: 1	Puducherry: 1
Himachal Pradesh: 3	Orissa: 10	National Capital: 3
Jammu and Kashmir: 4	Punjab: 7	
Jharkhand: 6	Rajasthan: 10	

Nominated by president: 12
Total membership: 245

Source: Government of India, Rajya Sabha, "Members of Rajya Sabha, Statewise," http://164.100.24.167:8080/members/StatewiseList.asp.

house has some special powers to correspond to the special powers of the lower house, although they are not of the magnitude of the powers of the lower house. And as noted previously, both houses participate in the elections of the president and the vice president of India.[34]

Political Parties and Elections

The Party System

India is the world's largest democracy, and it has been an active parliamentary democracy through recent history. With the exception of the period from June 1975 to March 1977 under Prime Minister **Indira Gandhi**,[35] when parliamentary elections for national and state governments were postponed and the Government assumed quite extraordinary emergency powers, India has been an open, sometimes tumultuously so, democratic system with a vigorous exchange of ideas and open access to political parties.

As noted earlier, India is a federal republic, and the political party structure reflects this fact by labeling parties as national or state organizations. Some parties, of course, have both national and state versions, just as some parties exist as national organizations and also as state organizations in more than one state.[36] A party recognized in four different states is automatically classified as a national party, as well. Prior to the 2005 elections in India, in addition to the dozens of political parties

Table 11.4   Representation by Political Parties in the Rajya Sabha, January 2018

Party	Number of Seats
All India Anna Dravida Munnetra Kazhagam (AIADMK)	13
All India Trinamool Congress (AITC)	12
Biju Janata Dal (BJD)	8
Bharatiya Janata Party (BJP)	58
Bodoland People's Front (BPF)	1
Bahujan Samaj Party (BSP)	5
Communist Party of India (CPI)	1
Communist Party of India (Marxist) (CPI(M))	7
Dravida Munnetra Kazhagam (DMK)	4
Indian National Congress (INC)	57
Independent and Others (Ind)	6
Indian National Lok Dal (INLD)	1
Indian Union Muslim League (IUML)	1
J&K Peoples Democratic Party (J&K PDP)	2
Janata Dal (Secular) (JD(S))	1
Janata Dal (United) (JD(U))	7
Jharkhand Mukti Morcha (JMM)	1
Kerala Congress (M) (KC(M))	1
Nationalist Congress Party (NCP)	5
Nominated (NOM)	8
Naga Peoples Front (NPF)	1
Rashtriya Janata Dal (RJD)	3
Republican Party of India (RPI)	1
Shiromani Akali Dal (SAD)	3
Sikkim Democratic Front	1
Samajwadi Party (SP)	18
Shiv Sena (SS)	3
Telugu Desam Party (TDP)	6
Telangana Rashtra Samithi (TRS)	3
Yuvajana Sramika Rythu Congress Party (YSRCP)	1
Open	6
Total	245

Source: Government of India, Rajya Sabha, "Alphabetical Party Position in the Rajya Sabha," http://164.100.47.5/Newmembers/partymemberlist.aspx.

that were recognized by the federal election commission, hundreds of political party organizations were classified as "unrecognized" because they had not won the necessary number of votes in any election to receive that designation.[37]

The period of the 1975–1977 "emergency" was very contentious in India.[38] Although "president's rule"—the name given in India to the prime minister exercising emergency powers—had been used often in

India's modern political history prior to 1975,[39] Prime Minister Indira Gandhi exercised emergency powers to a degree that had not been done previously in India.[40]

Gandhi said that India was facing a crisis of unmatched proportions domestically, as a result of strikes taking place in the country, economic inequality, and political stalemate in the nation's legislative bodies. Her argument was that if extraordinary measures were not taken—even "extraordinary" for a system in which emergency powers had been used often in the past—then Indian democracy might not survive. Using a process permitted by the Constitution, Gandhi consulted with President **Fakhruddin Ali Ahmed**, and asked the president to declare a state of emergency; she then assumed extraordinary political and economic powers for an eighteen-month period of time. During that time she undertook a massive suppression of the political opposition, jailing many and using government offices with the purported goal of bringing stability back to the nation. She undertook radical economic reforms through prime ministerial decree that she had been unable to get the Parliament to approve through the regular legislative process, enacting an economic reform program that permitted the government to regulate the economy far more rigorously than was the case in the past. The president permitted the continuation of Gandhi's emergency powers through late 1977, at which time she announced that India was ready to resume stable democratic government, although one of the last things she did under emergency powers was to issue legislation protecting herself from reprisals or legal punishment after democracy returned.[41]

Political Parties

India has dozens of political parties, and new parties are created on a regular basis. Even the Congress Party, which was so instrumental in the creation of the state of India,[42] has not survived in its original form through the past six decades of history as India's dominant party. Indeed, in 1980, following the period of emergency government, a bloc of the Congress Party renamed their organization "Congress (I)" after Indira Gandhi, with the motto "A government that works!" Today, the Congress Party is one of several parties with a substantial following nationwide, although it is no longer the dominant party on the Indian landscape.

The Congress movement brought India into existence, and it wholly dominated Indian politics through the late 1960s. It split in 1969, however, over disagreements dealing with Indira Gandhi's economic policies when she pushed through a program of land reform and "placed a ceiling on personal income, private property, and corporate profits. She also nationalized the major banks."[43] At that time the Congress became two different groups: the Congress (R) (Requisition) and the Congress (O) (Organization) factions. Although the party captured power after that time, it never regained its previous domination of the nation's political scene.[44] As late as the 1990s the renamed Congress (I) was the largest single party in the Lok Sabha, but it wasn't strong enough to form a government on its own, and it frequently found the process of coalition formation to be difficult.[45]

The 1967 election was the first time that the Congress really appeared vulnerable, with opposition parties winning control of state governments in Bihar, Kerala, Orissa, Punjab, and West Bengal. In the 1967 election in Rajasthan an opposition coalition was in control.[46] The Bharatiya Janata Party has been one of the major opposition forces. The BJP "is unique among India's political parties in that neither it nor its political predecessors were ever associated with the Congress. Instead, it grew out of an alternative nationalist organization—the Rashtriya Swayamsevak Sangh (RSS—National Volunteer Organisation). The BJP still is affiliated with the network of organizations popularly referred to as the RSS family."[47]

Elections

India had more than 834 million registered voters in 2014, leaving no doubt that it is, indeed, the world's largest democracy; of these, over 554 million voters actually cast votes in the 2014 election. These voters "travel to nearly 600,000 polling stations to choose from some 8,950 candidates representing roughly 162 parties."[48] Because of the sheer magnitude of India's electorate, the actual process of voting takes place over several weeks to allow electoral officials to move from one area to another.[49] An interesting marker of the 2014 parliamentary elections was that these were the first all-electronic elections in the history of the country. "One million electronic voting machines were deployed across the country to record every vote at the press of a button. Around five million people worked either as election officials or security personnel."[50]

> This was also the first time that a government, not run by Congress, the country's grand old party, had completed almost five years in office. The right-of-centre coalition of 22 parties, the National Democratic Alliance (NDA), led by the ruling Hindu-nationalist Bharatiya Janata Party (BJP), was seeking a second consecutive term in office. Its main challenger was the Indian National Congress (INC) led by Ms. Sonia Gandhi [the Italian-born widow of Indira Gandhi's son, Rajiv Gandhi, himself a past prime minister]. About 40 parties contested the elections, some regionally and some at national level. The BJP and Congress were directly pitted against each other, with no regional party in the race, in only 103 of the 543 constituencies.[51]

Today the Bharatiya Janata Party is the dominant bloc in Indian parliamentary politics, and in the May 2014 election the BJP received enough votes to form a parliamentary majority government on its own for the first time since 1984.[52]

Religion, Caste, and Social Class in India

Religion

When we look at politics and political behavior in India today we may be surprised to see the continuing influence of some very traditional forces in the determination of government and policy questions, including religion, caste, and social class. One student of Indian politics has noted that "it was long accepted by historians and other analysts of the past and present that religion would have a decreasing role in the modern world," and that "the great issues of political discourse would be constitutional arrangements, the solving of economic problems, and the resolution of conflicts of interests between nations."[53] Another student of India has observed

> The original vision of Indian democracy included a view of India as a secular polity, and in the nation's early days the feeling was that the goal of a secular polity was both reasonable and attainable. "With the adoption of 'one man, one vote' and the principle of secularism in the constitution, they hoped that the vote will replace religion as the legitimizer of political power and gradually the social functions of religion would be taken over by the secular institution—the state. . . . Secularism meant not only the absence of a state religion, but equal protection of all religions by the state."[54]

The interaction of religion and politics through modern Indian history has been problematic, however. Although it may have been the goal of many political leaders that India be a secular democracy, such certainly was not the goal of all political leaders (specifically, of course, the leaders of the religious groups). And in fact, religion has continued to be a very visible dimension of the political world in India's history.[55] Indeed, some leaders of different religious groups pressed as vigorously as they could for greater communalism, although it must be noted that the word *communalism* itself is problematic in this discussion: "Communalism is another Indian term that defies precise definition, but it is always used in a pejorative sense, implying that religious groups stress the importance of membership in their group over national identity, and that these groups seek their own advantage over those of other groups and of the nation as a whole."[56]

It is not clear exactly how successful the advocates of the two conflicting sets of goals have been. "It is frequently asserted that communalism in India has been increasing at an alarming pace; inter-community relations have dramatically worsened in recent years."[57] Although communal tension is typically thought of in terms of Hindu-Muslim conflict, in fact there are numerous other dimensions of conflict in India today, including between Christians and Sikhs. The issues of communalism that are related to the Kashmir conflict, and the issues of communalism that are related to the Punjab conflict—to which we will return later in this chapter—do tend to align along Hindu-Muslim lines and Hindu-Sikh lines, respectively. Muslim, Sikh, and Hindu orthodoxy are strong forces in their respective communities, and they find their way into politics.[58]

Caste

Caste is a concept that is often associated with Indian society and life.[59] As a religious concept, it is recognized by the *American Heritage Dictionary* as "each of the hereditary classes of Hindu society, distinguished by relative degrees of ritual purity or pollution and of social status" and as "any exclusive social class."[60] Although the government of India has sought to eliminate the caste system—and indeed the government has formally outlawed it—the concept and its implications have not disappeared. "Caste has undergone significant change since independence, but it still involves hundreds of millions of people. In its preamble, India's constitution forbids negative public discrimination on the basis of caste."[61] However, as many observers have noted, "Although some educated Indians tell non-Indians that caste has been abolished or that 'no one pays attention to caste anymore,' such statements do not reflect reality."[62]

> One irony of Indian politics is that its modern secular democracy has enhanced rather than reduced the political salience of traditional forms of social identity such as caste. Part of the explanation for this development is that India's political parties have found the caste-based selection of candidates and appeals to the caste-based interests of the Indian electorate to be an effective way to win popular support. More fundamental has been the economic development and social mobility of those groups officially designated as Backward Classes and Scheduled Castes. Accounting for 52 and 15 percent of the population, respectively, the Backward Classes and Scheduled Castes, or Dalits as they prefer to be called, constitute a diverse range of middle, lower, and outcaste groups who have come to wield substantial power in most states. Indeed, one of the dramas of modern Indian politics has been the Backward Classes and Dalits' jettisoning of their political subordination to upper castes and their assertion of their own interests.[63]

Social Class

Although there is an overlap between **social class** and caste—members of the lowest castes also tend to be members of the lowest social classes, but not all members of higher social classes are members of high castes—they really address different things. "In an analysis of class formation in India, anthropologist Harold A. Gould points out that a three-level system of stratification is taking shape across rural India. He calls the three levels Forward Classes (higher castes), Backward Classes (middle and lower castes), and Harijans (very low castes)."[64]

India's rapidly expanding economy, and its rush to produce a better-educated population that can address needs for new technology, have led to the rapid expansion of a new middle class in India. "The new middle class is booming, at least partially in response to a doubling of the salaries of some 4 million central government employees in 1986, followed by similar increases for state and district officers. Unprecedented liberalization and opening up of the economy in the 1980s and 1990s have been part of the picture."[65]

The Indian middle class today is estimated to include nearly 175 million people (out of over 1.3 billion, we should not forget).[66]

> Members of the upper class—around 1 percent of the population—are owners of large properties, members of exclusive clubs, and vacationers in foreign lands, and include industrialists, former maharajas, and top executives. Below the middle class is perhaps a third of the population—ordinary farmers, tradespeople, artisans, and workers. At the bottom of the economic scale are the poor—estimated at 320 million, some 45 percent of the population in 1988—who live in inadequate homes without adequate food, work for pittances, have undereducated and often sickly children, and are the victims of numerous social inequities.[67]

One of the key points to keep in mind is that, as one observer has noted, "one of the first priorities of these middle classes is a top-quality education for their children."[68] This has resulted in a significant demand for education—public and private—that has in turn had a result of making Indian students increasingly attractive on the global marketplace for education-intensive (i.e., technology-related) jobs.

Crises of National Unity: The Punjab and Kashmir

As noted earlier, one of the identifying characteristics of Indian politics has traditionally been what is called communalism, or a tendency of people to identify with "their" religious group rather than the nation as a whole. One scholar in the field has observed that "religion has continued to be a major source of socio-political identity as also of social cleavage both independently of and in association with language and caste."[69] Indeed, others have suggested that communalism "has been increasing at an alarming pace" and that "inter-community relations have dramatically worsened in recent years."[70] Traditionally this conflict has been seen in terms of the Hindu-Muslim tensions, described at the outset of this chapter, which led to the partition of India and the establishment of the nation of Pakistan. Today, however, the most frequently cited religion-based tension in India has been in the Punjab, where the increasing conflict between Hindu Indians and Sikh Indians has been the issue.

The Punjab

Tension in the state of **Punjab** has led to increasing conflict and outright violence, as the Sikh population there has increasingly called for the creation of a new state where the Sikhs would be the dominant group.[71] "The confrontation in Punjab began in 1973 when the Anandpur Sahib Resolution was announced, calling for the establishment of a 'Sikh Autonomous Region' with its own constitution. It also called for the transfer of Chandigarh, a union territory, to Punjab as the state's capital."[72]

This tension came to a head in June of 1984 when Prime Minister Indira Gandhi sent the Indian army into the Golden Temple in the city of Amritsar, a city in the Punjab, a site holy to the Sikhs. The army was sent in pursuit of Jarnail Singh Bhindranwale, a Sikh leader whom Gandhi saw as disloyal to India. The Indian army attacked the temple on June 3–6, 1984, and Bhindranwale, who was hiding in the temple, died during the fighting. The Golden Temple complex was damaged, as well.

One consequence of this conflict was that many Sikhs were outraged at what they saw as the desecration of their holiest shrine in the attack by the government of India. On October 31, 1984, Indira Gandhi was assassinated[73] by two of her Sikh bodyguards, Beant Singh and Satwant Singh, in retribution for the attack on Bhindranwale and the Golden Temple. The assassination of Gandhi led, in turn, to many anti-Sikh riots across the country, and as well to increasing sectarian tension between the majority Hindu population and the minority Sikh population. As one student noted, "To many Hindus, the imagery of a turban-wearing Indian has undergone a drastic change. He is anti-Indian, a secessionist, a Pakistani-collaborator, a killer of Mrs. Gandhi. He is an enemy or, to be moderate, a neighbor not trustworthy."[74]

This Hindu-Sikh tension continues to exist in India today. However, in what might be seen as an ironic twist, many commentators say that the "normal" tensions have been exacerbated by politicians.

Analysts from a variety of perspectives have commented on the increasing willingness of India's politicians to exploit religious and ethnic tensions for short-term political gain, regardless of their longer-term social consequences. Political scientist Rajni Kothari, for example, charges that there has been a general decline in the morality of Indian politicians. He alleges that politicians play a "numbers game," in which they appeal to chauvinistic caste and religious sentiments to win elections, despite the longer-term social tensions that their campaigns create. . . . The violence of religious militants in Punjab and Jammu and Kashmir has also contributed to sentiment among the Hindu majority that religious minorities employ aggressive tactics to win special concessions from the government.[75]

Kashmir

The status of **Kashmir**, and the history of events leading to its being part of India, have long been contested between India and Pakistan.[76]

The conflict assumes considerable symbolic as well as strategic importance because, as India's only Muslim-majority state, Jammu and Kashmir validates India's national identity as a religiously and culturally diverse society held together by a common history and cultural heritage. The roots of the Kashmir conflict extend at least as far back as 1947 when Maharaja Hari Singh, the princely state's Hindu ruler, decided to cede his domain with its predominantly Muslim population to the Indian Union at a time when Kashmir was under attack by a Muslim paramilitary force supported by Pakistan. Tensions persisted through the mid-1980s. . . . The status of Kashmir was the cause of two wars between India and Pakistan, in 1947 and 1965, and was an issue in the third war, in 1971.[77]

India claims that Kashmir legally became part of India in 1947 (with Singh's ceding the state to India), while Pakistan claims that the Kashmir citizens were denied their choice of which state to join when Maharaja Singh decided to cede Kashmir to India.[78] Discussions about a possible resolution of this conflict have been held periodically between India and Pakistan since 1972, but there have been no concrete negotiations. Unfortunately, there have as well been regular outbreaks of violence across the ceasefire line that has existed since 1948. The Pakistani-administered portion of Kashmir is almost exclusively Muslim, while the Indian-administered area is approximately two-thirds Muslim and one-third Hindu.

The significance of the Kashmir issue lies in the fact that it has been a continuous source of conflict between India and Pakistan, and that it continues to offer a reason for the governments dominated by two different religious groups to be in conflict.[79] Pakistan and India have a variety of issues that they need to work through, everything from economic relationships to atomic weapons, and the issue of who should control Kashmir has often served to both inflame the relationship between the two nations and also muddy the diplomatic waters when other important and complex issues need to be discussed.

The Indian System in Perspective

In recent years India has continued to appear on the world stage in a variety of key roles, ranging from being a key player in global information technology to being one of the world's leading markets for other economies. The increasingly global nature of the world's economies—highlighted in Thomas L. Friedman's book *The World Is Flat*[80]—has meant that when Americans telephone large US companies they are as likely to speak to telephone operators in India as someone in the United States. The Indian economy has grown enormously in recent years,[81] reflecting India's integration into a global marketplace.

Indeed, when Narasimha Rao became leader of Congress (I) and prime minister in 1991, he appointed Manmohan Singh (subsequently India's prime minister) to be his finance minister. Under Singh the Indian economy was transformed:

> Manmohan Singh's program of economic globalization, launched in June, 1991, had opened India's long-protected socialist economy to stimulating winds of world market investment and dramatic change, fueling what many hailed as India's economic "miracle." In less than five years India's economy grew as much as it had during the previous forty. Over ten billion dollars worth of foreign capital pumped up India's long-stalled, stagnating economy, giving it a vigorous jumpstart. Exports rocketed by more than 20 percent annually, industrial production jumped over 10 percent, and inflation fell to little more than 6 percent by the end of 1995. For the most affluent third of India's 960 million people, globalization brought hitherto undreamed-of levels of prosperity and material comfort.[82]

In the years since Narendra Modi has been prime minister, the Indian economy has continued to be strong. Modi is the first Indian prime minister to be born after India attained independence. Challenges of developing infrastructure have been daunting; India's population of 1.3 billion puts strains on roads, electricity, water delivery, health care, and other public services that most countries don't face. His extremely strong showing in the 2014 Indian election shows that he continues to be well connected to Indian voters.[83]

India prides itself on being "the world's largest democracy" today. While it clearly faces many of the challenges that developing nations must face—challenges that we identified in Chapter 3, on political development—the fact is that India has made remarkable progress in a number of key areas. Its economy is increasingly diversified, and the government continues to work on this. Its literacy rate is improving. At the time of independence Indian literacy was 14 percent (and female literacy was 8 percent); in 2011 the overall literacy rate for those over age seven years was 73 percent, with men at 81 percent and women at 65 percent.[84] India's middle class is expanding, although the lowest third of the population still live in dire circumstances. India does show, however, that a successful and stable democratic experience can be found in a developing nation. As Robert Hardgrave Jr. has written, "The institutions of government of India . . . were grounded in the structure of the British Raj. They were designed for administration and for the maintenance of stability; their purpose was to contain demands, not to respond to them. The fundamental problem of transition was to adapt these instruments of order to the needs of social change and democratic response."[85]

To a substantial degree, India has been a success story that can be emulated by many other nations that are today in the "developing" group of states seeking to become "developed" and democratic.

Discussion Questions

1. How did the history of British colonialism affect the current Indian political system? What were the most significant acts by Britain in the creation of the modern Indian state?
2. How does India's style of federal government compare with other federal governments that we have learned about? What are the most important differences? In what ways does India's brand of federalism reflect particularly Indian characteristics?
3. What political structures are particularly important in relation to religious cleavages in Indian society?
4. How powerful is the Indian prime minister today? Why is this so?
5. Given India's role as the world's largest democracy, what institutions are particularly important in the support of political stability there?

Notes

1. See, among others, Hermann Kulke and Dietmar Rothermund, *A History of India* (New York: Routledge, 2016); or D. D. Kosambi, *Ancient India* (New York: Meridian, 1965).

2. Robert L. Hardgrave Jr., *India: Government and Politics in a Developing Nation,* 3rd ed. (New York: Harcourt, Bracc, Jovanovich, 1980), p. 18. See also Emily Erikson,

Between Monopoly and Free Trade: The English East India Company, 1600–1757 (Princeton: Princeton University Press, 2014).

3. This is discussed in detail in Jim Masselos, *Nationalism on the Indian Subcontinent: An Introductory History* (London: Thomas Nelson, 1972), in chap. 2, "The Mutiny of 1857." See also Jill Bender, *The 1857 Indian Uprising and the British Empire* (Cambridge: Cambridge University Press, 2016).

4. A good general history can be found in John McLeod, *The History of India* (Santa Barbara: Greenwood, 2015).

5. This material is a summary of a quite substantial discussion, "Indian National Congress: From 1885 till 2017—A Brief History of Past Presidents," http://indianexpress.com/article/india/here-is-a-list-of-past-presidents-of-indian-national-congress-4967084. See also Richard Sisson and Stanley Wolpert, eds., *Congress and Indian Nationalism: The Pre-Independence Phase* (New Delhi: Oxford University Press, 1988); or Masselos, *Nationalism on the Indian Subcontinent,* chap. 5, "The Indian National Congress, 1885–1892."

6. A good discussion of this is in Judith Brown, *Gandhi and Civil Disobedience: The Mahatma in Indian Politics* (Cambridge: Cambridge University Press, 1977). See also Ramin Jahanbegloo, *The Gandhian Moment* (Cambridge: Harvard University Press, 2013); and Ajay Skaria, *Unconditional Equality: Gandhi's Religion of Resistance* (Minneapolis: University of Minnesota Press, 2016).

7. See "The Second World War and the Congress," https://www.inc.in/en/india-at-70/indiaat70-key-policies-brought-in-60-years-of-congress-rule-1940s-50s.

8. Ibid.

9. A good biography of Nehru is that by B. R. Nanda, *Jawaharlal Nehru: Rebel and Statesman* (New York: Oxford University Press, 1995).

10. See Masselos, *Nationalism on the Indian Subcontinent,* chap. 7, "Muslims and the Formation of the Muslim League."

11. See William Henderson, "The Refugees in India and Pakistan," *Journal of International Affairs* 7, no. 1 (1953): 57–65. See also Jisha Menon, *The Performance of Nationalism: India, Pakistan, and the Memory of Partition* (Cambridge: Cambridge University Press, 2013).

12. Hardgrave, *India,* p. 47. See also Narendra Chapalgaonker and Subhashchandra Wagholikar, *Mahatma Gandhi and the Indian Constitution* (Abingdon: Routledge, 2016).

13. Government of India, "The President of India: The Structure of the Government," http://presidentofindia.gov.in.

14. Supreme Court of India, "Supreme Court of India: Law, Courts, and the Constitution," http://supremecourtofindia.nic.in/constitution. See also Durga Das Basu, *Introduction to the Constitution of India* (Gurgaon: LexisNexis, 2015).

15. Hardgrave, *India,* p. 87. See also Subrata Kumar Mitra, *Politics in India: Structure, Process, and Policy* (New Delhi: Oxford University Press, 2014).

16. A good source for discussion of these types of issues is by Balveet Arora and Douglas Verney, *Multiple Identities in a Single State: Indian Federalism in Comparative Perspective* (New Delhi: Knoark, 1995).

17. This is the estimated population from 2018. See http://www.worldometers.info/world-population/india-population.

18. See https://www.loc.gov/item/96019266.

19. See James Manor, "India's Chief Ministers and the Problem of Governability," in Philip Oldenburg, ed., *India Briefing: Staying the Course* (Armonk, NY: Sharpe, 1995), pp. 48–49. See also Marcus F. Franda, *West Bengal and the Federalizing Process in India* (Princeton: Princeton University Press, 2016).

20. For discussions of federal-related political structures, see Atul Kohli, *The Success of India's Democracy* (New York: Cambridge University Press, 2001); Sankaran Krishna, "Constitutionalism, Democracy, and Political Culture in India," in Daniel Franklin and Michael Baun, eds., *Political Culture and Constitutionalism: A Comparative Approach* (Armonk, NY: Sharpe, 1995); or Akhtar Majeed, "Republic of India," in John Kincaid

and G. Alan Tarr, eds., *Constitutional Origins, Structure, and Change in Federal Countries* (Montreal: McGill-Queen's University Press, 2005).

21. A link to all state legislatures can be found on the Government of India website, https://www.india.gov.in/india-glance/states-india. See also K. L. Bhatia and Rudiger Wolfrum, *Federalism and Frictions in Centre-State Relations: A Comparative Review of Indian and German Constitutions* (New Delhi: Deep and Deep, 2001); or Partha Chatterjee, *State and Politics in India* (New York: Oxford University Press, 1998).

22. See Government of India website for the president of India, http://presidentofindia .gov.in.

23. See Abjul Gafoor Abdul Majeed Noorani, *Constitutional Questions in India: The President, Parliament, and the States* (New York: Oxford University Press, 2000).

24. See "Role and Power of India's President," *Hindustan Times,* July 25, 2012, http://www.hindustantimes.com/india/role-and-power-of-india-s-president/story-glu 9uyqsZLUtvgjyxO2cpK.html.

25. Government of India, "The Vice President of India," http://vicepresidentofindia .nic.in/homepage.

26. A good reference is by V. A. Pai Panandiker and Ajay K. Mehra, *The Indian Cabinet: A Study in Governance* (New Delhi: Konark, 1996).

27. On coalitions in India, see Katharine Adeney and Lawrence Saez, *Coalition Politics and Hindu Nationalism* (New York: Routledge, 2005); Sanjay Ruparelia, *Divided We Govern: Coalition Politics in Modern India* (New York: Oxford University Press, 2015); or Csaba Nikolenyi, *Minority Governments in India: The Puzzle of Elusive Majorities* (London: Routledge, 2012).

28. Parliament of India, "Council of States (Rajya Sabha)," http://rajyasabha.nic .in/rsnew/council_state/council_state.asp.

29. See Arthur Rubinoff, "The Decline of India's Parliament," in Nizam Ahmed and Philip Norton, eds., *Parliaments in Asia* (Portland: Cass, 1999); or R. B. Jain, "Implementing Public Policy in India," in Frederick Lazin, ed., *The Policy Implementation Process in Developing Nations* (Stamford: JAI, 1999).

30. See http://loksabha.nic.in. See also Suhas Palshikar, K. C. Suri, and Yogendra Yadav, *Party Competition in Indian States: Electoral Politics in Post-Congress Polity* (New Delhi: Oxford University Press, 2014).

31. See http://rajyasabha.nic.in.

32. See the Rajya Sabha website, "Questions on the History of the Rajya Sabha," http://rajyasabha.nic.in.

33. Ibid.

34. See http://rajyasabha.nic.in.

35. Although her name might suggest a relationship to Mahatma Gandhi, in fact Indira Gandhi was Jawarhalal Nehru's daughter.

36. One of the classic works on a state political party structure is the book by Paul Brass, *Factional Politics in an Indian State* (Berkeley: University of California Press, 1965).

37. See "Indian Elections," http://www.elections.in/political-parties-in-india, a page on political parties that not only lists the nationally competitive political parties but also provides links to electoral offices in each state's electoral office listing all parties competing in the states, as well.

38. See P. N. Dhar, *Indira Gandhi, the "Emergency," and Indian Democracy* (New York: Oxford University Press, 2000); or Bipan Chandra, *In the Name of Democracy: JP Movement and the Emergency* (New York: Penguin, 2003).

39. "President's Rule has been imposed frequently, and its use is often politically motivated. During the terms of prime ministers Nehru and Lal Bahadur Shastri, from 1947 to 1966, it was imposed ten times. Under Indira Gandhi's two tenures as prime minister (1966–1977 and 1980–1984), President's Rule was imposed forty-one times." Library of Congress, *Country Studies: India,* chap. 8, "Government and Politics," https:// www.loc.gov/item/96019266.

40. This included charges of mass forced sterilization, seizure of private property, and other violations of civil and political rights. See Sagarika Ghose, *Indira: India's Most Powerful Prime Minister* (New Delhi: Juggernaut, 2017); and David Lockwood, *The Communist Party of India and the Indian Emergency* (New Delhi: Sage, 2016).

41. Library of Congress, *Country Studies: India,* chap. 1, "Historical Setting," at https://www.loc.gov/item/96019266. See also Diego Maiorano, *Autumn of the Matriarch: Indira Gandhi's Final Term in Office* (New York: Oxford University Press, 2015).

42. Perhaps the classic work on the Congress Party of India is Stanley Kochanek, *The Congress Party of India: The Dynamics of One-Party Democracy* (Princeton: Princeton University Press, 1968). See also Zoya Hasan, *Parties and Party Politics in India* (New York: Oxford University Press, 2002); or Andrea Rommele, David Farrell, and Piero Ignazi, *Political Parties and Political Systems: The Concept of Linkage Revisited* (Westport: Praeger, 2005).

43. Library of Congress, *Country Studies: India,* "Historical Setting," https://www.loc.gov/item/96019266.

44. A very good discussion of the challenges facing the Congress as it tried to re-create its national appeal is found in Francine Frankel's chapter "Politics: The Failure to Rebuild Consensus" in Marshall Bouton, ed., *India Briefing, 1987* (Boulder: Westview, 1987), pp. 25–48.

45. See Amartya Mukhopadhyah, "Electoral Strategies of the Congress (I), the CPI (M), and Communalism," in Rakhahari Chatterji, ed., *Religion, Politics, and Communalism: The South Asian Experience* (New Delhi: South Asian Publishers, 1994), pp. 66–87.

46. Library of Congress, *Country Studies: India,* chap. 8, "Government and Politics," https://www.loc.gov/item/96019266.

47. Ibid. See also Yogendra K. Malik and V. B. Singh, *Hindu Nationalists in India: The Rise of the Bharatiya Janata Party* (Boulder: Westview, 1994); and Suhas Palshikar, Sanjay Kumar, and Sanjay Lodha, *Electoral Politics in India: The Resurgence of the Bharatiya Janata Party* (London: Routledge, 2017).

48. See the Inter-Parliamentary Union report "India—Lok Sabha," http://www.ipu.org/parline-e/reports/2145_E.htm.

49. Library of Congress, *Country Studies: India,* chap. 8, "Government and Politics." See Vani Kant Borooah, *Votes, Parties, and Seats: A Quantitative Analysis of Indian Parliamentary Elections, 1962–2014* (Basingstoke: Palgrave Macmillan, 2016).

50. See the Inter-Parliamentary Union report, "India—Lok Sabha."

51. Ibid.

52. See Paul Wallace, *India's 2014 Elections: A Modi-Led BJP Sweep* (New Delhi: Sage, 2015).

53. Ainslie T. Embree, "Religion and Politics," in Bouton, *India Briefing, 1987,* p. 49. See also Pradeep Chhibber, *Religious Practice and Democracy in India* (New York: Cambridge University Press, 2014).

54. Rakhahari Chatterji, "Religion, Politics, and Communalism in South Asia: Historical and Comparative Perspective," in Chatterji, *Religion, Politics, and Communalism,* p. 2.

55. See the section "Communalism"—including discussion of both Hindu communalism and Muslim communalism—in Hardgrave, *India,* pp. 120–124. See also Tanika Sarkar, *Hindu Wife, Hindu Nation: Community, Religion, and Cultural Nationalism* (Bloomington: Indiana University Press, 2001); or Harnik Deol, *Religion and Nationalism in India: The Case of the Punjab* (New York: Routledge, 2000).

56. Embree, "Religion and Politics," p. 51.

57. Satyabrata Chakraborty, "Communalism in India: The Changing Scenario," in Chatterji, *Religion, Politics, and Communalism,* p. 21.

58. See, for instance, Bonita Aleaz, "The Duality in the Sikh Identity and Its Communal Repercussions," in Chatterji, *Religion, Politics, and Communalism,* pp. 88–107.

59. See, for example, Rupa Viswanath, *The Pariah Problem: Caste, Religion, and the Social in Modern India* (New York: Columbia University Press, 2014); Christophe Jaf-

frelot, *Dr. Ambedkar and Untouchability: Fighting the Indian Caste System* (New York: Columbia University Press, 2005); or Paramjit Judge, *Mapping Social Exclusion in India: Caste, Religion, and Borderlands* (Cambridge: Cambridge University Press, 2014).

60. *American Heritage Dictionary of the English Language,* 4th ed. (Boston: Houghton Mifflin, 2000), entry "caste." See also Surinder Jodhka, *Caste in Contemporary India* (New Delhi: Routledge, 2015).

61. Library of Congress, *Country Studies: India,* chap. 5, "Social Systems," https://www.loc.gov/item/96019266.

62. Ibid.

63. Library of Congress, *Country Studies: India,* chap. 8, "Government and Politics."

64. Library of Congress, *Country Studies: India,* chap. 5, "Social Systems."

65. Ibid.

66. Ibid.

67. Ibid.

68. Joseph W. Elder, "Society," in Bouton, *India Briefing, 1987,* p. 116.

69. Rakhahari Chatterji, "Religion, Politics and Communalism in South Asia: Historical and Comparative Perspectives," in Chatterji, *Religion, Politics, and Communalism,* p. 1.

70. Satyabrata Chakraborty, "Communalism in India: The Changing Scenario," in Chatterji, *Religion, Politics, and Communalism,* p. 21.

71. See Anshu Malhotra and Farina Mir, *Punjab Reconsidered: History, Culture, and Practice* (New Delhi: Oxford University Press, 2012); Joyce Pettigrew, *The Sikhs of the Punjab: Unheard Voices of State and Guerrilla Violence* (Atlantic Highlands, NJ: Zed, 1995); or Pashaura Singh and Louis Fenech, eds., *The Oxford Handbook of Sikh Studies* (Oxford: Oxford University Press, 2014).

72. Library of Congress, *Country Studies: India,* chap. 8, "Government and Politics." The article "Religion and Politics" by Ainslie Embree has a very good section, "The Sikhs," pp. 67–71.

73. British Broadcasting Corporation, "The Assassination of Indira Gandhi," http://www.bbc.co.uk/programmes/p01k7vpm.

74. Chakraborty, "Communalism in India," p. 26.

75. Library of Congress, *Country Studies: India,* chap. 8, "Government and Politics." See also Bidisha Biswas, *Managing Conflicts in India: Policies of Coercion and Accommodation* (Lanham: Lexington, 2014).

76. See Mridu Rai, *Hindu Rulers, Muslim Subjects: Islam, Rights, and the History of Kashmir* (London: Hurst, 2004); "Kashmir Flashpoint," *BBC News,* November 1, 2006, http://news.bbc.co.uk/2/hi/in_depth/south_asia/2002/kashmir_flashpoint. See also Sumit Ganguly, *Deadly Impasse: Kashmir and Indo-Pakistani Relations at the Dawn of the New Century* (Cambridge: Cambridge University Press, 2016).

77. Library of Congress, *Country Studies: India,* chap. 8, "Government and Politics."

78. See Mushtaqur Rahman, *Divided Kashmir: Old Problems, New Opportunities for India, Pakistan, and the Kashmiri People* (Boulder: Lynne Rienner, 1996).

79. See Rekha Chowdhary, *Jammu and Kashmir: Politics of Identity and Separatism* (New York: Routledge, 2016); and Myla Ali Khan, *The Parchment of Kashmir: History, Society, and Polity* (New York: Palgrave Macmillan, 2012).

80. Thomas L. Friedman, *The World Is Flat: A Brief History of the Twenty-First Century* (New York: Farrar, Straus, and Giroux, 2006).

81. There is a substantial literature on Indian economic reform. One very good volume is that by Rob Jenkins, *Democratic Politics and Economic Reform in India* (New York: Cambridge University Press, 1996).

82. Stanley A. Wolpert, *A New History of India* (New York: Oxford University Press, 1997), pp. 445–446.

83. There is quite a literature on Modi, including the following: Rajiv Kumar, *Modi and His Challenges* (London: Bloomsbury India, 2016); Sreeram Sundar Chaulia, *Modi Doctrine: The Foreign Policy of India's Prime Minister* (London: Bloomsbury

India, 2016); and Ramesh Menon, *Modi Demystified: The Making of a Prime Minister* (Noida: HarperCollins India, 2014). See also "Know the PM," http://www.pmindia.gov .in/en/pms-profile, for more information on Modi.

84. See "CensusInfo India 2011," http://www.dataforall.org/dashboard/census infoindia_pca.

85. Hardgrave, *India,* p. 233.

12

Kenya

Learning Outcomes

After reading this chapter, you will be able to

- Appreciate Kenya as a leading African nation as it faces the same challenges as other African nations.
- Understand Kenya's constitutional makeup, and understand why Kenya has today the constitutional structures that it has.
- Explain Kenya's type of unitary government.
- Discuss the manner in which ethnic heterogeneity in Kenya is a political issue and how the government handles challenges related to ethnicity.
- Understand how Kenyan political structures, both executive and legislative, respond to Kenyan political needs.
- Explain the role that political parties have played in Kenya's political development, and the importance of parties for Kenyan politics today.

Kenya has a history of being one of East Africa's most stable political units, even though it has had challenges with issues of corruption and economic development. Kenya has functioned as East Africa's financial and communications center, and while it has had to deal with many of the same challenges as other developing nations in Africa, it has often been cited as the "major" political system of the region. As one author has noted,

> Until the 1980's Kenya was considered one of the continent's success stories, exemplifying stability, free-enterprise, and relatively benign leadership; a rare example of a state with a vibrant legislature, free

press, an independent judiciary, and institutionalized grass-roots political life—despite a cultural heterogeneity and socio-economic problems that had brought instability elsewhere in Africa.[1]

The elections that took place in Kenya in December 2007 led to violence, murder of hundreds, and a level of what was commonly interpreted as ethnic-based conflict that many found frightening. If this could happen in the most stable system in East Africa, what lessons were to be learned for other systems that were less stable and less secure? While some argued that the violence was not, in fact, based upon ethnic or tribal identity,[2] others are less sure, and many were afraid for the future of the nation. While the national elections of August 2017 were far less violent and far more orderly than the 2007 elections, it was still the case that the loser in those elections refused to accept the results of the election and contested them in court, eventually forcing a new presidential election to be held in October.

In this chapter we will look at Kenya's status today, and how it came to be where it is in terms of political and social development. Kenya's political heritage and its constitutional history will be briefly examined so that we might understand why its political institutions are as they currently are. Because a new constitution was ratified by the public in August 2010, much of what we will explore in this chapter is still relatively new, being worked out, and we will examine those structures and intentions, as well. Thus this chapter will be a combination of looking back at history and looking forward to the not-yet-certain future. We will examine Kenya's political structures and institutions, and then briefly observe political participation in recent events to draw some conclusions about the nature of the Kenyan political culture.

Kenya in an African Context

Africa is a vast continent, and making general observations about politics in such a varied region involves serious risks. With fifty-four independent states,[3] Africa has a staggering range of political institutions, political histories, political cultures, and political customs.

To lump these states together and talk about "African politics" is somewhat misleading because there are important differences between them. There is, for example, a wide cultural gap between the North African states and the Black African states south of the Sahara. The geographic and demographic differences are often striking, as witnessed by the huge Sudan and Zaire on the one hand, and the tiny Rwanda, Burundi and Swaziland on the other; within West Africa, oil-rich Nigeria—four times the size of Britain and with a population in 1999 of some 124 million—contrasts sharply with the Gambia, which, with an area of just over ten thousand square kilometers and a population of approximately 1.3 million, was once (in pre-independence days) described as "an eel wriggling its way through a slab of French territory."[4]

Our purpose here is not to attempt a comprehensive continental examination. Rather, here we seek to identify a few of the major themes or patterns of behavior that we can see as being significant in Africa, which will provide a context within which we can appreciate political developments in Kenya.

There are, in fact, some patterns that we can identify that most African states have in common.[5] Most African states were colonies of European powers and achieved independence from those colonial powers after 1960. Most states are still working to develop their own identities as nation-states. Most states are very poor and very rural, have significant public health problems (it has been estimated that over 14 percent of the adults of Zimbabwe have **AIDS**—the fifth worst in the world), and are very vulnerable to the world economy. Most states have a very heterogeneous political culture as a result of the number and variety of traditional tribal units within their borders.[6]

Contrary to what many think, elections and democratic politics do have a significant history in the African setting. "Elections have long been a conspicuous element of the political landscape of independent Africa. . . . Africans were elected to legislative councils in the 1920's in Ghana, Kenya, Nigeria, Sierra Leone, and Zambia."[7] In recent times, however, the conventional wisdom about the success and significance of elections in Africa has become more and more negative and pessimistic.

> Elections in much of contemporary Africa were widely regarded as irrelevant or a sham. There was growing evidence of elections which did not reflect democratic values; that those responsible followed neither the electoral procedures set out in the institutions bequeathed at independence nor other requirements of free and fair competition. Some concluded that the misuse and abuse of electoral institutions demonstrated that the process was ill-suited to Africa.[8]

One recent study of West African politics was subtitled "Seeking Unity in Diversity,"[9] and this, in brief, tells the trials of most African nations. As noted earlier, with the exception of Liberia, all of the states of West Africa, and most of the states of the rest of Africa, were the creation of colonial powers that divided the continent up during the late nineteenth century.

It is clear that the various **colonial powers** that ruled Africa into the twentieth century, including Italy, France, Germany, Portugal, and the United Kingdom, were concerned about the development of these nations as suppliers of goods and services; national integration was not a high priority on their political agendas. Thus, railroads and highways were designed to run from the hinterlands of the nations to the coast, so that raw materials could be shipped to the colonial power, but transportation within the African state, from one interior location to another interior location, might have remained underdeveloped and very difficult.

In addition to a lack of development of those infrastructures that could have promoted a sense of national integration, the borders of the African states were, themselves, entirely artificial creations. The primary units of loyalty in Africa, tribal units, have never corresponded to what we today look upon as national borders. British colonial officers may have decided to draw a national border between what today is Kenya and what today is Uganda, but as far as the people living in those regions were concerned, some of the soon-to-be Kenyans had more in common with soon-to-be Ugandans than they did with other soon-to-be Kenyans. This made it very difficult to develop any sense of what it meant to be a "Kenyan" for much of the population in that region.

In recent years we have seen prolonged and bloody civil wars in many nations in Africa, most recently resulting in the independence of the new nation of South Sudan in July 2011.[10] Where actual warfare hasn't broken out, we have seen situations of essentially authoritarian government that has been clear in its intention to remain in power, whatever the cost. The cost of these wars, of course, in addition to the thousands and thousands of lives that have been lost (the Council on Foreign Relations estimates that "well over 50,000 people have been killed and more than 1.6 million have been internally displaced since civil war broke out in South Sudan in December 2013"[11]), has been a lack of economic and political development. It has been hard enough for developing nations to make progress in their economic development when they have been able to focus all of their resources and efforts on the process of development itself. When their resources and efforts have been diverted to fighting to remain in power, or to drive someone else out of power, the nations have lost momentum in the development process, and some are almost hopelessly behind in the quest for political stability and economic progress.

Kenya's Political Heritage
Britain established its presence in East Africa in the middle of the nineteenth century, and the **British East African Protectorate** dates to 1895. It is worth noting that initially, Britain was more interested in ter-

ritories in what would become Uganda and Zanzibar than Kenya, because of their relation to the Nile River.

> To ensure its claims on Uganda and to ease communication with this interior region, as well as making certain any lingering elements of the slave trade were ended, Britain built the Uganda Railway, from the coastal city of Mombasa to Lake Victoria. Completed in 1901, it included, about halfway along, a railhead of workshops and offices that started as little more than a tented camp. . . . From these foundations the camp grew over the next three decades to become the city of Nairobi.[12]

In what was fairly typical British colonial practice, a small white minority became economically dominant in East Africa, farming and growing tea and coffee, and the native **Kikuyu** and other ethnic groups of the region (primarily the **Maasai** and **Kalenjin**) lost much of their land and standing.

Kenya officially became a British colony in 1920, but from then until independence in the early 1960s it was still run by and for British **expatriates**, British citizens who were residents of Kenya at the time.[13] Africans were not permitted to vote or to run for office, and it wasn't until 1944 that even a few appointed (not elected) native representatives were allowed to sit in the legislature. In the period including the years 1952 and 1959, primarily 1951 to 1954, Kenya operated in a continuing state of crisis as a result of the Mau Mau uprising against British colonialism.

The **Mau Mau** were a secret society, made up of ethnic Kikuyu who were unhappy with Kenya's colonial status, and were especially unhappy with the practice of white foreigners having control of much of Kenya's best land. (Indeed, **Jomo Kenyatta** [1891–1978], president of the Kenyan African National Union, was arrested in 1952 for Mau Mau activity and sentenced to seven years of hard labor for his activity.) Membership in the Mau Mau required the individual to take an oath to drive the white settlers out of Africa.[14] During the period of violence, over 70,000 suspected Mau Mau were arrested by the British, while over 13,000 were killed. Kenyatta was released from prison at age seventy-one, in 1961, and was elected Kenya's first prime minister in 1963. It was not until 2003 that the Mau Mau movement was legalized in Kenya.[15]

When Kenya became independent in 1963, power was highly centralized, and politics was dominated by one party: the **Kenyan African National Union** (KANU), run by President Kenyatta.[16] In 1978, when Kenyatta died, his vice president **Daniel arap Moi** (1924–) became president. Moi was shortly thereafter elected president of KANU and was its nominee for national president at the next election. He was elected at that time and in every succeeding presidential election until he finally stepped down from power in the election of 2002, when **Mwai Kibaki** was first elected president.[17]

Many argue that the dreams of Kenya's colonial leaders have not yet been achieved. There is no doubt about Kenya's independence; "what is debatable is whether the long-term goals of the nationalists, which included complete Africanization of the country's politics, economy and culture, have been realized."[18] The challenge is, as one student of Kenyan politics has observed, the process of "reconciling unity with self-determination"[19]—that is, finding a balance between national unity on one hand and individual rights and liberties on the other.

The Constitutional System

Kenya has had several different constitutions since its independence in 1963.[20] Like many or most members of the British Commonwealth— today referred to as the **Commonwealth of Nations**, not the *British* Commonwealth—Kenya's original independence constitution was negotiated with the colonial power over a several-year period of time at Lancaster House in London. Kenya's transition to independence under the British took place over a period of years, including several years of violence between the colonial government and the Mau Mau peoples who were seeking power. Its first constitution, in 1963, was very much a British-style, or "Westminster," constitution. Kenya had a parliamentary system of government with a head of state called the queen, who was the same person as the queen of England. When the queen was not in Kenya—which was almost all of the time—the monarchy would be represented by a British-appointed governor-general. The government had a two-chambered legislature, the National Assembly, with one chamber elected (the 117-member House of Representatives) and one appointed (the 41-member Senate, representing regional interests), and seven regions, each with its own assembly (although Kenya remained unitary, not federal). The leader of the elected chamber of the national legislature was to be the prime minister.

Shortly after independence, a year after independence, in fact, in 1964, the Kenyan constitution was changed to make Kenya a republic and a presidential system, cutting its constitutional ties to the British monarchy.[21] The upper house was abolished, making the National Assembly a unicameral body. And the old system of provinces was replaced by a new structure of regional government (although the regional governments were purely administrative, and Kenya never actually became federal in nature).

The 1964 Constitution was very centralized in terms of political power. It was typical in Kenya that most political institutions operated "at the pleasure" of the president, including Parliament, courts, electoral commissions, and so on. This practice of presidential dominance was, some observers have noted, "a holdover from the colonial period," and simply became standard operating procedure in Kenyan politics.[22]

Kenya had a major constitutional change in 1982 when, following the wishes of President Moi,[23] it officially became a one-party state, and the Kenyan African National Union legally took on constitutional status as a significant component of the government. Anyone wanting to run for office had to do so under the KANU umbrella and within the KANU party organization. KANU's role in politics was solidified in the elections of 1983 and 1988 when the one-party nature of Kenyan politics was further entrenched, and the party came to be increasingly identified with the state.

Jennifer Widner has argued[24] that KANU was transformed from a loose-knit group of politicians into a party-state dominated by President Moi. Her thesis was that an increased importance of ethnicity moved President Moi to move to a single-party system, to jail opponents, and to put a priority on national solidarity rather than democracy. This lasted for several years, but ultimately domestic support for multipartyism developed, and this domestic support, combined with pressure from foreign aid donors in the West, pressed for a change back to a multiparty state format.

In 1991 a new constitutional structure was established with some serious amendments made to the 1982 Constitution. Most important among the changes was that the one-party system of elections and government was repealed, and a multiparty system was established. Many different political parties participated in the elections of 1992, and the elections were essentially peaceful. Kenya was thereafter a multiparty state.

More recently, the demands of many increased that there be major constitutional change involving a diminution of presidential power. Many of the parties involved in the conversation suggested that political power had become too centralized in the hands of the president over the years, and that power "should be shifted from the executive branch to strengthen the judiciary and parliament."[25] The problem was that experts disagreed on how to actually make that shift happen, which was not made easier by the fact that the president of Kenya was certainly not in favor of a diminution of his power.

Kenya went through a period of serious constitutional self-evaluation and reflection between 2000 and 2004, although no significant changes were actually made to the Constitution.[26] Following the 1997 elections, Parliament had passed the Constitution of Kenya Review Act and had called for an active constitutional review, asking that comprehensive constitutional reforms be undertaken. Over the next five or so years there were many prolonged conversations about changes that were needed in Kenyan society and politics, and the Constitution of Kenya Review Commission (CKRC) was established to prepare the way for a new constitution.[27] A draft of a new constitutional structure was completed in 2002, but in a referendum in 2005 that draft constitution was rejected by a majority of the voters, primarily because some ethnic groups felt that advantages were being given to other ethnic groups. Although constitutional change was stopped temporarily, the process through the first five years of the decade did show that change was needed, and that there was substantial support for the idea of bringing about change, even if agreement had not been reached on exactly what that change should be.

Because the 2005 draft constitutional change was rejected, Kenya continued to be governed by the 1963 Constitution, as amended in 1982. Following the 2007 elections, as we will further explore later, regional and ethnic tensions led to a political crisis for the nation when substantial political violence and killing across the nation threatened national unity in a way that had not happened since independence. This led to a temporary power-sharing arrangement with a temporary appointment of a new prime minister to work with the president, and also to a national Committee of Experts being appointed to review issues of constitutional reform, and initially in November 2009 with later drafts following, a new draft constitution was presented to the public.[28]

After a period of time for the public to review the draft constitution and suggest proposed changes, a revised draft was sent to Parliament in January 2010; it was returned to the Committee of Experts, and was published and presented to Parliament on February 23, 2010. Parliament approved the new constitution on April 1, 2010. The new constitution was subjected to a referendum on August 4, 2010, and was approved by 67 percent of Kenyan voters.[29]

The new constitution continued Kenya's presidential model of government, but it established more opportunities to require the legislative branch to approve actions of the president before they would come into effect; presidential power was slightly reduced in the new plan.[30] The new constitution also brought back a second house of the legislature, with its focus being representation of *regions*. The plan suggested that each county should elect one senator and that the total number of elected and appointed senators would reach sixty. The new plan further suggested that there should be some **devolution of power** with some of the national legislative and administrative power devolving to county governmental structures, although the plan was very careful to make a distinction between this structure of devolution on one hand and the development of a federal system on the other, which it was explicitly not advancing. In a federal system the intermediate level of power has some sovereign power in some specific areas, power that cannot be limited or taken away by the central government.

This system specifically notes that the nation is to remain unitary, not federal, but that there will be some areas of authority that will be administered by the counties, and the central government is barred from interfering with those powers, unless Parliament deems such action necessary. The counties will oversee policy in the areas of agriculture, fisheries, county health, cultural activities, public entertainment, county transport, trade development, some education facilities, and implementation of specific national government policies on natural resources and environment conservation.[31]

It is worth noting that both President Mwai Kibaki and Prime Minister Raila Odinga campaigned in favor of the new constitution (although it should be noted that President Kibaki was not eligible to run for reelection again, so a new constitution that would limit the president's power would not affect him).

The new constitution includes provisions for multiparty elections; a strong system of entrenched freedoms and human rights, including freedom of expression, freedom of conscience and belief, equal opportunities for both genders, freedom of the media, and so on; a bicameral national legislature; a directly elected president with a cabinet that must be approved by the legislature; a developed system of courts, including a system of Islamic courts; and a system of regional government with some powers devolved from the center of politics.[32]

The new constitution is seen as a major improvement over its predecessor in a number of significant ways, highlighted in Box 12.1. Although the document was approved by an overwhelming majority of the public, and was supported by the two major contenders for the presidency in the 2007 election, it was not without opposition; many Christian clergy felt that the ban on abortions was not strong enough and were also unhappy about the constitutional retention of the existence of Muslim Kadhi courts.[33]

Regionalism and Unitary Government

As has been noted, Kenya today does not have a federal government but instead has a unitary government with some regional characteristics based in counties, which periodically lead some Kenyans to speculate about federalism. There is even a word in Swahili—*majimbo*—for a federal-like power-sharing structure that is advocated by some, most

---

Box 12.1   Kenya's Constitutional Reforms of August 2010

- Executive authority resides with a president rather than being shared between the president and the prime minister, as was the case following the 2007 presidential election and the "grand compromise" that was achieved to resolve the conflict that followed that election.
- Although authority resides with the president, much of the president's power and patronage ability are limited and require confirmation by the National Assembly. The president's power to suspend or dissolve the National Assembly has been removed, as well.
- The power of Parliament in relation to the president has been significantly increased. Included in its powers the Parliament will now be able to impeach the president.
- The National Assembly will have at least forty-seven elected women, at least one from each county. The newly elected Senate will have at least eighteen women members, 27 percent of the total membership.
- The new constitution created forty-seven elected county governments and guarantees that funding for these governments will be provided by the national government. This guarantees some level of equality among Kenya's forty-two ethnic groups by encouraging the devolution of power from the center to the regions and guaranteeing some access to financial resources.
- The new constitution includes a list of political, economic, and social rights, with specific rights for women, marginalized groups, and people with disabilities.

Source: Joel D. Barkan and Makau Mutua, "Turning the Corner in Kenya," *Foreign Affairs,* August 10, 2010, https://www.foreignaffairs.com/articles/east-africa/2010-08 -10/turning-corner-kenya.

---

notably former prime minister **Raila Odinga**. "**Majimboism**" has been in use in political vocabulary since the Lancaster House (London) Constitutional Conference in 1962, in fact. According to one source,

> Majimboism envisaged a system of government where executive, legislative and financial powers were shared between central and regional governments. The bulk of the power, however, still remained with the central government. The regional boundaries were loosely based on ethnic boundaries carved up by the British.
>
> The Majimbo issue had split the African leadership down the middle in the run-up to independence in 1963. To a large extent the system was predicated on the fear by the leaders of "smaller" ethnic groups that their communities would be dominated by the "larger" groups on national matters—economical or political.[34]

In the run-up to independence in the early 1960s, much discussion was focused on the debate over centralized and decentralized power. As noted earlier in this volume, one of the most common reasons for federal government is a large nation in which different regional groups want to retain some control over issues that are regionally important, issues that they do not want determined by a single national government for all regional groups in the same way. This tendency is exacerbated in political settings in which ethnic identities are regionally concentrated. This was clearly the case in Kenya in its early years.

In the constitution being planned in 1962 and early 1963, "there were to be 6 Jimbos (regions) constituted along ethnic lines. Tribes with close similarities were put under one region, e.g. Coast and North Eastern provinces were put under one state as the two are predominantly Muslim while Kikuyus, Embu, Meru were put in Central State."[35]

Following the election of Jomo Kenyatta in 1963, when Kenya attained self-governing status, the federalism/majimboism debate was ended, and a unitary and much more centralized approach to power was adopted. Kenyatta saw majimboism as a threat to national unity and wanted a unitary government structure.

In September 1982, President Moi led the government to adopt a strategy that started to make the regional districts the focal point of planning and implementation of development initiatives. One of the objectives of the new regional focus was to make administration more efficient, but another key goal was a political one: Moi felt that by decentralizing administrative action he could work around the Kikuyu-dominated state that he had inherited from Kenyatta. This strategy gave him the opportunity to work with other regions of the nation that were dominated by other ethnic groups (including the Kalenjin, his ethnic group).[36]

The 2010 Constitution includes a full chapter that focuses on the devolution of power to the counties, titled "Devolved Government" (Chapter 11). In the Constitution the argument is presented that "the objects of the devolution of government are" as follows:

(*a*) to promote democratic and accountable exercise of power;
(*b*) to foster national unity by recognising diversity;
(*c*) to give powers of self-governance to the people and enhance the participation of the people in the exercise of the powers of the State and in making decisions affecting them;
(*d*) to recognise the right of communities to manage their own affairs and to further their development;
(*e*) to protect and promote the interests and rights of minorities and marginalised communities;
(*f*) to promote social and economic development and the provision of proximate, easily accessible services throughout Kenya;

(g) to ensure equitable sharing of national and local resources throughout Kenya;

(h) to facilitate the decentralisation of State organs, their functions and services, from the capital of Kenya; and

(i) to enhance checks and balances and the separation of powers.[37]

Kenya today continues to be a unitary state, with sovereignty residing at the national capital, Nairobi. The nation is divided into administrative subdivisions, however, including 140 districts, joined to form seven rural provinces. The Nairobi area has special status. Under the new constitution, the primary administrative subdivisions are forty-seven counties, each with an elected governor. These counties are the basis of representation in the second chamber of the national legislature. Indeed, some other East African nations have wondered whether Kenyan-style federalism could work in their government as well as it does in Kenya.[38]

Ethnic and Tribal Tensions

As noted earlier, Kenya, as is the case for many nations in Africa, is an example of a political system whose national borders do not mirror traditional tribal and ethnic borders. That is, when the Western colonial powers were drawing national boundaries, they were more concerned about geopolitical issues involving their (the European nations') neighbors than they were in drawing borders that made sense in terms of tribal and ethnic population distributions. Many of Kenya's tribal groups spread across Kenya's borders, going into Ethiopia, Somalia, Tanzania, Sudan, or Uganda, for instance.

The multiethnic makeup of Kenya has periodically appeared to be significant when conflicts arise and ethnic groups start to feel vulnerable or are worried that "their" members are not getting the same resources as are members of other ethnic groups. There are today nearly forty different ethnic groups in Kenya, made up of three distinct linguistic families, the Bantu (including the Luhya, Kikuyu, Kamba, and Mijikenda groups); the Nilotic (the Luo, the Kalenjin, and the Masai groups); and the Cushitic (the Oromo and the Somali groups). The major ethnic groups are indicated in Table 12.1.

Many observers suggested that the violence that followed the 2007 presidential election was based upon ethnic group loyalty. Others have suggested that this isn't true.

> Contrary to prevailing attitudes, Kenyans have not traditionally identified themselves by ethnic group and studies have shown they do not have significant feelings of ethnic injustice. In a 2003 *Afrobarometer* survey, 70 percent said they would choose to be Kenyan if faced with a choice between a national identity and their ethnic group (28 percent

Table 12.1   Kenya's Major Ethnic Groups

Group	Percentage of Population
Kikuyu	22
Luhya	14
Luo	13
Kalenjin	12
Kamba	11
Kisii	6
Meru	6
Others	15

Source: Library of Congress, *Country Profile: Kenya*, http://www.refworld.org/docid/46f9134a0.html).

refused to identify themselves as anything but Kenyan). Analysts say much of the unrest that erupted after the December 2007 polls was just the latest display of politically organized violence. Political coalitions on both sides hired thugs to do their bidding, and ordinary Kenyans were caught in the cross fire, they say.[39]

Kenya's former prime minister, Raila Odinga, has indicated that in his view the normal day-to-day operation of politics in Kenya is not primarily based upon ethnic identity. His argument has been that it has been regionalism that is the real source of tension, since some regions have access to many resources and other regions do not. The fact that regions are associated with ethnic groups—many of Kenya's forty-two tribal groups are concentrated in one region of the nation rather than spread out across the nation—may make it seem that ethnic identity is the source of conflict, but it is really regionalism that is the source of conflict, he says.[40]

Although it may be possible to suggest that much of Kenya's ethnic violence can be attributed to short-term political explanation, the fact is that today there are many significant economic inequalities between some ethnic groups, and long-standing bitter disputes over land, particularly in the Rift Valley.[41] These regional variations result in some ethnic groups having many more resources than other ethnic groups, as a result of where they are. This has, understandably, exacerbated inter–ethnic group tensions.

Executive Structures

As noted earlier, ever since Kenya was granted independence in the early 1960s the Kenyan political system has been characterized by having a strong—we should say "dominant"—president. Originally Kenya constitutionally followed the British model, with a prime minister as the chief executive and the queen serving as the monarch of Kenya. Shortly after independence the British-model constitution was changed to a republican-style constitution with an elected president and no separate head of state, moving from a parliamentary system of government to a presidential system of government.

Starting in 1964, Kenyan politics was steered by the president. Jomo Kenyatta served as president from 1964 through 1978. Kenyatta was a remarkable national leader; the student should recall that he had already served time in prison for his Mau Mau sympathies and been released at age seventy before he became president. When he died at age eighty-six in 1978 he was succeeded by Daniel arap Moi, who had been the vice president of Kenya. Kenyatta had been criticized by many in his later years in office as being autocratic; Moi started to receive that same evaluation shortly after taking office.[42]

We noted earlier that shortly after Moi took office, in 1982, the Constitution of Kenya was amended to make Kenya a one-party state, helping to further cement Moi's power as president of KANU as well as being president of Kenya. Moi decreased the size of the military service in Kenya for a period of time and closed the universities to avoid structured opposition to his rule, and through the 1980s he continued to centralize power, despite the fact that he was receiving increased criticism from Western nations about his actions. More and more it was the case that Western nations were becoming critical of Moi, of corruption, and of Moi's pattern of rigid governance.

In 1991 Moi finally permitted an amendment to the Constitution so that multiparty elections could take place again, and in 1992 in the first multiparty elections in twenty-six years, the "ethnically fractured opposition failed to dislodge Moi and KANU from power."[43] Moi stayed in power through the next five years, and in the 1997 elections he again won the presidency, despite charges of electoral fraud.

The 1997 election was Moi's final election, however, because the Constitution prohibited him from seeking another election in December 2002. Despite the fact that Moi sought to—and did—get **Uhuru Kenyatta**, son of Kenya's first leader, chosen to be KANU's candidate for president, Moi wasn't successful in influencing the election. Mwai Kibaki, who ran against Moi in 1992 and 1997 and once was his vice president, won the majority of votes in 2002. Kibaki was the candidate of the largest opposition group, the National Rainbow Coalition (NARC). Not only did Kibaki win, but the National Rainbow Coalition won a parliamentary majority in the National Assembly. "The election, although not free of vote-rigging, was the most credible since independence."[44]

Starting shortly after the 2002 election, as noted earlier, there was popular support for a movement to modify—or replace—the Constitution, on the grounds that the president had become too powerful and a number of changes were needed in the constitutional structure of Kenya, including a bicameral legislature and devolution of some powers to regional levels. In 2005 the National Rainbow Coalition split over the issue of constitutional reform, with a result being the creation of a new opposition party, the Orange Democratic Movement (named after the oranges that had been the symbol of opposition to the proposed new constitution).

In the election of December 27, 2007, President Mwai Kibaki was reelected with 46 percent of the vote. The leader of the Orange coalition, Raila Odinga, received 44 percent of the vote, and Kalonzo Musyoka, Kibaki's vice president, received 9 percent of the vote. As noted earlier, the December 2007 election was dismissed by many as highly corrupt and rigged, and massive violence followed the election. A consequence of the disputed election—in which President Kibaki stayed in power—was the ultimate interim power-sharing agreement in February 2008 (see Box 12.2) between President Kibaki and the leader of the opposition, Raila Odinga, to create a position of prime minister that would be held by the leader of the opposition, Odinga, and the eventual (2010) approval of a new constitution.[45]

Legislative Structures

Prior to the August 2010 Constitution, the unicameral National Assembly consisted of 210 members, elected to a term of five years from single-member constituencies, plus twelve members nominated by political parties on a proportional representation basis.[46] The current National Assembly is described in Article 95 of the Constitution as follows:

> Two hundred and ninety members, each elected by the registered voters of single member constituencies; forty-seven women, each elected by the registered voters of the counties, each county constituting a single member constituency; twelve members nominated by parliamentary political parties according to their proportion of members of the National Assembly in accordance with Article 90, to represent special interests including the youth, persons with disabilities and workers; and the Speaker, who is an ex officio member.[47]

The first election for the National Assembly under the new constitution took place in 2013. At that time the people elected a bicameral parliament consisting of a National Assembly with over 300 members and a Senate with under 100 members; Parliament members were to serve five-year terms. The bicameral legislature was designed to offer

---

**Box 12.2   The February 2008
Power-Sharing Agreement**

- There will be a prime minister of the government of Kenya, with authority to coordinate and supervise the execution of the functions and affairs of the Government of Kenya.
- The prime minister will be an elected member of the National Assembly and the parliamentary leader of the largest party in the National Assembly, or of a coalition, if the largest party does not command a majority.
- Each member of the coalition shall nominate one person from the National Assembly to be appointed a deputy prime minister.
- The cabinet will consist of the president, the vice president, the prime minister, the two deputy prime ministers and the other ministers. The removal of any minister of the coalition will be subject to consultation and concurrence in writing by the leaders.
- The prime minister and deputy prime ministers can only be removed if the National Assembly passes a motion of no confidence with a majority vote.
- The composition of the coalition government will at all times take into account the principle of portfolio balance and will reflect their relative parliamentary strength.

Source: "Text of Kenya Power-Sharing Deal," *Christian Science Monitor,* February 29, 2008, http://www.csmonitor.com/World/Africa/2008/0229/p25s01-woaf.html.

---

more opportunities for representation of the regions than had been the case in the unicameral legislature of the previous several decades.

There are several very interesting structures that are part of the National Assembly in the new plan.[48] The vast majority (290) of members of the National Assembly are to be elected from single-member districts. In addition to these members, forty-seven women (one from each county) are elected to represent the counties in the National Assembly. In addition to these members, twelve members are to be nominated by political parties, in proportion to their support in the 290 single-member-district elections.

The new Senate is designed to represent the counties and "serves to protect the interests of the counties and their governments" (sec. 96, pt. 1). The Constitution indicates that the new Senate will be made up of

(*a*) forty-seven members each elected by the registered voters of the counties, each county constituting a single member constituency; and (*b*) sixteen women members who shall be nominated by political parties according to their proportion of members of the Senate elected under clause (*a*) in accordance with Article 90;

(*c*) two members, being one man and one woman, representing the youth; and

(*d*) two members, being one man and one woman, representing persons with disabilities.[49]

The Courts

The structure of courts is described in Chapter Ten of the August 2010 Constitution. The Constitution calls for a Supreme Court, a Court of Appeal and a High Court, and a structure of subordinate courts. These are usual structures and do not require more of our attention here.

The most interesting judicial structure to be described in the Constitution from the perspective of comparative political analysis is Section 170 of Chapter Ten that refers to **Kadhi courts**—courts of the Muslim religion. This was a controversial part of the new constitution; many in Kenya felt that the time had come to stop entrenching a place for the Muslim religion in the Kenyan Constitution. However, at the end of the day, more people felt that it was important to include the structure for those Kenyans of the Muslim religion.

The Constitution indicates that the jurisdiction of the Kadhi courts[50] "shall be limited to the determination of questions of Muslim law relating to personal status, marriage, divorce or inheritance in proceedings in which all the parties profess the Muslim religion and submit to the jurisdiction of the Kadhi courts" (sec. 170, pt. 5).

Kadhi courts are not new to Kenya.

Kadhis courts were in existence along the East Coast of Africa long before the coming of the British colonialists in the 19th century. The Kenyan coastal strip was then part of the territories controlled by the Sultan of Zanzibar. In 1895, the Sultan of Zanzibar authorised the British to administer the coastal strip as a protectorate, rather than a colony as distinct from the mainland, subject to certain conditions including the British agreeing to respect the judicial system then in existence in the said protectorate. The British agreed to these conditions and throughout their administration of the coastal strip this judicial system, which included the Kadhis courts, continued to exist.[51]

The Kadhi courts are not mosques; they are courts that are established to deal with a very specialized type of conflict. These courts have continued to provide an important function in terms of resolving personal status conflict for the approximately 10 percent of the Kenyan population who are Muslim; there are over 4 million Muslims in Kenya.

Political Parties and Elections

In its modern history—since independence in 1963—Kenya has had a lot of experience with elections and political parties. For much of this history, even though Kenya was holding elections, the elections took place in the context of single-party politics. As we have already noted, from 1982 through 1991 Kenya was constitutionally and legally a one-party system, and any political party activity that took place had to be activity of the Kenyan African National Union.

We should be careful to note here that just because the system involved only a single political party did not mean that there was no competition within the political system. Kenya could be considered to have a **competitive single-party system**. There were many elections that were strongly contested; the difference was that the competition took place within the KANU structure. This often meant that there were robust and strongly contested primary elections—contests to see who was going to be the candidate of the KANU party in a given election—and then once the candidate was chosen for the election the result would be certain.

Why do this? One answer is that it promotes national unity by keeping all politics within a single umbrella of KANU identity, so that any conflict that occurs does not occur within the context of national elections—there isn't any real opposition or conflict in the national elections, since there are only KANU candidates running for office—but the conflict that exists takes place within the party structure. This allows for a period of reconciliation and national unification in the final election following any contests that take place in the primary election.

Thus, in a given election there might have been a KANU-A candidate and a KANU-B candidate seeking the formal KANU nomination to run for the National Assembly. There would be a campaign that took place, people would have a choice, and eventually they would vote and select one of the two candidates. At that point the successful candidate would have to go through another campaign period without a serious opponent, knowing that they would be successful.

There is a history of elections being sources of tension and conflict in Kenya. There is a reason for this:

> Experts say elections are dominated by a winner-take-all mentality due to the consolidation of power in the executive branch. Though Kenya has had multiparty elections since 1992, the opposition has little power in the government. "If you lose the election, you have nothing to do." . . . As a result, opposition MPs often don't even show up to conduct the business of parliament.
>
> Because elections are such high-stakes affairs, political candidates are accustomed to hiring groups of young, armed men to protect

their interests (this practice is also common in Nigeria). Each poll since the introduction of multiparty elections—in 1992, 1997, and 2002—has been accompanied by low-level outbreaks of violence. Most experts trace this violence back to tactics that President Daniel arap Moi, who led the country from 1978 until 2002, used to divide the population and retain political power.[52]

We have already noted that Kenya has a large number of ethnic groups—over forty—with the Kikuyu being the largest with over 20 percent of the population. This could be inflamed by a political leader, like Moi, who knew how to play one group against another. "When Moi, who is Kalenjin, faced the prospect of losing power to an opposition party that contained many Kikuyu, he started an anti-Kikuyu campaign and incited land clashes in the Rift Valley between Kalenjins and Kikuyus in 1992 and 1997. Major rights groups such as Human Rights Watch and Amnesty International have reported extensively on the state-sponsored nature of this violence."[53]

Multipartyism in Kenya has a long history. Immediately upon receiving independence in 1963, Kenya was a multiparty state, and it stayed that way until 1982, when under the leadership of President Moi it legally banned all parties except KANU. By 1990, however, even KANU officials were arguing that Kenya would be better served by having opposition political parties, despite the objections of many that multipartyism would generate ethnic tensions and threaten political stability.[54] At the end of the day, the principle of multipartyism won out, and on December 10, 1991, Kenya's Parliament passed the constitutional amendment that ended KANU's legal monopoly on political power.[55]

The most recent Kenyan election for the National Assembly took place in August 2017,[56] at which time voters elected the president, members of the National Assembly and new Senate, as well as county governors and representatives. The Jubilee Party of Uhuru Kenyatta won a plurality of the seats in the Assembly, while Kenyatta was reelected with 54 percent of the votes. The major opponent for the presidency, Raila Odinga, announced that he would not accept the results of the election and challenged them in the Supreme Court; the results of the election were subsequently annulled by the Court on the grounds of electoral fraud, and new presidential elections were held on October 17, 2017. The results of the August election for the parliamentary and local elections, however, remained valid (see Tables 12.2 and 12.3).

Prior to the repeat election in October, the leading challenger, former prime minister Raila Odinga, announced that he was withdrawing from the election because it would not be a fair election. Many international observers expressed skepticism about the likelihood that the

Table 12.2   The Election of August 2017 for the Kenyan National Assembly

	Total Seats Won	Constituency- Based Seats Won	County Reserved Seats for Women Won	Nominated Seats Received
Jubilee Party (JP)	171	140	25	6
Orange Democratic Movement (ODM)	76	62	11	3
Wiper Democratic Movement– Kenya (WDM-K)	23	19	3	1
Amani National Congress (ANC)	14	12	1	1
Independents	14	13	1	0
Forum for Restoration of Democracy (FORD)	12	10	1	
Kenya African National Union (KANU)	10	8	2	
Economic Freedom Party (EFP)	5	4	1	
Maendeleo Chap Chap Party (MCCP)	4	3	1	
Party for Development and Reform (PDR)	4	3	1	
Chama Cha Mashinani (CCM)	2	2	0	
Kenya National Congress (KNC)	2	2		
Kenya Peoples' Party (KPP)	2	2		
People's Democratic Party (PDP)	2	2		
Chama Cha Uzalendo (CCU)	1	1		
MUUNGANO	1	1		
New Democrats (ND)	1	1		
Party of National Unity (PNU)	1	1		
Democratic Party (DP)	1	1		
Frontier Alliance Party (FAP)	1	1		
National Agenda Party of Kenya (NAPK)	1	1		

Number of men: 273
Number of women: 76
Percentage women: 21.78

Source: Inter-Parliamentary Union, "Parline Database: Kenya—National Assembly," http://www.ipu.org/parline-e/reports/2167_E.htm.

second election would be fair. The Independent Electoral and Bound-aries Commission (IEBC) of Kenya, designed to oversee elections, agreed, and the commissioner of the IEBC resigned, declaring that the second presidential election wouldn't be a fair election. She fled to the United States out of fear for her safety.[57]

On October 30 the IEBC declared Uhuru Kenyatta the winner of the second election, with an overwhelming 98.26 percent of the vote, and a

Table 12.3   The Election of August 2017 for the Kenyan Senate

	Total Seats Won	Constituency-Based Seats Won	Reserved Seats for Women Won	Youth Seats Won	Disability Reserved Seats Won
Jubilee Party (JP)	34	24	8	1	1
Orange Democratic Movement (ODM)	20	13	5	1	1
Wiper Democratic Movement–Kenya (WDM-K)	3	2	1	0	0
Amani National Congress (ANC)	3	2	1	0	0
Kenya African National Union (KANU)	3	2	1	0	0
Forum for the Restoration of Democracy (FORD-K)	1	1	0		
Independents	1	1			
Chama Cha Uzalendo (CCU)	1	1			
Party for Development and Reform (PDR)	1	1			

Number of men: 47
Number of women: 21
Percentage women: 30.88

Source: Inter-Parliamentary Union, "Parline Database: Kenya—Senate," http://www.ipu .org/parline-e/reports/2167_E.htm.

39 percent voter turnout—not surprising since Raila Odinga had pulled out of the election. Results are shown in Table 12.4.

The Kenyan System in Perspective

We started this chapter by observing that Kenya has played a leadership role among African nations over the years. The developing nations of Africa, Asia, and Latin America have a particular set of challenges that the developed nations of North America and Europe do not face: not only do they need to resolve all of the usual political structural challenges that face all other nations, but they need to do so in a way that allows for the most effective (and, they might hope, fair) opportunities for their citizens from a perspective of social and economic development. The challenges that the developed nations face in terms of providing their citizens with educations, with needed welfare resources, with medical care, and so on, all exist in the developing nations, too,

Table 12.4   The Election of October 2017 for the Kenyan Presidency

Candidate	Party	Number of Votes	Percentage of Vote
Uhuru Kenyatta	Jubilee Party of Kenya	7,483,895	98.26
Raila Odinga	National Super Alliance	73,228	0.96
Ekuru Aukot	Thirdway Alliance Kenya	21,333	0.28
Abduba Dida	Alliance for Real Change	14,107	0.19
Japheth Kaluyu	Independent	8,261	0.11
Michael Wainaina	Independent	6,007	0.08
Joseph Nyagah	Independent	5,554	0.07
Cyrus Jirongo	United Democratic Party	3,832	0.05
Invalid votes		37,713	
Total		7,616,217	100

Turnout: 38.84%

Source: Katharine Houreld and Duncan Miriri, "Kenyan President Kenyatta Wins 98 Percent of Vote in Repeat Election," Reuters, October 30, 2017, https://www.reuters.com/article/us -kenya-election-kenyatta/kenyan-president-kenyatta-wins-98-percent-of-vote-in-repeat -election-idUSKBN1CZ1SE.

only those nations need to work on the challenges with fewer resources and less developed infrastructure.

Following the December 2007 election, with the horrifying riots and murders that took place in January and February 2008, a power-sharing agreement was eventually worked out between the two major competing groups. It did bring peace, but with the hindsight of over three years it did not bring effective government. According to the country's former anticorruption tsar, "The grand coalition's most notable achievement is 'to have remained intact.'"[58] Changes were made, bringing a new constitution in 2010 and relatively peaceful—although not uncontested—elections after that. The August 2017 presidential election, with its objections by the individual who lost and a subsequent new election from which he withdrew, did not succeed in convincing all of the population that future elections would always be fair or untainted, but it did succeed in choosing a new leader with less violence than had been the case in the past.

Kenya is a political system that is finding its way. It started as a Westminster-model parliamentary regime, moved to become a presidential republic, and has struggled since that time three decades ago to find a formula that will allow its government to operate effectively while at the same time not exacerbate tensions between and among its many ethnic groups. Kenyans hope that the newest constitutional plan, approved in August 2010, will continue to make real progress in this regard. We will have to wait and see.

Discussion Questions

1. What are the key challenges that African nations have had to face over the past several decades? How has Kenya worked to control these challenges? Why do you think Kenya may have been more successful in this challenge than other nations?
2. What were the major forces that directed Kenya in its pre-independence period? Was the transition to independence similar to transitions elsewhere? What were the issues that motivated Kenyans in their most recent constitutional changes? Have the changes been effective?
3. How would you compare Kenya's unitary government with other unitary governments we have seen, such as governments in Britain or France, for example? Regionalism is very important in Kenyan public administration. Why? How does regionalism affect the way Kenyan politics operate?
4. How important an issue is ethnicity in Kenya? Why? What are illustrations of times when ethnicity became a flash point for domestic political conflict?
5. What are the key characteristics of the Kenyan political executive? How has it changed over time? Are there changes you can imagine that would make it more responsive to the Kenyan political system? How well does the Kenyan legislature meet the needs of the public? Can you imagine changes that would be helpful in this regard?
6. What does the case of Kenya show for the argument in favor of one-party states? Was the fact that Kenya was for many years a one-party state helpful or significant in Kenya's political development? How would you characterize the state of political parties in Kenya today?

Notes

1. Samuel Decalo, *The Stable Minority: Civilian Rule in Africa, 1960–1990* (Gainesville: Florida Academic Press, 1998), p. 175. Good general histories are Crawford Young, *The Post-Colonial State in Africa: Fifty Years of Independence, 1960–2010* (Madison: University of Wisconsin Press, 2012); and Robert Maxon, *East Africa: An Introductory History* (Morgantown: West Virginia University Press, 2009).

2. Stephanie Hanson, "Understanding Kenya's Politics," http://www.cfr.org/kenya /understanding-kenyas-politics/p15322.

3. South Sudan became the fifty-fourth independent state of Africa in July 2011.

4. William Tordoff, *Government and Politics in Africa,* 4th ed. (Bloomington: Indiana University Press, 2002), p. 1. See also David Booth and Diana Rose Cammack, *Governance for Development in Africa: Solving Collective Action Problems* (New York: Zed, 2013); Peter J. Bloom, Stephan Miescher, and Takyiwaa Manuh, *Modernization as*

Spectacle in Africa (Bloomington: Indiana University Press, 2014); and John Mukum
Mbaku and Pita Ogaba Agbese, *Ethnicity and Governance in the Third World* (Burlington, VT: Ashgate, 2001).

5. This paragraph is based upon a much longer section in Tordoff, *Government and
Politics in Africa*, pp. 1–3. See also Kelechi Amihe Kalu and Peyi Soyinka-Airewele,
eds., *Socio-Political Scaffolding and the Construction of Change: Constitutionalism and
Democratic Governance in Africa* (Trenton, NJ: Africa World, 2009); and Olusola Akin-
rinade and J. Kurt Barling, *Economic Development in Africa: International Efforts,
Issues, and Prospects* (London: Bloomsbury, 2013).

6. On AIDS in Zimbabwe, see *CIA World Factbook,* "People," https://www.cia.gov
/library/publications/the-world-factbook/geos/zi.html. See also Michael O'Neill and
Dennis Austin, *Democracy and Cultural Diversity* (New York: Oxford University Press,
2000), for an international perspective of these issues.

7. Fred Hayward, "Introduction," in Fred Hayward, ed., *Elections in Independent
Africa* (Boulder: Westview, 1987), p. 1. See also Jacky Bouju and Mirjam de Bruijn,
Ordinary Violence and Social Change in Africa (Boston: Brill, 2014).

8. Ibid. See also John Mukum Mbaku and Julius Omozuanvbo, eds., *Multiparty
Democracy and Political Change: Constraints to Democratization in Africa* (Trenton,
NJ: Africa World, 2006); and Kevin Ward and Emma Wild-Wood, *The East African
Revival: History and Legacies* (Burlington, VT: Ashgate, 2012).

9. *Global Studies: Africa* (Guilford, CT: Dushkin, 1991), p. 17. See also Sabelo J.
Ndlovu-Gatsheni, *Coloniality of Power in Postcolonial Africa: Myths of Decolonization*
(Oxford: African Books Collective, 2013).

10. See the coverage in "After Years of Struggle, South Sudan Becomes a New
Nation," *New York Times,* July 9, 2011, http://www.nytimes.com/2011/07/10/world
/africa/10sudan.html?_r=1&hp.

11. Council on Foreign Relations, "Global Conflict Tracker," https://www.cfr.org
/interactives/global-conflict-tracker#!/conflict/civil-war-in-south-sudan.

12. Neal Sobania, *Culture and Customs of Kenya* (Westport: Greenwood, 2003), pp.
18–19. See also S. H. Fazan and John Lonsdale, *Colonial Kenya Observed: British Rule,
Mau Mau, and the Wind of Change* (London: Tauris, 2015).

13. There is much written about the British colonial period in Kenya and the attitudes
of the colonial power. Wunyabario Maloba writes that "colonialism was a dictatorship. It
was imposed by violence and maintained by violence," and adds that the system "was
socially racist." See Wunyabario Maloba, "Decolonization: A Theoretical Perspective,"
in B. A. Ogot and W. R. Ochieng', *Decolonization and Independence in Kenya, 1940–
1993* (Athens: Ohio University Press, 1995), p. 9. See also W. O. Maloba, *The Anatomy
of Neo-Colonialism in Kenya: British Imperialism and Kenyatta, 1963–1978* (Cham,
Switzerland: Palgrave Macmillan, 2017).

14. See http://africanhistory.about.com/od/kenya/a/MauMauTimeline.htm. See also
Daniel Branch, *Defeating Mau Mau, Creating Kenya: Counterinsurgency, Civil War, and
Decolonization* (New York: Cambridge University Press, 2009); and Huw C. Bennett,
*Fighting the Mau Mau: The British Army and Counter-Insurgency in the Kenya Emer-
gency* (New York: Cambridge University Press, 2012).

15. See http://africanhistory.about.com/od/kenya/a/MauMauTimeline.htm. See also
Nicholas van der Bijl, *The Mau Mau Rebellion: The Emergency in Kenya, 1952–1956*
(Baarnsley, Yorkshire: Pen and Sword Military Press, 2017).

16. A very comprehensive study of the Kenya African Union is the volume by John
Spencer, *The Kenya African Union* (Boston: Routledge, 1985). See also David Sandgren,
Mau Mau's Children: The Making of Kenya's Postcolonial Elite (Madison: University
of Wisconsin Press, 2012).

17. See "Jomo Kenyatta: Kenya's First President," https://www.thoughtco.com/jomo
-kenyatta-early-days-43584. See also Charles Hornsby, *Kenya: A History Since Independence* (New York: Tauris, 2012).

18. W. R. Ochieng' and E. S. Atieno-Odhiambo, "On Decolonization," in Ogot and Ochieng', *Decolonization and Independence in Kenya,* p. xiii. See also Poppy Cullen, *Kenya and Britain After Independence: Beyond Neo-Colonialism* (Cham, Switzerland: Palgrave Macmillan, 2017).

19. Francis M. Deng, *Identity, Diversity, and Constitutionalism in Africa* (Washington, DC: US Institute of Peace, 2008), p. 197. See also the collection of essays by a group of anonymous authors titled *Independent Kenya* (London: Zed, 1982).

20. See http://www.constitutionnet.org/country/constitutional-history-kenya. A very good and comprehensive study is by Robert Maxon, *Kenya's Independence Constitution: Constitution-Making and End of Empire* (Madison: Fairleigh Dickinson University Press, 2011). See also Godwin R. Murunga, Duncan Okello, and Anders Sjogren, *Kenya: The Struggle for a New Constitutional Order* (London: Zed, 2014).

21. See Patrick Lumumba, *Kenya's Quest for a Constitution: The Postponed Promise* (Nairobi: Jomo Kenyatta Foundation, 2008); and Charles Oyaya and Nana Poku, *Constitutional Developments and Constitution-Making in Kenya: A Quest for Legitimacy* (London: Routledge, 2018).

22. Hanson, "Understanding Kenya's Politics."

23. See David Throup and Charles Hornsby, *Multi-Party Politics in Kenya* (Athens: Ohio University Press, 1998), especially chap. 3, "The Creation of the Moi State," pp. 26–50.

24. Jennifer Widner, *The Rise of a Party-State in Kenya: From "Harambee!" to "Nyayo!"* (Berkeley: University of California Press, 1992), p. 37.

25. Hanson, "Understanding Kenya's Politics." See also Patrick L. O. Lumumba and Luis Franceschi, *The Constitution of Kenya, 2010: An Introductory Commentary* (Nairobi: Strathmore University Press, 2014).

26. The volume by Makau Mutua, *Kenya's Quest for Democracy: Taming Leviathan* (Boulder: Lynne Rienner, 2008), is a good study of Kenya's attempts to establish a stable, effective government in the period after independence. Mutua focuses upon constitutional reform as the way to solve the problems of the KANU elite.

27. See the full text of the report of the Constitution of Kenya Review Commission at http://www.constitutionnet.org/vl/item/final-report-constitution-kenya-review-commission -final-draft.

28. The official final report of the Committee of Experts can be found at https:// katibaculturalrights.files.wordpress.com/2016/04/coe_final_report-2.pdf. See also Morris Kiwinda Mbondenya and J. Osogo Ambani, *New Constitutional Law of Kenya: Principles, Government, and Human Rights* (Nairobi: LawAfrica, 2012).

29. Mariama Diallo, "New Kenyan Constitution Ratified," *Voice of America News,* August 5, 2010, https://www.voanews.com/a/kenyas-new-constitution-ratified-100158209 /123395.html.

30. The full text of the new constitution can be found at http://www.parliament.go.ke /the-senate/the-constitution. The section on the new presidency can be found in chap. 9, sections 129–151.

31. See "Constitution of Kenya," http://www.klrc.go.ke/index.php/constitution-of -kenya. See also the publication by the Kenya Commission for the Implementation of the Constitution, *Effective Citizens' Participation: Broadening Citizens' Opportunities Under the Constitution of Kenya 2010* (Nairobi, 2015).

32. See "The Kenya Constitution," http://www.kenya-information-guide.com/kenya -constitution.html.

33. Joel D. Karkan and Makau Mutua, "Turning the Corner in Kenya," *Foreign Affairs,* August 10, 2010, http://www.foreignaffairs.com/articles/66510/joel-d-barkan -and-makau-mutua/turning-the-corner-in-kenya?page=show.

34. "Federalism in Kenya Popularly Known as 'Majimbo,'" *Muthumbi,* November 8, 2007, http://muthumbi.blogspot.com/2007/11/federalism-in-kenya-popularly-known-as .html. See also Dele Olowu and Paulos Chanie, *State Fragility and State Building in*

Africa: Cases from Eastern and Southern Africa (Cham, Switzerland: Springer, 2016); and Robert Maxon, *Majimbo in Kenya's Past: Federalism in the 1940s and 1950s* (Amherst, NY: Cambria, 2017).

35. "Federalism in Kenya." See also Fuankem Achankeng, *Nationalism and Intra-State Conflicts in the Postcolonial World* (Lanham: Lexington, 2015).

36. Tordoff, *Government and Politics in Africa*, p. 159. See also J. Andrew Grant and Fredrik Soderbaum, *The New Regionalism in Africa* (London: Routledge, 2017).

37. The full text of the new constitution is at http://www.parliament.go.ke.

38. Michael Madill, "Uganda: Why Federalism Can Work in Kenya but Fail Here," *The Independent* (Uganda), September 8, 2010, http://allafrica.com/stories /201009090963.html. See also Richard Simeon, John McGarry, and Karlo Basta, *Territorial Pluralism: Managing Difference in Multinational States* (Vancouver: University of British Columbia Press, 2015).

39. Stephanie Hanson, "Prime Minister Says Kenyan Politics 'Are Not Ethnic,'" http://www.cfr.org/democracy-and-human-rights/prime-minister-says-kenyan-politics-not -ethnic/p19586. See also Robert Maxon, *East Africa: An Introductory History* (Morgantown: West Virginia University Press, 2009); and Sebastian Elischer, *Political Parties in Africa: Ethnicity and Party Formation* (New York: Cambridge University Press, 2013).

40. Hanson, "Prime Minister Says Kenyan Politics 'Are Not Ethnic.'" See also Jon Holtzman, *Killing Your Neighbors: Friendship and Violence in Northern Kenya and Beyond* (Oakland: University of California Press, 2017); and the essay by Peter Kagwanja, "Courting Genocide: Populism, Ethno-Nationalism, and the Informalisation of Violence in Kenya's 2008 Post-Election Crisis," in the very good collection of essays edited by Mwangi Kagwanja and Roger Southall, *Kenya's Uncertain Democracy: The Electoral Crisis of 2008* (New York: Routledge, 2010).

41. Hanson, "Prime Minister Says Kenyan Politics 'Are Not Ethnic.'" An interesting collection is by Anke Weber, Wesley Hiers, and Anaid Flesken, *Politicized Ethnicity: A Comparative Perspective* (New York: Palgrave Macmillan, 2016).

42. See B. A. Ogot, "The Politics of Populism," in Ogot and Ochieng', *Decolonization and Independence in Kenya*, pp. 187–213.

43. Library of Congress, *Country Profile: Kenya*, https://www.loc.gov/rr/frd/cs/profiles /Kenya.pdf. See also Kimani Njogu, *Youth and Peaceful Elections in Kenya* (Oxford: Twaweza Communications, 2013); and Kimani Njogu, Catherine Bosire, and Alexander Luchetu Likaka, *Citizen Participation in Decision Making: Towards Inclusive Development in Kenya* (Nairobi: Twaweza, 2013).

44. Library of Congress, *Country Profile: Kenya*. See also Hervé Maupeu, Musambayi Katumanga, and W. V. Mitullah, eds., *The Moi Succession: The 2002 Elections in Kenya* (Nairobi: Transafrica, 2005).

45. Library of Congress, *Country Profile: Kenya*. See also *The Report of the Commission of Inquiry into Post Election Violence* (Nairobi: Government Printer, 2008). A very interesting study is by Bhekithemba Richard Mngomezulu, *The President-for-Life Pandemic in Africa: Kenya, Zimbabwe, Nigeria, Zambia, and Malawi* (London: Adonis and Abbey, 2013).

46. *CIA World Factbook,* "Kenya," https://www.cia.gov/library/publications/the -world-factbook/geos/ke.html. A very good chapter on the development of Kenya's legislature is by Joel Barkan and Fred Matiangi, "Kenya's Tortuous Path to Successful Legislative Development," in Joel Barkan, ed., *Legislative Power in Emerging African Democracies* (Boulder: Lynne Rienner, 2009).

47. Parliament of Kenya, "The National Assembly," http://www.parliament.go.ke /index.php/the-national-assembly.

48. See Section 97 of the Constitution. See also Charles Manga Fombad, *Separation of Powers in African Constitutionalism* (Oxford: Oxford University Press, 2016).

49. Constitution, Section 98.

50. See Joseph Oloka-Onyango, *When Courts Do Politics: Public Interest Law and Litigation in East Africa* (Newcastle-upon-Tyne: Cambridge Scholars, 2017).

51. "The Kadhis Courts," *Wajibu: A Journal of Social and Religious Concern,* no. 17, http://africa.peacelink.org/wajibu/articles/art_2120.html. On Muslim law in Africa, see the chapter by Abdulkadir Hashim, "Coping with Conflicts: Colonial Policy Towards Muslim Personal Law in Kenya and Post-Colonial Court Practice," in Shamil Jeppie, Ebrahim Moosa, and Richard Roberts, eds., *Muslim Family Law in Sub-Saharan Africa: Colonial Legacies and Post-Colonial Challenges* (Amsterdam: Amsterdam University Press, 2010).

52. Hanson, "Prime Minister Says Kenyan Politics 'Are Not Ethnic.'" See also Matthijs Bogaards, *Democracy and Social Peace in Divided Societies: Exploring Consociational Parties* (Basingstoke: Palgrave Macmillan, 2014); and Elischer, *Political Parties in Africa.*

53. Hanson, "Prime Minister Says Kenyan Politics 'Are Not Ethnic.'" See also Hassan Ndzovu, *Muslims in Kenyan Politics: Political Involvement, Marginalization, and Minority Status* (Evanston, IL: Northwestern University Press, 2014).

54. For discussion of the argument that multipartyism should be delayed until after fundamental stability is achieved, see John W. Harbeston, "Rethinking Democratic Transitions: Lessons from Eastern and Southern Africa," in Richard Joseph, ed., *State, Conflict, and Democracy in Africa* (Boulder: Lynne Rienner, 1999), p. 51: "Kenya thus provides one of the clearest examples in Africa of the precariousness of undertaking multiparty elections as the first step toward democracy before interparty agreement has been forged and the fundamental rules of the game reformed." See also Adrienne LeBas, *From Protest to Parties: Party-Building and Democratization in Africa* (Oxford: Oxford University Press, 2013).

55. B. A. Ogot, "Transition from Single-Party to Multiparty Political System," in Ogot and Ochieng', *Decolonization and Independence in Kenya,* pp. 239–261. See also Michael Chege, Gabriel Mukele, and Njeri Kabeberi, *The Electoral System and Multi-Partyism in Kenya* (Nairobi: African Research and Resource Forum, 2007).

56. See Inter-Parliamentary Union, "Parline Database: Kenya—National Assembly," http://archive.ipu.org/parline-e/reports/2167_E.htm.

57. See Robyn Dixon, "Kenyan Election Official Flees to U.S. in Fear for Her Life, Saying New Election Will Not Be Fair," *Los Angeles Times,* October 18, 2017, http://www.latimes.com/world/africa/la-fg-kenya-election-threats-20171018-story.html.

58. Karen Allen, "Has Kenya's Power-Sharing Worked?" *BBC News,* March 3, 2009, http://news.bbc.co.uk/2/hi/africa/7921007.stm. See also Nicholas Cheeseman and Daniel Branch, *Election Fever: Kenya's Crisis* (Abingdon: Routledge, 2008).

13

Mexico

Learning Outcomes

After reading this chapter, you will be able to

- Appreciate Mexico's political stability in the context of the third world nations and the political context of Latin America within which it operates.
- Discuss Mexican federalism, both in terms of its effect upon policymaking in Mexico and in terms of its similarity to and difference from other federal systems.
- Understand Mexico's version of a presidential executive and the position he holds in the political system.
- Describe the relation between Mexico's two legislative chambers, and explain how they compare with corresponding legislature structures elsewhere.
- Understand the operation of political parties in Mexico today.
- Appreciate the economic progress that Mexico has made over the past three decades.

Mexico—formally the United Mexican States—represents many variations from other nations we have already examined in this book. It is our first Latin American nation. And although it is a developing nation, it is a developing nation that has achieved a remarkable level of political stability over the years. These characteristics—among others—guarantee that in this chapter we shall note several differences in both political structure and political behavior from those we have observed so far.

Mexico's Political Heritage

Although Mexico has not had a revolution since early in the twentieth century (1910–1921), this should not be taken to suggest that there have been no issues of controversy in Mexican politics since that time, or that there has not been any significant political instability in domestic politics. Such is not the case. Indeed, Mexico's political culture is fragmented, and there are many issues of conflict in society.[1]

Mexico has, even in very recent years, experienced some very tense moments in the political arena. In 1968 several hundred students were killed in Mexico City while demonstrating against the government; massive land expropriation was undertaken in 1976; and an economic crisis was encountered in 1982. Indeed, many claimed that the 1988 presidential election was stolen by the forces of President Carlos Salina de Gortari when it was clear that the candidate of the Institutional Revolutionary Party might actually lose a presidential election for the first time in modern history. The same was true for the July 2006 election for president, which resulted in a highly contested electoral outcome when the Federal Electoral Court declared Felipe Calderón of the National Action Party (PAN) the winner of the election and president-elect.[2]

In the campaign for the August 1994 presidential election, the Institutional Revolutionary Party (the party of the government) candidate for the presidency associated with political reform, Luis Donaldo Colosio, was assassinated; another reform-oriented party leader, the secretary-general of the PRI, was assassinated in September 1994, shortly after the election. In both of these cases, the individuals identified as the assassins were tried and convicted, but feelings exist in Mexico that the full story behind the killings has not yet come out, and links with former president **Carlos Salinas de Gortari** (because of the involvement of his brother) continue to worry many.

Another significant point of instability relates to violence that broke out in the south of Mexico in the state of Chiapas in January 1994. The insurrection dealt with concerns about social issues—specifically dealing with land reform—and President de Gortari had to send the army against members of the Zapatista movement when they seized their state's second largest city, San Cristobal de las Casas, and three other sizable towns.[3] De Gortari eventually promised amnesty for the rebel leaders and government action on the issues related to poverty and land reform, but all of Mexico was shaken that such a level of violence took place. The government unilaterally declared a ceasefire in 1994, and active guerrilla warfare ended. In December 1997 a massacre of forty-five peasants took place in the state of Chiapas, again increasing tensions in the state. We shall return to further discussion of these issues later in the chapter.

In the early 1970s, Mexico seemed to have entered an era of rapid development and increasing prosperity. Mexico's oil industry was rapidly expanding and became the fourth largest in the world. Later, however, primarily as a result of the decline in world oil prices, Mexico's economy became a shambles, and domestic politics reflected the economic tensions in society.[4]

Mexico's political history falls into several broad eras.[5] Prior to 1521, Mexico was ruled by a series of Indian empires. Between 1521 and 1810, Mexico was under Spanish colonial power. Mexico first revolted against the Spanish on September 16, 1810; the struggle continued until 1821, when a stable independent government was installed. Between 1821 and 1877 there were a number of emperors, dictators, and presidents in power, and Mexico lost Texas (1836) and later (1846–1848) what today are California, Nevada, Utah, most of Arizona and New Mexico, and parts of Wyoming and Colorado, to the United States.

In 1855 the Indian leader **Benito Juárez** began to introduce political reforms in Mexico, but his leadership was short-lived, and between 1861 and 1867 Mexico fell under the rule of European powers. In 1867 Juárez again took power as president, and he executed Maximilian of Austria, who had become emperor of Mexico in 1864.

From 1877 to 1911, Mexican politics were dominated by the long and dictatorial presidency of **Porfirio Diaz** (1876–1880 and 1884–1911). The Diaz regime led to the social revolution of 1910–1921 and is regarded by most Mexicans as the beginning of modern Mexican politics. "The commonly accepted and most convenient symbol for the beginning of Mexico's modernization process is the Mexican Revolution of 1910."[6]

Political Stability

Mexico's stability has, over the past several decades, been the single most visible characteristic separating it from other Latin American nations. It has continued to operate under the same political structures for nearly a century, and it is the only major Latin American political system not to have had a military coup since the end of World War II. Also an exception to the general Latin American pattern, every Mexican president elected since the presidential election of 1934 has served out his full six-year term and participated in a peaceful transition of power rather than having his power seized by a coup or junta of one kind or another, something that has been much more common in Latin America, to the south of Mexico.

"Stability," as we use the term here, does not mean that Mexican society has not had social tensions, however. As recently as 1997, significant social tensions—including action labeled as an "insurrection"—

have arisen. Here, "stability" is used in a more restrictive sense to indicate the continuity of major political structures. One important example of this relative stability is the relation between the Mexican military and the civilian government. Whereas military coups are common in Central and South America, such is not the case in Mexico.[7]

Among the significant aspects of Mexican culture contributing to this pattern of stability is the process of political socialization there. It has been suggested that Mexico's socialization patterns have transformed in recent years, resulting in changes in the socialization process.[8] These include an expansion of mass education—today nearly one-third of Mexicans are in school, and an increasingly educated mass public wants to have more education. Student groups see increasing educational opportunities not only as avenues for advancement but also as means to further develop governmental expertise and legitimacy.[9]

For those who were adolescents in the early years of the twentieth century, the revolution was an event of overwhelming significance; for the post-revolutionary generation the most important characteristic of the environment in which they were reared was the prevalence of violence and instability. Thus, a stable contemporary regime is an important factor in the lives of most Mexican political elites today.

The Constitutional System

Mexico's contemporary political system was born in revolution. The new constitution, amending the Constitution of 1857, was announced in February 1917 and has been the constitution of Mexico since that time. Three key characteristics reflected in the Constitution are representative democracy, what has been called presidential dictatorship, and corporatism.[10]

Mexico's leadership in 1917 believed in the virtues of classical liberalism and established a constitution based upon **representative democracy**, guaranteeing equal rights for all citizens; providing for separation of powers in the legislative, executive, and judicial branches of government; and establishing representative government based upon popular sovereignty. It also produced a centralized federal government with significant political powers—for example, permitting the government to nationalize the petroleum industry in 1938 and allowing it to restrict foreign ownership of land in Mexico.[11]

While some aspects of the Constitution clearly were based upon fundamental principles of representative democracy, others are less so. Indeed, some have suggested that Mexico today has in essence a **presidential dictatorship**. The president has the right to issue executive decrees, which have the force of law; despite the notion of separation of powers, the president is permitted to introduce proposals in the legislature on his own authority (something that the US president, for example, is not permitted to do). This gives him a direct legislative power, in addition to his executive power. The president also has the power to appoint and remove judges, giving him clear judicial power as well. Thus, the president's power "is such that it absorbs and is complementary to the powers of the other two branches of government. In addition, the sovereignty of the states is found to be extremely limited by the Federation and subject to the discretionary powers of the president. The result is the establishment of a constitutional dictatorship of the presidential variety."[12]

The third theme of Mexican politics is that of corporatism, which we defined earlier in this book as implying a close interaction of groups and government whereby organizations are integrated into the governmental decisionmaking process. As the government's financial planning has come under increased pressures in recent years, tensions have begun to develop in the government-business relationship, and the government has anxiously sought ways to smooth over the sources of tension.[13]

Mexican labor law recognizes classes in society, and the Courts of Conciliation and Arbitration are given authority to resolve conflicts between labor and owners. There are many governmental boards and commissions that provide industrial and interest groups with a role in policymaking. These commissions can be referred to as "corporate" because through appointment of leaders of different social and economic groups to membership on the boards, these groups are indeed integrated into the government decisionmaking process.[14]

Federalism

Mexico is a federal system, including thirty-one states and one federal district, each of which has some policy jurisdiction. However, the Mexican states do not have the degree of power in relation to Mexico City that the German Lander have in relation to their respective national capital, for example. Each state has its own constitution and has the right to pass its own laws, within clearly defined parameters. Each state elects its own governor, who holds office for a term of six years. The state legislatures have three-year terms of office.[15]

It should be noted that despite the preeminence of the federal president, governors are significant political actors in Mexican politics, and charges of electoral fraud have been regularly leveled in gubernatorial elections as well as elections for the national presidency and Congress.

The overwhelming power of the president in the Mexican political system has done a great deal to weaken Mexican federalism. The president exercises control over state government, much as he exercises control over other branches of the federal government, through both constitutional and traditional justifications.[16]

Most frequently, however, the major source of presidential power, rather than coming exclusively from legal or constitutional structures, emanates from practical sources, such as the president's control (through legislation) of grant programs, federal financial aid to the states, and similar sources.

In recent years there has been an increasing policy of administrative decentralization in Mexico, something that reflects the challenges of political development and political modernization, as described in Box 13.1. This has been suggested by many to be necessary given recent "hyper-urbanization" in Mexico—the rush of so many rural residents to the urban area surrounding Mexico City, a topic to which we shall return later in the chapter. The government has become aware that educational, cultural, and health resources simply must be made available far more

---

Box 13.1   Political Development and Political Modernization

Individual nation-states do not spring fully-blossomed and mature into the contemporary political world. Political development and modernization are processes, and sometimes these processes are effectuated speedily, while at other times they take longer. Sometimes the evolution involved is gradual; other times it is abrupt, violent, and painful.[a]

Often the terms *modernization* and *development* are used interchangeably to refer to the movement of a nation-state from one evolutionary stage to another. Some scholars, however, distinguish between the two terms:

[Development is] an evolutionary process in which indigenous institutions adapt and control change and are not simply caught up in imitating and reacting to outside forces. Modernization is often contemporary, imported, and creates a dependency on the technologically advanced urban-industrial centers without helping local political and social institutions to grow and adapt. Development means that a system has some ability to be selective in the type and pace of changes, often imported, that occur in a country.[b]

Notes: a. A very good recent work in this area is Harry Eckstein, *Regarding Politics: Essays on Political Theory, Stability, and Change* (Berkeley: University of California Press, 1992).

b. Herbert Winter and Thomas Bellows, *People and Politics* (New York: Wiley, 1977), pp. 352–353.

broadly in contemporary Mexico; if not, some experts say, the rush to move to the urban areas will continue.[17]

Mexico's approach to federalism is, as noted earlier, far more centralized than that observed in Germany. Indeed, "the central government bureaucracy, dominated by the presidency, is the main source of public policy."[18] Thus, apart from the observation that states and state governments exist, our attention can remain focused on the national level of government if we are seeking an understanding of how political institutions and political behavior operate in Mexico.

Executive Structures

Simón Bolivar once observed that the new republics of the Americas needed kings who could be referred to as presidents and added that, in Mexico at least, these kings were kings for six-year periods.[19] The Mexican president is elected by direct popular vote in elections and can hold office for a single six-year term, after which time the individual can never be reelected. He must be at least thirty-five years of age and a native-born Mexican who is the son of native-born Mexicans. He must be male. He cannot be a clergyman. If he has been in either the military or the cabinet (which all recent presidents have been), he must have retired from that position at least six months prior to the election. The president is, very clearly, the single most powerful individual in Mexican politics.[20]

Power

Much of the president's power comes from his constitutional role in government; the president "encounters no effective restraint *within* government."[21] In that role he has very wide power to appoint and remove government officials (much broader fiscal powers than, say, the US president), the capacity to initiate and veto legislation, and the power to control the military. (Since the revolution, the military has been reorganized, and today it is restricted in its power to influence policy.) Although legislators in Mexico have the power to introduce legislation, legislation is typically introduced by the president.[22]

Nomination and Selection

The presidential election of 1988 was the first Mexican presidential election in modern history in which the outcome was truly in doubt, although by the time the votes were all counted (and rigged, opposition leaders charged) the PRI candidate again won.[23] While the PRI's hold on power continued thereafter, it was shaken, and in the election of 2000, after seventy-one years of the PRI being the party of power, for the first time another party won the presidency with the victory of the

National Action Party's **Vicente Fox**. The 2006 election saw the PRI finish third in the presidential race, so in hindsight the election of 2000 must be seen as the beginning of a manifestation of a truly competitive Mexican electoral system.[24]

The usual practice within the PRI through the 2000 election was to have the incumbent president handpick his successor, invariably from among those individuals who had been active in his cabinet. As noted earlier, the Constitution requires that a cabinet officer seeking the presidency must resign from office at least six months before the presidential elections, but this has not provided any difficulties for recent candidates. "There are some socioeconomic characteristics that are apparently valued by presidents when selecting their successors, including physical appearance, a neutral position in relation to organized religion, a middle-class background, and coming from a large state."[25] (For a list of recent presidents of Mexico, see Table 13.1.)

When recent incumbent presidents neared the final year of their six-year term of office, pressures began to be exerted on them to name a successor. Incumbents have tried to resist this pressure for as long as possible, however, because once an incumbent names the heir-apparent, he loses much of his own political power and will not be able to accomplish as much as he previously could for the duration of his time in office. One scholar, in fact, has identified nine different stages in the process of the selection of a new president. Although his work focused on one party—the PRI—it is applicable to all major Mexican parties.

Table 13.1 Recent Mexican Presidents

	Tenure	Party
Gustavo Diaz Ordaz	1964–1970	PRI
Luis Echeverría Alvarez	1970–1976	PRI
José López Portillo	1976–1982	PRI
Miguel de la Madrid Hurtado	1982–1988	PRI
Carlos Salinas de Gortari	1988–1994	PRI
Ernesto Zedillo Ponce de León	1994–2000	PRI
Vicente Fox Quesada	2000–2006	PAN
Felipe Calderón Hinojosa	2006–2012	PAN
Enrique Peña Nieto	2012–2018	PRI
Andrés Manuel López Obrador	2018–	MORENA

Sources: "Listing of Mexico's Presidents and Heads of State," http://www.mexconnect .com/articles/3186-listing-of-mexico-s-presidents-and-heads-of-state; "Lopez Obrador, an Atypical Leftist, Wins Mexico Presidency in Landslide," *New York Times,* July 1, 2018.

1. The president consults with advisers and colleagues as to acceptability of possible nominees.
2. The president announces his choice.
3. Power-seekers and political leaders in the PRI praise the candidate-designate.
4. The candidate is officially nominated at the PRI Rally.
5. The campaign takes place.
6. The election takes place.
7. The winning candidate officially accepts the election results.
8. The new president selects his advisers.
9. The new president selects an advantageous time to announce his appointments.[26]

Once the outgoing president had nominated his successor—who in recent elections had been a member of the cabinet and thus immediately resigned from the cabinet—the nominee of the PRI was expected to travel all over the country campaigning for office, meeting leaders of interest groups, local leaders, business leaders, community politicians, and so on, and in fact improve his knowledge of local problems at the same time that he was increasing his own visibility in the eyes of the electorate. Past experience has shown that even the most isolated of Mexican villages was visited—if not by the candidate himself then by one of his campaign workers—over the course of the campaign.

This process was violently disrupted in 1994 when the PRI candidate for the presidency, Luis Donaldo Colosio, who had been hand-picked by outgoing president Salinas de Gortari, was assassinated in early March as he was campaigning around the country. Picking Colosio's successor was especially difficult for the PRI because of a legal requirement that candidates could not have held public office during the six-month period prior to the election, which eliminated most of the possible candidates for the position. In late March 1994 the PRI nominated **Ernesto Zedillo Ponce de León**, a former cabinet minister and someone who had been Colosio's campaign manager, to serve as the party's new presidential candidate.

Some questioned why Mexico should even go through this ritual if the results of the election were certain. Of course, post-2000 the response to this question was that the results of the election were not certain: Vicente Fox Quesada of the Alliance for Change (which included the National Action Party and the Mexican Green Ecologist Party [PVEM]) won the 2000 presidential election. Even before this upset of the PRI, however, there were at least two reasons why the national campaign was useful, even if it contained no surprises. First, the act of campaigning itself helped to create support for the regime and thereby afforded the government greater legitimacy than it might otherwise have had without a campaign. Second, the presidential campaign could make a significant difference to candidates for the Senate and the Chamber of Deputies who were running for office, either on the same side as the presidential candidate or on an opposition ticket.

In the presidential election of August 1994, President Ernesto Zedillo Ponce de León of the Institutional Revolutionary Party was elected by a substantial margin, and he was sworn in on December 1, 1994. Zedillo was educated as an economist, with degrees from Yale, and had served in the prior Salinas administration as secretary of programming and budget as well as secretary of education prior to receiving the nomination for the presidency and running for the office.

President Zedillo pursued several goals as soon as he took office. Among these was to continue to open Mexico's political system so that groups and political parties that had in the past been shut out of participation could participate. He also targeted reform of the justice system, control of narcotics traffic, cutting corruption, and economic reform as needing a great deal of attention.

Six years later the situation was different. In July 1999, as the term of President Zedillo was coming to a close, one of the key questions in Mexican politics had to do with the issue of fraud and the PRI; the PRI was heartened, and its election chances were greatly increased, when a report was released at the end of July clearing the PRI of fraud. The opposition had hoped that the PRI would face serious charges that would affect its chances in the campaign. The leadership of the National Action Party and the Party of the Democratic Revolution (PRD) saw that victory might be possible if they could pool their resources to support a candidate together. By September it was clear that their policy preferences, and the fact that they each had a strong leader who wanted to be the nominee of the combined party, would prevent a coalition, and talks ended.

In November 1999 the PRI chose its candidate, Francisco Labastida, and PRI supporters were confident that victory would again be theirs. Within a week of receiving the PRI leadership position the former interior minister left on his first official tour abroad as the PRI presidential candidate, traveling to Argentina, Brazil, Uruguay, and Chile.

In December 1999 the head of the National Action Party, Vicente Fox, indicated that he wanted to renew efforts to create a national opposition alliance, and although Labastida and the PRI were in a comfortable leading position, Fox and his supporters continued to be enthusiastic. In April 2000 Fox was declared to be the winner of a six-way presidential debate, and his energy level and the energy level of his campaign increased; a month later he moved ahead in the opinion polls for the first time, giving increasing credibility to his claim that the PRI could be defeated if the opposition pulled together.

On election day the unthinkable happened, and the PRI lost, for the first time since 1929. Fox was sworn in on December 1, 2000. This was not only the first non-PRI president in Mexican history but also "the first peaceful democratic transfer of power ever in Mexican history."[27]

A year after his election, all was not going well for Fox. He had not made great progress on his campaign promises and was being seen as an ineffective leader. One commentator noted, "After Fox had brazenly predicted 7 percent economic growth this year, Mexico's economy has skidded to zero growth. After promising to create 1.3 million jobs, at least 250,000 jobs have been lost."[28] These were challenges that continued to face the Mexican president, and by the time of the presidential campaign in 2006 the PAN was in trouble.

The 2006 election was the closest in Mexican political history, and it took over two months for a definitive result to appear—and even then it was not "definitive" to all. The Justices of the Federal Electoral Institute—the government agency in charge of organizing the election—ruled that the election was fair and that the conservative candidate, former energy minister **Felipe Calderón Hinojosa** of the National Action Party, had won. The Party of the Democratic Revolution's candidate, **Andrés Manuel López Obrador**, came in a razor-close second, and the candidate of the Institutional Revolutionary Party, the party that had controlled power from 1929 to 2000 without stop, came in third.[29]

Six years later the PRI reclaimed the presidency with the election to office of **Enrique Peña Nieto**, former governor of the state of Mexico. After twelve years of having the PRI in the opposition, the Mexican population appeared tired of the policies of National Action Party rule since 2000 and was ready for a change. The global financial crisis of 2008 hit the Mexican economy hard and wiped out much of the progress of previous years, and although it might be argued that the government of President Calderón was not responsible for many of Mexico's economic challenges, the PAN *was* the party in charge, and people were ready for a change. At the same time, the rise of organized crime across Mexico—often driven by the drug trade—was proving to be a real challenge for the federal government, too.[30]

President Enrique Peña Nieto had to face issues of poverty, economic challenges caused by the drop in the price of oil leading to a much lower production of oil (which had been the largest source of

Mexican income), and drug-related violence, which has taken a heavy toll in Mexican society.

The election of 2018 was, apparently, a game-changer for Mexicans, and Andrés Manuel López Obrador—on his third try for the presidency— won a landslide victory in a result that the *New York Times* wrote

> puts a leftist leader at the helm of Latin America's second-largest economy for the first time in decades, a prospect that has filled millions of Mexicans with hope—and the nation's elites with trepidation.
>
> The outcome represents a clear rejection of the status quo in the nation, which for the last quarter century has been defined by a centrist vision and an embrace of globalization that many Mexicans feel has not served them.
>
> The core promises of Mr. López Obrador's campaign—to end corruption, reduce violence and address Mexico's endemic poverty— were immensely popular with voters, but they come with questions he and his new government may struggle to answer.[31]

In the 2018 presidential election López Obrador managed to defeat the major political parties of Mexico by "capturing more than half the vote, according to early returns, more than any candidate since the nation began its transition to democracy nearly 20 years ago. In a reflection of the lopsided vote, his main competitors conceded the race within 45 minutes of the polls' closing, another historical first. With his coalition partners, it is likely that he will hold a majority in Congress, potentially giving him more power to enact his policies."[32]

Observers of the election noted "five takeaways" from the election victory, many of which will be shaped by currents of history to come.[33] First, the election was a rejection of the Mexican status quo. Second, the "Trump factor" was apparent in the campaign, the seemingly unending assault by US president Donald Trump on Mexico since the US presidential election campaign in 2016—threatening to leave the North American Free Trade Agreement, threatening to make Mexico pay for a border wall between the two countries, and denigrating Mexican migrants to the United States. Mexicans apparently wanted someone to stand up to Trump. Third, Mexico's traditional challenges were not being resolved by the "traditional" parties, problems like corruption, violence, and the drug trade. Fourth, the victory may be a harbinger of a fundamental reshaping of the Mexican political system, with the first leftist government in decades in power. Finally, the election will have significant economic implications, although it is not completely clear what those will be. During the campaign the "traditional" parties claimed that the election of a leftist would destroy Mexico's economy. Only time will tell (see Table 13.2).

Table 13.2   Mexico's Presidential Election of July 2018

Candidate	Percentage of Vote
Andrés Manuel López Obrador (MORENA)	53.2
Ricardo Anaya Cortes (PAN)	22.3
José Antonio Meade Kuribreña (PRI)	16.4
Jaime Heliodoro Rodríguez Calderón	5.2

Source: Instituto Nacional Electoral, "Elecciones 2018," https://www.ine.mx.

Legislative Structures

The Mexican Congress is bicameral and consists of a **Chamber of Deputies** and a Senate. The Congress is inferior to the president in the structures of governmental power, and its consent to presidential legislative proposals can be counted upon. In fact, recent scholarship has indicated that presidential proposals have been approved unanimously 80 to 95 percent of the time in recent years, and they are normally opposed by less than 5 percent of the members of the Congress.[34]

The Senate

Senators are elected for six-year terms. The Senate is "frankly regarded in Mexico as a rubber stamp for presidential policy,"[35] and accordingly it is not looked upon as a highly significant structure in contemporary Mexican politics. Senators are elected by direct popular vote. The voting system is innovative and reflects Mexico's concern with making sure that significant minorities have some representation in the government. With the understanding that district-based representation tends to over-represent plurality parties and "hide" minority parties, the new electoral system was designed to make sure that significant minorities have representation by reserving seats for those minority parties.

The Senate has a total of 128 members, as reflected in Table 13.3, with thirty-two multimember constituencies of three senators, representing each of the thirty-one states and the federal district. Each party submits a list of two candidates for each state. Of the three senators for each state, two are allocated to the party that received the largest number of votes, and one is allocated to the party that received the second largest number of votes in that state. The final thirty-two seats are distributed by a proportional representation system based on party lists nationally; each national party submits a list of thirty-two candidates, and these are distributed according to the proportion of the

Table 13.3   Mexico's Senate Election of July 1, 2018

Political Group	Constituency Percentage	Constituency Number of Seats	Number of Proportional Seats	Total Number of Seats	Gain/Loss from 2012
National Regeneration Movement (MORENA)	37.5	44	14	58	+ 58
National Action Party (PAN)	17.7	16	6	22	− 12
Institutional Revolutionary Party (PRI)	15.8	8	6	14	− 41
Democratic Revolutionary Party (PRD)	5.4	7	2	9	+ 2
Citizens' Movement (MC)	4.6	5	2	7	+ 7
Green Party of Mexico (PVEM)	4.4	4	1	5	—
Labor	3.8	6	1	7	− 12
Others	6.7	6	0	6	− 2
Total		96	32	128	

Source: Instituto Nacional Electoral, "Elecciones Federales 2018—Senadurías National," https://p2018.ine.mx/#/senadurias/nacional/1/2/1/2.

national vote that the party receives; a party receiving 10 percent of the national vote will receive three Senate seats. The most recent election was in July 2018.

The senatorial election of 2018 was held simultaneously with elections for a new president and the House of Representatives, and other local elections, and these senators will hold office through August 2024. Voters elected all 128 members of the Senate. The presidential upset discussed earlier carried over into the Senate elections, with the National Regeneration Movement (MORENA) winning forty-four of the constituency-based ninety-six senator seats and fourteen of the proportional senator seats, for a total of fifty-eight seats in the Senate.[36]

The Chamber of Deputies

While senators are elected for six-year terms, the 500 deputies are elected for three-year terms according to a system of single-member-district voting and **partial proportional representation**, under which 200 of the 500 seats in the Chamber are elected by proportional representation, while the other 300 seats are elected from single-member districts. The proportional representation seats are distributed on the basis of national vote won by each party, with the proviso that the majority party cannot hold more than 300 seats overall; once the majority party hits 300 seats in the Chamber, any other seats that its proportional votes would give it are allocated to the next party.[37]

The 300 single-member-district seats are based upon population, but the Constitution guarantees each state at least two deputies. Although each state's number of seats is based upon the state's total population as a share of the national population, there is no constitutional provision that forces the states to divide their quota of seats into equally populated districts.

Electoral reform was introduced in 1977, raising the number of deputies from about 200 (the exact number depended upon how many minority party deputies were elected)[38] to 400, and this reform became effective with the 1979–1980 legislative session. For the 1988 election the total number of seats was raised to 500; the number of seats has remained 500 through the most recent—July 2018—election. Of these seats, 300 were elected by a single-member-district majority-vote system, with those districts based upon population similar to electoral systems we have seen in Britain or Germany (see Table 13.4).

Table 13.4   Mexico's Chamber of Deputies Election of July 2018

Political Group	Constituency Percentage	Constituency Number of Seats	Number of Proportional Seats	Total Number of Seats	Gain/Loss from 2012
National Regeneration Movement (MORENA)	37.2	109	84	193	+ 146
National Action Party (PAN)	18.1	38	41	79	– 28
Institutional Revolutionary Party (PRI)	16.4	6	36	42	– 162
Party of the Democratic Revolution (PRD)	5.4	11	12	23	– 30
Ecologist Green Party (PVEM)	4.7	7	10	17	– 21
Citizens' Movement (MC)	4.4	16	10	26	+ 5
Labor Party (PT)	3.9	54	7	61	+ 55
New Alliance Party (PNA)	2.5	1	0	1	– 11
Social Encounter Party (PES)	2.4	58	0	58	+ 46
Independents	.9	0	0	0	– 6
Total		300	200	500	

Source: Instituto Nacional Electoral, "Elecciones Federales 2018—Senadurías National," https://computos2018.ine.mx/#/diputaciones/nacional/1/3/1/1.

Mexico's electoral system strengthens the voice of the opposition parties in the Chamber of Deputies; as noted earlier, the majority party is not permitted to hold more than 300 seats in the 500-seat legislature, unless it wins over 60 percent of the votes, in which case it can hold up to 315 seats. The 200 at-large seats are distributed by proportional representation on the basis of the proportion of the national vote won by each party. All of the opposition parties together are guaranteed at least 150 of these 200 at-large proportional seats.

Thus, 30 percent of the seats in the Chamber of Deputies are guaranteed to opposition parties, as well as those seats they can win in the 300 district-based electoral races. This means that although the power of the Chamber of Deputies is limited, the opposition is guaranteed a significant presence there. Several smaller parties have benefited from the at-large proportional seats.[39]

In the election of July 2018, President Obrador's National Regeneration Movement won a majority, in a coalition called Juntos Haremos Historia (Together We Will Make History), along with the Labor Party (PT) and the Social Encounter Party (PES), winning 312 of the 500 seats. The National Action Party won under 16 percent of the seats, and the Institutional Revolutionary Party won only 8.4 percent of the seats, clearly showing that the Mexican voters wanted a change. These figures are indicated in Table 13.4.

The Bureaucracy

By the mid-1970s, the Mexican federal public sector included 1,075 agencies with nearly 3.4 million employees—nearly 17 percent of the country's total workforce. The administration of President de la Madrid sought to decentralize some of this bureaucracy, emphasizing regional programs and the increased participation of state and local governments in programs, especially those dealing with health care and education.[40]

We noted earlier that there are many quasi-governmental organizations in Mexico that complement the federal and state governments' efforts to enact policy. A recent study listed 123 decentralized agencies, 292 public enterprises, 187 commissions, and 160 development trusts, as well as 18 regular ministries and departments of state making up the federal bureaucratic infrastructure.[41]

As we shall see later, although the federal government has sought to decentralize the bureaucracy somewhat in recent years, it is still the case that massive bureaucracy affects the ability of the central government to enact policy, especially in central industrial areas such as oil, petroleum exploration and distribution (PEMEX), steel (SIDERMEX), fertilizers (FERTIMEX), and food purchasing, processing, and distribution (CONASUPO).[42]

Political Parties and Elections

Political Parties

A strong relationship exists between the dominant political party and the state in Mexico, but there remains a clear difference between the two. The primary function of the dominant party is to mobilize support and to legitimize the state.[43]

Although Mexico is often thought of as a one-party nation because of the history of the dominance of the PRI, such is clearly no longer the case; the years of PAN leadership, and most recently the national landslide for a leftist coalition, have shown not only that it is possible to defeat the PRI, but also that it can be done on a widespread scale.[44] Indeed, as noted earlier, the PRI candidate for president finished third in the 2006 election, and the PRI delivered its worst-ever performance at all three national levels (presidency, Senate, and Chamber of Deputies) in 2018. There are many opposition groups in society, made up of peasants, students, and workers.[45] With the leftist coalition MORENA capturing power in 2018 there is an indication of a functioning competitive party system, with credible performances by several party organizations.

The PRI was the major party in Mexico from the 1920s through the 2000 election. It was so well-entrenched and central to the operation of the government that through the end of the 1990s it had been seen as serving "as a subordinate extension of the presidency and central government bureaucracy."[46] The PRI had three major factions: an agrarian faction, a labor faction, and a "popular" faction, and it was governed by a national party congress called the National Assembly. Each of the three factions of the PRI vied for power on the Executive Committee, and although these three factions were ostensibly all on the same side in an election, there was often great competition between and among them for formal party leadership positions.

The PRI continued to play a very important role in Mexican politics through the 2018 election; its 2018 loss shows us that there is a major restructuring going on in the Mexican political arena, and there is some doubt about what the future will hold for the PRI. In the recent past the topic of fraud was one that was frequently associated with the PRI and elections at all levels—presidential, congressional, and state—and corruption was often cited in discussions of the results of the 2018 election.

In the 2006 presidential election the theme of fraud reappeared, with hundreds of thousands of Mexicans demonstrating in the Zocalo, Mexico City's main square, crying that the election had been stolen from the PRD's Obrador by the forces of the PAN's Calderón; ironically, the PRI was not involved in the crisis at all, because its candidate had finished third in the voting and was clearly not going to be the winner in the election.[47] Obrador did not disappear from competitive national elections, and finally on his third try for the presidency he won the election of 2018.

The National Democratic Front (FDN) was a new competing party in the 1988 election. Its roots were not new; they included the Mexican Communist Party (PCM),[48] which changed its name to the Unified Socialist Party of Mexico (PSUM) in 1981 when it joined with several smaller parties in a left-of-center coalition. The PSUM was able to provide the PRI with some serious competition at the state level of politics, although it was not very effective in federal elections until 1988.[49] The FDN is regarded by many as not really a true party but rather an electoral coalition whose roots include not only the communist PCM or PSUM but also a healthy noncommunist tradition. The FDN competed as the PRD, the Party of the Democratic Revolution, later, and was favored for a long while to win the 2006 presidential election, losing by less than one-tenth of 1 percent.

The major right-of-center parties include the Mexican Democratic Party (PDM) and the National Action Party. Both parties became more successful in elections following the 1977 reforms, which created the at-large proportional representation in the Chamber of Deputies, and they offered the PRI serious competition at the state level of politics through the end of the 1990s. The PDM was considered "the most conservative party with registration in Mexico,"[50] and it has its strongest political support in the countryside.

The PAN is considered the major party of the political right in Mexico today,[51] although following its substantial losses in the presidential, senatorial, and Chamber of Deputies elections of 2018 it will be doing some internal reorganization in the coming years. The major difference between the PAN and the PRI included the PAN's greater criticism of the United States and the PAN's desire to support the Catholic Church.[52] These changes allowed more members of the opposition parties to win election to the Chamber of Deputies. Thus, the president and the PRI were able to increase their perceived legitimacy by encouraging the opposition parties, without giving up any real political power at all.[53]

Even though the PRI had—until the 2000 presidential election—won nearly every federal election held since 1929, the broader Mexican electoral arena contained real electoral competition through 2000; with the PRI having lost both the 2000 and 2006 presidential elections it is certainly safe to say that the electoral arena is an open and competitive one today. And as noted earlier, with recent electoral reforms there seems to be real progress being made in offering Mexican voters real choices in the electoral setting, something that the elections of 2018 clearly demonstrated.[54]

A record 78 percent of registered voters participated in the 1994 presidential election, and 65 percent voted in the 2000 election. Almost 60 percent participated in the 2006 election, 63 percent voted in the 2012 presidential election, and 64 percent voted in 2018.[55]

The reforms of 1977 and 1988, alluded to earlier, were designed to increase political participation and to stimulate electoral competition. By just about any measure we might use, the reforms have to be considered to be effective; since they were enacted, in fact, opposition to the PRI has increased, and the PRI has moved from being the dominant party in the nation to being an "also-ran," well out of the lead for voter support.[56]

Political Development and Economics

Two distinct problem areas confront the Mexican government today. Both of these problems, it can be asserted, are a function of the economic crisis in Mexico.[57] One of these concerns is **urban migration**, with a unique set of problems facing Mexico City today. The massive pattern of migration from rural Mexico to the capital city is putting intolerable demands upon the infrastructure of Mexico City and has already had significant effects upon the quality of life there. The second problem has an international dimension and concerns the implications of the (illegal and) massive flow of Mexicans across Mexico's northern border with the United States.

Mexico City has suffered the same problems of urban migration as have the major cities of many developing nations, sometimes referred to as **hyper-urbanization**.[58] The crises of poverty and high unemployment often serve to push significant populations from rural areas to the urban capital area in search of jobs and better living conditions. Table 13.5 shows how significant this population movement to urban areas has been. In 1910, 28.7 percent of Mexico's population lived in an urban setting. In 2030 this is predicted to be 82.9 percent.[59] Ironically, the migrants usually find neither jobs nor better living conditions; rather, these migrations contribute to greater unemployment and worse living conditions.[60]

	1950	1960	1970	1980	1990	2000	2005	2016	2030 (predicted)
Table 13.5 Mexico's Urban Population (percentage of total population)									
	42.7	50.8	59.0	66.3	72.5	74.7	76.0	79.5	82.9

Source: Index Mundi, "Mexico—Urban Population," https://www.indexmundi.com/facts /mexico/urban-population.

Mexico City represents the worst of this general problem. In 2016 approximately 21 percent of Mexico's entire population lived in the greater Mexico City area—an increase of almost 3 percent over the year 2000—and a publication by the US Department of State refers to Mexico City as "the largest concentration of people in the world."[61]

Mexico City faces a wide range of environmental challenges. Over 2 million of its residents have no running water, sometimes living more than three city blocks from the nearest faucet. Over 3 million of its inhabitants have no sewage facilities. The city produces over 14,000 tons of garbage every day but can process only 8,000 tons of that. Breathing the polluted air of Mexico City (caused by 3 million cars, 7,000 buses, and over 13,000 factories) has been likened to smoking two packs of cigarettes a day, and the combination of chemical and biological poisons has been estimated to kill over 30,000 children annually through respiratory and gastrointestinal disease. "Overall," one study has noted, "pollution may account for the deaths of nearly 100,000 people a year."[62]

It is this type of situation that has contributed to the desire of many Mexicans to leave their homeland and head north to a country where, they have heard, there are jobs for those who want them and a better life for those who are willing to work for it. About half of Mexico's population is under twenty-one years of age, and many of these people see a future in the United States as preferable to a future in Mexico. The border between Mexico and the United States is nearly 2,000 miles long, and issues such as smuggling, illegal immigration, and the border's ecology (including air and water pollution) have proven to be a source of irritation in relations between the two countries.[63] Indeed, Donald Trump's successful campaign for president in the United States in 2016 had as a cornerstone the promise to "build a wall" to keep "Mexican criminals and murderers" out of the United States.

The **North American Free Trade Agreement** (NAFTA), ratified in November of 1993, was designed to do something about this latter problem. The agreement, negotiated by the governments of Mexico, the United States, and Canada, was designed to lower tariffs among the three nations and to improve trade opportunities among the three North American neighbors. One result of this agreement would be increased job opportunities in Mexico, with higher salaries offered to Mexican workers, to help them decide to stay in Mexico rather than looking north for their futures.

In the United States, critics of the agreement argued that while it might benefit Mexico, it would result in a significant loss of US jobs, as well as having a generally negative effect upon the continental environment, because Mexican environmental standards were significantly lower than US standards. Businesses, they said, would move from the United States to Mexico to find cheaper labor and less stringent environmental regulations.

Supporters of the plan countered that Mexico had promised to strengthen its environmental regulations so that there would be no "belt" of environmental disasters along the border between Mexico and the United States. As well, they argued, while it might be the case that some US jobs might be lost to Mexicans, the corresponding increase in US jobs because of the expanded market open to Americans would more than make up for the loss of other US jobs.

On balance, NAFTA has helped Mexico a great deal. According to one source, since the inception of NAFTA the trade relationship between the United States and Mexico has tripled, leaving Mexico the second largest business partner of the United States.[64] And recent data have shown a significant decrease in the number of young Mexicans trying to illegally cross the border to find jobs in the United States; the growth of good jobs on the Mexican side of the border has been a very effective way of keeping young educated Mexicans in Mexico.

NAFTA was another of President Trump's targets in his quest for the White House, and during the campaign he promised to "tear up" the agreement if he were elected. He was elected, and he continued in his first two years in office to bluster about doing away with the agreement. In September 2018 a new United States–Mexico–Canada trade agreement was announced (USMCA), although it is not clear at the time of this writing how its effects on the nations involved will differ from NAFTA.[65]

These trade-related problems were to some degree a function of Mexican economic stagnation.[66] A 1993 World Bank report indicated that Mexico's external debt increased from $57.4 billion in 1980 to $101.7 billion by 1991. This 1991 debt was equal to 36.9 percent of Mexico's gross national product (GNP), a staggering debt burden. By 1993 the external debt had grown to $165.7 billion, 69.9 percent of Mexico's GNP.[67] These challenges are illustrative of the general problems of international dependence, described in Box 13.2, faced by many economically developing nations today.

The situation was so bad by December 1994 that the United States decided that it had to respond positively to Mexico's requests for extraordinary assistance to what was called the peso crisis. A package of loans was assembled by the United States—under a presidential order of Bill Clinton, over some significant opposition from those in Congress who were afraid that the Mexican government would never be able to repay the loans—totaling nearly $50 billion.[68] Using these resources the government of Mexico was able to significantly improve its economic situation (see Table 13.6) and paid the loans back to the United States in full, and ahead of schedule.[69]

Box 13.2   Mexican Debt
in Perspective

The inequality between and among nations in their wealth and economic viability has led to a growing system of international dependence, in which the "have-not" nations have come to rely more and more upon the aid programs of the "have" nations in order to survive. In many respects "the history of the Third World is to a large extent the history of its incorporation into a global economy dominated by the 'core' industrialised countries of Western Europe and the United States."[a] The programs of these core nations include grants, loans, and in-kind assistance (such as wheat or tractors).

The economic dependence of the developing nations upon the developed nations has grown into a major international problem in recent years as the international debts of some of the have-not nations have skyrocketed, and the likelihood that they will ever be able to repay their loans has decreased. It is easy to see that Ecuador, a country with an external debt of over 23 percent of its GDP,[b] is going to have serious problems repaying its debts. Jamaica has worse problems, with an external debt of 77.8 percent of its GDP.[c]

Notes: a. Paul Cammack, David Pool, and William Tordoff, *Third World Politics: A Comparative Introduction* (Baltimore: Johns Hopkins University Press, 1988), p. 250.

b. World Bank, *World Development Indicators,* "Data: Ecuador," http://data.worldbank.org/country/ecuador.

c. World Bank, *World Development Indicators,* "Data: Jamaica," http://data.worldbank.org/country/jamaica.

Table 13.6   Growth of the Mexican Economy

	Gross Domestic Product
1999	$866 billion
2010	$1.0 trillion
2017 (estimated)	$2.4 trillion

Source: CIA World Factbook, "Mexico: Economy," https://www.cia.gov/library/publications /resources/the-world-factbook/geos/mx.html.

Mexico today is a country of contrasts. It is clearly a nation in which the vast majority of the resources are controlled by a small minority of the population. The proportion of the Mexican population living below the national poverty level increased from 49 percent in 2008 to 51 percent in 2016, a trend moving decidedly in the wrong direction.[70]

The Mexican System in Perspective

We have seen—albeit briefly—that the Mexican case provides us with the opportunity to view a type of political system different from others we have met in this volume, in many respects a significantly different system. Mexico was born in revolution and social upheaval, and in recent years it has been endeavoring to establish the kinds of social and political institutions that can ensure domestic stability and social harmony.

To a substantial degree, especially if we compare Mexico with its neighbors to the south, the endeavors have been successful if for no other reason than that Mexico has not experienced the regular military coups experienced so often by so many Latin American nations.

However, we must be less laudatory in other respects. Mexico is still suffering many of the problems faced by other nations in the developing world. Economic problems, distributional problems, and technological problems have meant that the general quality of life in Mexico has not improved as much as Mexico's leaders might have liked.

Some have argued that it is the system itself that is the real problem in Mexico. The relative stability of Mexico until recent times was based upon real reforms, particularly reforms in landownership, that occurred as a result of the revolution, and that were considered during the period from 1934 to 1940 when Lázaro Cárdenas was president. The PRI, it has been argued, dominated the Mexican political arena for so long precisely because it embodied those reforms. As those reforms began to become inadequate in more recent years, problems of stability (and stagnation and corruption) resulted.[71]

Discussion Questions

1. How would you compare Mexico's political stability with the stability of other Latin American nations? What is it that has helped Mexico be as stable as it has through its modern history?
2. How is Mexico similar to other federal political systems we have met in this book? How is it different? What are the major institutions that affect and reflect federalism in Mexico?
3. How does Mexico's presidency illustrate both the strengths and the weaknesses of presidential systems of government as described earlier in the text? Is Mexico a "typical" presidential system? Does the Mexican president have any unusual presidential powers?
4. What is the relationship between the Chamber of Deputies and the Senate in Mexico? Which has more political power? What are the special roles of the Senate? What functions does it perform in the political system?
5. What happened to the Institutional Revolutionary Party? What does its future appear to be today? How would you characterize the party system in Mexico today?
6. What do you view as the key economic challenges facing Mexico today? What economic crises has it managed to survive and work through in recent years? How has it made the progress that it has made? What does its future seem to hold?

Notes

1. L. Vincent Padgett, *The Mexican Political System* (Boston: Houghton Mifflin, 1976), p. 10. A good historical treatment of the Mexican political heritage can be found in Elisa Servin and Leticia Reina, *Cycles of Conflict, Centuries of Change: Crisis, Reform, and Revolution in Mexico* (Durham, NC: Duke University Press, 2007).

2. There was very widespread coverage of these charges in the foreign press. On the 2006 election see "Mass Protest over Mexican Election," BBC, July 9, 2006, http://news.bbc.co.uk/2/hi/americas/5161862.stm; or James C. McKinley Jr., "Throngs Call Loser Mexico's 'Legitimate' President," *New York Times,* September 17, 2006, http://select.nytimes.com/search/restricted/article?res=F20717F938550C748DDDA00894DE404482.

3. See Tim Golden, "In Remote Mexican Village, Roots of Rebellion Are Bared," *New York Times,* January 17, 1994, p. A1. See also Todd Eisenstadt, *Politics, Identity, and Mexico's Indigenous Rights Movements* (New York: Cambridge University Press, 2011).

4. Jorge Castañeda, "Mexico at the Brink," *Foreign Affairs* 64 (1985–1986): 287. See also Sidney Weintraub, *Unequal Partners: The United States and Mexico* (Pittsburgh: University of Pittsburgh Press, 2010).

5. A good historical overview can be found in Kenneth Johnson, *Mexican Democracy: A Critical View* (New York: Praeger, 1984), especially chap. 2, "The Aztec Legacy and Independence," and chap. 3, "Emerging Nationhood and the Great Revolution." A very good general history is that of Burton Kirkwood, *The History of Mexico* (New York: Palgrave Macmillan, 2005).

6. Robert Scott, "Mexico: The Established Revolution," in Lucian Pye and Sidney Verba, eds., *Political Culture and Political Development* (Princeton: Princeton University Press, 1965), p. 332. A good discussion of the revolution can be found in Alicia Hernandez Chavez, *Mexico: A Brief History* (Berkeley: University of California Press, 2006). See also Douglas Richmond, Sam Haynes, and Nicholas Villanueva, *The Mexican Revolution: Conflict and Consolidation, 1910–1940* (College Station: University of Texas Press, 2013).

7. A good discussion of this use of the term *stability* can be found in Daniel Levy and Gabriel Szekely, *Mexico: Paradoxes of Stability and Change,* 2nd ed. (Boulder: Westview, 1987); and in Larissa Lomnitz, Rodrigo Salazar Elena, and Ilya Adler, *Symbolism and Ritual in a One-Party Regime: Unveiling Mexico's Political Culture* (Tucson: University of Arizona Press, 2010). For more on this subject, see Jonathan D. Rosen and Hanna Samir Kassab, *Fragile States in the Americas* (Lanham: Lexington, 2017).

8. Daniel C. Levy, "The Political Consequences of Changing Socialization Patterns," in Roderic Camp, *Mexico's Political Stability: The Next Five Years* (Boulder: Westview, 1986), p. 19. See also Steven Levitsky, *Challenges of Party-Building in Latin America* (New York: Cambridge University Press, 2016).

9. This theme is discussed in Joe Foweraker and Ann Craig, eds., *Popular Movements and Political Change in Mexico* (Boulder: Lynne Rienner, 1990). See also Laura Randall, ed., *Changing Structure of Mexico: Political, Social, and Economic Prospects* (Armonk, NY: Sharpe, 2006).

10. Much of the discussion in the several paragraphs that follow is derived from much more extensive discussion in Juan Felipe Leal, "The Mexican State, 1915–1973: A Historical Interpretation," in Nora Hamilton and Timothy Harding, eds., *Modern Mexico: State, Economy, and Social Conflict* (Beverly Hills: Sage, 1986), pp. 29–32.

11. Barbara Stallings and Rogerio Studart, *Finance for Development: Latin America in Comparative Perspective* (Washington, DC: Brookings Institution, 2006). See also José Maria Serna de la Garza, *The Constitution of Mexico: A Contextual Analysis* (Portland: Hart, 2013).

12. Leal, "Mexican State," p. 30. See also Jorge Castañeda, *Perpetuating Power: How Mexican Presidents Were Chosen* (New York: New Press, 2000); and Nora Jaffary and Edward Osowski, *Mexican History: A Primary Source Reader* (Boulder: Westview, 2010).

13. John J. Bailey, *Governing Mexico: The Statecraft of Crisis Management* (London: Palgrave Macmillan, 1988), p. 139. See also Howard J. Wiarda, *Authoritarianism and Corporatism in Latin America—Revisited* (Gainesville: University Press of Florida, 2004).

14. See Francisco Zapata, "Mexican Labor in a Context of Political, Social, and Economic Change, 1982–2002," in Randall, *Changing Structure of Mexico.*

15. See Edward Gibson, *Federalism and Democracy in Latin America* (Baltimore: Johns Hopkins University Press, 2004). See also Aida Caldera Sánchez, *Improving Fiscal Federal Relations for a Stronger Mexico* (Paris: OECD Publishing, 2013).

16. Padgett, *Mexican Political System,* p. 204. See also Andrew Selee and Jacqueline Peschard, *Mexico's Democratic Challenges: Politics, Government, and Society* (Washington, DC: Woodrow Wilson Center, 2010).

17. William Glade, "Distributional and Sectoral Problems in the New Economic Policy," in Camp, *Mexico's Political Stability,* p. 95. See also Alberto Diaz-Cayeros, José Antonio Gonzá, and Fernando Rojas, "Mexico's Decentralization at a Crossroads," in T. N. Srinivasan and Jessica Wallack, eds., *Federalism and Economic Reform: International Perspectives* (New York: Cambridge University Press, 2006).

18. Bailey, *Governing Mexico,* p. 126.

19. Johnson, *Mexican Democracy,* p. 116. See also David Samuels and Matthew Shugart, *Presidents, Parties, and Prime Ministers: How the Separation of Powers Affects Party Organization and Behavior* (New York: Cambridge University Press, 2010).

20. Recent works on the Mexican presidency include Scott Mainwaring and Matthew Shugart, *Presidentialism and Democracy in Latin America* (New York: Cambridge Uni-

versity Press, 1997). See also Manuel Alcáantara Sáez, Jean Blondel, and Jean-Louis Thiébault, *Presidents and Democracy in Latin America* (New York: Routledge, 2018).

21. Bailey, *Governing Mexico,* p. 32. Emphasis his.

22. Padgett, *Mexican Political System,* p. 199.

23. Again, in addition to sources cited earlier, an example of these articles covering the presidential and congressional elections includes Alan Riding, "When the Bubble Burst for the Mexican Rulers," *New York Times,* July 9, 1988, p. 5. A good general study is that by Edgar Butler and Jorge Bustamante, eds., *Succesion Presidencial: The 1988 Mexican Presidential Election* (Boulder: Westview, 1990).

24. See Jorge I. Domínguez and Alejandro Poiré, *Toward Mexico's Democratization: Parties, Campaigns, Elections, and Public Opinion* (New York: Routledge, 2013). See also "Country Profile: Mexico," http://www.fco.gov.uk/servlet/Front?pagename =OpenMarket/Xcelerate/ShowPage&c=Page&cid=1007029394365&a=KCountryProfile &aid=1019744986727.

25. Padgett, *Mexican Political System,* pp. 188–189. See also Gretchen Helmke and Steven Levitsky, *Informal Institutions and Democracy: Lessons from Latin America* (Baltimore: Johns Hopkins University Press, 2006).

26. Frank Brandenburg, *The Making of Modern Mexico* (Englewood Cliffs, NJ: Prentice Hall, 1964), pp. 145–150. See also Randall, *Changing Structure of Mexico.*

27. Julia Preston, "The Mexico Election: The Overview—Challenger in Mexico Wins, Governing Party Concedes," *New York Times,* July 2, 2000, p. A1. See also "Fox Sworn In as President," *Facts on File,* December 1, 2000.

28. See S. Lynne Walker, "Fox Defends Record, Admits Much Work Left," *San Diego Union-Tribune,* September 2, 2001, p. A1. See also Sherry Beck Paprocki, *Vicente Fox* (New York: Chelsea House, 2013).

29. The quote on the 2006 election is from "Mexico Court Rejects Fraud Claim," *BBC News,* August 29, 2006, http://news.bbc.co.uk/2/hi/americas/5293796.stm. See also Jaime Suchlicki, *Mexico: From Montezuma to the Rise of the PAN* (Washington, DC: Potomac, 2008); and Matthew Cleary, *The Sources of Democratic Responsiveness in Mexico* (Notre Dame, IN: University of Notre Dame Press, 2010).

30. See Peter Katel, *Mexico's Future: Can the Country's New President Stop the Drug Cartels?* (Washington, DC: Congressional Quarterly, 2012); and Vanda Felbab-Brown, *Peña Nieto's Piñata: The Promise and Pitfalls of Mexico's New Security Policy Against Organized Crime* (Washington, DC: Brookings Institution, 2013).

31. Azam Ahmed and Paulina Villegas, "López Obrador, an Atypical Leftist, Wins Mexico Presidency in Landslide," *New York Times,* July 1, 2018, https://www.nytimes .com/2018/07/01/world/americas/mexico-election-andres-manuel-lope0z-obrador.html ?action=click&module=RelatedCoverage&pgtype=Article&region=Footer.

32. Ibid.

33. Azam Ahmed and Kirk Semple, "Mexico Elections: 5 Takeaways from Lopez Obrador's Victory," *New York Times,* July 2, 2018, https://www.nytimes.com/2018/07 /02/world/americas/mexico-election-lopez-obrador.html.

34. Merilee Serrill Grindle, *Bureaucrats, Politicians, and Peasants in Mexico: A Case Study in Public Policy* (Berkeley: University of California Press, 1977), p. 7. See Luis Carlos Ugalde, *The Mexican Congress: Old Player, New Power* (Washington, DC: CSIS, 2000); and Eduardo Alemán and George Tsebelis, *Legislative Institutions and Lawmaking in Latin America* (Oxford: Oxford University Press, 2016).

35. Judith Adler Hellman, *Mexico in Crisis* (New York: Holmes and Meier, 1978), p. 127.

36. Instituto Nacional Electoral, "Elecciones Federales 2018—Senadurías National," https://p2018.ine.mx/#/senadurias/nacional/1/2/1/2.

37. See Inter-Parliamentary Union, "Parline Database: Mexico—Chamber of Deputies," http://archive.ipu.org/parline-e/reports/2211_B.htm.

38. Under the system enacted in 1963, deputies were chosen by a combination of winner-take-all and proportional representation. "Under this system, opposition parties were

granted five seats in the Chamber of Deputies if they received at least 2.5 percent of the national vote and up to fifteen additional (twenty in all) deputies, one for each additional 0.5 percent of the national vote. In 1973 the threshold for representation in the Chamber was lowered from 2.5 to 1.5 percent and the maximum number of seats available to an opposition party under this 'party deputy' system was increased to twenty-five. This greatly improved the opposition's opportunities to win seats in the Chamber but also decreased the PRI's need to allow the opposition to win some district elections as a means of indicating the competitiveness of the political and electoral systems." Joseph Klesner, "Changing Patterns of Electoral Participation and Official Party Support in Mexico," in Judith Gentleman, ed., *Mexican Politics in Transition* (Boulder: Westview, 1987), p. 99.

39. Roderic Camp, "Potential Strengths of the Political Opposition and What It Means to the PRI," in Camp, *Mexico's Political Stability*, p. 187. See also Caroline Beer, *Electoral Competition and Institutional Change in Mexico* (Notre Dame, IN: University of Notre Dame Press, 2003).

40. Bailey, *Governing Mexico*, p. 62; discussion of this can be found in some detail at pp. 83–88. See also Eduardo Torres Espinosa, *Bureaucracy and Politics in Mexico* (Brookfield, VT: Ashgate, 1999).

41. Grindle, *Bureaucrats, Politicians, and Peasants*, p. 3. See Robert Wilson and Marta Santos, *Governance in the Americas: Decentralization, Democracy, and Subnational Government in Brazil, Mexico, and the USA* (Notre Dame, IN: University of Notre Dame Press, 2008).

42. Bailey, *Governing Mexico*, p. 61.

43. Todd Eisenstadt, *Courting Democracy in Mexico: Party Strategies and Electoral Institutions* (New York: Cambridge University Press, 2004). See Camp, *Politics in Mexico.*

44. See Yemile Mizrahi, *From Martyrdom to Power: The Partido Acción Nacional in Mexico* (Notre Dame, IN: University of Notre Dame Press, 2003); and Selee and Peschard, *Mexico's Democratic Challenges.*

45. See Jorge I. Domínguez and Alejandro Poiré, *Toward Mexico's Democratization: Parties, Campaigns, Elections, and Public Opinion* (New York: Routledge, 2013). See also Philip McMichael, ed., *Contesting Development: Critical Struggles for Social Change* (New York: Routledge, 2010).

46. C. E. Grimes and Charles E. P. Simmons, "Bureaucracy and Political Control in Mexico: Towards an Assessment," *Public Administration Review* 29, no. 1 (January–February 1969): 72. When the party was first organized in 1929 its name was the National Revolutionary Party; in 1938 it became the Mexican Revolutionary Party. In 1946 the name was changed for the third, and last, time to the PRI. A good discussion of the development of the PRI can be found in Hellman, *Mexico in Crisis*, pp. 33–57, chap. 2, "A Ruling Party Is Formed." See also Joy Langston, *Democratization and Authoritarian Party Survival: Mexico's PRI* (New York: Oxford University Press, 2017).

47. See the article published by the British Broadcasting Corporation, "Mexican Political Crisis Deepens," September 17, 2006, http://news.bbc.co.uk/2/hi/americas/5353074.stm.

48. Students interested in Marxism and communism in Mexico should consult Barry Carr, *Marxism and Communism in Twentieth-Century Mexico* (Lincoln: University of Nebraska Press, 1992); or Susana Nuccetelli and Ofelia Schutte, *A Companion to Latin American Philosophy* (Malden, MA: Wiley-Blackwell, 2010). See also Dag Drange Mossige, *Mexico's Left: The Paradox of the PRD* (Boulder: FirstForum, 2013).

49. See Barry Carr, "The PSUM: The Unification Process on the Mexican Left, 1981–1985," in Judith Gentleman, ed., *Mexican Politics in Transition* (Boulder: Westview, 1987), pp. 281–304. See also Alberto Diaz Cayeros, Federico Estevez, and Beatriz Magaloni, *The Logic of Poverty Relief: Electoral Strategies and Social Policy in Mexico* (New York: Cambridge University Press, 2016).

50. Klesner, "Changing Patterns," p. 101. See also Gavin O'Toole, *The Reinvention of Mexico: National Ideology in a Neoliberal Era* (Liverpool: Liverpool University Press, 2010).

51. See Dale Store, "The PAN, the Private Sector, and the Future of the Mexican Opposition," in Gentleman, *Mexican Politics in Transition*, pp. 261–273.

52. Johnson, *Mexican Democracy*, p. 145. See also Camp, "Potential Strengths," p. 186.

53. A very good discussion of this liberalization can be found in Wayne Cornelius, "Subnational Politics and Democratization," in Wayne A. Cornelius, Todd A. Eisenstadt, and Jane Hindley, eds., *Subnational Politics and Democratization in Mexico* (Boulder, CO: Lynne Rienner, 1999), pp. 15–40.

54. See Domínguez and Poiré, *Toward Mexico's Democratization*; or Michael Ard, *An Eternal Struggle: How the National Action Party Transformed Mexican Politics* (New York: Praeger, 2003).

55. Instituto Nacional Electoral, "Repositorio Documental," http://repositorio documental.ine.mx/xmlui. The 2018 data come from Instituto Nacional Electoral, "Computos Distritales 2018, Elecciones Federales," https://computos2018.ine.mx/#/presidencia/nacional/1/1/1/1.

56. Klesner, "Changing Patterns," pp. 95, 98.

57. A good discussion of this problem can be found in Randall, *Changing Structure of Mexico*.

58. See James B. Pick, *Mexico Megacity* (Boulder: Westview, 2000). See also Susan Eva Eckstein, *The Poverty of Revolution: The State and the Urban Poor in Mexico* (Princeton: Princeton University Press, 2014).

59. See Index Mundi, "Mexico—Urban Population," https://www.indexmundi.com /facts/mexico/urban-population.

60. Robert Long, "Urban Migration: The Dilemma of Mexico City," in Robert E. Long, ed., *Mexico* (New York: Wilson, 1986), p. 98. See also Daniel Hernandez, *Down and Delirious in Mexico City: The Aztec Metropolis in the Twenty-First Century* (New York: Scribner, 2011).

61. US Department of State, "Consular Information Sheet: Mexico," http://www .travel.state.gov/mexico.html. On the 2016 data, see World Bank, *World Development Report*, "Population in the Largest City," http://data.worldbank.org/indicator/EN.URB .LCTY.UR.ZS.

62. Otto Friedrich, "A Proud Capital's Distress," in Long, *Mexico*, p. 100.

63. Tony Payan, *The Three U.S.-Mexico Border Wars: Drugs, Immigration, and Homeland Security* (Westport: Praeger, 2006). By one estimate in 1980 more than 3 million Mexicans were in the United States illegally. Johnson, *Mexican Democracy*, p. 20.

64. "Mexico: President-Elect Meets with U.S. Leaders," *Facts on File*, August 24, 2000. See Lionello F. Punzo and Martin Anyul, *Mexico Beyond NAFTA* (London: Routledge, 2001); or Michael J. Boskin, *NAFTA at 20: The North American Free Trade Agreement's Achievements and Challenges* (Stanford: Hoover Institution, 2014).

65. Kimberly Amadeo, "Trump's NAFTA Changes: The USMCA Would Create US Jobs and Raise Auto Prices," *The Balance*, October 2, 2018, https://www.thebalance.com /donald-trump-nafta-4111368. See also Anne Applebaum, "Trump's New NAFTA Is Pretty Much the Same as the Old One—But at What Cost?" *Washington Post*, October 1, 2018, https://www.washingtonpost.com/news/global-opinions/wp/2018/10/01/trumps -new-nafta-is-pretty-much-the-same-as-the-old-one-but-at-what-cost/?noredirect =on&utm_term=.d15b77f36594.

66. Casteñada, "Mexico at the Brink," p. 287. See Francesco Duina, *The Social Construction of Free Trade: The European Union, NAFTA, and MERCOSUR* (Princeton: Princeton University Press, 2006).

67. World Bank, *World Development Report 1993* (New York, 1993), p. 279.

68. See Andres Oppenheimer, *Bordering on Chaos: Guerrillas, Stockbrokers, Politicians, and Mexico's Road to Prosperity* (Boston: Little, Brown, 1996).

69. See "Mexico: Early Repayment Set for U.S. Loan," *Facts on File*, June 18, 1996.

70. David Barkin, "Mexico's Albatross: The U.S. Economy," in Hamilton and Harding, *Modern Mexico,* p. 107; World Bank, *World Development Report 2011,* http://data .worldbank.org/topic/poverty.

71. This problem is discussed in Jaime E. Rodriguez, ed., *The Revolutionary Process in Mexico* (Berkeley: University of California Press, 1990). See also Santiago Levy, *Good Intentions, Bad Outcomes: Social Policy, Informality, and Economic Growth in Mexico* (Washington, DC: Brookings Institution, 2008).

14

Russia

Learning Outcomes

After reading this chapter, you will be able to

- See the impact of Russian history on the current Russian political system.
- Understand the real role of Russia's Constitution today.
- Compare Russia's current political system with other federalisms, and explain how Russian federalism is the same as, or different from, other federal systems.
- Discuss the role of ideology in Russia today and in the political systems that came before Russia.
- Understand the institutions of Russian government.
- Explain the relationship between the current president of Russia and the current prime minister of Russia.
- Understand the role of political parties in Russia, and appreciate the evolution of political parties from the time of the Communist Party of the Soviet Union (CPSU) to the parties in Russia today.

The study of politics in Russia, as well as Russia's political heritage, requires a deviation from the normal pattern of the area studies chapters preceding this one. Our fundamental premise in this volume has been that if we study the basic constitutional structures of a political regime we can develop some understanding of how the regime operates.

This is not to suggest that the detailed study of political parties in Britain, for example, would not contribute a great deal to a deeper understanding of the operation of the British political system. It would. What we have suggested, however, is that it is possible to understand how the British political system generally operates without a detailed examination of the Labour and Conservative Parties. Similarly, it is possible to become acquainted (and remember, our area studies do not claim to be comprehensive, but are simply designed as introductions) with the other political systems we have examined without detailed knowledge of their respective political parties.

This is all said by way of introduction to this chapter on the Russian political system because the Russian case poses an exception to the general patterns described earlier, one that is paralleled by the case of China as discussed earlier in this volume. While we can understand the essential pattern of operation of these other political systems by confining our examination to what might be called constitutional political structures, such an examination of the Russian political system would likely give us an inadequate image of political operations there. The Russian political system, while it has an extensive history, is a very new system in many important respects; we must appreciate its newness, and the circumstances from which it emerged, if we are to understand its operation.

Accordingly, after an examination of the Russian political heritage, we will turn our attention to a tentative examination of the new constitution and the system of constitutional political structures in the new political system that is called Russia. We must recall that modern Russia does not have a long and stable democratic history upon which to draw at moments of stress, and it does not have numerous democratic precedents to use as examples during moments of political crisis. Thus, while we may describe a number of (relatively new) political institutions, only time will tell us the degree to which they will endure and be effective.

Russia's Constitutional History

For many years—from 1917 through the breakup of the Soviet Union in 1991—the name "Russia" was used interchangeably by many with the **Union of Soviet Socialist Republics**, despite the fact that such a usage was incorrect. Russia was a part of the USSR—one of fifteen "independent" republics—but not the same as the USSR. The USSR was geographically the largest country in the world, making up nearly one-sixth of the planet's land mass—"more than twice the size of the United States, almost as big as the United States, Canada, and Mexico put together . . . only slightly smaller than the whole continent of Africa."[1] (This kind of comparison was slightly misleading, however, because a careful study of the Soviet map would have shown that a significant portion of the USSR was "not conducive to protracted habitation for sizeable populations.")[2] The Russian Federation today is an area of 6.5 million square miles, just under twice the size of the United States, and upon the demise of the USSR in 1991 the Russian Federation became the largest of the successor states to the USSR and inherited its permanent seat in the United Nations.

Russia's Political Heritage

Russia has existed for more than eleven centuries, under a variety of names and a variety of rulers. Under the Soviet regime many suggested that there were historical factors that had proven to be significant in influencing Soviet development in a non-Western direction;[3] clearly the same thing can be said about Russia. Patterns of behavior such as the "persistent tradition of absolutism in government, the recurrent use of revolutionary violence to solve political problems, and the lack of experience with democratic institutions and constitutional procedures"[4] all contributed to a political tradition in the Soviet Union—and now Russia—that was distinctly different from that shared by most Western (democratic) nations (see Table 14.1).

One major pattern in the Russian past was its history of revolutions, which led to the Revolution of 1917.[5] Among the earliest acts that can be called revolutions in Russian history was a shakeup in government

Table 14.1   Composition of the Former USSR

Name of Union Republic	Date Created	Capital	Area (square miles)	Population (millions)[a]
Russian SSR	November 1917	Moscow	6,592,800	146.1
Ukrainian SSR	December 1917	Kiev	233,100	49.2
Belorussian SSR	January 1919	Minsk	80,200	10.4
Uzbek SSR	October 1924	Tashkent	172,700	24.8
Kazakh SSR	December 1936	Alma-Ata	1,049,200	16.7
Georgian SSR	February 1921	Tbilisi	26,911	5.0
Azerbaijan SSR	April 1920	Baku	33,400	7.7
Lithuanian SSR	July 1940	Bilnius	26,173	3.6
Moldavian SSR	August 1940	Kishinev	13,012	4.4
Latvian SSR	July 1940	Riga	24,695	2.4
Kirghiz SSR	December 1936	Frunze	76,642	4.7
Tadzhik SSR	October 1929	Dushambe	54,019	6.4
Armenian SSR	November 1920	Erevan	11,306	3.4
Turkmenian SSR	October 1924	Ashkabad	188,417	4.5
Estonian SSR	July 1940	Tallin	17,413	1.4

Source: Soviet Union Information Bureau, *The Soviet Union: Facts, Descriptions, Statistics,* http://www.marxists.org/history/U.S.S.R./government/1928/sufds/index.htm.

Note: a. This is the population of the republics in 2000, following the breakup of the Soviet Union in 1991.

led by **Ivan the Terrible** in 1564. Ivan was rebelling not against the government (he was tsar at the time) but against the nobles in his regime, claiming that they were evil and traitorous. He agreed to maintain the throne only under the condition that he be given control of a secret police network called the Oprichnina, which he used to destroy the power of the nobles by arresting them, exiling them, and taking over their estates. Ivan's actions served to neutralize any threat that the nobility had posed to the power of the tsar.

The Revolt of December 1825, known as the Decembrist Uprising, was an attempt by the tsar's guards to overthrow the tsar (Nicholas I, 1825–1855) and do away with the restrictive, autocratic government of Russia. Partially because of the uncertainty of the revolutionaries, who could not agree on the kind of regime that they wanted to replace the tsar, the revolt was suppressed, and an increase in governmental repression took place at the hand of the tsar.

The oppressiveness of the tsar, however, did not check the spread of revolutionary ideas. Although the tsar freed the serfs in 1861 as a gesture to placate public unrest, revolutionary fervor continued to spread. Political organization was begun by a revolutionary intelligentsia, primarily organized in the Narodnik movement. The Narodniki were originally intellectually based—drawn from student and intellectual groups. The movement had as its goal the promotion of a socialist society, maintaining that the traditional Russian village was socialist in orientation. The Narodniki argued that "once the aristocratic system and the feudal order were destroyed, Russia would spontaneously be recognized as a vast association of agrarian cooperative communities."[6]

The first Marxist organization in Russia, called the Emancipation of Labor, was founded in 1883 by a group led by George Plekhanov. Between 1883 and 1894 this kind of group was formed in most major Russian cities, including one formed in St. Petersburg in 1895 led by a young revolutionary named **Vladimir Lenin** (1870–1924). Both **Joseph Stalin** (1878–1953) (whose real name was Joseph Dzhugashvili) and **Leon Trotsky** (whose real name was Leon Bronstein) became active in politics during this period of time. In 1898 the first Russian Social Democratic party convention was held, in Minsk, its goal being to consolidate various factions of Marxists.

The second Russian Social Democratic party convention was held in 1903, meeting first in Brussels (because it was not permitted to operate in Russia), then moving to London. In London the party divided into two factions over the issue of organization. Some party members wanted a European-style social democratic party. Lenin argued against that form of party, saying that the tsar's secret police would not permit such an open party to operate freely. He argued in favor of a restricted, tightly organized party of dedicated revolutionaries. The party split into two factions over this question on a vote of thirty-three to eighteen.[7] Lenin was leader of the majority faction, called the Bolsheviks. The labels **Bolshevik** ("majority") and **Menshevik** ("minority") stuck to the two factions of the party, and the two factions of the Russian Social Democratic Party were thereafter known as the Bolsheviks and the Mensheviks.

At this time Lenin presented his proposals, which he had introduced in his earlier publication *What Is to Be Done?* (published in 1902). In that work he called for a new kind of nonelectoral party organization, designed not so much to compete for power in elections but "to seize power on behalf of the working class and to establish a 'dictatorship of the proletariat.'"[8]

At the turn of the twentieth century, Russia was again near the point of revolution. Strikes and industrial unrest spread throughout the country as a result of yet another economic crisis. On January 9, 1905, a day that came to be known as Bloody Sunday, soldiers fired on a procession of workers bringing a list of grievances to the tsar (Nicholas II), killing hundreds and causing a revolt. Worker councils, called soviets, were formed in many cities to direct strike activities. Leon Trotsky, a leader of the St. Petersburg soviet, issued a call for constitutional reforms, free elections, a parliament, and freedom for political parties to form.

The tsar managed to put down the revolt, but he acceded to many of the requests in an effort to promote the stability of his regime. In the **October Manifesto**, he promised a national parliament (called the Duma), a constitution, free elections, and protection of civil liberties. After 1905 Russia was a much more liberal and less oppressive society than it had been previously, although the tsar was still the most significant political actor because of his power of absolute veto over the Duma and his power to dismiss the Duma at will.[9]

The year 1917 saw new revolution in Russia. Russia's performance in World War I, coupled with continued poor economic growth and increased governmental repressiveness, led to more rebellions. The tsar was overthrown in March 1917, and the Duma became the provisional government, granting amnesty to most of the Bolshevik leaders who had been exiled (like Lenin) or sent to Siberia (like Stalin) by the tsar, and allowing them to return to the political scene. From the beginning of the revolution, the worker councils played central roles in the coordination of revolutionary activity. The soviet of Petrograd (the new name for St. Petersburg) in fact rivaled the provisional government (the Duma) as a source of leadership.

In April 1917, Lenin returned to Russia and issued his "April Theses," calling for the overthrow of the provisional government and the transformation of the "bourgeois democratic revolution" into a revolution sponsored by the "proletarian class."[10] The provisional government, headed by Alexander Kerensky, opposed Lenin's policies, but in the end it could not stand up to the Bolshevik organization. On the nights of November 6–7, 1917, all members of the provisional government were arrested by the Red Guard, on order of Lenin. Lenin announced that the former government was dissolved and that the Petrograd soviet, headed by its Central Executive Committee, was now in control. The new government was headed by a Council of Peoples' Commissars, led by Lenin as chairman, Stalin as commissar of nationalities, and Trotsky as commissar of foreign affairs.

From 1917 through 1991 the Soviet Union existed as a Marxist-Leninist political system, moving through a number of different leaders, through varying degrees of authoritarian government, and through varying degrees of aggressiveness about spreading the doctrine of Marxism-Leninism to other political systems.[11] With the coming to power of **Mikhail Gorbachev** (1931–) in 1985, a new era began. This included a gradual relaxation of the degree to which the Communist Party of the Soviet Union ran the government and, equally important, a corresponding increase in human rights tolerated by the central government as well as a corresponding diminution in the amount of control Moscow insisted on having over the fifteen "independent republics" of the Soviet Union.[12]

In November 1989 the wall dividing Germany's East and West Berlin was opened, and shortly thereafter it physically came down.[13] In 1990, East and West Germany were reunified. This reunification, combined with other effects of the centrifugal forces of nationalism, had a critical impact upon the Soviet Union and its satellite governments in Eastern Europe. In 1991, under Gorbachev, discussions were undertaken about a restructuring of the Soviet Union into a new confederation, giving more power—returning sovereignty—to the individual republics. This led, as we shall further discuss below, to the creation of the **Commonwealth of Independent States** (CIS) and the death of the Union of Soviet Socialist Republics. It was, indeed, a "new world order."[14] This rapid change in the structure and evolution of the Soviet Union is outlined in Box 14.1.

The Devolution of the Soviet Union

The USSR was composed of fifteen union republics and consisted of "more than a hundred large and small ethnic groups with their own dis-

Box 14.1 Important Landmarks in Russian History

1237–1240	Mongol (Tatar) conquest of Russia begins 200 years of Mongol rule
1480	Ivan III frees Muscovy from Mongol rule
1712	Peter the Great moves capital of Russia to St. Petersburg (now Leningrad) for a "window to the West"
1861	Emancipation of the serfs by Alexander II
1905	Revolution forces Nicholas II to grant token reform, including establishment of a parliament (the Duma)
1917	March Revolution overthrows monarchy and establishes socialist government
1917	November Revolution brings Lenin's Bolsheviks to power
1917–1921	Development of a kind of communism called "War Communism"
1921–1928	"New Economic Policy"
1924–1938	Death of Lenin in 1924 leads to a struggle for power; Stalin emerges on top and then ruthlessly consolidates his control
1953	Death of Stalin
1957	Consolidation of power by Nikita Khrushchev
1964	Khrushchev ousted; replaced by Leonid Brezhnev and Alexei Kosygin
1982	Brezhnev dies; succeeded by Yuri Andropov
1984	Andropov dies; succeeded by Konstantin Chernenko
1985	Chernenko dies; succeeded by Mikhail Gorbachev Gorbachev elected to new presidency of Soviet Union
1991	Boris Yeltsin elected president of Russia (June); Attempted coup/overthrow of Gorbachev (August 19); Gorbachev resigns from Communist Party (August 24); Commonwealth of Independent States treaty signed (December 21); Breakup of USSR; Gorbachev resigns as USSR president (December 25)
1993	Current Russian Constitution promulgated
1996	Yeltsin reelected president
2000	Vladimir Putin elected president
2004	Putin reelected president
2008	Dmitry Medvedev elected president, and appoints Putin as premier
2012	Putin reelected president
2018	Putin reelected president

Source: Adapted from David Roth and Frank Wilson, *The Comparative Study of Politics* (Englewood Cliffs, NJ: Prentice Hall, 1980), p. 24; recent data from *New York Times,* December 11, 2017.

tinct cultural heritages. Many, but not all, ethnic groups [had] their own territories within the U.S.S.R. These territories were designated, in descending order of importance, as 'Union Republics' [15], 'autonomous republics' [11], 'autonomous regions' [8], and 'autonomous areas' [10]."[15]

In the late 1980s the heterogeneous nature of the Soviet Union became the cause of tension—and open violence—in Soviet politics. The nationality question[16] was the cause of many deaths in 1989 as various ethnic groups protested that their ethnic groups were not receiving adequate attention from Moscow.[17] The goals of these ethnic groups were often territorial but occasionally involved unhappiness with religious, political, or economic policies. According to the US State Department, about thirty-five borders within the Soviet Union were being disputed between different national groups in the Soviet Union in early 1989, including conflicts in Armenia, Azerbaijan, Kazakhstan, Uzbekistan, Lithuania, and Georgia, to name just a few.[18]

The largest single geographic component of the USSR was the Russian Soviet Federative Socialist Republic (RSFSR), making up over three-fourths of the USSR. The fourteen other union republics apart from Russia were each called Soviet Socialist Republics (SSRs) and were Armenian SSR, Azerbaijanian SSR, Belorussian SSR, Estonian SSR, Georgian SSR, Latvian SSR, Lithuanian SSR, Kazakh SSR, Kirghiz SSR, Moldavian SSR, Tadzhik SSR, Turkmenian SSR, Ukrainian SSR, and Uzbek SSR.

The 1936 Soviet Constitution, and later the 1977 Soviet Constitution, both suggested that the USSR was a "federal" political system. The federal relationship, as it has been described earlier in this book, proved to be more imaginary than real, however. In reality, the Soviet Union was a very centralized unitary system with a number of component units that had no real powers of their own, and thus the larger entity could not be called "federal" in any meaningful sense of the term.

Soviet federalism was developed by Lenin and Stalin as a vehicle for keeping many of the "independent republics" that had been included in the Russian Empire under control. In the Revolution of 1917 the Bolsheviks had promised self-determination to the various national minorities, and military conquest did not appear to them to be a preferential strategy, if they had any choice. By making the new state a "federation" it was possible to at least maintain the impression that the member units retained some autonomy, albeit token autonomy.

The Constitution of 1924 contained a number of clauses reflecting the "federal" nature of the regime. In addition to the usual powers granted federal governments (found in federal regimes of the day including Canada, West Germany, the United States, and Australia, for example) such as the power to coin money, to have an army, and the like, the Soviet Constitution gave the federal government a great number of economic planning powers, central to Marxist ideology. The Constitution had no bill of rights and no electoral laws, leaving these areas of concern, as well as the areas of civil and criminal law, to the member republics.[19] In practice, however, things didn't work out this way.

It is interesting to note that the 1977 Constitution, in an early draft, suggested doing away with the Soviet federation and creating a unitary state. The plan was turned down and deleted from the final draft of the Constitution. The 1977 Constitution referred to the USSR as a "unitary, federal, and multinational state, formed on the basis of the principle of socialist federalism and as a result of the free self-determination of nations and the voluntary union of equal Soviet Socialist Republics."[20]

The Soviet federal structure was partially reflected in the constitutional structure of the government in one of the two houses of the Soviet legislature, which was called the **Supreme Soviet.** Under the 1988 amendment to the Constitution, 750 members of the Supreme Soviet were to be elected on the basis of governmental units, with each of the country's republics having the same representation in the legislature; thus Estonia's 1.5 million citizens had the same number of representatives as the Ukraine's 50 million citizens.[21]

As noted earlier, by 1991 the gradually increasing spirit of nationalism that had begun to reassert its presence in a variety of the "independent" republics was too strong to ignore any longer. The Union of Soviet Socialist Republics was dissolved,[22] and a new structure of association, the Commonwealth of Independent States, emerged to replace the USSR as a vehicle for the association of a number of truly independent republics, all of which had been union republics within the USSR.[23]

Not all of the former union republics of the USSR chose to join the CIS; Estonia, Latvia, and Lithuania, the Baltic republics of the USSR, were not interested in prolonging a formal association with the other states. They left. The other states had been willing in 1991 to stay within the USSR and to create a looser confederation, still calling the association the Union of Soviet Socialist Republics. Following an attempted overthrow of the government in Moscow in 1991 by ultraconservative forces opposed to these changes,[24] however, and the resignation of President Gorbachev from the Communist Party,[25] the other republics decided that more independence from Moscow, rather than less, was the better course to follow in the future. The CIS did not prove to be a terribly effective political structure to succeed the USSR, however, and coordination of policy among the former Soviet republics was not consistent. This is not inconsistent with our discussion earlier in this volume about the relative advantages and disadvantages of federations and confederations; the CIS was much more similar to a confederation than to a federation, with all of the advantages and disadvantages this suggests. Today there remain nine members of the CIS: Armenia, Azerbaijan, Belarus, Kazakhstan, Kyrgyzstan, Moldova, Russia, Tajikistan, and Uzbekistan.[26]

The Constitutional System

For the person studying US politics, the US Constitution is a highly significant document. On the other hand, studies of Soviet politics traditionally did not spend a great deal of time or attention explaining the Soviet Constitution because it was not a meaningful or significant document in the Soviet political regime.

The Russian constitutional system following its most recent constitutional modification in 1993 is one that appears to be developing a number of democratic political structures.[27] This development, however, is often slow, and frequently painful. As we will see later in this chapter, a pluralistic system of political parties has tried to develop in modern Russia today, only to be frustrated by the government of **Vladimir Putin**, and debate over what should be the new constitutional institutions of the regime is very intense and visible in the public arena, even to the point of leading to public violence.

Indeed, part of the violence in Russia in mid-1993, including what the leaders of Parliament referred to as a coup by President **Boris Yeltsin** (1931–2007), and what Yeltsin referred to as "unconstitutional behavior" by the leaders of Parliament, was caused precisely because both sides of the debate were firmly committed to what they called "constitutional government"; they simply couldn't agree on what kind of constitution Russia ought to have.[28] Thus we should note that it is very clear that many in the new generation of Russian leaders consider their constitutional institutions to be very important, even if they cannot agree on precisely what those institutions should be.

One problem that has made the development of constitutional consensus more difficult in Russia is that there has been no tradition of stable constitutional government in Russia or the Soviet Union.[29] Yet it is clear that the existence of a constitution must have been important to the Bolsheviks, and to their political successors: the Soviet Union had a number of constitutions, and political leaders would not have invested the effort to create the constitutions if they did not feel that the exercise would be worth their while. Indeed, as recently as the fall of 1988 the Soviet government devoted significant time and effort to the process of constitutional reform.

Since the Revolution of 1917 there have been six constitutional eras in the USSR and Russia. First, on July 10, 1918, a new constitution was put into force in Russia. This was followed by the second era, with the arrival of the first constitution of the USSR in January 1924. In 1935 a third era came about when a constitutional commission was appointed and instructed to draft a new constitution for the USSR, to replace its original 1924 constitution. The new constitution was approved late in 1936.[30]

After Stalin's death, movements were launched to create a new constitution, but progress was slow. In 1962 Khrushchev began efforts to draft a new constitution, but his ouster in 1964 stalled the project. Although Brezhnev became chairman of the constitutional commission upon his accession to power, the project was not one of high priority for Brezhnev at the time. A fourth constitutional era came when, "without the usual advance clues, there came the abrupt announcement in May, 1977 that the new Draft Constitution would soon be published for nationwide discussion."[31]

Under Mikhail Gorbachev a new constitutional balance of power, a fifth era, was brought about in 1988 and 1989 with a new Supreme Soviet and Soviet presidency, which will be described later. With the resignation of President Gorbachev[32] and the dissolution of the Soviet Union in 1991, a new constitutional era began for Russia, although it was still evolving in September 1993 when some argued that a civil war was narrowly averted involving a conflict between Boris Yeltsin[33] and the more conservative Russian Parliament.

By September 1993 Yeltsin and the Russian Parliament had been in conflict for a good while, with the Parliament controlled by Communist conservative elements—those not supporting Yeltsin's efforts to reform the system both in terms of economic policy and in terms of efforts to speed up democratization. After some supporters of the Parliament tried to mount an armed uprising, Yeltsin called out the army to recapture the Parliament building from the rebels. Yeltsin remained in control, with his power stabilized for the time being.[34]

In November 1993 President Yeltsin announced that a new constitution for Russia would be placed before the Russian voters on December 12, 1993, to replace the constitution originally adopted in April 1978 but amended on numerous occasions since that time. At the same time, Yeltsin indicated that Russian voters would be asked to vote for members of the new Parliament. The new constitution would give the president the right, under limited conditions, to issue decrees having the force of law, to dissolve Parliament, to declare a state of emergency, and to temporarily curb civil rights; it would also give Russians a number of unprecedented guarantees of personal freedoms and entrench a number of reforms of Communist-era economic policies.

In the December 1993 election the new constitution was approved by a significant majority of voters in a nationwide plebiscite, but Yeltsin's party did not win a majority in the new Parliament.[35] While many debated whether this was a result of the unpopularity of his economic policies, his ineffective campaigning before the election, or a personal rejection of Yeltsin himself, the outcome was a state of uncertainty. Although Yeltsin vowed to press on with his economic and political reforms, it appeared that his policies would have as much difficulty in the new Parliament as they had experienced in the old Parliament.

In the 1993 "Yeltsin" Constitution the president has a great deal of power.[36] The president nominates the prime minister, who must be confirmed by the Duma. However, if the Duma rejects the president's nominee three times, he then has the power to dissolve the Duma and call for new elections. Although some claimed that the 1993 Constitution would not last long following its promulgation, at the time of this writing (2018) it has endured, and although we will see later in this chapter that the presidency has become extremely powerful, the constitutional system itself has endured.

The question can be asked, Why did Soviet leaders continue for so many years the "constitutional ruse" as it could be called, having constitutions that were primarily of symbolic significance? The answer appears to be that the Soviets had an ambivalent attitude toward constitutions. On one hand, in terms of Marxist ideology, they saw both the state and its structures such as a constitution as evils. On the other hand, they were willing to recognize constitutions as necessary evils, necessary for providing external and internal legitimacy, and for helping to run the regime in the transitional period during which time the state "evolves" from capitalism to socialism to communism.

Even though Lenin and his fellow revolutionary leaders were in the middle of a significant domestic battle with other Soviet political leaders, they still believed that it was important to have a constitutional framework for their new government.[37] The role of a constitution in the USSR was to give "legal expression to the basic ideological norms of Soviet doctrine."[38]

Federalism

As noted earlier, there is a long and well-entrenched history of federal structures in Russia. Long before the Soviet Union was created in the early years of the twentieth century as a federal structure, Russia could be characterized as having characteristics of a more or less federal regime.

Even when it was ruled by the tsar as the Russian Empire, there were characteristics of federal government that could be seen in Russia, although whether it was actually federal government—in the sense of shared sovereignty—is really a different matter; the history of the nation is a history of centralized power, whether it was called unitary government or whether it was called federal government. The appearance of federal-like structures was, as suggested earlier in this book is often the case in extremely large nations, because of the sheer size and heterogeneity of Russia. It was not possible to govern all of Russia from a completely centralized perspective, simply as a function of geography and distance.

When the Union of Soviet Socialist Republics was created, it had to operate under a model of being federal because the "independent" republics that were drawn into the USSR would not have voluntarily joined otherwise. While some might argue that the member republics did not come voluntarily in any event, it was far more politically palatable to the actors involved to use the language of federalism to describe the nature of government in the USSR. Many of the member republics were themselves "federative socialist republics," including states within their borders, reflecting the fact that each republic, in turn, was made up of member units with which power was shared.

Once the Soviet Union dissolved, and the member republics decided to walk away from the Union, Russia maintained its federal governmental nature. Today the Russian Federation is made up of eighty-three "federal subjects," each represented in the Federal Council of the legislature. There are forty-six oblasts (provinces); twenty-one component republics, nominally autonomous with each their own constitution, president, and legislature; nine krais (territories); four autonomous okrugs (districts); one Jewish autonomous oblast; and two federal cities (Moscow and St. Petersburg) that function as separate governmental regions. The eighty-three federal subjects are grouped into eight federal districts, each administered individually by a representative of the Russian president.[39]

Ideology

The political regime that was referred to as the USSR had an ideological foundation officially referred to as **Marxism-Leninism**.[40] Ultimately, Marxism-Leninism was based upon the *Communist Manifesto* (written in 1848) and subsequent writings of Karl Marx and Friedrich Engels. More directly, however, political ideology in the Soviet Union could be explained as Marxism interpreted and applied by Soviet leaders of the day, including Lenin, Stalin, Khrushchev, and Brezhnev. Each of these leaders in turn interpreted and revised Marx's ideas so that the particular version of Marxism would support the regime of the day and provide a rationalization for the policies of the government in power.[41]

The perspectives of Marx were, in fact, different from those of Lenin, Stalin, Khrushchev, Brezhnev, or even Gorbachev. Marx was a theorist, dealing with philosophies and ideas. Lenin and his followers were pragmatists, political actors, interested in the philosophy suggested by Marx, but faced with the challenge of putting the theories into concrete form, of operationalizing the ideology.

As the economic, social, and political characteristics of the Soviet Union changed, Marx's ideas had to be revised to fit the times. Lenin, for example, revised Marxian theory to justify its relevance to the conditions of the Soviet Union during the period between 1917 and 1924.[42] Lenin died in January 1924. Following his death there was a major power struggle to decide who would be the next leader. The two major contestants were Joseph Stalin and Leon Trotsky. Stalin's position emerged as the stronger of the two; as secretary-general of the Communist Party of the Soviet Union he had been able to build a strong base of power.

In 1936 Stalin had a new constitution written that he proclaimed to be the most democratic in the world. He created a new Parliament, and a bill of rights (although it did not effectively protect individual rights from governmental abuses), and at the same time centralized power to guarantee that no one would be able to challenge his control. After securing his hold on power, Stalin claimed that the Marxist revolution was completed within the USSR.[43] Stalin, accordingly, turned his attention away from the revolution within the state to revolution in other states, looking at the concept of revolution in the world. Stalin felt that the Soviet system could assist Marxist revolutions in other parts of the world, after it had developed into a militarily powerful regime.

In terms of major modifications of Marxism (or of "Marxism-Leninism-Stalinism" as he preferred to call it), Stalin's contributions were neither as many nor as significant as those of Lenin. However, he did make some contributions to the Soviet polity, including the creation of the structure of the five-year plan to direct the development of the Soviet state and the introduction of the concept of "enemy of the people" into Soviet ideology.[44]

Nikita Khrushchev emerged as Soviet leader in 1957. In a manner similar to Lenin and Stalin, Khrushchev was said by students of Marxism to have contributed several major theoretical modifications to the Marxism-Leninism-Stalinism of his day.[45]

Less than ten years later, while Chairman and First Secretary Khrushchev was vacationing, he was "deposed" by a team headed by Leonid Brezhnev and **Alexei Kosygin** in October 1964. The post-

Khrushchev leadership, primarily **Leonid Brezhnev**, undertook somewhat of a retrenchment following the ouster of Khrushchev. The liberalization by Khrushchev of restrictions in the areas of arts, literature, and education was again tightened; the Soviet Union's apparent relaxation of its control over its satellites also was reversed, with the 1968 crushing of the Czechoslovakian uprising.[46]

Following the death of Leonid Brezhnev in November 1982, the future direction of Soviet ideology was uncertain. **Yuri Andropov**, former head of the KGB (the State Security Committee) and Politburo member was selected to take over as secretary-general of the Communist party, but his period of leadership was brief and did not contribute anything in the way of ideological significance, primarily due to his age and illness.[47] When Andropov died two years later in 1984 he was replaced by **Konstantin Chernenko**, another senior party leader, who also died in office after a very brief period of leadership. The accession to office of Mikhail Gorbachev in 1985 suggested the promise of significant change in what, exactly, a "Marxist" ideology meant,[48] but in 1985 no observer of the Soviet system would have imagined the degree of change that would come within the next decade, through the Gorbachev years and into the period of leadership of Boris Yeltsin.[49]

Structures of the Government

The Former Congress of People's Deputies
The idea for change of the **Congress of People's Deputies** was first suggested by Mikhail Gorbachev in the late fall of 1988 as part of a package of reforms for the Soviet Union's government. One observer noted that Gorbachev had become "increasingly frustrated and angry at the resistance being mounted to his reforms by Party and state bureaucrats. He holds these officials to blame for the economic stagnation and moral decline from which his country suffers, and accuses them of stifling the initiative of the population."[50] This legislative body, the first elections for which were held in March 1989, was intended to be a more active legislature than had been the case with the Supreme Soviet in the past; its members would be elected from competitive elections, and it would elect from among its 2,250 members 542 members of a new, much more active and more powerful, Supreme Soviet.

The exact role of the new Congress of People's Deputies was still being negotiated at its first meeting in June 1989. Among the agreements reached at that time were that the Congress would convene twice a year instead of once, as originally proposed by Gorbachev; deputies of the 2,250-member Congress who were not elected to the 542-member

Supreme Soviet or its commissions or committees could participate in
the sessions and have access to the information and documents made
available to the Supreme Soviet; and the Congress would retain the
"right to cancel or change any document, any legislative act, and any
decision taken by the Supreme Soviet."[51]

The Former Supreme Soviet

Prior to the constitutional amendment proposed by Mikhail Gorbachev
in late 1988, the Supreme Soviet was a very weak, essentially rubber
stamp legislative body that approved whatever legislation was placed
before it by Communist Party officials, despite the fact that it was
described in Chapter 15 of the Constitution as "the supreme body of
state power in the U.S.S.R. . . . empowered to resolve all questions
placed within the jurisdiction of the U.S.S.R. by this constitution."[52]

The Supreme Soviet was a bicameral body, composed of the Soviet of
the Union and the Soviet of Nationalities, members of which were all
elected at the same time for four-year terms. Members of the Soviet of the
Union were elected on the basis of population in the component republics.
Members of the Soviet of Nationalities represented the "federal" nature of
the political system, with each union republic having thirty-two seats, each
autonomous republic having eleven seats, each autonomous region having five seats, and each national area having one seat. The two houses of
the Supreme Soviet had over 1,500 representatives.

As noted earlier, in 1988 Mikhail Gorbachev proposed a fundamental change in the institution, asking the Supreme Soviet to "abolish
itself,"[53] and to create a new institution in its place, the new Congress of
People's Deputies. As part of his package of proposals, Gorbachev proposed that the new Congress of People's Deputies would elect from
among its own members a new Supreme Soviet, one that would "act as
a full-time legislature for the nearly eight months it will be in session,"[54] meeting for two sessions each year, one in the spring and one in
the fall, each lasting three or four months. On paper, at least, the new
Supreme Soviet was to be much more active, and important, than its
predecessor had been.[55]

At the same time that new institutions were being created at the
level of the USSR government, new institutions were proposed and created for Russian government, too. Institutions of the Russian Republic
were essentially parallel to those of the Soviet government, with a
Russian Federation Supreme Soviet made up of a Council of the
Republic and a Council of Nationalities. The executive branch was to
be led by a president, assisted by a Government (a chairman and a

number of ministers) drawn from the Supreme Soviet. In essence the Russian government was very much a French-model government led by a strong president.[56]

The New Federal Assembly

In the fall of 1993 when Boris Yeltsin won his "battle for supremacy between the executive and legislative branches," and called for new legislative elections, he also ordered replacement of all of the regional and territorial legislatures, demanding that they "submit to new elections and face a drastic reduction in their size." The new councils were called State Dumas—a term used in tsarist Russia—and were to be made up of fifteen to fifty full-time legislators. They replaced the existing councils, which had been called soviets.[57] The Russian Federation today has eighty-nine units, including two federal cities, Moscow and St. Petersburg.

Yeltsin's new legislative structure[58] included an upper house called the **Federation Council** and a lower house called the **State Duma**. The State Duma had 450 members, elected for a four-year term. Of these, 225 members were elected by simple majority from single-member-district constituencies. The other 225 members were elected by a party-list proportional representation system, in which the entire nation would be treated as a single constituency, with only federal lists receiving at least 5 percent of the popular vote eligible to receive seats. Voters cast two separate ballots for the two groups of legislators.

The electoral system was changed for the State Duma elections that took place on December 2, 2007. Under the new system, adopted in 2005 and designed by President Vladimir Putin, elections were completely based upon proportional representation, replacing the mixed electoral system initiated by Boris Yeltsin. In this proportional representation system a party would have to obtain at least 7 percent of the votes (up from 5 percent) to win representation in the State Duma, although this requirement was changed in 2011 to a 5 percent threshold. At the time of the 2007 election, thirty-five political parties applied to contest the elections, but the Central Electoral Commission (CEC) permitted only eleven parties to participate. Critics of the new electoral system with a 7 percent threshold argued that the measures prevented small parties from entering the Parliament,[59] but President Putin insisted that the tougher standard was necessary to stop extremist parties from running for elections.

In the next elections, on December 4, 2011, Putin's United Russia Party again—to the surprise of no one—received the largest bloc of votes, receiving just under 50 percent of the popular votes but still winning a majority of seats in the Duma. The election was called in August by President **Dmitry Medvedev**, and seven parties submitted candidate lists. Overall, 60 percent of the registered voters submitted ballots. The Communist Party of the Russian Federation received over 19 percent of the votes, and the Liberal Democratic Party of Russia received just under 12 percent of the votes.[60] This Parliament was the first elected to serve a five-year term rather than a four-year term; the 7 percent threshold rule still applied in this election, with the 5 percent threshold to come into effect starting in the 2016 parliamentary elections.

The most recent parliamentary elections were held in September 2016. In these elections the United Russia Party, again led by Prime Minister Medvedev, won a clear victory and increased its seats in the Duma from 53 percent to 76 percent of the total. Again the Communist Party and the Liberal Democratic Party were represented in the Duma, as was the Just Russia Party, and the main opposition parties Yabloko and the People's Freedom Party failed to reach to threshold for representation. Election results are indicated in Table 14.2.

The Council of the Federation has 178 appointed members, with 89 multimember (two-member) constituencies that correspond to the various units of the Russian federal government. Two members are appointed by the executive and legislature of each of the units of the government, the regions and the local governments.[61]

The New Presidency

Until the 1989 changes in the power of the Supreme Soviet, one of its most important structures was the Presidium (its full title was the Presidium of the Supreme Soviet of the USSR), which had thirty-nine

Table 14.2   The Duma Election of 2016

Political Group	Number of Seats	Percentage of Seats
United Russia	343	76.2
Communist Party	42	9.3
Liberal Democratic Party of Russia	39	8.7
A Just Russia	23	5.1
Other	3	0.7
Total	450	100.0
Number of women: 57/450 (12.7%)		

Source: Inter-Parliamentary Union, "Parline Database: Russian Federation—State Duma," http://archive.ipu.org/parline-e/reports/2263.

members, including a chairman, a first vice chairman, fifteen vice chairmen (one from each union republic supreme soviet), a secretary, and twenty-one members. Members of the Presidium were elected by the USSR Supreme Soviet "at a joint meeting of its chambers," from among its members in both houses. The Presidium was referred to as "the continuously functioning agency of the U.S.S.R. Supreme Soviet, accountable to the latter for all its activity, and exercising . . . the functions of supreme body of state power of the U.S.S.R. in intervals between sessions of the Supreme Soviet."[62]

Thus, although the legislative function may have rested de jure with the 1,517-member Supreme Soviet, it was possible to say that this function was usually exercised by the Presidium's chairman and a few assistants in the name of the Presidium, carrying out "most of the legislative functions of the government."[63] The chairman of the Presidium was most visible of the thirty-nine members, however, and he usually acted in the name of the complete body. Until 1989 the chairman of the Presidium was often referred to by Western media as the president of the USSR.

In October 1988 **Andrei Gromyko** was forced to retire from the position of chairman of the Presidium, and he was replaced by Mikhail Gorbachev. As part of Gorbachev's package of reforms for the Supreme Soviet, he suggested the creation of a new position of an executive president, called the chairman of the USSR Supreme Soviet, who would be elected by the Congress of People's Deputies. Gorbachev "made no secret of his intention to become the first holder of the new, extremely powerful post of executive president." On May 23, 1989, Gorbachev was nominated in the newly created Council of People's Deputies for the new position, and on May 26 he was elected president by 96 percent of the deputies voting.[64]

The Russian presidency occupied by Boris Yeltsin, as earlier noted, was created at the same time as Gorbachev's Soviet presidency. Yeltsin was elected president of Russia on June 12, 1991.[65] Much of his effort in his first two years in office was spent fighting with the Russian Parliament, many members of which were a remnant from the days of Communist control of the institutions of the Soviet Union. Following his battle with the Parliament in the fall of 1993, Yeltsin was confident that the elections in December 1993 would produce a new constitution with increased power for the president, and a Parliament more sympathetic to his economic and political goals. The constitution was approved; the sympathetic Parliament did not come into being.

Yeltsin was reelected in a two-part election on June 16, 1996. In the first stage of the election he barely won a plurality of the votes. In the runoff election between the two top vote-getters he received a majority of the votes and won a second term in office. His term was troubled by serious domestic and economic problems. The bureaucracy was huge and had to be significantly cut back. There was a serious challenge to the government by "mob"-like racketeers, and many reports indicated that the government was unable to enforce the law over the racketeers. The Russian economy virtually collapsed, with the ruble being halved in value and imports falling by nearly 45 percent.[66] In August 1998 the government floated the ruble, significantly devaluing it, imposed strong currency controls, and tried to regain control of the economy. This caused an enormous backlash as Russians criticized the government and indicated that they had been better off under an oppressive Communist state, but Yeltsin stayed the course.

Yeltsin had numerous challenges as the end of the decade arrived. In 1999, the former Russian satellites of Poland, Hungary, and the Czech Republic all joined the North Atlantic Treaty Organization, something that Russia took to be a challenge, since accepting these nations as equal international partners emphasized the change in Russia's status in the preceding decade. This was exacerbated when it was made clear that Lithuania, Latvia, and Estonia, all of which had also at one time been part of the Soviet Union, wanted to join the organization in the future. As well, just three years after the Chechen-Russian war (1994–1996) ended in a virtual stalemate, the fighting started again in 1999, with Russia launching air strikes and following up with significant deployments of ground troops. By the end of November 1999, Russian troops had surrounded Chechnya's capital, Grozny, and about 215,000 Chechen refugees had fled to neighboring territories.

These challenges in Russia's strategic environment, combined with Yeltsin's significant health problems in his second term in office, led him to announce that he intended to step down at the end of his term. This was seen by many outside of Russia as a real test of the democratic system established by Yeltsin, based upon the foundation laid by Gorbachev: Would the system be able to handle a transition to someone who was not intimately involved with the creation of the current Russian democratic institutions?

The answer was, apparently, yes. In the presidential election of April 7, 2000, over 68 percent of registered voters participated in the contest, and Vladimir Putin won the election with a significant margin of victory, approximately of the same magnitude on the first ballot that Yeltsin had won on the second round of the election of 1996. Putin had a number of serious economic and political challenges to face immediately after assuming office, and while he clearly was not able to resolve all of the problems that had been in existence for literally decades, he did make a real contribution[67] to the goal of having a stable transition from one government to another and to the goal of demonstrating to the Russian population as well as those watching from elsewhere in the world that stable government in Russia could be achieved.

During his first term, Putin moved to recentralize power and cut back the positions of regional governments and big business. He also pushed forward an ambitious program of domestic reforms, particularly in the economic sphere, including banking reforms, tax reform, anti-money-laundering legislation, and administrative and judicial reform.

Putin was elected to a second term as Russian president by a landslide in March 2004 with over 70 percent of the vote. His nearest rival, the Communist candidate, drew less than 14 percent. As Putin's second term drew to an end, outside observers were convinced that he was not going to give up power easily and were watching closely to see what he would do. As things turned out, Putin followed the letter of the law in the Constitution scrupulously and did not stand for reelection in the 2008 presidential election. As the election approached, he announced that his first deputy prime minister, Dmitry Medvedev, was his preferred choice to be the next president of Russia, and he campaigned for Medvedev in the elections.[68]

Immediately after being endorsed by Putin, Medvedev announced that if he were elected in 2008 he would appoint Putin to be his premier, and Putin announced that he would accept that position if it were offered. Although the Constitution did not permit Putin to serve a third consecutive term as president, it did not bar him from serving as premier, in which position he could continue to play an extremely influential role in Russian government.

Medvedev was elected president on March 2, 2008, winning 71.2 percent of the vote. Gennady Zyuganov of the Communist Party received 18 percent of the vote and Vladimir Zhirinovsky of the Liberal Democratic Party of Russia received 9.5 percent of the vote. The Organization for Security and Cooperation in Europe (OSCE), which provides election-monitoring groups for national elections in its member states, did not provide a monitoring group for this election because of what it labeled as Russian governmental "limitations that are not conducive to undertaking election observation."[69] Medvedev promptly appointed Putin to be his premier.

During Medvedev's presidency there continued to be much speculation about the power relationship between Medvedev and Putin, and whether Medvedev was simply a four-year "placeholder" for Putin, allowing him to stay at the center of power until he would be eligible to be president again. In changes made to electoral law during Putin's second term as president, the length of a term of office of the president would increase from four years to six years, effective with the president elected in 2012. This, in fact, turned out to be the case; at the United Russia Party Congress in Moscow in September 2011, President Medvedev proposed that Putin should run again for president in 2012, and Putin immediately announced that he would do so, and that if elected he would appoint Medvedev as his premier. The election returned Putin to power with a reported 64 percent of the vote, although there were widespread charges of the election being rigged and of widespread vote fraud.[70]

To the surprise of very few international observers, President Putin announced in late 2017 that he would participate in the 2018 presidential election (see Table 14.3) for an unprecedented fourth term as Russian president. Also to the surprise of none, he won an easy and overwhelming victory in the election, which was helped when the main opposition leader, Alexei Navalny, was barred from participating in the competition, supposedly because of an embezzlement conviction that he said was manufactured by the Kremlin.[71] Outside election monitors found a substantial number of violations, "including ballot-stuffing, bloated voter rolls, 'voting' by dead people, coercion by employers, expulsion of election observers and multiple vote-casting."[72]

The Constitutional Court

The Constitutional Court of the Russian Federation has been described as "the first independent court to be established in Russia since the Bolshevik Revolution."[73] The court was established in October 1991 by the fourth Russian Congress of People's Deputies. While the law that created

Table 14.3   Russia's Presidential Election of 2018

Candidate	Percentage of Vote
Vladimir Putin (United Russia Party)	77.5
Pavel Grudinin (Communist Party of the Russian Federation)	11.9
Vladimir Zhirinovsky (Liberal Democratic Party of Russia)	5.7
Other	5.8
Total	100.9

Source: CIA World Factbook, "Russia," https://www.cia.gov/library/publications/the-world-factbook/geos/rs.html.

the Court indicated that the Court was "prohibited from considering political questions," it was frequently caught in the middle of explicitly political quarrels between President Yeltsin and the Russian Parliament. The Court is authorized in the 1995 Constitution to rule on violations of constitutional rights, to hear appeals from lower courts, and to participate in impeachment proceedings against the president.

In fact, although the Court initially tried to walk a very narrow line and offend neither the Parliament nor the president, its decisions favored the Parliament significantly more frequently than they did the president.[74] Yeltsin suspended the Constitutional Court in October 1993 but reconvened it in March 1995.

Political Parties and Elections

In the old Soviet system, when one thought of political parties one thought only of the Communist Party of the Soviet Union. This party was in essence a governing organization in the USSR, and it was "by far the most important political institution in that country."[75] While the role of the Communist Party of the Soviet Union went over a relatively short period of time from one of absolute dominance to one of being outlawed,[76] the structure of the political party has come to play a much more realistic role in Russian politics.

In recent years, a number of significant political parties and movements have come into existence, some more democratically oriented than others.[77] Some of these parties have roots in earlier democratic movements. On the other hand, other parties are direct descendants of the CPSU itself. It is clear from recent presidential and legislative elections, however, that the Communist Party is no longer the dominant force in Russian politics that it was only a couple of decades ago.

The dominant political party in recent years has been the party of Vladimir Putin, the United Russia Party.[78] Although other parties do exist in Russia, and do compete in parliamentary elections, the United Russia Party is clearly the dominant party of the era. The Liberal Democratic Party of Russia (LDPR) is an ultranationalistic party, led by the Deputy Speaker of the Duma, Vladimir Zhirinovsky. The Communist Party of the Russian Federation (KPRF) continues to support the traditional economic policies of the old Communist regime, and it is headed by Gennady Zyuganov. The Communist Party is especially strong in rural areas of Russia, and it campaigns with the platform that it will nationalize key industries and improve health care, public education, and public housing. Another major party is the Russian United Democratic Party (Yabloko), which claims that it is the party of "freedom and justice."

Political Succession, Russian-Style

The issue of the succession of leadership in the Soviet Union and Russia illustrates the problem mentioned earlier about a lack of established democratic traditions and commitment to peaceful democratic transitions from one leader to another.[79]

Leonid Brezhnev was able to arrange the ouster of Nikita Khrushchev through political alliances in the Politburo; in 1977 he expanded his base of power by acquiring the position of chairman of the Presidium of the Supreme Soviet in addition to his position as general secretary of the Communist Party. The leaders who followed Brezhnev to the post of party general secretary, Yuri Andropov and Konstantin Chernenko, were both old party functionaries, and because of their ages (seventy-nine and eighty-two years, respectively) and accompanying illness, their opportunities to lead and to suggest significant policy innovations were few.

Many Sovietologists were keenly interested in what would happen in the process of succession of Brezhnev. Some thought it would introduce conflict and instability, some thought it would simply maintain the status quo, and some thought that it would open up significant avenues for reform in Soviet politics.[80]

Andropov's ill health made him a weak leader, and he placed a special emphasis on what was called "collective leadership" during his brief time in office. He was not able to create a new cabinet to reflect his own preferences, but was forced to permit the existing members of the Politburo, the Party Secretariat, and most top government functionaries to retain their positions. This was to no small degree because he "owed his election as general secretary primarily to [Defense Minister Marshal] Ustinov and [Foreign Minister Alexi] Gromyko." As well, he "also had to show consideration for that part of the 'Brezhnev faction,' . . . who had voted for him."[81]

When Chernenko succeeded to the position of general secretary, he was able to arrange for himself to be elected chairman of the Presidium of the Supreme Soviet relatively quickly, in June 1983. As with Andropov, his health very quickly limited his ability to exercise the potential power of his office. At this time Mikhail Gorbachev rose to the position of second secretary of the Central Committee, and he frequently substituted for Chernenko when the latter's health forced him to take lengthy breaks from activity.

When Gorbachev assumed the USSR's top position in the spring of 1985, some suggested that his assumption of power might "well prove to be a major turning point in Soviet history";[82] others asked if he would "make a difference" in the way the Soviet regime functioned.[83] As we have already noted, he introduced a number of very significant structural changes in his first few years in office, even though he continued to face strong resistance from the entrenched bureaucracy to his call for a new kind of society.

Gorbachev led Soviet politics from 1985 through 1991, and the **perestroika** ("restructuring"), **glasnost** ("openness"), and **demokratizatsiya** ("democratization") that were associated with his regime were highly significant in changing the tenor and direction of Soviet—and post-Soviet—politics. Under his leadership the fundamental structural changes of USSR governmental institutions discussed in this chapter took place, including changes in legislative and executive structures and a significant change in the role of the Communist Party in the political system.

In 1990 the Congress of the Russian Soviet Federated Socialist Republic declared that its laws would take precedence over Soviet laws. This contributed significantly to the demise of the USSR. In April 1991 the Russian Federation created the position of president, and two months later Boris Yeltsin became Russia's first democratically elected president.

Yeltsin's political fortunes varied drastically between the date he came to power in June 1991 and the end of the decade. While at times both he and the political and economic reforms he advocated had wide support, at other times his governments suffered dramatically. Indeed, the conflict between Yeltsin and the Russian Parliament that took place in September 1993—to which we have already referred—was illustrative of some of the problems from which his governments suffered.

The most remarkable legacy of the Yeltsin presidency, however, may be what came after Yeltsin's term: a peaceful transition to a democratically elected successor. It is customary to observe that in a country that is new to democracy it is not the first democratic election that is crucial to watch, but the second. A despot may decide to bring about reform and may order a "democratic" election to take place, and it may be the case that the culture will not support that reform and in the election after the one ordered by the authoritarian ruler serious problems will develop. While Vladimir Putin's campaign and election were not without problems and charges of improprieties, the international observers who were on hand indicated that the election was free and fair and that the election of Putin in 2000 was a legitimate one.

We noted earlier that Putin "finessed" the Russian electoral law by designating a loyal handpicked successor—Dmitry Medvedev—to run for president in 2008, who in turn promised to appoint Putin to serve as premier during his term of office as president, and that Medvedev in fact served as a "placeholder" for Putin for four years when he was constitutionally ineligible to serve as president, returning the presidency to Putin in 2012. Putin, of course, was easily elected in 2012, with a six-year term, and Putin's reelection was seen as "guaranteed" in 2018. Some observers said that the issue in the 2018 election was succession, and life after Putin, and not the reelection of Putin himself: the interesting question will be what happens as the end of Putin's six-year term approaches in 2024. "With the victory of President Vladimir V. Putin assured, the real contest, they say, is the bare-knuckled, no-holds-barred fight to determine who or what comes after him by the end of his next six years in office, in 2024. What might be called the Court of Putin—the top 40 to 50 people in the Kremlin and their oligarch allies—will spend the next presidential term brawling over that future."[84]

The Russian System in Perspective

The Russian system provides an interesting case study, both in its own right and in a comparative perspective. Russia is a political system that is actively evolving from one period and style of politics to another. We can see that the changes from Soviet institutions and political behavior to Russian institutions and behavior have been, and will continue to be, both dramatic and traumatic. Indeed, no one knows at this point in time whether Russia's recent experiences with democracy will, in fact, endure.

The Russian case is an illustration of a society without a history of democratic institutions and political behavior attempting to establish democratic institutions and behavior. The transition to stable, Western-style parliamentary democracy will not come without a long period of tension and effort on the part of the Russian people, but if they can achieve all of the goals they are seeking to achieve, much will have been accomplished.

In short, the Russian system is quite different from other political systems we have met over the course of our studies. Nations in flux, as we see in the case of Russia, are nations with significant potential, but ones that have to worry about the potential for violence and self-destruction as well as the potential for accomplishment. The single most important lesson we should draw from our studies is that we cannot walk into any new political study with the assumption that all politics operate in the same fashion as they do in the United States. In this manner, we can see the value of cross-national political inquiry. Our new perspectives provide us with a better ability to make our own observations in the future and to draw our own conclusions as we continue our studies.

Discussion Questions

1. How did the long and difficult history of governmental transitions affect the current Russian political system? What do you think were the most significant historical events in this evolution?
2. We have seen that constitutions may be more or less significant in a political system. Has the role of Russia's Constitution varied over time? What is its role today?
3. Is Russia federal in the same way that Germany and Canada are federal? What are the differences that you see? How is Russia different? How does this affect the power of the president of Russia?
4. The Soviet Union was born in a complex and rigid ideological context. How would you characterize the role of ideology in the creation of Russia? Was ideology the driving force, or was it pragmatic politics? How much is ideology steering policy and politics in Russia today?
5. What are the key differences between Russian political institutions today and the political institutions of the Union of Soviet Socialist Republics and the Commonwealth of Independent States that preceded it? Should Russia be classified as a parliamentary regime, a presidential regime, or something else? Why?
6. What is the power of President Putin in Russia today? Has he moved Russian leadership back toward the past style of Russian authoritarian leadership, or is he simply a very successful leader?
7. Given the importance of political parties to the Soviet Union, are parties as important to Russia? What is the role of political parties in Russia today?

Notes

1. Vadim Medish, *The Soviet Union* (Englewood Cliffs, NJ: Prentice Hall, 1981), p. 1.
2. John S. Reshetar, *The Soviet Polity* (New York: Harper and Row, 1978), p. 21.
3. Geoffrey Hosking, *Russia and the Russians: A History* (Cambridge: Harvard University Press, 2001) is a good reference in this area. See also Nicholas Riasanovsky and Mark Steinberg, *A History of Russia* (New York: Oxford University Press, 2011).
4. Gwendolen M. Carter, *The Government of the Soviet Union* (New York: Harcourt, Brace, Jovanovich, 1972), p. 14. See also A. I. Polunov, Thomas Owen, and L. G. Zakharova, *Russia in the Nineteenth Century: Autocracy, Reform, and Social Change, 1814–1914* (Armonk, NY: Sharpe, 2005).
5. This section is based upon a much longer section written by Vernon V. Aspaturian, "Soviet Politics," in Roy C. Macridis, *Modern Political Systems: Europe* (Englewood Cliffs, NJ: Prentice Hall, 1978), pp. 335–340. See also the discussions of Russia's revolutionary heritage in Paul Buskovitch, *A Concise History of Russia* (New York: Cambridge University Press, 2012).
6. Aspaturian, "Soviet Politics," p. 336.
7. Michael G. Roskin, *Countries and Concepts* (Englewood Cliffs, NJ: Prentice Hall, 1982), p. 219.

8. Aspaturian, "Soviet Politics," p. 338. Some good recent studies of Lenin include the following: William Fuller, *Civil-Military Conflict in Imperial Russia, 1881–1914* (Princeton: Princeton University Press, 2014); and Christopher Read, *Lenin: A Revolutionary Life* (New York: Routledge, 2005).

9. Adam B. Ulam, *The Russian Political System* (New York: Random, 1974), p. 27.

10. See David Marples, *Lenin's Revolution: Russia, 1917–1921* (Harlow: Longman, 2000).

11. A very good general history is that by Theodore Link, *Communism: A Primary Source Analysis* (New York: Rosen, 2005). More specialized studies are by Adam B. Ulam, *The Bolsheviks: The Intellectual and Political History of the Triumph of Communism in Russia* (Cambridge: Harvard University Press, 1998); and Terry Fiehn and Chris Corin, *Communist Russia Under Lenin and Stalin* (London: Murray, 2000).

12. A good history looking at the relative impact of Mikhail Gorbachev in historical context is by Kevin O'Connor, *Intellectuals and Apparatchiks: Russian Nationalism and the Gorbachev Revolution* (Lanham: Lexington, 2006). See also M. S. Gorbachev, *Gorbachev: On My Country and the World* (New York: Columbia University Press, 1999); Iulia Shevchenko, *The Central Government of Russia: From Gorbachev to Putin* (Burlington, VT: Ashgate, 2004); and Jonathan Harris, *Subverting the System: Gorbachev's Reform of the Party's Apparat, 1986–1991* (Lanham: Rowman and Littlefield, 2005).

13. See David Marples, *The Collapse of the Soviet Union: 1985–1991* (New York: Pearson, 2004); Ruth Starkman, *Transformations of the New Germany* (New York: Palgrave Macmillan, 2006).

14. In September 1990, President George H. W. Bush discussed the Persian Gulf crisis and international relations in a speech titled "Toward a New World Order" (*US Department of State Dispatch,* September 17, 1990, v. 1, no. 3, p. 91). More recently, and related to the Soviet Union, in May 1991 Bush gave the speech "The Possibility of New World Order: Unlocking the Promise of Freedom" (*Vital Speeches,* May 15, 1991, v. 57, n. 15, p. 450). A recent study of Russia is that by J. L. Black, *Vladimir Putin and the New World Order: Looking East, Looking West?* (Lanham: Rowman and Littlefield, 2004).

15. Medish, *The Soviet Union,* pp. 29–30.

16. Ronald Grigor Suny, "The Nationality Question," in Janet Podell and Steven Anzovin, eds., *The Soviet Union* (New York: Wilson, 1988), p. 136. See also Goran Grgic, *Ethnic Conflict in Asymmetric Federations: Comparative Experience of the Former Soviet and Yugoslav Regions* (New York: Routledge, 2017).

17. Indeed, "in his closing speech to the first session of the new Congress of People's Deputies, Mikhail Gorbachev commented that no single issue had been so widely discussed by the Congress as that of interethnic relations." *Radio Liberty: Report on the U.S.S.R.,* June 16, 1989, p. 21.

18. Celestine Bohlen, "The Soviets and the Enmities Within," *New York Times,* April 16, 1989, p. E1.

19. John N. Hazard, *The Soviet System of Government* (Chicago: University of Chicago Press, 1980), pp. 98–99. See Cameron Ross, *Federalism and Democratisation in Russia* (New York: Manchester University Press, 2013).

20. See Robert Sharlet, *The New Soviet Constitution of 1977* (Brunswick, OH: King's Court Communications, 1978), p. 97. This has a copy of the complete text of the Constitution.

21. Felicity Barringer, "Soviets Draft Plans for Government Change," *New York Times,* October 22, 1988, p. 3.

22. Adam Ulam's essay "Looking at the Past: The Unraveling of the Soviet Union," *Current History* 91, no. 567 (1992): 339–347, is very good in this regard. See the publication by the Organization for Economic Cooperation and Development, *Russian Federation: Key Issues and Policies* (Paris, 2015).

23. "Commonwealth of Independent States Treaty Signed," *New York Times,* December 23, 1991, p. A10. On the CIS, see Zbigniew Brzezinski and Paige Sullivan, *Russia*

and the Commonwealth of Independent States: Documents, Data, and Analysis (Armonk, NY: Sharpe, 1997); and *The Territories of the Russian Federation 2017* (London: Routledge, 2017).

24. "Soviet Coup Started," *Los Angeles Times,* August 30, 1991, p. A1. See also Andrew Langley, *The Collapse of the Soviet Union: The End of an Empire* (Minneapolis, MN: Compass Point, 2006).

25."Gorbachev Resigns from C.P.S.U.," *New York Times,* August 25, 1991, p. 1.

26. The Belarus description of the CIS can be found on the Foreign Ministry of the Government of Belarus website, http://mfa.gov.by/en/organizations/membership/list /c2bd4cebdf6bd9f9.html. See Eric Engle, *Russia, the European Union, and the CIS* (Portland: International Specialized Book Service, 2012).

27. Michael McFaul, Nikolai Petrov, and Andrei Riabov, *Between Dictatorship and Democracy: Russian Post-Communist Political Reform* (Washington, DC: Carnegie Endowment for International Peace, 2004). See also Jane Henderson, *The Constitution of the Russian Federation: A Contextual Analysis* (Portland: Hart, 2011).

28. See Steven Erlanger's article "Now Yeltsin Must Govern: Struggle with Hard-Liners over for Now, Talk Is of 'A Second Russian Revolution,'" *New York Times,* October 10, 1993, p. 1. See also Thomas Remington, *The Russian Parliament: Institutional Evolution in a Transitional Regime, 1989–1999* (New Haven: Yale University Press, 2001).

29. Ulam, *Russian Political System,* p. 59.

30. See Samantha Lomb, *Stalin's Constitution: Soviet Participatory Politics and the Discussion of the 1939 Draft Constitution* (New York: Routledge, 2018).

31. Sharlet, *New Soviet Constitution of 1977,* p. 5. See also Robert Sharlet, *Soviet Constitutional Crisis: From De-Stalinization to Disintegration* (New York: Routledge, 2015).

32. "Resignation of President Mikhail Gorbachev," *Vital Speeches* 58, no. 7 (January 15, 1992): 194. Gorbachev wrote a very interesting book describing his views on the direction of Russia in 2016 titled *The New Russia* (Cambridge: Polity, 2016).

33. See Leon R. Aron, *Yeltsin: A Revolutionary Life* (New York: St. Martin's, 2000); and Roy Medvedev, *Post-Soviet Russia: A Journey Through the Yeltsin Era* (New York: Columbia University Press, 2000).

34. See Boris Kagarlitsky, *Russia Under Yeltsin and Putin: Neo-Liberal Autocracy* (Sterling, VA: Pluto, 2002). On the new Russian Constitution, see Gordon Smith and Robert Sharlet, *Russia and Its Constitution: Promise and Political Reality* (Boston: Martinus Nijhoff, 2008); or Henderson, *Constitution of the Russian Federation.*

35. See Anton Steen and Vladimir Gelman, *Elites and Democratic Development in Russia* (New York: Routledge, 2003). See also Victor Leontovitsch, Parmen Leontovitsch, and Aleksandr Solzhenitsyn, *The History of Liberalism in Russia* (Pittsburgh: University of Pittsburgh Press, 2012).

36. Eugene Huskey, *Presidential Power in Russia* (Armonk, NY: Sharpe, 1999). See also Thomas Remington, *Politics in Russia* (Hoboken, NJ: Taylor and Francis, 2015).

37. Reshetar, *The Soviet Polity,* p. 172.

38. Aspaturian, "Soviet Politics," p. 401. See also Sharlet, *New Soviet Constitution of 1977,* pp. 73–132.

39. On Russian federalism, see Jeffrey Kahn, *Federalism, Democratization, and the Rule of Law in Russia* (New York: Oxford University Press, 2008); or Cameron Ross and Adrian Campbell, *Federalism and Local Politics in Russia* (New York: Routledge, 2009). A more focused study is by Cameron Ross, *Federalism and Democratisation in Russia* (New York: Manchester University Press, 2013). See also A. Starodubtsev, *Federalism, and Regional Policy in Contemporary Russia* (New York: Routledge, 2018).

40. A very good collection on ideology in the former Soviet Union is Stephen J. Lee, *Russia and the U.S.S.R., 1855–1991: Autocracy and Dictatorship* (New York: Routledge, 2006). See also Bertram Wolfe, *An Ideology in Power: Reflections on the Russian Revolution* (New York: Routledge, 2017).

41. Sam C. Sarkesian and James Buck, *Comparative Politics* (Sherman Oaks, CA: Alfred Publishing, 1979), pp. 97–98. Marxism is a highly elaborate theoretical framework, far beyond our level of analysis here in any detail. See Gustav Wetter, *Soviet Ideology* (New York: Praeger, 1962), for a very good introduction to the ideas of Marxism as interpreted in the Soviet Union.

42. Medish, *Soviet Union*, pp. 67–68. See James Ryan, *Lenin's Terror: The Ideological Origins of Early Soviet State Violence* (New York: Routledge, 2012).

43. Sarkesian and Buck, *Comparative Politics*, p. 101. Recent analyses of Stalin include Robert Service, *Stalin: A Biography* (Cambridge: Harvard University Press, 2005).

44. Sarkesian and Buck. *Comparative Politics*. See also Aspaturian, "Soviet Politics," p. 356; and David Brandenberger, *Propaganda State in Crisis: Soviet Ideology, Indoctrination, and Terror Under Stalin, 1927–1941* (New Haven: Yale University Press, 2011).

45. Aspaturian, "Soviet Politics," p. 358. On Khrushchev, see William Taubman and Sergei Khrushchev, *Nikita Khrushchev* (New Haven: Yale University Press, 2000); and Nikita Sergevich Khrushchev, *Memoirs of Nikita Khrushchev* (University Park: Pennsylvania State University Press, 2004).

46. Carter, *Government of the Soviet Union*, p. 13. See also Matthew Ouimet, *The Rise and Fall of the Brezhnev Doctrine in Soviet Foreign Policy* (Chapel Hill: University of North Carolina Press, 2003).

47. Dmitri Volkogonov, trans. Harold Shukman, *Autopsy for an Empire: The Seven Leaders Who Built the Soviet Regime* (New York: Free Press, 1998); and John W. Parker, *Kremlin in Transition,* vol. 1, *From Brezhnev to Chernenko, 1978 to 1985* (Boston: Unwin Hyman, 1991).

48. See Christopher Xenakis, *What Happened to the Soviet Union? How and Why American Sovietologists Were Caught by Surprise* (Westport: Praeger, 2002). See also Remington, *Politics in Russia*. More recently there has been discussion of the impact of Vladimir Putin on the theory of Russian power; see Walter Laqueur, *Putin: Russia and Its Future with the West* (New York: Thomas Dunne, 2015).

49. George W. Breslauer, *Gorbachev and Yeltsin as Leaders* (New York: Cambridge University Press, 2002); or Stephen Kotkin, *Armageddon Averted: The Soviet Collapse, 1970–2000* (New York: Oxford University Press, 2008). See also Jonathan Haslam, *Russia's Cold War: From the October Revolution to the Fall of the Wall* (New Haven: Yale University Press, 2011).

50. Elizabeth Teague, "Gorbachev's First Four Years," *Radio Liberty: Report on the U.S.S.R.,* March 3, 1989, pp. 3–4.

51. See Dawn Mann, "The Opening of the Congress," *Radio Liberty: Report on the U.S.S.R.,* June 9, 1989, pp. 1–2.

52. Sharlet, *New Soviet Constitution of 1977,* p. 108.

53. Paul Quinn-Judge, "Gorbachev Dominance Displayed in Parliament," *Christian Science Monitor,* December 1988, p. 1.

54. David Remnick, "New Soviet Congress Tackles Procedure," *Washington Post,* May 27, 1989, p. A15.

55. Bill Keller, "A Guide to the Election Process," *New York Times,* March 26, 1989, p. E3. See also Dawn Mann and Julia Wishnevsky, "Composition of Congress of People's Deputies," *Radio Liberty: Report on the U.S.S.R.,* May 5, 1989, p. 6.

56. See *Radio Free Europe/Radio Liberty Research Report,* May 14, 1992, pp. 112–119.

57. Celestine Bohlen, "Yeltsin Orders Replacement of Legislatures of Regions," *New York Times,* October 9, 1993, p. 9. See also Richard Sakwa, *Russian Politics and Society* (New York: Routledge, 2008).

58. See Tiffany Troxel, *Parliamentary Power in Russia, 1994–2001: President vs. Parliament* (London: Palgrave Macmillan, 2003). See also Julie Newton and William Tompson, eds., *Institutions, Ideas, and Leadership in Russian Politics* (New York: Palgrave Macmillan, 2010); and Steven S. Smith and Thomas Remington, *The Politics of*

Institutional Choice: The Formation of the Russian State Duma (Princeton: Princeton University Press, 2016).

59. See "OSCE Slams 'Unfair' Russian Elections," *Der Spiegel,* December 2007, http://www.spiegel.de/international/world/0,1518,521063,00.html; Richard Sakwa, ed., *Power and Policy in Putin's Russia,* 2nd ed. (Hoboken, NJ: Taylor and Francis, 2013); and Regina Smyth, *Candidate Strategies and Electoral Competition in the Russian Federation: Democracy Without Foundation* (Cambridge: Cambridge University Press, 2011).

60. Inter-Parliamentary Union, "Parline Database: Russian Federation (State Duma), Elections in 2011," http://archive.ipu.org/parline-e/reports/arc/2263_11.htm.

61. For more information on the Council of the Federation, see the Inter-Parliamentary Union's "Parline Database," http://archive.ipu.org/parline-e/reports/2264_B.htm.

62. Sharlet, *New Soviet Constitution of 1977,* p. 112.

63. D. Richard Little, *Governing the Soviet Union* (London: Longman, 1989), p. 157.

64. Teague, "Gorbachev's First Four Years," p. 4. See also Michael Parks, "Party Picks Gorbachev as Nominee for President at People's Congress," *Los Angeles Times,* May 23, 1989, p. 8; and Michael Parks, "New Russian Congress Elects Gorbachev to Presidency," *Los Angeles Times,* May 26, 1989, p. 1.

65. See "Yeltsin Elected President," *U.S. News and World Report,* June 17, 1991, pp. 36–38. On the presidency, see Richard Rose, *Russia Elects a President* (Glasgow: Centre for the Study of Public Policy, 2000). On Yeltsin, see Timothy Colton, *Yeltsin: A Life* (New York: Basic, 2008).

66. See Barry Turner, ed., *The Statesman's Yearbook* (Basingstoke: Palgrave, 2000), pp. 1329–1330.

67. See Peter Baker, *Kremlin Rising: Vladimir Putin's Russia and the End of Revolution* (New York: Scribner, 2005). See also Michael Stuermer, *Putin and the Rise of Russia* (New York: Pegasus, 2009). On Putin's power, see Stephen White, *Politics and the Ruling Group in Putin's Russia* (New York: Palgrave Macmillan, 2008); and Sakwa, *Power and Policy in Putin's Russia.*

68. See "Putin Sees Medvedev as Successor," *BBC News,* December 10, 2007, http://news.bbc.co.uk/2/hi/europe/7136347.stm. See also Richard Sakwa, *The Crisis of Russian Democracy: The Dual State, Factionalism, and the Medvedev Succession* (New York: Cambridge University Press, 2011).

69. "OSCE/ODIHR Regrets That Restrictions Force Cancellation of Election Observation Mission to Russian Federation," http://www.osce.org/odihr/elections/49438.

70. See Kathy Lally and Will Englund, "Putin Wins Election as Russian President; Opponents Claim Widespread Fraud," *Washington Post,* March 4, 2012, https://www.washingtonpost.com/world/russians-voting-and-watching/2012/03/04/gIQA3j6CqR_story.html?utm_term=.37f1d78f632d.

71. See "Russia Election: Vladimir Putin Wins by Big Margin," *BBC News,* March 19, 2018, https://www.bbc.com/news/world-europe-43452449.

72. Vladimir Kara-Murza, "Why Putin's Sham Election Shows What He's Afraid Of," *Washington Post,* March 20, 2018, https://www.washingtonpost.com/news/democracy-post/wp/2018/03/20/why-putins-sham-election-shows-what-hes-afraid-of/?utm_term=.61d329480c91.

73. This section is based upon a more detailed discussion in *Radio Free Europe/Radio Liberty Research Report,* May 14, 1992, p. 14. See also Alexei Trochev, *Judging Russia: Constitutional Court in Russian Politics: 1990–2006* (New York: Cambridge University Press, 2008).

74. *Radio Free Europe/Radio Liberty Research Report,* May 14, 1992. See Alexei Trochev, *Judging Russia: Constitutional Court in Russian Politics, 1990–2006* (Cambridge: Cambridge University Press, 2011); and Carla Thorson, *Politics, Judicial Review, and the Russian Constitutional Court* (New York: Palgrave Macmillan, 2012).

75. Ronald Hill and Peter Frank, *The Soviet Communist Party* (London: Allen and Unwin, 1981), p. 1. See John Lowenhardt *Party Politics in Post-Communist Russia* (Hoboken, NJ: Taylor and Francis, 2013).

76. See Rita DiLeo, "The Soviet Communist Party, 1988–1991: From Power to Ostracism," *Coexistence* 29, no. 4 (1992): 321–334. See also S. P. Roberts, *Putin's United Russia Party* (New York: Routledge, 2011).

77. See the essay Roy Medvedev, "After the Communist Collapse: New Political Tendencies in Russia," *Dissent* 39, no. 4 (Fall 1992): 489–498. See Stephen White, *Understanding Russian Politics* (New York: Cambridge University Press, 2011); and Derek Hutcheson, *Twenty Years of Post-Communist Elections: The Voters' Perspective* (Aberdeen: University of Aberdeen Press, 2010).

78. See Roberts, *Putin's United Russia Party*; and Ora John Reuter, *The Origins of Dominant Parties: Building Authoritarian Institutions in Post-Soviet Russia* (Cambridge: Cambridge University Press, 2017).

79. Much of the material in the next few paragraphs is based upon much more extensive analysis in Boris Meissner, "Implications of Leadership and Social Change for Soviet Policies," in Kinya Niiseki, ed., *The Soviet Union in Transition* (Boulder: Westview, 1987), pp. 50–56. See also Vladimir Gelman, *Authoritarian Russia: Analyzing Post-Soviet Regime Change* (Pittsburgh: University of Pittsburg Press, 2015).

80. Timothy Colton, *The Dilemma of Reform in the Soviet Union* (New York: Council on Foreign Relations, 1986), pp. 68–69.

81. Meissner, "Implications of Leadership," p. 52.

82. Herbert J. Ellison, "Gorbachev and Reform: An Introduction," in Lawrence W. Lerner and Donald W. Treadgold, eds., *Gorbachev and the Soviet Future* (Boulder: Westview, 1988), p. 1.

83. There is an absolutely massive literature on Gorbachev. See, among others, A. S. Cherniaev, Robert English, and Elizabeth Tucker, *My Six Years with Gorbachev* (University Park: Pennsylvania State University Press, 2000); and Jack F. Matlock, *Reagan and Gorbachev: How the Cold War Ended* (New York: Random, 2004).

84. Neil Mac Farquahar, "Putin's Reelection Is Assured: Let the Succession Fight Begin," *New York Times,* December 11, 2017, https://www.nytimes.com/2017/12/11 /world/europe/russia-vladimir-putin-election.html. See also William Zimmerman, *Ruling Russia: Authoritarianism from the Revolution to Putin* (Princeton: Princeton University Press, 2014); Tina Burrett, *Television and Presidential Power in Putin's Russia* (New York: Routledge, 2011); or Ben Judah, *Fragile Empire: How Russia Fell in and out of Love with Vladimir Putin* (New Haven: Yale University Press, 2013).

15

The United Kingdom

The British political system is regarded by many as the "mother" of modern democracies. The institution of Parliament developed in Great Britain, and the role of the monarchy in Britain devolved to a point that it could exist in harmony with democratic political norms. The Westminster model of parliamentary government to which we have referred again and again in this book is derived, of course, from the parliamentary system that evolved in Britain at Westminster.

Many students are confused about the names **England**, **(Great) Britain**, and the **United Kingdom**. These three names are not, in fact, interchangeable; they refer to different political systems. The United Kingdom is a country in Western Europe with a population of over 66 million people (in 2017) and a national capital in London. The formal name of the United Kingdom is the United Kingdom of Great Britain and Northern Ireland. (The "Northern" part of this is only since 1922; prior to 1922, when Ireland was divided into Northern Ireland and the Republic of Ireland, the formal name of the UK was the United Kingdom of Great Britain and Ireland.) Great Britain is the principal island of the United Kingdom, and it includes England, Scotland, and Wales. England is an administrative unit of the United Kingdom of Great Britain and Northern Ireland, and it occupies most of the southern half of the island of Great Britain: Wales is to the west, and Scotland is to the north. Having said all of this we should note that today the term *Britain* is generally used interchangeably with *United Kingdom* or *England,* as we have frequently done in this volume, even though they do not technically refer to the same thing.

The Constitutional System

Earlier we discussed the distinction between governments with written constitutions and those with constitutional government, and we pointed out that a political system need not have a written document in order to be referred to as a constitutional regime. Indeed, the example that we used at that time was the case of Britain. Students of British politics agree that for all intents and purposes there is a British constitution, in the sense that there is a body of fundamental precepts underlying the British political regime and consequent British political behavior. The fact that Britain does not have a specific document called the Royal Constitution has led some to say that Britain has no constitution. This error "confuses the constitution with what is usually only one of its sources."[1]

Britain's lack of a written constitution is not a result of British inexperience with the writing of constitutions. The British government has written constitutions for many former possessions that are today independent nations, most in the Commonwealth of Nations. For example, in 1867, the British North America Act was passed by the British Parliament. It united what was then called Canada (today Ontario and Quebec) with Nova Scotia and New Brunswick to form the Dominion of Canada. Australia received its constitution in 1901. The Union of South Africa's constitution was passed in 1909. New Zealand was granted "responsible" government in 1852.[2] India's independent status and relations with the British Commonwealth were defined at the London conference of prime ministers in April 1949, and its new constitution became effective in January 1950.[3] Many other constitutions have been written for newly independent countries—formerly members of the British Empire—since that time.

Constitutions of political regimes can frequently be said to have several components, and these all apply in Britain: (1) written charters or collections of historical documents, (2) legislative statutes of "constitutional" significance, (3) judicial interpretation, and (4) customs and precedents. "The 'written' constitutions acquire many unwritten parts and through the years they become overlaid with legislative amplifications, judicial interpretations, and customary provisions. The 'unwritten' ones usually have important parts committed to paper as charters or broad constitutional statutes. In the course of time the two types come more and more to resemble one another."[4]

One scholar of the British Constitution has suggested that there are many sources from which it emanates: statutory law (acts of Parliament), common law and judicial decisions, and "the customs of the Constitution."[5] Although there is no single document that can be called the British Constitution, scholars agree that fundamentally this is not significant; whether there is a single document or not, Britain has a constitution in the sense that there are fundamental principles underlying British government and limiting the behavior of the British government.

Statutory law is law that derives from acts of Parliament. We should note that while not all acts of Parliament can or should be regarded as constitutional acts, "there is scarcely a session of Parliament that does not contribute to the constitutional structure statutes that add to or alter the basic law of the land."[6] Acts that are usually considered to be part of the unwritten British Constitution are the Magna Carta (1215), the Petition of Right (1626), the Habeas Corpus Act (1679), the Bill of Rights (1689), the Act of Settlement (1701), the Acts of Union with Scotland (1707) and Ireland (1800), the Great Reform Act (1832), the Parliament Act (1911), and the Statute of Westminster (1931), among many others.[7]

Common law sources of constitutional doctrines are harder to pin down. Common law, by definition, is concerned with customs; according to **William Blackstone** (1723–1780), the eighteenth-century scholar whose work on British law is seen as being authoritative, laws of this nature are "not set down in any written statute or ordinance, but depending on immemorial usage for their support."[8] Many judicial decisions eventually become part of the body of common law and acquire "constitutional" status over time. Generally speaking, judicial interpretation is of less significance in Britain than in the United States. Because Britain operates under a system of legislative supremacy, with no regular judicial review of legislative statutes, the British judiciary has a lower profile than its US counterpart. As one observer has noted, "The British courts, however, in interpreting and clarifying the law frequently declare what the constitution is. The civil liberties of British subjects are largely embedded in the common law and thus have been defined and protected by the courts."[9]

The third source of British constitutional doctrine has been referred to as "customs of the Constitution." A number of these customs may be highlighted here:

1. The Cabinet consists of members of, and is responsible to, Parliament.
2. The Sovereign [today, the Queen] does not attend Cabinet meetings.
3. The Sovereign does not withhold assent from (veto) Bills which have passed the two Houses of Parliament.
4. The Speaker (presiding officer) of the House of Commons takes no part in political controversy.[10]

These four points illustrate the customs of behavior that have evolved over the years in Britain and are referred to as being "constitutional" in nature today. Although the monarch today may legally retain the right to veto or withhold assent from an act of the British Parliament, it would be regarded as unconstitutional to do so.[11] Similarly, while the monarch legally can appoint anyone to be prime minister, constitutionally they can only appoint someone who can command the support of a majority of the House of Commons. This distinction may strike many as being curious, that an action may be at the same time both legal and unconstitutional, but it is nonetheless the case that in the United Kingdom the law may permit an action that has, through custom over time, become impermissible. This is a valid distinction, and an important one to recall.

It is also important to distinguish "between the Constitution and the principles that underlie it. The Principles are in one sense more important than the Constitution itself."[12] Constitutions may change, through statutory acts, common law, judicial decisions, or custom—but principles remain. Two fundamental principles are said to underlie the British Constitution. The first principle involves the rule of law. Citizens are entitled to the protection of law, and both individuals and the government of the state are to be limited in what they can do by the law of the regime. The second principle is that of **parliamentary sovereignty**, a principle suggested earlier in this chapter. This point can be further stated to mean that (1) there is no law of an earlier Parliament that the current Parliament cannot change if it wishes to do so; (2) there is no clear distinction between "constitutional" acts of Parliament and acts of Parliament that are not "constitutional"; and (3) no person or body (for example, the courts) can nullify an act of Parliament on the grounds that the act is opposed to the Constitution.[13] Anything the British Parliament does, by definition, is constitutional, even though it is possible to imagine legislation that it might—legally—pass that individuals might see as violating customs and traditions to the extent that they might call the legislation "unconstitutional."

A number of structural characteristics of the British political system can be regarded as almost constitutional in their significance for the regime.[14] First, the United Kingdom is a unitary political system, not a federal system, a point to which we shall return shortly. Centralized power is something that is, and has been, part of British constitutional life.

In addition to the United Kingdom being a unitary political system, the second structural characteristic, as noted earlier, is that the **Westminster model of government** generally is composed of four parts. First, the chief executive is not the same as the head of state. Second, the executive powers of government are exercised by the chief executive and their cabinet, not by the head of state. Third, the chief executive and the cabinet come from and are part of the legislature. Fourth, the chief executive and the cabinet are responsible to, and can be fired by, the legislature. This model of government differs significantly from the US system in that in Britain there is no clear separation of powers between the legislative and executive branches, which is so important to the US political culture. The concern of the American Founding Fathers over "checks and balances" simply is not found in the Westminster political structure; the British legislature "checks" the British executive in a different way from that found in the United States. The political executive is actually part of the legislature, and the courts do not have the power to limit what the legislature does.

A third political structure identified with the British Constitution is that the prime minister and cabinet are drawn from and are responsible to the national legislature. ("Responsible to" here means "answerable to"—the legislature has the right to hire and fire the prime minister.) Although occasionally some cabinet members may not be from the legislature, the prime minister and the bulk of the cabinet will invariably be from the House of Commons (or whatever the name of the lower, elected house of the national legislature is in other systems modeled after the British Parliament). They remain in office as long as they continue to be supported by a majority of the lower house of the national legislature.

A fourth major significant political structure in the British system is that of political parties. Political parties are so much a part of the British political system that we cannot imagine British politics operating in their absence. Institutions and patterns of behavior such as "responsible government," "party discipline," and "votes of confidence," among others, require healthy political parties. Parliamentary government could not exist without a rigorous system of political parties.

Unitary Government

Britain is unitary. There is no sharing of sovereignty between the national government and some intermediate level of government; indeed, there are no sovereign intermediate levels of government in the United Kingdom to correspond to states in the United States or Mexico, provinces in Canada, or Lander in Germany (although there are administrative units of government). This is significant in that Parliament thereby becomes more relevant to the daily routine of life in Britain because it influences many aspects of life affected by intermediate levels of government in other political systems.

We should note, however, that in 1997, the start of a devolution of power from Westminster to the regions took place. Two different referenda were held in the United Kingdom to give Scotland and Wales an opportunity to reclaim some of the political power that had developed in Westminster over the years. The Government of **Tony Blair** was committed to giving the Scots and the Welsh the option of having their own parliaments with wide—but not exclusive—powers to govern in their respective areas. Blair pledged in the 1997 parliamentary campaign to institute a broad devolution of powers from the central government at Westminster in London to Scotland, Wales, and Northern Ireland.[15]

The constitutional structures of the United Kingdom are reflected in the governmental structure. Welsh affairs are handled at the British national level by the secretary of state for Wales, working with members of Parliament elected from Wales. The secretary of state for Scotland is also a cabinet member who works with members of Parliament from that area. A secretary of state for Northern Ireland works with its eighteen members of Parliament to represent that territory.

In September 1997 referenda were held in both Scotland and Wales on the issue of devolution.[16] In Scotland, voters responded to two questions—whether they wanted to set up their own parliament in Edinburgh with wide powers, and whether they wanted this parliament to have the power to raise extra taxes—with 74 percent of the voters saying yes to the first question and 63 percent saying yes to the second.

A week later the Welsh voted on a single question: whether they wanted their own assembly with the power to administer public services. The assembly would not have the power to levy taxes or pass laws, so it was not called a parliament. The Welsh voted 50.3 percent yes, which was enough for Prime Minister Blair to claim support for this policy and indicate that he would pursue that direction in future policy.

In 1998 the Parliament of the United Kingdom passed three distinct devolution acts: the Scotland Act 1998, the Northern Ireland Act 1998, and the Government of Wales Act 1998 (which was later amended by the Government of Wales Act 2006). These acts formally established the three devolved legislatures and authorized them to exercise some powers previously held at Westminster.

On December 2, 1999, Britain officially created a new provincial government in Northern Ireland, and devolution took another step forward. Northern Ireland on that day received home rule for the first time in many years. The devolution issue in relation to Northern Ireland had been wrapped up in the history of religious violence there, with Protestant and Catholic paramilitary groups there fighting since 1922, so devolution could proceed only as far as the status of the peace process would permit it. Under what was called the **Mitchell Agreement**— named after former US senator George Mitchell, who chaired a committee that worked on a peace agreement for Northern Ireland—much authority over policy in Northern Ireland would move from London to Belfast, and government of the province would come from a new local assembly and cabinet.[17]

There are some important differences between Parliament and the devolved legislatures, the key one being the way members are elected. All members of the Parliament are elected by what we called earlier a single-member-district plurality system, or "first past the post" election, where the person who receives the most votes in a given riding (district) is the winner. In both the Scottish Parliament and the National Assembly for Wales, members of the legislatures are elected using either a district and the single-member-district plurality structure, or a region using proportional voting. No matter how they are elected, they have equal roles. All members in the Northern Ireland Assembly are elected on the basis of what is called the single transferable vote version of proportional representation.[18]

It is important to note, though, that even after the movement for devolution, the national Parliament in London remains the ultimate sovereign power. This is the key distinction between a federal system on one hand and a unitary system with devolved power on the other. In the latter case the national legislature "retains the power to amend the devo-lution Acts or to legislate on anything that has been devolved. That said, the government has made clear it will not normally legislate on a devolved matter without the consent of the devolved legislature, which requires a Legislative Consent Motion."[19]

Executive Structures

The British case is the source of the "split executive" parliamentary model that was described earlier in this text. The role of the monarch is one that has evolved over a long period of time; its function is one of both substance and style. Indeed, the noted English author George Orwell observed in 1944 that "in a dictatorship the power and the glory belong to the same person. In England the real power belongs to unpre-possessing men in bowler hats: the creature who rides in a gilded coach behind soldiers in steel breast-plates is really a waxwork. It is at any rate possible that while this division of functions exists a Hitler or a Stalin cannot come to power."[20]

The Monarch

In our discussion of the political executive in Chapter 4, a brief outline of the evolution—and perhaps *devolution* is the more appropriate term—of the power of the British monarchy was presented. We saw that while at one point the monarch had absolute power to promulgate laws, fire the legislature, and imprison political opponents, the situation changed radically (but gradually) over time. As democratic institutions became popular, they also became powerful, and the ability of the monarch who happened to be in power at the time to resist reform diminished. Monarchs more sympathetic to liberal ideas, such as William and Mary (proclaimed king and queen by Parliament in 1688), helped the process to maintain, and to increase, its momentum.

Today, not even William and Mary would recognize the relationship that exists between the monarch and the Parliament. De jure, under law, most powers of British government are still exercised in the name of the king or queen, but in reality, de facto, today they are almost all exer-cised "on the advice" of the chief executive, the prime minister. And in reality, the monarch would not reject that advice.

In the eighteenth century, the king relied more and more on his cab-inet—a group of advisers—for guidance. In the early eighteenth cen-tury, the role of the cabinet was only that of providing advice; the king still did as he pleased. As ideas of democratic government grew over the next two centuries, the power relationship changed so that the king was obligated in terms of history and culture (although not legally required) to accept the advice of his cabinet. Cabinet members now were exclusively drawn from the house of Parliament that was chosen by the public, namely, the House of Commons. Now the cabinet was in reality governing in the name of the king without consulting him.

> The monarch has the constitutional right, as Bagehot put it, to be consulted, to advise, and to warn. When Anthony Eden resigned as Foreign Secretary in 1938, King George VI protested to **Neville Chamberlain**, the Prime Minister, that he had not been kept properly informed. It is clearly a valuable safeguard that Prime Ministers should be under such an obligation, and should have to bear it in mind when they may be tempted to arbitrary action. Cabinet papers, Foreign Office dispatches from overseas posts, and major departmental memoranda are sent to the Monarch.[21]

"The elaborate pretense that the Queen is still the real ruler of Britain still decorates the machinery of British government," has noted one observer. Two examples of what can be called a **royal pretense** can be offered here by way of illustration. All Royal Commissions begin with a message from the monarch: "Greeting! Now Know Ye That We, reposing great trust and confidence in your knowledge and ability." And legislative acts begin with the words "Be it enacted by the Queen's most Excellent Majesty, by and with the advice and consent of the Lords Spiritual and Temporal, and Commons, in this present Parliament assembled."[22] While both of these messages seem to be indicating that the monarch really is considering alternatives, in fact this is not the case, and the monarch has no real decision in the matter at all.

One of the most visible examples of the royal pretense occurs on an annual basis when the monarch opens the session of Parliament, seated on her throne in the House of Lords. She "summons the Commons" to the chamber of the House of Lords and reads her **Speech from the Throne**, in which she outlines the plans she has for "her" government, what she wants "her" government to do in the coming parliamentary session.[23] The fraud here, of course, is that the speech that she reads is written by the prime minister and cabinet; like a puppet, she says what she is told to say.[24]

Selection of the Chief Executive

Among the most striking characteristics of British parliamentary government today is the duality of its executive leadership. The monarch is the official or legal (de jure) head of state, the head of state in law, but the active (de facto) head of government, *the* head of government in fact, is the prime minister. Appointments are made, acts of Parliament are proclaimed, policy is proposed, and all government is carried on in the name of the monarch. It is the prime minister and his or her cabinet, however, who make all the selections for appointments, who author or sponsor legislative proposals, and who make the administrative decisions that keep government running.

The legal claim to power of the cabinet rests in the fact that, since the seventeenth century, the monarch has had a Privy Council to advise him or her—a kind of present-day cabinet. In the earliest days of British government, the Privy Council was the focus of governmental power, but as the British Constitution has evolved over the years, so, too, has the Privy Council. Today, although the Privy Council is no longer active, cabinet members must first be made members of the Privy Council, and then are appointed to the cabinet. There are today over 650 Privy Councilors, since appointment to the Privy Council is a lifetime designation.[25] Cabinet membership may change frequently, and individuals may leave the cabinet; they do not leave the Privy Council. Today the Privy Council continues to meet, but its day-to-day business is done by cabinet members.

Normally the Privy Council meets once each month, but the student can discern how important the meetings really are by the fact that a quorum—the minimum number of members required to be in attendance to do business—is three (out of over 650 members), and in some special cases business can be transacted with only two members in attendance. Typically these are both members of the cabinet. Customarily the meetings take place with the sovereign in attendance, and the sovereign remains standing so that meetings will be kept short.[26]

As noted earlier, the cabinet meets as a subcommittee of the (inactive) Privy Council and acts in the name of the Privy Council. "The Privy Council has survived as the formal machinery through which the monarch exercises her prerogative powers when necessary. Although membership of the Privy Council is extensive . . . its working character is that of a small number of ministers who are called together to witness the signature by the monarch of some formal document."[27]

Although long ago the British monarch was free to choose whomever he or she wanted as advisers, this is no longer the case today. As soon as election returns are in, if an incumbent prime minister's party has lost its majority, that person submits their resignation to the queen, and subsequently the new majority leader in the House of Commons is "invited" to form a Government. Symbolically the act is described as "the Queen has invited Mrs. May to form a Government." This is not a realistic description of the process today; there really is no alternative for the queen to the invitation that is issued.

"In theory, the Queen has the right both to dissolve parliament and to choose the prime minister"—however, the first power has not really been exercised in the past hundred years; the second power "only recently has become a fiction."[28] This lack of real power in the selection of a prime minister is the result of clear majorities existing in the House of Commons with "obvious" prime ministerial choices. Should some future election produce an inconclusive result, with no clear majority present in the House of Commons, the monarch may again be called upon to take a meaningful and substantive part in the selection process.

The Cabinet and the Prime Minister

In his classic work on the British Cabinet, Sir Ivor Jennings wrote in 1951 that "it is a peculiarity of our Constitution that the principles governing the formation and working of the Cabinet and its relations with Parliament can be stated with hardly any reference to the law."[29] In 1937, the British Parliament finally took statutory notice of the cabinet when it passed the Ministers of the Crown Act, naming a number of "cabinet rank" positions.[30]

The development of the position of prime minister has followed the evolution of the cabinet itself. As suggested earlier, the earliest of cabinets were collections of advisers to monarchs. Cabinet members held little real power, and none was first among the group of equals. George I (who ruled from 1714 to 1727) started the practice of having his cabinet meet in his absence. The result of this "was to transform what had been a mere inner group of royal advisors into a board of government with an independent existence of its own. Having lost its natural president [the King], it was inevitable that it should find one of its own, a 'prime minister' in fact, upon whom would fall the task of coordinating policy, which before had been the King's."[31]

The first "modern" British prime minister is usually cited as being **Sir Robert Walpole**, who held office from 1721 to 1742. Ever since World War II, the styles of prime ministers have varied, and the range of roles played by the prime minister "has prompted a long-running debate about the power of the Prime Minister between 'the presidential school' and 'the chairmanship school.'"[32]

The prime minister is first minister of the cabinet, but the power of that position varies widely depending upon the political environment of the time. Some British prime ministers have had much power; others have simply been in the role of "chairman of the board," coordinating action among a number of powerful actors. "Viewed from the top, British government looks more like a mountain range than a single pyramid of power. The Prime Minister is preeminent among these peaks, but the political significance of this preeminence is ambiguous."[33]

Although the prime minister has traditionally received the bulk of the attention of scholarship related to the executive branch of government in Britain, there has been some scholarship in recent years focusing upon the cabinet itself. It is the ministers, after all, who are responsible for gathering resources for public programs. And it is the ministers who are in a position to oversee and—to some degree—direct the vast civil service, a subject to which we shall return momentarily.[34]

The individual ministries are also important because they may serve as a step on the way to the prime ministership for a given individual. Some ministries (such as Treasury or Defense) have more status than others (such as Agriculture or the Welsh Office).[35] In any event, it is rare that individuals become prime minister without having served in other cabinet capacities first.

Individual ministers have several different constituencies that must be kept in mind as they perform their jobs. First, they must direct their own specific ministries, thus being in a position of responsibility for a vast network of civil service employees. Second, they must be aware of and responsible to Parliament, for the Government as a whole is responsible to Parliament for what it does. Third, they must respond to the needs and desires of the public outside of Westminster, including their own political parties, trade unions, chambers of commerce, professional organizations and interest groups, as well as international factors.[36]

The cabinet has varied in size in this century, ranging from just over a dozen to over two dozen members. As of 2018 it has twenty-three full members,[37] although in 2009 under Labour prime minister **Gordon Brown** it reached thirty-one members in size and was criticized as being "too big to make decisions."[38] Current membership of the cabinet is illustrated in Box 15.1. The prime minister is guided in cabinet selections by a number of factors:

- The need to include as many of the leading members of his party as possible and to represent the various groups and shades of opinion.
- The convenience of having a reasonable number of reliable friends and close supporters.
- The need to achieve adequate coordination between departments.
- The desirability of avoiding friction and jealousy between the "ins" and the "outs" as well as to silence potential critics.[39]

The role of the prime minister in the British political system can be analytically broken down into seven different components.[40] First, the prime minister is concerned with party management. The prime minister holds that office precisely because he or she is head of their party in

---

Box 15.1   The British Cabinet

Prime Minister, First Lord of the Treasury, and Minister for
the Civil Service: Theresa May
First Secretary of State, Minister for the Cabinet Office:
Damian Green
Chancellor of the Exchequer: Philip Hammond
Secretary of State for the Home Department: Amber Rudd
Secretary of State for Foreign and Commonwealth Affairs:
Boris Johnson
Secretary of State for Exiting the European Union: David Davis
Secretary of State for Defence: Gavin Williamson
Secretary of State for Health: Jeremy Hunt
Lord Chancellor and Secretary of State for Justice: David Lidington
Secretary of State for Education, Minister for Women and Equalities:
Justine Greening
Secretary of State for International Trade and President of the
Board of Trade: Liam Fox
Secretary of State for Business, Energy, and Industrial Strategy:
Greg Clark
Secretary of State for Environment, Food, and Rural Affairs:
Michael Gove
Secretary of State for Transport: Chris Grayling
Secretary of State for Communities and Local Government:
Sajid Javid
Leader of the House of Lords, Lord Privy Seal: Baroness Evans of
Bowes Park
Secretary of State for Scotland: David Mundell
Secretary of State for Wales: Alun Cairns
Secretary of State for Northern Ireland: James Brokenshire
Secretary of State for International Development: Penny Mordaunt
Secretary of State for Digital, Culture, Media, and Sport:
Karen Bradley
Secretary of State for Work and Pensions: David Gauke
Chancellor of the Duchy of Lancaster: Sir Patrick McLoughlin

Source: Government of the United Kingdom, "Gov.UK: Ministers," https://www
.gov.uk/government/ministers.

---

the House of Commons, and prime ministers must be careful to maintain party support. One way to do this is through party patronage—
appointments to either cabinet-level or subcabinet-level positions. A
majority of the 650 members currently serving in the House of Commons is 326; by the time a prime minister appoints about twenty MPs to

cabinet positions, and another sixty to subcabinet-rank positions, and yet another two to three dozen to positions of parliamentary private secretary, this individual has a bloc of almost one-third of the votes necessary for remaining in office.

The Government exists because it controls a majority in the House of Commons. The ultimate weapon of the Government to keep its party members in control is the power of dissolution, but this is too severe a threat to bandy about lightly. "The majority must be treated with respect and given reasonably full information in response to questions. . . . Even the strongest Governments have been known to bow to 'the sense of the House.'"[41]

The second major job of a prime minister involves the timing and winning of a general election. Winning a national election is necessary for a prime minister to retain their power. (The current prime minister, **Theresa May**, was first elected Conservative MP for Maidenhead in 1997, served as home secretary from 2010 to 2016, and became prime minister in July 2016 when **David Cameron** resigned following the British vote to leave the European Community. The election of 2017 was her first as prime minister.) Only the prime minister has the power to choose a date for a national election (and to advise the queen to dissolve Parliament and call for an election on a given day). Prime ministers want to set election dates such that balloting day corresponds to their parties' popular periods, not with inevitable slippages in popularity.

A third dimension of activity for the prime minister involves their image in Parliament. Contacts in both the majority and opposition parties must be nurtured. Until World War II, the prime minister was personally "Leader of the House of Commons." Since that time other requirements have prevented the prime minister from holding this position personally, but the prime minister must still be aware of, and concerned with, happenings in the House of Commons.

Related to this is a fourth facet of the prime minister's role, participating in **parliamentary question time**. Twice a week the prime minister appears in the House of Commons to answer parliamentary questions, primarily from the members of the Opposition. Prime ministers take this activity seriously, as a poor performance can affect both their image in Parliament and their image with the public. One student of this phenomenon indicated that "on two nights a week the Prime Minister receives up to three boxes of files in preparation for the next day's ordeal, reading these ahead of Cabinet papers or Foreign Office telegrams."[42]

Yet another dimension of the prime minister's activity involves debating policy. Research has shown that in a typical year the prime minister will participate in only six major debates, which are usually on only three issues: international affairs, the economy, and the business of the Government.[43] As far as general debate is concerned, the prime minister usually has ministers in charge of relevant departments articulate the Government's position in a debate.

Prime ministers are also concerned with press publicity. The prime minister, after all, must worry about the general image of their Government. Generally speaking, the press is happy to oblige the prime minister with media attention; this is an example of a symbiotic relationship in which both the prime minister and the press profit from media coverage of the prime minister.

The seventh and final component of behavior of the prime minister is one to which we have already alluded: chairing the cabinet. The once or twice a week that the prime minister sits down with the heads of the various departments of government allows for crucial policy discussion to take place, as well as for communication of problems from ministers to the prime minister. All cabinet members are affected by the principle of "collective responsibility." This means that the cabinet as a whole is responsible for acts of the Government, and no member of cabinet may attack or criticize actions of the Government after a collective policy decision has been made.

Margaret Thatcher, Thatcherism, and the Prime Minister's Position

The arrival of **Margaret Thatcher** as prime minister in May 1979 affected British politics significantly and "changed the nature of contemporary Conservatism" in Britain.[44] Thatcher's strong antisocialist and antiunion style was not an example of a consensual style of leadership. She knew what she wanted to accomplish, and she worked in a determined manner to accomplish it. She introduced a style to contemporary British politics that came to be known first as "conviction politics," and subsequently as **Thatcherism**.[45] If this meant engaging in an ideological battle within her own party, she was quite willing to do so. Indeed, many observers of British politics indicated that "the main feature of the first Thatcher administration was the Prime Minister's near total dominance over economic policy formation."[46]

When Thatcher moved into 10 Downing Street (the official home of the prime minister) in 1979 the British economy was weak. She sought to turn the economy around, to a substantial degree through legislation nullifying many of the socialist policies that had been guiding the economy for years under a Labour government, and engaging in direct conflict with the powerful labor unions.[47]

The Thatcher Government privatized (sold off to private business interests) a number of government-owned industries, for instance overseeing the conversion of British Telecom from a government-run business to being a private corporation with stockholders.[48] Her Government cut subsidies, reduced services, and fought with local governments that—often still controlled by the Labour opposition party—sought to move into policy areas vacated by the central government.

Ultimately, Thatcher's "conviction style" of politics—specifically her insistence on new taxes and her opposition to further integrating Britain into the European economy—alienated even most of her supporters in the Conservative Party. In November 1990, Thatcher's leadership of the Conservative Party was challenged by former (Conservative) defense minister Michael Heseltine. Heseltine received enough votes on the first ballot of the party leadership vote to convince Thatcher that she would not win, and she indicated that she would resign as leader and prime minister once the party selected a new leader. On the next ballot, it was not Heseltine, but Thatcher's handpicked successor, **John Major**, who was elected leader of the Conservative Party. The day after that vote, Margaret Thatcher visited the queen to submit her resignation, and the queen "invited" John Major to form a Government.

John Major tried to steer a more moderate Conservative line. The Conservative Party was reelected under Major's leadership in April 1992. That reelection—the fourth straight win for the Conservative Party—showed that a substantial proportion of the British public supported his record.

Unfortunately for Major and the Conservatives—perhaps simply as a result of the Conservative Party being in power for so long—the public's support for Major's Government and his leadership started to decline, sharply, by the middle 1990s. This trend was intensified by the change in the leadership of the Labour Party and the very skillful campaigning of Tony Blair as a "new" (that is, moderate) Labour leader. Blair called for a "national renewal," and moved the Labour Party closer to the political center of British politics. He emphasized that after eighteen years of rule the Conservative Party "was tired," and he worked hard to tie John Major to the policies of Margaret Thatcher. At the time of the 1997 election, he was able to convince a substantial majority of British voters that Labour no longer represented the "threat" to Britain that Margaret Thatcher had described years earlier, and that Labour would be more responsive to the contemporary needs of the British public than the entrenched leadership of the Conservative Party. Labour won the 1997 election handily, and Blair became, at age forty-three, the youngest prime minister since the early nineteenth century, serving until June 2007.[49]

Blair was a successful prime minister, serving longer than any other Labour Party PM (the next longest-serving Labour PM was **Clement Attlee**, who served from 1945 to 1951) and leading the party to three consecutive general election victories. He presided over a moderated Labour Party, which likely was why he managed to stay in power for as long as he did. Although his Government increased spending on health and education during his tenure in office, it also was careful about significant tax increases during its time in office, too. Blair also opposed adopting the euro as the currency to replace the British pound, a policy position that was supported by the British public. Blair oversaw the signing of the Belfast Agreement, a peace agreement and framework for government of Northern Ireland. Other significant acts during Blair's term as prime minister included constitutional change with the Human Rights Act of 1998, devolution of power with a Scottish Parliament and a Welsh Assembly, and the removal of most hereditary peers from the House of Lords in 1999. He emphasized the importance of the National Health Service and public education.

In 2007, after serving two full terms as prime minister (1997–2001, 2001–2005, and being reelected in 2005 for a third term), Blair announced that after ten years he thought he had served long enough, and stepped down in September 2007. As had been the case with his Conservative predecessor, Blair's popularity in office was bound to start to fade; in local elections held in May 2006 the Labour Party had lost over 300 local council seats around the UK, and Blair felt that it was time that he step down.

Blair was succeeded as Labour leader and prime minister by Gordon Brown, who had served as Blair's chancellor of the Exchequer. Unfortunately for Brown, despite his being a different individual from Tony Blair, the public was ready for a change in party control of government. In May 2008 Labour was dealt another clear blow in local elections, suffering its worst loss in over four decades and receiving only 24 percent of the vote.[50] In April 2010 Brown asked the queen for an early dissolution of Parliament and new elections, and those elections led in May 2010 to a coalition government—the first **hung Parliament**, in which no party received a majority, since 1974—led by David Cameron of the Conservative Party and **Nick Clegg** of the Liberal Democratic Party. Labour found itself serving as the Loyal Opposition.

David Cameron stood for reelection as prime minister in May 2015, and the Conservative Party won 331 seats in Parliament—up from 306 in the 2010 election—compared with 232 for Labour (down from 258 in 2010). On June 23, 2016, a referendum took place on whether Britain should pull out of the European Union—commonly known as **Brexit**, a combination of "British" and "exit," with Cameron campaigning for the no side, arguing that Britain would be better off in Europe than outside of Europe. The yes votes won by 52 percent to 48 percent, and the next day Cameron announced that he would resign as prime minister since a majority of the voters had rejected his position, stating, "I do not think it would be right for me to try to be the captain that steers our country to its next destination."[51]

In July 2016, Theresa May won a leadership election at a Conservative Party meeting, and she was appointed by the queen to be prime minister, facing the challenge of guiding the United Kingdom in its exit from Europe. In April 2017 she announced an early general election to take place the next month, with the goal of an increased Conservative majority, since she was still operating with Cameron's 50.9 percent of the seats in the House of Commons from the 2015 election. When the election took place on June 8, 2017, the Conservative Party ended up losing seats, going from 331 to 318, while Labour went from 232 to 262 and the Liberal Democrats went from 8 to 12,[52] generating another hung Parliament in which the Conservatives combined with Northern Ireland's Democratic Unionist Party to create a minority Government.

Legislative Structures

In the British case, a bicameral national legislature is not a reflection of a federal regime as is the case in the United States, Germany, Mexico, India, Australia, or Canada. Instead, it is a result of a class-conscious society and political evolution. Recall that for a brief period of time, from 1649 to 1660, the **House of Commons** declared that the **House of Lords** "was useless and dangerous," and it was accordingly "wholly abolished and taken away."[53] The House of Lords was revived in 1660, and since that time the relationship between the two houses has passed through three distinct phases. The first phase, from 1660 to 1810, saw a period of general predominance of the House of Lords, although the House of Commons was not without influence.

Between 1811 and 1911 a number of changes took place that affected the relationship between the two houses. The Reform Acts of 1832, 1867, and 1884 strengthened the House of Commons in relation to the House of Lords. These reflected the idea that the cabinet should be responsible to the House of Commons (and should, therefore, resign if the House of Commons should fail to support its policies) and clearly limited the future role of the House of Lords.

When the House of Lords rejected a number of Government bills that had passed the House of Commons in 1910, the Government pushed through the Parliament Act of 1911, which limited the power of the Lords in two very significant aspects: (1) money bills could only be delayed by the House of Lords for one month after being approved by the House of Commons, and then they became law even without the approval of the Lords; and (2) other public bills could be delayed for up to two years, after which time they would become law with only the approval of the Commons. (This period was shortened to one year by the Parliament Act of 1949.) The Parliament Act of 1911, which institutionalized these two radical limitations on the power of the House of Lords, was approved by the Lords only after it became clear that if they failed to do so the king was prepared to appoint enough new members of the House of Lords sympathetic to the bill to guarantee its passage.[54]

The third phase, from 1911 to the present time, has seen the House of Commons as the clearly dominant power in the relationship. The House of Lords no longer challenges major legislative policy of the Government. It may occasionally revise or amend bills, and it has been known to oppose outright acts of the Commons, but under the Parliament Act of 1911 its power to influence policy of the Government is severely limited.[55]

The House of Lords

One of the major roles of the House of Lords historically has been not legislative at all, but judicial.[56] The House of Lords inherited a number of judicial functions from the Curia Regis, and until 2009 (when the Supreme Court of the United Kingdom came into existence) a subgroup of the House of Lords served as the supreme judicial tribunal of the United Kingdom. Originally, the entire House of Lords acted as an appeals court; in 1876 an act was passed (the Appellate Jurisdiction Act) allowing for the appointment to the House of Lords of "Lords of Appeal in Ordinary," holding peerage for life—essentially the equivalent of justices on the US Supreme Court, who are appointed for life—called **Law Lords**. They were required to have held high judicial office for at least two years or to have been practicing for at least fifteen years. Their membership in the House of Lords was only for those individuals and would not be hereditary and thereby passed to their children.

The functions of the House of Lords today can be said to have four components:

1. The examination and revision of Bills brought from the House of Commons. . . .
2. The initiation of Bills dealing with subjects of a comparatively non-controversial character. . . .

3. The interposition of so much delay (and no more) in the passing of a Bill into law as may be needed to enable the opinion of the nation to be adequately expressed upon it. . . .
4. Full and free discussion of large and important questions.[57]

Much of the time of the House of Lords is devoted to the review of legislation, as indicated in Box 15.2.

Early in its existence, prior to the seventeenth century, "there were usually between seventy and one hundred persons who sat in the House of Lords in response to the King's writ of summons."[58] As of December 2017 there are 802 members of the House of Lords, made up of three groups: elected hereditary peers, archbishops and bishops, and life peers, as indicated in Table 15.1.

One response to the demand for reform of the House of Lords was the introduction of the **life peerage**. Since the late nineteenth century, more and more members of the House of Lords were appointed as life peers. They served as members of the House of Lords as long as they lived, but their titles were not passed to their heirs as was the case with normal peerages. The Life Peerages Act of 1958 resulted in a great

---

Box 15.2   Tasks of the House of Lords

Key functions of the House of Lords include

- Working on behalf of the UK public.
- Making effective laws.
- Holding the Government to account.
- Investigating and influencing public policy
- Reaching out to connect people with the House of Lords.
- Representing the United Kingdom on the international stage.

How time is spent:

- Legislation: 57 percent (bills 47 percent, statutory instruments 10 percent).
- Scrutiny: 40 percent (debates 30 percent, questions 6 percent, statements 4 percent).
- Other: 3 percent.

Sources: House of Lords, *Work of the House of Lords* 2016–2017 (London, 2017), p. 40; Government of the United Kingdom, "Work of the House of Lords, 2016–2017," http://www.parliament.uk/business/lords/work-of-the-house-of-lords/work-of-the-house-of-lords-2016-17.

Table 15.1   The House of Lords, December 2017

By Party	Number	Women	By Type	Number
Conservative	253	63	Life Peers[a]	718
Labour	201	63	Excepted Hereditary Peers[b]	92
Liberal-Democrat	102	35	Bishops[c]	25
Crossbench	177	42	Not sitting	25 leave-of-absence
Bishops	25	2		8 senior members of judiciary
Other	44	4		
Total	802	209 (26%)		802
Women: 147 (20%)				

Sources: Government of the United Kingdom, House of Lords, *Work of the House of Lords, 2016–2017* (London, 2017), p. 40; "Members of the House of Lords," http://www.parliament .uk/mps-lords-and-offices/lords/?amp;type=0&sort=2&type=0.

Notes: a. Life Peers are appointed for their lifetime only; these Lords' titles are not passed on to their children; the queen formally appoints Life Peers on the advice and recommendation of the prime minister.

b. The right of Hereditary Peers to sit and vote in the House of Lords was ended in 1999 by the House of Lords Act, but 92 members were elected internally to remain until the next stage of the Lords reform process.

c. A limited number of 25 Church of England archbishops and bishops sit in the House, passing their membership on to the next most senior bishop when they retire. The archbishops of Canterbury and York traditionally get life peerages on retirement.

increase in the number of life peers in the House of Lords, with few new hereditary peerages being created after 1964. As noted in Table 15.1, the appointment of hereditary peers—where children would inherit their parents' seats—to sit in the House of Lords was ended in 1999 by the House of Lords Act, but at that time 92 of the more than 700 members were elected by their fellows in the Lords to stay as members for the duration of their terms (their lives).[59]

In 1948 many in British society suggested that women should be permitted to serve in the House of Lords, but the tradition-conscious House of Lords opposed the idea. Peeresses, women who inherited a seat in the House of Lords from their fathers in the absence of a male heir, were forbidden from sitting and voting in the House of Lords. This policy has since been changed, and today over 25 percent of the Lords are women.[60]

Only since 1963 has it been possible for individuals to resign from the House of Lords, to renounce their peerages. Traditionally, one could not renounce one's title, and since the law forbade individuals from serving in both houses of Parliament, if a member of the House of Commons had a father who was a peer in the House of Lords, and his father died, that Commons member had to resign his seat in the Commons and take his father's seat in the Lords. He could not simply renounce his new peerage and stay in the Commons (which was the more important of the two legislative houses). In 1948, party leaders in Parliament agreed to allow peers to renounce their positions, thus allowing members of the House of Commons who "accidentally" became peers to retain their elected positions.[61]

Reform of the House of Lords has continued over time. In 1999 the House of Lords Act removed the right of most hereditary peers to remain as members of the House and reduced the size of the Lords from 1,330 (October 1999) to 669 (March 2000). An amendment to that act permitted ninety-two hereditary peers to remain until the House was fully reformed. Today there are several different ways that an individual can become a member of the House of Lords, including

> a. House of Lords Appointments Commission: Set up in May 2000, this independent, public body recommends individuals for appointment as non-party-political life peers and vets nominations for life peers to ensure the highest standards of propriety.
> b. Dissolution Honours: Takes place at the end of a Parliament, when peerages can be given to MPs—from all parties—who are leaving the House of Commons.
> c. Resignation Honours: Resigning Prime Ministers can recommend peerages for fellow politicians, political advisors or others who have supported them.
> d. Political lists/"working Peers": Lords appointed to boost the strengths of the three main parties. Regular attendance in the House is expected, usually on the frontbench as a spokesman or whip. The media has dubbed these Members "working Peers."
> e. Ad hoc announcements: Used to announce someone appointed as a Minister who is not already a Lord.
> f. Archbishops and bishops: The number of bishops in the House has been limited to 26 since the mid-nineteenth century. If a vacancy comes up the most senior serving bishop is appointed. The Archbishops of Canterbury and York usually get life peerages on retirement.
> g. Speakers: Traditionally, peerages are awarded to former Speakers of the House of Commons.[62]

The House of Commons

We saw earlier that the original reason for being of the House of Commons was a fund-raising one; the king needed to raise more money than the House of Lords could provide for the nation's budget, and politically he could do so only by summoning representatives of the public to Parliament. Early Parliaments were primarily concerned with two tasks: first, they agreed to requests from the king for money; second, as a quid pro quo for giving the king money, they presented the king with petitions of grievances.

The nineteenth century was a century of reform for the House of Commons. The Reform Act of 1867 allowed all householders to vote, as well as all persons occupying lodgings of an annual value of 10 pounds sterling or more. Similar measures were enacted for Scotland and Ireland in 1868. The Ballot Act of 1872 brought secret voting, and a Reform Act of 1884 further expanded suffrage. (Women over age thirty were first allowed to vote in 1918; in 1928 requirements for women to vote were made the same as those for men.)[63]

The development of the cabinet in the eighteenth century greatly changed the role of the House of Commons.[64] The Speaker was originally perceived as the king's representative in the House; by 1640 the Speaker was the representative of the House of Commons to the king. Today, the Speaker has great power to control debate and legislation. Speakers are elected by a new House of Commons immediately after a general election: the majority party nominates a candidate who invariably wins on a party-line vote.

Legislation

There are a number of different types of legislation in the British House of Commons. We can initially distinguish in Britain between Government bills and private members' bills, something that we introduced in Chapter 3. Government bills are bills that are introduced and sponsored by the cabinet, and to which strong party discipline is applied. Private members' bills are proposals for legislation that are introduced by non-cabinet members (including members of the majority party who are not in the cabinet, as well as by members of all of the opposition parties).

Private members' bills are legally restricted in only one way: they may not deal with money, either raising it or spending it. Moreover, private member bills are placed on a separate calendar, usually handled only on Friday afternoons, and few members of Parliament even have the opportunity to introduce their own proposals over the course of a legislative session due to the limitation of time.[65]

Since there would not be time in a legislative session for all members of Parliament who wanted to submit private members' bills of their own to do so, a "ballot," or drawing, is held at the beginning of each session to determine which members of Parliament will have the opportunity to introduce their own pieces of legislation.[66]

Besides distinguishing between bills on the basis of who introduces them in the House of Commons, we can also distinguish between bills in terms of their subject: What do the proposed pieces of legislation intend to do? Public bills are drafts of new laws that would affect the country as a whole, such as tax law, criminal law, regulation policy, and so on. Private bills have individual application only, such as a special act of citizenship.[67]

The legislative process in the House of Commons involves the "standard" parliamentary procedure that we covered earlier in this text.[68] After bills are passed in the House of Commons they are sent to the House of Lords. As indicated earlier, if the House of Lords does not approve a bill, it no longer can kill the bill but can only delay its eventual passage.

A final, special procedure should be mentioned here that relates again to the royal pretense mentioned earlier. Bills approved by both houses of Parliament must be given the **royal assent** (approval by the queen) before they become law. Ever since 1707 this royal assent has not been refused to a bill that has passed both houses of Parliament. The monarch has not given the royal assent in person since 1854; today it is done by a commission.

> The title of each Bill which is to receive the Assent is read, and the Assent is signified by the Clerk of the Parliaments. The assenting formula is still given in Norman French. For Public Bills, and Private Bills of a local character, it is "La reine le veult" (the Queen wishes it). For Private Bills of a personal character the formula is "Soit fait comme il est desire" (let what is desired be done). The formula for Bills granting supply or imposing taxation is "La reine remercie ses bons sujets, accepte leur benevolence, et ainsi le veult" (the Queen thanks her good subjects, accepts their benevolence, and so wishes it). The formula for refusing the assent was formerly "La reine s'avisera" (the Queen will consider the matter).[69]

The Civil Service

The civil service is an integral part of British government and politics. When cabinet ministers seek to have policy put into operation, it is through the civil service that they operate. The civil service is, ostensibly, nonpolitical, and its function is to administer the policies of the government of the day.[70]

Over time it has been made clear that the civil servant is an apolitical employee of the government. As of the end of June 2017, nearly 392,000 civil servants work for the British government (down from a high of 732,000 in 1979), about one-sixth of them working in the inner London area.[71] Since 2010 the size of the civil service has been reduced by 95,000 positions, or about 20 percent. Women make up 54 percent of the civil service.[72]

Members of the civil service focus on providing services directly to the public, including paying benefits and pensions, running employment services, running prisons, issuing driving licenses, as well as policy analysis, project management, and legal and economic analysis.[73] Only a small proportion of them are high-ranking policymakers; the vast majority are individuals working in offices of government agencies around the nation. A recent study of the British civil service recognized twenty-eight professions included within it (see Box 15.3).

Box 15.3   The British Civil Service

Corporate finance
Counter-fraud standards
Digital, data, and technology
Government communication
Government economic service
Government finance
Government information technology
Government knowledge and information management
Government legal service
Government occupational psychology
Government operational research
Government planning
Government planning inspection
Government property
Government science and engineering
Government security
Government social research
Government statistical service
Government tax profession
Government veterinary profession
Human resources
Intelligence analysis
Internal audit
Medical profession
Operational delivery
Policy
Procurement
Project delivery

Source: Government of the United Kingdom, "Civil Service: About Us," https://www.gov.uk/government/organisations/civil-service/about.

Recent Governments have been concerned with the higher ranks of the civil service because "civil service and administrative reforms have been seen as intimately linked to the 'sharp end' of the Government's policy outputs."[74] The high-ranking civil servants, sometimes referred to as "Mandarins" (the term comes from China, where *Mandarens* were "Manchu officials"), play an important role in government.[75] One study of this relationship has concluded that "civil servants have more influence, and ministers less, than constitutional theory suggests."[76]

Local Government

Another level of government in Great Britain that cannot be ignored is the local level. Although we earlier referred to Britain as a unitary and not a federal government because all sovereignty is based at Westminster, the central government has decentralized many governmental functions, and local government is often significant in Britain because it is the level of the administration of much domestic policy.

A significant role for local government has a long history in Britain, going back to the early nineteenth century. The role of local government became more political after the arrival of Thatcherism began to reshape many fundamental domestic policies of the central government. In regions of Britain where Thatcher's Conservative Party was very unpopular, local governments sought to continue many of the programs that Thatcher was discontinuing or cutting back at the national level.[77]

The Supreme Court

The Supreme Court of the United Kingdom was created in the Constitutional Reform Act of 2005 and took effect in October 2009. Through this legislation the new Court took over the functions that had been exercised by the House of Lords for over 600 years, more precisely exercised by the subgroup of the House of Lords referred to as the Law Lords, who were appointed specifically for that purpose. The role of the Supreme Court is to "play an important role in the development of United Kingdom law,"[78] as well as being the final court of appeal in the United Kingdom. According to the Supreme Court itself, its role includes the following:

- it is the final court of appeal for all United Kingdom civil cases, and criminal cases from England, Wales, and Northern Ireland;
- it hears appeals on arguable points of law of general public importance;

- it concentrates on cases of the greatest public and constitutional importance;
- it maintains and develops the role of the highest court in the United Kingdom as a leader in the common law world.[79]

The transfer of judicial functions from a subgroup of the House of Lords to an independent Supreme Court was meant to be significant in British constitutional development. "The Supreme Court was established to achieve a complete separation between the United Kingdom's senior Judges and the Upper House of Parliament, emphasizing the independence of the Law Lords and increasing the transparency between Parliament and the courts."[80] It even moved out of the building where the Law Lords had been sitting to a new site in its own building, across Parliament Square from the House of Lords.

The separation of the Supreme Court from the House of Lords did not change one very important characteristic of British politics, however: there still is no power of judicial review exercised by the Supreme Court, and laws passed by Parliament cannot be nullified by the Court. Many educated observers of the British (unwritten) Constitution believe, however, that this birth of a new constitutional structure in the United Kingdom has opened the door for major constitutional change. As one commentator has noted,

> No one suggests yet that the UK Supreme Court will follow its namesakes in the United States and Israel by declaring statutes unconstitutional. It is worth remembering, however, that the US Supreme Court justices did so in 1803 without explicit powers under their country's constitution and so did their Israeli counterparts in 1995, without a written constitution at all. Lord Collins, however, one of the law lords who will move to the new court in October, predicts that his colleagues will evolve over time into a different type of body—"perhaps not so pivotal as the American Supreme Court, but certainly playing a much more central role in the legal system and approaching the American ideal of a government of laws and not of men."[81]

Political Parties and Elections

It has been suggested by a noted scholar that "British government is party government."[82] Parties organize electoral activity, including the selection of candidates in elections, the construction of programs, and the operation of election campaigns. In the general elections, voters vote not so much for the individual candidates whose names appear on the ballot papers, but rather for the party "team" with which the candidate is affiliated.

Politics in Britain has also often been referred to as "the politics of class,"[83] so it should come as no surprise that support for political parties in Britain has frequently been explained in terms of class allegiances. In recent years the allegiances have been described as "Labour, representing the working community, versus the Conservatives, representing capital."[84]

However, British political parties are "unknown to the constitutional law."[85] Parties originally developed in Britain over the issue of royal power, with the Tories (later to be called the Conservatives) favoring the royalty, and the Whigs (later to become the Liberals and Labour) opposing the royalists. Around the time of their development, in 1688 or so, neither the Tories nor the Whigs could have been called political *parties* in the contemporary sense of the word.[86]

One of the early developmental problems of British political parties involved the question of opposition to the monarch.[87] The concept of a "loyal opposition" developed slowly, and not without a great deal of friction, because early on it was difficult for many to accept the notion that it was possible to be against a Government in power without being against the regime itself.[88]

By the middle of the eighteenth century the concept of a "loyal opposition" was accepted. Edmund Burke, a great British politician of his time, argued that to combine to oppose or topple the Government was not treason: "when bad men combine, the good must associate; else they will fall, one by one."[89] Parties contribute a great deal of stability to the political system, by providing the basis for the formation of Governments and by "enabling the Government, as leaders of the most powerful party in the House of Commons, to secure the passage of their programme of legislation."[90]

In the past, Britain has usually been regarded as a two-party political system. Strictly speaking, though, this is not correct. Britain was often said to have a two-party system by one measure only: the number of political parties that had formed a Government since 1945 are two—Conservative and Labour. This changed in 2010, however, with the participation in the coalition government of the Liberal Democratic Party. So, by any measure today we would have to say that Britain has a multiparty system.

This misperception about the British party system is largely a result of the relationship between electoral systems and party systems, as discussed earlier. Britain has a single-member-district plurality voting electoral system—what we earlier called a "first past the post" system. It doesn't matter whether a given candidate receives a majority of votes in a constituency as long as he or she has a plurality—more votes than any other candidate.

In the period immediately prior to the 2010 national election there was much discussion in Britain about electoral reform.

> In February 2010, the House of Commons approved government plans to hold a nationwide referendum on changing the electoral system from "first-past-the-post" to "alternative votes." . . . The Labour Party, which had pledged electoral reform in its 1997 election manifesto, argued that the new voting system was needed to restore trust in politics. The Liberal Democrats led by Mr. Nick Clegg, which have historically been a strong proponent of electoral reform, supported the plan. On the contrary, the Conservative Party argued that the current system had ensured a stable government and kept out extremists. It pledged to abolish the referendum plan if it won the general elections. Finally, the outgoing House of Commons was dissolved before the Bill could become law. . . . In the alternative votes system, voters rank candidates in order of preference. A candidate obtaining more than 50 per cent of the first choice votes is declared elected. If no candidate secures more than 50 per cent of the votes, the candidate with the fewest number of votes is eliminated and voters' second choices are allocated to the remaining candidates. This process continues until a winner emerges.[91]

There has not been a single political party that has won over half of the votes in a British parliamentary election since 1935. The closest that any party has come to a majority of the votes was in 1955 when the Conservative Party won 49.7 percent of the vote. The extreme bias of the single-member-district plurality system can be illustrated by the October 1974 election in which the Labour Party won a bare majority in the House of Commons of 319 seats (out of 635, a bare majority since 318 is the minimum number of seats that is over half of 635) with 39.2 percent of the vote, while the Liberal Party had 18.3 percent of the vote (almost half of the Labour vote), and yet received only 13 seats in the House of Commons (4 percent of the Labour total).[92]

The same general phenomenon happened in the 1997, 2001, and 2005 elections, too. In all of these elections, Labour received substantial majorities in terms of the seats in the House of Commons, but considerably less popular support. To take just one illustration, in the 2005 election results, Labour received 55 percent of the seats in the House of Commons in exchange for 35 percent of the popular vote, while the Liberal Democratic Party received less than 10 percent of the seats in exchange for 22 percent of the vote.

As can be seen from Table 15.2, this bias of vote concentration continues to exist. In the 2010 and 2015 elections both of the larger parties, Conservative and Labour, received more seats in the House of Commons than they deserved on the basis of vote percentage, while the

Table 15.2 The Bias of the British Electoral System

Party	% Vote	% Seats	Difference
2010 Election			
Conservative	36.1	47.2	+ 11.1
Labour	29.0	39.8	+ 10.8
Lib-Dem	23.0	8.0	− 15.0
Other	11.9	4.2	− 7.7
2015 Election			
Conservative	36.9	50.9	+ 14.0
Labour	30.4	35.7	+ 5.3
Lib-Dem	7.9	1.2	− 6.7
Other	24.8	12.2	− 12.6
2017 Election			
Conservative	42.4	48.9	+ 6.5
Labour	40.0	40.3	+ 0.3
Lib-Dem	7.4	1.8	− 5.6
Other	10.2	8.9	− 1.3

Source: "British Governments and Elections Since 1945," http://www.politicsresources.net/area/uk/uktable.htm.

smaller Liberal Democratic Party, other smaller parties, and the regional parties (Scottish Nationalists, Sinn Fein, Plaid Cymru) received fewer seats than they deserved.

It was indicated earlier that Theresa May became prime minister when David Cameron resigned as prime minister following the Brexit referendum in 2016. She was not elected in a national vote but was chosen by the Conservative Party to become prime minister while it controlled a majority (331 seats) in the House of Commons. Although May indicated her willingness to pursue the Brexit policy direction, she felt limited in her ability to negotiate withdrawal terms with Europe because of the narrow nature of the Brexit margin (52 percent to 48 percent) and the narrow nature of the Conservative majority in the House of Commons that had been elected in Cameron's reelection as prime minister in 2015, 50.9 percent of the seats. She decided to call a very early election, anticipating that she could increase the Conservative majority in the Commons. She called on voters to give her "a strong and stable government to get the best Brexit deal,"[93] but that isn't what happened.

As we noted earlier when the election took place on June 8, 2017, the Conservative Party ended up losing seats, going from 331 to 318 (48.9 percent of the seats), while Labour went from 232 to 262 (40.3

percent) and the Liberal Democrats went from 8 to 12 (1.8 percent),[94] generating another hung Parliament in which the Conservatives were forced to combine with Northern Ireland's Democratic Unionist Party to create a minority government, one in which the prime minister doesn't lead a majority of members of the House of Commons, but in which she leads nearly a majority. Election results are shown in Table 15.3.

Constitutionally, elections for the House of Commons must be held at least every five years. As we have seen, however, since the British Constitution is "unwritten," the constitutional parameters relating to elections are whatever the House of Commons says they should be. In 1694, the Commons passed the Triennial Act, setting the maximum term of the House at three years; in 1716 the maximum term was extended to seven years by the Septennial Act. It wasn't until 1911 that the present five-year constitutional limitation was set. Since 1911 it has usually been the case that elections have been called before the five-year limit on the life of a Parliament. Article 1(3) of the Fixed-Term Parliaments Act of 2011 indicates that "the next general elections will be held on the first Thursday in May in the fifth calendar year."[95] There have been two noteworthy exceptions to this, however. During both World War I and

Table 15.3   The 2017 British General Election

Party	Percentage of Votes	Number of Seats	Percentage of Seats
Conservative	42.4	317	48.7
Labour	40.0	262	40.3
Scottish National	3.0[a]	35[a]	5.4
Liberal Democrats	7.4[a]	12[a]	1.8
Democratic Unionist	0.9[a]	10[a]	1.5
Sinn Fein	0.7[a]	7[a]	1.0
Plaid Cymru	0.5[a]	4[a]	0.6
Green	1.6	1	0.2
Independent/Other	3.5	1	0.2
The Speaker	(runs unopposed)	1	0.2
Total		650	99.9

Source: Inter-Parliamentary Union, "Parline Database: United Kingdom—House of Commons," http://archive.ipu.org/parline-e/reports/2335_E.htm.

Note: a. The very regional parties—the Scottish National Party, the (Northern Ireland) Democratic Unionist Party, the (Northern Ireland) Sinn Fein, and the (Welsh) Plaid Cymru—received far more representation in the House of Commons than did the Liberal Democrats on a seats-per-vote basis because they are more regionally concentrated; they ran candidates in fewer districts, and their candidates came in first in more districts even though their total votes received were fewer than those of the Liberal Democrats.

World War II, Parliament decided—and legislated accordingly—to postpone elections because of the feeling that electoral uncertainty would not help the war efforts. Consequently, "the Parliament chosen in 1910 was not dissolved until the end of 1918, and there was no general election in Britain between 1935 and 1945."[96]

Essentially it can be argued that one person, the prime minister, decides when a national election will take place. Although since 1911 the Constitution has required (with the two exceptions noted) that elections be held at least every five years, in point of fact the prime minister has felt free over the years to request that the monarch dissolve Parliament and call for new elections at a time earlier than required that is an advantage to the Government in power. This was what May did in the summer of 2017, although her strategy backfired when the Conservatives lost, rather than gained, seats. Tradition requires (although technically the law does not) that the monarch grant a dissolution when one is requested by the prime minister.

One of the most remarkable differences between the British electoral process and many other electoral processes is the relative brevity of the campaign period in Britain. In the US system, for example, primaries sometimes start as much as eleven months before elections, and informal campaigning may begin significantly before that. In Britain, the Government's ability to call a "surprise" election may be a real strategic advantage; "approximately three weeks after a dissolution, the entire electorate of Britain goes to the polls."[97] Vacancies arising between general elections are filled through by-elections, elections that take place in individual "ridings," or electoral districts, as needed.[98]

The British System in Perspective

This chapter has presented few major deviations from what we learned in earlier chapters. The British political system *is* the Westminster model that we met earlier. In this presentation of the major structures in the British political system, we have briefly shown the manner in which it is possible to look at a political system using the general approach we introduced at the beginning of this text.

We have seen in this chapter that in a nation's constitutional makeup, custom and tradition may be just as important as written statutes, if not more so. The fact that it is even possible to imagine actions in the British political system that might be legal, yet unconstitutional, attests to the relative importance of the unwritten law of tradition. Britain offers a clear example of a political system in which one must be familiar with the political environment and political history of a nation before one can seriously attempt to understand how public policy is made there.

Discussion Questions

1. How would you explain to someone who has never studied this region the relationship between "England" and "Great Britain" and "United Kingdom"? Do they refer to the same thing? What are the differences?
2. What are the especially important components of the British unwritten constitution? What would be the significance if Britain had a written constitution? What would be different?
3. Britain is the model for parliamentary government. What are the key components of the British model?
4. The positions of head of state and chief executive evolved over a long period of time in British politics. Which is most significant today? Why?
5. What is the political role of the prime minister in British politics? How does the prime minister relate to other actors?
6. What would you say was the most important way that Margaret Thatcher played a crucial and possibly transformative role in modern British politics?
7. What are the differences in roles between the House of Commons and the House of Lords? Does the House of Lords play any important functions in British politics today?
8. Give an example of the importance of the concept of party discipline in British parliamentary government today.

Notes

1. Max Beloff and Gillian Peele, *The Government of the United Kingdom* (New York: Norton, 1980), p. 10. See also Elizabeth Wicks, *The Evolution of a Constitution: Eight Key Moments in British Constitutional History* (Portland: Hart, 2006); and Martin Loughlin, *The British Constitution: A Very Short Introduction* (Oxford: Oxford University Press, 2013).

2. George W. Keeton, *Government in Action in the United Kingdom* (London: Ernest Benn, 1970), pp. 29–30. See also Peter Oliver, *The Development of Constitutional Theory in Australia, Canada, and New Zealand* (Oxford: Oxford University Press, 2004); and Rodney Brazier, *Constitutional Reform* (Oxford: Oxford University Press, 2008).

3. See Zoya Hasan and Eswaran Sridharan, *India's Living Constitution: Ideas, Practices, Controversies* (London: Anthem, 2005). See also Herbert Vere Evatt, *The King and His Dominion Governors: A Study of the Reserve Powers of the Crown in Great Britain and the Dominions* (London: Routledge, 2013).

4. Hiram Stout, *British Government* (New York: Oxford University Press, 1953), p. 19. See also Peter Leyland, *The Constitution of the United Kingdom: A Contextual Analysis* (Oxford: Hart, 2016).

5. Sydney D. Bailey, *British Parliamentary Democracy* (Boston: Houghton Mifflin, 1958), p. 2. See also Jeffrey Jowell and Dawn Oliver, *The Changing Constitution* (New York: Oxford University Press, 2011).

6. Stout, *British Government,* pp. 20–21. See also Javier Garcia Oliva and Helen Hall, *Religion, Law, and the Constitution: Balancing Beliefs in Britain* (New York: Routledge, 2018).

7. Stout, *British Government*, p. 20. See also Robert Hazell and James Melton, *Magna Carta and Its Modern Legacy* (Cambridge: Cambridge University Press, 2015); and Andrew Blick, *Beyond Magna Carta: A Constitution for the United Kingdom* (Oxford: Hart, 2015).

8. Quoted in Beloff and Peele, *Government of the United Kingdom*, pp. 10–11; Bailey, *British Parliamentary Democracy*, p. 3. See also John Laws, *The Common Law Constitution* (New York: Cambridge University Press, 2014).

9. Stout, *British Government*, p. 21. See also Vernon Bogdanor, *The British Constitution in the Twentieth Century* (Oxford: Oxford University Press, 2003); and Richard Stone, *Textbook on Civil Liberties and Human Rights* (Oxford: Oxford University Press, 2012).

10. Bailey, *British Parliamentary Democracy*, p. 4. See T. R. S. Allan, *The Sovereignty of Law: Freedom, Constitution, and Common Law* (Oxford: Oxford University Press, 2013).

11. See *The Monarchy in Britain* (London: Her Majesty's Stationery Office, 1981), pp. 8–11; or Charles Douglas-Home and Saul Kelly, *Dignified and Efficient: The British Monarchy in the Twentieth Century* (Brinkworth: Claridge, 2000). See also Michael Gordon, *Parliamentary Sovereignty in the UK Constitution: Process, Politics, and Democracy* (Oxford: Hart, 2015).

12. Bailey, *British Parliamentary Democracy*, p. 5. See also Dan Jones, *Magna Carta: The Birth of Liberty* (New York: Viking, 2015).

13. Bailey, *British Parliamentary Democracy*, p. 6. See also Graham Gee, Robert Hazell, Kate Malleson, and Patrick O'Brien, *The Politics of Judicial Independence in the UK's Changing Constitution* (Cambridge: Cambridge University Press, 2015).

14. Stout, *British Government*, pp. 26–27. See also Roger Masterman, *The Separation of Powers in the Contemporary Constitution: Judicial Competence and Independence in the United Kingdom* (New York: Cambridge University Press, 2011).

15. In July 1997 the British Government released plans to create a 129-seat Scottish parliament to be located in Edinburgh, as well as plans to create a 60-seat Welsh legislative assembly, to be located in Cardiff. The Scottish parliament would be more powerful than the Welsh body because it would have some taxation and legislative powers—including the power to decide whether to raise or lower income taxes by up to 3 percent—while the Welsh body would not have taxation powers, but would be able to legislate on issues such as health, transportation, the environment, and education. This devolution plan would not have permitted either the Scottish or Welsh bodies to vote on full independence. See Russell Deacon, *Devolution in the United Kingdom* (Edinburgh: Edinburgh University Press, 2012); or Karyn Stapleton and John Wilson, *Devolution and Identity* (London: Routledge, 2016).

16. See Michael O'Neill, *Devolution and British Politics* (New York: Pearson/Longman, 2013); Kenneth O. Morgan, *Revolution to Devolution: Reflections on Welsh Democracy* (Cardiff: University of Wales Press, 2014); and Iain McLean, Jim Gallagher, and Guy Lodge, *Scotland's Choices: The Referendum and What Happens Afterwards* (Edinburgh: Edinburgh University Press, 2014).

17. See Grenfell Morton, *Home Rule and the Irish Question* (Hoboken, NJ: Taylor and Francis, 2014).

18. Government of the United Kingdom, "Guidance: Devolution of Powers to Scotland, Wales, and Northern Ireland," February 18, 2013, https://www.gov.uk/guidance/devolution-of-powers-to-scotland-wales-and-northern-ireland.

19. Ibid.

20. Quoted in Anthony Sampson, *The New Anatomy of Britain* (New York: Stein and Day, 1972), p. 215.

21. Max Nicholson, *The System* (New York: McGraw-Hill, 1967), p. 158. See Douglas-Home and Kelly, *Dignified and Efficient*.

22. Sampson, *New Anatomy of Britain*, p. 215. See also Kelly Grotke and Markus Josef Prutsch, *Constitutionalism, Legitimacy, and Power* (New York: Oxford University Press, 2014).

23. At the time of this writing, the monarch is Queen Elizabeth II, who has held the British throne since February 1952, longer than any other British monarch. The heir apparent is her oldest son, Charles, Prince of Wales, born in 1948.

24. Sampson, *New Anatomy of Britain*, p. 215. See also Bill Jones and Dennis Kavanagh, *British Politics Today* (New York: Manchester University Press, 2003), especially chap. 12, "The Monarchy and the House of Lords." The text of the Throne speech of Queen Elizabeth II that was delivered on June 28, 2017, can be found at http://www.bbc.com/news/uk-politics-40448814.

25. See http://privycouncil.independent.gov.uk/privy-council/privy-council-members.

26. Privy Council Office, "Privy Council Office FAQs," https://privycouncil .independent.gov.uk/work-of-the-privy-council-office/faqs.

27. Beloff and Peele, *Government of the United Kingdom,* p. 67.

28. Sampson, *New Anatomy of Britain,* pp. 217–218. See Patrick Diamond, *Governing Britain: Power, Politics, and the Prime Minister* (London: Tauris, 2014).

29. Sir Ivor Jennings, *Cabinet Government* (Cambridge: Cambridge University Press, 1951), p. 79.

30. Stout, *British Government,* p. 77. See also Simon James, *British Cabinet Government* (London: Routledge, 1999); and Dennis Kavanagh and Anthony Seldon, *The Powers Behind the Prime Minister: The Hidden Influence of Number Ten* (London: HarperCollins, 2008).

31. K. R. MacKenzie, *The English Parliament* (New York: Penguin, 1950), p. 81. See also Byrum Carter, *The Office of Prime Minister* (Princeton: Princeton University Press, 2015).

32. James Barber, "The Power of the Prime Minister," in R. L. Borthwick and J. E. Spence, *British Politics in Perspective* (New York: St. Martin's, 1984), p. 73. See also Thomas Poguntke and Paul Webb, *The Presidentialization of Politics: A Comparative Study of Modern Democracies* (New York: Oxford University Press, 2005); and Peter Hennessy, *The Prime Minister: The Office and Its Holders Since 1945* (New York: Palgrave, 2001).

33. Richard Rose, "British Government: The Job at the Top," in Richard Rose and Ezra Suleiman, eds., *Presidents and Prime Ministers* (Washington, DC: American Enterprise Institute, 1980), p. 1. An interesting comparative study is by Mark Bennister, *Prime Ministers in Power: Political Leadership in Britain and Australia* (New York: Palgrave Macmillan, 2012).

34. Richard Rose, *Ministers and Ministries: A Functional Analysis* (Oxford: Clarendon, 1987), p. 4. See also John Hutton and Leigh Lewis, *How to Be a Minister: A 21st Century Guide* (New York: Biteback, 2014).

35. A table ranking the political status of the many cabinet portfolios can be found in Rose, *Ministers and Ministries,* p. 86.

36. Peter Hennessy, *Cabinet* (Oxford: Basil Blackwell, 1986), pp. 1–15. See also Reginald Bassett, *Essentials of Parliamentary Democracy* (Hoboken, NJ: Taylor and Francis, 2013).

37. See http://www.parliament.uk/mps-lords-and-offices/government-and-opposition1 /her-majestys-government.

38. David Barrett, "Cabinet 'Too Big to Make Decisions,'" *The Telegraph* (London), June 20, 2009, p. 1.

39. H. Victor Wiseman, *Politics in Everyday Life* (Oxford: Basil Blackwell, 1966), pp. 167–169.

40. Rose, "Job at the Top," pp. 3–26. See also Andrew Blick and G. W. Jones, *Premiership: The Development, Nature, and Power of the British Prime Minister* (Charlottesville, VA: Imprint Academic, 2010). A good series of portraits can be found in Vernon Bogdanor, *From New Jerusalem to New Labour: British Prime Ministers from Attlee to Blair* (Basingstoke: Palgrave Macmillan, 2010).

41. Wiseman, *Politics in Everyday Life,* p. 159. This is also discussed in R. A. Rhodes, *Everyday Life in British Government* (New York: Oxford University Press, 2011).

42. Rose, "Job at the Top," pp. 12–13. See also Peter Riddell, *The Unfulfilled Prime Minister: Tony Blair's Quest for a Legacy* (London: Politico, 2005).

43. Rose, "Job at the Top," pp. 12–13. See also Tony Blair, *A Journey: My Political Life* (New York: Knopf, 2010).

44. Martin Holmes, *The First Thatcher Government, 1979–1983: Contemporary Conservatism and Economic Change* (Boulder: Westview, 1985), p. 1. See also Eric Evans, *Thatcher and Thatcherism* (New York: Routledge, 2004); and Ben Jackson and Robert Saunders, *Making Thatcher's Britain* (Cambridge: Cambridge University Press, 2012).

45. Peter Jenkins, *Mrs. Thatcher's Revolution: The Ending of the Socialist Era* (Cambridge: Harvard University Press, 1988), p. 81. Two good studies are Tim Bale, *Margaret Thatcher* (New York: Routledge, 2015); and Andrew Crines, Timothy Heppell, and Peter Dorey, *The Political Rhetoric and Oratory of Margaret Thatcher* (London: Palgrave Macmillan, 2016).

46. Indeed, the Thatcher government's goal of lowering inflation at almost any cost "brought about a fundamental division of opinion within the Conservative Cabinet, backbench MPs and the party itself. The conflict between the political monetarists, or dries, and the left-wing Conservatives, or wets, was a marked feature of the whole of the period from 1979 to 1983"; Holmes, *First Thatcher Government*, pp. 74, 199. See also Duncan Needham and Anthony Hotson, *Expansionary Fiscal Contraction: The Thatcher Government's 1981 Budget in Perspective* (Cambridge: Cambridge University Press, 2014).

47. A good description of this relationship is in Dave Marsh and Jeff King, "The Unions Under Thatcher," in Lynton Robins, ed., *Political Institutions in Britain: Development and Change* (New York: Longman, 1987), pp. 213–229. See also Margaret Thatcher, *Margaret Thatcher: The Autobiography* (New York: Harper, 2013).

48. On recent directions of policy, see Tony Baldry and Jane Ewart-Biggs, *Social Policy* (London: Wroxton Papers in Politics, 1990).

49. See Philip Stephens, *Tony Blair: The Making of a World Leader* (New York: Viking, 2004). Blair's autobiography is Blair, *A Journey*.

50. See "Brown 'Disappointed' by Poll Loss," *BBC News,* May 2, 2008, http://news.bbc.co.uk/2/hi/uk_news/politics/7372860.stm.

51. "Brexit: David Cameron to Quit After UK Votes to Leave EU," *BBC News,* June 24, 2016, http://www.bbc.com/news/uk-politics-36615028. There is a huge and growing literature on Brexit, including Roger Liddle, *The Risk of Brexit: The Politics of a Referendum* (London: Rowman and Littlefield, 2015); and Philip Whyman and Alina Petrescu, *The Economics of Brexit: A Cost-Benefit Analysis of the UK's Economic Relationship* (New York: Palgrave Macmillan, 2017).

52. See "British Governments and Elections Since 1945," http://www.politicsresources.net/area/uk/uktable.htm.

53. Bailey, *British Parliamentary Democracy,* p. 35. See also Janice Morphet, *Modern Local Government* (London: Sage, 2008); and J. A. Chandler, *Local Government Today* (New York: Manchester University Press, 2009).

54. Frank Stacey, *British Government* (London: Oxford University Press, 1975), p. 72.

55. Bailey, *British Parliamentary Government,* pp. 36–37, 41. See Meg Russell, *Reforming the House of Lords: Lessons from Overseas* (New York: Oxford University Press, 2000).

56. See Maxwell Barrett, *The Law Lords: An Account of the Workings of Britain's Highest Judicial Body and the Men Who Preside over It* (Hampshire: Macmillan, 2000). See also A. P. LeSueur, *Building the UK's New Supreme Court: National and Comparative Perspectives* (New York: Oxford University Press, 2004); Louis Jacques Blom-Cooper, Brice Dickson, and Gavin Drewry, eds., *The Judicial House of Lords* (New York: Oxford University Press, 2009); and James Lee, *From House of Lords to Supreme Court: Judges, Jurists, and the Process of Judging* (Oxford: Hart, 2011).

57. Bailey, *British Parliamentary Government,* p. 38. See also Emma Crewe, *Lords of Parliament: Manners, Rituals, and Politics* (New York: Manchester University Press,

2005); and Peter Dorey and Alexandra Kelso, *House of Lords Reform Since 1911: Must the Lords Go?* (New York: Palgrave Macmillan, 2011).

58. Bailey, *British Parliamentary Government,* p. 42.

59. Nicholson, *The System,* p. 153. See also the study by the Government of Great Britain, *A House for the Future: A Summary* (London: London Royal Commission on the Reform of the House of Lords, 2000); and Meg Russell and Robert Hazell, *Next Steps in Lords Reform: Response to the September 2003 White Paper* (London: University College of London, 2003).

60. See http://www.parliament.uk/mps-lords-and-offices/lords/?amp;type=0&sort =2&type=0.

61. Nicholson, *The System,* p. 153. See also Frank Pakenham, Earl of Longford, *A History of the House of Lords* (London: Sutton, 1999).

62. See House of Lords, "How Do You Become a Member of the House of Lords?" http://www.parliament.uk/about/mps-and-lords/about-lords/lords-appointment. See also Chris Ballinger, *The House of Lords, 1911–2011: A Century of Non-Reform* (Oxford: Hart, 2012); and the very impressive four-volume study of the reform of the House of Lords by Peter Raina, *House of Lords Reform* (Oxford: Lang, 2011, 2013, 2014, 2015).

63. Bailey, *British Parliamentary Democracy,* pp. 65–69. The evolution of the institution is chronicled in Christopher Taucar, *The British System of Government and Its Historical Development* (Montreal: McGill-Queen's University Press, 2014). See also John Robert Maddicott, *The Origins of the English Parliament, 924–1327* (New York: Oxford University Press, 2010); and Philip Norton, *Parliament in British Politics* (New York: Palgrave Macmillan, 2005).

64. See Jowell and Oliver, *The Changing Constitution.* A very good description of the development of parliamentary government and the role of the Parliament can be found in Michael Rush, *Parliamentary Government in Britain* (New York: Holmes and Meier, 1981), pp. 19–47. See also Anna Manasco Dionne, *Women, Men, and the Representation of Women in the British Parliaments: Magic Numbers?* (Manchester: Manchester University Press, 2010).

65. Wiseman, *Politics in Everyday Life,* p. 147.

66. Stacey, *British Government,* p. 56. See also Robert Hazell and Richard Rawlings, *Devolution, Law Making, and the Constitution* (Charlottesville, VA: Imprint Academic, 2005). For those who like trivia: members' names are put on pieces of paper and put into a bag, from which names are drawn of members who will be allowed to introduce legislation. The expression "it's in the bag" that indicates a sure thing comes from this process and this bag.

67. Stout, *British Government,* pp. 128–137.

68. Wiseman, *Politics in Everyday Life,* p. 148. For a very good cross-national treatment of this subject, see David Olson, *The Legislative Process: A Comparative Approach* (New York: Harper and Row, 1980), p. 346.

69. Bailey, *British Parliamentary Democracy,* p. 108.

70. See Gavin Drewry and Tony Butcher, *The Civil Service Today* (Oxford: Basil Blackwell, 1988), pp. 1–8. See also David Marsh, David Richards, and Martin J. Smith, *Changing Patterns of Governance in the United Kingdom: Reinventing Whitehall?* (New York: Palgrave, 2001); and Brian Unwin, *With Respect, Minister: A View from Inside Whitehall* (London: Tauris, 2017).

71. See John Gretton and Anthony Harrison, eds., *Reshaping Central Government* (New Brunswick: Transaction, 1987), p. 2. See also June Burnham and Robert Pyper, *Britain's Modernised Civil Service* (New York: Palgrave Macmillan, 2008).

72. "Civil Service Employment," https://www.gov.uk/government/uploads/system /uploads/attachment_data/file/647454/civil_service_workforce_infographics_june_2017 .pdf. See Hazel Conley and Margaret Page, *Gender Equality in Public Services: Chasing the Dream* (New York: Routledge, 2015).

73. "Civil Service: About Us," https://www.gov.uk/government/organisations/civil -service/about. A good study is by James Rees and David Mullins, *The Third Sector*

Delivering Public Services: Developments, Innovations, and Challenges (Briston: Policy Press, 2016).

74. John R. Greenaway, "The Higher Civil Service at the Crossroads: The Impact of the Thatcher Government," in Lynton Robins, ed., *Political Institutions in Britain: Development and Change* (New York: Longman, 1987), p. 49. See also Rodney Lowe, *The Official History of the British Civil Service: Reforming the Civil Service* (New York: Routledge, 2011).

75. Anthony Sampson as quoted in Drewry and Butcher, *Civil Service Today,* p. 151. See Richard Chapman, *Ethics in the British Civil Service* (London: Routledge, 2010); and Jenny Manson, *Public Service on the Brink* (Luton: Andrews UK, 2012).

76. John Greenwood and David Wilson, *Public Administration in Britain* (London: Allen and Unwin, 1984), p. 84.

77. A very good discussion of this is by Lawrence Pratchett, *Renewing Local Democracy: The Modernisation Agenda in British Local Government* (New York: Routledge, 2013). See also Colin Copus, Mark Roberts, and Rachel Wall, *Local Government in England: Centralisation, Autonomy, and Control* (London: Palgrave Macmillan, 2017); and Steve Leach, *Local Government Reorganisation: The Review and Its Aftermath* (New York: Routledge, 2013).

78. See "The Role of the Supreme Court," https://www.supremecourt.uk/about/role -of-the-supreme-court.html. See also Gee et al., *Politics of Judicial Independence.*

79. See "Significance to the UK," https://www.supremecourt.uk/about/significance -to-the-uk.html. See also Alan Paterson, *Final Judgment: The Last Law Lords and the Supreme Court* (Oxford: Hart, 2013).

80. See Joshua Rozenberg's column in *The Times/Sunday Times Literary Supplement* titled "Britain's New Supreme Court: Why Has a Fundamental Change in the Constitution Been So Little Reported and Debated?" September 2, 2009, https://www.the-tls.co .uk/articles/private/britains-new-supreme-court.

81. Richard Rose, *Politics in England* (Boston: Little, Brown, 1980), p. 249. See also UCL Judicial Institute, *The UK Supreme Court: Taking Stock Two Years On* (London, 2011).

82. J. Denis Derbyshire and Ian Derbyshire, *Politics in Britain: From Callaghan to Thatcher* (Edinburgh: Chambers, 1990), p. 5. See also K. D. Ewing, Jacob Rowbottom, and Joo-Cheong Tham, *The Funding of Political Parties: Where Now?* (New York: Routledge, 2012).

83. Derbyshire, *Politics in Britain,* p. 5. There is a much longer discussion of the nature of the interparty differences in economic and social policy here, pp. 6–14.

84. Keeton, *Government in Action in the United Kingdom,* p. 90. See also Matthew Cole, *Political Parties in Britain* (Edinburgh: Edinburgh University Press, 2012).

85. Stout, *British Government,* p. 163. See Alistair Clark, *Political Parties in the UK* (New York: Palgrave Macmillan, 2012).

86. A very good discussion of the evolution of British parties can be found in H. M. Crucker, "The Evolution of the Political Parties," in R. L. Borthwick and J. E. Spence, *British Politics in Perspective* (New York: St. Martin's, 1984), pp. 104–121.

87. Bailey, *British Parliamentary Democracy,* p. 138.

88. Ibid.

89. Quoted in Keeton, *Government in Action in the United Kingdom,* p. 93. See also Paul Whiteley and Patrick Seyd, *High-Intensity Participation: The Dynamics of Party Activism in Britain* (Ann Arbor: University of Michigan Press, 2002); and Colin Copus, *Party Politics and Local Government* (New York: Manchester University Press, 2004).

90. Keeton, *Government in Action in the United Kingdom,* p. 93. See also Danny Rye, *Political Parties and the Concept of Power: A Theoretical Framework* (Basingstoke: Palgrave Macmillan, 2014).

91. Inter-Parliamentary Union, "Parline Database: United Kingdom—House of Commons," http://www.ipu.org/parline-e/reports/2335_arc.htm. See also Adam Boulton and

Joey Jones, *Right Honourable Housemates: The 2010 Election and the Coalition Government* (New York: Simon and Schuster, 2010).

92. Rose, *Politics in England,* p. 256. See also Christopher Kam, *Party Discipline and Parliamentary Politics* (New York: Cambridge University Press, 2009); and Ian Lamond, *2015 UK General Election and the 2016 EU Referendum: Towards a Democracy of the Spectacle* (New York: Palgrave Macmillan, 2017).

93. Inter-Parliamentary Union, "Parline Database: United Kingdom—House of Commons."

94. See "British Governments and Elections Since 1945," http://archive.ipu.org/parline-e/reports/2335_E.htm.

95. Inter-Parliamentary Union, "Parline Database: United Kingdom—House of Commons."

96. Stout, *British Government,* p. 200. See also Stephen Ingle, *The British Party System: An Introduction* (New York: Routledge, 2008); and Simon Griffiths and Kevin Hickson, *British Party Politics and Ideology After New Labour* (New York: Palgrave Macmillan, 2010).

97. Stout, *British Government,* p. 211.

98. Chris Cook and John Ramsden, *By-Elections in British Politics* (Hoboken, NJ: Taylor and Francis, 2013).

16

The United States

Learning Outcomes

After reading this chapter, you will be able to

- Understand how US political history has helped to shape the creation of current US politics.
- Appreciate the nature of US federalism.
- Understand the unique nature of the US presidency and its powers.
- Explain the special characteristics of the US national legislative structures and why they have evolved to their current status.
- Be aware of the Supreme Court's powers today and how the Supreme Court's role in US politics has changed over time.
- Understand how the role of political parties has changed over time and how the nature of the US party system affects federal policymaking today.

The purpose of this chapter is to illustrate how the major institutional structures of the US political system fit together and to show what some of the major consequences of those institutions are. The US system is different from those that we have seen prior to this point, even though it shares *some* characteristics with *some* of the systems we have seen, such as sharing a presidential structure with Mexico or a federal structure with Germany.

The Constitutional System

The US Constitution, created in 1787 (see Table 16.1), was really the second US constitution. The first constitution, strictly speaking, was the document called the **Articles of Confederation**, which was sent to the

---

Table 16.1   Key Events in the Development of the US Constitution

September 1774	Meeting of the First Continental Congress
May 1775	Meeting of the Second Continental Congress
July 1776	Congress adopts the Declaration of Independence
November 1777	Congress adopts the Articles of Confederation
March 1781	Articles of Confederation ratified by required number of states
October 1781	British General Cornwallis surrenders at Yorktown
September 1786	Annapolis Convention decides that Articles of Confederation need to be fixed
May 1787	Constitutional Convention meets in Philadelphia
September 1787	Constitution signed
June 1788	New Hampshire is the ninth state to ratify the new Constitution
March 1789	New Constitution takes effect

Source: Based upon William Bianco and David Canon, *American Politics Today* (New York: Norton, 2017), pp. 30–31.

---

states for ratification in 1777 and which took effect when the last state ratified the document in 1781. The articles, coming as they did at the end of the Revolutionary War when the American colonies were rebelling against the British monarchy, put an emphasis on **limited government**— and ended up creating a government that was *so* limited that it simply wasn't able to govern. The Articles of Confederation had no executive structure; all national powers were exercised by the Congress, in which each state had a single vote. There was no national judicial structure, as all judicial matters were left to the states. Most challenging of all, to limit the power of government, and because of a general suspicion of centralized power, each state had a veto over any changes to the articles, and any legislation required the approval of nine of the thirteen states. Congress had no power to force states to pay taxes, which limited the ability of the national government to act, too.

In May 1787 the Constitutional Convention met in Philadelphia to "devise such further provisions as shall appear to them necessary to render the Constitution of the Federal Government adequate to the exigencies of the Union."[1] When the delegates met, they brought with them consensus on three broad principles for the final product of their discussions: popular control of government, a rejection of monarchy, and limited government and an emphasis on individual rights. The idea of the importance of government receiving "the consent of the governed" was a radical one at the time, but it, along with an emphasis on "natural rights," was key. These principles had been clearly expressed in the

Declaration of Independence eleven years earlier: "We hold these truths to be self-evident, that all men are created equal, that they are endowed by their Creator with certain unalienable Rights, that among these are Life, Liberty, and the pursuit of Happiness. That to secure these rights, Governments are instituted among Men, deriving their just powers from the consent of the governed."

The process of having the new Constitution approved was not a quick one or an easy one. Having recently fought a war against Britain and a centralized monarchy, people were very suspicious of the idea of governmental power.[2] A series of essays written by James Madison, Alexander Hamilton, and John Jay titled the **Federalist Papers** sought to justify the new plan and sought to generate public support for the new arrangement. Both **Federalists** and **Anti-Federalists** fought hard, and the final Constitution was a document of compromise in key areas of conflict such as those between advocates of majority rule against advocates of minority rights, small states against large states, those advocating legislative domination against those advocating executive power, those advocating national power against those advocating state power, and those supporting slavery against those opposing it, among other issues (see Table 16.2).[3]

The plan approved in Philadelphia required the approval of nine of the thirteen states, specifically in special state conventions and not the state legislatures (which were expected to be more opposed to the new ideas), to bring the new system into effect; it took until June 21 of 1788 for nine state conventions to ratify the plan. New York and Virginia

Table 16.2 Constitutional Compromise in Philadelphia

Issue	Challenge	Compromise
Representation	Based on population, or based on equal representation for states	Bicameral legislature with one house based on each
President	Popularly elected, or elected by states	Electoral College, based on states
Representation of slaves	To be counted like citizens, or not counted at all	Three-Fifths Compromise
Individual rights	Guaranteed in state constitutions, or national bill of rights	Bill of Rights passed by First Congress

Source: Based upon William Bianco and David Canon, *American Politics Today* (New York: Norton, 2017), p. 37.

approved the plan within months following that date, but Rhode Island and North Carolina refused to ratify the new Constitution until after the First Congress passed a Bill of Rights.[4]

The framework that finally emerged from the constitution-drafting process included a range of powers that were divided between the central government and the states in different ways: some exclusive powers, some shared powers, and some checking powers, as illustrated in Table 16.3.[5]

Federal Government

One of the key principles of US politics is that the United States is a federal political system. We noted in Chapter 2 that "in a federal system there are two levels of government above the local level, both enjoying sovereignty in certain areas."[6] In this context, sovereignty refers to the ability to determine public policy without interference from, or approval of, the other level of government. We further noted in our earlier description that federalism is fundamentally about intergovernmental relations—relations between the national government and the state governments—and political power: What decisions are to be made by the central government, and what decisions are to be made by the states?

The nation-state balance of power has shifted over time in US politics. Originally the state governments in the United States were far more powerful than was the national government. This has changed over time, and today the federal government can affect peoples' lives in many, many more ways than was the case almost 250 years ago, and, because of the federal government's "power of the purse" it is able to influence a good deal of policy coming out of the states, too. While some areas of federal jurisdiction today have always been the jurisdiction of the national government, such as national defense, or foreign policy, other areas have shifted over time from being the responsibility of the states to being the responsibility of the nation, or have shifted from being outside the realm of government policymaking at all to being the responsibility of either the state or the nation. For example, there was a time when the federal government was not involved in education policy, or medical care for retirees; those are clearly regulated by the federal government today.

Through the nineteenth century the jurisdiction of the federal government was restrained compared to the jurisdictions of the states, because the courts ruled that the Tenth Amendment of the Constitution directed residual power to the states, not the federal government: "The powers not delegated to the United States by the Constitution, nor prohibited by it to the States, are reserved to the States respectively, or to the people." The key actor in this growth of federal power was the

Table 16.3   The US Constitution's Distribution of Powers

Type	Branch	Examples
Exclusive powers	Congress	• Raise revenue through taxes and borrowing, and spend money through the budget process • Regulate interstate and foreign commerce • Coin money • Establish post offices and roads • Grant patents • Create a system of federal courts • Declare war • "Raise and support armies" • "Elastic clause": "make all laws which shall be necessary and proper"
	President	• Serve as commander-in-chief • Receive ambassadors • Issue pardons • "The executive power shall be vested in the President"
	Supreme Court	• Lifetime appointment of justices
Shared powers		• President has power to negotiate treaties and make appointments, but Senate must give its "advice and consent," meaning approval • Only Congress can declare war, but president as commander-in-chief can commit troops overseas
Checking powers	Congress	• Congress can impeach the president, vice president, federal judges • Congress controls budget, so can affect behavior of other branches
	President	• President can veto legislation • President can appoint justices (but not fire them)
	Supreme Court	• Principle of judicial review established in 1803 gives Court the ability to strike down laws passed by Congress or actions by the executive branch

Supreme Court of the United States, which decided that the grant of power to Congress in Article 1, Section 8, through the "necessary and proper" clause of the Constitution ("The Congress shall have Power . . . To make all Laws which shall be *necessary and proper* for carrying into Execution the foregoing Powers, and all other Powers vested by this Constitution in the Government of the United States") was more important than the Tenth Amendment's suggested balance, and that it opened the door for the federal government to regulate, and fund, much more than had been the case in the nation's early years.

Different names have been utilized for the different federal-state relations that have been dominant over the years. Originally, from the founding of the republic in 1789 through 1937, the relationship was referred to as one of "dual federalism," which meant that there was very little overlap between the national and the state governments. Federal government jurisdiction was very limited, and the federal government did not try to expand its powers a great deal. From 1937 through the present time the federal-state balance has been referred to as "cooperative federalism" or "fiscal federalism," and the relationship has been described as showing greater coordination and cooperation between levels of government.[7] The federal government frequently uses its "power of the purse" to get states to enact specific policies by offering various levels of block grants and conditional grants to the states if they will pass legislation and policy that does what the federal government wants.[8]

The key to appreciating US federalism is the degree to which it has permitted both of the levels of government, national and state, to play a key role in policymaking over the years. This has permitted each level of government to have an opportunity to contribute to public policy. The states argue that they are closer to the people than the national government and, therefore, can be more responsive to public demands.[9] They also suggest that they can provide more of an opportunity for people to participate in government. And states are in a better position to play a role as a check on the national government abusing its power than private individuals would be. On the other hand, as we can see in contemporary US society today, some argue that providing the states with too much power would promote even greater inequality across the nation as richer states provide their citizens with more services and goods than poorer states. As well, the argument is made that if states had been left to their own devices there likely would not have been an end to the practice of slavery in the American South, or even later the systematic discrimination of a significant population simply based upon race. That is, the influence of a national political morality has on many occasions pressed state and local practices to change and adapt to modern times.

Federal-state tensions over policy jurisdiction—the question of which level of government is best able to legislate in policy areas—occurs in a huge range of policymaking areas, from environmental legislation to health policy to energy management and federal spending, not to mention criminal law (which has been primarily the jurisdiction of the states).[10] The question of which level of government should legislate, and who should decide which level of government should legislate, has continued to be a matter of some conflict.[11]

The Presidency

While the parliamentary model of government is characterized by a dual executive—in Britain a monarch and a prime minister—one of the major characteristics of US politics is its single executive. The responsibilities of the president of the United States have increased tremendously since the office first appeared with President George Washington. At the Philadelphia Convention in 1787 some of the delegates suggested having a "multiple executive," several people sharing the responsibilities of the presidency, on the grounds that such an arrangement would divide power and would protect against too much power being concentrated in the hands of a single individual. The dominant view at the time, however, was that greater energy was needed in the office, and that a multiple executive could lead to a lack of clarity about who was in charge of what. At the end of the day the forces arguing for a single executive actor won.[12]

Even the title of the chief executive office was the subject of much discussion at the time. Given the immediate past history of the time, there was no desire to use the title "king," but there was much give and take about what would work in its place. Ultimately, the title "president" seemed like the most realistic option.[13]

Article 2 of the Constitution begins quite simply, stating, "The executive power shall be vested in a President of the United States of America." However, it never actually states what, exactly, the "executive power" is meant to include, which makes sense given that the power of the office has changed so much over the years and the range of issues in which the office is involved has grown. The Constitution sets the term of office for the president at four years and spends a great deal of time focused on how the president shall be chosen.[14] Subsequent sections of Article 2 deal with the powers of the president (Section 2), the duties of the president (Section 3), and the removal of the president from office (Section 4).

Originally the issue of term limits was not a major one, and there were no limitations on reelection for the presidency until after Franklin Roosevelt broke the precedent set by George Washington of limiting himself to two terms in office and ran (and was elected) for a third term in 1940. In 1947 Congress formally proposed the Twenty-Second Amendment, stating that "no person shall be elected to the office of President more than twice,"[15] and the amendment was declared ratified in February 1951.

Presidential elections are discussed later, but it is worth noting here that much of the attention devoted to the creation of the office of the president involved how the president would be selected. The debate in 1787 was primarily between those who wanted the president to be directly elected by the people (remembering that at the time "the people" meant white male property holders, only a small minority of the total population) and those who wanted the president to be chosen by (and thus responsible to) the national Congress. Ultimately the decision was made to not have the president chosen by Congress, but also to not have the president directly elected by the people, using instead an indirect electoral structure called the **Electoral College**. The Electoral College was to be made up of a group of political elites—"electors"— chosen by "the people," although it is worth noting that electors were not at the time and are not today always required to cast their votes for the candidates with whom they are associated; they can cast their electoral ballot for whomever they want to.[16]

The individual who is credited with the creation of the modern US presidency is the thirty-second president, Franklin Delano Roosevelt, who used the powers of the presidency during a period of tremendous national crisis—the Great Depression, followed by World War II—to vastly expand the range of domestic political arenas in which the federal government was involved. Under Roosevelt the powers of the federal government grew enormously, over the objection of many who were opposed to the growth of federal power, and of presidential power.

At one point, after the Supreme Court ruled the National Industrial Recovery Act unconstitutional (1935) because it improperly expanded federal political power, he introduced the Judicial Procedures Reform Bill of 1937, which would have allowed him to appoint an additional justice for each incumbent justice over the age of seventy (and in 1937 there were six Supreme Court justices over that age), thus likely changing the majority opinion of the Court. Roosevelt's **court packing** plan ran into intense political opposition and was not passed by Congress, but shortly afterward the Court started to change its mind and ruled many of Roosevelt's proposals to be constitutional, thus opening the way for a vast expansion of federal power.[17]

As noted in Chapter 4, the US presidency has been said to include a number of distinct, identifiable roles that the president is expected to play in the political arena. The extent to which each of these roles is highlighted by an individual president has varied, of course, depending upon the interests and skills of the individual.[18]

The presidency has a number of bases of power. We mentioned the **expressed powers of the president**, those powers that are actually established in the language of the Constitution (for example, the power of the president to grant pardons). In addition to these powers are what are called the **implied powers of the president**, which are powers that are necessary to allow the president to exercise expressed powers. The **delegated powers of the president** include those given to the president by Congress, for example when Congress established Social Security, or Medicare, or the Affordable Care Act of Barack Obama: Congress sets some general policy guidelines, and then the president as chief of the executive branch of government is responsible for seeing those policies carried out. The **military power of the president** as commander-in-chief is established through the Constitution,[19] and the president also has significant (although vastly less transparent and open) power as chief executive and head of national intelligence, thereby directing the National Security Council, the Central Intelligence Agency, the National Security Agency, the Federal Bureau of Investigation, the Defense Intelligence Agency, and a number of other domestic and international security and intelligence structures. And of course, during times of crisis presidents have claimed an emergency power that enables them to move quickly and dramatically to undertake action required by the challenges of the moment.[20]

The president also has other powers. The powers to grant pardons and appoint federal judges (although the latter must be ratified by the Senate) constitute the **judicial power of the president**. He has diplomatic power through the Department of State, and while many international treaties and agreements are made by the State Department and ratified by the Senate, many very significant "treaties" have not been treaties at all but have been executive agreements. They may look very much like treaties, and even be negotiated in the same way, but do not have to be approved by the Senate.[21]

The **legislative power of the president** is very different from the legislative power that chief executives have in parliamentary systems. The British prime minister is at the same time the prime minister and commander-in-chief, and also a member of the House of Commons. As such, the prime minister has legislative power as well as executive power; we have noted how the prime minister is both leader of the executive branch and also leader of the legislative branch. The US president is not—and cannot be—a member of either the House of Representatives or the Senate and, therefore, does not strictly speaking have any legislative power of his own. He cannot introduce any legislation in either house of the legislature but needs to have either a senator or a representative do so. This means that if he cannot find a representative or a senator to introduce a bill, the bill cannot be introduced (although it is extremely unlikely that this would actually happen). The president does have a negative legislative power, however, through the **veto**, the constitutional power to reject acts of Congress. His veto is not what we would call absolute, however, because after the president vetoes a bill it can still become law if it is approved by a two-thirds vote in both the House and the Senate. Since the nation's earliest days, presidents have vetoed legislation over 3,000 times, but their vetoes have been overridden only 111 times.[22]

Finally, the president also has demonstrated presidential initiative through the **executive order**, which has become in recent years an option for presidents when they cannot convince Congress to pass legislation. This was especially important for Barack Obama after the Republicans came to control both houses of Congress in his final term of office; he used executive orders to achieve policy initiatives that could not be accomplished through the legislative process.[23]

Executive orders have the status of formal legislation in areas in which the president already has some jurisdiction. When presidents do not have success in having legislation passed by Congress—such as Donald Trump currently—they tend to rely on executive orders to affect policy through the president's ability to directly instruct officers of the executive branch of government how to enact policy.[24] Where no policy exists, this is difficult, but in any area in which there has been previous legislation that is being administered by a part of the executive branch, the president can affect policy through an executive order. For example, while Trump was unable to actually convince Congress to do away with Barack Obama's Affordable Care Act, he was able to direct offices in the federal bureaucracy dealing with health policy to not enforce policies that the act had created.

Most of the president's authority comes by way of the area of delegated power, however, when Congress has passed some general policy statement and has left the details of that policy and the enforcement of that general policy up to the executive branch of government. Whether this involves policy dealing with health, education, housing, transportation, taxes, banking regulation, environmental policy, or any of a number of different areas, over the years Congress has found that it is simply impossible to legislate for all eventualities, or to legislate to solve all social problems. Congress has found that what it is able to do is to set some broad guidelines and refer policy execution to the executive branch of government, which happens to be headed by the chief executive, the president.

While legislatures in the sixteenth century found it easy to pass laws prohibiting hunting on the monarch's property, legislatures in the nineteenth and twentieth centuries found it much more difficult to pass laws prohibiting poverty, or illness, or racial hatred. This was what led to the growth of executive power, with the legislature passing some very general policy statements to be enacted by the executive, and the more specialized executive agencies creating policy in areas in which they had expertise.

In many instances, therefore, congressional legislation is not very detailed. Often, Congress defines a broad goal or objective and delegates enormous discretionary power to administrators to determine how that goal is to be achieved. Agency administrators have enormous discretionary power to draft rules and regulations that have the effect of law. Indeed, on many occasions the courts have treated these administrative rules like congressional statutes. For all intents and purposes, when Congress creates an agency such as the Department of Homeland Security, members of Congress don't even know all of the details of what the laws need to include, so their response is to give the law a broad mandate to achieve some desirable outcome and, therefore, transfer its own legislative power to the executive branch.[25]

Other Executive Structures

Although we refer to the president as chief executive, and there is no doubt that he is chief of the executive branch of government, he is by no means the only leader of the executive branch of government. Although members of the cabinet have no constitutional status beyond a reference in Article 2, Section 2, each is responsible for leadership of vast governmental bureaucracies, and they also serve as presidential advisers.[26] Members of the cabinet are appointed by the president but must be confirmed by the Senate. They serve at the pleasure of the president, and presidents have asked for resignations of their cabinet members (or simply announced their departures via Twitter) when they no longer have confidence in them as members of their "teams." President Trump's executive team, the Cabinet, is listed in Box 16.1.

The Executive Office of the President was created in 1939 by President Franklin Roosevelt to support the needs of modern government. It has nearly 2,000 employees, about one-third of whom are found in two distinct offices: the Office of Management and Budget, and the Office of the US Trade Representative, which is responsible for negotiating trade agreements with other nations. Organizations that are included in the Executive Office of the President are shown in Box 16.2.[27]

The vice president, although his is a portfolio without many specific powers, plays a very significant constitutional role in the executive branch of government. Constitutionally, the vice president exists for two

---

**Box 16.1   The Cabinet of
President Donald Trump, December 1, 2018**

Acting Administrator of the Environmental Protection Agency	Andrew Wheeler
Administrator of the Small Business Administration	Linda E. McMahon
Acting Attorney General	Matthew Whitaker
Director of National Intelligence	Daniel Coats
Director of the Central Intelligence Agency	Gina Haspel
Director of the Office of Management and Budget	Mick Mulvaney
Representative of the United States to the United Nations	Nikki R. Haley
Secretary of Agriculture	Sonny Perdue
Secretary of Commerce	Wilbur L. Ross Jr.
Secretary of Defense	James Mattis
Secretary of Education	Elisabeth Prince DeVos
Secretary of Energy	James Richard Perry
Secretary of Health and Human Services	Alex Azar
Secretary of Homeland Security	Kirstjen Nielsen
Secretary of Housing and Urban Development	Benjamin S. Carson Sr.
Secretary of the Interior	Ryan Zinke
Secretary of Labor	Alexander Acosta
Secretary of State	Mike Pompeo
Secretary of Transportation	Elaine L. Chao
Secretary of the Treasury	Steven T. Mnuchin
US Trade Representative	Robert Lighthizer
Vice President	Michael R. Pence
White House Chief of Staff	John F. Kelly

Source: White House, "The Cabinet," https://www.whitehouse.gov/the-trump-administration/the-cabinet.

---

distinct roles: to succeed the president in case of death, resignation, or incapacity, and to preside over the Senate, casting a tie-breaking vote when needed. The first vice president, John Adams, is reported to have stated, "I am Vice President. In this I am nothing, but I may be everything." He also reportedly said, "My country has in its wisdom contrived for me the most insignificant office that ever the invention of man contrived or his imagination conceived."[28]

Following the assassination of President John F. Kennedy, some in Congress were concerned that the constitutional law about presidential

---

Box 16.2   The Executive Office of the President

Chair: White House Chief of Staff
Council of Economic Advisers
Council on Environmental Quality
National Security Council
Office of Administration
Office of Management and Budget
Office of National Drug Control Policy
Office of the US Trade Representative
Office of the Vice President
Domestic Policy Council (includes Office of National AIDS Policy, Office of Faith-Based and Neighborhood Partnerships, Office of Social Innovation and Civic Participation, and White House Rural Council)
National Economic Council
Office of the Press Secretary
Office of the First Lady
Office of Public Engagement
Office of Intergovernmental Affairs
Office of Urban Affairs

Source: White House, "The Administration," https://www.whitehouse.gov/the-trump-administration.

---

succession was not clear. What if Kennedy had been incapacitated by being shot in the head, and not killed? How incapacitated would he need to have been for the vice president to assume the powers of the presidency? Would the vice president become acting president, or actually president? In response to these questions, the Twenty-Fifth Amendment to the Constitution was proposed by Congress in July 1965, and it was ratified in February 1967:

- In case of the removal of the president from office, or his death or resignation, the vice president "shall become President" (the language in Article 2, Section 1, had indicated that in case of the removal of the president from office or his death, resignation, or inability to discharge his powers and duties, "the same shall devolve on the Vice President," but it did not clarify whether the vice president would actually become president).
- It allowed for the president to decide on his own that he was "unable to discharge the powers and duties of his office" on a temporary basis, and provided a process both for him to hand his

powers to the vice president to be "acting president," and to reclaim the powers at a later time.

• It allowed for a situation in which the vice president and a majority of the cabinet might declare the president unable to discharge his duties, and described a process for the president to reclaim his powers, or to contest the assertion that he was unable to discharge his duties.

However ambiguous the powers of the vice presidency may be, the fact of the matter is that a number of vice presidents—eight—have become president through succession; most recently Gerald Ford assumed the presidency when Richard Nixon resigned from office. As well, of course, even more have gone on to run for president themselves and win office.

Legislative Structures
One of the characteristics of a presidential system of government, such as one finds in the United States, is **legislative independence**: the legislature is independent *of* the executive. The independence of the legislature from the executive, and the corresponding independence of the executive from the legislature, are core to the political behavior of a presidential government.

The US legislative branch of government is a **bicameral legislature**. That is, it has two separate and independent houses, one called the House of Representatives and the other called the Senate. The two houses are organizationally and behaviorally distinct from each other; they derive from the Great Compromise that produced US federal government in 1787, when larger states favored a system of representation based upon population, and smaller states favored a system of representation based upon equal treatment of all states. The compromise produced a two-house legislature in which the upper house was based upon equal representation for the states—the Senate with two senators per state, whatever the population of the state—and the lower house was based upon population of the states.[29]

As far as the House of Representatives is concerned, Article 1, Section 2, of the Constitution originally said that the "number of Representatives shall not exceed one for every thirty Thousand, but each State shall have at least one Representative." This produced fifty-nine members of the House. Over the years, every ten years following a census, the number of members of the House of Representatives grew until the size of the House reached 435 members (each representing 30,000 citizens) in 1911. At that time the Constitution was amended to permanently set the size of the House at 435 members and let the ratio of voters per representative grow as time went by.[30] Today the average population of a congressional district is about 710,000 people, and some have argued that that ratio is simply too large to fulfill the intention of the Founding Fathers that members of the House of Representatives should know the members of their districts well. They argue that the size of the House should be expanded significantly to take representation back to something closer to the original representation, although it is worth noting that even if the ratio were to grow from 1 per 30,000 to 1 per 50,000, the current population of the United States (over 325 million) is such that it would require a House of over 6,000 members.[31]

Table 16.4 shows some of the differences between the House of Representatives and the Senate. It is clear that the two chambers have different cultures, and different styles of operation, with the Senate being more deliberative and more collegial, with procedure being much more formalized in the House of Representatives. Differences in the length of terms of office, with members of the House serving two-year terms and members of the Senate serving six-year terms, are significant, too, as members of the House need to start to run for reelection almost as soon as they are elected.

While the notion of representation is the key to any legislative structure, we should note that demographic representation is not a strength of either house of Congress: the pattern of domination by older, white males is long-standing (see Table 16.5), although gender balance has changed in recent years.[32] Following the election of 2018, the House of Representatives had 85 women members out of 435 (about 19.5 percent, up from 82 women in the preceding House), and the Senate had 23

Table 16.4   Structural Characteristics of the US House of Representatives and Senate

Characteristic	House of Representatives	Senate
Minimum age	25	30
Length of term	2 years	6 years
Total size	435	100
Number per state	1 to 53 (varying with state population)	2
Focus of representation	Local	State
US citizenship	At least 7 years	At least 9 years
Elected by	Popular vote	Popular vote (originally elected by state legislatures)

Source: US Constitution, Article 1, Section 2 (House) and Section 3 (Senate).

women members (or 23 percent, up from 21 percent in the preceding Senate), both all-time-high figures.

Political parties are the key structure of organization in both houses of Congress, although US political parties are clearly different from those we have seen in other nations in terms of the extent to which they can be counted upon to act cohesively. Each house is controlled by the majority party of the day, with all committee chair positions controlled by the majority party and the majority party controlling a majority on each committee. In recent years the level of partisanship has increased significantly in each house, so that it is increasingly correct to say that there is little intraparty cooperation in either the legislative process or committee work.

The committee system is the key to the operation of each house of Congress. Woodrow Wilson once wrote that "it is not far from the truth to say that Congress in session is Congress on public exhibition, whilst Congress in its committee rooms is Congress at work." Congress has four different kinds of committees—standing (see Table 16.6), select,

Table 16.5   Representation in the US House of Representatives and Senate, 2015 (percentages)

	House of Representatives	Senate	US Population
Gender			
Women	20	20	51
Party			
Republican	56	54	25
Democrat	44	44	33
Independent	0	2	36
Race			
White	79	97	64
Black	10	2	13
Hispanic	8	4	16
Asian	2.5	1	5
Native American	0.5	0	1
Religion			
Protestant	57	55	51
Catholic	31	26	24
Jewish	4	9	2
Mormon	2	7	2
Other	6	3	21
Foreign-born	3	3	13
Military service	18	20	13

Source: Benjamin Ginsberg, Theodore Lowi, Margaret Weir, and Caroline Tolbert, *We The People,* 11th ed. (New York: Norton, 2016), p. 362.

joint, and conference—and through these structures Congress does the majority of its work.

A **standing committee** is a permanent committee in either house in which the bulk of legislative work takes place. They propose legislation, write legislation, hold hearings on legislation, and may, at the end of the process, vote legislation out to the full house for consideration and approval.

A **select committee** usually is temporary in life and most often is not designed to present legislation for the consideration of the full house. These committees are created in response to a specific need, or crisis, and hold hearings to permit a public airing of problems and possible solutions. Typically they deal with areas that are not within the jurisdiction of a standing committee.

A **joint committee** has membership coming from both houses of Congress. Joint committees are permanent, but they are not focused on preparing legislation for the two houses of Congress. Rather, they are important in holding hearings and collecting information that is referred to standing committees for action. The four joint committees existing today are economic, taxation, library, and printing.

Table 16.6 US Congressional Standing Committees

House of Representatives	Senate
Agriculture	Agriculture, Nutrition, and Forestry
Appropriations	Appropriations
Armed Services	Armed Services
Budget	Banking, Housing, and Urban Affairs
Education and the Workforce	Budget
Energy and Commerce	Commerce, Science, and Transportation
Ethics	Energy and Natural Resources
Financial Services	Environment and Public Works
Foreign Affairs	Finance
Homeland Security	Foreign Relations
House Administration	Health, Education, Labor, Pensions
Intelligence	Homeland Security and Governmental Affairs
Judiciary	Intelligence
Natural Resources	Judiciary
Oversight/Government Reform	Rules and Administration
Rules	Small Business and Entrepreneurship
Science, Space, and Technology	Veterans' Affairs
Small Business	
Transportation and Infrastructure	
Veterans' Affairs	
Ways and Means	

Source: Benjamin Ginsberg, Theodore Lowi, Margaret Weir, and Caroline Tolbert, *We The People,* 11th ed. (New York: Norton, 2016), p. 362.

A **conference committee** is a temporary committee made up of members of both houses whose members are appointed by the Speaker of the House (for the House of Representatives) and the presiding officer (for the Senate); they typically appoint members of the respective chambers who have worked on the piece of legislation in question and are most well-informed about the bills. The work of these committees is to find a compromise between legislation that has passed the House and legislation that has passed the Senate, because in order for a bill to become a law it must be passed in identical form in both houses. It is rarely the case that legislation is passed by both the House and the Senate in identical form, so conference committees are appointed to create final versions of the legislation.

Both houses of Congress value the principle of **seniority** in their internal organization. Committee chair positions are typically given to the majority member who has continuously served on that particular committee the longest. (If a member leaves a committee and subsequently returns, they return with no credit for previous time served.) Leadership positions in both houses of Congress are typically determined on the basis of seniority, as well.

The Legislative Process

The most important action associated with legislatures, of course, is legislation—passing laws—and both the House and the Senate take this action quite seriously. Generally speaking there are four types of legislation that can be passed. These are bills, simple resolutions, concurrent resolutions, and joint resolutions.

A **bill** is a legislative proposal that becomes law if passed by both houses in identical form and if it is approved by the president. Bills that originate in the House have titles that begin "H.R." and bills that originate in the Senate have titles that begin "S."

A **simple resolution** is a piece of legislation that is intended to express the sense of the house; these are not signed by the president, and they do not take on the force of law. They are labeled either "H. Res." or "S. Res." depending upon the house in which they originate. This type of resolution is most often of a symbolic nature, for example H. Res. 128 in the 115th Congress (2017–2018) was titled "Supporting respect for human rights and encouraging inclusive governance in Ethiopia."[33]

A **concurrent resolution** is an effort in which both chambers want to express their views on a nonlegislative issue, and there is a desire to have both chambers act together rather than pass a simple resolution. These are labeled either "H. Con. Res." or "S. Con. Res.," depending upon their chamber of origin. A recent example would be S. Con. Res. 3, "A concurrent resolution setting forth the congressional budget for the United States Government for fiscal year 2017 and setting forth the appropriate budgetary levels for fiscal years 2018 through 2026."[34]

A **joint resolution** is legislation that passes both chambers in identical form and is signed by the president, so these are essentially the same as a bill. "The joint resolution is generally used for continuing or emergency appropriations. Joint resolutions are also used for proposing amendments to the Constitution; such resolutions must be approved by two-thirds of both Chambers and three-fourths of the states, but do not require the president's signature to become part of the Constitution."[35]

The legislative process itself is quite complicated, although the general steps in the process of legislation can be enumerated simply, as shown in Box 16.3.[36]

As indicated earlier, the House and the Senate have different styles of operation, primarily as a function of their size. The House has a substantial number of rules and procedures that govern the legislative process, and the Rules Committee has great control over the legislative

---

Box 16.3   The Legislative Process in the United States

- A member of Congress introduces the bill.
- The bill is referred by the Speaker or the president of the Senate to a committee. In the House of Representatives a bill may be sent to more than one committee.
- Committee chair assigns the bill to a subcommittee. Eighty to ninety percent of bills die in subcommittee or committee.
- If bill is approved by subcommittee it is sent back to full committee, where it must be approved before being sent to the full house.
- Floor action on the bill takes place. Typically only a limited number of legislators participate in debate.
- If the bill passes it is referred to the second chamber, where it goes through committee, subcommittee, and full-chamber steps.
- If the bill passes it is sent to a conference committee to work out any differences between the two chambers, if they exist. If differences cannot be worked out, the bill dies.
- If the bill is approved by both chambers, it is sent to the president for a signature or a veto.
- If the bill is vetoed, the Congress can attempt to override the veto with a two-thirds vote in both chambers.

Source: US House of Representatives, "The Legislative Process," https://www .house.gov/the-house-explained/the-legislative-process.

process in which debate is controlled.[37] On the other hand, the Senate tends to be much less structured and tends to rely more upon individual agreements between and among senators.[38]

The Supreme Court

We noted earlier that in most political systems around the world the courts are not seen as political actors. Indeed, in the earliest days of the American republic that was the case, too, and the power of the Supreme Court as a significant political actor is a characteristic that has evolved over time. Article 3 of the Constitution—dealing with the Court—was brief and did not appear to foresee the Court's current role in the political realm. The Supreme Court had a very limited **original jurisdiction** (areas in which cases would begin in the Supreme Court), composed of cases involving ambassadors, public ministers, and consuls, and cases to which a state was a party. Otherwise the Supreme Court's work came from its **appellate jurisdiction** (cases that had been to lower federal courts that were being appealed to the Supreme Court).[39]

In 1789 Congress passed the **Judiciary Act of 1789**, which described the structure of the Supreme Court, as well as laid out a vision for the system of lower federal courts. The Supreme Court was set at six justices, a chief justice plus five associate justices at the time. By the time of the Civil War this had increased to ten justices, then it was revised to nine in 1869, where it has remained since. The Judiciary Act established thirteen federal district courts—the lowest level of federal court—and three circuit courts (today called appeals courts)—courts with appellate jurisdiction.[40]

The man responsible for the growth of the political role of the Supreme Court was Chief Justice John Marshall, who was a supporter of the idea of judicial activism and of an increased role for the Supreme Court in the political arena. Marshall was the individual most closely associated with the principle of judicial review; his basic assertion was that the Supreme Court had the power to determine when acts of Congress were unconstitutional (and this later was expanded to include actions of the executive branch of government).

The condensed description of the case of *Marbury v. Madison* (1803), in which the Supreme Court asserted a power of judicial review, is helpful in order to understand the principles involved. Thomas Jefferson and the Democratic-Republican Party had just defeated the Federalists in the election of 1800, and in their final months in power the Federalists in the lame-duck Congress gave departing president John Adams an opportunity to appoint forty-two new justices of the peace for the District of Columbia and Alexandria, Virginia, before he left office. This action was loudly opposed by the incoming majority party of Democratic-Republicans, but they could not prevent it from taking place. As it turned out, not all of the judicial commissions were actually delivered before midnight on Adams's last night in power, and when President Jefferson took office he had his new secretary of state, James Madison, block delivery of remaining commissions. William Marbury was one of the individuals who was on the list of those scheduled to receive judicial appointments, but he did not receive his expected judicial commission, and he asked the Supreme Court to issue an order to the Department of Justice that he be given his position.

Marshall did not want to support Jefferson, because they were political opponents associated with the two different political parties, but he felt that if he ordered Jefferson to have the commissions delivered, Jefferson would simply ignore his order, consequently weakening the influence of the Supreme Court. Marshall's recourse was to turn to the idea of judicial review. The Court's opinion said that Marbury should have been given his commission, but said that the Court did not have the power to order Jefferson to do so because the part of the Judiciary Act of 1789 that gave the Court the power to issue orders was unconstitutional; thereby Marshall claimed for the Court the power to be able to interpret the constitutionality of acts of Congress in a way that Jefferson would support. Marshall wrote that the part of the Judiciary Act that gave the Court the power to issue orders to anyone holding federal office went beyond the original jurisdiction of the Court in the Constitution, and he claimed that any attempt by Congress to change the jurisdiction of the Court would be unconstitutional, unless it did so through constitutional amendment. "It is emphatically the province and duty of the judicial department to say what the law is. . . . If two laws conflict with each other, the courts must decide on the operation of each. So if a law be in opposition to the Constitution . . . the court must determine which of these conflicting rules governs the case. This is of the very essence of judicial duty."[41] By using this previously unclaimed power of judicial review to say whether an act of Congress was constitutional, Marshall positioned the Supreme Court to become a significant actor in future governmental policy.[42]

The US judicial system reflects the federal nature of the republic, in that there is a federal network of courts that deals with federal law and practices, and there are state networks of courts that deal with state laws and practices. Because of the "supremacy clause" of the Constitution, the federal Constitution and national laws take precedence over state laws and state constitutions if and when they conflict, and over the years the Supreme Court has heard many challenges to state laws by the federal government, and to federal law and administration by state governments.[43]

District courts are the lowest level of federal court. There are eighty-nine federal districts in the fifty states, with at least one district in each state, and other districts in the Virgin Islands, Guam, the Northern Mariana Islands, and the District of Columbia, bringing the total to ninety-four judicial districts with 677 judges.[44]

Federal **appeals courts** (called circuit courts until 1948) are courts of appeals for cases coming out of district courts. Today there are twelve regional courts as well as the Court of Appeals for the Federal Circuit (in Washington, D.C.), with a total of 179 appeals court judges and 84 senior judges, who are semi-retired judges who help out with the overall workload of the courts.

The **Supreme Court** is at the top of the federal judicial pyramid, although in practice the appeals courts are the courts of last resort for most cases. It also has appellate jurisdiction for cases coming out of state courts if they deal with federal law. The Supreme Court has been hearing about seventy-five to eighty-five cases a year in recent years, and when it makes a decision its decision will be announced by one of a variety of alternatives, including majority opinions, concurring opinions, dissents, and *per curiam* ("by the court") opinions.

Many scholars have argued that appointing a justice to the Supreme Court may be the single most important thing that a president will do during his term of office, since justices serve "during good behavior," and regularly have stayed on the Court into their eighties. A president who appoints an activist Supreme Court justice who is either very liberal or very conservative can affect federal politics and policies for thirty or forty years.[45]

While the two major political parties have shared, or exchanged, control of Congress over the years, it has often been the Supreme Court through its power of interpretation of Congressional legislation that has ultimately shaped the nature of governmental policy in the United States. Whether the topic includes religious liberty, free speech, race, a right to privacy, same-sex marriage, or specific application of federalism to government, it has been the Supreme Court through its power of judicial review that has guided the government.[46]

Political Parties and Elections

Earlier in this volume we described the significance of the type of political party system for the politics of a nation, and we indicated that the United States had a single-member-district voting system with its resultant characteristic: a two-party system (because it is very difficult for third parties to win enough votes to get representation in the legislatures). In this section of this chapter we want to explore the role of political parties in the United States, as well as the type of elections that take place. This will include discussion of the Electoral College in presidential elections and the impact that it has had in recent years.

As indicated earlier, political parties come from a variety of sources. In the US case, the original two parties—the Federalists and the Democratic-Republicans—were factions in national politics, primarily differing over matters of national finances. Parties were not formally recognized at the time, and indeed in his Farewell Address, President George Washington warned against the negative effect of parties, stating that "they are likely, in the course of time and things, to become potent engines, by which cunning, ambitious, and unprincipled men will be enabled to subvert the power of the people and to usurp for themselves the reins of government, destroying afterwards the very engines which have lifted them to unjust domination."[47]

There have been a number of different periods of party competition in the United States over time, including the already mentioned Federalists and Democratic-Republicans (from 1789 to 1828); an era of competition between the Democrats and the Whigs (from 1829 to 1856, primarily differing over tariffs and slavery); an era of competition between the Democrats and the Republicans, dominated by the Republicans (1857–1896, primarily differing over slavery before the Civil War, and differing on Reconstruction after the Civil War); an era of competition between the Democrats and the Republicans dominated by the Republicans (1897–1932, focusing on industrialization and immigration); an era of competition between the Democrats and the Republicans, dominated by the Democrats (1933 to 1968, with major debates over the size and scope of the federal government); and the current era of competition between the Democrats and the Republicans, in which neither party has proven to be dominant.

The history of the United States shows the impact of **realignment of political parties** when a significant bloc of voters shifts from "permanent" loyalty to one party, to loyalty to another party. Students of elections have identified several different kinds of elections based upon the type of realignment that takes place at the time, including "maintaining" elections, "deviating" elections, and "critical" elections (see Box 16.4). A **maintaining election** is one in which voters essentially keep their party identity. A **deviating election** is one in which primary identities are not changed, but short-term forces may result in the other party winning the election *this* time; voters still think of themselves as they did before the election. A **critical election** reflects a fundamental shift in the way the electorate sees itself and suggests that new realities are in place that will be evident for years to come.

Box 16.4   Types of Election Outcomes

Maintaining Election

When the past majority political party continues to win a majority in the election. Roosevelt's election in 1932 showed a fundamental realignment of the electorate, and the elections of 1936, 1940, 1944, and 1948 were all "maintaining" elections in which the Democratic majority continued to control power.

Deviating Election

When the past majority political party loses an election for short-term causes but the fundamental identity of the electorate does not change, so that the past majority comes back to power soon. In 1952 and 1956, Republican candidate Dwight Eisenhower won the presidency, but the fundamental attitudes of the electorate didn't change; Democrat John F. Kennedy came to power in 1960.

Critical Election

When the past majority political party ceases to be a majority political party and the fundamental attitudes and identities of the electorate shift. The 1932 election of Franklin Roosevelt was a critical election in that an electorate that had been dominant Republican prior to the election was converted to a dominant Democratic electorate.

Source: Walter Dean Burnham, *Critical Elections and the Mainsprings of American Politics* (New York: Norton, 1970).

While political parties are important for a number of reasons in democratic government, including serving as political linkage mechanisms, recruiting mechanisms, and the like, among their most visible roles is in organizing and competing in elections, and then organizing the behavior of elected officials. As we have seen, parties provide the language and the structure for the operation of both houses of Congress,[48] and it is parties that provide the mechanisms for nomination for elections and competition in elections. It is impossible to imagine, George Washington's admonition notwithstanding, US politics operating without the existence of political parties.[49]

The US federal political system is federal in elections, too, with both national and state electoral structures. Each of the fifty states governs and regulates its own electoral system; states determine whether they are going to be unicameral or bicameral, and they determine the number of representatives that will exist in their legislatures and how those representatives will be elected. Within the United States today only the state of Nebraska is unicameral; all the rest of the states have bicameral legislative systems. Nebraska's state legislature is also non-partisan, which is not a practice duplicated elsewhere. State practices for nomination for elections, for carrying out elections, for the size of their respective state legislatures, and so on, all vary, and all are regulated by state constitutions.[50]

The national electoral system has three foci: elections for the House of Representatives, elections for the Senate, and elections for the presidency. Each of these is affected by the national two-party system, and each has evolved over time (and continues to evolve) to respond to the demands of the day in which it operates.

Members of the House of Representatives, as we noted earlier, are elected for two-year terms of office. The House of Representatives sitting in 2018 is known as the 115th Congress because there have been 115 elections for the House since the first House of Representatives met from March 4, 1789, to March 4, 1791.[51] We noted earlier that the size of the House grew from under 60 members at the time of its creation to 435 in 1911, and in 1911 its maximum size was set at 435. Every ten years, following the US Census, a **reapportionment** takes place in which it is determined how many representatives each state will receive; the total population of the nation is divided by 435, and that figure is then used against individual state populations to determine how many districts each state will receive. Today each of the 435 seats represents approximately 710,000 individuals. As state populations shift, their representation in Congress changes. Today the state of California has fifty-three seats in the House of Representatives, the largest in the nation; Vermont has one seat in the House of Representatives.

After it is determined how many seats a state will have, districts are drawn by state commissions (these are state decisions, not federal decisions); districts are supposed to come as close as possible to being equal size in population. Since early years of the republic, though, there has been a practice by those in power of trying to draw districts to maximize support for whichever political party controls a majority in the state legislature. In 1812 in Massachusetts, Governor Elbridge Gerry signed a bill that redistricted Massachusetts and that helped his Democratic-Republican Party by designing districts to give the Democratic-Republican candidates easier majorities. Opponents said that one of the districts looked like a salamander, and the term *gerrymandering* came to refer to the practice of drawing district boundaries so that the resulting district is the right size in terms of population, but also so that it has a majority of the party in control (see Figure 16.1).[52]

We noted earlier that while representation in the House of Representatives is based upon population, representation in the Senate is based upon the principle of equal representation for each state, with every state having two senators, no matter what its population is. Thus California has two senators, and so does Vermont. Since the electoral districts involved are the entire state, the issue of gerrymandering doesn't apply; population doesn't count, and districts aren't redrawn every ten years. Senators serve terms of six years, and senators are referred to as being in the A class, the B class, and the C class in terms of elections, with one-third of the Senate in each class, and with one of the classes being elected every two years along with all of the members of the House of Representatives.[53] Thus in 2018 all 435 representatives were elected, along with one-third of the Senate. Looked at from a different perspective, every two years California has elections for all fifty-three of its representatives and one of its senators, although in one election out of three there is no senatorial election.

In the elections that took place in November 2018 (see Table 16.7), the Republican Party won 199 seats in the House of Representatives, a loss of 36 seats from the 235 it controlled in the previous Congress, and the Democratic Party won 235 seats, a gain of 42 from the 193 it controlled in the previous Congress (there were 7 vacant seats at the time of the election). In the Senate, 35 seats were at stake (one-third of the 100 seats in the Senate plus one special election), of which the Republicans won 10 and the Democrats won 25, ending up with a partisan balance of

Figure 16.1   Gerrymandering for a US House of Representatives Electoral District

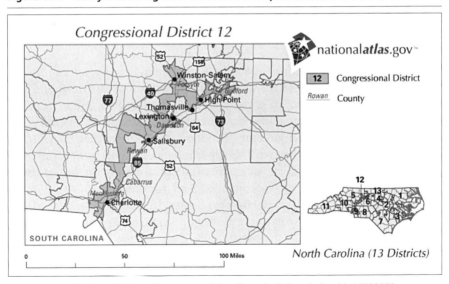

Table 16.7   The US Legislative Elections of 2018

	House of Representatives	Senate
Republicans	199[a]	53
Democrats	235	47

Source: CNN Politics: National Results, https://edition.cnn.com/election/2018/results/house, and https://edition.cnn.com/election/2018/results/senate. Accessed December 2, 2018. *Note:* a. At the time of writing, one House seat was still undeclared.

53 Republicans (a gain of 2) and 47 Democrats and Independents (a loss of 2) to bring the total to 100.

Presidential elections are more complicated because of the existence of the **Electoral College**, as mentioned earlier in this chapter. Because the Founding Fathers did not fundamentally trust "average voters" (and that term had very little meaning in 1787), and because there was a fundamental disagreement between those who wanted the president chosen by state political leaders and those who wanted the president chosen directly by the people, the Founders created the institution called the Electoral College in the new Constitution. On election day, voters in each state do not vote for the presidential candidates themselves, but actually technically vote for lists of **presidential electors**, individuals associated with one of the two major political parties who will, if chosen, cast their electoral votes for the party's nominee for the presidency. Elections are technically held state by state, and in each state whichever list of electors receives the most votes wins all of the electoral positions. That is, if the Republicans receive 51 percent of the vote in California, all of the fifty-five Republican elector candidates (fifty-three because of the number of congressional districts, and two because of the number of senators) are declared elected, and none of the Democratic elector candidates are elected. In some states the names of the electors are actually on the presidential ballot under the name of the candidate they are pledged to support, and in other states only the names of the parties' presidential candidates are on the ballot (even though the public is not technically voting for them).

The total number of **electoral votes** is 538, which is the total of 435 from the number of seats in the House of Representatives plus 100 from the number of seats in the Senate, plus three for the District of Columbia. To be elected president a candidate must receive one more than half of the electoral votes, or 270 electoral votes. To use the examples we've used before, California would have fifty-five electoral votes (from fifty-three representatives and two senators), and Vermont would have three electoral votes (from one representative and two senators). In most states electoral votes are awarded on a winner-take-all basis: in California in 2016 Hillary Clinton won 61.7 percent of the vote and Donald Trump won 31.6 percent of the vote, but Clinton received all of California's electoral votes, and Trump received none. Maine and Nebraska allocate electors based upon congressional districts, where the candidate who wins the most votes in each congressional district receives that electoral vote, and the two electoral votes from Senate seats go to the individual who received the most votes statewide.

After the November election determines which electoral voters have been chosen in each state, in December the presidential electors meet in each of the state capitals and cast written votes. In most states it is entirely legal for the electors to not vote for the candidate they were elected to support, or not vote at all, although most Americans never know how their electors actually vote.

Article 2, Section 1, of the Constitution describes the technical operation of the Electoral College. If no candidate receives a majority of the votes, the members of the House of Representatives are to meet to choose the winner. This is a process that hasn't happened since 1824, and one that clearly can happen only if there are more than two political parties competing in the election.

Another interesting dimension of the Electoral College that has been visible in recent years is the possibility that a presidential candidate could win a majority of the electoral votes without winning a majority of the popular vote, such as happened in 2016 with the election of Donald Trump, and before that in 2000 with the election of George W. Bush. This is made possible by the winner-take-all nature of the electoral vote. Donald Trump could win the "red" states by small margins—for instance, Arizona at 45.5 percent compared to 45.4 percent for Clinton, or Florida at 49.1 percent compared to Clinton's 47.8—and he would win all of the electoral votes from those states. Clinton won some of the very large states by huge margins—for example, California by 62 percent to 33 percent for Trump—and won all of California's electoral votes. When the electoral votes were tallied, Clinton won about 2.9 million votes more than Trump won, about 2.1 percent of the vote; Trump won the vote that counted by winning thirty states with 306 electoral votes (see Table 16.8).

The US System in Perspective

With respect to many of the structural characteristics identified in the first part of this book, the US system is an outlier: it is federal, not unitary; it

Table 16.8   The US Presidential Election of 2016

	Electoral Vote (%)	Popular Vote (%)	Gain/Loss (%)
Donald Trump (Republican)	306 (57.4)	62,984,825 (46.1)	+ 11.3
Hillary Clinton (Democrat)	227 (42.6)	65,853,516 (48.2)	– 5.6
Gary Johnson (Libertarian)	0	4,488,931 (3.3)	
Jill Stein (Green)	0	1,457,050 (1.1)	
D. Evan McMullin (Independent)	0	731,788 (0.5)	
Total	533[a]	136,669,237	

Source: Federal Election Commission, "Official 2016 Presidential General Election Results," https://www.fec.gov/pubrec/fe2016/2016presgeresults.pdf.
Note: a. Five electors chose not to cast ballots.

is presidential, not parliamentary; it has a single-member-district representation system in its lower house and a multiple-member-district system in its upper house (with two senators per state, even if they are elected one at a time); it has active judicial review; and it has a two-party system that has entrenched itself deeply into the political culture. Nevertheless, it is clear that, as with the other political systems examined in this text, political structures affect political behavior in the United States, and those structures and behaviors affect policies and practices.

Discussion Questions

1. What were major factors in US political history that have affected the operation of US politics today?
2. What are the special federal institutions and political practices in the United States? How does America's style of federal government influence US politics? How would this compare with federal government in other systems you have met?
3. What is special about the US president? What special powers does he have? How would you characterize his relationship with the Congress and the Supreme Court?
4. What is the relationship between the House of Representatives and the Senate in the legislative process? Do they have equal roles? What is particularly representative of the principle of federalism in their procedures?
5. How would you compare the nature and role of political parties in the United States today to those in other developed democracies?

Notes

1. William Bianco and David Canon, *American Politics Today* (New York: Norton, 2017), p. 31.

2. See Pauline Maier, *Ratification: The People Debate the Constitution, 1787–1788* (New York: Simon and Schuster, 2010); and Gordon S. Wood, *The Idea of America: Reflections on the Birth of the United States* (New York: Penguin, 2012).

3. Sean Wilson, *The Flexible Constitution* (Lanham: Lexington, 2013).

4. This was a very important principle for many at the time. See Eric Kasper, *To Secure the Liberty of the People: James Madison's Bill of Rights and the Supreme Court's Interpretation* (DeKalb: Northern Illinois University Press, 2010).

5. See *The Constitution of the United States: With Index and the Declaration of Independence* (Washington, DC: US Government Printing Office, 2012).

6. See Erin Ryan, *Federalism and the Tug of War Within* (New York: Oxford University Press, 2011).

7. See Sean Nicholson-Crotty, *Governors, Grants, and Elections: Fiscal Federalism in the American States* (Baltimore: Johns Hopkins University Press, 2015); and Ballard Campbell, *The Growth of American Government: Governance from the Cleveland Era to the Present* (Bloomington: Indiana University Press, 2015).

8. See Gilliam Glidden, *Congress and the Fourteenth Amendment: Enforcing Liberty and Equality in the States* (Lanham: Lexington, 2013).

9. But see Sotirios Barber, *The Fallacies of States' Rights* (Cambridge: Harvard University Press, 2013).

10. See Joseph Francis Zimmerman, *Congress and Crime: The Impact of Federalization of State Criminal Laws* (Lanham: Lexington, 2014); Michael Rebell and Arthur Block, *Equality and Education: Federal Civil Rights Enforcement in the New York City School System* (Princeton: Princeton University Press, 2014); David Konisky, *Failed Promises: Evaluating the Federal Government's Response to Environmental Justice* (Cambridge: Massachusetts Institute of Technology Press, 2015); R. Allen Hays, *The Federal Government and Urban Housing* (Albany: State University of New York Press, 2012); or Amelia Williams, *Federal Energy Management and Government Efficiency Goals* (New York: Nova Science, 2010).

11. John Kincaid and Nicholas Aroney, *Courts in Federal Countries: Federalists or Unitarists?* (Toronto: University of Toronto Press, 2017); and Richard Allen Epstein, *The Classical Liberal Constitution: The Uncertain Quest for Limited Government* (Cambridge: Harvard University Press, 2014).

12. See Ryan Barilleaux and Christopher Kelley, *The Unitary Executive and the Modern Presidency* (College Station: Texas A&M University Press, 2010); and Michael Nelson, *Guide to the Presidency and the Executive Branch* (Thousand Oaks, CA: Congressional Quarterly, 2013).

13. Kathleen Bartoloni-Tuazon, *For Fear of an Elective King: George Washington and the Presidential Title Controversy of 1789* (Ithaca: Cornell University Press, 2014).

14. The text of the Constitution uses the pronoun "he" in reference to the president. This made sense at the time of the writing of the Constitution since women were neither allowed to vote nor allowed to hold public office. This is clearly no longer the case today.

15. See Michael Korzi, *Presidential Term Limits in American History: Power, Principles, and Politics* (College Station: Texas A&M University Press, 2011).

16. Gary Bugh, *Electoral College Reform: Challenges and Possibilities* (Burlington, VT: Ashgate, 2010). See also Robert T. Miller, *The Electoral College: An Analysis* (Hauppauge, NY: Nova Science, 2011); and David Schultz and Stacey Hunter Hecht, *Presidential Swing States: Why Only Ten Matter* (Lanham: Rowman and Littlefield, 2015).

17. See Jeff Shesol, *Supreme Power: Franklin Roosevelt vs. the Supreme Court* (New York: Norton, 2010); and Stephen Shaw, William Pederson, and Franklin Williams, *Franklin D. Roosevelt and the Transformation of the Supreme Court* (London: Routledge, 2015).

18. See also Michael Nelson, *The Evolving Presidency: Landmark Documents, 1787–2015* (Thousand Oaks, CA: Congressional Quarterly, 2016); and Robert J. Spitzer, *The President and Public Policy: The Four Arenas of Presidential Power* (Tuscaloosa: University of Alabama Press, 2012).

19. See Ryan C. Hendrickson, *Obama at War: Congress and the Imperial Presidency* (Lexington: University Press of Kentucky, 2015).

20. Chris Edelson, *Emergency Presidential Power: From the Drafting of the Constitution to the War on Terror* (Madison: University of Wisconsin Press, 2013). See also David Coleman, *The Fourteenth Day: JFK and the Aftermath of the Cuban Missile Crisis* (New York: Norton, 2012); Chris Edelson, *Power Without Constraint: The Post-9/11 Presidency and National Security* (Madison: University of Wisconsin Press, 2016); and Donald Kelley and Todd Shields, *Taking the Measure: The Presidency of George W. Bush* (College Station: Texas A&M University Press, 2013).

21. Lee Hamilton, *Congress, Presidents, and American Politics: Fifty Years of Writings and Reflections* (Bloomington: Indiana University Press, 2016).

22. Benjamin Ginsberg, Theodore J. Lowi, Caroline J. Tolbert, and Margaret Weir, *We the People,* 11th ed. (New York: Norton, 2017), p. 514.

23. See Robert P. Watson, *The Obama Presidency: A Preliminary Assessment* (Albany: State University of New York Press, 2012); Bert Rockman, Andrew Rudalevige, and Colin Campbell, *The Obama Presidency: Appraisals and Prospects* (Los Angeles: Sage/Congressional Quarterly, 2012); and Derrick E. White and Kenneth Alan Osgood, *Winning While Losing? Civil Rights, the Conservative Movement, and the Presidency from Nixon to Obama* (Gainesville: University Press of Florida, 2013).

24. See Graham Dodds, *Take Up Your Pen: Unilateral Presidential Directives in American Politics* (Philadelphia: University of Pennsylvania Press, 2013).

25. Ginsberg et al., *We the People,* p. 516.

26. Article 2, Section 2, states that the president "may require the Opinion, in writing, of the principal Officer in each of the executive Departments, upon any Subject relating to the Duties of their respective Office," but doesn't provide any more detail than this about either what the executive departments will be or what the powers of the principal officers will be.

27. See *The Executive Office of the President, 1939–2012* (Washington, DC: Congressional Quarterly, 2013).

28. Lucius Wilmerding Jr., "The Presidential Succession," *Atlantic Monthly,* May 1947, https://www.theatlantic.com/past/docs/unbound/flashbks/pres/wilmer.htm. There is a significant literature on presidential succession, including the following: Kate Anderson Brower, *First in Line: Presidents, Vice Presidents, and the Pursuit of Power* (New York: Harper, 2018); Jody Baumgartner and Thomas Crumblin, *The American Vice Presidency: From the Shadow to the Spotlight* (Lanham: Rowman and Littlefield, 2015); Joel K. Goldstein, *The White House Vice Presidency: The Path to Significance, Mondale to Biden* (Lawrence: University Press of Kansas, 2016); and John D. Feerick, *The Twenty-Fifth Amendment: Its Complete History and Applications* (New York: Fordham University Press, 2014).

29. See Andrew J. Taylor, *Congress: A Performance Appraisal* (Boulder: Westview, 2013).

30. In 1959 when Hawaii and Alaska were added as states the number of representatives was temporarily raised to 437—with one representative for each new state—but the number was rolled back to 435 following the 1960 Census.

31. See "Return the House of Representatives to the People," http://www.thirty-thousand.org.

32. See Richard Fenno, *The Challenge of Congressional Representation* (Cambridge: Harvard University Press, 2013).

33. US House of Representatives, H. Res. 128, https://www.congress.gov/bill/115th-congress/house-resolution/128.

34. US Senate, S. Con. Res. 3, https://www.congress.gov/bill/115th-congress/senate-concurrent-resolution/3.

35. US Senate, "Legislation, Laws, and Acts," https://www.senate.gov/legislative/common/briefing/leg_laws_acts.htm. See Mark Grossman and Scott Derks, *Constitutional Amendments: Encyclopedia of the People, Procedures, Politics, Primary Documents Relating to the 27 Amendments to the U.S. Constitution* (New York: Grey, 2017).

36. Shannon Jenkins, *The Context of Legislating: Constraints on the Legislative Process in the United States* (Abingdon: Taylor and Francis, 2016); and John Castellano, *The Legislative Process in the United States Congress: An Introduction* (New York: Nova Science, 2013).

37. See Jeffery Jenkins and Charles Haines Stewart, *Fighting for the Speakership: The House and the Rise of Party Government* (Princeton: Princeton University Press, 2012); and Matthew N. Green, *Underdog Politics: The Minority Party in the U.S. House of Representatives* (New Haven: Yale University Press, 2015).

38. Neil MacNeil and Richard Baker, *The American Senate: An Insider's History* (Oxford: Oxford University Press, 2013); Martin Gold, *Senate Procedure and Practice* (Lanham: Rowman and Littlefield, 2013); and Richard Arenberg, Robert Dove, and Olympia J. Snowe, *Defending the Filibuster: The Soul of the Senate* (Bloomington: Indiana University Press, 2014).

39. Matthew Eric Kane Hall, *The Nature of Supreme Court Power* (Leiden: Cambridge University Press, 2010); and Richard J. Regan, *A Constitutional History of the U.S. Supreme Court* (Washington, DC: Catholic University of America Press, 2015).

40. See Regan, *Constitutional History of the U.S. Supreme Court.*

41. *Marbury v. Madison,* 5 U.S. 1 Cranch 137 (1803).

42. See Linda Greenhouse, *The U.S. Supreme Court: A Very Short Introduction* (New York: Oxford University Press, 2012); and Steven J. Kautz, *The Supreme Court and the Idea of Constitutionalism* (Philadelphia: University of Pennsylvania Press, 2011).

43. Article 6, Clause 2: "This Constitution, and the Laws of the United States which shall be made in Pursuance thereof, and all Treaties made, or which shall be made, under the Authority of the United States, shall be the supreme Law of the Land, and the Judges in every State shall be bound thereby, any Thing in the Constitution or Laws of any State to the Contrary notwithstanding."

44. "Judges and Judgeships," http://www.uscourts.gov/judges-judgeships.

45. See Dian Farganis and Justin Wedeking, *Supreme Court Confirmation Hearings in the U.S. Senate: Reconsidering the Charade* (Ann Arbor: University of Michigan Press, 2014).

46. Vincent Phillip Munoz, *Religious Liberty and the American Supreme Court: The Essential Cases and Documents* (Lanham: Rowman and Littlefield, 2015); David O'Brien and Ronald Collins, *Congress Shall Make No Law: The First Amendment, Unprotected Expression, and the Supreme Court* (Lanham: Rowman and Littlefield, 2010); Jeffrey Hockett, *A Storm over This Court: Law, Politics, and Supreme Court Decision-Making in Brown v. Board of Education* (Charlottesville: University of Virginia Press, 2013); Christopher Waldrep, *Jury Discrimination: The Supreme Court, Public Opinion, and a Grassroots Fight for Racial Equality in Mississippi* (Athens: University of Georgia Press, 2010); and Christopher P. Banks and John C. Blakeman, *The U.S. Supreme Court and New Federalism: From the Rehnquist to the Roberts Court* (Lanham: Rowman and Littlefield, 2012).

47. Washington's *Farewell Address,* para. 18, sentence 1.

48. Jacob R. Straus, *Party and Procedure in the United States Congress* (Lanham: Rowman and Littlefield, 2012).

49. Marjorie Randon Hershey, Barry Burden, Christina Wolbrecht, *U.S. Political Parties* (Thousand Oaks, CA: Congressional Quarterly, 2014); L. Sandy Maisel and Mark Brewer, *Parties and Elections in America: The Electoral Process* (Lanham: Rowman and Littlefield, 2012); and L. Sandy Maisel and Jeffrey Berry, eds., *The Oxford Handbook of American Political Parties and Interest Groups* (New York: Oxford University Press, 2010).

50. See Jamie Carson, *Legislative Politics and Policy-Making: Ambition, Competition, and Electoral Reform in the Politics of Congressional Elections Across Time* (Ann Arbor: University of Michigan Press, 2013).

51. The year 1789 was 229 years prior to the year 2018. At two years per House, that makes the House of 2018 the 115th House.

52. A wonderful explanation of how gerrymandering works can be found in the article by Christopher Ingraham in the *Washington Post* titled "This Is the Best Explanation of Gerrymandering You Will Ever See," https://www.washingtonpost.com/news/wonk/wp/2015/03/01/this-is-the-best-explanation-of-gerrymandering-you-will-ever-see/?utm_term=.d95d4e0bfc74. See also William Miller et al., *The Political Battle over Congressional Redistricting* (Lanham: Lexington, 2013); and Erik J. Engstrom, *Partisan Gerrymandering and the Construction of American Democracy* (Ann Arbor: University of Michigan Press, 2013).

53. Although the Seventeenth Amendment, ratified in 1913, changed the electoral system for the Senate from having senators elected by the state legislatures to having senators be directly elected by voters in the states. See Wendy Schiller and Charles Haines Stewart, *Electing the Senate: Indirect Democracy Before the Seventeenth Amendment* (Princeton: Princeton University Press, 2015).

Glossary

absolute veto. The complete blockage of a piece of legislation. In the legislative context, a case in which a legislative chamber's refusal to approve legislation completely stops the progress of that legislation, resulting in failure of the legislation in question.

AIDS. Acquired immunodeficiency syndrome. One of Africa's largest killer diseases, caused by the human immunodeficiency virus (HIV), which is transmitted through bodily fluids and significantly reduces the body's ability to resist infections.

analytic systems. Groups of objects that are connected with one another in an analytic way.

anarchism. A belief that all forms of government interfere with individual rights and freedoms and should therefore be abolished.

Andropov, Yuri Vladimirovich. Soviet politician and the fourth general secretary of the Communist Party of the Soviet Union. Served only fifteen months, from November 1982 until his death in February 1984.

Anti-Federalists. In the early days of the United States, a group opposing the new constitutional proposals of 1787.

appeals court. In a network of courts, a court that reviews the decisions of lower courts.

appellate jurisdiction. See *appeals court*

Arab Spring. From December 2010 through the summer of 2011 people protested authoritarian rule in Tunisia, Egypt, Libya, Bahrain, Syria, Jordan, to as far west as Morocco. Almost no country in the Arab Middle East was untouched by calls for democratic government.

Article 16 powers. Under the French Constitution, part of the emergency powers at the disposal of the president.

Articles of Confederation. In the United States the first constitution, ratified in 1781. The constitution so limited the power of the central government that it proved to be ineffective, leading to a new Constitutional Convention being called in 1787.

Attlee, Clement. British Labour Party leader who served as prime minister of the United Kingdom.

backbencher. Name deriving from positions in the British House of Commons in which seats are arranged in two sets of rows facing each other. Party leaders sit on the frontbenches of their respective sides; nonleaders, or followers, sit on the backbenches— hence backbenchers are not party leaders.

Basic Law. An alternative structure to a constitution in postwar Germany.

bicameral legislature. A legislature with two legislative houses, or chambers.

bill. Typically a legislative proposal that becomes law if passed by the legislature and approved by the executive.

Bill of Rights. First ten amendments of the US Constitution. Ratified by the states in December 1791. Also refers to a component of British constitutional law.

467

Blackstone, William (1723–1780). Eighteenth-century scholar whose work on British law is seen as being authoritative.

Blair, Tony. British Labour Party leader who served as prime minister of the United Kingdom, 1997–2007.

blocked vote. Legislative possibility in France that requires the legislative chambers to vote on a bill in its original text, incorporating only those amendments proposed or accepted by the government.

Bolshevik. The Bolsheviks were the majority faction in an internal party conflict of the Russian Social Democratic Party at its 1903 convention. The leader of the majority faction was Vladimir Lenin.

Brexit. The process of Britain exiting from the European Union. In June 2016, 52 percent of the British population voted to leave the EU. The specific terms of Britain's withdrawal, including new customs details, are currently being negotiated.

Brezhnev, Leonid. Soviet politician who served as General Secretary of the Communist Party, 1964–1982.

Britain. See *Great Britain*

British East African Protectorate. In Kenya, dating to 1895, also known as British East Africa, this was the name of territory in East Africa controlled by Britain. It remained a protectorate until 1920, when it became the Colony of Kenya.

British East India Company. Founded in London in 1600, it exercised much influence around the world in the development of British colonial trade.

British Raj. In India, referring to the period of time of direct rule by Britain.

Brown, Gordon. British Labour Party leader who served as prime minister of the United Kingdom, 2007–2010.

Bundesrat. Upper house of the German bicameral legislature.

Bundestag. Lower house of the German bicameral legislature.

bureaucracy. Administrative structure of government, including organizational perspective, focusing upon structures, organizational charts, lines of communication, hierarchical organization, formal rules, and how government operates.

cabinet. Formal body of advisers to the head of state in a parliamentary system. Head of the cabinet is the prime minister or other appropriate title. The name also applies to the group of senior advisers and heads of executive agencies in a presidential system.

Calderón Hinojosa, Felipe. Leader of the Mexican National Action Party and president of Mexico, 2006–2012.

Cameron, David. British Conservative Party leader who served as prime minister of the United Kingdom, 2005–2010.

capitalism. Economic system in which the major means of production are owned by individuals, not by the government of the state. The economic philosophy emphasizes private ownership and a market economy—that is, nonregulation of the marketplace by the government.

case study method of inquiry. Intensive study of individual cases.

caste. In India, referring to the hereditary classes of Hindu society, perceived to be distinguished by relative degrees of ritual purity or pollution, and of social status.

Central Committee of the Chinese Communist Party. In China, the Central Committee of the Chinese Communist Party is a body of about 200 individuals—most recently documented at 204 members—elected by the Party Congress, to act in the name of the Communist Party when it is not in session.

centralized federation. Federal system in which the central government has more power than the intermediate (e.g., state- or provincial-level) governments, although to be considered a federation there must be some policy jurisdictions that are under the control of the intermediate governments.

Chamberlain, Neville. British Conservative Party leader who served as prime minister of the United Kingdom, 1937–1940. Best known for his policy of "appeasement" with Germany in the period leading up to World War II.

Chamber of Deputies. Name for the lower house in many bicameral legislatures, including (in this volume) Mexico and France.

chancellor. Title of the chief executive of the Federal Republic of Germany.

Chernenko, Konstantin. Soviet political leader, chairman of the Presidium of the Supreme Soviet and general secretary of the Communist Party of the Soviet Union, February 1984–March 1985.

Chiang Kai-shek (1887–1975). Chinese political and military leader. Chiang was an ally and successor of Sun Yat-sen. Led the Chinese Nationalists in the civil war against the Chinese Communist Party following World War II, ultimately retreating to Taiwan where he served as president of the Republic of China and director of the Guomindang until his death in 1975.

chief executive. Head of the executive branch of government. Typically in parliamentary systems this is the prime minister, elected as a member of the legislature, just as all other members of the legislature are elected. Head of cabinet. In presidential systems, this role is played by the president.

Chinese Communist Party (CCP). Ruling party organization in China.

Chirac, Jacques. President of France, May 1995–May 2007; prime minister of France, March 1986–May 1988.

civil society. How the population of a nation organizes into associations or organizations that are independent of formal institutions of the state; how people organize groups to define their interests.

Clegg, Nick. British Liberal Democratic Party leader who participated in a British coalition government, 2010–2015.

coalition government. Two or more nonmajority parties pooling their legislative seats to form a majority parliamentary bloc.

Code Napoleon. Body of laws assembled during the time of Emperor Napoleon, intended to standardize law and legal structures from Europe through Asia.

cohabitation. In France, the situation of having a president from one political party and a prime minister from another political party.

collective good. Any good that, if available to one person in a group, cannot feasibly be withheld from the others in that group.

colonial powers. In Africa, referring to the nations that had a colonial relationship with an African territory, in which the (typically European) nation established and maintained colonies in African territory, exercised sovereignty over that territory, and ran the social, political, and economic institutions of that nation. Also applies to settings outside of Africa in which native populations were directed and governmentally administered by European powers.

committee of the whole. Technical device used in a legislature to establish a different set of procedural rules; a legislative body can dissolve itself into a committee of the whole.

common law system. Sometimes called Anglo-American law, and referred to as judge-made law. This is not to suggest that today's laws in common law political systems are not made by the legislatures of those systems, or conversely that today's laws are made by judges in those systems. This type of law is more culturally sensitive and more flexible, relying more upon judicial interpretation than legislative design.

Commonwealth of Independent States (CIS). Emerged in December 1991 to serve as a structure to replace the Soviet Union.

Commonwealth of Nations. Voluntary association of nations that were part of the British Empire at some point in their history. Today the Commonwealth functions as a political "family" with no requirement of formal or constitutional linkages.

communes. Part of the Chinese Great Leap Forward (1958–1961). Communes were groups of about 5,000 families that would work together for greater efficiency than had been previously possible if working separately.

communism. Belief in government ownership of the major means of production, and of the general primacy of politics over economics; the government should actively regulate and control all sectors of the economy with little or no private property.

comparative method of inquiry. Comparison of two or more case studies.

competitive single-party system. In Kenya under one-party government from 1982 to 1991, there were competitive elections, but they took place as primary elections within the framework of the Kenyan African National Union party. While national elections nominally had one political party, there were competitive factions within the party that participated in primary elections.

concrete, or real system. A set of objects that we can actually see (or touch, or feel, or measure).

concurrent power. Both the federal and the state governments may act in a given policy area. In Germany the Lander may legislate in areas of concurrent power, "as long as, and to the extent that, the Federation does not exercise its right to legislate."

concurrent resolution. In the United States, concurrent resolutions are efforts in which both chambers of the Congress want to express their views on a nonlegislative issue, and there is a desire to have both chambers act together rather than pass simple resolutions.

confederal system. Union of sovereign states that each retain their powers but agree to coordinate their activities in certain respects.

conference committees. In the United States, temporary committees made up of members of both houses of the Congress whose members are appointed by the Speaker of the House (for the House of Representatives) and the presiding officer (for the Senate); they typically appoint members of the respective chambers who have worked on the piece of legislation in question and are most well-informed about the bills.

Confucius (Kung Fu-tzu, c. 551–479 B.C.E.). Chinese philosopher. While the emperors based their power on a "mandate of heaven"—a Chinese variation on what would be known in Europe much later as the "divine right of kings" theory—Confucian theory suggested that even emperors had to follow ethical principles, including moral leadership.

Congress of People's Deputies. Name of legislature of the Soviet Union from 1989 to 1991, succeeding the Supreme Soviet of the Soviet Union, and succeeded by the State Council of the Soviet Union. Also the name of the supreme government institution in the Russian Federation from 1990 to 1993.

conservative ideology. Position described as being most satisfied with the way society is operating, satisfied with the status quo. Classical conservatives do not share the optimism of liberals that individuals can improve society. They are more skeptical of human nature and believe that human nature may be selfish. They place more emphasis on respecting institutions and traditions and are not sure that they (or others) are capable of devising a better system. They believe in elitism.

constituency vote. In Germany the vote that focuses on candidates running for office from districts, not the "at large" candidates.

constitution. Expression of the ideas and organization of a government that is formally presented in one document and describes how power is distributed among the actors.

constitutional government. Limited government, specifically an absolute limitation on governmental power in specific areas.

constructive vote of no confidence. See *positive vote*

cooperative federalism. In Germany and other systems, a relationship in federal government in which both the central government and the intermediate-level governments can share jurisdiction over and responsibility for policy issues.

corporatism. Belief that advocates a close degree of cooperation and coordination between the government and labor and business groups in the formation of economic policy.

Council of Ministers. In India the collective executive body, which corresponds to the cabinet in Britain and other parliamentary systems, that is responsible to the legislature.

coup d'état. Revolution from above.

court packing. In the United States, name given to President Franklin Roosevelt's proposal to appoint extra justices to the Supreme Court; his plan would have allowed him to appoint an additional justice for each incumbent justice over the age of seventy.

critical election. When the past majority political party ceases to be a majority political party, and the fundamental attitudes and identities of the electorate shift.

Cultural Revolution. In China, collective purging of individuals who were seen as not being "good" Communists, took place between 1966 and 1976.

de Gaulle, Charles. Leader of the French Resistance against Nazi Germany in World War II; chairman of the Provisional Government of France, 1944–1946; founder of the Fifth Republic in 1958; and president of France, 1958–1969.

de Gaulle constitution. The French Constitution of the Fifth Republic. Although it wasn't literally authored by Charles de Gaulle (substantial credit is given to Michel Debré), it reflected de Gaulle's views of needed structures and relationships that shaped the document.

Debré, Michel. French political leader, member of the National Assembly, minister of defense, minister of foreign affairs, and prime minister of France, 1959–1962. Credited with being the driving force behind the current Constitution of France.

Declaration of Independence. In the American colonies, a document expressing key principles of those calling for separation from Britain in 1776.

delegated powers of the president. These include powers given to the president by Congress as part of legislation.

democratic centralism. In China the theory that key decisions are made at the center, and then moved out to the more democratic bodies and structures to be ratified.

demokratizatsiya ("democratization"). One of three key principles of Soviet politics under Mikhail Gorbachev from 1985 through 1991.

Deng Xiaoping (1904–1997). In China, statesman and leader of the Communist Party. While Deng never held office as the head of state, head of government, or General Secretary of the Party, he served as the Supreme Leader of the People's Republic of China from 1978 to 1992. Best known as being a reformer who led China toward permitting a market economy to develop.

deviating election. When the past majority political party loses an election for short-term causes but the fundamental identity of the electorate does not change, so that the past majority comes back to power soon.

devolution of power. Political power flowing from the center to more distant areas of the nation. In Britain, moving power from the political center (London) to regional administration (Cardiff, Wales, and Edinburgh, Scotland).

Diaz, Porfirio. Mexican political leader who served as president of Mexico, 1876–1880 and 1884–1911.

divine law. Guidelines based upon the religious or theological conceptual framework from which law and political power are said to be derived.

divine right of kings. Belief that the monarch derives his power directly from God, not from the people.

ecological level of analysis. Relates to observations and measurements focusing on groups, not individuals, and the types of conclusions that can be drawn from those observations and measurements.

Electoral College. In the United States the structure designed to elect the president, involving political elites voting for the president, as distinct from direct popular election, which the Founding Fathers did not trust.

electoral votes. In the United States the number of votes each state has in the presidential election. The number of electoral votes each state has is the total of the number of representatives it has in the House of Representatives (ranging from one to fifty-three) plus the number of senators it has (two).

empirical approach to inquiry. Relies on measurement and observation.

England. Administrative unit of the United Kingdom of Great Britain and Northern Ireland, part of the island of Great Britain along with Scotland and Wales.

executive order. Has the status of formal legislation in areas in which the president already has some jurisdiction. This has become in recent years an option for US presidents when they cannot get Congress to pass legislation.

expatriates. Individuals who temporarily or permanently live in a country other than the one in which they were born, or in which they have citizenship—British residents of Kenya, or India, for example.

experimental method of inquiry. Method of inquiry in which one manipulates one variable in order to observe its effect upon another variable.

expressed powers of the president. In the United States those powers actually established by the language of the Constitution—for example, the power of the president to grant pardons.

extraterritorial rights. In China, the rights of foreigners to operate under their own national legal systems rather than under Chinese law.

Fakhruddin, Ali Ahmed. President of India, 1974–1977.

fascism. A belief (that includes national socialism) that usually is said to include seven components: irrationalism, social Darwinism, nationalism, glorification of the state, the leadership principle, racism (more important in national socialism than in fascism), and anticommunism.

Federalist Papers. Series of essays written by James Madison, Alexander Hamilton, and John Jay that sought to justify the proposed new US Constitution in 1787 and sought to generate public support for the new plan.

Federalists. Starting in 1787, a political position in the United States supporting the new constitutional proposals of 1787, which were ratified in 1788.

federal system. When government operates on two levels above the local level, with both the central government and state or provincial level of government enjoying sovereignty in certain areas.

Federation Council. Upper house of the Federal Assembly (the bicameral legislature) of Russia following adoption of the 1993 constitution of the Russian Federation.

feminism. System of beliefs that has emerged primarily in the West in opposition to oppression of women, and opposition to sexism in general. Has developed different schools including liberal or reform feminism, Marxist feminism, socialist feminism, and radical feminism.

Five Percent Clause. In Germany the characteristic of voting indicating that parties can win seats from the proportional representation second votes only if they poll at least 5 percent of the second votes cast.

Fourth Republic. Period in French history, following the end of World War II, when France attempted to reestablish stable democratic government. Lasted until June 1958, when the government of Charles de Gaulle became the first government of the Fifth Republic.

Fox Quesada, Vicente. Mexican political leader, leader of the National Action Party, and president of Mexico, 2000–2006.

frontbencher. Name derives from positions in the British House of Commons in which seats are arranged in two sets of rows facing each other. Party leaders sit on the frontbenches of their respective sides.

Gandhi, Indira. Indian political leader, leader of the Indian National Congress, and the third prime minister of India, 1966–1977, and from 1980 until her assassination in 1984.

Gandhi, Mohandas. Indian political leader, leader of the Indian independence movement against British rule, president of the Indian National Congress.

Gaullism. French movement of support for Charles de Gaulle that claimed to be an alternative to divisive political parties.

General Secretary of the Party. In China, formal leader of the secretariat of the Central Committee of the Chinese Communist Party.

gerrymandering. In the United States the practice of drawing in extremely irregular ways the boundaries of electoral districts to maximize support for whichever political party controls a majority in the state legislature.

Giscard d'Estaing, Valérie. French political leader and president of France, 1974–1981.

glasnost ("openness"). One of three key principles of Soviet politics under Mikhail Gorbachev from 1985 through 1991.

Gorbachev, Mikhail (1931–). General secretary of the Communist Party of the Soviet Union from 1985 to 1991, and last head of state of the USSR, serving from 1988 until its end in 1991.

Government bill. In Britain, bill originating in the Government frontbench—where the members of the cabinet sit. Typically these bills come from various ministries and are passed up to cabinet, then ratified by cabinet and introduced in the legislature as a Government bill.

Great Britain. Principal island of the United Kingdom, which includes England, Scotland, and Wales.

Great Leap Forward. In China the name given to a five-year plan announced in 1958 by Mao Zedong.

Gromyko, Andrei. Soviet political leader and chairman of the Presidium of the Union of Soviet Socialist Republics, 1985–1988.

guerrilla warfare. Focuses attention on government targets, usually military targets, rather than the often random civilian targets focused upon by terrorists.

Guomindang (GMD). Chinese name of the Nationalist Party led by Sun Yat-sen.

head of state. Person who symbolizes the state and the dignity of the political regime, as distinct from the chief executive, who serves as the operational head of the executive branch of government.

Hollande, François. French political leader and president of France, 2012–2017.

House of Commons. Name of the lower chamber of the Parliament of the United Kingdom and many other national legislatures.

House of Lords. Name of the upper chamber of the Parliament of the United Kingdom.

Hundred Flowers Movement. In China, based upon a saying of Confucius: "Let a hundred flowers bloom, let a hundred schools of thought contend." Based on the idea that the free and open exchange of ideas would be supported by Mao.

hung Parliament. In Britain and other parliamentary systems, describes a Parliament in which there is no majority party, which requires either a coalition Government to be created or a minority Government to be formed, in which the Government does not quite have a majority but has nearly a majority and can operate that way.

hyper-urbanization. Practice of substantial populations moving from rural areas in a nation to the major cities in search of a better life, often creating substantial health and environmental problems.

immobilism. Where two or more political structures each have enough power to block the other, but not enough to achieve their own objectives, which means that it is possible that nothing will be accomplished.

implied powers of the president. In the United States, powers that are necessary to allow the president to exercise expressed powers.

Indian National Congress. Organization that led resistance to British colonial rule. Following India's independence, the Congress became the Congress Party.

individual level of analysis. Relates to the types of observations and measurements in analysis, focusing upon individuals, not groups, and the types of conclusions that can be drawn from those observations and measurements.

input-output analysis. David Easton's analytic framework viewed the political system as a continuously operating mechanism, with demands and supports going in (inputs), and authoritative decisions and actions coming out (outputs).

interest group. Collection of individuals who share common beliefs, attitudes, values, or concerns.

Ivan the Terrible. Russian tsar, 1533–1584.

jacquerie. Revolution from below.

Jiang Zemin (1926–). General Secretary of the Communist Party of China from 1989 to 2002, president of the People's Republic of China from 1993 to 2003.

Jinnah, Muhammed Ali. Founding leader of Pakistan and leader of the All-India Muslim League from 1913 until Pakistan became independent in August 1947. Served as Pakistan's first governor-general, 1947–1948.

joint committee. Legislative committee made up of members from both houses in a bicameral legislature.

joint resolution. In the United States, legislation that passes both chambers in identical form and is signed by the president; essentially the same as a bill.

Juárez, Benito. President of Mexico, 1858–1872.

judicial power of the president. In the United States the power to grant pardons and appoint federal justices.

judicial precedent. Courts referring to previous decisions when they make decisions. The process is referred to as *stare decisis* ("to stand by things decided").

judicial review. Process by which courts rule upon the propriety or legality of action of the legislative and executive branches of government.

Judiciary Act of 1789. In the United States, legislation passed by Congress in 1789 that described the structure of the Supreme Court, as well as laid out a vision for the system of lower federal courts.

jurisdiction. Determination of which court (or level of court) has authority to adjudicate a specific question.

Kadhi courts. In Kenya a system of Muslim courts that deal with issues of personal status.

Kalenjin. Ethnic group of people in western Kenya and eastern Uganda, numbering nearly 4.4 million total.

Kashmir. Province in the north of India that is the country's only Muslim-majority state; has been a source of conflict because a majority of its population wants to become part of Pakistan.

Kenyan African National Union (KANU). Political party in Kenya that served as the basis of government for forty years, from the time of independence from Britain in 1962 to its electoral loss in 2002.

Kenyatta, Jomo (1891–1978). Kenyan nationalist leader, served as the first prime minister (1963–1964), then as president (1964–1978). Served as president of the Kenyan African National Union, the political movement associated with driving the British out of Kenya.

Kenyatta, Uhuru Muigai. Kenyan political leader and president of Kenya, 2013 to the present.

Khrushchev, Nikita. Soviet political leader, first secretary of the Communist Party of the Soviet Union, 1953–1964, and chairman of the Council of Ministers of the Soviet Union, 1958–1964.

Kibaki, Mwai. Kenyan political leader and president of Kenya, 2002–2013.

Kikuyu. In Kenya the most populous ethnic group, comprising about 5.3 million people, about 23 percent of the country's population.

Kohl, Helmut. German political leader, leader of the Christian Democratic Union, and chancellor of Germany (West Germany until 1990), 1982–1998.

Kosygin, Alexei. Soviet political leader and chairman of the Council of Ministers of the Soviet Union, 1964–1980.

Kovind, Shri Ram Nath. Indian political leader and fourteenth president of India. Assumed office in July 2017.

Lander. Units of the national territory in Germany. The Lander are the equivalent of provinces in Canada or cantons in Switzerland or states in the United States.

Law Lords. Members of the House of Lords who served as the high court for the United Kingdom; in 2009 the Law Lords' power was transferred from the House of Lords to the Supreme Court of the United Kingdom.

legal culture. Focuses upon the beliefs, attitudes, and values of society relative to the law and politics.

legislative independence. Independence of the legislature from the executive, as in the United States. Unlike the relationship that exists in parliamentary legislatures, where the head of the executive branch is also the head of the legislative branch.

legislative power of the president. In the United States the president can block legislation with a veto (although vetoes can be overridden by Congress); the president cannot introduce legislation directly. In Mexico the president is permitted to be involved in the legislative process.

legislative supremacy. Idea that the legislature "hires" the chief executive (although the head of state may "nominate" them) or invests them with power.

Lenin, Vladimir (1870–1924). Creator of the Soviet Communist Party and leader of the 1917 October Revolution; founder of the Union of Soviet Socialist Republics. His interpretation of and contributions to classical Marxist theory produced a distinct body of political theory referred to as Leninism.

levels of analysis. The way we look at political problems, either from a broad, societal perspective (the ecological level) or from a more narrow, individual perspective (the individual level).

liberal ideology. Position that is more content with society than is that of the radical, but still believes that reform is possible, perhaps necessary. Liberalism includes a belief in human potential, in the ability of individuals to change institutions for the better, in human rationality, and in human equality.

life peerage. Historical pattern of the House of Lords in Britain in which an individual was appointed to the Lords and would keep that seat for the duration of his life. A similar phenomenon existed in the Canadian Senate, in which members were appointed by the head of state (on the advice of the prime minister) and would keep their positions as long as they lived.

limited government. Criterion by which we measure whether a government can be called constitutional or not. Are there absolutely limits to what the government can do? Are there some things (e.g., restricting free speech) that the government absolutely cannot do?

linkage mechanism. Political structure that serves to connect the voice and opinions of the people to the political leaders of the regime.

Lok Sabha. Lower house of India's bicameral parliament.

Long March. In China a massive military retreat led by Mao Zedong in 1934 to avoid capture and defeat by the Nationalist Chinese (Guomindang) forces led by Chiang Kai-shek. Mao's forces walked over 8,000 miles in 370 days. The Long March marked the beginning of the ascent to power of Mao and a generation of Chinese Communist leaders.

López Obrador, Andrés Manuel. Mexican political leader and president of Mexico. Assumed office in December 2018.

lower house of a legislature. That house in a bicameral system most directly elected by the people.

Maasai. In Kenya an ethnic group of people numbering over 800,000 as of 2009, located primarily in Kenya but also in northern Tanzania.

Macron, Emmanuel. French political leader, founder of the En Marche! movement in France, and president of France. Assumed office in May 2017.

maintaining election. When the past majority political party continues to win a majority in the election.

Majimboism. Regional administrative decentralization in Kenya.

Major, John. British political leader, leader of the Conservative Party, and prime minister of the United Kingdom, 1990–1997.

Mao Zedong (1893–1976). Leader of Chinese Communist Party and chairman of the CCP from 1949 until his death in 1976. Creator and developer of Chinese Communist ideology.

Marbury v. Madison (1803). Supreme Court case in the United States in which the principle of judicial review was established.

Marxism. Ideological structure based upon the Communist Manifesto (written in 1848) and subsequent writings of Karl Marx and Friedrich Engels.

Marxism-Leninism. Complex framework describing the economic system and the inevitable conflict between the working class and the owners of the means of production. Suggested the inevitability of class conflict, and was adopted and modified by Lenin to create Soviet Communism.

Mau Mau. Secret society of Kikuyu Kenyans who were seeking independence from British colonial power.

May, Theresa. British political leader, leader of the Conservative Party, and prime minister of the United Kingdom. Assumed office in July 2016.

Medvedev, Dmitry. Russian political leader; served as prime minister of Russia under Vladimir Putin, 1999–2008; served as president of Russia, 2008–2012; and again as prime minister of Russia since 2012.

Menshevik. Minority faction in an internal party conflict of the Russian Social Democratic Party at its 1903 convention. The leader of the majority faction was Vladimir Lenin.

Merkel, Angela. German political leader, leader of the Christian Democratic Union, and chancellor of Germany since 2005.

metropolitan France. Refers to the twenty-two administrative regions of France, containing ninety-six departments. Metropolitan France does not include the overseas territories and possessions of the country.

Middle Kingdom. In China, can also be translated as the "center of civilization." A name that is often used in China for its traditional name.

military coup. Sometimes called a generals' coup, involves military leaders taking over a government because of their dissatisfaction with civilian control.

military power of the president. In the United States the president serves as commander-in-chief of the armed forces.

ministerial instability. Refers to the pattern in France of regular cabinet turnover in the Fourth Republic, of cabinets coming into existence and not lasting very long.

minority government. Prime minister does not control over 50 percent of the seats in the legislature.

Mitchell Agreement. In Britain the agreement in 1998 (also known as the Good Friday Agreement), named after US senator George Mitchell, that much authority over policy in Northern Ireland would move from London to Belfast.

Mitterrand, François. French political leader, leader of the French Socialist Party, and president of France, 1981–1995.

Moi, Daniel arap (1924–). Second president of Kenya, serving from 1978 to 2002.

moral law. Refers to precepts or guidelines that are based upon subjective values, beliefs, and attitudes, focusing upon behavior.

most different systems design. Instead of looking for differences between two or more essentially similar nations, this focuses upon similarities between two or more essentially different nations.

most similar systems design. Investigators take two systems that are essentially similar, and subsequently study differences that exist between the two basically similar systems.

Mountbatten, Louis, First Earl Mountbatten of Burma. British royal family member and international leader, serving as the last viceroy of India in 1947 and the first governor-general of independent India, 1947–1948.

Mountbatten Plan. In India, refers to the plan by Viscount Lord Louis Mountbatten, the last British governor-general of India, to partition what was then called India into two new nations, a Hindu India and a Muslim Pakistan.

multinational corporations (MNCs). Business enterprises that operate in more than one nation. They can be very large and can have significant economic (and political) influence upon the countries in which they operate. Some MNCs are economically larger and more powerful than some of the nations in which they operate.

multiple-member-district voting system. More than one representative per electoral district. Voters cast ballots and the top more-than-one vote-getters are elected.

Nanjing Massacre. In China, also known as the Rape of Nanjing. In December 1937 the Japanese attacked Nanjing and hundreds of thousands of Chinese civilians and disarmed soldiers were murdered, and 20,000–80,000 women were raped by soldiers of the Imperial Japanese Army. The International Military Tribunal of the Far East estimates more than 200,000 casualties in the incident; China's official estimate is about 300,000 casualties.

Narasimha Rao, Pamulaparti Venkata. Indian political leader, leader of the Indian National Congress, and prime minister of India, 1991–1996.

nation. Used in this book interchangeably with *nation-state,* but can also be used in an anthropological way to denote a group of people with shared characteristics, perhaps a shared language, history, or culture, who exist within a defined state. See *nation-state*

National Assembly. Lower house of the bicameral French Parliament.

nationalism. Includes identification with a national group and support for actions that will support and benefit the national group. This may or may not correspond to borders of a particular state.

nationalist movement. Special case of a social movement in which a group of individuals who are articulating a common set of beliefs (for example, that India should become independent of Britain) starts to act within the political system to influence political policy.

Nationalist Party. Group that overthrew the Qing Dynasty and established the Republic of China in 1912. Fought with Chinese Communist Party and eventually was driven off of mainland China to island of Taiwan.

National Party Congress. Chinese Communist Party organization of 4,000 to 5,000 members that formally elects the Communist leadership body, the Central Committee. (Not to be confused with the National People's Congress.)

National People's Congress (NPC). In China, the legislative branch of the national government of the People's Republic of China. (Not to be confused with the National Party Congress.)

nation-state. Involves an instance in which the nation and the state overlap.

natural law. Refers to a body of precepts governing human behavior that is more basic than human-made law, and one that is said to be based on fundamental principles of justice.

navette. In France, the sending of a bill back and forth between the two chambers of the national legislature until they agree on a compromise version.

Nehru, Jawaharlal (1889–1964). One of India's founders, leader of the National Congress Party, and prime minister of India.

neocorporatism. Takes up where the theory of pluralism leaves off. Suggests that groups and group interaction with government are highly significant for the political system.

normative approach to inquiry. Focuses on philosophies, or "shoulds."

North American Free Trade Agreement (NAFTA). Treaty between Mexico, the United States, and Canada in 1993 guaranteeing free trade among the three nations. Nullified by US president Donald Trump in 2018 and replaced by the United States–Mexico–Canada Agreement (USMCA).

October Manifesto. Declaration by Russian tsar Nicholas II as a response to the Russian Revolution of 1905. The manifesto pledged to grant civil liberties to the people, grant power to the legislature (the Duma), and make other concessions to critics of the tsar's rule.

Odinga, Raila. Kenyan political leader, second prime minister of Kenya from 2008 to 2013, and current leader of the Opposition in Kenya.

Opium War (1839–1842). In China, when outside forces pressed Chinese authorities to make concessions that resulted in China suffering from foreign interference in its domestic policy.

original jurisdiction. In the United States, refers to the very limited number of legal situations in which cases would actually be heard first in the Supreme Court. The vast majority of the work of the Supreme Court comes through its appellate jurisdiction rather than through its original jurisdiction.

palace coup. Forces behind the coup are typically members of a royal family; one member of the royal family tries to push out those in office so that he or she can take power.

parliamentary executive. Executive political structures in a parliamentary regime, including the head of state and the chief executive. More complex than its presidential alternative, if for no other reason than it is a multiple executive.

parliamentary question time. In Britain, twice a week the prime minister appears in the House of Commons to answer parliamentary questions, primarily from the members of the Opposition. In other parliamentary systems may occur less frequently.

parliamentary sovereignty. In Britain the principle that whatever Parliament does is constitutional and becomes part of constitutional law.

partial proportional representation. Structure in the Mexican Chamber of Deputies by which only some of the members of the Chamber are elected from electoral districts, and others are chosen as a function of how many deputies each party won in the district-based races.

Party Congress. Formal leadership structure of the Chinese government, with over 3,000 members elected indirectly from regional congresses. The Party Congress in turn elects a president and a State Council (the cabinet/executive structure), and the State Council then elects a premier.

party discipline. Relates to the cohesion of the body of party members within a legislature.

Peña Nieto, Enrique. Mexican political leader, leader of the Institutional Revolutionary Party, former governor of the state of Mexico, and fifty-seventh president of Mexico, 2012–2018.

People's Liberation Army (PLA). In China, military organization of all land, sea, and air forces of the People's Republic of China.

perestroika ("restructuring"). One of three key principles of Soviet politics under Mikhail Gorbachev from 1985 through 1991.

peripheral federation. Type of federal government in which more power is based in the member units of the federation than in the central government, although in order to be considered a federal government there must be some policy jurisdictions that are under the control of the center.

plenum. The major arena of the legislative house.

pluralism. Idea that competing groups in society determine public policy through bargaining and compromise.

plurality. In a legislature or an election, having more votes than any other party, although it may be less than a majority.

Politburo (Political Bureau). The most important political group within the Chinese Communist Party comprising the top political leaders (about nine) in the nation. Many Soviet-model states have or had politburos.

political culture. Set of concepts focusing upon the environment in which political action takes place.

political elite. Those who have relatively high levels of interest in politics and relatively high levels of involvement in the political process.

political ethnocentrism. For Westerners to assume that because political institutions or relationships or behavior work one way in stable Western democracies, they must work the same way in all political systems.

political party. Long-lived organization that seeks to influence political process, and that seeks to control power (or at least participate in governance) in the polity. These tend to be more permanent and institutionalized than are interest groups and are concerned with a larger number of issues than interest groups.

political recruitment. Processes that select or draw into politics those individuals who reach positions of significant national influence.

political role. Pattern of expected behavior for individuals holding particular positions in a system.

political socialization. Process by which the individual acquires attitudes, beliefs, and values relating to the political system.

Pompidou, Georges. French political leader; leader for the Union for the New Republic (until 1968) and the Union of Democrats for the Republic (1968–1974); prime minister of France, 1962–1968; and president of France, 1969–1974.

positive law. Legislation that has three major identifiable characteristics: it is human-made law, it is designed to govern human behavior, and it is enforceable by appropriate governmental action.

positive or **constructive vote of no confidence**. In Germany, in order to dismiss a chancellor, not only does a majority of the Bundestag need to vote against the incumbent ("no confidence"), but it also must agree in the same vote on a successor.

premier. Leadership title that varies with different political systems. The position of premier is typically the prime minister or leader of the executive branch (as distinct from the head of state). In China today the Party Congress has over 3,000 members elected indirectly from regional congresses. The Party Congress in turn elects a president and a State Council (the cabinet/executive structure), and the State Council then elects a premier.

presidential dictatorship. Non-literal characterization of Mexican political leadership in which the president has the right to issue executive decrees that have the force of law; despite the notion of separation of powers, the president is permitted to introduce proposals in the legislature on his own authority.

presidential electors. Those individuals chosen in a presidential election in the United States to be part of the Electoral College. These individuals are associated with one of the political parties and will, if chosen, cast their electoral votes for the party's nominee for the presidency.

presidential model. Centralizes both political power and symbolic authority of the executive branch in one individual, the president.

pressure group. Narrower in scope than an interest group, usually related to a single issue. Goal is to affect public policy.

private members' bill. In Britain a bill originating from any member of Parliament, either in the Government backbenches or the Opposition frontbenches or backbenches, who is not a member of the cabinet.

Privy Council. Antecedent of a parliamentary cabinet, starting in the seventeenth century, a group of advisers to the British head of state.

proportional representation voting system. Voters in an election vote for the party they prefer, not for candidates. The proportion of votes that a party receives determines the proportion of seats it will receive in the legislature.

Punjab. Indian state that has seen conflict in recent years because of tension between the Sikh population and the Hindu-dominated central government.

Putin, Vladimir. Russian political leader; leader of the All-Russia People's Front; president of Russia, 2000–2008; prime minister of Russia, 2008–2012; and president of Russia again from 2012 to the present.

quasi-presidential or **quasi-parliamentary executive**. Refers to the French model political executive, which is a significant deviation from the British "Westminster" model.

radical ideology. Often associated with violence, although that need not be the case. Generally, radicals are extremely dissatisfied with the way society (and politics) is organized and are impatient to undertake fundamental changes in society.

Rajya Sabha. Upper house in India's bicameral legislature.

rational choice theory. Individuals will participate when it is in their personal interest to do so, when their individual participation will make a difference in terms of benefits (e.g., public policies) to them; personalized interests will necessarily join those groups.

reactionary ideology. Corresponds to that of the radical, only on the right end of the spectrum. The reactionary position proposes radical change backward—that is, retrogressive change favoring a policy that would return the society to a previous condition or even a former value system.

realignment of political parties. When a significant block of voters shifts from "permanent" loyalty to one party, to loyalty to another party.

real system. A set of objects that we can actually see (or touch, or feel, or measure).

reapportionment. In the United States, every ten years (following the administration of the national census), once the national population is known and the populations of each state are known, the number of seats that will be allotted to each state for representation in the House of Representatives is calculated.

Red Guard. In China a mass movement of civilians, mostly students and other young people who were mobilized by Mao Zedong in 1966 and 1967, during the Cultural Revolution.

Red Versus Expert Debate. In China one of the most divisive issues in the early 1960s. Pragmatic party leaders were labeled as the "experts," and the more radical supporters of Mao and the People's Liberation Army were labeled as the "red" faction, and they disagreed over the appropriate strategy for China's ongoing economic development after the Great Leap Forward failed. Eventually the "experts" triumphed.

referendum. Situation in which political questions are submitted to the public for a vote rather than being resolved in the legislature.

reform coup. Political takeover often done in the name of reform, and seizure of power may be undertaken by a labor leader or someone holding political office. Not a member of the military (see *military coup*) or member of the royal family (see *palace coup*).

representative democracy. Kind of democracy that uses elected officials representing the population, rather than direct participation by the population, as the means of governing and making political decisions.

republic. Form of democratic government that does not have a monarchy. Major political leadership positions are not inherited. Political leadership should be a "public thing," or in Latin a "*res publica,*" not something belonging to a royal family.

Republic of China. Created in 1949 as an independent China on the island of Taiwan by the Nationalist Party led by Sun Yat-sen when the Nationalist forces were driven off the Chinese mainland by the forces of Communist China, which established the People's Republic of China at the same time.

residual powers. In Germany the Lander are given these powers in Article 70 of the Constitution. Any powers not specifically given to the central government remain with the states. In the original US Constitution the residual powers were reserved for the states.

responsible government. In parliamentary systems, refers to the Government's ability to deliver on its promises. Because of the existence of party discipline, and the fact that the legislative branch of government is led by the same individual as is the executive branch, parliamentary governments tend to be more responsible than presidential governments.

Romano-Germanic approach to law. Sometimes referred to as code law, has developed from the basis of Roman law at the time of Justinian (C.E. 533). This type of law, as contrasted with common law, is based upon comprehensively written legislative statutes, often bound together as codes.

royal assent. Traditional act by which the monarch in Britain approved legislation passed by Parliament. Today royal assent is given by a commission, not by the monarch.

royal pretense. Idea that the queen is still the real ruler of Britain, rather than a recognition that the monarchy is now primarily of symbolic importance.

rubber stamp power. Situation in which a legislative body may have formal power in the legislative process, but in fact it must go along with the other chamber.

Salinas de Gortari, Carlos. Mexican political leader, leader of the Institutional Revolutionary Party, and president of Mexico, 1988–1994.

Sarkozy, Nicolas. French political leader, leader of the Union for a Popular Movement (until 2015) and the Republicans (after 2015), and president of France, 2007–2012.

Schmidt, Helmut. West German political leader, leader of the Social Democratic Party, and chancellor of West Germany, 1974–1982.

Schröder, Gerhard. German political leader, leader of the Social Democratic Party, and chancellor of Germany, 1998–2005.

scientific law. Refers to observations and measurements that have been empirically determined and that focus upon physical, biological, and chemical concepts, not social questions.

select committee. Legislative committee that tends to be given a specific scope of inquiry, or a special problem to address, as well as a specific duration.

Senate. Name for the upper house of many bicameral legislatures, including (in this volume) France, Mexico, and the United States.

seniority. In the United States the principle that positions in Congress are associated with the number of years of continuous service in the house.

separation of powers. Notion that centralized power is dangerous, and that political power in the state should be divided so that power can be a check on power.

simple resolution. In the United States, legislation that is intended to express the sense of the house; these are not signed by the president, and they do not take on the force of law.

simple vote of no confidence. Expression by the German Bundestag that it no longer supports the chancellor, but cannot agree on a successor. This does not result in the chancellor being dismissed.

single-member-district plurality voting system. In this kind of system the nation is divided into a number of electoral districts. Each district corresponds to one seat in the legislative chamber, and its representative is elected by plurality rather than majority voting: the person receiving the most votes wins and does not need to receive more than half of the total votes cast.

Sinification of Marxism. In China the practice of rooting the abstract formulations of Marxism-Leninism in the specific reality of China; modifying Marxism to work in China.

social class. Refers to some kind of ordering of groups in society, usually including such characteristics as income, education, occupation, values, expectations, and affects.

socialism. Ideology that developed out of the industrial revolution advocating governmental concern with individuals' quality of life, including education, medical care, and standard of living. May be found in democratic versions—as in Great Britain or Sweden—or in authoritarian versions—as in Nazi Germany or fascist Italy.

socialist law. Assumption that law is a tool of the state and should be used to help the people.

social movement. A broad group of individuals who share an interest in a given social issue and who mobilize to act on those common interests.

social policy. Government policy in relation to income, housing, medical care, education, and the like.

sovereignty. The real power to make political decisions, and those decisions do not need to be approved by another actor in the political system.

Soviet federalism. Idea of "independent republics" coming together into a unified political system. Developed by Lenin and Stalin as a vehicle for keeping many of the so-called independent republics within a single political unit, the USSR.

Speech from the Throne. Speech the queen delivers in Britain (and other heads of state deliver in their respective nations) in which she outlines plans for "her" Government for the year. The important consideration to recall is that the speech is written by the prime minister and cabinet, not the monarch.

Stalin, Joseph (1878–1953). Premier of the Soviet Union from 1941 to 1953 and first general secretary of the Communist Party from 1922 to 1953.

standing or permanent committee. Legislative committee established at the opening of the legislative term that lasts for the life of the legislature.

Standing Committee of the National People's Congress. In China the leadership group of the 3,000-member National People's Congress. Consists of a chairman, fifteen vice chairmen, a secretary-general, and 153 members.

Standing Committee of the Politburo. In China, senior leadership of the Politburo. About twenty members.

stare decisis ("to stand by things decided"). Practice of courts referring to previous decisions when they make decisions.

state. Explicitly political entity, created and alterable by people, based upon accepted geographic boundaries.

State Council. In China the equivalent of the cabinet in parliamentary systems.

State Duma. Lower house of the Federal Assembly (the bicameral legislature) of Russia following adoption of the 1993 constitution of the Russian Federation.

statistical method of inquiry. Involves more sophisticated forms of measurement and observation than is the case with the empirical method of inquiry.

structural-functional analysis. Focuses upon what Gabriel Almond referred to as political "structures," by which he means either political institutions or behavior, and political "functions," by which he means the consequences of the institutions or the behavior. This kind of analysis asks the basic question, "What structures perform what functions and under what conditions in a political system?"

Sun Yat-sen (1866–1925). Chinese revolutionary and political leader. Played a key role in the overthrow of the Qing Dynasty and the establishment of the Republic of China in 1912. Later cofounded the Guomindang (Chinese National People's Party) and served as its first leader.

Supreme Court. Highest court in the judicial structure of a nation.

Supreme Leader. Leader of the Chinese Communist Party.

Supreme Soviet. Highest legislative body in the Union of Soviet Socialist Republics. Made up of the Soviet of Nationalities and the Soviet of the Union. First established in 1938 and disbanded in 1991 with the breakup of the Soviet Union.

suspensory veto. Structure in which a legislative chamber's refusal to approve legislation from the other house can only slow the legislative process down, not block the legislation from coming into effect.

systems theory. See *input-output analysis*

terrorism. Political behavior that uses violence, the threat of violence, or coercion to influence political behavior.

Thatcherism. Style of contemporary British politics introduced by Prime Minister Margaret Thatcher known first as "conviction politics." Thatcher's brand of Conservative ideology was strongly antisocialist and antiunion.

Thatcher, Margaret. British political leader, leader of the Conservative Party, and prime minister of the United Kingdom, 1979–1990.

Third Republic. French constitutional regime from 1870 to 1940. Came into existence at the end of the Second French Empire in the Franco-Prussian War, and ended with the German occupation of France at the start of World War II.

Three Represents. Theory of Chinese philosophy of Jiang Zemin, general secretary of the Communist Party from 1989 to 2002. This thought is a continuation and development of Marxism-Leninism, Mao Zedong thought, and Deng Xiaoping theory.

Tiananmen Square massacre. In China, critical demonstrations that took place in 1989 in Beijing in which hundreds of thousands of Chinese demonstrated in favor of economic and political reforms, and were attacked by the Chinese government.

totalitarianism. System in which the government controls individual political behavior and political thought. Totalitarianism is said to go beyond authoritarianism because it seeks to control thought, too, not only political behavior, which is the goal of authoritarian polities.

Trotsky, Leon. Early Soviet political leader and People's Commissar of Military and Naval Affairs of the Soviet Union, 1918–1925.

unicameral legislature. Legislature with one legislative house or chamber.

Union of Soviet Socialist Republics (USSR). Communist state that existed between 1922 and 1991, including Russia and fourteen other Soviet republics, dominated by the Communist Party of the Soviet Union. Its capital was in Moscow.

unitary system. A system in which significant power resides at the national level. There is no intermediate level of government between the national level and the local level.

United Kingdom. Political system made up of Northern Ireland and the political units of Great Britain, including England, Scotland, and Wales.

unwritten constitution. Collection of constitutional principles widely accepted in the regime as fundamental and authoritative that are not formally approved as law or are not labeled in one document as "the constitution."

upper house of a legislature. That house in a bicameral system further from direct public control. Often appointed, although today many upper houses are elected directly by the public as well.

urban migration. In the modern world describes the process of segments of the population moving from rural settings to large cities in hopes of finding a better life.

veto. Ability to block legislation. In the United States the president has the power to veto legislation, although if Congress passes the legislation again by a two-thirds margin it becomes law.

vote of confidence. Vote by a majority of the legislature indicating its confidence in, or support for, the prime minister and his or her cabinet.

vote of no confidence. The legislature voting that it does not want to be led by a specific prime minister and cabinet.

Walpole, Robert. Early prime minister of Great Britain, 1721–1742, and considered to be the first "modern" British prime minister.

warlords. Political leaders outside of government who use private armies to maintain their strength.

Weimar Republic. Parliamentary republic established in 1919 in Germany to replace the imperial government that had preceded it.

Westminster model of government. In Britain and other nations, generally considered to be composed of four parts. First, the chief executive is not the same as the head of state. Second, the executive powers of government are exercised by the chief executive and their cabinet, not the head of state. Third, the chief executive and the cabinet come from and are part of the legislature. Fourth, the chief executive and the cabinet are responsible to, and can be fired by, the legislature.

writ of dissolution. Head of state may dissolve the legislature—fire the legislature—and call for new elections by issuing such a writ.

Xi Jinping. Chinese political leader, president of China since 2013, general secretary of the CPC, chairman of the Central Military Commission, chairman of the National Security Committee, full member of the Central Committee of the CCP, and commander-in-chief of the People's Liberation Army.

Yeltsin, Boris (1931–2007). First president of the Russian Federation, 1991–1999.

Zedillo Ponce de León, Ernesto. Mexican political leader, leader of the Institutional Revolutionary Party, and president of Mexico, 1994–2000.

Selected Bibliography

Aberbach, Joel, and Peterson, Mark, eds. *The Executive Branch.* New York: Oxford University Press, 2005.

Achankeng, Fuankem. *Nationalism and Intra-State Conflicts in the Postcolonial World.* Lanham, MD: Lexington, 2015.

Ahlquist, John, and Levi, Margaret. *In the Interest of Others: Organizations and Social Activism.* Princeton: Princeton University Press, 2013.

Alemán, Eduardo, and Tsebelis, George. *Legislative Institutions and Lawmaking in Latin America.* Oxford: Oxford University Press, 2016.

Almond, Gabriel, and Coleman, James, eds. *The Politics of the Developing Areas.* Princeton: Princeton University Press, 1960.

Anderson, Owen J. *The Natural Moral Law: The Good After Modernity.* New York: Cambridge University Press, 2012.

Arendt, Hannah. *The Origins of Totalitarianism.* New York: Schocken, 2004.

Arter, David. *Comparing and Classifying Legislatures.* Hoboken, NJ: Taylor and Francis, 2013.

Atkins, Nicholas. *The Fifth French Republic.* New York: Palgrave Macmillan, 2004.

Badinter, Robert, and Breyer, Stephen. *Judges in Contemporary Democracy: An International Conversation.* New York: New York University Press, 2004.

Baker, Ernest, ed. *Social Contract: Essays by Locke, Hume and Rousseau.* New York: Oxford University Press, 1970.

Baldwin, Nicholas. *Legislatures of Small States: A Comparative Study.* London: Routledge, 2013.

Baradat, Leon. *Political Ideologies: Their Origins and Impact.* Englewood Cliffs, NJ: Prentice Hall, 2009.

Barilleaux, Ryan, and Kelley, Christopher. *The Unitary Executive and the Modern Presidency.* College Station: Texas A&M University Press, 2010.

Barkan, Joel, ed. *Legislative Power in Emerging African Democracies.* Boulder: Lynne Rienner, 2009.

Barker, David C., and Carman, Christopher. *Political Representation in Red and Blue America: How Cultural Differences Shape Democratic Expectations and Outcomes.* New York: Oxford University Press, 2012.

Barker, Ernest, ed. and trans. *The Politics of Aristotle.* New York: Oxford University Press, 1970.

Bauer, Gretchen, and Tremblay, Manon. *Women in Executive Power: A Global Overview.* New York: Routledge, 2011.

Bauman, Richard, and Kahana, Tsvi, eds. *The Least Examined Branch: The Role of Legislatures in the Constitutional State.* New York: Cambridge University Press, 2006.

Bell, David. *Parties and Democracy in France.* Brookfield, VT: Ashgate, 2000.

Bell, David, and Gaffney, John. *The Presidents of the French Fifth Republic.* Houndmills: Palgrave Macmillan, 2013.

Bell, John. *Judiciaries Within Europe: A Comparative Review.* Cambridge: Cambridge University Press, 2010.

Bennister, Mark. *Prime Ministers in Power: Political Leadership in Britain and Australia.* New York: Palgrave Macmillan, 2012.

Berenson, Edward, Duclert, Vincent, and Prochasson, Christophe. *The French Republic: History, Values, Debates.* Ithaca: Cornell University Press, 2011.

Birnir, Johanna. *Ethnicity and Electoral Politics.* New York: Cambridge University Press, 2007.

Biswas, Bidisha. *Managing Conflicts in India: Policies of Coercion and Accommodation.* Lanham: Lexington, 2014.

Blomgren, Magnus, and Rozenberg, Olivier. *Parliamentary Roles in Modern Legislatures.* New York: Routledge, 2012.

Blondel, Jean. *Comparative Legislatures.* Englewood Cliffs, NJ: Prentice Hall, 1973.

Booth, David, and Cammack, Diana Rose. *Governance for Development in Africa: Solving Collective Action Problems.* New York: Zed, 2013.

Bouju, Jacky, and de Bruijn, Mirjam. *Ordinary Violence and Social Change in Africa.* Boston: Brill, 2014.

Boyron, Sophie. *The Constitution of France: A Contextual Analysis.* Portland, OR: Hart, 2013.

Brower, Kate Anderson. *First in Line: Presidents, Vice Presidents, and the Pursuit of Power.* New York: Harper, 2018.

Burgess, Michael. *Comparative Federalism: Theory and Practice.* New York: Routledge, 2006.

Burnham, June, and Pyper, Robert. *Britain's Modernised Civil Service.* New York: Palgrave Macmillan, 2008.

Burton, Guy, and Goertzel, Ted. *Presidential Leadership in the Americas Since Independence.* Lanham: Lexington, 2016.

Camp, Roderic. *Politics in Mexico: Democratic Consolidation or Decline.* New York: Oxford University Press, 2014.

Carter, Byrum. *The Office of Prime Minister.* Princeton: Princeton University Press, 2015.

Castellano, John. *The Legislative Process in the United States Congress: An Introduction.* New York: Nova Science, 2013.

Chapalgaonker, Narendra, and Wagholikar, Subhashchandra. *Mahatma Gandhi and the Indian Constitution.* Abingdon: Routledge, 2016.

Cheeseman, Nicholas, and Branch, Daniel. *Election Fever: Kenya's Crisis.* Abingdon: Routledge, 2008.

Chemerinsky, Erwin. *Enhancing Government: Federalism for the 21st Century.* Stanford: Stanford University Press, 2008.

Chenoweth, Erica. *Political Violence.* Los Angeles: Sage, 2014.

Chhibber, Pradeep. *Religious Practice and Democracy in India.* New York: Cambridge University Press, 2014.

Clayton, Anthony. *The Wars of French Decolonization.* London: Routledge, 2013.

Cleary, Matthew. *The Sources of Democratic Responsiveness in Mexico.* Notre Dame, IN: University of Notre Dame Press, 2010.

Cole, Matthew. *Political Parties in Britain.* Edinburgh: Edinburgh University Press, 2012.

Conway, Margaret, Steuernagel, Gertrude, and Ahern, David. *Women and Political Participation: Cultural Change in the Political Arena.* Washington, DC: Congressional Quarterly, 2005.

Costa, Olivier. *Parliamentary Representation in France.* London: Routledge, 2013.

Covert, Tawnya J. Adkins. *Making Citizens: Political Socialization Research and Beyond.* New York: Palgrave Macmillan, 2017.

Crosby, Margaret. *The Making of the German Constitution: A Slow Revolution.* Oxford: Berg, 2004.

Cullen, Poppy. *Kenya and Britain After Independence: Beyond Neo-Colonialism.* Cham, Switzerland: Palgrave Macmillan, 2017.

Dahlerup, Drude. *Women, Quotas, and Politics.* New York: Routledge, 2006.

Diamond, Larry, and Plattner, Marc, eds. *Electoral Systems and Democracy.* Baltimore: Johns Hopkins University Press, 2006.

Docherty, David. *Legislatures.* Vancouver: University of British Columbia Press, 2014.

Dogan, Mattei, and Pélassy, Dominique. *How to Compare Nations: Strategies in Comparative Politics.* Chatham, NJ: Chatham House, 1990.

Domínguez, Jorge, and Poiré, Alejandro. *Toward Mexico's Democratization: Parties, Campaigns, Elections, and Public Opinion.* New York: Routledge, 2013.

Drake, Michael. *Problematics of Military Power: Government, Discipline, and the Subject of Violence.* Portland: Cass, 2002.

Duchacek, Ivo. *Comparative Federalism: The Territorial Dimension of Politics.* New York: Holt, Rinehart, and Winston, 1970.

Duchacek, Ivo. *Power Maps: Comparative Politics of Constitutions.* Santa Barbara: Clio, 1973.

Easton, David. *A Framework for Political Analysis.* Englewood Cliffs, NJ: Prentice Hall, 1965.

Easton, David. *A Systems Analysis of Political Life.* New York: Wiley, 1965.

Ebenstein, Alan, Ebenstein, William, and Fogelman, Edwin. *Today's ISMs: Socialism, Capitalism, Fascism, Communism, Libertarianism.* Upper Saddle River, NJ: Prentice Hall, 2000.

Edelson, Chris. *Emergency Presidential Power: From the Drafting of the Constitution to the War on Terror.* Madison: University of Wisconsin Press, 2013.

Eisenstadt, Todd. *Politics, Identity, and Mexico's Indigenous Rights Movements.* New York: Cambridge University Press, 2011.

Elischer, Sebastian. *Political Parties in Africa: Ethnicity and Party Formation.* New York: Cambridge University Press, 2013.

Engle, Eric. *Russia, the European Union, and the CIS.* Portland: International Specialized Book Service, 2012.

Epstein, Richard Allen. *The Classical Liberal Constitution: The Uncertain Quest for Limited Government.* Cambridge: Harvard University Press, 2014.

Evennett, Heather. *Second Chambers.* London: House of Lords Library, 2014.

Ferree, Myra Marx. *Varieties of Feminism: German Gender Politics in Global Perspective.* Stanford: Stanford University Press, 2012.

Ferreira da Cunha, Paulo. *Rethinking Natural Law.* New York: Springer, 2013.

Fish, M. Steven, and Kroenig, Matthew. *The Handbook of National Legislatures: A Global Survey.* New York: Cambridge University Press, 2009.

Franda, Marcus F. *West Bengal and the Federalizing Process in India.* Princeton: Princeton University Press, 2016.

Freedman, Thomas. *The World Is Flat: A Brief History of the Twenty-First Century.* New York: Farrar, Straus, and Giroux, 2005.

Freeman, Mark. *Making Reconciliation Work: The Role of Parliaments.* Geneva: Inter-Parliamentary Union, 2005.

Friedrich, Carl. *Totalitarianism in Perspective.* New York: Praeger, 1969.

Gerhardt, Michael. *The Power of Precedent.* New York: Oxford University Press, 2008.

Gibson, Edward. *Federalism and Democracy in Latin America.* Baltimore: Johns Hopkins University Press, 2004.

Ginsburg, Tom, and Moustafa, Tamir, eds. *Rule by Law: The Politics of Courts in Authoritarian Regimes.* New York: Cambridge University Press, 2008.

Godwin, Ken, Ainsworth, Scott, and Godwin, Erik. *Lobbying and Policymaking: The Public Pursuit of Private Interests.* Thousand Oaks, CA: Sage/Congressional Quarterly, 2013.

Gordon, Michael. *Parliamentary Sovereignty in the UK Constitution: Process, Politics, and Democracy.* Oxford: Hart, 2015.

Grant, J. Andrew, and Soderbaum, Fredrik. *The New Regionalism in Africa.* London: Routledge, 2017.

Grazio, Luigi. *Lobbying, Pluralism, and Democracy.* New York: Palgrave, 2001.

Green, Simon, and Paterson, William, eds. *Governance in Contemporary Germany: The Semisovereign State Revisited.* New York: Cambridge University Press, 2005.

Greenawalt, Kent. *Religion and the Constitution.* Princeton: Princeton University Press, 2006.

Greenberg, Edward S. *Political Socialization.* New York: Routledge, 2017.

Grossmann, Matthew. *The Not-So-Special Interests: Interest Groups, Public Representation, and American Governance.* Stanford: Stanford University Press, 2012.

Hagemann, Karen, Michel, Sonya, and Budde, Gunilla. *Civil Society and Gender Justice: Historical and Comparative Perspectives.* New York: Berghahn, 2008.

Hall, Kermit, and McGuire, Kevin. *The Judicial Branch.* New York: Oxford University Press, 2005.

Hartz, Louis. *The Liberal Tradition in America: An Interpretation of American Political Thought Since the Revolution.* New York: Harcourt, Brace, 1955.

Hayes, Christine. *What's Divine About Divine Law? Early Perspectives.* Princeton: Princeton University Press, 2015.

Hazan, Reuven. *Cohesion and Discipline in Legislatures: Political Parties, Party Leadership, Parliamentary Committees, and Governance.* New York: Routledge, 2013.

Heilmann, Sebastian. *China's Political System.* Lanham: Rowman and Littlefield, 2017.

Helleringer, Genevieve, and Purnhagen, Kai. *Towards a European Legal Culture.* Portland: Hart, 2014.

Henderson, Jane. *The Constitution of the Russian Federation: A Contextual Analysis.* Portland: Hart, 2011.

Henneberg, Susan. *Gender Politics.* New York: Greenhaven, 2017.

Herring, Pendleton, and Pearson, Sidney. *Presidential Leadership: The Political Relations of Congress and the Chief Executive.* New York: Routledge, 2017.

Herrnson, Paul, Deering, Christopher, and Wilcox, Clyde. *Interest Groups Unleashed.* Thousand Oaks, CA: Sage/Congressional Quarterly, 2013.

Hershey, Marjorie, Burden, Barry, and Wolbrecht, Christina. *U.S. Political Parties.* Thousand Oaks, CA: Congressional Quarterly, 2014.

Heun, Werner. *The Constitution of Germany: A Contextual Analysis.* Oxford: Hart, 2011.

Hornsby, Charles. *Kenya: A History Since Independence.* New York: Tauris, 2012.

Hudson, James R. *Special Interest Society: How Membership-Based Organizations Shape America.* Lanham: Lexington, 2013.

Ingle, Stephen. *The British Party System: An Introduction.* New York: Routledge, 2008.

James, Peter. *The German Electoral System.* London: Taylor and Francis, 2017.

Jodhka, Surinder. *Caste in Contemporary India.* New Delhi: Routledge, 2015.

Johnson, Nevil. *Government in the Federal Republic of Germany: The Executive at Work.* New York: Pergamon, 2013.

Joseph, William. *Politics in China: An Introduction.* New York: Oxford University Press, 2014.

Kallhoff, Angela. *Why Democracy Needs Public Goods.* Lanham: Lexington, 2011.

Kautz, Steven J. *The Supreme Court and the Idea of Constitutionalism.* Philadelphia: University of Pennsylvania Press, 2011.

Keleman, R. Daniel. *The Rules of Federalism: Institutions and Regulatory Politics in the EU and Beyond.* Cambridge: Harvard University Press, 2004.

Kenny, Meryl. *Gender and Political Recruitment: Theorizing Institutional Change.* Basingstoke: Palgrave Macmillan, 2013.

Kincaid, John, Renzsch, Wolfgang, and Detterbeck, Klaus. *Political Parties and Civil Society in Federal Countries.* Don Mills, Ontario: Oxford University Press, 2015.

Kirkwood, Burton. *The History of Mexico.* New York: Palgrave Macmillan, 2005.

Krook, Mona Lena, and Childs, Sarah. *Women, Gender, and Politics: A Reader.* New York: Oxford University Press, 2010.

Kulke, Hermann, and Rothermund, Dietmar. *A History of India.* New York: Routledge, 2016.

Kundnani, Hans. *The Paradox of German Power.* New York: Oxford University Press, 2015.

Landman, Todd. *Issues and Methods in Comparative Politics: An Introduction.* New York: Routledge, 2008.

Langston, Joy. *Democratization and Authoritarian Party Survival: Mexico's PRI.* New York: Oxford University Press, 2017.

LaPalombara, Joseph, and Weiner, Myron, eds. *Political Parties and Political Development.* Princeton: Princeton University Press, 2015.

Lasswell, Harold. *Politics: Who Gets What, When, How?* New York: McGraw-Hill, 1936.

Lawson, Kay. *The Comparative Study of Political Parties.* New York: St. Martin's, 1976.

Lawson, Kay. *Political Parties and Democracy.* Santa Barbara: Praeger, 2010.

Lazardeux, Sebastien. *Cohabitation and Conflicting Politics in French Policymaking.* New York: Palgrave Macmillan, 2015.

Lazaridis, Gabriella, Campani, Giovanna, and Benveniste, Annie. *Rise of the Far Right in Europe: Populist Shifts and "Othering."* London: Palgrave Macmillan, 2016.

LeBas, Adrienne. *From Protest to Parties: Party-Building and Democratization in Africa.* Oxford: Oxford University Press, 2013.

Lee, James. *From House of Lords to Supreme Court: Judges, Jurists, and the Process of Judging.* Oxford: Hart, 2011.

Leston-Bandeira, Cristina. *Parliaments and Citizens.* London: Routledge, 2014.

Levitsky, Steven. *Challenges of Party-Building in Latin America.* New York: Cambridge University Press, 2016.

Li, Cheng. *Chinese Politics in the Xi Jinping Era: Reassessing Collective Leadership.* Washington, DC: Brookings Institution Press, 2016.

Li, Xiaobing, and Tian, Xiansheng. *Evolution of Power: China's Struggle, Survival, and Success.* Lanham: Lexington, 2014.

Li, Yuwen. *The Judicial System and Reform in Post-Mao China: Stumbling Towards Justice.* Burlington, VT: Ashgate, 2014.

Lijphart, Arend. *Parliamentary vs. Presidential Government.* New York: Oxford University Press, 1992.

Lijphart, Arend. *Patterns of Democracy: Government Forms and Performance in Thirty-Six Countries.* New Haven: Yale University Press, 2012.

Loewenberg, Gerhard. *British and French Parliaments in Comparative Perspective.* New Brunswick, NJ: Aldine, 2010.

Loughlin, Martin. *The British Constitution: A Very Short Introduction.* Oxford: Oxford University Press, 2013.

Madison, James. *Notes on Debates in the Federal Convention of 1787.* Athens: Ohio University Press, 1966.

Mahler, Gregory. *Politics and Government in Israel: The Maturation of a Modern State,* 3rd ed. Lanham: Rowman and Littlefield, 2016.

Maisel, L. Sandy, and Barry, Jeffrey, eds. *The Oxford Handbook of American Political Parties and Interest Groups.* New York: Oxford University Press, 2010.

Maisel, L. Sandy, and Brewer, Mark. *Parties and Elections in America: The Electoral Process.* Lanham: Rowman and Littlefield, 2012.

Malleson, Kate. *The Legal System.* New York: Oxford University Press, 2005.

Maloba, W. O. *The Anatomy of Neo-Colonialism in Kenya: British Imperialism and Kenyatta, 1963–1978.* Cham, Switzerland: Palgrave Macmillan, 2017.

Marples, David. *The Collapse of the Soviet Union: 1985–1991.* New York: Pearson, 2004.

Martin, Shane, Saalfeld, Thomas, and Strøm, Kaare W., eds. *Oxford Handbook of Legislative Studies.* Oxford: Oxford University Press, 2016.

Menon, Jisha. *The Performance of Nationalism: India, Pakistan, and the Memory of Partition.* Cambridge: Cambridge University Press, 2013.

Mershon, Carol, and Shvetsova, Olga. *Party System Change in Legislatures Worldwide: Moving Outside the Electoral Arena.* Cambridge: Cambridge University Press, 2013.

Miller, Mark. *Judicial Politics in the United States.* Boulder: Westview, 2015.

Mngomezulu, Bhekithemba Richard. *The President-for-Life Pandemic in Africa: Kenya, Zimbabwe, Nigeria, Zambia, and Malawi.* London: Adonis and Abbey, 2013.

Mossige, Dag Drange. *Mexico's Left: The Paradox of the PRD.* Boulder: FirstForum, 2013.

Muniz-Fraticelli, Victor M. *The Structure of Pluralism: On the Authority of Associations.* Oxford: Oxford University Press, 2014.

Murphy, James. *The Philosophy of Positive Law: Foundations of Jurisprudence.* New Haven: Yale University Press, 2005.

Mushaben, Joyce Marie. *Becoming Madam Chancellor: Angela Merkel and the Berlin Republic.* Cambridge: Cambridge University Press, 2017.

Nelken, David. *Using Legal Culture.* London: Wildy, Simmonds, and Hill, 2012.

Nelson, Michael. *Guide to the Presidency and the Executive Branch.* Thousand Oaks, CA: Congressional Quarterly, 2013.

Nester, William R. *DeGaulle's Legacy: The Art of Power in France's Fifth Republic.* New York: Palgrave Macmillan, 2014.

Neustadt, Richard. *Presidential Power and the Modern Presidents: The Politics of Leadership from Roosevelt to Reagan.* New York: Free Press, 1990.

Newton, Julie, and Tompson, William, eds. *Institutions, Ideas, and Leadership in Russian Politics.* New York: Palgrave Macmillan, 2010.

Nicholson-Crotty, Sean. *Governors, Grants, and Elections: Fiscal Federalism in the American States.* Baltimore: Johns Hopkins University Press, 2015.

Ninet, Antoni Abat I. *Constitutional Violence: Legitimacy, Democracy, and Human Rights.* Edinburgh: Edinburgh University Press, 2013.

Nordlinger, Eric. *Soldiers in Politics: Military Coups and Governments.* Englewood Cliffs, NJ: Prentice Hall, 1977.

Norton, Philip. *Parliament in British Politics.* New York: Palgrave Macmillan, 2005.

O'Connor, Kevin. *Intellectuals and Apparatchiks: Russian Nationalism and the Gorbachev Revolution.* Lanham: Lexington, 2006.

Oliva, Javier Garcia, and Hall, Helen. *Religion, Law, and the Constitution: Balancing Beliefs in Britain.* New York: Routledge, 2018.

Olson, David. *Democratic Legislative Institutions: A Comparative View.* New York: Routledge, 2015.

Olson, Mancur. *The Logic of Collective Action: Public Goods and the Theory of Groups.* Cambridge: Harvard University Press, 1965.

O'Neill, Michael. *Devolution and British Politics.* New York: Pearson/Longman, 2013.

Palshikar, Suhas, Kumar, Sanjay, and Lodha, Sanjay. *Electoral Politics in India: The Resurgence of the Bharatiya Janata Party.* London: Routledge, 2017.

Palshikar, Suhas, Suri, K. C., and Yadav, Yogendra. *Party Competition in Indian States: Electoral Politics in Post-Congress Polity.* New Delhi: Oxford University Press, 2014.

Patton, David. *Out of the East: From PDS to Left Party in Unified Germany.* Albany: State University of New York Press, 2011.

Pelizzo, Riccardo, and Stapenhurst, Frederick. *Parliamentary Oversight Tools: A Comparative Analysis.* New York: Routledge, 2012.

Peters, B. Guy, and Pierre, Jon. *Handbook of Public Administration.* Thousand Oaks, CA: Sage, 2003.

Pratchett, Lawrence. *Renewing Local Democracy: The Modernisation Agenda in British Local Government.* New York: Routledge, 2013.

Przeworski, Adam, and Teune, Henry. *The Logic of Comparative Social Inquiry.* New York: Wiley, 1970.

Putnam, Robert. *Bowling Alone: The Collapse and Revival of American Community.* New York: Simon and Schuster, 2000.

Pye, Lucian, and Verba, Sidney, eds. *Political Culture and Political Development.* Princeton: Princeton University Press, 1965.

Rawls, John. *Justice as Fairness.* Cambridge: Harvard University Press, 2001.

Regan, Richard J. *A Constitutional History of the U.S. Supreme Court.* Washington, DC: Catholic University of America Press, 2015.

Remington, Thomas. *Politics in Russia.* Hoboken, NJ: Taylor and Francis, 2015.

Riasanovsky, Nicholas, and Steinberg, Mark. *A History of Russia.* New York: Oxford University Press, 2011.

Riker, William. *Federalism: Origin, Operation, Significance.* Boston: Little, Brown, 1964.

Riley, Dennis, and Brophy-Baermann, Bryan. *Bureaucracy and the Policy Process.* Lanham: Rowman and Littlefield, 2006.

Roberts, Geoffrey K. *German Electoral Politics.* Manchester: Manchester University Press, 2013.

Rogowski, Ralf, and Gawron, Thomas. *Constitutional Courts in Comparison: The U.S. Supreme Court and the German Federal Constitutional Court.* New York: Berghahn, 2016.

Ross, Cameron. *Federalism and Democratisation in Russia.* New York: Manchester University Press, 2013.

Rossiter, Clinton. *The American Presidency.* New York: Mentor, 1960.

Rowe, Carolyn, and Jacoby, Wade. *German Federalism in Transition: Reforms in a Consensual State.* New York: Routledge, 2010.

Rozell, Mark. *Executive Privilege: Presidential Power, Secrecy, and Accountability.* Lawrence: University Press of Kansas, 2010.

Ruedin, Didier. *Why Aren't They There? The Political Representation of Women, Ethnic Groups, and Issue Positions in Legislatures.* Colchester, UK: ECPR, 2013.

Ruparelia, Sanjay. *Divided We Govern: Coalition Politics in Modern India.* New York: Oxford University Press, 2015.

Ryan, Erin. *Federalism and the Tug of War Within.* New York: Oxford University Press, 2011.

Rye, Danny. *Political Parties and the Concept of Power: A Theoretical Framework.* Basingstoke: Palgrave Macmillan, 2014.

Sáez, Manuel Alcáantara, Blondel, Jean, and Thiébault, Jean-Louis. *Presidents and Democracy in Latin America.* New York: Routledge, 2018.

Sagar, D. J. *Political Parties of the World.* London: Harper, 2009.

Sakwa, Richard, ed. *Power and Policy in Putin's Russia,* 2nd ed. Hoboken, NJ: Taylor and Francis, 2013.

Sarat, Austin, and Douglas, Lawrence. *The Limits of Law.* Stanford: Stanford University Press, 2005.

Sasaki, Masamichi. *Elites: New Comparative Perspectives.* Boston: Brill, 2008.

Schoen, Harald. *Voters and Voting in Context: Multiple Contexts and the Heterogeneous German Electorate.* Oxford: Oxford University Press, 2017.

Schofield, Norman. *Multiparty Democracy: Elections and Legislative Politics.* New York: Cambridge University Press, 2006.

Selee, Andrew, and Peschard, Jacqueline. *Mexico's Democratic Challenges: Politics, Government, and Society.* Washington, DC: Woodrow Wilson Center, 2010.

Serna de la Garza, José Maria. *The Constitution of Mexico: A Contextual Analysis.* Portland: Hart, 2013.

Shao, Binhong. *China Under Xi Jinping: Its Economic Challenges and Foreign Policy Initiatives.* Leiden: Brill, 2015.

Sharlet, Robert. *Soviet Constitutional Crisis: From De-Stalinization to Disintegration.* New York: Routledge, 2015.

Shaw, Stephen, Pederson, William, and Williams, Franklin. *Franklin D. Roosevelt and the Transformation of the Supreme Court.* London: Routledge, 2015.

Skaria, Ajay. *Unconditional Equality: Gandhi's Religion of Resistance.* Minneapolis: University of Minnesota Press, 2016.

Smith, Jennifer. *Federalism.* Vancouver: UBC Press, 2014.

Solzhenitsyn, Aleksandr. *The History of Liberalism in Russia.* Pittsburgh: University of Pittsburgh Press, 2012.

Strøm, Kaare, Müller, Wolfgang, and Bergman, Torbjörn, eds. *Cabinets and Coalition Bargaining: The Democratic Life Cycle in Western Europe.* New York: Oxford University Press, 2008.

Sturm, Roland, Jeffery, Charlie, and Benz, Arthur. *Federalism, Unification, and European Integration.* New York: Routledge, 2013.

Tang, Wenfang. *Populist Authoritarianism: Chinese Political Culture and Regime Sustainability.* New York: Oxford University Press, 2016.

Taylor, Andrew J. *Congress: A Performance Appraisal.* Boulder: Westview, 2013.

Taylor, Stephen, and Wykes, David. *Parliament and Dissent.* Edinburgh: Edinburgh University Press, 2005.

Thomas, Sue, and Wilcox, Clyde. *Women and Elective Office: Past, Present, and Future.* New York: Oxford University Press, 2005.

Thorson, Carla. *Politics, Judicial Review, and the Russian Constitutional Court.* New York: Palgrave Macmillan, 2012.

Thorson, Esther. *Political Socialization in a Media-Saturated World.* New York: Lang, 2016.

Tomsic, Matevz. *Elites in the New Democracies.* New York: Lang, 2016.

Unwin, Brian. *With Respect, Minister: A View from Inside Whitehall.* London: Tauris, 2017.

Vilas, Carlos Maria. *Shaky Democracies and Popular Fury: From Military Coups to Peoples' Coups.* Tampa: University of South Florida Press, 2004.

Wall, Rachel. *Local Government in England: Centralisation, Autonomy, and Control.* London: Palgrave Macmillan, 2017.

Warber, Adam L. *Executive Orders and the Modern Presidency: Legislating from the Oval Office.* Boulder: Lynne Rienner, 2006.

Ward, Kevin, and Wild-Wood, Emma. *The East African Revival: History and Legacies.* Burlington, VT: Ashgate, 2012.

Weintraub, Sidney. *Unequal Partners: The United States and Mexico.* Pittsburgh: University of Pittsburgh Press, 2010.

Werbner, Pnina. *The Making of an African Working Class: Politics, Law, and Cultural Protest in the Manual Workers Union of Botswana.* London: Pluto, 2014.

Whitaker, Lois Duke. *Voting the Gender Gap.* Urbana: University of Illinois Press, 2008.

Whittaker, David. *The Terrorism Reader.* New York: Routledge, 2007.

Wiarda, Howard J. *Authoritarianism and Corporatism in Latin America—Revisited.* Gainesville: University Press of Florida, 2004.

Wiarda, Howard J. *Corporatism and Comparative Politics: The Other Great "Ism."* Florence: Taylor and Francis, 2016.

Wilson, Sean. *The Flexible Constitution.* Lanham: Lexington, 2013.

Wolfe, Bertram. *An Ideology in Power: Reflections on the Russian Revolution.* New York: Routledge, 2017.

Wright, Teresa. *Party and State in Post-Mao China.* Malden, MA: Polity, 2015.

Wu, Guoguang. *China's Party Congress: Power, Legitimacy, and Institutional Manipulation.* Cambridge: Cambridge University Press, 2015.

Young, Crawford. *The Post-Colonial State in Africa: Fifty Years of Independence, 1960–2010.* Madison: University of Wisconsin Press, 2012.

Yu, Yingshi, Duke, Michael, and Chiu-Duke, Josephine. *Chinese History and Culture.* New York: Columbia University Press, 2016.

Zhao, Suisheng. *Debating Political Reform in China: Rule of Law vs. Democratization.* Hoboken, NJ: Taylor and Francis, 2014.

Zheng, Yongnian. *Contemporary China: A History Since 1978.* Hoboken, NJ: Wiley, 2014.

Zimmerman, William. *Ruling Russia: Authoritarianism from the Revolution to Putin.* Princeton: Princeton University Press, 2014.

Zweigenhaft, Richard, and Domhoff, G. William. *Diversity in the Political Elite: How It Happened, Why It Matters.* Lanham: Rowman and Littlefield, 2006.

Index

294–295; emergency rule, 292–293; executive structures, 283–285; federalism, 281–283; Gandhi, Indira, Prime Minister, 292–293; Gandhi, Mohandas, 279; Home Rule, 279; Indian National Congress and independence, 279; Indian Rebellion (1857), 278–279; Kashmir, 299–300; language, 282; legislative structures, 285–291; Lok Sabha, 282, 286–290; Mountbatten, Viscount Lord Louis, Governor-General, 280; Narasimha Rao, P.V., Prime Minister, 284; Kovind, Shri Ram Nath, President, 283; Nehru, Jawaharlal, Prime Minister, 280; political heritage, 278–280; political parties, 291–294; presidency, 283–285; Prime Minister's Office, 284–285; Punjab, 297–298; Quit India Movement, 279; Rajya Sabha, 286–287, 290–291; religion and politics, 295–296; Republic, 281; social class and politics, 297; state governments, 281–283; Union Government, 280–281
Indian National Congress, and independence movement, 279
Individual level of analysis, 10–11
Individualistic fallacy, 12
Input-output analysis, 16, 39
Inquiry, methods of, 5–6
Interest groups, 163–166; defined, 164; political parties and, 167
Israel: proportional representation voting, 64–65; unwritten constitution, 31
Ivan the Terrible, in Russia, 366

Jacquerie, political violence, 148–149
James I, 87; and religion as a source of law, 116–117
James II, 88
Japanese Americans, and lack of constitutional protections, 32
Jaros, Dean, and political socialization research, 134
Jiang Zemin, 188
Joint committee in legislature, 71, 450
Judicial functions, 121
Judicial powers of the US president, 442
Judicial precedent, 115
Judicial review, 122–123; France, 230
Judicial structures, federal, 120
Judiciaries, 110–124; China, 203–204; democracy, 121; France, 230–231; Germany, 252–253; Kenya, 323; politics and, 121–124; as source of

law, 117; Russia, 384–385; United Kingdom, 420–421; United States 453–455
Judiciary Act of 1789, United States, 453
Jurisdiction, judicial, 119
Justice, idea of, 112

Kadhi courts, in Kenya, 323
Kalenjin, in Kenya, 311
Kashmir, in Indian politics, 299–300
Kenya, 307–329; African patterns, 308–310; AIDS, 309; bicameralism, 321–323; British East African protectorate, 310–311; Commonwealth of Nations, 312; competitive single-party system, 324–325; Constitution of Kenya Review Commission, 314; Constitution of Kenya (2010), 317–318; constitutional system, 312–315; courts, 323; decentralized power, 317; devolution of power, 314; ethnic conflict and political parties, 318–319, 325; executive structures, 319–321; expatriates, 311; Kadhi courts, 323; Kalenjin, 311; Kenyan African National Union (KANU), 311; Kenyatta, Jomo, President, 311, 317; Kibaki, Mwai, President, 312, 315; Kikuyu, 311; legislative structures 321–323; Maasai, 311; Majimbo, 315–316; Mau Mau, 311; Moi, Daniel arap, President, 311, 313, 317; multipartyism, 325; National Assembly, 321–323; Odinga, Raila, Prime Minister, 315, 316, 319; one-party state, 320; political heritage, 310–312; political parties, 324–326; presidential power, 313, 319–321; Queen, 312; regionalism, 315–318
Kenyan African National Union, 311
Kenyatta, Jomo, 311, 317
Kerensky, Alexander, in Russia, 368
Khrushchev, Nikita, and Soviet ideology, 376
Kibaki, Mwai, President of Kenya, 312, 3 15
Kikuyu, in Kenya, 311
Kingship, 47
Knesset, Israeli, size, 59
Kohl, Helmut, Chancellor of Germany, 256, 269
Kosygin, Alexi, and Soviet ideology, 376
Kovind, Shri Ram Nath, President of India, 283

About the Book

Among the many tools available for teaching comparative politics, Gregory Mahler's text stands out for its unique exploration of concepts, structures, and illustrative cases.

Part 1 of the book, after setting the stage with a discussion of comparison as a method of inquiry, focuses on the core institutions that affect politics within nations, as well as on political behavior and civil society. In Part 2, those same topics are systematically revisited as they interact in the context of nine detailed, up-to-date (through 2018) country studies.

This well-integrated, cross-national, and accessible approach serves perfectly to provide students with the tools and perspectives that they need to better understand the diverse political systems of today's world.

Gregory S. Mahler is academic dean emeritus and research professor of politics at Earlham College.